Germany

FODOR'S TRAVEL PUBLICATIONS

are compiled, researched, and edited by an international team of travel writers, field correspondents, and editors. The series, which now almost covers the globe, was founded by Eugene Fodor in 1936.

OFFICES
New York & London

Fodor's Germany

Contributors: Robert Brown, Kathy Ewald, Birgit Gericke, George W. Hamilton, Andrew Heritage, Nicholas Law, Pamela Vandyke Price, Robert Tilley
Drawings: Beryl Sanders
Maps: Roger Gorringe, Swanston Graphics
Cover Photograph: Owen Franken

Cover Design: Vignelli Associates

Fodor's 89

Germany

FODOR'S TRAVEL PUBLICATIONS, INC.
New York & London

ISBN 0–679–01639–2

MANUFACTURED IN THE UNITED STATES OF AMERICA
10 9 8 7 6 5 4 3 2

CONTENTS

EAST GERMANY

Map of East Germany 474

FACTS AT YOUR FINGERTIPS
Travel Formalities 475; When to Go 476; Seasonal Events 476; Currency 476;
Language 477; Getting to East Germany 477; Customs on Arrival 478; Hotels
478; Camping 479; Restaurants 479; Tipping 480; Mail 480; Telephones 480;
Closing Times 480; Getting Around East Germany 480.

FOREWORD

For fully three decades Germany has been a key country in our series of Guides. Year by year we have charted its progress—its emergence from the terrible devastation of the last World War, the sad consolidation of its sundered statehood and the gradual climb of the Western part back to affluence. During those heady years of upward mobility West Germany luxuriated in its economic miracle and became one of Europe's most expensive countries. Today, though still enjoying an admirably high standard of living, Germany need not be an overly expensive destination for the visitor. That is not to say that the country is down there in the bargain basement. Rather, that the Germans, thorough and practical as ever, have made a number of imaginative efforts to help visitors keep costs within reasonable bounds. The vagaries of the exchange rate apart, there is every reason to believe that Germany will continue to offer highly competitive vacations for the visitor to Europe.

We would like to stress that the hotel and restaurant listings are selective. We do not profess to provide a complete listing for accommodations or for eating places. We select those that we feel would interest our readers and change the listings year by year so as to include new ones that have surfaced. Space alone prevents us being more comprehensive and there could well be twice the number of acceptable places in any given town than we have been able to list.

The task of creating this edition would not have been possible without the help of many friends both around Germany and in tourist offices abroad. We would especially like to express our gratitude to Mr. Günther Nischwitz, the Director of the German National Tourist Office in London and his staff; to the many staff members of local tourist offices throughout Germany who have provided us with so much information; the German Wine Institute in Mainz; and Swanston Graphics for their cartography.

While every care has been taken to assure the accuracy of the information in this guide, the passage of time will always bring change, and consequently, the publisher cannot accept responsibility for errors that may occur.

All prices and opening times quoted here are based on information available to us at press time. Hours and admission fees may change, however, and the prudent traveler will avoid inconvenience by calling ahead.

Fodor's wants to hear about your travel experiences, both pleasant and unpleasant. When a hotel or restaurant fails to live up to its billing, let us know and we will investigate the complaint and revise our entries where the facts warrant it.

Send your letters to the editors of Fodor's Travel Publications, 201 E. 50th Street, New York, NY 10022, or 30–32 Bedford Square, London WC1B 3SG, England.

FACTS AT
YOUR FINGERTIPS

FACTS AT YOUR FINGERTIPS

For specific information on East Germany vacation-planning, see the East Germany Facts at Your Fingertips *section.*

Planning Your Trip

SOURCES OF INFORMATION. The major source of information for all aspects of travel to Germany is the German National Tourist Office. They produce a wealth of tourist literature, the bulk of it free and all of it useful. They are a strikingly efficient organization and should be the first people to contact when planning your vacation.

Their addresses are:

In the U.S.: 747 Third Ave., New York, N.Y. 10017 (212–308–3300); 444 South Flower St., Suite 2230, Los Angeles, CA 90017 (213–688–7332).

In Canada: P.O. Box 417, 2 Fundy, Place Bonaventure, Montreal, H5A 1B8 (514–878–9885).

In the U.K.: 61 Conduit St., London W.1 (01–734–2600).

Within Germany, almost every town of any significance has its own local tourist office (*Verkehrsamt*), and there are also a series of larger, regional tourist offices located throughout the country. Generally located at the City Hall (Rathaus) or main rail station (Hauptbahnhof), all these offices produce an abundance of material on their regions (what to see, how to get around, special discount travel tickets, where to eat, accommodations, etc.). Though be warned that in smaller towns, most of the pamphlets are in German only. But every office will also have at least one fluent English speaker, if not more. Most offices also run accommodations services (*Zimmernachweis*).

We give addresses of all the major offices in the *Practical Information* sections for every chapter, following the hotel and restaurant listings.

PACKAGE TOURS OR INDEPENDENT TRAVEL? The best and most economical way to visit Germany, especially from the States and Canada, is on a package tour. The number and variety of these is immense and most offer excellent value for money. The principal advantage of any

1

package tour is that the two single most expensive components of any vacation—getting there and accommodations—will generally be competitively priced and will be arranged for you.

At the same time, most packages offer considerable flexibility. You can, for example, buy an all-inclusive, pre-paid package, which gives you flight, accommodations, meals and excursions—all at a fixed price—leaving only incidental expenditure (drinks, shopping, mail etc.) for you to pay for during your trip. For those making a first visit and unsure of where to visit or how to get around, this is frequently an excellent introduction to a country. Many, however, might find this type of trip too stifling or regimented. There is also the drawback that you might find your fellow packagees—from whom there is no escape—dull, though of course at the same time you might get on fine.

Alternatively, therefore, there are packages which give you flight and accommodations only, with optional pre-paid meals and excursions. To a large extent, this sort of semi-independent package gives you the best of both worlds. Accordingly, it tends to be the most popular.

Other options available include fly-drive, which is particularly suitable for those who want the maximum independence, though here costs tend to be steeper, or a rail-air combination. Similarly, special interest packages, again offering varying degrees of flexibility and independence, are also available. Popular themes include sailing, bird-watching, castle touring, painting, photography, art tours, gourmet tours, sporting activities of all kinds, farm vacations, and much else besides.

However, if you do plump for a package, be very sure to find out in advance exactly what is included in the price and how much you will have to pay for once in Germany. For example, how many meals are included? How tied to the tour are you? If it is a bus tour, do you have to stay with the tour city by city or can you leave and rejoin it at will? If you have a car, is the rate included in the package or is there an additional fee per mile? Is the car exactly what you want? Air-conditioning is certainly unnecessary at any time of year in Germany, and there is a substantial difference between the charge for standard and automatic shifts. Can you drive a standard? What is the tour operator's responsibility for getting you home on time?

In other words, be absolutely certain you know what you are paying for, *and read the fine print very carefully.*

Independent travel, on the other hand, has the great advantage of allowing you to do precisely as you please, but it also has the drawback of almost always being more expensive than a comparable package tour. That is not to say it can't be better value for money. For instance, while dinner and meals on a package tour may generally be very inexpensive, this is normally because the tour operator has struck a cut-price rate with your hotel or restaurant. Accordingly, you will tend to get cut-price food and service, while anyone traveling on their own will almost certainly get both better food and better service. Is this better value for money? Possibly, but individual preference is clearly the dominant factor in choosing any vacation and it is up to you to decide.

TRAVEL AGENTS. Regardless of whether you plan to visit Germany independently or take a package, it is advisable to consult a reputable travel agent. If you are only after an inexpensive flight, at the very least he will be able to guide you through the impenetrable maze of trans-Atlantic air fares. But if you want to buy a complete package, or even have an entire itinerary devised (which will prove expensive) he will be able to recommend the most appropriate for your particular needs. He will also be able to arrange insurance and passports. A good travel agent can save you time, money and a good deal of inconvenience, and is an invaluable extra source of information.

If you are in any doubt which agent to contact, consult the American Society of Travel Agents, 1101 King St., Alexandria, VA 22314, or the British Association of Travel Agents, 53 Newman St., London W.1. Both will point you in the right direction.

TOUR OPERATORS. Full details of the many operators offering trips to Germany are available from the German National Tourist Office, Lufthansa and of course your travel agent. But such is the range of tours and vacations on offer from both the States and the U.K., that a summary of one or two of the more typical should provide you with a handy pointer to availability. Bear in mind, however, that the few we list here are only the tip of the iceberg and that many, many more are available. All details quoted below are for 1988 only—check latest information with your travel agent.

From the U.S. U.S.-based operators offering packages to Germany include:

American Express, 822 Lexington Ave., New York, N.Y. 10021 (212–758–6510 or 800–241–1700).

Cosmos/Globus Gateway, 95–25 Queens Blvd., Rego Park, N.Y. 11374 (718–268–1700).

Lufthansa, 680 Fifth Ave., New York, N.Y. 10010 (718–895–1277).

Maupintour, 1515 St. Andrews Dr., Lawrence, KS 66044 (913–843–1211 or 800–255–4266).

Olson Travelworld, P.O. Box 92734, Los Angeles, CA 90009 (213–670–7100).

WHEN TO GO. The main tourist season in Germany runs from May to late October, when the weather is naturally at its best. As well as many tourist events, this period has many hundreds of folk festivals. The winter sports season in the Bavarian Alps runs from Christmas to mid-March.

Prices everywhere are generally higher during the summer, so you may find considerable advantages in visiting Germany during the low season. Most large resorts offer special low season *(Zwischensaison)* or "edge of season" *(Nebensaison)* rates, for example, and tourist offices can provide lists of hotels offering special low-price inclusive weekly packages *(Pauschalangebote).* Similarly, many winter resorts offer special winter off-season rates *(Weisse Wochen)* for the periods immediately before and after the high season. These are normally inclusive of seven days' bed-and-breakfast and skiing lessons. The other major advantage of off-season travel is that crowds, which in the major tourist destinations are often otherwise thick on the ground, are very much less in evidence.

However, there are a number of disadvantages. First, the weather, which during the summer is normally delightful throughout the country, is pretty miserable in the winter. Secondly, many major tourist attractions, especially in rural areas, close down.

Climate. The German climate is generally temperate and mild. Winters, as we say, are often quite gloomy, though, away from the Alps, never particularly cold, except perhaps in the Harz region of Lower Saxony and the higher regions of Northern Franconia; rather they are dull and mostly wet. Summers, however, are usually excellent and warm, though be prepared for cloudy and wet days from time to time. The south is normally quite a bit warmer than the north, but as you get nearer the Alps, summers are much shorter lived, starting in May. Spring and fall are often delightful, though they, too, can be wet.

The only real exception to the above is the strikingly variable weather in southern Bavaria caused by the *Föhn*, an Alpine wind that gives rise to very clear but rather oppressive conditions in summer, and can cause the snow in the alpine regions to disappear overnight.

Average afternoon temperatures in degrees Fahrenheit and centigrade:

	Jan.	Feb.	Mar.	Apr.	May	June	July	Aug.	Sept.	Oct.	Nov.	Dec.
Berlin												
F°	35	38	46	55	65	70	74	72	66	55	43	37
C°	2	3	8	13	18	21	23	22	19	13	6	3
Munich												
F°	33	37	45	54	63	69	72	71	64	53	42	36
C°	1	3	7	12	17	21	22	22	18	12	6	2

SEASONAL EVENTS. January sees the outstanding event in the winter sports year, the International Winter Sports Week at Garmisch-Partenkirchen. Berlin's Green Week gets under way with the traditional agricultural and garden show accompanied by social and sports events.

February. Nürnberg holds its famous toy fair early in the month, Frankfurt International Trade Fair for consumer goods takes place mid-month, and Berlin has its well-known film festival later in the month. The Fasching season (carnival season) has its peak events such as Enthronement of Carnival Princes and Princesses, Fool's Congresses, masked balls and masked parades in January and February, particularly in Cologne, Munich, Mainz, Augsburg, Düsseldorf, Aachen, Bonn, Wiesbaden, Frankfurt, and in hundreds of smaller localities reaching its peak on *Rosenmontag* (the Monday before Ash Wednesday) in the Rhineland, and on *Faschingsdienstag* (Shrove Tuesday) in Munich and Bavaria.

March. Munich's International Fashion Fair "Mode Woche" (open to members of the trade only, but hotels will be full) is usually at the beginning of the month, and the Strong Beer Festival (*Starkbier Fest*) takes place at the Nockherberg.

April. Walpurgis festivals occur throughout the Harz Mountains on the last day of the month, while Frankfurt holds its Fur Fair. Mannheim begins its traditional May Market, with a parade of flower floats; Stuttgart and Munich have Spring Festivals; toward the end of April Marburg has a special May festival on the Market Square. The Hannover Industrial Fair begins the end of April and lasts into early May. In Furth-im-Wald in East Bavaria the *Leonhardiritt* equestrian procession takes place.

May also signals the opening of the festival season, with Wiesbaden staging its annual panorama of opera, drama, concerts and ballet, with the participation of foreign artists and companies, during the first three weeks of the month. Bonn's season of summer theater, music and folklore also begins in May, as does the Stuttgart ballet week and the Killisberg Park summer theater. At Pentecost, Rothenburg-on-Tauber commemorates a famous event in its history by putting on the traditional *Meister Trunk* play, followed by equally traditional shepherds' dances and the comic Hans Sachs Plays. On Corpus Christi Day there are parades at Freiburg and Berchtesgaden, and colorful religious processions take place in all the Catholic regions of Germany.

June sees Kiel Week, a great time for yachtsmen. The Augsburg season of openair opera and operetta starts in the middle of the month and continues into September, while in Munich the ballet festival begins, as do the Munich Film Festival and the Nymphenburg Palace summer concerts. In Heidelberg the first of the summer castle illuminations takes place.

July is the festival month for children: the Biberach festival with 3,000 children in historical costumes; the Children's Festival at Dinkelsbühl; and the oldest Bavarian children's festival at Kaufbeuren. It is also the month of the Bach Week at Ansbach, which takes place in alternate years, the Lorelei Festival at St. Goarshausen on the Rhine, the world's largest marksmen's festival (Schutzenfest) in Hannover, and the horse racing week at Bad Harzburg. But the big dates for this month are Germany's most famous musical drawing cards, the Wagner Festival at Bayreuth and Munich Opera Festival.

August. Horse race addicts have a big fixture at the end of August, the international contests at Baden-Baden's Iffezheim Week. The German Grand Prix takes place either on the Nürburgring in the Eifel or at Hochenheim in southern Rhineland in early August, also the month of the Kulmbach beer festival, Stuttgart's European Music Festival, Augsburg's annual Peace Festival, and Heidelberg's openair theater at the castle. Meanwhile, at Mainz, the Wine Market anticipates by a few days the wine festivals which break out all over the Rhineland early in September.

September itself, however, sees the bulk of the wine festivals which succeed or overlap one another all the way into the first few days of November. There are too many of them to list, but of particular note are those of Bad Dürkheim, about the middle of the month, confusingly known as the Sausage Fair, the *Backfischfest* in Worms, and the one at Neustadt, which doesn't get under way until September 30. Before that, though, four other events in September deserve mention—the second of Frankfurt's big trade fairs, early in the month, and, about the middle, one of the most spectacular sights of the year, the Rhine in Flames illuminations, which bathe the river in fire from St. Goar on one bank to St. Goarshausen on the other, at the very point where the Lorelei used to wreck the Rhine boats before James Watt thwarted her by inventing the steam engine. There is also international show-jumping in Aachen and Munich. Finally, and running on into October, the Cannstatt Folk Festival in Stuttgart, which dates back to 1811, gets under way.

The second half of September is also noted for the inception of the Oktoberfest in Munich, which, to justify its name, does continue for a few days into October. Dating back to 1810 when King Ludwig I of Bavaria got married, this festival attracts as many as 6,000,000 visitors from Germany and abroad for two weeks of beer drinking, parades, fun-fair amusements, sideshows, dancing, and general merrymaking, plus a few congresses and exhibitions.

October. The International Book Fair in Frankfurt also gets under way in October, as does the Bremen Freimarkt, the oldest Folk Festival in Germany, dating back to 965.

November sees St. Martin's Day parades in, among other places, Heidelberg. Another November event is the Leonhardiritt, parades honoring St. Leonard, the patron saint of cattle and horses, in Bad Füssing. In Munich the six-day indoor bicycle race (*Sechs Tage Rennen*) begins in the Rudi Sedlmayer Halle. On November 11, at 11.11 A.M. the new Carnival Season begins officially.

December. As the regular theater and entertainment season sets in, the number of special events falls off, but there is one more of great importance, the Christkindlmarkt, or Christ Child's Market, a fair that begins in the second week of the month in Nürnberg, Rothenburg, Munich, Stuttgart, and some other cities.

National Holidays 1989. Jan. 1 (New Year's Day); Mar. 24, 27 (Easter); May 1 (Labor Day); May 4 (Ascension); May 15 (Pentecost Monday); May 25 (Corpus Christi, southern Germany only); June 17 (German Unity Day); Aug. 15 (Assumption Day, Bavaria and Saarland only); Nov. 1 (All Saints); Nov. 22 (Day of Prayer and Repentance); Dec. 25, 26 (Christmas).

WHAT TO PACK. The golden rule is to travel light; generally, try not to take more than you can carry yourself. Not only are porters more or less wholly extinct in Europe these days (where you can find them they're very expensive anyway), the less luggage you take the easier checking in and out of hotels becomes, similarly airports (increasingly the number one nightmare of all modern travel) became much easier to get through, and if you only take one piece of luggage, the less risk there is of your luggage being lost en route, and, in theory anyway, the less time you need to wait for it to appear when you get off the plane. Remember also that there are strict regulations governing the amount of luggage you can take with you on the plane. Each passenger is allowed two pieces of luggage, neither of which must exceed 62" (height × width × length) and which together do not exceed 106". Penalties for excess baggage are high. In theory, you may also take only one piece of hand luggage onto the plane, though most airlines usually turn a blind eye to this.

Clothes. The German climate is comparable to that of New England, so take along the sort of clothes you would wear there, depending of course on the sort of vacation you plan to have. A light rain coat is essential, however. If you are going to the Alps, remember that evenings are cool, even at the height of summer, so take along some good warm sweaters. Real mountain enthusiasts should wait until they get to Germany to get their hiking/climbing trousers and then splash out on a pair of *Kniebundhosen,* just about the best and certainly most practical hiking trousers there are.

Most hotels expect you to be reasonably smartly dressed for dinner but evening dress, for example, is not going to be expected anywhere but in a handful of the most expensive hotels and restaurants.

If you wear glasses, take along a prescription. Otherwise, there is no difficulty in getting medicines, but if you have to take a special preparation take along your own supply.

Don't forget your swim cap if you think you might swim in either indoor or outdoor pools. They're obligatory in Germany.

COSTS IN GERMANY. Germany has an admirably high standard of living—among the highest in Europe—and can unquestionably be an expensive country to visit, particularly if you spend time in the cities. You will also find that many items—gas, food, hotels and trains, to name but a few—are probably more expensive here than in the States. Similarly, the present disadvantageous exchange rate has certainly not helped. However, the vagaries of exchange rates being what they are, the situation could easily change, so it is essential to check them carefully both before and during your trip. However, a number of crucial factors are on your side.

First, the country's low rate of inflation—itself an admirable testimony to the affluence and efficiency of the Germans—has helped keep costs well within manageable bounds, with the result that many of the staples of tourism have increased only slightly in price for many years and remain very competitive.

Secondly, naturally conscious of their high-price-tag reputation, the Germans have made significant efforts in offering a host of special-offer deals. Hotels, restaurants, transport, sports—all have many excellent-value deals available of one sort or another. We give details of many in the following sections. But both your travel agent and the German National Tourist Office should also be able to help you. And once in Germany, you'll find that local tourist offices have a wealth of literature, and a great deal of practical advice, on cost cutting.

Thirdly, you can cut your budget considerably by visiting less-known cities, towns and summer and winter resorts. All along the Main and Neckar rivers you will find small towns as charming, if not as well known, but less expensive than Rothenburg and Heidelberg; Westphalia offers similar atmosphere at cheaper prices than the fabled Rhine towns and cities; wine lovers should explore the Palatinate instead of the classical Rhine-Mosel tour; in northern Germany the East Frisian islands from Emden on are less crowded than their more expensive sisters along the North Frisian coast; and ski enthusiasts would do well to investigate the advantages of the Harz and Eifel mountains, the Allgäu with charming resorts like Kleinwalsertal, the mountains and forests of Swabia, the Black Forest and, most particularly, Oberpfalz and Bayerischer Wald in East Bavaria. Known as the step-child of German tourism, East Bavaria offers excellent quality at truly bargain rates.

Sample costs. Museum entrance DM. 3–8; cinema DM. 15; opera, anywhere from DM. 30–200; subway or bus DM. 2.30; one-mile taxi ride DM 7; glass of whiskey DM. 8; bottle of beer DM. 3 (more in a restaurant); bottle of wine DM. 8 (more in a restaurant); cup of coffee (in café) DM. 3; cigarettes DM. 3–4.

TAKING MONEY ABROAD. Traveler's checks are the safest and simplest way to take money abroad. The best-known are American Express, Bank of America, Cook's and Barclay's, but practically all banks issue them and you will have no difficulty cashing them throughout Germany (see *Changing Money* below). It is, however, hard to say if it is more advantageous to take checks in dollars or marks; the former stand a chance of making or losing you a little if the exchange rate changes, the latter will of course retain their value throughout your time in Germany.

Britons holding a Uniform Eurocheque card and checkbook—apply for them at your bank—can cash up to £100 a day at banks participating in the scheme, or use the checks for services—shops, hotels, restaurants— again up to £100.

Credit cards. All the major credit cards are generally, though by no means universally, accepted throughout Germany. In our hotel and restaurant recommendations we list which of the major cards—American Express, Diner's Club, MasterCard (incorporating Access and EuroCard), and Visa—are accepted by each establishment. But always be sure to check before reserving your room or ordering a meal that your particular piece of plastic is accepted. As a general rule, Visa is probably the most widely-accepted, while practically all larger and more expensive establishments will take American Express. In the event of losing your credit card, immediately register the loss at one of the following offices: *American Express* tel. 069–720016; *Diners Club* tel. 069–26030; *MasterCard/Access* tel. 069–79330; *Visa* tel. 069–7562537.

GERMAN CURRENCY. The unit of currency in Germany is the Deutschmark, written as DM. It is divided into 100 pfennigs. There are bills to the value of 1,000, 500, 50, 20, and 10 DM, and coins to the value of 5, 2 and 1 DM and 50, 10, 5, 2 and 1 pfennigs.

At the time of writing (mid-1988), the mark stood at around 1.80 to the U.S. dollar and around 3.11 to the pound sterling. However, these rates will change both before and during 1989, and it is essential to keep a sharp eye on exchange rates during your trip.

Changing Money. All international airports and many larger rail stations in Germany have exchange offices operated by bona fide banks, all offering the official rate of exchange and most open outside normal banking hours (see below). Otherwise, outside banking hours, you can normally change money at tourist offices, some travel agents, most hotels and at any one of the growing number of private exchange kiosks *(Wechelstuben)* found in larger towns and cities. All, however, charge well above the official rate and should be used in emergencies only.

The best place to change money anywhere in Germany is at a bank. Times vary from state to state and city to city, but banks are generally open weekdays from 8.30 or 9 to 3 or 4 (5 or 6 on Thursday). Branches at airports and main train stations open as early as 6.30 A.M. and close as late as 10.30 P.M.

If you think you are going to arrive in Germany outside banking hours, or know that there will not be an airport or rail station exchange office where you arrive, take along enough German money to get you through the first day or so. All banks in both the U.S. and U.K. can supply small quantities of Deutschmarks, though some may require a few days' notice.

PASSPORTS. Americans. All U.S. citizens require a valid passport to enter West Germany. Visas are not required. If you do not have a passport, apply in person at U.S. Passport Agency Offices, local county courthouses or selected Post Offices. If you have a passport not more than 12 years old you may apply by mail; otherwise you will need:

—proof of citizenship, such as a birth certificate.

—two identical photographs, two inches square, in either black and white or color, on non-glossy paper and taken within the past six months,

—$42 for the passport itself plus a $7 processing fee if you are applying in person (no processing fee when applying by mail) for those 18 years and older, or if you are under 18, $27 for the passport plus a $7 processing fee if you are applying in person (again, no extra fee when applying by mail).

—proof of identity that includes a photo and signature, such as a driver's license, previous passport, or any governmental ID card.

Adult passports are valid for 10 years, others for five years; they are not renewable. Allow four to six weeks for your application to be processed, but in an emergency, Passport Agency offices can have a passport readied within 24–48 hours, and even the postal authorities can indicate "Rush" when necessary.

If you expect to travel extensively, request a 48- or 96-page passport rather than the usual 24-page one. There is no extra charge. When you receive your passport, write down its number, date and place of issue separately; if it is later lost or stolen, notify either the nearest American Consul or the Passport Office, Department of State, 1425 K St. NW, Washington DC 20524, as well as the local police.

Canadians. Canadian citizens apply in person to regional passport offices, post offices or by mail to Bureau of Passports, Complexe Guy Favreau, 200 Dorchester West, Montreal, P.Q. H2Z 1X4 (514–283–2152). A $25 fee, two photographs, a guarantor, and evidence of citizenship are required. Canadian passports are valid for five years and are non-renewable.

Britons. British subjects should apply for passports on special forms obtainable from main post offices or a travel agent. The application should be sent or taken to the Passport Office according to residential area (as indicated on the guidance form) or lodged with them through a travel agent. It is best to apply for the passport 4–5 weeks before it is required, although in some cases it will be issued sooner. The regional Passport Offices are located in London, Liverpool, Peterborough, Glasgow and Newport. The application must be countersigned by your bank manager or by a solicitor, barrister, doctor, clergyman or justice of the peace who knows you personally. You will need two full-face photos. The fee is £15; passport valid for 10 years.

British Visitor's Passport. This simplified form of passport has advantages for the once-in-a-while tourist to most European countries (including West Germany). Valid for one year and not renewable, it costs £7.50. Application may be made at main post offices in England, Scotland and Wales, and in Northern Ireland at the Passport Office in Belfast. Birth certificate or medical card for identification and two passport photographs are required—no other formalities.

HEALTH AND INSURANCE. The different varieties of travel insurance cover everything from health and accident costs, to lost baggage and trip cancelation. Sometimes they can all be obtained with one blanket policy; other times they overlap with existing coverage you might have for health and/or home; still other times it is best to buy policies that are tailored to very specific needs. Insurance is available from many sources, however, and many travelers unwittingly end up with redundant coverage. Before purchasing separate travel insurance of any kind, be sure to check your regular policies carefully.

Generally, it is best to take care of your insurance needs before embarking on your trip. You'll pay more for less coverage—and have less chance to read the fine print—if you wait until the last minute and make your purchases from, say, an airport vending machine or insurance company counter. If you have a regular insurance agent, he or she is the person to consult first.

Flight insurance, which is often included in the price of the ticket when the fare is paid via American Express, Visa or certain other major credit cards, is also often included in package policies providing accident coverage as well. These policies are available from most tour operators and insurance companies. But while it is a good idea to have health and accident insurance when traveling, be careful not to spend money to duplicate coverage you may already have . . . or to neglect some eventuality which could end up costing a small fortune.

For example, basic Blue Cross-Blue Shield policies do cover health costs incurred while traveling. They will not, however, cover the cost of emergency transportation, which can often add up to several thousand dollars. Emergency transportation *is* covered, in part at least, by many major medical policies such as those underwritten by Prudential, Metropolitan and New York Life. Again, we can't urge you too strongly that in order to be sure you are getting the coverage you need, check any policy carefully before buying. And bear in mind also that most insurance issued specifically for travel will not cover pre-existing conditions, such as a heart condition.

Several organizations offer coverage designed to supplement existing health insurance and to help defray costs not covered by many standard policies, such as emergency transportation. Some of the more prominent are:

Carefree Travel Insurance, c/o ARM Coverage Inc., 120 Mineola Blvd., Box 310, Mineola, N.Y. 11510 (516–294–0220 or 800–645–2424), offers insurance, legal and financial assistance, and medical evacuation throughout Europe arranged by Inter. Claim. Carefree coverage is available from many travel agents.

International SOS Assistance Inc. does not offer medical insurance but provides medical evacuation services to its clients, who are often international corporations (215–244–1500 or 800–523–8930).

IAMAT (International Association for Medical Assistance to Travelers), 736 Center St., Lewiston, N.Y. 14092 (716–754–4883) in the U.S.; or 188 Nicklin Rd., Guelph, Ont. N1H 7L5, (519–836–0102).

Travel Assistance International, the American arm of Europ Assistance, offers a comprehensive program providing medical and personal emergency services and offering immediate, on-the-spot medical, personal and financial help. Trip protection ranges from $35 for an individual for up to eight days to $220 for an entire family for a year. Full details from travel agents or insurance brokers, or from *Europ Assistance Worldwide Services, Inc.,* 1133 15th St. N.W., Suite 400, Washington, D.C. 20005

(800–821–2828). In the U.K., contact *Europ Assistance Ltd.,* 252 High St., Croydon, Surrey (01–680 1234).

The Association of British Insurers, Aldermary House, Queen St., London E.C.4 (01–248 4477), will give comprehensive advice on all aspects of vacation travel insurance from the U.K.

Another frequent inconvenience to travelers is the loss of baggage. It is possible, though often a complicated affair, to insure your luggage against loss through theft or negligence. Insurance companies are reluctant to sell such coverage alone, however, since it is often a losing proposition for them. Instead, this type of coverage is usually included as part of a package that also covers accidents or health. Should you lose your luggage or some other personal possession, it is essential to report it to the local police immediately. Without documentation of such a report, your insurance company might be very stingy. Also, before buying baggage insurance, check your homeowner's policy. Some such policies offer "off-premises theft" coverage, including the loss of luggage while traveling.

Trip cancellation coverage is especially important to travelers on APEX or charter flights. Should you be unable to continue your trip during your vacation, you may be stuck having to buy a new one-way fare home, plus paying for the charter you're not using. You can guard against this with "trip cancellation insurance." Most of these policies will also cover last minute cancellations.

STUDENT AND YOUTH TRAVEL. All student travelers should obtain an *International Student Identity Card,* which is generally needed to get student discounts, youth rail passes, and Intra-European Student Charter Flights. Apply to *Council On International Educational Exchange,* 205 East 42 St., New York, N.Y. 10017 (212–661–1414); or 312 Sutter St., San Francisco, CA 94108. Canadian students should apply to the *Association of Student Councils,* 187 College St., Toronto, Ont. M5T 1P7 (416–979–2406).

The following organizations can also be helpful in finding student flights, educational opportunities and other information. Most deal with international student travel generally, but materials for those listed cover Scandinavia.

American Youth Hostels, PO Box 37613, Washington, DC 20013 (202–783–6161). Members are eligible to use the worldwide network of youth hostels. The organization publishes an extensive directory on same.

Council on International Educational Exchange (CIEE), 205 East 42 St., New York, N.Y. 10017 (212–661–1414); and 312 Sutter St., San Francisco, CA 94108, provides information on summer study, work/travel programs and travel services for college and high school students, and a free Charter Flights Guide booklet. Their *Whole World Handbook* ($8.95 plus $1 postage) is the best listing of both work and study possibilities.

Institute of International Education, 809 United Nations Plaza, New York, N.Y. 10017 (212–883–8200) is primarily concerned with study opportunities and administers scholarships and fellowships for international study and training. The New York office has a visitor's information center; satellite offices are located in Chicago, Denver, Houston, San Francisco and Washington.

Also worth contacting is *Educational Travel Center,* 438 North Frances, Madison, WI 53703 (608–256–5551).

HINTS FOR HANDICAPPED TRAVELERS. Facilities for the handicapped in Germany are generally good if variable, though where are they not? The German National Tourist Office detail facilities of those hotels with special amenities for handicapped visitors in their hotel listings. Similarly, many regional tourist offices also give details of hotels in their areas with facilities for the handicapped. In addition, the German Association for Autobahn Services (GFN) in Bonn (at Poppelsdorfer Allee 24) also produce a leaflet—*Autobahn Service fuer Behinderte*—detailing all stopping places on the German autobahn network with facilities for the handicapped. Similarly, German Railways have introduced special jumbo-sized carriages in a number of Inter-City express trains to accommodate wheelchairs; details from German Railways. However, the principal source of information within Germany is the *BAG Hilfe fuer Behinderte e. V.* (German Disabled Association), Kirchfeldstrasse 149, 4000-Dusseldorf 1, Germany.

Otherwise, major sources of information are: *Access to the World: A Travel Guide for the Handicapped,* by Louise Weiss, an outstanding book covering all aspects of travel for anyone with health or medical problems; it features extensive listings and suggestions on everything from availability of special diets to wheelchair accessibility. Order from *Facts On File,* 460 Park Ave. South, New York, N.Y. 10016 (212–683–2244); the guide costs $14.95. The *Moss Rehabilitation Hospital,* 12th St. and Tabor Rd., Philadelphia, PA 19141 (215–329–5715), gives information on facilities for the handicapped in many countries and also provides toll-free numbers of airlines with special lines for the hearing impaired; they can also provide listings of tour operators who arrange vacations for the handicapped. But for a complete list of tour operators, write to the *Society for the Advancement of Travel for the Handicapped,* 26 Court St., Brooklyn, N.Y. 11242 (718–858–5483).

In the U.K., contact *Mobility International,* 43 Dorset St., London W.1; the *National Society for Mentally Handicapped Children,* 117 Golden Lane, London E.C.1; the *Across Trust,* Crown House, Morden, Surrey (they have an amazing series of "Jumbulances," huge articulated ambulances, staffed by volunteer doctors and nurses, that can whisk even the most seriously handicapped across Europe in comfort and safety). But the main source in Britain for all advice on handicapped travel is the *Royal Association for Disability and Rehabilitation* (RADAR), 25 Mortimer St., London W.1.

LANGUAGE. The Germans are great linguists and you will find English spoken in all hotels, restaurants, airports and stations, museums and other places of interest. Similarly, tourist offices, both national and regional, will have at least one member of staff who speaks fluent English, though all of the staff will probably be similarly fluent. However, don't assume that everyone you deal with will automatically speak English. It is not always widely spoken in rural areas, and it is in any case only common courtesy to ask beforehand if the person you are dealing with speaks English. Needless to say, the Germans respond warmly to anyone who makes the effort to master a few words or phrases in German (we give a basic vocabulary at the end of the Guide), but the odds are that the reply will be in perfect English.

TIME. During the summer (dates vary every year, but generally this means from the end of March to the end of September), Germany is six hours ahead of Eastern Standard Time, seven hours ahead of Central Time, eight hours ahead of Mountain Time and nine hours ahead of Pacific Time. During the winter, Germany puts her clocks back one hour, but as all America does likewise, the time difference remains the same.

Similarly, Germany is one hour ahead of British Summer Time and, during the winter, one hour ahead of Greenwich Mean Time.

Getting to Germany

FROM THE U.S. By air. Flights from major departure points in the U.S. to all principal German cities are frequent and generally easy to arrange. And, given the perpetual battle for business among the major airlines flying the Atlantic, fares are generally inexpensive. We give details of sample fares to Germany below.

However, be warned that though fares may be low and flights numerous, long-distance flying today is no bed of roses. Lines and delays at ever-more-crowded airports, perfunctory in-flight service and shrinking legroom on board a giant jet with some 400 other people, followed by interminable waits for your luggage when you arrive, are the clearest possible signals that the glamor of air travel—if it ever existed—is very much a thing of the past.

Unfortunately, these problems are compounded when flying to Europe by the fact that most flights from the States are scheduled to arrive first thing in the morning. Not only are you in for a night's discomfort on the plane, but you arrive at the start of a new day to be greeted by the confusion (some would say chaos) of a modern airport. To make life even more difficult for the weary traveler, many hotels will not allow you to check in before noon or even 1 P.M. giving you as much as six hours with nothing to do and nowhere to go.

There are a number of steps you can take, however, in order to lessen the traumas of long-distance flying. The first and possibly the most important of all is to harbor no illusions about the supposed luxury. If you approach your flight knowing that you are going to be cooped up for a long time and will have to face delays and discomforts of all kinds, the odds are that you will get through it without doing terrible things to your blood pressure or being disillusioned—but there's no point expecting comfort, good service and efficiency because you won't get them.

The right attitude is half the battle, but there are a number of other practical points to follow. Wear comfortable, loose-fitting clothes and take off your shoes. Try to sleep as much as possible, especially on the night flights; this can very often mean not watching the movie (they are invariably dull anyway) as it will probably be shown during the only period when meals are not being served and you can sleep. If you have difficulty sleeping, or think you might, take along a light sedative and try to get a window seat in order to avoid being woken up to let the person next to you get to the toilet or being bashed by people walking down the aisle. Above all, avoid alcohol, or at least drink only a little. The dry air of a pressurized airplane causes rapid dehydration, exaggerating the effects of drink and jet lag. Similarly, drink as much water as possible. Finally, once you arrive, try to take things easily for a day or so. In the excitement of being in a new place, especially for the first time, you can very often not realize how tired you are and optimistically set out sightseeing, only to come down to earth with a bump. Whatever you do, don't have any business meetings for at least 24 hours after arriving.

Fares. With air fares in a constant state of flux, the best advice for any-one planning to fly to Germany independently (rather than as part of a package tour, in which case your flight will have been arranged for you) is to check with a travel agent and let him make your reservations for you. Nonetheless, there are a number of points to bear in mind.

The best bet is to buy either an Apex or Super Apex ticket. First Class, Business and even the misleadingly-named Economy, though giving maximum flexibility on flying dates and cancellations, as well as permitting stop overs, are extremely expensive. Apex and Super Apex, by contrast, are reasonably priced and offer the all-important security of fixed return dates (all Apex tickets are round trip). In addition, you get exactly the same service as flying Economy. However, there are a number of restrictions; you must book, and pay for, your ticket 21 days or more in advance; you can stay in Germany no less than and no longer than a stated period (usually six days and six months); if you miss your flight, you forfeit the fare. But from the point of view of price and convenience, these tickets certainly represent the best value for money.

If your plans are sufficiently flexible and tighter budgeting is important, you can sometimes benefit from the last-minute bargains offered by tour operators otherwise unable to fill their plane or quota of seats. A number of brokers specializing in these discount sales have sprung up who can book seats of this type. All charge an annual membership fee, usually around $35–45.

Among them are: *Stand-Buys Ltd.,* 311 West Superior St., Suite 414, Chicago, IL 60610 (312–943–5737). *Moments Notice,* 40 East 49th St., New York, N.Y. 10017 (212–486–0503). *Discount Travel Intl.,* 114 Forest Ave., Narberth, PA 19072 (215–668–2182), and *Worldwide Discount Travel Club,* 1674 Meridian Ave., Miami Beach, FL 33139 (305–534–2082).

Charter flights are also available to Germany, though their number has decreased in recent years. Again, a travel agent will be able to recommend the most reliable. You might also consider, though this too should be done via a travel agent, buying a package tour to Germany, but using only the plane ticket. As packagers are able to get substantial discounts on fares through block booking seats, the price of the total package can sometimes be less than an ordinary air fare alone.

Typical fares as of mid-1988 for New York to Frankfurt were: $3,030 First Class, round-trip (year round); $713–$760 Apex, roundtrip (fares vary according to season). Charter fares are about the same, or possibly slightly lower than Apex.

Please note that these fares will probably change either before or during 1988.

By boat. There are no direct liner sailings from either the U.S. or Canada to Germany, though those with salt in their veins may feel inclined to sail to England on the *QE2* and continue from there—expensive and slow.

Alternatively, there are a limited number of freighter sailings to Germany, though you may have to wait up to a year for a berth. For details, contact *Air Marine Travel Service,* 501 Madison Ave., New York, N.Y. 10022 (212–661–7777 or 800–221–4770), publisher of the *Trip Log Quick Reference Freighter Guide.*

FROM THE U.K. By air. There are excellent air connections, in general operated by *British Airways* and *Lufthansa,* between the U.K. and all major German cities, principally from London's Heathrow and Gatwick airports. Berlin, Bremen, Köln, Düsseldorf, Frankfurt, Hamburg, Hannover, Munich, Saarbrücken, and Stuttgart all have at least three flights daily, many more in some cases—Berlin, for example, has no less than nine flights daily—and flying time is between about one hour 15 minutes and one hour 45 minutes. In addition, an even larger number of West German destinations can be reached via Frankfurt, hub of Germany's internal air network. Similarly, both Basel and Zurich in Switzerland are useful bases from which to reach many places in south Germany.

Fares. European air fares are high, disproportionately so in many cases, and flights to Germany are unfortunately no exception. About the cheapest fares offered by the major carriers on scheduled flights are SuperApex or Apex. To Berlin a SuperApex roundtrip fare costs around £124 while Club works out at around £354. Quite strict booking conditions are attached to Apex fares—you must book at least two weeks to a month in advance and must stay at least one Saturday night, and no cancellations or stopovers are allowed—but in all they represent quite good value for money, certainly in comparison to the so-called Economy fares, which are generally about twice the cost. Details from the airlines or your travel agent.

At long last a secondary network of "scheduled charter" flights has been developed to compete with and undercut the main carriers. The prime movers are *German Tourist Facilities,* 184–186 Kensington Church St., London W8 4DP (01–792 1260); example return fares as at mid-1988— Berlin £99, Frankfurt £79, Munich £94. They also operate inclusive tours and seasonal short break holidays at amazingly low prices.

For last minute seat-only bookings on charter flights check the classified columns of *The Standard, The Times* and *Sunday Times,* and *The Mail on Sunday.* However, you are unlikely to find anything much cheaper than the above, except at the beginning and end of the main holiday periods.

By train. There are three main routes to Germany from London. The quickest is from London (Victoria) to Dover, then across the Channel by Jetfoil to Ostend, from where trains run across Belgium, via Brussels, to Germany, plugging into the German Inter-City network at Köln. Destinations in both south and north Germany can easily be reached by mid-evening without an unduly early start from London. However, there are also trains from London in the afternoon that connect with overnight trains from Ostend. Additionally, there are conventional ferry services from Dover to Ostend, but these are naturally slower than the Jetfoil and arrivals in Germany consequently considerably delayed. In all cases it is essential to reserve seats in advance; a £6 supplement is also payable for the Jetfoil.

Secondly, there is the classic route from London (Liverpool Street) to Harwich, and then across the North Sea via British Ferries to the Hook of Holland, from where the EuroCity train the "Loreley" runs into Germany, calling at Köln, Frankfurt, Karlsruhe, Baden-Baden, Freibourg, and Basel. There are excellent connecting InterCity services to all parts of Germany from Köln. The journey is best made on the overnight ferry crossing—though book well in advance—which arrives in Holland early in the morning. First class is available on both train and ship and is well worth the extra cost.

The third and final route is from London (Liverpool St.) to Harwich and then by DFDS/Prins ferry to Hamburg. Though rather slower than either of the above routes and running only every other day, the ferry crossing is on board a superbly-appointed ship—more a mini-liner than a humble ferry. It is popular, however, so book well in advance.

Fares. Note that all fares quoted below were for mid-1987; for up-to-the-minute details on all train travel to Germany, consult the German National Tourist Office or your travel agent.

London—Köln via Dover and Ostend, including the Jetfoil supplement, is around £93.50 round-trip second class. Also on offer was a "5-day special," giving four nights on the Continent for £64.50, including the Jetfoil supplement.

London—Köln via the Hook of Holland was around £101.60, but not including a berth in a cabin on the ferry.

London—Hamburg using the Sealink ferry, and again traveling via the Hook of Holland was around £126.60 round trip, while a "5-day special" was around £80.50, again not including a berth.

London—Hamburg on the DFDS sailing, again with a berth, was around £165 round trip.

For first class, add roughly 50% to all fares, but note that on all routes except those via the Hook of Holland ships are one class.

Note also that young people under 26 should investigate the greatly reduced fares on offer from *Transalpino,* 71–75 Buckingham Palace Gardens, London S.W.1, and *Eurotrain,* 52 Grosvenor Gardens, London S.W.1. Break of journey en route is permitted, and to most destinations a choice of route is available.

For journey planning, the *British Rail Europe International Timetable* is very useful. It is clearly laid out, easy to understand and a real bargain at £1.50 ($1.25). It is available from all British Rail Travel Centers. For more detailed planning the *Thomas Cook Continental Timetable* is essential; this is published monthly. Be sure to buy the issue covering the period of your trip as the summer schedules of the European railways are very different to the winter.

The timetable can be bought in the U.S. from *Forsyth Travel Library Dept TCT,* P.O. Box 2975, 9154 West 57th St., Shawnee Mission, KA 66201, or in the U.K. from any branch of Thomas Cook or by post from Thomas Cook, P.O. Box 36, Peterborough, PE 368B.

By car. There is a wide choice of ferry services to Germany from the U.K., and, depending on your final destination, these will generally select themselves (see Ferry Chart).

For destinations in north Germany, the choice is between one of the direct sailings by DFDS/Prins Ferries to Hamburg and one of the shorter North Sea routes. On the direct DFDS route, the ferries are extremely comfortable and offer excellent accommodations and food. The crossing, which takes 21 hours, is from Harwich and operates every other day. On the shorter routes, there are two crossings which are ideal for north Germany and the Rhur, both of them long enough to allow a good night's sleep. These are the Sealink service from Harwich to the Hook of Holland, and the Olau Line service from Sheerness to Vlissingen. Both these Dutch ports have excellent motorway links across Holland. Day sailings are also available. If traveling from northern England, the North Sea Ferries service from Hull to Rotterdam is worth considering, as is the summmer-only DFDS sailing from Newcastle to Esbjerg (Denmark) from where there are good road connections down into Germany.

For access to all regions of Germany, there is a wide range of short cross-Channel routes to Ostend and Zeebruge in Belgium by Townsend Thoresen/R.T.M. joint service and from Ramsgate to Dunkirk by Sally Viking. The crossing times on these routes are around 4½ hours, making them only really suitable for day-crossings. However, the service on these routes has declined markedly, with only two conveniently scheduled daytime sailings to Zeebruge, and three to Ostend. It's best to take a morning crossing and stay overnight in either Holland or Belgium close to the German border. Motorways from both Ostend and Zeebruge are excellent.

Note that the Channel ports of Calais and Boulogne are of limited value for Germany. Their motorway connections are oriented largely toward Paris. Even for Basel and the southwest of Germany, it is best to go via Ostend or Zeebruge and then via Brussels, Luxembourg and Strasbourg.

Fares. Harwich—Hamburg on DFDS with an average car plus driver and one passenger works out from around £200 one way including a cabin.

Harwich—Hook of Holland on Sealink and Sheerness—Vlissingen on Olau work out from around £136 one way, again with an average car, driver and one passenger, including a cabin berth overnight.

Dover or Ramsgate—Ostend, Zeebruge or Dunkirk work out from around £80 one way, again with an average car, driver and one passenger.

Fares may well increase before and during 1989. For latest information, consult your travel agent.

By bus. A wide range of services is operated by a group of companies promoted under the banner of *International Express.* The majority of the routes run by Translines serve the army bases in the northern half of the country. Eurolines run daily throughout the summer to Köln, Frankfurt, and Munich. Leaving London Victoria Coach Station at 7.30 P.M., Köln is reached before 10 A.M. the following morning, and Munich around 7 P.M. that evening. Fares are not cheap at around £100 return to Munich. In the U.K. their details are available from all National Express coach stations and appointed travel agents. In London contact International Express, The Coach Travel Center, 13 Regent St., London SW1Y 4LR (01–439 9368).

CUSTOMS ON ARRIVAL. There are three levels of duty free allowance for people entering Germany. For those entering Germany from outside Europe the allowances are 400 cigarettes or 100 cigars or 500 grams of tobacco; plus, 1 liter of spirits more than 22% proof or 2 liters of spirits less than 22% proof, plus 2 liters of wine; plus, a reasonable quantity of perfume (the Germans are uncharacteristically imprecise as to the definition of "reasonable", but it should not exceed 50 grams of perfume and ¼ liter of toilet water); plus, other goods to the value of DM. 115.

Entering Germany from a country belonging to the EEC, the allowances are 200 cigarettes (300 if not bought in a duty-free shop) or 75 cigars or 400 grams of tobacco; plus, one liter of spirits more than 22% proof (1.5 liters if not bought in a duty-free shop) or three liters of spirits less than 22% proof; plus five liters of wine; plus 75 grams of perfume and one-third of a liter of toilet water; plus, other goods to the value of DM. 780.

For those entering Germany from a European country not belonging to the EEC, the allowances are 200 cigarettes or 50 cigars or 250 grams of tobacco; plus, 1 liter of spirits more than 22% proof or 2 liters less than 22% proof and 2 liters of wine; plus, a reasonable quantity of perfume; plus, other goods to the value of DM. 115.

All tobacco and alcohol allowances are for those of 17 or over. All items intended for personal use may be imported and exported freely. There are no restrictions on the import and export of German currency.

Staying in Germany

HOTELS. The standard of German hotels—from topnotch luxury spots (of which the country has more than its fair share) to the humblest Pension—is generally excellent. Prices are high (see below for details), but not disproportionately so in comparison to other north European countries. But you can nearly always expect courteous and polite service, clean and comfortable rooms and not a little atmosphere. Note, however, that there is no official grading system within the country.

In addition to hotels proper, the country also has numerous *Gasthöfe* or *Gasthäuser,* which are principally country inns but which normally also have rooms; Pensions or *Fremdenheime* (guest houses); and, at the lowest end of the scale, *Zimmer,* meaning, quite simply, rooms, normally in private houses: look for the sign reading *Zimmer frei* or *zu vermieten* on a green background, meaning "to let." A red sign reading *besetzt* means there are no vacancies.

Lists of German hotels are available from the German National Tourist Office and all regional and local tourist offices. (Most hotels have restaurants, but those listed as *Garni* will provide breakfast only). Tourist offices will also make bookings for you at a nominal fee, but may have difficulty doing so after 4 P.M. in the high season and at weekends, so don't leave it too late in the day before looking for your accommodations. (If you do get stuck, ask someone who looks local—a postman, policeman, waitress, etc.—for a *Zimmer zu vermieten* or a *Gasthof;* in rural areas especially you'll find that people are genuinely helpful). A hotel reservation service is also operated by *ADZ,* Beethovenstr. 61, 6000 Frankfurt/Main

(069–740767). They are able to make reservations in any hotel in the country. The reservation fee is DM. 3 per person.

Many major American hotel chains—Hilton, Sheraton, Holiday Inn, Arabella, Canadian Pacific, Ramada, Preferred—have hotels in most larger German cities. Similarly, European chains are well represented.

Prices. Service charges and taxes are automatically included in all quoted room rates. Similarly, Continental breakfast is usually but not always included—larger breakfasts are always extra—so check this before you book. The price system is by no means inflexible, however, and depends very much on supply and demand. Major hotels in large cities can request higher room prices during trade fair and congress periods than, for example, at weekends or when business is quiet. On these "off days," a room that would normally cost DM. 390 a night might only cost you DM. 111 for a weekend arrangement. Also, rooms that are booked after 10 P.M. are usually cheaper on the principle that an occupied room at a reduced rate is better than a vacant one. This is not an advisable alternative during high season, however!

Credit cards. Note also that not all German hotels, and few pensions and the like, accept credit cards, even the major ones. However, both American Express and Visa are usually accepted in city hotels. The letters following hotel entries refer to the credit cards accepted by that establishment: AE–American Express; DC–Diners Club; MC–MasterCard/Access; V–Visa/Barclaycard.

We have divided all the hotels in our listings into four categories: Deluxe (L), Expensive (E), Moderate (M) and Inexpensive (I)—based on price.

Two people in a double room can expect to pay in DM:

	Major Cities and Resorts	Smaller Towns	Small Resorts, Rural Areas
Deluxe (L)	250—450	100—175	———
Expensive (E)	180—250	80—100	70—90
Moderate (M)	120—180	60—80	50—70
Inexpensive (I)	60—120	40—60	30—50

ROMANTIK HOTELS. Among the most delightful places to stay—and eat—in Germany are the aptly-named Romantik Hotels and Restaurants. The Romantik group now have establishments throughout northern Europe (and even a few in the States), including around 60 in Germany itself. All are in atmospheric and historic buildings—an essential precondition of membership—and are personally-run by the owners, with the emphasis on excellent food and service. Prices vary considerably from deluxe to moderate, but in general are not over expensive, particularly for special week-ends and short holidays of three or four days where, for example, half-board (including excellent food) is available at around DM. 225 to 400 per person.

In addition, German Railways offer a special Romantik Hotel Rail program, in conjunction with a German Rail Tourist Ticket giving nine days' unlimited travel. Youdon't need to plan your route in advance, only your first night's accommodations need to be reserved before you leave. The remaining nights can be reserved as you go. The package also includes sightseeing trips, a Rhine/Moselle cruise, bicycle hire, and the like.

A detailed brochure listing all Romantik Hotels and Restaurants is available at $7.50 (including mailing) from *Romantik Hotels Reservations,* P.O. Box 1278, Woodinville, WA 98072 (206–485–6985). For reservations call 800–826–0015.

CASTLE HOTELS. Of comparable interest and value are Germany's Castle Hotels, all privately-owned and run and all overflowing with atmosphere. A number of the simpler ones lack a little in the way of comfort, but the majority are delightful places to stay, with valuable antique furnishings, tennis courts, hunting and fishing. Nearly all are located away from main centers. Prices range from about DM. 50 to 160 per person per night, but average around DM. 60.

The German National Tourist Office issue a *Castle Hotels in Germany* brochure. They, and your travel agent, can also advise on a number of packages available for Castle Hotels, including four to six night tours.

SPAS AND BEAUTY FARMS. Taking the waters in Germany, whether for curing the body or merely beautifying it, has been popular since Roman times. There are around 250 health resorts and mineral springs— the word *Bad* before the name of a place is a sure sign that it's a spa— offering treatments, normally at fairly high prices. Beauty farms in particular, a growth industry if ever there was one, are normally found only in deluxe spa hotels.

There are four main groups of spas and health resorts. The mineral and moorland spas, where treatments are based on natural warm-water springs; those by the sea on the Baltic and North Sea coasts; hydropathic spas, which use an invigorating process developed in the 19th century; and climatic health resorts, which depend on their climates—usually mountainous—for their health-giving properties.

Average cost for three weeks' treatment is from DM. 800 to 2,100; for four weeks', DM. 1,300 to 3,200. This includes board and lodging, doctor's fees, treatments and tax. A complete list of spas, giving full details of their springs and treatments is available from the German National Tourist Office, or from the German Health Resort and Spa Association (*Deutsche Bäderverband*), Schumannstr. 111, 5300 Bonn 1.

SELF-CATERING. Bungalows or apartments (*Ferienwohungen* or *Ferienapartments*), usually accommodating two to eight people, can be rented throughout Germany. Rates are low, with reductions for longer stays. Gas and electricity, and sometimes water, are usually charged extra. There is also normally a charge for linen, though you may also bring your own.

Details of self-catering in all regions of the country are available from the relevant regional and local tourist offices (see *Practical Information* sections for addresses). In addition, the German Automobile Association also issue listings of family holiday apartments; write *ADAC Reisen,* Am Westpark 8, 8000 Munich 70.

FARM VACATIONS. *Urlaub auf dem Bauernhof,* or vacations down on the farm, have increased dramatically in popularity throughout Germany over the past two or three years, and almost every regional tourist office now produces a brochure listing farms in their area offering bed and break-fast, apartments or whole farmhouses to let. The German Agricultural Association (DLG) also produces an illustrated brochure listing over 1,500 farms, all inspected and graded, from the Alps to the North Sea, offering accommodations. It's available for DM. 7.50 (send an international reply coupon if writing from the States) and is available from *DLG Reisedenst, Agratour,* Rüsterstr. 13, D–6000 Frankfurt/Main 1.

CAMPING. Camp sites—some 2,000 in all—are scattered the length and breadth of Germany. The German Camping Club (*DCC,* Mandlstr. 28, D–8000, Munich 40) produces an annual listing of 1,600 sites; this guide, which also includes the whole of Europe, is available at DM. 19.80, and lists details of sites where trailers and mobile homes can be rented. Similarly, the German Automobile Association (see *Self-Catering* above for address) publishes a listing of all camp sites located at Autobahn exits. In addition, the German National Tourist Office publishes a comprehensive and graded listing of camp sites.

Sites are generally open from May to September, though about 400 are open all year round for the very rugged. They tend to get very crowded during the high season, however. Prices range from around DM. 10 to 15 for a car, trailer, and two adults; less for tents. If you want to camp outside a site, you must get permission from the land owner beforehand; ask the police if you can't track him down. Drivers of mobile homes may park for one night only on roadsides and in motorway recreation areas, but may not set up camping equipment.

YOUTH HOSTELS. Germany's youth hostels *(Jugendherbergen)* are probably the most efficient, up-to-date and proportionately numerous of any country in the world. There are some 600 in all, many located in castles that add a touch of romance to otherwise utiliterian accommodations. Other than in Bavaria, where there is an age limit of 27, there are no restrictions on age, though those under 20 take preference when space is limited. You should, however, have an International Youth Hostel card, valid one year, for reduced rates, usually about DM. 3.20 to 4, or, for adults 10.50 and families 20. These are available from the *American Youth Hostels Association,* PO Box 37613, Washington DC 20013, the *Canadian Hostelling Association,* 333 River Rd., Ottawa, Ont. K1L 8H9.

For listings of German youth hostels, contact the *Deutsches Jugendhergerbswerk Hauptverband,* 26 Bülowstr., D–4930 Detmold (05231–74010), or the German National Tourist Office.

RESTAURANTS. The selection of eating places in Germany is extremely varied both in style and price, and there is a broad spectrum of establishments ranging from the simple everyday spot to the highest class of international cuisine. The grandest and smartest spots—and the most expensive—are naturally found principally in cities. Munich, for example, boasts the only 3-star restaurant in Germany, but Köln, Düsseldorf, Frankfurt, Hamburg, Aachen, Wiesbaden and Berlin are close on its heels. But at the opposite end of the scale almost every street has its *Gaststätte,* a sort of combination diner and pub, and every village its *Gasthof,* or inn. The emphasis in both is on the characteristic German preference for *gut bürgerliche Küche,* or good home cooking, with simple but generally delicious food, wholesome rather than sophisticated, at very reasonable prices. These are also places where people meet in the evening for a chat, a beer and a game of cards, so you needn't feel compelled to leave as soon as you have eaten. They normally serve hot meals from 11.30 A.M. to 8.30 or 9 P.M., after which cold snacks are usually available. Interestingly, it's lunch rather than dinner that is the main meal in Germany, a fact reflected in almost universal appearance of a *Tageskarte,* or suggested menu, every lunchtime. And at around DM. 8 to 15 in either a *Gaststätte* or *Gasthof* for soup, a main course and simple dessert (though this is not always offered) it's excellent value. Coffee, however, even in expensive restaurants, is not usually served, and even when it is it's often not particularly good. Go to a cafe after your meal and have your coffee there. Some, though not all, expensive restaurants also offer a *table d'hote* (suggested or special) daily menu. Prices will be much higher than in a *Gaststätte* or *Gasthof,* but considerably cheaper than *à la carte.* In fact, as far as *à la carte* eating in Germany is concerned, there's normally not much difference between lunch and dinner prices.

All restaurants, other than the least expensive, display their menus outside, and all prices on them will include tax and service, so shop around a bit before plumping for the one that takes your fancy. Note that all wine lists also automatically include tax and service in quoted prices.

Credit Cards. The letters following restaurant entries refer to the credit cards the establishment accepts: AE–American Express; DC–Diners Club; MC–MasterCard/Access; V–Visa/Barclaycard. Note that credit cards are by no means universally accepted: check before ordering your meal that your own pieces of plastic are accepted.

Prices. We have divided the restaurants in our lists into three categories: Expensive (E), Moderate (M) and Inexpensive (I). These grades are determined solely by price for a three-course dinner (lunch will be much less).

Approximate prices, per person and excluding drinks, in DM. are:

	Major Cities	*Rural Areas*
Expensive (E)	65 and up	50—75
Moderate (M)	45—65	25—50
Inexpensive (I)	25—45	15—25

Budget Eating Tips. Foreign restaurants. Germany has a vast selection of moderately priced Italian, Greek, Chinese and—largely as a result of the numbers of Yugoslav and Turkish workers in Germany—Balkan restaurants. All are good value, though you may find the Balkan restaurants a little over liberal with the garlic. Italian restaurants are about the most popular of all the specialty restaurants in Germany. Indeed the pizza-to-go is as much a part of the German's diet as *Bratwürst* or the Hamburger. You'll find that Chinese restaurants in particular offer special tourist and lunch menus.

Stand-up snack bars *(Imbiss).* Often on wheels or in pedestrian zones these can be found in almost every busy shopping street, at car parks, railway stations, near markets or outdoor activities and often just on the street corner. They serve Würst (sausages) grilled, roasted or boiled, of every shape and size, and rolls filled with cheese, cold meat or fish, usually accompanied by French fries. Prices range from DM. 3 to DM. 6 per portion.

Department stores *(Kaufhäuser)*. For lunch the restaurants in local department stores are especially recommended. Their meals are wholesome, appetizing and inexpensive. Kaufhof, Karstadt, Horton and Hertie are some names to note, as well as the enormous Ka-De-We in Berlin, particularly famous for its food, and the Kaufmarkt in Munich's suburb of Oberföhring.

Butcher's shops *(Metzgerei)*. These often have a corner serving warm snacks. The Vincenz-Murr chain in Munich and Bavaria have particularly good-value food. Try *Warmer Leberkäs mit Kartoffelsalat,* a typical Bavarian specialty, which is a sort of baked meat loaf (sold per 100 grams) served with sweet mustard and potato salad; or in northern Germany, try *Bouletten,* small hamburgers, or *Currywürst* (sausages in piquant curry sauce).

Fast food. A number of good fast food chains exist all over the country, of which the best are Wienerwald, McDonald's and Wendy's, serving grilled chicken (in the case of Wienerwald) and hamburgers and salads. Also good are the Nordsee fish bars, serving hot and cold fish dishes for lunch.

Picnics. Buy some wine or beer and some cold cuts and rolls *(Brötchen)* from a department store, supermarket or delicatessen and turn lunchtimes into picnics. You'll not only save money, but you'll also be able to enjoy Germany's beautiful scenery. Or leave out the beer and take your picnic to a beer garden, sit down at one of the long wooden tables and order a *Mass* (liter) of beer. You'll quickly strike up conversation with your neighbors.

TIPPING. The service charges on hotel bills suffice, except for bell hops and porters (DM. 2 per bag or service). Whether you tip the hotel concierge depends on whether he or she has given you any special service.

Service charges are included in restaurant bills (listed as *Bedienung*), as well as tax (listed as *MWST*), but it is customary to round up the bill to the nearest mark or give about 5% to the waiter or waitress at the same time as paying the bill. You don't leave it on or under the plate as is customary in the U.S.

In taxis, round the fare up to the nearest full mark as a tip. More is not expected, except of course for special favors or if you have particularly cumbersome or heavy luggage (though you will be charged .50 pfennigs for each piece of luggage anyway).

MAIL. Post offices *(Postamt)* are identified by a yellow sign bearing a post-horn; mail-boxes are also yellow, with the same symbol. Postage stamps can be purchased from vending machines (make sure you have some small change handy) bearing the words *Postwertzeichen* or *Briefmarken* or at the appropriate counter at the post office. At the time of writing (mid-1988) mail costs are as follows, although increases for 1989 are scheduled. Airmail letters to the U.S.A. and Canada cost DM. 1.40, postcards 90 pfennigs. Airmail letters to the U.K. cost 80 pfennigs, postcards 60 pfennigs.

Telegrams. File your telegram at the post office. Charges to New York are DM. 1.20 per word; to London 60 pfennigs a word.

TELEPHONES. As in most European countries the Post Office operates the telephone service. Local phone calls from pay stations (yellow kiosks) cost 20 to 30 pfennigs. Cheap rates on long distance calls within the
Federal Republic operate between 6 P.M. and 8 A.M. and at weekends. Foreign calls can be made from call-boxes bearing the sign *Inlands und Aus-
landsgespräche*. But as you will probably need such a large amount of
small change, it is more convenient to inquire at a post office. Phone calls
from hotels are considerably more expensive (often as much as four times
the normal price).

Newly introduced in Germany are telephone kiosks which can *receive*
calls. They are recognizable by their telephone numbers (Rufnummer)
clearly visible on the outside of the doors, and a sign bearing a ringing
telephone.

To call the operator dial 1188 for local directory information and 00118
for international directory inquiries.

CLOSING TIMES. Shops are generally open from 9.00 to 6 or 6.30
Monday to Friday, and closed on Saturday afternoons (larger department
stores often remain open until 2.00 P.M.) and on Sundays. On the first Saturday of every month shops in large towns stay open all day. Longer hours
may apply at important holiday resorts, and there is a general move to
bring about one late-night shopping evening per week by 1988. At railway
stations in larger cities travel provisions can be bought in the evenings and
over weekends.

All shops and banks close over public holidays. For bank opening hours,
see *Changing Money* under *German Currency*.

ELECTRICITY. In nearly all areas, the voltage is 220, AC current, 50
cycles. Better check before plugging in, however. Transformers to step
down too-high voltage can be bought in special shops everywhere, along
with adaptors for German sockets and plugs, which differ from the American and British varieties. It's always best to take along a battery-operated
razor.

MUSEUMS AND HISTORIC BUILDINGS. There are literally hundreds of museums and galleries in Germany, to be found not only in the
large cities, but also in smaller towns. In addition, nearly every region and
town has a local history collection, *Heimatmuseum*.

The thousands of castles and stately homes often house valuable collections, and are worth seeing just for their romantic exteriors. The churches
and cathedrals bear handsome witness to many bygone architectural
styles.

Most of these sights have an admission charge, sometimes as high as
DM. 8.00. Average prices are DM. 3–3.50. However, many museums and
galleries have free days and also give reductions to children, students and
old-age pensioners. There are also special prices for groups. So it's worth
checking with the local tourist office.

Many museums and galleries are closed on Mondays, and open late
(usually until 9.00 P.M.) on one evening of the week. Opening times are
normally listed in the monthly calendar of events, issued by the tourist
offices of most large towns and cities, so check with the local tourist office.

SPORTS. The Germans are nothing if not sports mad, there is practically no sport, however arcane, except perhaps cricket, that cannot easily be arranged almost anywhere in the country. A good number of sports packages—sail boats, riding, tennis, climbing, walking, horseback riding, to name only a few—are also available. Consult the German National Tourist Office or your travel agent for details. Below, we give details of some of the more popular participant sports. Details of important sporting events are also published every month by regional and local tourist offices.

Fishing. Fishing is available at many locations in Germany, but a permit, valid for one year and costing DM. 10 to 20, from the local authority, is required, as is a local permit to fish in a particular spot. These last are available from the owner of the stretch of water you plan to fish. Details from local tourist offices or from *Verband der Deutschen Sportfischer,* Bahnhofstr. 37, 605 Offenbach.

A number of hotels also have fishing for guests, but you will normally be expected to deliver your catch—if any—to the hotel.

Golf. Golf in Germany is rapidly increasing in popularity and there are growing numbers of courses round the country. Clubs will usually allow non-members to play if they are not too busy; charges will be about DM. 30 during the week, up to DM. 60 at weekends and on public holidays. For information, write the *German Golf Association,* Rheinblickstr. 24, 6202 Wiesbaden Biebrich.

Hiking and mountaineering. Germany's hill and mountain regions have around 132,000 km. (82,000 miles) of marked hiking and mountain-walking tracks. They are administered by regional hiking clubs and, where appropriate, mountaineering groups, all of which are affiliated to the *Verband Deutscher Gebirgs- und Wandervereine e. V.,* (Association of German Mountain and Touring Clubs), Hospitalstrasse 21b, D–7000 Stuttgart 1. They can provide information on routes, hiking paths, overnight accommodations and mountain huts; addresses of individual clubs are also available from local tourist offices.

For specifically alpine walking, contact the *Deutsche Alpenverein* (DAV), Praterinsel 5, D–8000 Munich 22. They administer over 250 mountain huts and about 15,000 km. (9,500 miles) of Alpine paths. In addition, they can provide courses in mountaineering and touring suggestions for routes in both winter and summer. They will admit foreign members.

There are also various mountaineering schools, which offer week long courses ranging from basic techniques for beginners to advanced mountaineering. Contact the *Verband Deutscher Ski- und Bergführer,* Lindenstrasse 16, D-8980 Oberstdorf.

Local tourist offices and sports shops can usually supply details of mountain guides.

Horseback riding. Riding schools and clubs can be found throughout Germany. Rates are generally high and most schools will insist on a minimum standard of competence before allowing novices out. Alternatively, pony treks are available in many parts of the country. Contact the German National Tourist Office or local tourist offices.

Sailing. A wide variety of sailing holidays and possibilities are available throughout Germany. Most North Sea and Baltic resorts and harbors will have either sailing schools or sail boats of varying types to rent. Lake sailing is equally popular, particularly on Chiemsee in Bavaria and Steinhuder

Meer. For details, write *Verband Deutscher Segelschulen,* Graelstr. 45, 44 Münster in Lower Saxony.

In addition, there are large numbers of companies renting motorboats on Germany's principal rivers. Contact the German National Tourist Office.

Swimming. Almost all larger towns and resorts have both openair and indoor pools, the former frequently heated, the latter often with wave or whirlpool machines. In addition, practically all coastal resorts have indoor seawater pools, as well as good, if bracing, beaches. Similarly, all German spas have thermal and mineral water indoor pools. Finally, Bavaria's Alpine lakes and large numbers of manmade lakes elsewhere have marked off swimming and sun bathing areas.

Note that swimming in rivers, especially the larger ones, is not recommended and in some cases is positively forbidden—look for the *Baden Verboten* signs—either because of shipping or pollution, or both.

Remember also that bathing caps are obligatory at all indoor and outdoor pools; if you don't have your own you can hire one. And bear in mind that the Germans are rather given to nudism. Many pools will have special days for nude bathing only and on certain beaches nude bathing is also allowed. Signs reading *FKK* mean nudity is allowed.

Tennis. Courts are available practically everywhere both summer and winter. Local tourist offices will supply details of where to play, charges and how to book, the latter being essential in most areas. Charges vary between DM. 16 to 22 for outdoor courts and DM. 25 to 35 for indoor courts.

Windsurfing. This has become so popular, particularly on the Bavarian lakes, that it has had to be restricted on some beaches as a result of collisions between windsurfers and swimmers. Nonetheless there are still many places where it is possible, and where windsurfers can easily be hired. Lessons, at around DM. 25 per hour, are also generally available. For further information, contact the German National Tourist Office or *VDWS,* Fasserstr. 30, 8120 Weilheim, Oberbayern.

WINTER SPORTS. Southern Bavaria is the big winter sports region, with Garmisch-Partenkirchen, where the Olympic Stadium is located, the best known center. There are also winter sports resorts in the Black Forest, the Harz region, the Bavarian Forest, Rhön Mountains, Fichtelgebirge, Sauerland and the Swabian mountains. From the middle of December to the end of March is the normal skiing season, but at the higher altitudes such as Zugspitze (near Garmisch), you can usually ski from as early as the end of November to as late as the middle of May. There's no need to bring skis with you—you can rent them or buy them on the spot. Look out for the special winter off-season rates *(Weisse Wochen)* offered by most winter sports resorts for cross-country and downhill skiing holidays. Prices include seven days' bed and breakfast (or half-board) plus skiing course.

For cross-country (or *Langlauf*) skiing, which is becoming increasingly popular (the equipment is considerably cheaper and there is no waiting at ski-lifts) as opposed to downhill (or *Alpin*) skiing, there are stretches of prepared tracks (or *Loipen*) to be found in the valleys and foothills of most winter-sports centers as well as in the suburbs of larger towns in Southern Bavaria.

Ski-bobbing is on the increase here. There are runs and schools teaching the sport at Bayrischzell, Berchtesgaden, Garmisch-Partenkirchen, Füssen, and Oberstdorf in the Alps, as well as at Altglashütten, Bernau, and Feldberg in the Black Forest. Ice rinks, many open all year, are prolific.

Getting Around Germany

BY AIR. Germany's internal air network is excellent, with frequent flights linking all major cities. Services are operated by Lufthansa, and Germany's leading charter company, *LTU,* from Dusseldorf, except for flights to Berlin, which are operated by British Airways and Pan Am. In addition, three small airlines operate services between a limited number of northern cities and the East and North Frisian Islands, though many of these flights operate only in the summer. Details of all internal services are available from travel agents.

Lufthansa also run an excellent train, the "Lufthansa Express," linking Düsseldorf, Köln, Bonn and Frankfurt airports and acting as a supplement to existing air services. Only passengers holding air tickets may use the train, but there is no extra charge for it. Service is first class. Moreover, luggage is automatically transferred to your plane on arrival at the airport. German Railways operate a similar service called "Rail-Fly", and trains on the Köln-Munich line stop at Frankfurt airport instead of at Wiesbaden for connections with flights to and from Frankfurt.

Fares. These can be high, but Lufthansa has a wide range of fares on internal services with excellent bargains at off-peak times, such as the *Flieg und Spar* arrangement, and reduced fares for those under 26.

BY TRAIN. German Federal Railways—or D.B. *(Deutsche Bundesbahn)* as it is usually referred to—is one of the most comprehensive rail systems in Europe, and in common with all the rest makes a massive loss! Nonetheless, services are reliable, fast and comfortable.

1985 saw a major reorganization and improvement in the IC network, with increased services and several new inclusive package deals. Further improvements took place in 1987. On the main line passenger service, connecting main towns and cities, there is now a group of six basic Inter City routes—look for the IC logo—and the number of trains traveling daily the length and breadth of Germany has been increased from 156 to 219.

On all the IC routes there is an hourly service and all trains have both first and second class. However, a supplement, currently around DM. 6 (irrespective of distance traveled or whether a change of trains is required) is payable. The service gives excellent connections between IC trains at the main nodal points—Hannover, Dortmund, Köln, Mannhein, Würzburg and Frankfurt Airport—and changing trains couldn't be easier. You only have to cross to the other side of the platform, and if you have reserved your seats the carriage you will board will stop exactly opposite the one you have got off. Before boarding your train look at the notice board on the platform which will show how the train is made up; for example, where the first and second class carriages and buffet car are in the train. Then look for the carriage identification letters (A–E) which hang from the station roof. These show where each pair of carriages will come to a halt, and will also correspond with the carriage letters on your reservation. It is possible to check in your baggage for Frankfurt Airport from any of 52 stations throughout Germany; except on the weekends, there is guaranteed overnight delivery.

If you buy your ticket in advance, the cost of the seat reservation is included in the IC supplement—so think ahead, have a seat and save money!

Rail passengers in possession of a valid round-trip air ticket can buy a *Rail and Fly* ticket for DB trains to major German airports: Hamburg, Bremen, Hannover, Dusseldorf, Köln/Bonn, Saabrucken, Stuttgart, Nürnberg and Munich. The price is around DM.90 second class and DM.140 first class. This includes IC and EC surcharges as well as subway connections.

The IC network is complemented by FD trains *(Fernexpresszüge)*, which are long distance express trains, and D trains *(Schnellzüge)*, which are the ordinary fast trains. On both these types of train a small supplement—currently DM. 5—must be paid if you are traveling under 50 km. (30 miles). No supplements are necessary for traveling on the semi-fast E trains *(Eilzuge)* or the very local services. The moral of the tale is simple: don't use fast trains for short hops and check the type of train you are catching before you get on board!

Fares. At press time (mid-1988), German Federal Railways had just introduced a new fares system under the slogan "the new fares for the new railway." However, the system of special "saver" and "companion" tickets is fiendishly complicated, and is likely to be altered for 1989. Our best advice is to contact the nearest German Rail office for an English language leaflet explaining the system in detail closer to the time of your visit.

A word of warning: in the high season you will frequently encounter lines at ticket offices for seat reservations. Unless you are prepared to board the train without a reserved seat, taking a (slender) chance of a seat being available, the only way to avoid these lines is to make an advance telephone seat reservation, calling the Ticket Office *(Fahrkarten Schalter)* of the rail station from which you plan to depart. Here again, you will probably have to make several attempts before you get through to the Reservations' Section *(Reservierungen–Platzkarten)* but you will then be able to collect your seat ticket from a special counter without having to wait in line.

Tourist Rail Cards. Holders of British Rail Senior Citizens' Rail Cards can now buy an "add on" European Senior Citizens' Rail Card which gives half price rail travel in most European countries—including West Germany. Senior Citizens from other countries who intend staying in Germany for some time may consider buying the D.B. *Senioren Pass.* This is available in two forms: the Senioren Pass "A" gives half price travel for distances over 50 km. (30 miles) from Monday to Saturday for DM. 75, while the Senioren Pass "B" gives half price travel on any day of the week for around DM. 110. Both are valid for a year and can be bought before going to Germany.

There is a wide range of Rail Rover and special offer tickets for West Germany, all of which provide substantial savings. First, if you intend to travel widely in Europe as well as Germany, the Eurail Pass is an unbeatable bargain. It gives unlimited rail travel in 16 European countries (not including the U.K.), as well as discounts on many lake steamers and river boats. However, it is available only to residents of non-European countries and must be purchased before you leave for Europe (contact the German National Tourist Office—see page 1 for addresses—or your travel agent). Costs are $308 for 15 days, $385 for 21 days, $484 for one month, $682 for two months and $836 for three months.

Secondly, for travel within Germany only there is the DB, "Germanrail", Tourist Card. This covers the complete German rail network and the Europabus services along the Romantic Road (Frankfurt, Würzburg, Augsburg, Munich, Füssen) and the Rhine–Moselle line (Frankfurt–Trier). In addition the card entitles you to a reduced fare to cross East Germany and visit West Berlin, with a free coach tour thrown in, and gives you a reduction on the fares of the K.D. Rhine line steamers (on the River Rhine). Costs are around DM 260 for 9 days, and DM 355 for 16 days in second class.

Thirdly, there are the DB Regional Rail Rovers *(Tourenkarten)* which cover some 73 areas, including all the main tourist regions (the Black Forest, Bavaria and the Rhineland etc.). They are excellent value for money and are valid for any 10 days within a 21-day vacation period. Unless you are going to Germany on a holiday run by the railways themselves, the Tourenkarte has to be bought when you arrive in Germany. However, there is one catch: to be eligible you must have traveled at least 250 km. (155 miles) by DB to reach your holiday area (and intend to travel 250 km. on departure). So check distances carefully on your map—it may be worth making a slight detour to qualify!

For young visitors from outside Europe there is the Eurail Youthpass. Conditions are the same as for the Eurailpass, with the following differences: it is available only to those between 12 and 22, or students under 26, is valid for second class travel only and is issued only for periods of one or two months. Costs are $320 for one month and $420 for two months. Secondly, there is the Inter Rail Card. This is valid for one month and gives half-price rail travel in the country in which it is bought and free travel throughout most of the rest of Europe. The card can be purchased by people under 26 and costs around £145. New in 1987 was the *Taschengeld Pass* (literally "Pocket Money Pass") which is issued to children and youngsters between 12 and 17 and allows half-price fares on all DB routes in Germany; cost DM. 40 for one year.

In 1987 an entirely new system of fares was introduced, with special economy fares—Sparpreis and Super-Sparpreis—for many types of journey, and these are excellent value for money. These are available to single travelers, accompanying travelers, and to family groups. However, the system is quite complex; special conditions apply, which are explained in a leaflet available from German Rail.

BY BUS. Germany has a good bus network. A large proportion of services are operated by the railways *(Bahnbus)* and are closely integrated with train services, while on less busy rail lines services are run by buses in off-peak periods—normally mid-day and weekends—and rail tickets are valid on these services. The railways, in the guise of *Deutsche Touring*, also operate the German sections of the Europabus network. Contact *Deutsche Touring*, Am Römerhof 17, 6000-Frankfurt/Main 90, for details. Most other bus services are operated by the Post Office.

One of the best services is provided by the Romantic Road Bus between Würzburg (with connections to and from Frankfurt and Wiesbaden) and Füssen (with connections to and from Munich, Augsburg and Garmisch-Partenkirchen at Echelsbacher Brücke); this is an all-reserved-seats bus with a stewardess and one daily service in each direction, leaving in the morning and arriving in the evening. Details from the German National Tourist Office or local tourist offices.

Urban services exist in all towns of any size and consist for the most part of an interconnecting service of local buses, trams (street-cars), electric railway services (S-Bahn) and sometimes subway services (U-Bahn). Fares vary according to distance, but a ticket usually allows you to transfer freely between the various routes. Some cities issue Rover, or 24-hour, tickets at special rates.

BY BIKE. Information on all aspects of cycling in Germany is available from the *Bund Deutscher Radfahrer* (Association of German Cyclists), Otto Fleck Schneise 4, 6000 Frankfurt 71. There are no formalities governing the importation of bikes into Germany, and no duty is payable. Bikes can also be carried on trains, though *not* on InterCity trains, on purchase of a *Fahrradkarte,* or bicycle ticket. These cost DM. 5 per journey and can be bought at any rail station. Those under 26 with a *Tramper Ticket*—a monthly rover which costs DM. 228—can take their bikes free of charge. Full details in the railway's pamphlet *Fahrrad am Bahnhof.*

Bicycles are also available to rent at over 270 rail stations throughout the country, most of them in Southern Germany, for DM. 10 per day (DM. 5 if you have a rail ticket). They can be returned at any other station.

BY BOAT. River and lake trips are among the most potent delights of a vacation in Germany, nowhere more so than along the Rhine, Germany's longest river. The Rhine may be viewed at a variety of paces: by fast hydrofoil, by express boat, by large sedate motorship or by romantic paddle steamer. For those in a hurry there is a daily hydrofoil service from Düsseldorf right through to Mainz. It is advisable to book in advance for this. For gentler souls there is a wide range of more leisurely cruises. German cruising ships also operate on the Upper Rhine as far as Basel; on the Main between Frankfurt and Mainz; on the Danube to Linz and on to Vienna; on the Europe Canal joining the Main and the Danube; on the Elbe and Weser and their estuaries; on the Inn and Ilz; and on the lakes Ammersee, Chiemsee, Königsee, and Lake Konstanz, as well as on Kiel Fjord.

Eurail passes are valid on the services on the KD Rhineline and on the Moselle between Trier and Koblenz. If you use the fast hydrofoil an excess will have to be paid. DB Tourist Card holders are given a 50% reduction. Happily, standard rail tickets are also accepted by KD Rhineline, so you can go one way by ship and return by train. All you have to do is pay a small surcharge to KD Rhineline and get the ticket endorsed at one of the landing stage offices. But note that you buy the rail ticket first and *then* get it changed.

Ever felt like pampering yourself? KD Rhineline have the package for you. They offer a program of luxury tours ranging from a five-day cruise along the Rhine from Amsterdam to Basel, to a four-day "Four Country Cruise" which visits Amsterdam, Köln, Strasbourg and Basel among other cities, and costs DM. 1,110 first class. On these cruises, extra staff are taken on board to cater for your every need and the food is magnificent! The ships even cruise more slowly to give you more time to appreciate the landscape. The tours can be booked either for the cruise only to fit in with your own program, or as a complete holiday. However, one of the best and most attractive ways of seeing the glories of the Rhine and Mosel is on one of the traditional KD old-time paddle steamers or one of their large modern motor vessels. During the summer there are good services between Bonn and Koblenz and between Koblenz and Birgen; both trips take around five hours.

KD have several budget deals too; for example on Sundays or holidays children between 4 and 14 accompanied by adults pay only DM. 5; half-price for senior citizens on Mondays; free trip if it's your birthday!

German Federal Railways in conjunction with *Fränkische Personenschiffart* also offer through rail and boat trips between Nürnberg and Aschaffenburg (50 km.—30 miles—from Frankfurt). The same company has regular services from Erlangen, Fürth, Furchteim, Bamberg, Würzburg, Wurtheim and Gemünden.

Ferries. During the summer boat and ferry services on and around the North Sea and Baltic coasts are good. For example, there is a daily service between Cuxhaven and Helgoland. A daily service also operates (May–Sept.) from Bremerhaven (Columbus Bahnhof) to Helgoland. To connect with these sailings a through train operates from Hannover to Bremen. The crossing itself takes around 3¼ hours. A faster service, with a cruising time of 2½–3 hours, operates from Bremen to meet this service. There is also a daily sailing between Helgoland and Hornum on the island of Sylt, and Büsum on the coast of Schleswig Holstein. Several other lines connect the East Frisian islands with the mainland. The main services are between Reede, on the island of Borkum, Emden, and Eemshaven in Holland; between Westanleger, on Wangerooge, and Harle, to the north of Wilhelmshaven; and between Norddeich north of Norden and the islands of Juist, Norderney and Baltrum. The islands of Langeoog and Spiekeroog are served by the ports of Bensersiel and Neuharlingersiel. All these mainland ports have rail connections timed to serve the ferries. The North Frisian Islands are equally well served. Westerland on Sylt is served by a railway which crosses a causeway to reach the island. The island of Amrum is best reached via the ferry from Dagebüll which serves the port of Wittdün. There is a private railway from the Federal Rail Station at Niebull to the quayside at Dagebüll.

BY CAR. Entry formalities for motorists are very simple, and only an international car registration and international drivers' license are required, but *not* if your car or your license are from an EEC country or Austria, Norway, Switzerland, Sweden or Portugal. Then, only your domestic license, plus proof of insurance, are required. All foreign cars must have a country sticker and have liability insurance. The green international insurance card is not required; it is, however, advisable.

German roads are generally excellent. All larger roads are both well-maintained and fast, while an endless network of smaller roads makes getting off the beaten track both easy and desirable.

There are three principal automobile clubs: *ADAC (Allegmeiner Deutscher Automobil-Club),* Am Westpark 8, D–8000, Munich 70; *AvD,* Lyonerstr. 16, Frankfurt/Niederrad; *DTC,* Amalienburgstr. 23, Munich 60.

ADAC and AvD operate breakdown trucks on all autobahns, as well as having emergency telephones every 7½ miles. On minor roads, go to the nearest call box and dial 19211, the unified telephone number for local breakdown services. Ask, in English, for "road service assistance," if you have to use the service. Help is free, but all materials have to be paid for.

Scenic routes. Germany boasts 26 specially-designated tourist roads, all covering areas of particular scenic and/or historic interest. The longest is the Deutsche Ferienstrasse, the German Holiday Road, which runs from the Baltic to the Alps, a distance of around 1,715 km. (1,070 miles). The most famous, however, and also the oldest, is the Romantische Strasse, the Romantic Road, that runs from Würzburg in Franconia to Füssen in the Alps, in all around 350 km. (220 miles) through some of the most beautiful sites in Germany.

Among other notable touring routes—all with expressive and descriptive names—are the Grüne Küstenstrasse (Green Coast Road), that follows the North Sea coast from Denmark to Emden; the Burgenstrasse (Castle Road), running from Mannheim to Nürnberg; the Deutsche Weinstrasse (German Wine Road), running through the heartland of German wine country; and the Deutsche Alpenstrasse (German Alpine Road), running the length of the country's southern border. In addition, there many other equally delightful, if less well-known, routes, such as the Märchenstrasse (the Fairytale Road), the Schwarwald Hochstrasse (the Black Forest Mountain Road), and the Deutsche Edelsteinstrasse (German Gem Road).

We give details, and, in the case of the most famous, maps too, of each road in the "By Car" entries of the relevant *Practical Information* sections after every chapter. Similarly, we list addresses of the tourist authorities responsible for each road, all of whom will be happy to supply further information, as well as being able to help with accommodations en route.

Regulations. In built up areas, the speed limit is 50 km.p.h. (30 m.p.h.) while on all other roads except autobahns the limit is 100 km.p.h. (60 m.p.h.). At the time of writing there is no speed limit on the autobahns, a fact that the Germans, among the most aggressive drivers in Europe, take full advantage of. However, there is a recommended limit of 130 km.p.h. (80 m.p.h.).

Note that seat belts must be worn at all times by front *and* back seat passengers.

Fuel. Gasoline (petrol) costs have fluctuated considerably, and at present lie between DM. 1.03 and 1.20 per liter, (roughly equivalent to one U.S. quart), a lower price than in many other European countries. West German fuel contains less lead than is customary elsewhere on the Continent, and it has been found that some elderly cars object to this, but it makes no difference at all to the performance of the newer models. German filling stations are highly competitive, but avoid autobahn filling stations as these are considerably more expensive. Self-service or *SB-Tanken* stations are cheapest. Pumps marked *Bleifrei* contain unleaded petrol.

Conversion chart. If you want to convert from miles (m) into kilometers (km), read from the center column to the right; if from kilometers into miles, from the center column to the left. Example—5 miles = 8 kilometers, 5 kilometers = 3 miles.

m	km		m		km
0.6	1	1.6	37.2	60	96.5
1.2	2	3.2	43.4	70	112.2
1.8	3	4.8	49.7	80	128.7
2.4	4	6.3	55.9	90	144.8
3.1	5	8.0	62.1	100	160.9
3.7	6	9.6	124.2	200	321.8
4.3	7	11.2	186.4	300	482.8
4.9	8	12.8	248.5	400	643.7
5.5	9	14.4	310.6	500	804.6
6.2	10	16.0	372.8	600	965.6
12.4	20	32.1	434.9	700	1,126.5
18.6	30	48.2	497.1	800	1,287.4
24.8	40	64.3	559.2	900	1,448.4
31.0	50	80.4	621.3	1,000	1,609.3

Road gradings. All *autobahns* in the Federal Republic are distinguished from the main roads by the letter "A" followed by the motorway number. Other main roads, *Bundesstrassen,* are preceded by "B." In addition, there is a network of major European highways criss-crossing West Germany, incorporating the autobahns but preceded by "E" for Europaroute. Do not get confused if a particular stretch of autobahn appears with an "E" number. For example, the autobahn A9 (Hof–Munich) is also Europaroute E51/45. Major renumbering of the Europaroutes which took place in 1987 has only added to the confusion—best follow "A" signs for major towns.

CUSTOMS ON RETURNING HOME. If you propose to take on your holiday any *foreign-made* articles, such as cameras, binoculars, expensive timepieces and the like, it is wise to put with your travel documents the receipt from the retailer or some other evidence that the item was bought in your home country. If you bought the article on a previous holiday abroad and have already paid duty on it, carry with you the receipt for this. Otherwise, on returning home, you may be charged duty (for British residents, Value Added Tax as well). In other words, unless you can prove prior possession, foreign-made articles are dutiable *each time* they enter the U.S. The details below are correct as we go to press. It would be wise to check in case of change.

U.S. residents. You may bring in $400 worth of foreign merchandise as gifts or for personal use without having to pay duty, provided you have been out of the country more than 48 hours and provided you have not claimed a similar exemption within the previous 30 days. Every member of the family is entitled to the same exemption, regardless of age, and the exemptions can be pooled.

The $400 figure is based on the fair retail value of the goods in the country where acquired. Included for travelers over the age of 21 are one liter of alcohol, 100 cigars (non-Cuban) and 200 cigarettes. Any amount in excess of those limits will be taxed at the port of entry, and may additionally be taxed in the traveler's home state. Only one bottle of perfume trade-marked in the U.S. may be brought in. You may not bring home meats, fruits, plants, soil or other agricultural items.

Gifts valued at under $50 may be mailed to friends or relatives at home, but nor more than one per day (of receipt) to any one addressee. These gifts must not include perfumes costing more than $5, tobacco or liquor.

Canadian residents. In addition to personal effects, the following articles may be brought in duty free: a maximum of 50 cigars, 200 cigarettes, 2 pounds of tobacco and 40 ounces of liquor, provided these are declared in writing to customs on arrival and accompany the traveler in hand or checked-through baggage. These are included in the basic exemption of $300 a year. Personal gifts should be mailed as "Unsolicited Gift—Value Under $40."

British residents. There are two levels of duty free allowance for people entering the U.K.; one, for goods bought outside the EEC or for goods bought in a duty free shop within the EEC; two, for goods bought in an EEC country but not in a duty free shop.

In the first category you may import duty free: 200 cigarettes or 100 cigarillos or 50 cigars or 250 grams of tobacco (*Note* if you live outside Europe, these allowances are doubled); plus one liter of alcoholic drinks over 22% volume (38.8% proof) or two liters of alcoholic drinks not over 22% volume or fortified or sparkling or still table wine; plus two liters of still table wine; plus 50 grams of perfume; plus nine fluid ounces of toilet water; plus other goods to the value of £32.

In the second category you may import duty free: 300 cigarettes or 150 cigarillos or 75 cigars or 400 grams of tobacco; plus 1½ liters of alcoholic drinks over 22% volume (38.8% proof) or three liters of alcoholic drinks not over 22% volume or fortified or sparkling or still table wine; plus five liters of still table wine; plus 75 grams of perfume; plus 13 fluid ounces of toilet water; plus other goods to the value of £250. (*Note* though it is not classified as an alcoholic drink by EEC countries for Customs' purposes and is thus considered part of the "other goods" allowance, you may not import more than 50 liters of beer).

In addition, no animals or pets of any kind may be brought into the U.K. The penalties for doing so are severe and are strictly enforced; there are *no* exceptions (though if you wish you can make arrangements to have your pet put into six months quarantine—at a price.) Similarly, fresh meats, plants and vegetables, controlled drugs and firearms and ammunition may not be brought into the U.K. There are no restrictions on the import or export of British and foreign currencies.

GERMANY AND THE
GERMANS

The Enjoyment of Success

by
ROBERT TILLEY

*Robert Tilley is a British freelance journalist who has lived and worked
in Germany for over 18 years. He is a regular contributor to the* Sunday
Telegraph *in Britain, and a noted radio journalist in Germany itself. He
is married with four children and today lives in Munich.*

First of all, let's sweep away some popular misconceptions: the Germans
are not militaristic, inflexible or authoritarian, and they do have a sense
of humor. Why else should the West German Army, the *Bundeswehr,*
have recruiting problems, and whence came that anarchic and anti-
authoritarian streak that is unmistakably present in the German character? And why, if humor is absent, is the cabaret tradition so strong, and
political and social satire so trenchant?

Two world wars and an accumulation of superficial comic-book obser-
vations of the German people have created a catalogue of prejudices as
fictitious as any of the Grimm fairy tales. An opinion poll commissioned

in Britain by the mass-circulation German magazine *Stern* found that only 42 percent of those questioned liked the Germans, while 20 percent expressed active dislike. *Stern* organized a similar questionnaire in the United States, where the results were more favorable for the Germans: 71 percent of the polled Americans said they liked the Germans, while only seven percent expressed dislike.

Opinion polls of this nature are an invidious and possibly highly inaccurate affair, of course, and in moving instinctively to the defense of the maligned Germans one runs the risk of being found guilty of the same prejudice and generalization—albeit in reverse. The fact of the matter is that the typical German is an elusive phantom, and that's the way it should be.

Of course, the comic-book, beer-swilling Bavarian in *lederhosen* and climbing boots can be seen in many an Alpine village, but the Berliner would disown him as a representative of the German race. But then at the same time, the tall, elegant Prussian who dominates the Berlin street scene would be regarded as an envoy from another nation when abroad in any town south of the river Main.

North versus South

This north–south division in Germany is almost as perceptible as the fortified frontier that divides the country into two ideological halves. The rivalry between the English and the Scots is schoolboy stuff compared to the hearty animosity separating the Bavarians and the "Prussians."

Like the English–Scottish rivalry, it is rooted in a shared history scarred by internecine quarrels, although the most traumatic event occurred when Prussians and Bavarians were united in one of their many alliances against Austria. The Prussian command reputedly manned the front line with untrained Bavarian peasants, many armed only with pitchforks. Thousands are said to have been slaughtered. "It was a massacre," sighed my Munich taxi driver, tracing the roots of Prussian–Bavarian hostility to this one battle.

Certainly, there are other causes, also rooted in history. The Bavarians are proud that their royal dynasty—the Wittelsbachs—is older than the Prussian house of Hohenzollern, and moreover actually outlasted it. The fact that two of Bavaria's latter-day rulers were insane is smilingly dismissed as a slight deviation in the Wittelsbach line. Indeed the much celebrated insanity of young King Ludwig II is welcomed as *Gluck im Ungluck* (a prevalent German expression meaning "Fortune in misfortune"), for the eccentric king built a collection of castles which bankrupted the Royal purse but which now reap large sums of money in tourist expenditures. Similarly, Ludwig's munificent patronage of Wagner cost the Bavarians dearly in terms of hard cash—but what an investment!

Liquidity Problems

But there are other more visible differences that distinguish the Bavarian from his fellow German to the north or, for that matter, the Berliner from the Rhinelander, and both of these from the Saarlander. You've only got to join them at table to sort out one from another. This applies not only to the food they eat, but above all to their liquid refreshment.

The Berliner really does drink, and apparently enjoy, beer sweetened with fruit juice, and the Bavarian really does quaff what he calls his "hop-juice" from outsize, liter mugs. Each regards the drinking habits of the other with amusement and some distaste. The Rhinelander, on the other hand, is the country's wine connoisseur, and the humblest Rhineland home often hides a cellar full of the finest vintages. At the modest sitting-room table of a Saarland coal-miner's home, I've been served the rarest of *Trockenbeerenauslese* wines, taken from a rack stacked with bottles bearing labels that read like a guide to the best wines of Germany.

But fine as its wine indisputably is, beer is Germany's drink and its emblem. It has more breweries—1,300—than the rest of Western Europe put together, and the tiniest village is often dominated by a massive brewery producing a beer of world-class but consumed only by a small circle of lucky initiates who happen to live there. An English colleague of mine spends blissful holidays touring the country breweries of Bavaria on a bicycle. "I won't live long enough to sample them all," he says, recommending his tour to anyone who wants to get to know Germany and the Germans at close hand; which, in this case, means at eye-level over the foaming rim of a full beer glass.

Of Beer and Beer Gardens

This is the time to put to rest another misconception. The Germans are not the world's greatest beer-drinkers. In Europe alone they lag behind the Belgians and the Czechoslovaks, and in fact they drink less beer than coffee. But beer nonetheless occupies a central role in German popular mythology and culture, and, in Bavaria at any rate, dominates not only social life but working life, too. Crates of beer arrive simultaneously with the bricks at any building site. The employees at my own place of work accumulate enough empty beer bottles to finance a wild annual Christmas party. Doctors prescribe it for hospital patients, Augustinian monks supplement their Lenten diet with it (Munich's *Augustiner* beer is one of Germany's finest), while the award for the best Bavarian brewer recently went to a retiring nun, who produces her excellent brew for her convent!

The beer is not only very good, it is pure, kept that way in Bavaria at least by a strict purity code established nearly five centuries ago by Duke William IV. How long the code will stand is questionable, for the Bavarians are fighting a rearguard action against Common Market bureaucrats who want to standardize German beer with that of other community countries. The rot has already set in, the Bavarians complain, with the replacement of wooden barrels by pressurized containers in the beer gardens and even in the hallowed pavilions of the Munich Oktoberfest. "Is nothing sacred?" sighed my neighbor at a table groaning with the burden of many liter mugs of beer, beneath the shade of a chestnut tree in one of Munich's innumerable beer gardens.

These beer gardens are the center of Bavarian life in the summer months, which in a good year means the long, balmy span between Easter and the first cold snap of October. This is the time to visit Munich, when the velvety southern German nights draw families out, like moths to a candle, to the lantern-hung, throbbing beer gardens. Baskets bursting with home-baked delicacies are emptied onto rough wooden tables, jostling for room with liter mugs and glasses. Join one of these tables and your glass will still be half full by the time you are drawn into the magic circle and invited to share a *Leberkäs* or to try a slice of pungent, white radish. This is the Bavarian at home; there's no need to court an invitation to his house.

The Bavarians, of course, enjoy no monopoly in outdoor delights like these. In Frankfurt, the cider pubs of Sachsenhausen are where to find the city's businessmen on off-duty summer nights; in Berlin the pavement cafes are an extension of the German living-room; while along the Rhine the arrival of the first new wine after the grape harvest is party time for all.

The Seriousness of Pleasure

It's said that the German takes even his pleasures seriously, and the truth of that observation is clear to anyone who watches the people at play. The loving care and attention with which the picnic basket is packed for the beer garden, the studied jollity with which the beer mugs are lifted and clattered against each other in toasts to good health and long life, the frenetic but indefinably well-ordered abandon of Fasching and Carnival revelers; all embody an unmistakable seriousness of purpose.

Fasching, the German carnival period which reaches its peak on the eve of Lent, starts with disciplined precision at the eleventh hour of the eleventh day of the eleventh month. You can't take your pleasures much more seriously than that!

The German carnival not only has a strict calendar but a rigid social framework within which almost anything goes. Staid old hotels open up their ballrooms, which for much of the rest of the year serve as serious conference centers. On the crowded dancefloor business tycoons dressed as tramps bump elbows with bus-drivers passing as princes. At nearby tables office staff on a night out drop convention for a few hours, slip into the *"Du"* form of address and call the boss by his first name. Slipping into the *"Du"* form, by the way, is by no means as straightforward as it sounds; it usually involves a formal ritual in which the two parties drink to each other while entwining their arms in a contortion well-nigh impossible to perform. Perhaps that's the point of the exercise. The night after the ball, the social code will have been restored, the *"Du"* form will have been dusted and put away for another year and colleagues of many years standing will be addressing each other again as *"Sie, Herr Schmidt"* and *"Sie, Frau Braun."*

Fasching, with its centuries of tradition, has accumulated a mythology of its own, and for the sake of the uninitiated at least one of these myths should be laid to rest. It used to be said that no German divorce court judge would recognize a dalliance during Fasching as grounds for ending a marriage, and everybody appears to have a neighbor who knows somebody who knows a married couple who go separate ways at Fasching and never meet up at the same ball. The reality of Fasching is usually less uninhibited, and even the titillating promise of the masked balls of the Saarland and Rhineland, when otherwise retiring ladies are allowed to hunt down eligible men in a Leap Year-like splurge, compressed into the evening hours, rarely yields anything more exciting than a stolen kiss or two.

Christmas and Forests

Before we are tempted to smile indulgently at the well-organized excesses of the German carnival, it should be pointed out that the Germans chuckle at the sublimated Fasching celebrated in the English-speaking world: Christmas. The garish decorations, the mincemeat pies and the funny hats, the parties and the party games—all are as foreign and as forced to the German as Fasching is to the Englishman for whom carnival means a procession of floats through the high street and a marquee on the village green. Although Germany gave the English-speaking world many yuletide traditions—not least the Christmas tree—it kept for itself its own private style of celebrating Christmas.

Christmas in Germany sums up much of the German character and culture, but for the outsider it's difficult to partake of this rite because the Germans celebrate it within a closed circle of family and friends. Those lucky enough to break into this circle cannot fail to be impressed, and even moved by the subdued but perceptible joy which takes hold of a German family on Christmas Eve. German carols are indisputably among the richest and most beautiful of the genre, and to hear them picked out carefully on the keys of a sitting room piano or sung in a snow-swathed town square is an experience that makes a visit to Germany at this time of year particularly worthwhile.

German folk songs of all kinds are a fascinating guide to what for want of a better word must be called the soul of the people. The close identification of the people with the beauty of their homeland is the chief characteristic of the German *Folkslied,* in which can be detected an atavistic fascination with the forests that cover a quarter of the land. The German forest, however, is dying, with one third of its trees probably irreversibly sick, victims of industrial pollution. It's significant that this pernicious threat to the German forest has mobilized the people like no other post-war force and given Europe's own viable, truly ecological political movement, the Greens, a big thrust forward. Walking in the dense, dark forests that wrap themselves around most German cities is a national pastime, which takes on added purpose in the fall when half the population, or so it appears, comb the woodlands for mushrooms. The identification and gathering of mushrooms and their preparation for the table is a very German pursuit, and a delectable one too given the fine mushroom recipes that abound in this part of the world.

Athletics and Aerobics

Walking in the woods, hiking in the hills or over the wild, wide heaths, the German is a very outdoor person. Around 40 percent of all adult Germans claim to participate actively in one sport or another, and Germany's wide variety of climate and terrain ensures a wide choice. As in all leisure-time activities, the German tackles his sport, whether it's the weekend round of golf or the daily bout in the gym, with a seriousness of purpose that takes both enjoyment and success for granted. In East Germany, this approach, exploited by a political system that seeks prestige in physical prowess, has pushed a nation-state of 22 million people into a premier position on the sports fields of the world. In West Germany, it has given impulse to capitalist-minded sports goods manufacturers eager to encourage each new leisure-time craze and not beyond creating one of their own when business flags. West Germans have run athletically through them all: skate-boards, roller-skates, frisbees, jogging and aerobics. Other nations followed the fads as well of course, but none could have devoted so much concentrated energy on each one as the West Germans. Fortunes were made by manufacturers who recognized the potential of the craze early on, and were lost by those who joined in when it was already on the way out.

The big money-spinner these days is cross-country skiing, not really to be dismissed as a fad because the Germans have been skiing along the flat for much longer than the hedonists among them have been racing downhill. But cross-country skiing is now Germany's fastest growing popular sport, both in terms of numbers and sales of equipment. Enthusiasts who once argued among themselves over the ideal length, weight, material and bindings of a pair of downhill skis now debate the optimum characteristics of the cross-country variety. And the manufacturers are only too pleased to join in with the offer of an endless variety of products that change with whim and season.

In summer, cycling is the mass sport, for the health-conscious German has rediscovered the freedom of two wheels. Bicycles far outnumber cars in the major cities, although the preponderance is never very evident, particularly during the rush-hour. Yet official statistics show that 67 percent of West German homes own at least one bicycle, whereas 65 percent have a car. Municipalities throughout the country have reacted to the trend by providing cycle-paths, a refinement of city planning which can hold unexpected perils for the uninitiated. Many of these paths are demarcations of, or extensions of, pedestrian pavements, and woe betide the unwary who strays from one to the other. The German motorist is notoriously aggressive, but he (or she) pales before the livid anger of a cyclist whose rights have been transgressed.

A Home of Your Own

The manufacturers of bicycles and other sports equipment face stiff competition from another rapidly growing industry: gardening tools and furniture, the accessories of a leisure activity that disclose a lot about the longings of the German for a home of his own, and a lot of land around it. "There's no happiness like a home of your own," declares a big building society from the hoarding-hung walls of underground rail stations packed with people who, for the most part, are returning to rented apartments in city blocks and suburbs where private gardens are an expensive privilege. The building society's bid for business has found a response within the German breast, for more and more people are finding the not inconsiderable means to move into their own four walls.

When the German moves into that most precious of possessions, his own home, he moves in to stay. The country's housing market is very static, with little mobility, and the renowned British practice of changing homes like a suit of clothes is regarded as another example of the eccentricities that abound on the other side of the Channel. The German develops an attachment to his home that reaches far deeper than its foundations, possibly because he has not only struggled so hard to put together the required cash but has also lent a hand in its actual construction. There are villages and towns, particularly in industrial and relatively poorer regions of Germany, where the majority of homes have been built by their owners, with some help from friends and relatives. My wife carried bricks for her father at an age when she was scarcely able to carry her satchel to school. In those post-war years, when all Germany resembled a building site, the family home rose floor by floor, from the cellar up, with the family moving into each level as it was completed. The ties that now bind that modest house with those who built it are so strong that just the hint that one day it may have to come under the hammer in public auction is enough to kindle a family quarrel of visceral passions.

All Mod-Cons

It is perhaps significant that the wood most often used by the German householder to furnish his home and panel its walls is oak, that most noble and lasting of forest products. If the real thing is too expensive, veneers and "oak-like" surfaces are accepted, giving baronial bombast to built-in kitchens and the enormous, all-embracing cupboards which dominate so many German living rooms. Not surprisingly, the average German family is well served by the products of the country's advanced electrical and electronics industries (and those, of course, of Japan, Germany's main competitor in this field). Eight out of ten West German kitchens have a washing machine and a refrigerator, and a quarter of them have a dishwasher, too. Only four percent of West German homes are without an electric vacuum-cleaner, while only 12 percent have no telephone. Color televisions are to be found in nearly three quarters of West German homes, while approaching ten percent of West German families have now succumbed to video. Statistics for East German homes are unavailable, but they obviously lag far beyond those on record in the much more prosperous Western half of the divided country.

The increasing accessibility of labor-saving devices in the home and moves within industry to cut the length of the working week to 35 hours are giving the Germans an unprecedented amount of leisure time, and they are putting it to good use, and not only on ski slopes and tennis courts. More people visit museums and art galleries on a weekend than pack the country's soccer stadiums.

Art cinemas, theaters, concert halls and opera houses consistently play to full houses. The serious German cinema, whose pre-war preeminence was smashed by the Nazis, is enjoying a glorious renaissance after the doldrums of the '50s and '60s. Festivals abound, and Munich is now challenging Berlin as the major German film festival city.

Help from Their Friends

So there it is, Germany at work and play. Mostly seen at play, for that is how most visitors experience the country and its customs. But mention of work brings us to one final myth that must be dispelled: the German workaholic is not a national type but an aberration. Individual productivity in industry is certainly among the highest in the world, but it is achieved with the help of the modern plant and technology that arose from the rubble of a devastating war. No open-minded German—and I like to think he represents the majority of the nation—will deny the magnitude of the American contribution to postwar German reconstruction, particularly the aid so wisely and generously channeled through the Marshall Plan. Yet, at the same time, no open-minded non-German should be blind to the role played by individual effort and the ingenuity that springs from necessity. The Germans rebuilt their country as so many of them build their own homes, from the foundations up, with their own hands, and with a lot of help from their friends.

Johann Wolfgang von Goethe
1749-1832

GERMAN HISTORY
AND CULTURE

From Pax Romana to Ostpolitik

For anyone stumbling across Germany's history for the first time, its confusions and complexities can seem legion, frequently well-nigh impossible to unravel. The problem, essentially, is what exactly is meant by "Germany"? The country today, for instance, bears little resemblance to that newly and aggressively united by Bismarck in the 19th century, its borders having shrunk, expanded and then contracted violently in the turbulence of two world wars and the head-on collision of the 20th century's two most malevolent political systems.

Earlier German history may not always have been so violent, but a similarly confused picture emerges. Germany is a country with few natural borders and a language extending across both political and geographical frontiers. As a result, it has almost of necessity remained a somewhat fluid entity. Its story is littered with numerous rulers, both petty and powerful, ruling areas both large and small. In the 9th century for example, much of present day Germany was united under one ruler; in the 18th, when the country had grown enormously, there were more than 300. In the intervening periods, Popes and Emperors, Spaniards and Austrians, Swedes and Frenchmen, Poles and Italians have ruled, or hoped to rule, all or part of this disputed, shifting land.

The regionalism that naturally resulted has remained a central characteristic of the country, and the most casual visitor is likely to be aware
of the sense of passing into another land as you travel from the Rhineland
to Franconia, or Baden to Bavaria, say. If you travel from West to East
Germany, of course, this becomes literally true.

Thus a good deal of German history means two things. One is that it
is the history of various parts of the country, most often quite independent
of one another. Second, it means central European history. France, the
Lowlands, Denmark, Austria, Hungary, Czechoslovakia and Poland have
all at one time or another been united with all or parts of Germany, sometimes peacefully, sometimes not. The resulting story may not always be
easy to follow, but it is certainly not lacking in drama.

From Romans to Romanesque

The four great glaciations of the Pleistocene Age, lasting from about
two and a half million to 10,000 years ago, almost excluded primitive man
from northern Europe. But, by about 5,000 B.C., tribes had begun to settle
in the Rhine and Danube valleys, paving the way for the greater sophistication of the Bronze Age (2,000 to 800 B.C.) and the Iron Age.

Among the most successful of these later Iron-Age peoples were a tribe
from the Salzkammergut, today in Upper Austria, whose prosperity was
based on abundant salt deposits. Their widespread trading brought them
into contact with Greeks and Etruscans, elements of whose cultures they
absorbed, while their mastery of iron in weapon-making enabled them to
dominate less well-armed neighboring tribes. They expanded north to Belgium and east and south through France. By the time prehistory merges
with history, their descendants, mixed with local inhabitants and other
migrants, had become the "barbarians," who were eventually to confront
the Romans.

In this, they were remarkably successful. By the middle of the first century B.C., Julius Caesar had already written off the Germans as a rather
ill-defined group of tribes, no match for the might of Rome's legions. By
9 B.C. this assessment seemed to have been proved accurate as the Romans
under Augustus marched into Germany, reaching the Elbe. Eighteen years
later, however, the Germans inflicted a stunning defeat on the Romans,
who, giving up the unequal struggle, prudently withdrew, establishing a
300-mile-long frontier west of the Rhine that remained the northeastern
border of their Empire for around 300 years.

As the Roman Empire crumbled, besieged by Huns and Visigoths alike,
so its brief presence in Germany faded to no more than a memory. In the
four turbulent centuries that followed, marauding German tribes swept
over what had been the Roman frontier into France, sparking violent and
random warfare between themselves and the Gauls—the Dark Ages with
a vengeance.

The chaos that was Europe in the 7th century A.D., was to undergo a
near miraculous transformation in the next 120 years, ultimately leading
to the foundation of the Germanic Empire. The key figure here was Charlemagne, who by dint of political sophistication and military success, eventually presided over an immense and unified European Empire that
stretched from northern Germany to northern Spain. Charlemagne's
dreams of establishing a second Western Empire, based on that of the Ro-

mans, were realized more completely still by his coronation as Emperor of Rome by the Pope in 800 and the recognition of his Imperial status by the eastern Byzantine Empire.

But to some extent, it is possible to argue that Charlemagne's quite remarkable political and military achievements were overshadowed by the even more extraordinary artistic renaissance he fostered. Charlemagne's passion for learning, spurred on by his companion and tutor Alcuin, sparked an unprecedented interest in the lost classical world. In short, Charlemagne reinstituted the fashion for scholarship. Pre-Romanesque, or Carolingian, architecture was born, based on Byzantine models and adopting from them both the basilica form for buildings and the technology of stone and rounded arch. Exceptionally, however, the cathedral in Aix-la-Chapelle, or Aachen, just inside Belgium, was octagonal in shape. The Byzantine influence is evident too in decorative mosaics and fine stone and ivory carving. In addition, Christian missionaries drawn to Charlemagne's court, presented manuscripts that were copied and illuminated by local scribes. The acanthus leaf, derived from Roman capitals, reappeared as a decorative feature. Two of the finest examples of Carolingian illuminated manuscripts are the *Gospels of Aix* and the *Ada Gospels,* both dating from around 800.

The Carolingian Empire disintegrated on Charlemagne's death, battered by Viking and Magyar invasions, and soon divided into three kingdoms (from west to east, West Francia, Lotharingia and East Francia) by the Treaty of Verdun in 843. The election of Conrad, an Eastern Frank, as King in 911 furthered the breakup of Charlemagne's Empire, alienating the Western Franks, whose history thereafter becomes the history of France. The possession of the central kingdom of Lotharingia, later Lorraine, was henceforth to be the subject of almost permanent dispute between France and Germany.

Within the eastern half of the Empire, which broadly corresponds to much of present-day Germany, local rivalries, carefully manipulated by the ever more powerful church, persisted. Nonetheless, Henry the Saxon, who succeeded Conrad in 918, was able to outmaneuver both the squabbling local rulers and the church and bequeath to his son, Otto I, an Empire of remarkable unity.

Yet the Ottonian Empire presided over by Otto I, despite its new-found strength, was to hold within it the seed of a power struggle of immense proportions, as the Church, ambitious for temporal as well as spiritual authority, attempted to wrest more and more influence away from the Emperors. By granting gifts of land to the German bishops, Otto invested the German church with its first really substantial power. The reforming zeal of the shrewd Cluniac popes of the 11th century, their task simplified after the death of Otto by a succession of less than able Emperors, helped forge ever stronger links between Rome and its German outposts, transforming the Papacy into an international power at the expense of the hapless German Emperors. This power was consolidated when the German Emperors lost first the power to nominate the Pope and then, at the Concordat of Worms in 1122, even the right to nominate German bishops.

But if this period witnessed the erosion of Imperial power, it also saw the establishment of a flourishing and vigorous artistic tradition. Early Romanesque art developed in Germany under the patronage of the Ottonian Emperors. Otto III, like his grandfather, Otto I, entered Charlemagne's tomb at Aachen as if to seek personal inspiration with which to fertilize the flourishing renaissance around him. The center of the Germanic world had by now, under earlier Viking pressure, shifted east and south away from Aachen to Reichenau, Regensberg and Fulda. The maturity of the barbarian tradition of linear ornamentation can be seen in the illuminated manuscripts such as the *Egbert Codex,* produced at Reichenau around 980, and the *Gospels of Otto III* from Munich. In architecture—the other great artistic triumph of the period—the Romanesque produced heavy, monumental buildings, with emphatically-rounded arches and elaborately-carved capitals. St. Michael's in Hildesheim, begun around 1015, is an excellent early example; later examples include all of the great Rhineland cathedrals of Speyer, Trier, Mainz and Worms.

Emperors and Princes

By the middle of the 12th century, the German Emperors' struggles with the Pope had both intensified and shifted to northern Italy, distracting the Emperors from Germany itself. The first Hohenstaufen Emperor, Frederick Barbarossa, for example, who ruled from 1152–1190, made energetic efforts to reassert his authority over the Pope, but these came to little. Humiliated by the Pope in Venice, he died, drowned on the Third Crusade. His grandson Frederick II, crowned Emperor in 1220, paid even less attention to Germany. He grew up and died (1250) in Sicilly—a Hohenstaufen inheritance through his Norman mother Constance—almost a foreigner, although popular, in Germany.

Local princes within Germany, taking advantage of these long periods of Imperial non-interference, enlarged their own estates and increasingly directed the affairs of the rapidly expanding Germany of the 12th and 13th centuries. The Teutonic Knights, a military order founded in Jerusalem in 1128, crossed the Vistula in 1231, so beginning the assimilation of Prussia into the Germanic Empire. The increasing power of the local princes was further strengthened when Charles IV (1347–78) was obliged to concede in 1356 by the terms of the "Golden Bull" the exclusive right of electing the king and Emperor to seven German rulers, or "electors."

Despite the political divisions in the country, Germany nonetheless continued to bloom artistically and intellectually in the 12th and 13th centuries. The Crusades had broadened the horizons of Europe. Frederick II, who had kept a harem in Sicily, was not the only European sympathetic to Islam. One of the best known of the Minnesingers—knight-poets who traveled the Empire singing of knightly love—was Walter von der Vogelweide (c.1160–1230), widely thought of as the father of German lyric poetry: he considered that the Christian, Muslim and Jew worshipped one and the same God. This was the age of chivalry, and the spirituality of Wolfram von Eschenbach's *Parsifal* and the knightly ideals of Godfrey von Strassburg's *Tristan* (c.1210) are its very essence.

Yet, by the 14th century other influences were at work. Merchants returned from the Middle East with new exotic spices, dyes, silks, oils and fruits—and Arab numerals. The ideals of chivalry were soon lost in the new age of international commerce. Prosperous merchants and artisans banded together in *hanses*—associations and guilds—and towns grew rapidly in wealth and population. Lübeck and Hamburg in north Germany agreed in 1241 to protect each other's trading operations and later the

DENMARK

Baltic Sea

North Sea

Hedeby

Holstein

† Lübeck

Altmark

Hamburg

POMERANIA
to Germany 995

Stettin

FRIESLAND

Bremen

† Utrecht

S A X O N Y

Lorraine

R. Weser

▲ Goslar

Lusatia

Meissen

R. Elbe

R. Oder

POLAND

R. Vistula

† Bruges

Ghent †

Aachen

□ Cologne

Brabant
Liège †

LOTHAIRINGIA

Thuringia

▲ Altenburg

† Erfurt

Breslau

Frankfurt

Gelnhausen ▲

Mainz †

R. Main

Egar

† Prague

KINGDOM OF
BOHEMIA

Reims ‡

R. Mosel

Trier ▲

Worms ▲ Würzburg

Kaiserslautern ▲

Metz †

R. Rhine

FRANCONIA

Heidelberg ▲

Trifels ▲ Hohenstaufen ▲

Nuremberg □

Regensburg †

R. Danube

Moravia

Vienna † ‡

Hagenau

FRANCE

Besançon ‡

Alsace

Tübingen □

SWABIA

Augsburg †

▲ Munich

AUSTRIA

Basel □

Zurich □

BAVARIA

† Salzburg

HUNGARY

BURGUNDY

R. Rhone

CARINTHIA

Styria

STYRIA

Lyons †

† Bozen

Trent †

Friuli

‡ Aquileia

Carniola

Fünfkirchen †

Grenoble □

s

P

□ Milan

□ Vicenza

□ Padua

□ Venice

CROATIA

R. Po

Pavia □

KINGDOM OF ITALY

Modena □

† Ferrara

□ Bologna

□ Ravenna

Avignon †

Montpellier ‡

† Arles

Provence

□ Florence

Pisa †

□ Perugia

Siena □

BOSNIA

Adriatic Sea

Corsica

PAPAL
STATES

† Rome

Mediterranean Sea

Sardinia

KINGDOM

OF

SICILY

The Holy Roman Empire 950–1400

- (shaded) Kingdom of Otto I 950
- —— Holy Roman Empire 1100
- (hatched) area lost by 1360
- ▲ Hohenstaufen centres
- † Bishopric by 1400
- ‡ Archbishopric by 1400
- □ University towns

ports of the Hanseatic League they founded grew to dominate trade in the Baltic and North Seas.

A more specifically European influence was that of Gothic architecture, imported from northern France in the 13th century and characterized by the pointed arch and rib vault. St. George's Cathedral in Limburg is still Romanesque on the outside but Gothic inside. Köln Cathedral, begun in 1248 (although completed only in the last century), is both more wholly Gothic and specifically German. St. Elizabeth in Marburg and later "hall" churches—with naves and aisles of equal height—followed. Their rib vaulting and flying buttresses made the massive pillars and arches of the Romanesque redundant. Nave and aisle soared, buttressed walls no longer bore weight but were irradiated by beautiful stained glass. Similarly, sculpture underwent a radical transformation, with free-standing figures emerging from the stonework. The new Gothic style also found expression in military and civil architecture such as the Teutonic Knights' castle at Marienburg and the town halls of Brunswick, Lübeck and Hannover.

Prince and Burghers

By the 15th century, the troubled German Emperors had yet another unhappy problem to confront. Bohemia (modern Czechoslovakia) was in open revolt following the death at the stake of the religious reformer and nationalist John Huss in 1415, surrendered to the Pope by the Emperor Sigismund. It took until 1436 to bring the Bohemians to heel, and then only after a series of crushing defeats. The heretical preaching of Huss was to prove no more than a foretaste of what was to follow, however.

The sale of indulgences by the Church, sins pardoned in return for cash, was now big business, immensely profitable for Rome. Originally designed to finance the Crusades, the money was now used to fund anything and everything, even crusades that never took place. A young Augustinian priest, Martin Luther, rejected this cynical practise as a direct contradiction of the scriptual doctrine of salvation by faith. As Luther opposed the Roman Church, so the Habsburg Emperor Charles V supported it, determined to stamp out the heretical movement. Luther's refusal to recant when they met at the Diet of Worms in 1521 led to his banishment from the Empire. But the Reformation movement, its ideas transmitted rapidly round Europe not least as a result of the new technology of printing, had taken root.

Luther's ideas heartened the peasants, depressed more than ever by the recent reduction of their status to that of slaves within the newly adopted legal framework of Roman law, and their negligible share in the new urban prosperity. They attacked and destroyed hundreds of monasteries and castles. However, their violence alienated Luther and united a well-disciplined army under princely command which routed them. The Swabian League pursued its own private grudge against the peasants, turning the princes' victory into a massacre. More than 100,000 peasants perished and many more were dispossessed. Different reforming sects, however, multiplied everywhere, pouring through the breach in centralized authority so dramatically opened by Luther.

The reformed churches won an important victory in 1526 at the Diet of Spires when Charles V conceded the right of the Lutheran princes to practise their own religions within their own lands. Three years later, however, this was withdrawn, leading to the formal "protest" of the princes, the original Protestants. Their cause advanced with the open support of at least three of the seven Imperial electors and the princes regained the right previously withdrawn, this a severe blow to the power of the civic authorities, at the Peace of Augsburg in 1555 precipitating the abdication of Charles V, entirely frustrated in his attempts to rebuild the Roman church in Germany. On his abdication he divided his empire in two, passing on the Germanic Empire to his brother, Ferdinand I, and Spain and the Low Countries to his son, Philip II, a division that led to a divergence of Austrian and Spanish Habsburg interests. Charles then retired to die in Spain. The princes had gained at the expense of the Empire.

The Reformation was but part of the wider Renaissance, the great revolution of thought and critical re-examination of contemporary standards and values and the position of the individual. The Humanist philosophy of the Renaissance reversed the tortured mysticism of the High Gothic, still very visible in the dramatic figure of the crucified Christ in *The Isenheim Altarpiece* by Grünewald (c.1475–1528), although that painter had been influenced by the latest styles in Italy. Few new churches were built and cathedrals remained unfinished—the rich burghers would no longer pay for them, spending their money instead on the new status symbols of comfortable town houses and prestigious town halls. The domestic architecture of the German Renaissance is essentially an earthy, and much less mystical Gothic. The upward Gothic lift survives in the height of many of the buildings of this period, but is grounded and interrupted by the introduction of the horizontal in ground floor arcades, heavy cornices, jutting dormers and the "compromise" of the gable.

A changing awareness is expressed in the works of poets and painters too, both in their message and in their form. Albrecht Dürer (1471–1528), the first giant of northern European painting, brilliant technical virtuoso and intellectual, returned to Germany from Italy with a new understanding of space, perspective, light and color in painting. Yet he employed these devices in a distinctly north European manner, not least to promote the Reformed churches. His *Four Apostles* relegates St. Peter, symbol of the Roman church, to the background, for instance. Similar concerns influenced Lucas Cranach the Elder (1472–1553), another central figure in the effloresence of painting in 16th-century Germany. He portrayed the Roman church as it was, the Pope with the princes at his feet, and as it should have been, Christ washing his disciples' feet. He too was a busy publisher of Reformation literature and Luther was godfather to one of his children. Cranach painted many religious subjects, but is remembered principally for his development of the full-length portrait and his interest in landscape as a subject worthy of the painter's attention. Altdorfer (1480–1538) shared Cranach's interest in landscape and effectively fathered the northern European tradition of pure landscape painting.

The great philospher Erasmus (1469–1536), perhaps the key figure in the development of Humanism in northern Europe, also took as a starting point opposition to the Roman church, ridiculing it for its corrupt and absurd practises in *The Praise of Folly,* significantly illustrated by Hans Holbein the Younger (c.1498–1543). Holbein's portraits of Erasmus marked his emergence as a major painter and it was through Erasmus that he secured an introduction to Sir Thomas More, the leading English humanist. In 1532, upset by the turmoil of the Reformation, Holbein left

Switzerland permanently for London. His appointment as court painter
to Henry VIII won him a salary of £20 a year and the king even sent him
abroad to paint Anne of Cleves so that he might judge her beauty before
he married her.

The increasing demand for portraits by Emperors, Kings, princes and
rich bourgeois patrons throughout the Renaissance period is a direct reflection of the growing status of the individual. Patrons—Imperial, Royal
or otherwise—were no longer pictured as tiny, pious donors in an Adora-
tion scene but were now the subjects of the paintings. Similarly, figurative
sculpture achieved a new emancipation from architecture. Peter Parler's
self-portrait c.1380 in Prague Cathedral marks a sure step in that struggle
for liberation. Tilmann Riemenschneider (c.1460–1531) left behind the
anonymous medieval collective personality of the earlier, free-standing
Gothic figure, creating instead an exquisite, intensely individual awareness.

The Changing Empire

In the 20 years following Charles V's abdication, Protestantism pros-
pered throughout Germany. Indeed the whole country might well have
become entirely Protestant but for serious divisions among the Protestants
themselves, into followers of Calvin on the one hand, and Luther on the
other, and the determined efforts made by the Roman church—the Counter Reformation—after the Council of Trent (1545–1563) to regain its preeminent position. The new "militant" Roman church, its message carried
principally by the Jesuits, did much to stem the growth of Protestantism,
and was responsible also for the withdrawal of Protestants' rights in many
parts of Germany in the latter part of the 16th century. This in turn provoked the Protestants into forming the Protestant Union in 1608, a move
which in turn provoked the creation of an opposing Holy Catholic League,
headed by Maximilian of Bavaria, whose elder brother was the Jesuit
Archbishop of Köln.

The continuing problems caused by the Reformation dragged on into
the 17th century, culminating in the appalling devastation of the Thirty
Years' War (1618–1648). Ferdinand II—Emperor from 1617—detested
Protestantism as much as Charles V had, and, like the Emperor Sigismund
in the early-15th century, enflamed Bohemian national feeling, persecuting
Bohemian Calvinists. Enraged Bohemian nobles threw two Catholic min-
isters and their secretary from a window of the Hradchin fortress in
Prague (their survival was miraculous according to Catholics but due to
a landing on a dung hill according to Protestants), deposed Ferdinand and
declared the Calvinist Palatinate Elector, Frederick V, King. Maximilian
of Bavaria, a more experienced commander, won a decisive victory over
Frederick, for which he was given the Palatinate in western Germany by
a grateful Emperor, a foolish gift which spread the war to the west.

The Protestant princes stirred at last, enlisting first the aid of King
Christian of Denmark. After his defeat, by the two great military leaders,
Tilly and Wallenstein, they turned to King Gustavus Adolphus of Sweden
for support. The Swede had financial backing from Cardinal Richelieu,
then chief minister of France, who, although no lover of Protestants,
hoped to destroy the power of the Holy Roman Empire, now firmly identified with the Habsburg family. The Swedes fared better than the Danes,

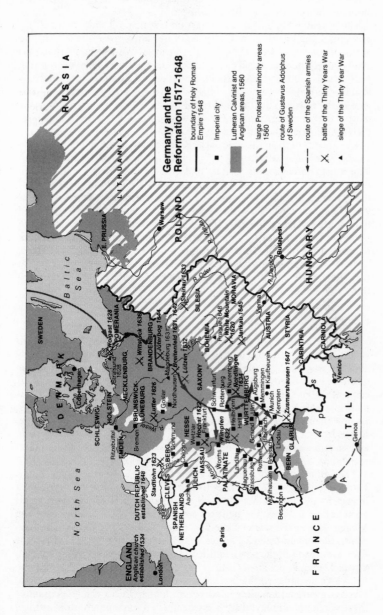

Germany and the Reformation 1517–1648

- —— boundary of Holy Roman Empire 1648
- ■ Imperial city
- Lutheran Calvinist and Anglican areas, 1560
- ⫰ large Protestant minority areas 1560
- → route of Gustavus Adolphus of Sweden
- ⇢ route of the Spanish armies
- ✕ battle of the Thirty Years War
- ▲ siege of the Thirty Year War

reaching Mainz and Worms in the west and Prague in the east, but finally withdrew almost completely from Germany after the death of their king and desertion by their Lutheran armies.

Thirty years of inconclusive warfare on German soil shattered the Empire into a patchwork of well over 300 tiny states, some—mainly in the north—Protestant, some Catholic. The Peace of Westphalia in 1648 that finally ended the war, confirmed the independence of Switzerland and the Netherlands, and granted parts of Pomerania to Sweden, and Alsace to France; the Rhine became the French-German boundary, from the Palatinate in the north to Switzerland in the south. The Habsburgs' hold over most of the surviving German Empire was now only nominal, though their presence in Bohemia, Hungary and Austria was real enough.

The upheavals from the time of the Reformation to the end of the Thirty Years' War had a catastrophic effect on German arts, driving many German artists abroad, some to Italy and others to the Netherlands. Adam Elsheimer (1578–1610) and Johann Liss (1579–1630) both spent most of their working lives in Italy and died there. Elsheimer's paintings such as *The Flight into Egypt* show the results of his experimentation with varied light sources. Georg Flegel (1566–1638) left behind the disturbances of his native Bohemia, settling in Frankfurt, and was the first German painter to concentrate on still-life. Architecture was even more seriously affected, and few buildings of note were constructed until the close of the 17th century, Elias Holl's town hall in Augsburg (1615–1620) being a rare exception.

Baroque and Rococo

If the devastations of the Thirty Years' War had turned Germany into a cultural wasteland, the country was later to witness an astonishing revival of the arts, which in the fields of architecture and, above all, music was to assure her a central, almost dominant role in Europe. The first stirrings came at the end of the 17th century, when the economic and political climate had stabilized sufficently to permit patronage and encourage the arts. By now the Baroque, imported from Italy, had become the dominant style. Being Italian, however, it was generally associated with the Catholic church and was accordingly never popular in the Protestant north of Germany.

The first buildings of significance date from the end of the 17th century. Leopold I (1640–1705), seeking to emulate the grandiose and absolutist monarchy of Louis XIV in France, most particularly as expressed in his great palace at Versailles, built his own Versailles, Schönbrunn palace in Vienna. It was the work of the first major architect of the German Baroque, the Italian-trained Fischer von Erlach (1656–1723). Likewise, the dynastic dreams of the powerful Elector of Saxony provided work for Matthaeus Daniel Poppleman (1662–1736) in Dresden, today in East Germany, where he designed the fantastic Zwinger, which resembles nothing so much as a gargantuan piece of porcelain. Johann Lucas von Hildebrandt's more spacious and playful style, owing much to Italian influences, evident in the Upper Belvedere in Vienna (the roof of the lower hall is supported on the backs of huge crouching giants), looks forward to the exuberance of the Rococo. Hildebrandt (1668–1745) also worked with Balthasar Neumann (1687–1753), the genius of the German Rococo, who was chiefly responsible for the Wurzburg Residenz with its magnificent ceremonial staircase, later decorated by Tiepolo. Of the many churches built by Neumann, that of Vierzehnheiligen near Bamberg in Bavaria, begun in 1743, is his masterpiece combining spatial effects with exquisite decoration.

Further Italian influences are apparent in the wholehearted German adoption of the Italian concept of *unisono*, the ellision, as it were, of the dividing lines between painting, sculpture, decoration and architecture. This is most obvious in the work of the Asam brothers, Egid Quirin (1692–1750) and Cosmas Damian (1686–1739), whose church of St. John Nepomuk in Munich (1733–1746) for example—designed, decorated, painted and even paid for by the Asams—mixes all the arts together in frothy profusion. The Zimmerman brothers, Dominikus (1685–1766) and Johann Baptist (1680–1758) were equally versatile. Their greatest work, Die Wies church in Bavaria, built by Dominikus and painted by Johann Baptist, is both a further example of *unisono* and a highpoint in the story of German Rococo. Andreas Schluter's work marks him as another of the leading Baroque architects, although his court career (1694–1707) in the service of the Elector of Brandenburg terminated prematurely when a water tower he built fell down.

Architects were not the only beneficiaries of royal and princely patronage. Many courts retained the services of musicians and it was at that of Weimar that, in 1708, Johann Sebastian Bach (1685–1750) obtained the post of court organist. He was the greatest musician of the prodigious Bach dynasty, itself synonymous with German musical development. The nature of his output was determined by his employment as organist, chapel-master and cantor, which involved working with the organ, the choir and the small orchestra; his greatest achievements are perhaps his church works, the *Mass in B Minor* and the *Passion according to St. Matthew.* Their scale and tragic grandeur, their representation of the faith and hope of the human spirit transcends Bach's own dour and parochial, if ardent, Protestantism. The lighter, more popular Italian style of *Messiah,* on the other hand, and a wide variety of occasional music and operas reveal George Friederich Handel (1685–1759), a contemporary, who had left Germany for England, as the much more worldly man that he was.

The Rise of Prussia

The artistic triumphs of the first half of the 18th century in Germany belie the fact that politically the period also witnessed a major shift in the balance of power within the Germanic Empire: the gradual erosion of Habsburgs' influence and the growing importance of Prussia.

The Habsburg's hold over Germany had already been loosened by the Treaty of Westphalia in 1648. Weakened further by the Turkish siege of Vienna in 1683 and Louis XIV's attacks on the Rhineland Palatinate in 1702, the Habsburgs then found themselves drawn into what were to become the Wars of Spanish Succession with France, the result of Louis' aggressive moves toward Spain, still integrally linked with the Austrian Habsburgs. Despite Louis' eventual defeat—principally the result of English intervention on the side of the Habsburgs—the Treaty of Utrecht that ended the war in 1713 saw the final separation of the Spanish and Austrian Habsburg Empires. The consequence of this was to turn the attention of the Austrian Habsburgs away from Germany toward their Austrian and Hungarian lands.

The removal of the Habsburgs from the center of the German political arena was the signal for the rise of Prussia. The first act in the long drama that was eventually to see the emergence of Prussia as a European power, however, dates from well before this time, when, in 1415, the then Emperor gave Brandenburg in Prussia to Frederick Hohenzollern. By 1618 this original territory had expanded considerably to include Brandenburg, the Duchies of Prussia and Cleves, and Mark and Ravensburg in the Rhineland. By 1656, Frederick William, the Great Elector, had established full sovereignty over Prussia and had secured Pomerania from the Swedes as well as small estates that almost linked Berlin, his capital, with his properties in the Rhineland.

The next two Hohenzollerns strengthened Prussia further. The first confirmed the dynasty's rising fortunes by crowning himself King Frederick I at Konigsberg. In 1701 the second, the boisterous but dull "Soldier King" Frederick William I, transformed Berlin from the Athens of the north into its Sparta, as his son Frederick was later to write. This same son, later Frederick the Great (ruled 1740–1786), thus inherited from his father a powerfully armed though not yet territorially unified Protestant state organized on wholly military lines.

The future of the Habsburgs, faced with an ever more powerful Prussia, was jeopardized further by the fact that the Emperor Charles VI had no son. His desire to see his daughter Maria Theresa inherit the throne was not easily fulfilled, women being excluded from the succession. The eventual assent of the rest of Europe to the so-called Pragmatic Sanction which paved the way for Maria Theresa to come to the throne in 1740 was to cost Austria dear, however, and lead to a series of conflicts—the Wars of Austrian Succession—which were to result in a further weakening of Austria's influence on German affairs, and a corresponding gain by Prussia. By 1763 in fact, Prussia under Frederick had won large areas of Poland and had secured West Prussia, thereby linking the Duchy of Prussia with Brandenburg.

The Age of Enlightenment

French fashions had come to dominate Europe in the 18th century, and nowhere was this more strongly felt than in Prussia. As a child and young man Frederick the Great had longed to escape the philistine boredom of his father's court and he even planned to run away to France; his plans failed, so he brought France to himself. He devoured French classics, books on art, history, science and politics—speaking French at court and entertaining Voltaire at his palace of Sanssouci at Potsdam, a gem of German Rococo.

The first reaction against the excesses of the Baroque, the frivolity and escapism of the Rococo, and indeed the French themselves, came in the form of neo-Classicism. This style was inspired by discoveries such as those of the ruins of Pompeii and Herculaneum in 1748 and was in large measure guided by the essays on the subject written by the scholar Johann Joachim Winckelmann (1717–1768). The best-known proponent of neo-Classicism in painting was Anton Raffael Mengs (1728–1779). In architecture the revival of classicism came, not surprisingly, in the Protestant north, with the work of Gilly (1772–1800), a French Huguenot.

Frederick's life spanned the age of the *Aufklarung* or "Enlightenment," a period of increasing toleration and liberalism, to which he made not inconsiderable contributions. He abolished torture except for treasonable and other serious offences, the press had never been so free and Catholicism was tolerated in Berlin. German literature too caught the mood: the intense religiosity in the writings of Jakob Bohme (1575–1624) and the black pessimism and distress of Andreas Gryphius (1616–64) became outmoded. Gottfried Wilhelm von Leibniz (1646–1716), the philosopher and physicist, had been instrumental in the foundation of the Berlin Academy whose purpose was to promote "German culture"; Johann Herder (1744–1803) and Heinrich Heine (1797–1825) found new grounds for optimism; and the move away from rationalism started with the deeply felt emotion in the works of Friedrich Gottlieb Klopstock (1724–1803), while the penetrating intelligence and clear thought of Gotthold Ephraim Lessing (1729–81), the playwright and critic, made him the first figure of European stature in modern German literature.

However, it was in the field of music that late-18th-century Germany's contributions to both the Age of Enlightenment and the burgeoning Romantic movement were made most gloriously resonant. Indeed, Germany boasted the three key figures in the development of classical music: Haydn, Mozart and Beethoven.

Josef Haydn (1732–1809), the first great classicist, spent much of his active life as composer and conductor to Prince Eszterhazy in his palace in Eisenstadt. At the age of eight he came to Vienna as one of the Court Choristers, but after his voice broke, he had to spend eight wretched years as a music teacher. He originated chamber music, the string quartet and the sonata and stood as a major paternal figure—Papa Haydn—to his own and succeeding generations of musicians.

Wolfgang Amadeus Mozart (1756–91), who more than any other artist set Baroque Salzburg to music, was composing minuets at five years of age. He was perhaps the most purely inspired of all composers, a genius no superlatives can properly describe. Though he played before the Empress Maria Theresa as a boy, his prolific work was not appreciated by the Austrians (certainly not to the extent it was in Bohemia and England); he died at the tragically early age of 35, and was buried in a pauper's grave, all trace of which was lost forever.

Ludwig van Beethoven (1770–1827) was born in Bonn on the Rhine but lived most of his life in Vienna, where he composed the bulk of his music. Through his numerous compositions, especially through his nine symphonies, Beethoven gradually and increasingly changed into Romantic tonality, entering the Romantic period with a grandeur that many of his successors strove to emulate but few equaled.

Revolution and the Dissolution of Empire

The close attention paid by the Austrian and Prussian monarchs to the early stages of the French Revolution in 1789 changed swiftly to alarm as the republican National Assembly proclaimed the *Declaration of the Rights of Man* and then effectively confiscated land in Alsace still nominally owned by German bishops and princes. The alarm quickened to panic at the arrest of Louis XVI and his wife Marie Antoinette, the Emperor's sister. Monarchy had to be defended, as neither the Emperor nor the Prussian king, enlightened despots though they were, could seriously countenance republican sentiment. The efforts they made to secure the restoration of the French monarchy were as pathetic as were their consequences: Louis and Marie Antoinette lost their heads to the guillotine in 1793. The Germans stood by helplessly while the Revolution deteriorated into the Terror, and their relief at Bonaparte's *coup d'etat* in 1799 was to be short-lived.

Bonaparte continued the revolutionaries' policy of war-mongering and his consecration as Emperor of the French by the Pope in Paris in 1804 signalled quite clearly his intention to substitute a French for a German Empire. Austria, deserted by the Prussians, lost first the crucial battle of Austerlitz (1805) and then the Holy Roman Empire to Napoleon in 1806. His formation of the Rhineland Confederation (under his own presidency) parted the Austrian Empire from her German states; Francis II's abdication as Emperor Elect on 6 August 1806 formally parted the Austrian Empire from her extinct Holy Roman Empire and marked the end of the First Reich. His assumption of the title of Emperor of Austria more accurately described the lands still under Habsburg control.

After crushing Austria, Napoleon turned on Prussia, whom he defeated on the fields of Jena and Auerstadt. The provisions of the Peace of Tilsit (1807) completed Frederick William's humiliation; Prussia was carved up and more than halved in size. But Napoleon fell to his own ambition; his catastrophic Russian campaign was compounded by defeat at the battle of the Nations at Leipzig (1813). The Congress of Vienna (1814–1815), rudely disturbed by Napoleon's return from exile in Elba and final collapse at Waterloo, dismembered the French empire and recreated Prussia and Austria. Some 35 separate free states formed a German Confederation, which met under Metternich's Austrian presidency in Frankfurt.

Liberation and Unity

The great days of French power and influence were over, and the stage was set for the rise of German nationalism in tandem with the Romantic movement, in part a reaction against French classicism and rationalism. Its most influential forerunner was Johann Wolfgang von Goethe (1749–1832), recognized by Europe even before the start of the French Revolution as the literary giant of his age. His early adoption of neo-Classicism led him to the introspection of *Werther,* so seminal in the rebellious *Sturm und Drang* movement of German literature, and his masterpiece, *Faust,* looked back to a Germany of the past. The breadth and depth of his writings mark him as the true "universal" man and perfectly span the passing age of enlightenment and the dawning age of Romanticism. Goethe, passionately anti-Prussian and an admirer of Napoleon, though neither republican nor nationalist in spirit, firmly established a wholly "German" literature. Friedrich Schiller (1759–1805), Goethe's close friend and associate at the court in Weimar, then the literary center of Germany, was more overtly Romantic and is remembered chiefly for his dramas on such popular subjects as *Don Carlos* and *Maria Stuart* (Mary, Queen of Scots).

Much of the art of this period was influenced by an emphasis on the romantic experience of nature, and was linked to that of Germany in the 15th and 16th centuries. The work of a group of painters, mockingly called the Nazarenes, was to influence the English Pre-Raphaelites. This historicism, allied to the rediscovery of the poetry of the medieval Minnesingers, led to the depiction of "heroic pastorals," as in the paintings of Joseph Anton Koch (1768–1839); and the typical visionary quality and somber melancholy are both present in the landscapes of Caspar David Friedrich (1774–1840), the most important Romantic painter of his time.

The recovery of Germany from the Napoleonic wars, exemplified by this upsurge of nationalist feeling transmuted into art, was boosted by Prussia's creation, in 1818, of a customs union, the *Zollverein*, which introduced a trade tariff common to all the different parts of Prussia. It proved such a stimulus to trade and commerce that within 25 years almost all the German states had joined it (the Austrian Empire did not).

Thus Prussia became the natural focus for the tendency towards German unity. Georg Friedrich Hegel (1770–1831), the foremost of her philosophers, viewed history as a dialectic sequence of thesis, antithesis and synthesis and the state as the ultimate expression of reality; he approved of the developments in Prussia. In contrast, the central theme in the pessimistic work of Arthur Schopenhauer (1788–1860) is his perception of the will as evil and yet the guiding force of destiny.

But change was in the air; German Romantic literature bypassed the existential intensity of Johann Holderlin (1770–1843), outgrew the fairy tales of the brothers Grimm and found political expression in the pessimism of Karl Georg Buchner (1813–37) and other radicals agitating for reform following the Paris revolution of 1830. The German Confederation had been hamstrung from the outset, consisting as it did of so many independent states with divergent interests, and paralysed by Metternich (1773–1859) who remained a stubborn defender of Austrian preeminence. The shock waves of the next Paris revolution (1848), which toppled the restored French monarchy, spread quickly to the Confederation, the Austrian Empire and Prussia: the Confederation organized an embryonic parliament; in Vienna, Metternich resigned even as an Austrian constitution was being promulgated; Prince William fled from Berlin to England and Frederick William IV was suitably impressed by the need for a Prussian constitution.

Bismarck (1815–98), premier of Prussia from 1862, prepared from the start for the inevitable struggle for leadership of a German Union with Austria, cynically intent on destroying her. Helped by Napoleon III's championship of Italian nationalism against the Austrians, his creation of a highly efficient army backed up by an expanding arms industry, and the involvement of Austria over the Duchies of Schleswig and Holstein, he forced the Austrians into war and defeated them at Sadowa (1866). With the road to Vienna open, they had no option but to acquiesce in the formation of a north German Confederation under Prussian control. Bismarck was elected chancellor of the *Reichstag*—the parliament of the Confederation—and then cleverly won the remnant of doubting south German states to the cause of unity by provoking war with France (1870). Napoleon III was taken prisoner at the battle of Sedan and the Prussians quickly took Paris; Alsace and Lorraine again became German. William I's proclamation as German Emperor the following year in the palace of Versailles

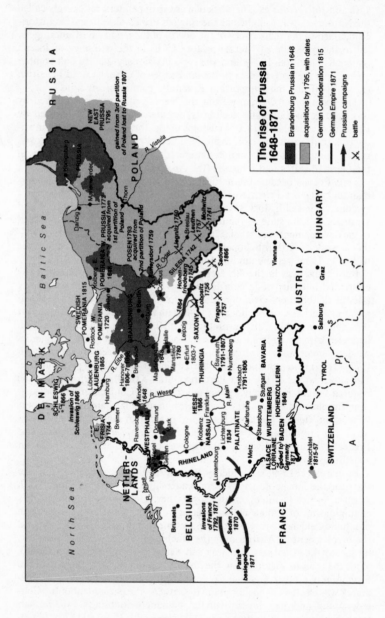

The rise of Prussia 1648-1871

Brandenburg Prussia in 1648

acquisitions by 1795, with dates

German Confederation 1815

German Empire 1871

Prussian campaigns

battle

inaugurated the *Deutsches Reich* and intensified a violent German nationalism. The Second Reich was Hohenzollern and Prussian, where the First
had been Habsburg and Austrian.

This was to be reflected in the arts; the light-heartedness and delicacy
of Franz Schubert (1797–1828), Robert Schumann (1810–56), the peripa-
tetic Felix Mendelssohn (1809–47) and the charming Biedermeier furniture were still the creations of Vienna; but as militarism and the emphasis
on Germany's historic past increased so were these tendencies mirrored
by a new historicism and didactic heaviness in both painting and architecture. While introspection still marks the work of some portraitists, such
as Anselm Feuerbach (1829–1880), the influence of the rediscovered medieval texts became increasingly apparent. The heavy Doric style of the architect Karl-Friedrich Schinkel (1781–1841), Gilly's pupil, evident in the
long colonnades of the Old Museum and the Old Guard House in Berlin,
was replaced by neo-Gothicism. Alfred Rethel (1816–1859) was commissioned to paint a series of frescos depicting the life of Charlemagne for
Aachen Town Hall (left incomplete); the life of Frederick the Great is a
recurring theme in the work of Adolf von Menzel (1815–1905) who was
also commissioned to document contemporary events of propaganda
value.

Nationalism and War

The defeats of both Austria and France were triumphs for Bismarck,
who from his power base in Prussia thus became the architect of German
unity. But to hold this fragile edifice together he had to impose a regime
of "blood and iron," and the constitution he promulgated was little more
than a facade for absolutism. At first, frightened that Catholic loyalties,
aroused by the proclamation of Papal Infallibility in 1869 would kill German unity in its infancy, he launched his *Kulturkampf* against the Catholic
church. The rapid growth of industrialization—in part paid for by repara-
tions from the French—and a new degree of centralized administration
led to the emergence of both a new class of capitalists and an urban prole-
tariat. The latter's awakening political consciousness gave rise to the formation of trade unions, and Bismarck found himself forced to take repres-
sive measures against the Socialists.

Karl Marx (1818–83) and Friedrich Engels (1820–95), the co-authors
of the Communist Party manifesto (1848) had long since fled Germany
for safer foreign parts, having advocated the violent overthrow of the existing social order. Bismarck could, however, do nothing to stem the growth
of the Socialist Party in the Reichstag, and conceded social reforms including the introduction in 1883–4 of national insurance for sickness and accident, and pensions (1889) in the vain hope of stealing the Socialists' fire.

Friedrich Wilhelm Nietzsche (1844–1900) made criticisms of a different
kind: *Also sprach Zarathustra* is a devastating critique of contemporary
bourgeois values and preaches the need for a race of "supermen" capable
of saving and remoulding human civilization. The methods the Nazis used
when they embarked on their solution of society's "evils" would no doubt
have horrified Nietzsche, although they found justification in his work for
acting as they did. Richard Wagner (1813–83) glorified Germany's past
in his massive operatic works while his patron King Ludwig II of Bavaria
lived a fantasy life in his dream castles at Neuschwanstein, Hohenschwan-

gau, Linderhof and Herrenchiemsee. Wagner's *Der Ring des Nibelungen*, based on Germanic myths and legends, has profound moral and political themes, while *Die Meistersinger von Nurnburg* hymns the holiness of German art. Johannes Brahms, (1833–97), the last of the 19th-century classicists, did not compose for the theater. Wagner's methods, though not his preoccupation with legend and politics, found their greatest disciples in Richard Strauss (1864–1969) and the symphonist, Gustav Mahler (1860–1911).

Bismarck, disinclined to liberalize the voting system and faced with growing political discontent at home, turned, like so many before him, to an aggressive foreign policy. He involved the government in the scramble for territory in Africa, previously the concern of private entrepreneurs, and major German colonies were established in southwest and east Africa. He also supported the ever-growing armaments industry and created a powerful navy. These threats aroused the hostility of the French and English, who moved towards a new *entente* with each other.

But by 1890 Bismarck's system had failed, and faced with the alternative of abrogating the constitution, which the Kaiser was unwilling to do, he was forced to resign. He had unified Germany, but left behind him a militaristic regime which had bred, among the working classes, a pacifist reaction, the combination of which were to bring Germany to her knees in the next decades.

Reaction against the middle class and the bourgeois values enshrined by the capitalists was reflected in the works of painters such as Emil Nolde (1867–1956) and Paula Modersohn-Becker (1876–1907), who used violent forms and harsh, discordant colors to portray their view of a corrupt, distorted society. Though they had no stated programme, two groups of painters, *Der Blaue Reiter,* founded by Wassily Kandinsky (1866–1944), and *Die Brucke,* were the leading exponents of pre-war Expressionism.

After several years of unease and mounting tension over crises such as that of Morocco in 1905–06, when war had been narrowly averted, flashpoint was reached in the Balkans. There Prussia found it in German interests to support Austria as a bulwark against the Russians, and there Austria knew Germany would bear the brunt of any fighting that resulted from attempts to quell the rebellious Slavs. The assassination of the Archduke Franz Ferdinand and his wife at Sarajevo on 28 June 1914 was the trigger for a war that was to embroil Europe for the next four years.

Austria declared war on 28 July; Germany, in the first two days of August, occupied Luxemburg and entered Belgium. France and England mobilized and declared war on 4 August, and general hostilities broke out. But the French, standing firm at the battle of the Marne, frustrated German expectations of rapid victory, and a terrible war of attrition followed, with both German and Allied troops entrenched, and dying in their hundreds of thousands. The entry of the Americans on the side of the Allies in 1917, together with growing unrest within Germany herself, led to the termination of the war in 1918, leaving the Second Reich defeated and disillusioned.

The revolutionary tendencies in Germany, endemic since 1848 and left unresolved by Bismarck, were now aggravated, despite the promises held out by President Wilson's "Fourteen Points," by the ill-judged peace terms and their application by the Allies and by the absence of any German statesmen of stature. Civil war, fired by the mutiny of the navy at Kiel in 1919, raged for three months. The Weimar Republic was proclaimed by the Social Democrats, in the city of Goethe and Schiller, after the abdication of the Kaiser, but it became more and more preoccupied with the maintenance of law and order at the expense of real reform.

Economic collapse, leading to hyper-inflation, combined with fear of Russian-inspired bolshevism, resulted in a series of coalition governments of the center-right. The drastic financial reforms of Schacht encouraged a new flow of foreign investment, and this helped stabilize German politics between 1924 and 1929. In 1926 Germany joined the League of Nations but the death of the foreign minister, Stresemann, who had brought this about, the great recession, and then the Wall Street crash of 1929 were disasters on the road to World War II.

The arts moved away from Expressionism to a new Realism in keeping with the times. Max Beckmann (1884–1969) and Otto Dix (1891–1960) were the dominant painters of the *Neue Sachlichkeit* (New Objectivity), which was virtually co-terminous with the Weimar Republic. The frenetic life of a society knowing itself to be on the edge of calamity was reflected in the savage satires of George Grosz (1893–1969) and in the doom-laden music of Kurt Weill (1900–50).

The slump and inflation had ruined the middle classes and by 1933 one man in three was out of work. Then an instant solution to the country's ills was offered by way of nationalism, militarism and anti-semitism, by Adolf Hitler, a demagogue of compelling power, who by joining the National Socialist party was to bring it from insignificance to the preeminent political force in Germany. His success had not been without difficulty; his *putsch* at Munich in 1923 had failed and he spent some time in prison, where he wrote the blueprint for Nazism, *Mein Kampf*. It was not until after 1929 that he and his party gained real support. Although he became Chancellor in 1933 by constitutional means, his rise to power was achieved by a mixture of brilliant propaganda, specious promises, violence and intimidation which effectively silenced all opposition, including that of the Communists.

In the following years, by draconian measures—close control of the economy, and a massive program of rearmament—he achieved the revival so necessary to Germany's recovery. But it was a recovery brought about at untold human cost, for, hand-in-hand with his economic measures, he put vicious concepts of racial purity into practice, creating death, misery and exile on a hitherto unbelievable scale. The nightmare of the Holocaust had arrived to haunt the world.

In 1936 Hitler marched his troops into the Rhineland, demilitarized under the Treaty of Versailles. His alliances with Mussolini in Italy and with the Japanese, and his support for General Franco in the Spanish civil war, led some elements in France and England to recognize the same situation as in the years before World War I.

The tension and fear of war created by the re-militarization of the Rhineland and the annexation of Austria (the *Anschluss*) were temporarily and partially dispersed by the Munich agreement signed by Hitler and Neville Chamberlain in September 1938. There remained many in England and France who were totally opposed to the agreement and the price paid for peace in the dismemberment of Czechoslovakia. There has been much controversy since about whether Germany or the Allies put the few months of preparation between the outbreak of war in September 1939 to better use, and whether when it came to the point, Hitler would have been willing to risk war in 1938.

Hitler rounded off his diplomatic *blitzkrieg* by signing a pact with Soviet Russia in August 1939, thus ensuring that Germany would not have to fight the now inevitable war on two fronts. This alliance with a long-despised regime confounded foreign apologists for communism and fascism alike, but ideology regained the upper hand in June 1941 when Germany invaded Soviet Russia.

Meanwhile, fresh from his triumph in Czechoslovakia, Hitler advanced on Poland in September 1939, but this time the Allies did not hesitate and in line with the guarantees given to Poland, declared war. The swift advance to the North Sea of German mechanized (Panzer) divisions overwhelmed the ill-prepared Allied armies; the British were compelled to evacuate the remains of their expeditionary force from the beaches of Dunkirk and the French to submit to the installation of a puppet government in Vichy while Hitler paraded victorious through the streets of Paris.

Convinced that Britain, now alone, could not last long, Hitler recklessly turned on Soviet Russia, at first with a success comparable to that gained in the west. But with the entry of the United States into the war following the Japanese attack on Pearl Harbor in December 1941, Allied war supplies to Russia enabled the Russians to counterattack at the gates of Stalingrad as well as laying the material foundations for the Allies' own initiatives in North Africa, Sicily, Italy, and, finally in June 1944, for D-day and the invasion of Europe.

The three victorious powers met at the Yalta conference but the reunification of Germany there envisaged never came about owing to the failure of the occupying powers (the U.S.A., the U.S.S.R., Great Britain and France) to agree. Crisis point came in 1948 when Russia attempted by blockade to exclude the other three allies from their agreed zones in Berlin, geographically isolated in the middle of the Soviet zone, but was frustrated by a massive allied airlift.

Realities were faced in 1949 when the Federal Republic, West Germany, was proclaimed in May with its seat in Bonn, while the Soviet-occupied zone, East Germany, was named as the German Democratic Republic.

Under the chancellorship of the veteran Rhineland politician Konrad Adenauer and his finance minister Ludwig Erhardt, West Germany made astonishingly rapid economic progress. Currency reform following the collapse of 1945–6, the infusion of large sums of American aid under the Marshall plan, and a plentiful supply of skilled labor boosted by the influx of refugees from the east (only halted finally in 1961 by the erection of the Berlin Wall) together with the astutely *laissez-faire* policies of Erhardt had already by 1950 brought German industrial production back to the level of 1938.

The Federal constitution gives carefully defined powers to the Landtags, the local governments of the ten *Lander* into which the state is divided and which send representatives to the Bundestag in Bonn, to whom both the chancellor, in effect prime minister, and the president, who is head of state, are responsible. The occupying powers, having satisfied themselves that the mistakes of the Treaty of Versailles had been avoided, agreed to Germany's being declared a sovereign state in 1955. In 1958 she became a founder-member of the Common Market (the EEC) and in 1973, joined the United Nations.

The West German economic miracle *(Wirtschaftswunder)* continued to gather pace over these 15 years, until the onset of world recession in 1973 overtook a country enjoying unprecedented prosperity and arguably once more—at least in economic terms—the most powerful in Europe. The inhibitions imposed by recent history had kept Germany, though an economic giant, a political pygmy. But the *entente* within the EEC between Adenauer and President de Gaulle and the improvement after 1969 in relations with the East brought about by Chancellor Willy Brandt have increasingly ensured that modern Germany has begun, since the recovery of 1974–5, to punch its weight in world politics.

EATING IN GERMANY

A Guide to German Food

There's just no getting around the fact that the staple diet of practically the entire German nation revolves around starch. In fact, that's just the starting point. Combine the two words "food" and "German" and immediately a splendid caricature of a red-faced, knee-slapping, endomorphic specimen tucking into a giant sized plate of *Eisbein mit Sauerkraut,* frothing stein of beer close at hand, leaps to mind. One has only to realize that there are 200 different types of bread alone baked in Germany—most of it delicious, by the way—or to consider the veritable tons of *Knödel* (dumplings) consumed in Bavaria, swimming in gravy and accompanying the obligatory *Sonntagsbraten,* or Sunday roast, and it doesn't take too long to begin to feel that perhaps our jovial German isn't such a cliche. Similarly, the predominance of thick, rich soups, the platefuls of pasta, the many hundreds of different cakes and pastries, and the beer—above all perhaps, the beer—all seem to point to the fact that the guzzling German is not such a mythical figure after all.

Unfortunately, however, he is. Up to a point anyway. German food if it is anything is unquestionably *deftig,* literally "heavy." But the Germans today are probably every bit as health-conscious as their counterparts in California. The statistics show that every third German has an almost fanatical dedication to some species of *Diät,* or diet, while sports and every type of fitness and body-care facility under the sun abound. You have only to step onto a tennis court or go to a swimming pool in Germany to realise that the all-so-obvious evidence of a surfeit of bread, *Knödel* and beer is generally not on show.

So what then do the Germans eat? The immediate answer is certainly not as much as most visitors imagine, or indeed eat themselves while in Germany. But, beyond this simple fact, the question becomes much harder to answer than one might at first sight imagine.

The basic complication is that German cuisine as such does not really exist. That is, there is no readily identifiable body of cooking in Germany that one can point to and confidently label as such, unlike French cuisine, for example, or Italian. There are, it is true, certain general characteristics that can be indentified, particularly the emphasis on starch. But for the most part German cooking consists of an amalgam of regional dishes that are not generally found outside their own areas. Of course you will find specialty restaurants throughout the country that serve dishes from other regions, much as you might find a Chinese restaurant in Italy or even an English restaurant in France. And it's important also to realize that many regional dishes represent no more than local variants of foods found in other parts of Germany. Yet for the most part, it has to be admitted that German cuisine as such does not really exist.

Say It with Sausages

There is, however, one very important exception. It may not quite rate with the soufflé or *turbot à la reine* in terms of delicacy, finesse or sophistication, but it *is* found all over Germany. This is the sausage, the ambassador of German cooking and the one universal foodstuff over which the Germans can claim undisputed mastery.

The most famous German sausage is the Frankfurter, found throughout the world and so well-known that it is doubtful whether more than a tiny percentage of the hundreds of thousands who eat them daily pause to think that its name derives from the city where they originated. Frankfurt sausages should be cooked in hot water, but must never be boiled, only allowed to cook through gently. They are then eaten with bread and mustard or horseradish. A smaller variety of the Frankfurter found in southern Germany and made from identical ingredients is called, perversely, a *Wienerwurst*. In the U.S. and Britain they are known as Wieners or Vienna sausages, while in Austria itself they're known as frankfurters!

A quick lunchtime snack in Bavaria is *Ein Paar Wiener mit Kartofelsalat,* which means a "pair" of Wienerwurst sausages. These are sold only in multiples of two: "ein Paar, dwei Paar, drei Paar" and so on. Anyone who asks for them in any other way immediately identifies himself as either a foreigner or a "Prussian."

The number and variety of other types of German sausage are immense. There is *Fleischwurst, Gelbwurst, Rindsbratwurst,* and *Wollwurst,* not to mention the typical Munich specialty, *Weisswurst,* a delicate white sausage made from veal, calves' brains and spleen, and traditionally eaten only between midnight and noon. Small wonder that it's a favorite breakfast for Carnival revelers returning home in the early hours after a *Faschingsfest.* Everyone has heard of *Leberwurst;* it is a specialty of Hesse (they call it *Zeppelinwurst* in Frankfurt). *Nürnberger Bratwurst,* the pork sausage of Nürnberg, usually served fried or, better still, grilled, is similarly famous, so much so in fact that you will find restaurants all over the country called

Bratwurststube that specialize in them. A favorite between-meal snack in Mainz is *Weck, Worscht und Wein,* a roll, sausage and wine. Coburg serves sausages roasted; Soest in Westphalia bakes them in dough. Westphalia is the place for *Rinderwurst* and *Blutwurst,* beef sausage and blood sausage (which unappetizing as it may sound is really very tasty). The *Bouillon-wurst* of Hannover is served with mustard and horseradish; *Milzwurst,* a spleen sausage found along the Danube, is very good sliced and fried in golden breadcrumbs. Stuttgart has the *Saiten,* a juicy sausage served with lentils. Braunschweig has a whole army of sausage specialties. This is the city that gave cervelat sausage to the world, along with *Mettwurst* and *Knackwurst.*

But, as we say, the sausage aside, German cooking really means regional cooking. So the best and most convenient way to arrange our overview of German food is by region.

Bavaria

Our gastronomic tour begins in Bavaria. Traditionally a poor area of the country, the Bavarians have always taken pride in using simple ingredients and making them decidedly appetizing. The best known example of this labor of love is the dumpling, a humble dish raised to something approaching an art form. The array of dumplings is positively stupendous. The basic dumpling is the *Kartoffelknödel* or *Kartoffelkloss,* the classic version of which is made from roughly one-third boiled potatoes and two-thirds raw potatoes. But in addition there are also *Leber-* (liver), *Semmel-* (bread), *Böhmische-* (dough) and *Speck-* (bacon) dumplings, the last two having their origins in Czechoslovakia and the Austrian Tyrol respectively. The dumpling is most often served with *Schweinebraten,* roast pork, which all Germans love, though perhaps none more so than the Bavarians. Also popular in Bavaria is *Schweinshax'n,* roast knuckle of pork, and *Kal-bshax'n,* veal shank, both of which are served with dumplings—of course—or potato salad. Other Bavarian specialties include *Leberkäs,* pork roast loaf, particularly popular in Munich and served piping hot like *Weisswurst* with sweet mustard and crisp pretzels or rolls. The natural accompaniment to all these dishes, needless to say, is a large glass of cold beer.

Before leaving central southern Bavaria, a mention should also be made of the excellent trout, *Forelle,* most usually caught in mountain rivers, the freshwater salmon-trout, *Lachsforelle, Bachsaibling* found throughout upper Bavaria, and the Chiemsee *Renke,* a type of whitefish from the Chiemsee.

Among East Bavarian specialties that shouldn't be missed is the *Regens-burger,* a short, thick, spicy sausage made in Regensburg and comparable to Nürnberg's famous *Bratwurst.* (Like them, they should be grilled.) Another local sausage specialty is the *Bauernseufzer,* the "farmer's sigh," which hails from Amberg. The Danube also provides a number of tasty fish, among them the *Donawaller,* or Danube sheatfish, served *blau* (boiled) or *gebacken* (breaded and fried). Carp, or *Karpfen,* are found in abundance in Tirschenreuth, slightly farther to the north. East Bavaria also boasts a fine radish, the *Weichser Rettiche,* again best when washed down with the good locally-produced beers.

Passing westwards across Southern Bavaria and heading into the Allgäu, you'll find that cows and cheese are as integral a part of the region as mountains and meadows. Surprisingly, the art of cheesemaking in the Allgäu does not date back all that far, only about 150 years when an enterprising Allgäuer brought the secret of the famous Swiss cheeses to the region, subsequently called *Allgäuer Emmantal.* Kempten, the capital of the Allgäu, is the home of the Cheese Exchange *(Käsebörse),* and in numerous cheese dairies, or *Käskuchä,* you can watch top cheese-masters at work. Another Allgäuer import, introduced to the region by French soldiers, is *Böfflamott,* a German corruption of *Boeuf à la mode.* It's a form of marinated beef casserole cooked in red wine and lemon, served with lettuce and potatoes. A genuinely local Allgäu dish, both popular and delicious, is *Kässpatzen,* cheese noodles; not recommended for those on a stricter *diät,* however.

Continuing westwards again toward Bodensee, or Lake Constance, you'll find that fish specialties top the list. There are 35 different types of fish in the lake, the *Felchen* being the most highly prized. It belongs to the salmon family and is best eaten *blau* (poached) in rosemary sauce or baked in almonds *(Müllerin)* and accompanied by a top quality Meersburg white wine.

Swabia and Franconia

We are now in Swabia, the land of the *Pfannkuchen* and the *Spätzle,* both flour-and-egg dishes, and both essentially rather thrifty dishes, as is only appropriate to a region known for its economizing inhabitants. Hence the various noodle dishes. *Pfannkuchen,* pancakes, are generally filled with meat, cheese, jam, or sultanas, or chopped into fine strips and scattered in a clear consommé soup known as *Flädlesupp. Spätzle,* golden-yellow egg noodles, are the usual accompaniment for the Swabian Sunday roast beef lunch of *Riderbraten.* Perhaps one of the best known dishes is the Swabian version of ravioli, *Maultaschen,* again usually served floating in a broth strewn with chives.

Everyone has probably heard of the delicious Black Forest Cherry cake, *Schwarzwälderkirschtorte,* and certainly at some time or another have sampled the *Kirschwasser,* Black Forest cherry brandy. Locally it is called *Chriesewässerle,* which comes from the French *cerise* (cherry), proof of the region's culinary affinity with nearby France. The region also has a number of excellent brandies, or *Schnaps,* made from plums, raspberries and pears, all identified by the name *Schwarzwälder,* followed by the kind of fruit "water" *(Wasser).*

But the inhabitants of the Black Forest don't just eat cake and drink *Schnaps.* They also have delicious smoked bacon or *Speck* known as *Schwarzwaldgeräuchertes,* the genuine article being smoked over Black Forest fir cones. This, together with a hearty chunk of farmhouse bread and a glass of chilled white wine, constitutes the local farmers' "second breakfast" (served at around 9 A.M.!) and known as *z'Nuni.*

Heading northeast towards Franconia, a visit to Würzburg must, necessarily, put wine before food. The delicious dry white wines from the river Main in their specially-shaped bulbous green bottles known as *Bocksbeutel* number among the finest in Germany. The people of Franconia like good, strong food so plain homely fare is much in demand. *Schlachtplatte* consists of several types of fresh sausages, meat and *Leberwurst,* and it may be served with *Fränkische Klösse*—yet another type of dumpling. *Bamberger Krautbraten* is a white cabbage stuffed with meat filling, served with—you guessed it—potato dumplings and washed down with a glass of good Franconian beer such as *Kulmbacher* or the smokey *Rauchbier* from Bamberg.

Central Germany

Proceeding northwest, we enter Hesse. Although the region has no local specialties as such, fine dishes are made with simple ingredients such as bacon, pork, potatoes, turnips, leeks, apples or pears. *Weckewerk,* for example, is pork mixed with softened bread-rolls and baked in a mould, while *Sulperknocken* is made from pickled and boiled pigs' ears and trotters served with sauerkraut and a puree of green peas. And you really cannot say you have been to Hesse, or indeed to nearby Mainz as well, without trying the *Hankäs mit Musik. Handkäs* is a Mainz cheese, which is round and rather waxlike in appearance. It should only be eaten when fully ripened, the ripe cheese being distinguished principally by its extreme smelliness. In the Rheingau it is eaten with potatoes in their jackets, and in Rheinhesse it is accompanied by white wine from the local vineyards. The *Musik* is a liberal portion of sliced onions in a mixture of oil and vinegar which is poured over the cheese.

The Saarland borders directly onto France, giving rise to a distinct French influence on Saarland cuisine. However, while the region's very high standard of cooking is undeniable—the number of three-star restaurants makes this only too clear—Saarland haute cuisine should not be confused with everyday Saarland specialties, most of which are based on potatoes. In addition, Saarland also produces excellent cider made from wild apples and pears shaken from the trees, traditionally drunk with *Stinkes,* an exceedingly aptly-named Limburg cheese served with onions that outdoes even the *Hankäs* for sheer odor impact.

Higher up in the Palatinate, the people are reputed to have a particular weakness for sausage—even more so than other Germans—the herb-flavored *Pfälzer* being a special favorite. The basic reason for this sausage mania is believed to be that sausages are an excellent way of building up a thirst, the Palatinate being of course one of the very best wine-producing areas of Germany. The ideal combination of wine and sausage is found at the annual *Dürkheimer Wurstmarkt* (Dürkheim Sausage Fair) held each September.

Entering the Rhineland, look out for *Hase im Topf,* a delicious and highly-flavored rabbit pâté made with port, Madeira, brandy and red wine, baked for hours in an earthenware pot. A specialty of the Lower Rhineland and the Bergisch Land is *Panhas,* a meat paste prepared with sausage gravy, blood and buckwheat meal.

But it is Rhenish pickled beef, or *Sauerbraten,* one of the most popular dishes in Germany, that is perhaps best known of all the Rhineland specialties. It's marinated for at least three days in spiced vinegar, then simmered in red wine. Traditional accompaniments are stewed apples, Brussel sprouts, or *Rotkohl* (red cabbage), plus *Knödel*—dumplings—and local beer.

Continuing on again, be on the look-out for Westphalian ham, famous for more than 2,000 years. The hams can weigh as much as 33 pounds and are considered particularly good for breakfast, when a huge slice is served on a wooden board with rich, dark pumpernickel bread baked for 20 hours (and tasting considerably better than its reputation), and, for the sturdy, a glass of strong, clear *Steinhäger Schnaps.* A favorite main course is *Pfefferpothast,* a sort of goulash with lots of pepper and heavily browned. The "hast" at the end of the name is from the old German word *Harst,* or roasting pan. In Hameln and its surroundings, home of the famous Pied Piper and, further into the Weserbergland, setting for the Grimms' fairy-tales, you will come across rivers and streams abundant with trout and eels.

Traveling through the Weserbergland, you must sample some *Göttinger Speckkuchen* from the town of the same name. It's similar to the southern German *Zwiebelkuchen,* or onion tart, and unquestionably numbers among the more *deftig* lunchtime dishes.

Heading up into the mountainous Harz, you'll find an abundance of fresh-water fish and excellent game dishes, particularly venison. However, the Harz is probably best known for its cheese—*Harzer,* to be exact—a round, sharp-tasting cheese seasoned with caraway seeds and covered in a bluish mould. It is best eaten with black bread spread with *Gänseschmalz,* goosefat.

Lower Saxony and the North

The Lüneberger Heide, a vast area of rolling heathland between Celle and Lüneberg in Lower Saxony, is particularly famed for the delicious lamb it produces from the small sheep that roam the great heath in their thousands. The best known of the area's many lamb dishes is *Heidschnückenbraten,* roast lamb with an unusual flavor halfway between mutton and game. It is a delicacy which on no account should be missed when you are in this area. Other specialties of Lower Saxony include the strange-sounding and originally Frisian *Grünkohl mit Pinkel.* It consists of kale or cabbage with *Pinkelwurst,* the local sausage made out of finely-chopped fatty pork. In order to digest the fat, you should wash the whole lot down with a measure of ice-cold *Korn Schnaps,* traditionally drunk out of a pewter spoon.

Approaching the coast, German gastronomy undergoes a radical change. In Bremen, for example, a must in summer is *Aalsuppe grün,* eel soup seasoned with dozens of herbs. Smoked eel, *Räucheraal,* is equally delicious, while in the fall you should try *Bunte oder Gepflückte Finten,* a wonderful dish of green and white beans, carrots and apples. A dish available at any time of year is *Bremer Küken ragout,* a fabulous concoction of sweetbreads, spring chicken, tiny veal meatballs, asparagus, clams and fresh peas cooked in a white sauce.

Along the popular resorts of the East Frisian Islands, fish—boiled, fried, baked or smoked—reigns supreme. In addition there is fresh crab galore, *Granat* or *Garnelen* (shrimp), and even seagulls' eggs.

Schleswig Holstein is also a paradise for seafood. A particular regional specialty is *Labskaus,* much favored by sailors. This is a stew made from pickled meat, potatoes, herring (sometimes) and garnished with a fried egg, sour pickles and lots of beetroot. *Holstein Schnitzel,* found throughout

Germany but invented and best in Schleswig Holstein, is a golden-fried, breaded veal cutlet, somewhat like the Austrian *Wienerschnitzel,* the whole topped with a fried egg and anchovy. A much more unusual regional specialty, however, is *Gefüllte Schweinerippchen,* pork chops stuffed with toast, raisins, apples, and laced with rum. In Büsum you should try *Krabben,* a sort of tiny shrimp, while Lübeck is famous for its marzipan.

We have now reached the most northerly point of Germany—Flensburg—home of Schleswig Holstein rum. Why this most unlikely spot should be famed for rum of all unlikely drinks is easily explained by the fact that until the mid-19th century Flensburg belonged to Denmark, whose merchant fleets then spread far and wide around the world bringing back, among their varied cargoes, large quantities of Caribbean rum. But rum, famous and delightful though it is, is by no means the extent of Flensburg's specialties. *Schweinebauch,* roast belly-pork, *Schweinebacken,* pigs cheek, *Speck,* bacon, and *Schinken,* ham, are all commonly found here. There is also a local ham, *Holstein Katenschinken,* that is a real delicacy. And in addition to rum, try the *Holsteiner* beer, best drunk with juniper-scented *Korn* or *Bommerlunder* brandy; it should see you through nobly.

There is just one corner of the Federal Republic whose cuisine we have not yet considered: Berlin, home of the infamous and fabled German national dish—*Eisbein mit Sauerkraut.* This is a heavily-spiced pork shank, served with Sauerkraut and mashed potatoes or pease pudding, a very thick pea puree. This dish—along with *Bockwurst,* a chubby Frankfurter, and *Bockwurst,* usually served with *Erbsensuppe* (yellow pea soup)—form the Berliner's staple diet, and you will find them on menus throughout the city. In fact, *Bockwurst* stands are as common as hotdog stands in the States. But Berliners also like *Schlesisches Himmelreich,* roast goose or pork with potato dumplings, cooked with fried fruit in a rich gravy. *Königsberger Klopse,* and *Berliner Bouletten,* the former a small meatball with herring and capers, the latter Berlin's variant of the Hamburger—the American rather than the German version—are also common and very popular. Finally, look out for *Kasseler Rippenspeer,* not a dish from the town of that name in Hesse, but salted pork, fried golden in butter then slowly cooked, the recipe concocted originally by a Berlin butcher named Cassel.

Last but Not Least

This gastronomical tour should not be concluded without a bow to the herring. If you are fond of herring, Germany will make you very happy. Herrings are eaten here in every imaginable way: there's "Green" herring, fried fresh; rollmops, or "Bismarck" herrings, rolled up around pickles, gherkins, and onions; *Brathering,* sour, pickled herring; *Matjeshering,* herring with potatoes boiled in their skins, plus lots of butter; and even a herring salad with diced cucumber potatoes and much seasoning. In Emden, in fact, they'll give you a whole herring lunch, with hors d'oeuvre, main dish and salad all provided by this protein-rich fish.

A couple of final tips should also be noted. Wherever you go in Germany, sooner or later you will be confronted with a *Brotzeit*—an in-between or second breakfast, and as important a meal to the Germans as any other. As they start their day relatively early, usually around 7, by about 10 most Germans' thoughts begin to turn toward their stomachs. Out come the rolls and sausage, a piece of cheese or *Leberwurst,* a slice of *Sulze* (chopped meat in aspic) or a piece of *Kasseler,* washed down with—no, not always beer, more often than not it's mineral water, of which there are almost as many kinds as there are wines, or *Apfelsaft* (apple juice). But as a visitor you can *Brotzeit* whenever you feel like it. Many taverns and restaurants have a special *Brotzeitkarte* supplement to their menus, or serve a *Brotzeit-teller,* a platter of cold meat with cheese and bread and a glass of *Schnaps.*

And finally, if, after lunch, you are still hungry, there is always the oblig-atory *Kaffee und Kuchen,* coffee and cake taken in one of the many cafes found in all towns. A cup of fresh ground coffee is accompanied by a por-tion of one of the mouth-watering cakes like *Schwarzwalderkirsch* or *Käsekuchen,* though the Germans are also very fond of less elaborate cakes such as Madeira cake, known variously as *Englischer Kuchen, Mar-morkuchen,* or even *Sandkuchen.*

At the end of the day it's onto the bathroom scales again and time to start thinking about *abspecken,* literally, if rather bluntly, "getting the fat off." As a tourist, however, when you have completed your typical Ger-man gastronomic day, whether in the north, south, east or west, with or without *Knödel, Eisbein, Würst, Pumpernickel* or *Schwarzwälderkirsch-torte,* you will just have to forget the excess pounds. Tomorrow will bring more opportunities for sampling Germany's culinary delights. You can always *diät* when you get home.

GERMAN WINE

Weinfests and Carousels

by
PAMELA VANDYKE PRICE

Pamela Vandyke Price is a noted British writer on wine. She has published 21 books on the subject. Her writing, broadcasting and lecturing on wine and wine-related subjects have won her several awards, both French and British.

Germany produces some of the most famous, and indeed most expensive, wines in the world. Moreover, her wine-producing regions are among the most beautiful in the country, with imposing castle ruins on rocky crags, black-and-white gabled houses filling the villages, and elegant spas abounding. You need only sit on a terrace overlooking a river and a vineyard and sample the local wine for the romantic magic of Germany and her wines to become dreamily clear.

Yet there's a paradox here, for Germany doesn't, or at any rate shouldn't, seem an obvious wine producing country. For one thing, the wine regions are relatively far north, on the same latitude as Vancouver and Winnipeg, with cold winters and unreliable summers. To this extent the existence, and, even more to the point, the quality of German wines is in large measure a tribute both to the high caliber of the vines and the skill and dedication of those who devote their lives to making fine wine.

The paradoxes do not end here, however, for the curious seeker after German wine is in for a couple of further surprises. The first is that, unlike in France for example, the very finest wines are seldom drunk with meals. Rather, they are reserved for leisurely sipping in appreciative company, often with no food at all or perhaps just a few biscuits or plain sponge cake. The delicacy and complexity of these great wines is such that they deserve the whole attention of the drinker in a clean and fresh atmosphere. This isn't affectation. Their wonderful bouquet and lingering flavor merit the sort of attention that you simply can't give them in a crowded dining room, particularly when they have to compete with the conflicting smells of food and, likely as not, smoke. Of course, there are plenty of pleasant wines you can, indeed should, drink with meals, especially carafe wines or *offener weine* (literally, "open wines"). But even then it's not necessary to order a meal if you want to try a selection of open wines; you need merely order a range of glasses and then compose a mini-tasting of your own.

The second surprise concerns Liebfraumilch. Though unquestionably the best-known German wine, you'll seldom see it on a wine list in Germany itself. The reason is simply that although the original Liebfraumilch came from the vineyard surrounding the Liebfraukirche (the Church of Our Lady) at Worms, it has long since been a general term, used to describe a style of German wine. Though subject to legislation, and a "quality" white wine, it was originally created as a general *type* of wine, intended specifically for export, as the ambassador of German wines if you like. So don't expect to find it in Germany itself; instead make the most of the chance to try other wines in their birthplace. Not only will they be less expensive here, but some, produced only in small quantities, will never be found outside the country.

2,000 Years of Wine

The history of Germany's wines begins with the Romans, whose armies placed a high priority on their wine ration, using it for disinfectant and medicinal purposes—wine was often used to make a doubtful water supply safe—as well as for refreshment. How much of the wine consumed by the Romans in Germany was actually produced there is unknown, and it seems likely that it was only in the reign of Charlemagne in the 9th century that significant quantities of wine began to be produced in Germany itself. It was Charlemagne, or so the story goes, who noticed that certain south facing slopes shed their winter snows early and who suggested that vines be planted on them. The success of these early wine-producers, and the importance of the rivers along which all the important vineyards were situated, is made clear by the famous medieval relief of a wine ship in the Landesmuseum in Trier transporting wine casks along the Mosel.

Later, the great medieval monasteries, who needed wine for sacramental as well as medicinal purposes, were to exert a significant influence on the development of German wines, not least by introducing more systematic methods of cultivation. But in addition, merchants, bankers, scholars, diplomats and the nobility all helped promote German wines, which by the Renaissance had become not only an important export but had improved dramatically in quality. By the 19th century, the fame of German wine had spread even farther afield, even to the New World, with political and religious refugees and the hoardes of immigrants who settled in America all helping to spread the message abroad. Queen Victoria, who loved everything German, also helped boost the reputation of the country's wines, and following a visit to Hocheim in 1850 even permitted the use of her name for the Könegin Viktoria-Berg site.

By the middle of the 19th century, German wine production had become significantly more scientific and exact, a process that has continued and accelerated throughout the 20th century. Much of this work has been carried out by the world-famous German Wine Institute at Geisenheim, which has played a vital role in evolving new strains of vines, improving fermentation techniques, soil analysis, and the like. In addition, they have advised many of the great estates on the laying out of their vineyards. A great many wine producers have also helped in the ever more precise and productive methods used in Germany today, not least by banding together to form winegrowers' co-operatives—there are several hundred today—and pooling their resources and expertise. The most modern and expensive equipment is now commonplace, and the co-operatives supply wine to hundreds of outlets.

BASIC WINE FACTS

German wine means, first and foremost, white wine. There are a number of pale wines (generally very pale in color), some sparkling wines, and even a few red wines, but essentially the vast bulk of German wines—almost 90%—and all the really great ones, are white. Secondly, like all wines, particularly the very finest, an almost infinite number of factors can influence the final product. Even supposedly similar wines can vary tremendously. Every bottler, shipper and importer, every change in the weather, every different type of grape, every tiny difference in the soil, all these factors and many more beside influence and alter every bottle of wine in a thousand subtle ways. The difficulties facing the would-be connoisseur are made all the more extreme by the fact that tastes also vary greatly, and that one man's "dry" can easily be another's "medium dry," to take just one simple example.

So short of going out and actually drinking the stuff, which is of course the ultimate object of the exercise, what do you need to know to guide you through the initially daunting world of German wines? Below we list the salient facts.

Bottles and Glasses

There are five basic types of bottle. Mosel wines come in slender, dark green bottles, Rhine wines in slender brown bottles. Red wines come in slightly fatter, sloping-shouldered bottles. Franconian *steinwein* is bottled in dumpy flagons of green glass known as a *bocksbeutel*. Its origins can be traced back to the Middle Ages when leather skins, hung from a saddle or belt, were used to transport wine. Finally, sparkling wines come in a traditionally-shaped Champagne bottle.

The standard German wine glass has a long stem, to ensure that your hand does not warm the wine, and a bowl shaped somewhat like an onion with the top cut off. This inward curving shape catches the bouquet and directs it to the drinker's nose. There are also a number of variations on this standard type. Mosel glasses, for example, often have green stems, while Rhine glasses can have brown stems. Similarly, the finest Mosel wines are sometimes drunk from a glass known as a "Treviris," after Trier, whose bowl is cut with a special pattern. You may also find that the very best wines of all, from whatever region, are drunk from a smaller glass so that more can be shared around. Sparkling wines are served in a deep-ish, triangular-shaped stemmed bowl. At wine festivals and some tastings, a miniature tumbler is used. Finally, you may also encounter all or any of these types in tinted glass. These were very much more common in the last century and owe their existence to the same mock-modesty that led the Victorians to put petticoats on piano legs so as not to offend, the offending article in this case being the "flyers," or little bits of cork, grit or grape that are occasionally found in wine and which, it was felt, affronted the gaze of the drinker.

Tasting

Although many inexpensive German wines are very pleasant to drink, and can be swallowed casually for the immediate enjoyment they afford, the finer wines should be sampled in a much more deliberate way. First, look at the color; for most of the young white wines it will be a light, lemony-gilt. But for all white wines it should be brilliantly clear. Then sniff the wine as you twirl it around in the glass. If you fill your glass to the brim you won't be able to do this and will cheat yourself of the bouquet. The fragrance of German wine is usually quite marked: wafting, delicate, and charming, tempting you to drink . . . and then drink more. The flavor tends to be light, the dry wines refreshing the palate, the sweeter wines appealing by the luscious way they linger, trailing slowly away so that the final impression is enchanting.

The finest wines should be drunk at leisure. Sample them with deliberate care. They are masterpieces of the wine makers' art and deserve your undivided attention, even for a short time, and should not be drunk at meals.

Label Language

German wine labels are often magnificent specimens of intricate design, delightful in themselves. They provide detailed information about the contents of the bottle and everything on them is strictly controlled by law. Understanding them is an essential step in coming to grips with German wine. Unfortunately, they can also often appear difficult to decipher, in some cases positively impenetrable. Names can be disconcertingly long, and the famous Gothic script apparently used specifically to obscure.

In fact most labels are much easier to read than they might seem. Long names are often only those of growers and shippers run together. The monster "Winzergenossenschaft," for example, only means "Wine Growers' Co-operative." Similarly, the suffix "er" is often attached to place names, meaning "of," thus Oppenheim becomes Oppenheimer—of Oppenheim— Rüdesheim becomes Rüdesheimer. Anything appearing after "Schloss" is just the name of a castle, while "Graf von Hatushka-Greiffenclau" means no more than the "Count of Hatushka-Greiffenclau." The secret is not to panic but to sort out the different names calmly. You'll find everything falls into place surprisingly quickly.

A Typical German Wine Label

Wine region —————— RHEINPFALZ   Vintage

1982

Site name ————— **Winzerdorfer Rebberg**

Riesling ———— Grape name

Halbtrocken

Taste or style —— Qualitätswein b.A. A.P.Nr. 5 16 98 7 83 —— A P # (see below)

Erzeugerabfüllung Winzer Bacchus, Winzerdorf

Wine Quality   Grower and bottler

Amlitiche Prüfungsnummer

5	16	98	7	83
# of testing station	# identifying location of bottler	bottler's identification #	# of a particular lot or bottling	year of test

General Label Terms. Grape names. A number of different grapes are used in Germany. For white wine, the most important are: Riesling, specifically Rheinriesling which should not be confused with certain other wines from other countries that may be labeled Riesling; Muller-Thurgau; Sylvaner, which makes some of the finer Franken wines; Traminer; Scheurebe; Sigerrebe; Morio-Muskat; Ruländer, also known as Pinot Gris; Kerner; Trollinger; Gutedel.

For red wines, the principal grapes are: Portugieser; Blauer Trollinger; Blauer Spätburgunder, also known as Pinot Noir.

Don't forget that Riesling should be pronounced so that the first syllable rhymes with "geese" rather than "rice." The prestige of the Riesling is such that, though it will have been used on the very finest Rhine and Mosel wines, its name will not appear on the label. Confusingly, on cheaper bottles you will also find that no grape name appears.

Vintage dates. Everyone can read a date, but if no date appears it should be assumed that the wine should be drunk soon.

Trocken and **Halb Trocken.** These mean that the wine will be dry or medium dry respectively.

Site names. These will appear on quality wines, such as the "Goldtröpfchen" at Piesport, the "Doktor" at Bernkastel or the "Gutes Domtal" at Nierstein. The situation is slightly confused, however, by the fact that even a small site may be owned by several concerns—there are three owners of the Doktor site for example—but at the same time the particular owner's name will always appear on the label. Similarly, one owner may also have sites in a number of different vineyards.

A.P. This is an abbreviation of *Amlitiche Prüfungsnummer,* meaning that the wine has met with the approval of a qualified body of authorities. Once the wine has this official approval, it is issued with a number which appears on the label. Two sealed bottles are then deposited with the authorities who, in the event of any dispute as to the authenticity or quality of the wine, are able to trace the history of the wine and, if need be, sample the bottles. See our specimen label for a breakdown of these numbers.

Erzeugerabfüllung or **Aus Eigneneum Lesegut.** This means that the wine was produced and bottled on the same estate where the grapes were grown.

Süssreserve. A system whereby unfermented grape juice can be added, under strict control, to wines that are otherwise tart or too sharp. It may not be used for any of the finer wines. It should also not be confused with the French system of *chaptalization,* the addition of sugar to the unfermented grape juice to promote the action of the yeasts.

Oechsle. A system of measuring grape sugar in the "must," the unfermented grape juice. For the sweetest German wines, the higher the percentage the better, and if a grower announces the percentage his wine has reached, congratulate him.

Wine Quality. All German wines fall into two basic categories— *Deutsche Tafelwein* or *Deutsche Landwein* and *Qualitätswein*—both strictly monitored. In either case, all relevant information detailing the wine will appear on the label.

Deutsche Tafelwein. Essentially a simple table wine, for the most part drunk only in Germany, made from a blend of different wines from one of the four Tafelwein regions.

Tafelwein. A blend of simple everyday wines from other EEC countries which may or may not contain German wines, but generally bottled in Germany.

Deutsche Landwein. A category of Deutscher Tafelwein introduced after the 1982 vintage and made with rather more ripe grapes than those used for simple Deutsche Tafelwein. It is usually dry or medium dry and the grapes must come from one of the 15 Landwein regions.

Qualitätswein bestimmer Anbaugebiete. Usually shortened to "QbA," this category comprises the bulk of Germany's wines and represents something of a halfway house between the cheapest and the finest wines. It must come from one of the 11 specified wine regions (see below) and the grapes must have been allowed to ripen fully. These wines are best consumed young.

Qualitätswein mit Prädikat. Usually shortened to QmP, meaning "quality wine with a special attribute." This is the top category of German wine. It is divided into one of six types. In ascending order of quality these are:

—*Kabinett:* generally the driest of the QmP wines and made from fully ripened grapes; the label will normally mention the specific plot in the vineyard in which the grapes were grown.

—*Spätlese:* literally, "late harvest," that is the grapes have been picked late, though the wine is not necessarily particularly sweet. However, it will have an intense flavor.

—*Auslese:* the grapes will have been picked late and selected bunch by bunch with only the finest going into the vat; generally very sweet and very special.

—*Beerenauslese:* not only will the grapes have been picked very late, they will have been selected grape by grape; moreover, they will also have been subjected to the fungus *botrytis cinerea* (*edelfaüle* or "noble rot") which makes the flavor more intense still. This is a very fine wine.

—*Eiswein:* made from Beerenauslese grapes that are frozen at the moment of picking and go into the vat with a coating of ice; very sweet, very fine, and very expensive.

—*Trockenbeerenauslese:* Beerenauslese grapes that have been left on the vine until they dry and shrivel, leaving no more than a single drop of intensely luscious juice in each grape; this wine is very sweet and rich, and very, very rare.

The Wine Regions

As we have already mentioned, there are 11 officially-designated wine-producing regions in Germany, each producing wines typical of their own area (i.e. similar in taste) and different from wine produced elsewhere in the country. All are located along rivers or around lakes, the importance of which are vital to successful wine production. The presence of water helps temper the climate in the immediate area by providing generally less variable day- and night-time temperatures than in other parts of the country, as well as reflecting the rays of the sun and helping the grapes to ripen. Moreover, the fogs and mists that rise from the waters in the fall protect the precious crop from frost at its most vunerable moment, most German grapes being picked relatively late (October and November) to let them ripen fully.

Particularly outstanding years for German wines were 1983 and 1985 for Southern Baden and Alsatian wines, and 1985 for Franken (Bocksbeutel), Palatinate and North Baden (Bergstrasse region) wines. 1983 was also a good year for Moselle, Rhine, Saar/Ruwer, Ahr and Nahe wines.

Bus tours and other sightseeing trips can be easily arranged through all the main regions—contact local tourist offices for details—while for the less active there are ferries and steamers that journey from vineyard to vineyard, many providing refreshments of one sort or another.

It is not normally possible to visit the great estates without having made prior arrangements, but all wine villages have plenty of *weinstube,* cafes and delightful restaurants where the local produce can be sampled in appropriate surroundings. There are also a number of important wine museums, while tourist offices can provide excellent guides and brochures to their own regions. They will also be able to advise on the all-important matter of wine tasting, though note that we give details of this in the *Practical Information* for each chapter.

Remember that in high season and during local festivals, accommodations can be very difficult to arrange and that roads and transport will be crowded.

We list the wine regions by size (area under cultivation), beginning with the largest.

Rheinhessen. This is the largest wine-producing area in Germany. It is bordered on the west by the river Nahe and on the north and east by the Rhine. The two largest towns here are Mainz and Worms, the latter the site of the Liebfrauenkirche, the Church of Our Lady.

Wines from here are generally rather full and fruity, and for the most part are pleasant and inexpensive, though a number of quality wines are also produced.

Rheinpfalz. Though smaller than the Rheinhessen, the Rheinpfalz nonetheless produces more wine than any other area of the country. The region runs along the west bank of the Rhine for 80 km. (50 miles) to Neustadt and the French border, with the Deutscher Weinstrasse (the German Wine Road) running its length. It is also one of the most attractive of Germany's wine regions, with an abundance of little villages dotting the countryside, their buildings sporting traditional black-and-white gables.

The wines here are generally fairly robust and are particularly good with many of the local specialties, particularly sausages, to which whole festivals, notably that at Bad Durkheim, are devoted. Weinstube here also commonly have a "carousel," an iron frame holding six, nine or 12 glasses in numbered slots. Fill them up and sample as many as you can manage.

Detour if possible to Speyer where, opposite the Cathedral, there is an important museum, a large section of which is devoted to wine and where the oldest wine in the world, dating from the third century A.D., is preserved in an amphora.

Baden. The southernmost of the wine regions and the most diverse, both in landscapes and wines. The region extends from near Heidelburg in the north to Bodensee (Lake Constance) in the south. Local wine consumption is significantly higher than in other regions of the country, with the result that very little wine is exported.

Much pink wine is made, produced by fermenting white and black grapes together. It's known as Schillerwein, though it has nothing to do with the 19th-century Romantic writer of that name, being derived instead from the word "schillern," meaning to shimmer or glitter. An unusual white wine from here, Weissherbst, is a white wine made from black grapes, whose skins—which provide the color—are removed early in the fermentation.

Mosel-Saar-Ruwer. The wine-growing regions of the Mosel, with its tributaries the Saar and the Ruwer (pronounced "Roover"), run from just south of Trier to Koblenz on the Rhine. They produce some of the most famous wines in Germany: crisp, fresh and charming, with a glorious bouquet. They are also often highly individual, the result of the extraordinary meanderings of the Mosel, so that even neighboring plots face in quite different directions and produce quite different wines. The banks of the river are also extremely steep, and you'll often see no more than a single row of vines on a precipitous ledge apparently accessible only to a mountain goat.

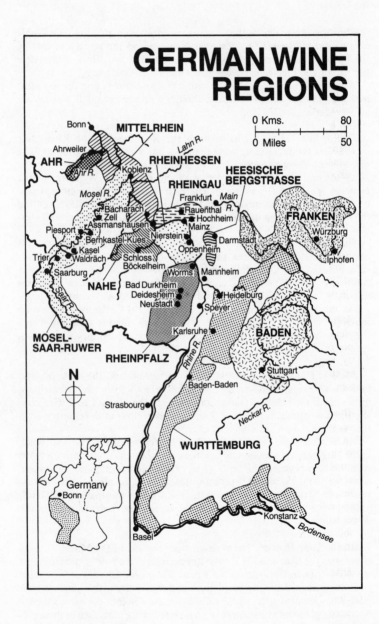

GERMAN WINE REGIONS

0 Kms. 80

0 Miles 50

Bonn

MITTELRHEIN

Ahrweiler

Lahn R.

AHR

Ahr R.

Koblenz

RHEINHESSEN

HEESISCHE BERGSTRASSE

RHEINGAU

Mosel R.

Frankfurt *Main*

Bacharach   Rauenthal *R.*

Zell   Hochheim

Assmanshausen   Mainz

Piesport   Nierstein   **FRANKEN**

Bernkastel-Kues   Würzburg

Kasel   Oppenheim

Trier Waldräch   Darmstadt   Iphofen

Saarburg   Schloss   Worms   Mannheim

Böckelheim

NAHE   Bad Durkheim   Heidelburg

Deidesheim   Speyer

Neustadt

Karlsruhe   **BADEN**

MOSEL-SAAR-RUWER

Saar R.

Stuttgart

RHEINPFALZ

N   Baden-Baden

Rhine R.

Strasbourg   *Neckar R.*

WURTTEMBURG

Germany   Konstanz

Bonn   *Bodensee*

Basel

The famous sites are generally clearly marked, even from the river, so that relaxing on board one of the many steamers you can identify villages and vineyards bearing such renowned names as Piesport, Zell, and Graach, with its Nimmelreich vineyard. Bernkastel, site of the famous "Doktor" vineyard, makes an excellent center from which to explore the region.

Württemburg. This is the most important red wine region in Germany. These range in quality from everyday Tafelweins to some very elegant specimens. A quantity of white wine is also produced here, however, most being generally vigorous and hearty. Like their neighbors in Baden, the people of Württemburg do not export much wine, and local consumption is high. The vineyards are mostly along the river Neckar and its many tributaries. Stuttgart is the most important town in the region and makes an excellent base.

Franken. Franken, or Franconia, is the most easterly of the German wine regions, and lies in undulating countryside, its vineyards strung along the length of the river Main and its tributaries. The region's wines are generally earthy and rather dry, even "masculine." Franconia also boasts the famous "Stein" site at Würzburg, principal city of Franconia, which gave rise to the general term for Franconian wines, Steinwein. Traditionally, most Franconian wines are bottled in a squat, green flagon, the bocksbeutel. A very little red wine ia also produced in Franconia.

Nahe. The Nahe region is sandwiched between Rheinhessen, which it borders to the west, and the Mosel, to the east, and lies along the steep slopes of the river Nahe. Its wines tend to be fruity and slightly "fat" or spicy, with a number of them among the very best in the country. Those from the north of the region are generally similar to those from Rheinhessen.

Rheingau. This is the aristocrat of Germany's wine producing regions. Here, some of the most famous white wines in the world are produced. It's a small area, extending from Hocheim in the east to Lorch in the west with the Rhine running the length of its southern side, the whole area forming a shallow crescent. Both climate and soil are ideal for the region's most famous grape, the Riesling, which produces delicate, highly flavored wines, as noble as they are elegant. The region also has a distinguished wine-producing history. The term Kabinett is believed to have originated here, while the Rheingauers also discovered the value of *Botrytis Cinera,* "noble rot." A quantity of fine red wines are also produced here, notably from the steep vineyards around Assmannshausen.

Mittelrhein. The Mittelrhein is perhaps the most beautiful of the wine regions of Germany. It begins just below Bonn and extends south for some 100 km. (60 miles) on both banks of the Rhine. It is a region of steep, terraced vineyards, crowned with medieval castles, and many delightful little villages. The famed Lorelei, a lonely rock in the middle of the Rhine said to lure fishermen to their death, is also in the Mittelrhein, at Kaub at the southern end of the region. The wines here, very little of which are exported, are generally pert and fresh and rather fruity.

Ahr. This is the most northerly wine region in Germany. It produces predominantly red wines that are both light and fruity, the bulk of which is consumed locally. Charming, winding roads and pleasant scenery make this a delightful region to explore.

Hessische Bergstrasse. The literal translation of this, the smallest of the wine regions, is the Hesse Mountain Road, and the area, bordered by the Rhine to the east and the Odenwald Forest to the east, is delightful. Its wines tend to be rich and fragrant, verging on the hearty. Practically none is exported, giving a visit here added purpose.

Sparkling Wines

In addition to the vast quantities of ordinary wine—white, pink and red—produced in Germany, the Germans are also exceedingly fond of Schaumwein, or Sekt as it is more commonly known. Some of this could accurately be described as Champagne, though it may not legally be labeled as such (only French sparkling wines have that honor, a peculiarity made all the more bizarre for having been written into the Treaty of Versailles in 1919). However, much of the German variety is not made according to the Champagne method, but follows a slightly less time-consuming and hence more inexpensive process known as "sealed vat," or *Tank Vergämung.*

The name Sekt apparently owes its origins to the great early-19th-century actor Ludwig Devrient. Echoing his stage character, he would habitually call for "A cup of sack," in his favorite weinstube after performances when playing Falstaff. The nickname, suitably Germanized, caught on.

As with all German wines, the production of Sekt is strictly controlled. Bottles labeled Sekt, or even Deutscher Sekt, may be made from grapes grown outside Germany, though they must have been produced and bottled in Germany. However, bottles labeled more specifically, Mosel Sekt or Rhein Sekt for example, will be the genuine article, in these instances coming from the Mosel and the Rhine respectively. If the name of a particular estate, such as Schloss Saarfels in the Mosel, is used, then only wine from that estate may be in that bottle.

In addition to Sekt, there is also a semi-sparkling wine called Perlwein. This is distinguished also by the fact that it comes in bottles made of thicker than normal glass to resist the pressure inside.

Wine Festivals

Throughout the summer and fall, numerous wine festivals are held in the wine-producing regions. Complete lists are available from the *Deutsche Wein-Information,* Postfach 1707, D–6500 Mainz 1. The German National Tourist Office and regional tourist offices are also able to provide information on these festivals.

The term *weinfest* is self-explanatory. However, a *winzerfest* is a growers' festival; a *weinmarkt* is an occasion when both the trade and the public may sample wines from stalls; a *weinlesefest* is a vintage celebration; a *weindorf* is a wine village *en fête;* a *weinblütenfest* is a festival celebrating the flowering of the vines in early summer.

Wine Courses

A number of courses on wine are arranged in the various regions, most in German. However, the German Wine Academy arrange a program in English for both beginners and the more advanced. Contact the German Wine Academy, Postfach 1705, D–6500 Mainz 1, or the German National Tourist Office for details.

SOUTHEAST GERMANY

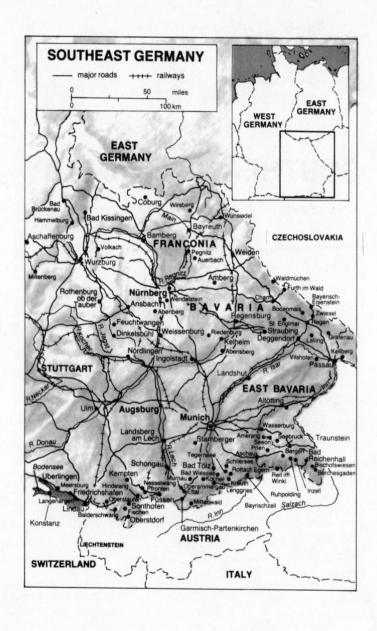

MUNICH

City of Beer and Baroque

If there really is a capital of Germany, it's Munich (München), capital of the free state of Bavaria (Bayern) and the third largest city in the Federal Republic. Dating from 1158, beer capital of the world and cultural center of West Germany, it is an intellectual, entertaining and earthy meeting place which attracts the young much as does the West Coast in the U.S. or the Riviera in France. The city has about it an air of permissiveness which contrasts sharply with the puritanical uprightness of the Prussians in the north. The people of Munich are goodnatured and easygoing and possess an almost infinite capacity for fun and laughter. This bonhomie reaches its peak during Fasching, the carnival that runs from Epiphany on January 6 to Mardi Gras and which encompasses some 2,000 masked balls of every imaginable kind.

Real Fasching enthusiasts end these wild nights only the next morning with a *Weisswürst* breakfast (Munich white sausage) before going straight to work. It's not unusual to see costumed crowds walking the streets in the early morning, especially on Shrove Tuesday (Faschingsdienstag) when the shops close early and throngs of costumed revelers fill the city to ring out the carnival period in style.

Munich is a city bursting with atmosphere; it's exciting and easy to explore and is plentifully supplied with accommodations. Even though terribly ravaged by the war, its revival has been remarkable. With its operas and theaters, galleries and old buildings, parks and squares, splendid countryside within easy reach and wide variety of nightlife, Munich is too good for the vacationer to miss.

Exploring Munich

To explore the city, you should take your time. Munich's motto is *Gemütlichkeit*. It can't be translated exactly, but roughly speaking it means something like easygoing and relaxed. And that's exactly the approach you should adopt. Try sitting in one of the beer gardens, strolling through the pedestrian streets and generally watching the world go by, as the Münchners do. In between, you can take your sightseeing more seriously.

The heart of the city is the Karlsplatz, a square popularly known as Stachus. From here there is an area of some 100,000 square yards stretching between the Hauptbahnhof, the rail station in Schützenstrasse, and continuing through the Karlstor Gate, Marienplatz and Odeonsplatz. Now, it is virtually all one vast pedestrian zone, separated by a broad shopping avenue, the Sonnenstrasse, where it meets the Dachauerstrasse at Lenbachplatz. At the corner of Karlsplatz and Prielmayerstrasse is the grey Palace of Justice (Justizpalast), and on the other side there's the Sonnenstrasse, which leads down to Sendlingertor Platz. Here, there's another new pedestrian shopping zone running the length of the Sendlingerstrasse. The small, dazzlingly-decorated Baroque church of St. John Nepomuk is here. It's better known as the Asamkirche, after the two brothers Asam who built it with love (and their own money) in the 18th century. It's next door to the house where they used to live.

But our tour begins at the Karlstor, in front of which a graceful fountain plays. This is one of the old city gates. Beneath the Karlsplatz there's an underground shopping plaza, which stretches as far as the Hauptbahnhof. There are numerous escalator exits to all corners of the square and adjoining streets. Passing through the Karlstor, you enter the main thoroughfare of the old city, the bulk of which was sadly destroyed in the war. Today, it's a vast pedestrian mall, variously known as the Neuhauserstrasse and the Kaufingerstrasse. It reaches the center of the city at Marienplatz, but just before Marienplatz, on a small side square, is the Frauenkirche—the cathedral of Munich and the Parish Church of Our Lady—whose onion-shaped domes are the symbol of Munich. Built from 1468 in Bavarian Gothic style, it was largely destroyed in the war, but, like so many other important buildings in Munich, has been lovingly rebuilt. Indeed, the modern interior, immensely dignified in its simplicity, forms a striking contrast to the worn red-brick exterior. The interior is also remarkable for its great height, a characteristic exaggerated by the thin, white pillars that line the length of the nave. At the rear of the church is the elaborate Baroque tomb of the Emperor Ludwig of Bavaria, dating from the early-17th century. There are also an interesting series of photographs of the church before and after it was bombed, which make only too clear the near destruction of the building and its subsequent remarkable restoration.

Two other buildings in the Neuhauserstrasse are of interest: the small Bürgersaal Chapel, which has some lovely frescos and sculptures in its Rococo interior; and the Renaissance Michaelskirche, the Church of St. Michael. The latter is a magnificent building, spacious and handsome, and decorated throughout in plain white stucco. It was built originally for the Jesuits in the late-16th century and is closely modeled on the Gesù in

Rome. Like the Frauenkirche, it too was restored after bomb damage. Among much else of interest it contains the tomb of Napoleon's stepson, Eugène de Beauharnais, a suitably grave neo-Classical monument in the north transept, while in the crypt Ludwig II, doomed Dream King of Bavaria, lies buried. Next to the Michaelskirche is the former Augustine Church, now housing the hunting and fishing museum.

The Marienplatz

Continue along the Kaufingenstrasse to the Marienplatz, site of the city's market in the Middle Ages. On one side is the Gothic Neues Rathaus, the New Town Hall, built like so many of the city's more fanciful creations by Ludwig II towards the end of the 19th century. The central tower contains a superb Glockenspiel. Every day in summer at 11 and 5 two levels of performing figures—knights on horseback and folk dancers—revolve to the music of this giant musical box 90 meters (280 ft.) above the Marienplatz. The knights in fact represent a tournament held on the occasion of the marriage of Duke William V and Renate of Lorraine in 1567. There's a lift to the summit of the tower which, as well as giving fine views of the city, also gives the best external view of the Frauenkirche, otherwise obscured by the cluster of buildings surrounding it. A brief but telling inscription on the facade of the Town Hall states simply that the building was "Built in 1867–1874, Enlarged 1888–1908, Destroyed 1944–1945, Rebuilt 1952–1956."

In the center of the Marienplatz is a marble column, the Mariensäule, topped by a statue of the Madonna—hence the name of the square—that was built by the elector of Bavaria in 1638. It was put up to commemorate the sparing of the city by the occupying Swedish forces in the Thirty Years' War.

Across from the Town Hall is the Gothic Peterskirche, another landmark of the old city and dating originally from the 11th century. Its tower, over 90 meters (300 ft.) and offering an excellent view, is fondly called Der Alte Peter, Old Peter. Climb the tower if a white disc is posted on the north side of the platform; it means the view is clear all the way to the Alps. A red disc means visibility is limited to Munich.

Behind Peterskirche is the Tal, a street lined with furniture shops and also boasting the best umbrella shop in the city. It ends at the Isartor, built in 1337 and the one city gate that has remained largely as it was when originally built. However, before heading off down here, leave Marienplatz by its southeast corner and take a look at the Viktualienmarkt, the food market. Here, in the small beer garden, between the pretty stalls of fresh and inviting local produce, people meet and grumble about prices and politics or the day's events. The market women are as strong-armed and direct as ever and their regular customers much the same: self-confident, straight-forward, distrustful, good-humored, sly and ready to lend a hand. The famous Munich comedian, Karl Valentin, has his memorial fountain and statue on the Viktualienmarkt, standing with a bouquet of flowers in one hand; an anonymous tribute of love.

Another side trip from the Marienplatz also reveals one of the city's most famous and delightful treasures, the little Asamkirche, otherwise known as the church of St. John Nepomuk. Head south down Sendlingerstrasse, an excellent shopping street, for 200 or 300 yards. The church is

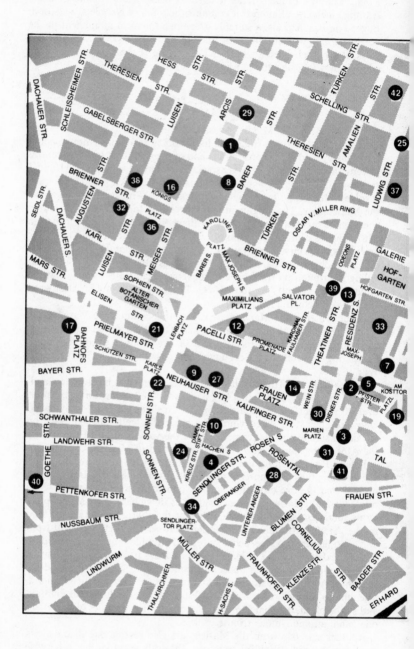

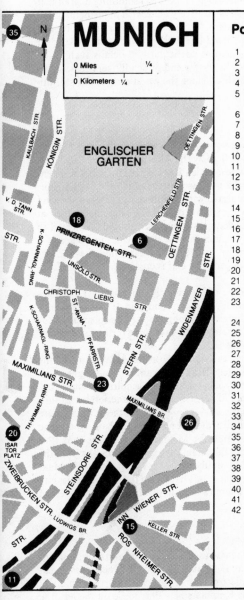

MUNICH

0 Miles ¼

0 Kilometers ¼

ENGLISCHER GARTEN

Points of Interest

1 Alte Pinakothek
2 Alter Hof
3 Altes Rathaus
4 Asamkirche
5 Bayerisches Hauptmünzamt (State Mint)
6 Bayerisches Nationalmuseum
7 Bayerisches Nationaltheater
8 Bayerisches Staatsarchiv
9 Bügersaal Kirche
10 Damenstiftskirche
11 Deutsches Museum
12 Dreifaltgkeitskirche
13 Feldherrnhalle and Preysing Palais
14 Frauenkirche
15 Gasteig Kulturzentrum
16 Glyptothek
17 Hauptbahnhof
18 Haus der Kunst
19 Hofbräuhaus
20 Isartor
21 Justizpalast
22 Karlstor
23 Kleine Komödie am Max II Denkmal
24 Kreuzkirche
25 Ludwigskirche
26 Maximilianeum
27 Michaelskirche
28 Münchner Stadtmuseum
29 Neue Pinakothek
30 Neues Rathaus
31 Peterskirche
32 Propyläen
33 Residenz
34 Sendlinger Tor
35 Siegestor
36 Staatliche Antikensammlungen
37 Staatsbibliothek
38 Stadtische Galerie
39 Theatinerkirche
40 Theresienwiese
41 Viktualienmarkt
42 Universität

on the right and, despite its small scale, its charming early-Rococo facade is easy to spot. It was built by the brothers Asam—Cosmos Damian and Egid Quirin—around 1730. Small though it is, it lacks nothing in grandeur of conception and execution, and is positively alive with movement, color, painting and statuary. To some extent, it may strike many as no more than a preposterously over-decorated jewel box, but repeated visits make clear an extraordinary depth of imagination, particularly in details such as the cunningly-lit bay over the altar. At the far end of Sendlingerstrasse is the Sendlingertor itself, much remodeled since the Middle Ages but still imposing.

Along the Isar

Returning to Marienplatz, head down to the river and the Isartor along Tal. As you leave the square, you'll go by the Altes Rathaus, or Old Town Hall, a 15th-century building whose lavish Renaissance interiors were entirely destroyed at the end of the war, as was the adjoining Rathaustor, or gate tower. The Isartor is decorated with a 19th-century fresco showing the victorious return of Ludwig of Bavaria in 1322 after his victory at Ampfing. The tower of the gate contains a curious museum, dedicated to Karl Valentin and bearing his name: the Valentin Museum. There's a handy and attractive coffee bar on the top floor. Continue down Zweibrückenstrasse and the river is ahead. The Isar is crossed here by the Ludwigsbrücke.

On the big island in the middle of the river is the colossal Deutsches Museum of Science and Technology. It was founded in 1903 by the engineer Oskar von Miller and for long was among the very finest science museums in the world. However, you may find that some of the exhibits are showing their age now somewhat.

Continuing downstream from the museum on the right bank of the river, you will pass the new Gasteig Kulturzentrum on your right, a recently completed mammoth, red-brick, multi-purpose cultural center conceived as a sort of Lincoln-Pompidou center. Its main function is the philharmonic hall, but there is also a library, conservatoire, theater playhouse and evening-class establishment. Further along the right bank you come to the circular Maximilianeum, built for Maximilian II in the mid-19th century and today the seat of the Bavarian Parliament. Cross back to the left bank of the river over the Maximiliansbrücke, which leads into Maximiliansstrasse, a broad avenue that heads back into the center of the city and is, together with the Theatinerstrasse, one of Munich's most elegant (and expensive) shopping streets.

Toward the Residenz

In the center of the Maximiliansstrasse is the large bronze monument to Emperor Maximilian, the Max II Denkmal, opposite which is the small comedy theater, Kleine Komödie am Max II Denkmal. Further on down the Maximiliansstrasse, past the Kammerspiele Playhouse on the left, the narrow Am Kosttor takes you into the tiny square called Platzl where you'll find the Hofbräuhaus. It was founded in 1589 by Duke Wilhelm V and is today a state brewery. This is the place where all your dreams (or nightmares) of throngs of jolly Germans at long tables clasping what seem to be buckets full of beer, shouting, singing and drinking—above all, drinking—as buxom wenches sway toward them with yet more foamy beer, will come true. Though be warned that you'll find more tourists in here than Germans. Still, the huge tap room is an absolute must, though don't be shocked by the bawdy atmosphere. It wouldn't be half as much fun if it wasn't noisy. You won't be able to drink anything other than beer—it comes by the liter—downstairs, but in the gallery above there's a quiet restaurant. Close by, via Pfisterstrasse, is the Alter Hof, the medieval residence of the Bavarian Dukes and the Emperor Ludwig.

Back on Maximiliansstrasse, you now enter Max-Joseph-Platz. Here, you are faced by the Residenz on one side and the National Theater with the Bavarian State Opera on the other. A large complex of buildings, the Residenz has been the home of the dukes, princes and kings of the House of Wittelsbach for over 650 years. Built on from the 16th to the 19th centuries, it was almost totally destroyed in the war. But enough of the rich furnishings were saved to enable a successful restoration to take place. The Residenz is divided into four sections: the Alte Residenz and central sections of the palace, which include the Cuvilliés Theater, the one-time court theater and a delightful specimen of Rococo architecture; the Königsbau, which houses the Schatzkammer or Treasury of the Wittelsbachs (containing, among its many treasures, a small Renaissance statue of St. George, studded with 2,291 diamonds, 209 pearls and 406 rubies); the Residence Museum itself, a vast complex brimming with paintings and tapestries; and the Festsaalbau, which includes the Herkules Saal concert hall, and, behind the palace, the Hofgarten, framed by arcades and full of flowers.

At the west end of the Hofgarten is Odeonsplatz, scene of the doomed putsch of 1923. Its southern end is dominated by the Feldernhalle, an open loggia built by Ludwig I in the mid-19th century and modeled on the early-Renaissance Loggia dei Lanzi in Florence. To one side of it is the Theatinerkirche, built at the end of the 16th century but with a facade added in the latter 18th century by Francois Cuvilliés. Its twin towers and high Baroque dome are a distinctive feature of the Munich skyline. Leading north away from Odeonsplatz, with a fine equestrian statue of Ludwig I marking the beginning, is Ludwigstrasse, an imposing and grandiose neo-Classical boulevard, with the State Library, the University and Ludwigskirche among its more notable buildings. Ludwigstrasse ends at the Siegestor, the Arch of Victory, also built by Ludwig I and copied from the Arch of Constantine in Rome. Beyond, is the district of Schwabing.

Schwabing and the Englischer Garten

What Greenwich Village is to Manhattan, Schwabing is to Munich. It is not a quaint old quarter, however, but a modern district and favored residential area. The main artery through Schwabing is the Leopoldstrasse, which in summer abounds with artists selling their work at open stalls (candlelit at night), cafés, ice cream parlors, and crowds of tourists.

Lying along the east side of Schwabing is the Englischer Garten. It's Munich's most famous park and the largest city-park in Europe. It was established by royal commission as long ago as 1790 by the American-Briton, Sir Benjamin Thompson, later Count Romford. The Garden covers a huge area and includes a Chinese pagoda (the Chinesicher Turm), the Monopteros (a small Greek temple with a fine view over the city), a boating lake, a lakeside café/restaurant with summer beer-garden, and endless walks. There is no better (or cheaper) way of experiencing a true Munich summer evening than to buy your own picnic supper *(Brotzeit)* from a butcher or supermarket and bear it off to the beer garden at the Chinese pagoda. After buying your mug of beer from the Ausschank, take a seat at one of the long wooden trestle tables and enjoy your supper. You will soon begin talking *Bayerisch,* the Bavarian dialect. You needn't feel self-conscious, for no German stands on formality before getting into conversation with a stranger here. Everyone greets everyone else with a jolly *Grüss Got* (God's greeting to you) and, given a liter of beer, the Bavarians are always keen to introduce any foreigner into the secrets of their language. This is the real Munich.

Munich's Major Museums

The city has a number of superb museums, of which several are of outstanding importance. Perhaps the two foremost are the Alte and Neue Pinakotheks (meaning old and new picture galleries). They are located opposite each other on the Barerstrasse just to the west of the Ludwigstrasse. The Alte Pinakothek, built between 1826 and 1836 (and badly damaged in the war, as is only too obvious from the exterior), houses a magnificent collection of Old Masters, with particular emphasis on North European works. The collection was begun by Duke Wilhelm IV (another of the myriad Wittelsbachs) in the 16th century and continued by his family in the succeeding centuries. A visit here should be a highlight of any trip to Munich. The Neue Pinakothek was founded shortly after the completion of the Alte Pinakothek, in 1846 to be exact, its purpose being to house modern—that is, 19th-century—works, carrying on, if you like, where the Alte Pinakothek left off. Though the collection contains a small number of 18th-century English paintings, it is accordingly rich in Impressionists and works of the Munich school. However, the originally 19th-century building that housed the collection was so severely damaged in the war that it eventually had to be demolished and the collection is now housed in a brand new and extremely lavish building on the site of its predecessor.

Until the new building was opened, the collection was temporarily housed in the Haus der Kunst in the Prinzregentstrasse, where today you will find the Staatsgalerie Moderner Kunst, a splendid collection of 20th-century works. In addition, important modern art exhibitions are held here, as well as annual antique and book fairs.

The Theresienwiese

Munich is probably most immediately associated in most people's minds with the Oktoberfest, the annual beer drinking festival that takes place every year around the end of September. It's an immensely popular event and attracts serious beer drinkers from all over the world, with Australians and Scots—deadly rivals in the beer drinking stakes—well to the fore. The city gets horribly crowded during the festival, however, so if you plan to visit then book well ahead.

The Oktoberfest dates from the celebrations held to mark the engagement of 1810 of Crown Prince Ludwig, later Ludwig I, to Princess Theresa, after whom the site of the festival is named. Today's celebrations have come a long way since then, however. Yet in spite of the very obvious commercialization, the crowds, the high prices and the frankly sordid atmosphere in most of the great beer tents, each of which holds several thousand people, most of them drunk, there is still something exhilarating about the festival, something that unquestionably captures the easy-going bonhomie of this very likeable city.

It all takes place at the Theresienwiese, a former horse-racing track to the southwest of the city center. The field itself is overlooked by a monumental statue of *Bavaria*—a sort of mini Statue of Liberty—some 35 meters or so (100 ft.) high. Like her cousin in New York, the bronze statue has a hollow head which you can climb up to, if you can manage the 130 steps. But don't go in the afternoon; the interior becomes positively furnace-like as the day heats up.

Palaces and Parks

Munich has a series of delightful palaces and castles surrounding it, the most famous of which is that at Nymphenburg in the northwest suburbs of the city, built as a summer residence by the rulers of Bavaria. The central and oldest part of the building dates from 1664, while the buildings and arcades that flank it were added over the next 100 years, the bulk of the work being undertaken in the reign of Max-Emmanuel between about 1680 and 1730. The gardens, a mixture of formal French parterres and English parkland, were landscaped over a similar period. The interiors are exceptional, especially the Banqueting Hall—a Rococo masterpiece in green and gold. But perhaps the greatest delight is the Hunting Lodge—the Amalienburg—in the grounds, the work of Cuvilliés, who was also responsible for the Residenz Theater in Munich itself. That the "hunting" the lodge was designed for was not necessarily always an outdoor pursuit, can be easily guessed by the decoration and atmosphere of courtly high life.

Also within easy reach of the city is Schlessheim, noted for the Neues Schloss, with frescoed hall and staircase and the beautiful Baroque Festival and Victory Halls, where concerts of Baroque music are given in the summer. The French Empire-style gardens contain a hunting lodge of their own, the Jagschloss, which today houses the largest collection of Meissen porcelain in Germany.

Nearby is Schloss Haimhausen, with a permanent exhibition of antiques, while, back in the suburbs at Obermenzing on the river Würm, there is Schloss Blutenburg, a moated castle and today home of the International Children's Book Library. Here too concerts are held in the summer in either the chapel or the Baroque hall.

Excursions from Munich

Taking advantage of the tentacle-like arms of the S-Bahn, stretching considerable distances into the countryside around Munich, it's easy to get out of the city and deep into the rolling hills of Upper Bavaria in as little as 30 minutes. Take a bicycle with you (they travel free on the S-Bahn at weekends) or hire one from any station once you get there, and you can get well off the beaten track. This is ideal country for cycling and walking.

The Funf-Seen-Land (literally, "Five Lakes Land") southwest of Munich is one of the most popular destinations; the lungs of the city. The lakes in question are the Starnbergersee, Ammersee, Wörthsee, Wesslingersee, and Pilsensee, all offering bathing, boating, walking and picnicking. There is also a peaceful cycle track from the city.

The largest is Starnbergersee. You can hire rowboats here, and there is also a steamer that makes a regular circuit of the lake. The town of Starnberg, rising from terraces from the lakeside, is itself of interest. It is primarily an elegant lakeside resort with a small yacht harbor, lakeside cafes, villas and hotels, and an expensive shopping center. However, there is also a 16th-century castle (it belonged originally to the Princes of Bavaria) and an 18th-century parish church, as well as an interesting Heimatmuseum (Local Museum). At the southern end of the lake is Seeshaupt, another popular little lakeside resort, dramatically framed by the snow-clad Alpine peaks behind it. Close by Seeshaupt is a small group of marshy lakes—the Ostersee lakes—that contain a wealth of animal and bird life.

Ammersee, though smaller than Starnbergersee, is perhaps more lovely still, being in mountainous country and further from the bustle of the city. There are a number of good beaches all round the lake, but the attractions here also include the Benedictine priory of Andechs on the Heiliger Berg (Holy Mountain). After climbing the 710 meters (2,333 ft.) to the summit, quench your thirst with the special dark beer brewed by the monks. At the southern end of the lake is the summer resort and market town of Diessen, with a fine Bavarian Rococo church and attractive craftsmen's quarter (the potteries and studios can be visited).

The Isar valley south of Munich is also an excellent region to visit, with plenty of good value accommodations for longer stays. From Munich, the first place you reach (some 10 km.—6 miles—from the city and easily accessible by S-Bahn or bus in about 20 minutes) is Grosshesselohe, famous principally for its magnificent iron railway bridge over the Isar. A marvel of engineering when it was built in 1857, sadly it has now been replaced by a new bridge. There is a good view along the valley from the bridge, but it's worth crossing also to get to Grünwald, opposite Grosshesselohe. Here you'll find Burg Grünwald, a fine 13th-century castle, renovated of late and today home to special exhibitions from the Munich Prehistoric Collection. Continuing down the Isar valley toward the Alps, some 16 km. (10 miles) from Grosshesselohe and Grünwald you reach Wolfrathausen, a picturesque old market town with the Alps towering impressively beyond it.

The most popular destination to the north of the city is Dachau, 18 km. (11 miles) from Munich and again easily reached by S-Bahn. The town is famous, or infamous, principally as the site of one of the Nazis' more notorious concentration camps (which can be visited). With the obvious exception of the camp, however, Dachau is actually rather a charming place. Its location is scenic and picturesque, while the origins of the town can be traced back as far as 800. 30 km. (19 miles) north of Dachau is Altömunster, with a convent dating from 730 and a fine 18th-century church. If you go by road, stop off at Indersdorf, halfway between Dachau and Altömunster, to visit the old monastery and fine 13th-century church.

Finally, if you feel like venturing a good bit further afield from Munich and penetrating into the Alps themselves, take one of the frequent excursion buses from the city (details from the tourist office) that go to the magnificent fairy-tale castles built by Ludwig II at Linderhof, Herrenchiemsee and, most famously, Neuschwanstein (see the next chapter). Buses also run to Berchtesgaden, site of Hitler's Alpine retreat—the Eagle's Nest— and to Garmisch Partenkirchen, Germany's premier winter sports resort and host to the 1936 and 1972 Winter Olympics.

(For further details of the German Alps, see the next chapter, *Along the Alps*).

PRACTICAL INFORMATION FOR MUNICH

TELEPHONES. The telephone code for Munich is 089. To call any number in this chapter, unless otherwise specified, this prefix must be used. Within the city, no prefix is required.

HOTELS. Munich is well supplied with hotels, but it is nonetheless advisable to book in advance, particularly during the Oktoberfest and the Fashion Weeks—*Mode Woche*—in March and October, and also on account of the many other trade fairs, exhibitions and international events which take place throughout the year.

The reservation service, *Zimmervermittlung,* of the tourist office will be glad to assist you, if you write to them in advance at *Fremdenverkehrsamt Müchen,* Zimmervermittlung Postfach, 8000 München 1. They do not accept telephone reservations. If you arrive in Munich without a reservation go to the accommodations service at Riem Airport or at the Hauptbahnhof (main station).

Munich hotels are among the highest priced in Germany, but tourist deflation in the past years has created panic among many, particularly the new American chain-hotels, who were among the first to join the special all-inclusive, out-of-season "Munich Weekend" package, which includes city and countryside tours, museum fees, etc.

These low-price arrangements include such packages as: "Munich Weekend Key," "Munich Christkindl Key" (valid from Nov. 28 to Dec. 24), "Munich's New Year's Eve Key" (valid from Dec. 25 to Jan. 6), "Munich Theater Key" (valid from Oct. 31 for one year), "Munich Summer Stop" (valid from June 11 to Aug. 30), and "Munich Easter Key" (valid from Holy Thursday for one week). (There are some exempted weekends when trade fares are held). In addition to the reduced hotel prices, they include breakfast, city sightseeing tour or an afternoon excursion to one of the Bavarian lakes, free ride to the top of the Olympic tower, shopping coupons, free admission to all museums and galleries as well as to Schloss Nymphenburg Palace and the Botanical Gardens. German Federal Railways *(Bundesbahn)* offer a considerable reduction on train fares in conjunction with these packages. The special arrangements offered by the City of Munich can be booked on all railroad stations or through a travel agency. Information from the tourist office *(Fremdenverkehrsamt),* tel. 23911.

Deluxe

Bayerischer Hof. Promenadeplatz 2–6 (21200). 700 beds, all rooms with bath or shower, some with large floor-level bath; studio rooms and suites also available. Sauna bath and heated rooftop swimming pool. Service is not always compatible with modern deluxe standards, though. Bayerischer Hof acquired the famous *Montgelas Palais* next door, had it restored and reopened as a hotel annex containing elegant period-furnished apartments and banquet and private dining rooms, some fashionable shops, and the rustic-style *Palais-Keller.* Restaurants include the *Grill* and *Trader Vic's* (pseudo-Polynesian), and the (loud) *Nightclub* with dancing. AE, DC, MC, V.

Grand Hotel Continental. Max-Joseph-Str. 5 (551570). 200 beds, all rooms with bath; private suites available. Near Maximilianplatz. Furnishings include antiques and art objects. Fine food in atmospheric *Conti Grill* and in rooftop restaurant. Cocktail lounge; terrace garden. AE, DC, MC, V.

Hilton. Tucherpark 7 (38450). 500 rooms, each with private bath and balcony, T.V. and other amenities. Between the Englischer Garten and the Isar. Swimming pool, sauna, shopping arcade, underground parking. Several restaurants: *Tivoli Grill* for "international" food, *Bayernstube* for Bavarian, *Isar-Café* for pastries; small beer garden overlooking little Eisbach river; rooftop *Marco Polo* with bar, for dining and dancing. AE, DC, MC, V.

Königshof. Karlsplatz 25 (551360). 120 rooms, all sound-proof, air-conditioned, most with bath. First-class food in restaurant overlooking Stachus (Karlsplatz). Underground parking. AE, DC, MC, V.

Romantik Hotel Insel-Muhle. Von-Kahr-Str. 87 (81010). 37 rooms with bath. This former mill on the banks of the Wurm river, in Munich's leafy Untermenzing suburb, is one of the most appealing of what, to many, is the best hotel chain in the country. Impeccable service, atmospheric restaurant, and riverside beer-garden. AE, DC, MC, V.

Vier Jahreszeiten. Maximilianstr. 17 (230390). Palatial, it has served royalty and other important international figures, and is still Munich's leading hotel. Now owned by the Kempinski chain, it has a new wing at the back with rooftop pool and convention facilities. Several restaurants, with *Vier Jahreszeiten Bar* for dining and dancing, and the fine *Walterspiel,* which bears the name of the famous chef who used to own the place. AE, DC, MC, V.

Expensive

Ambassador. Mozartstr. 4 (530840). 100 beds, studio suites only, all with bath, radio, T.V. and kitchenette. In quiet spot near Theresienwiese. Good Italian restaurant *Alfredo.* AE, DC, MC.

Arabella. Arabellastr. 5 (92321). 400 beds on upper floors of super-modern 22-story apartment building in Arabella Park, Bogenhausen suburb. Restaurant and indoor pool with sauna on top floor with magnificent view. AE, DC, MC, V.

Deutscher Kaiser. Arnulfstr. 2 (558321). 300 beds, most rooms with bath (those without have inconvenient facilities). Near main station. Fine view from 15th-floor restaurant and café. Underground parking. AE, MC, V.

Eden-Hotel-Wolff. Arnulfstr. 4–8 (551150). 210 rooms with bath. Very comfortable hotel with a long tradition. Next to main station. Rustic *Zirbelstube* restaurant serves old-Munich specialties. No credit cards.

Excelsior. Schützenstr. 11 (551370). 180 beds, all rooms with bath and radio, top-floor terrace suites with T.V. On quiet pedestrian mall opposite main station. Game specialties in atmospheric *St. Hubertus* restaurant. AE, DC, MC, V.

Holiday Inn. Leopoldstr. 194 (340971). 400 rooms and series of suites, in three buildings connected by huge hotel hall. On outer edge of Schwabing, well-located for Nuremberg autobahn. Modern and comfortable; swimming pool; several restaurants and cocktail lounges; *Aquarius* nightclub; *Almstube* with zither player. AE, DC, MC, V.

Orbis. Karl Marx Ring 87 (63270). 185 rooms, pool, sauna, two restaurants and bar. In Perlach suburb, close to airport and with good public transport to city center. AE, DC, MC, V.

Palace. Trogerstr. 21 (4705091). 73 rooms and suites with bath. A modern hotel with old-fashioned elegance and decor. Four miles from the airport, 10-minute tram ride to downtown Munich. Roof garden, Jacuzzi, sauna, gym. No restaurant. AE, DC, MC, V.

Penta. Hochstr. 3 (4485555). 600 rooms, including some in the Deluxe range. On the Rosenheimer Berg, the hotel forms part of "Motorama" with car exhibitions and shopping center. Rooftop swimming pool. Cocktail lounge, self-service restaurant. *Münchner-Kindl-Stuben,* open to 2 A.M., offers Bavarian and international cuisine. AE, DC, MC, V.

Preysing. Preysingstr. 1 (481011). 60 rooms, all with bath, airconditioning, radio, T.V. Apartments available, also on monthly basis. Underground garage. One of Munich's best run and respected hotels. No restaurant in the hotel, but with first-class cellar-restaurant in same building. DC.

Prinzregent. Ismaningerstr. 42–44 (4702081). 70 rooms with bath. Excellently renovated Bavarian-style hotel centrally located off Prinzregentenstr.; comfortable and attractive. No restaurant, but good bar and breakfast room, plus sauna, pool, and garden. AE, DC, MC, V.

Residence. Artur-Kutscher-Platz 4 (399041). 300 beds. The latest in architecture, in quiet side-street in Schwabing. Swimming pool in basement. Restaurant *Die Kutsche.* AE, DC, MC, V.

Sheraton. Arabellastr. 6, Effnerplatz (924011). 650 rooms (1,300 beds). Arabella Park, Bogenhausen suburb. Top three floors, with outstanding view of the city, now devoted to business and convention guests. Several restaurants, including *Bayern Stube;* bar, nightclub. AE, DC, MC, V.

Teletap-Hotel-Drei-Löwen. Schillerstr. 8 (595521). 130 rooms, most with bath. 3 min. walk from station. Well-run, comfortable hotel, recently renovated. Private car-parking. *Strawberry* restaurant. AE, DC, MC, V.

Trustee Park Hotel. Parkstr. 31, near the Fair Grounds (5195421). 40 rooms with bath. Primarily a businessperson's hotel. Special family deals are often available. Restaurant, bar. AE, DC, MC, V.

Moderate

Ariston. Unsöldstr. 10 (222691). 100 beds, all rooms with bath or shower. Modern, garni. Quiet location, near Haus der Kunst. AE, DC, MC.

Arosa. Hotterstr. 2 (222691). 86 rooms with bath or shower. Central, garni, underground garage. AE, DC, MC, V.

Biederstein. Keferstr. 18 (395072). Small modern villa in Schwabing next to the Englischer Garten. Quiet, yet near Schwabing center. AE, V.

Braunauer Hof. Frauenstr. 40 (223613). 22 beds. Well-known Bavarian eating-place with a few rooms. Centrally located near Viktualien food market.

Bräupfanne. Oberföhringerstr. 107a (951095). 25 rooms, all with bath. In northeast suburb of Oberföhring, with bus service to city. Good value, and good restaurant. AE, DC, MC, V.

Central. Schwanthalerstr. 111 (510830). 50 rooms and 18 apartments. On Theresienhöhe in the Hacker-Pschorr-Zentrum. AE, DC, MC, V.

Daniel. Sonnenstr. 5 (554945). 80 rooms with bath. Modern, comfortable rooms with a good downtown location. No restaurant. AE, DC, MC, V.

Domus. St.-Anna-Str. 31 (221704). All rooms with bath and balcony. Near Haus der Kunst. Garni, underground garage. AE, DC, MC, V. Closed Christmas.

Edelweiss Park-Hotel. Menzingerstr. 103 (8111001). Small, modern, garni; in quiet residential area not far from Nymphenburg Gardens. AE, DC, MC, V.

Gästehaus Englischer Garten. Liebergesellstr. 8 (392034). 24 rooms, some next door and less comfortable. Renovated watermill with antique furnishings; central, yet idyllic location next to Englischer Garten. No credit cards.

Leopold. Leopold Str. 119 (367061). 120 beds, many single rooms. In Schwabing, garni, with old-fashioned Gasthaus in front, modern wing at the back. Parking. AE, DC, MC, V.

Hotel Pension am Markt. Heiliggeiststr. 6 (226844). 30 rooms, most with bath. Located in one of Munich's prettiest and quietest squares. No credit cards.

Metropol. Bayerstr. 43 (530764). 200 rooms, most with bath, all with radio. Opposite south exit of main station. Large underground garage. AE, DC, MC, V.

Moorbad-Wetterstein. Grünwalder Str. 16 (650051). 100 beds, all rooms with bath or shower. In suburb of Grünwald. Heated pool, mudpack and Kneipp cures. Garage.

Nymphenburg. Nymphenburger Str. 141 (181086). 80 beds, all with bath or shower. Half-way between Hauptbahnhof and Nymphenburg Palace. Restaurant. AE, DC, MC.

Platzl. Munzstr. 8 (293101). 200 beds, 100 baths. Opposite the Hofbräuhaus—rooms on this side are noisy. Indoor pool, own parking lot. Bavarian folklore shows presented nightly in large beer restaurant. AE, MC.

Reinbold. Adolf-Kolping-Str. 11 (597945). 74 rooms, small but well-appointed; airconditioned, with ice-box and drinks. Recent, near Hauptbahnhof and Stachus (Karlsplatz). AE, DC, MC, V.

Schweiz-Gebhardt. Goethestr. 26 (539585). Near Hauptbahnhof. Good restaurant. AE, DC, V.

Splendid. Maximilianstr. 54 (296606). 64 beds. Small, plush hotel, ideally located for sightseeing, entertainment, shopping. AE.

Inexpensive

Ariane. Pettenkoferstr. 44 (535529). 12 rooms, most with bath. Reserve well in advance for this small pension, with high standards of comfort and excellent central location. No credit cards.

Beck. Thierschstr. 36 (225768). 50 rooms, most with bath. In a handsome art nouveau building in Lehel, within easy walking distance of downtown. No credit cards.

Grobner. Herrnstr. 44 (293939). 30 rooms, some with bath. Friendly, family-run hotel with good central location. No credit cards.

Kriemhild. Gunterstr. 16 (170077). Pension. 40 rooms, half with bath. No restaurant. In western suburb, 30 minutes from downtown. Not far from Schloss Nymphenburg park. MC.

Lettl. Amalienstr. 53 (283026). Pension. In Schwabing, centrally-located and very good value. Rooms in old building not so good.

Monarchia. Senefeldstr. 3 (555281). 65 beds, most rooms with bath or shower. Quiet, with good restaurant.

Zur Mühle. Kirchplatz 5 (965042). 100 beds, all with bath or shower. In Ismaning suburb, about 20 minutes' drive from center; 5 minutes' from S-Bahn station. A newly reopened historic hostelry, this *Romantik Hotel* has a waterside terrace, beer garden, and restaurant with Bavarian specialties.

Camping

For full details write to either the Munich *Fremdenverkehrsamt* or the German Camping Club, *Deutsche Campingclub e.V.,* Mandlstr. 28, 8000 München 40 (tel. 334021). The *ADAC* (German Automobile Club) also issues maps showing Munich camping sites (tel. 76761). There are four main campsites in and around Munich, also equipped for caravans and camping buses.

Campingplatz am Langwieder See (tel. 8141566). North, at Langwieder See exit from Stuttgart autobahn. Open Apr.–15 Oct.

Camping Nordwest in Ludwigsfeld (tel. 1506936 or 1503790 after 9 P.M.). North, off Dachauer Str. Open May–15 Oct.

Camping Thalkirchen (tel. 7231707). In Isar Valley nature park, near Hellabrunn Zoo on Isar Canal. Open Mar.–Oct. Popular and crowded. Also winter camping.

Internationaler Wald-Campingplatz Obermenzing (tel. 8112235). Near beginning of Stuttgart autobahn. Very good. Open all year.

Youth Hostels

General information may be obtained from the *Jugend Informations-zentrum,* Paul-Heyse-Str. 22 (tel. 531655). There are three Youth Hostels *(Jugendherberge).* A YH card is needed, and the upper age limit is 27, as all over Bavaria. Hostels tend to get very full in summer, so reservations are advisable.

DJH Jugendherberge. Wendl-Dietrich-Str. 20 (131156). Nearest tram stop, Rotkreuzplatz. Fully modernized. Check-in times 6–9 A.M. and 12 A.M.–11.30 P.M.

DJH Jugendgästehaus Thalkirchen. Miesingstr. 4 (7236550). Near zoo, tram stop Boschetsriederstr. Check-in time 7 A.M.–11 P.M.

DJH Jugendherberge Burg Schwaneck. Burgweg 4–6 (7932381). 130 beds. In Pullach, about 12 km. (8 miles) south of city center. Renovated castle (1834) on hill above romantic Isar valley. Popular. Garden, sauna, tennis, bowling, bicycles for hire. Check-in time 5–11 P.M.

Youth Hotels

Christlicher Verein Junger Männer (YMCA and YWCA). Landwehrstr. 13 (555941). Very near main station; restaurant evenings only; age limit 27.

Haus International. Elisabethstr. 87 (185081). Good location near Schwabing, tram stop Nordbad; disco and swimming pool; no age limit.

Jugendheim Marienherberge. Goethestr. 9 (555891). Age limit 25, girls only.

HOW TO GET AROUND. From the airport. Munich's international airport—*Flughafen Riem*—is located about 10 km. (6 miles) from the city center. A bus leaves from outside the arrivals *(Ankunft)* building for the Hauptbahnhof, the main rail station in the center of Munich every half hour between 6 A.M. and 8 A.M., and every 15 minutes between 8 A.M. and 9 P.M.; thereafter, they run according to aircraft arrivals. A bus leaves the station for the airport every 15 minutes between 5 A.M. and 9 P.M. Either way, the 30-minute ride costs DM. 5.

A regular bus service, no. 37, goes from the airport to Riem S-Bahn station, where line S6 will take you directly to the Hauptbahnhof. Bus no. 37 also connects, at Steinhausen, with tram no. 19 to the city center.

A taxi from the airport to the main rail station will cost you about DM.25, luggage extra.

City transportation. In common with most large West German cities, Munich has an efficient, well-integrated system of buses, trams (streetcars), electric suburban railway (S-Bahn) and metro or subway (U-Bahn), which operates from about 5 A.M. to 1 A.M. Fares are uniform for the entire system and as long as you are traveling in the same direction, you can transfer from one system to another using the same ticket.

A single ticket *(Einzelfahrkarte)* for a ride in the inner, metropolitan, area costs DM.2.40, or DM.1.86 for a short journey of a few blocks.

Strip tickets *(Mehrfahrtenkarten)* can save you money. A strip of 7 (red) tickets for short journeys in the inner zone and for children costs DM.5; 8 (blue) for longer rides DM.6.50; 13 (blue) DM.12 (including the outer area). You must cancel your ticket—minimum of 2 sections for each journey in the inner area—in one of the blue machines marked with a yellow "E" *(Entwerterautomaten),* found on platforms and inside buses and trams. Failure to do this *before* starting your journey may cost a DM.40 fine.

The best deal for you may be the *24-Stunden-Ticket,* valid on all forms of transport for 24 hours. It costs DM.6.50 (children 4-14 years, DM.2) for the inner area (blue zone), and DM.12 (children DM.4) for the suburban and *S-Bahn* network (blue and green zones) as well.

All tickets can be obtained from the blue dispensers at U- and S-Bahn stations, some bus and tram stops, kiosks with the sign *"Mehrfahrtenkarten"* and a white "K" on a green background, bus and tram drivers displaying the same sign, or from tourist offices.

Note that if you already hold a Youth Pass, EurailPass, Inter-Rail Card, or DB Tourist Card, you can travel free on the S-Bahn network.

By taxi. Usually Mercedes and always cream-colored, taxis are easily hailed in the street or at any one of the numerous cab ranks or telephone 2161 (there's an extra charge for the drive to the pick-up point). Rates start at DM.2.90 for the first mile. There are additional charges of 50 pf. for every piece of luggage. Figure on paying DM.7–DM.10 for a short trip within the city. However, especially in view of the excellent public transport in the city, save taxis for emergencies; charges quickly mount up.

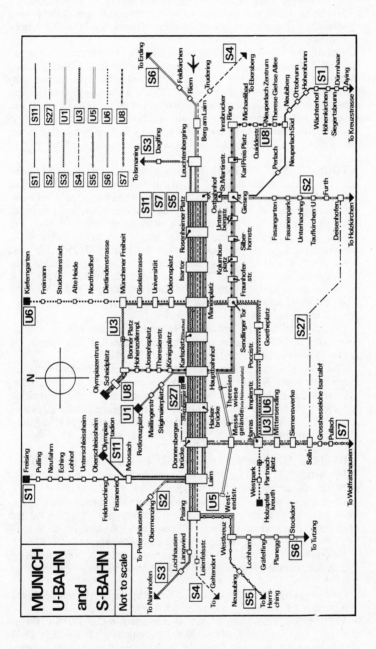

By bicycle. Cycling is an excellent way of seeing Munich as the city and its environs are well endowed with cycle tracks. A map of them, with suggested tours, may be obtained free from all branches of the *Bayerische Vereinsbank.*

Bicycles can be hired at the Englischer Garten, at the corner of Königin-str. and Veterinärstr. (tel. 397016), for DM.5 an hour, DM.15 a day (May–Oct., Sat. and Sun. in good weather). Lothar Borucki, Hans-Sachs-Str. 7 (tel. 266506) hires them out for DM.50 a week, and also has tandems. Bicycles can also be hired at S-Bahn stations for DM.5 a day if you have used public transport to reach the station (show your ticket), otherwise DM.10. For cycling further afield you may find the brochure *Fahrrad am Bahnhof* useful—from *DB* (German Railways) ticket offices.

TOURIST INFORMATION. The *Fremdenverkehrsamt* (central tourist office) is located in the heart of the city at Sendlingerstr. 1 (23911), just around the corner from Marienplatz. This office can help with room reservations; if you arrive out of hours, call the number above for a recorded message detailing hotel vacancies. It's open Mon.–Thurs. 8.30–3, Fri. 8.30–2. Longer opening hours are kept by the city tourist office at the Hauptbahnhof, at the south entrance on Bayerstr. (2391256). It's open Mon.–Sat. 8.30 A.M.–10 P.M., Sun. and holidays 1–9.30. There are also tourist offices at Riem Airport (907256), open Mon.–Sat. 9 A.M.–10 P.M., Sun. 11–7; and in the Rathaus (city hall) on Marienplatz (open Mon.–Fri. 9–5). The municipal information office (Stadtbüro) is in the Stachus underground shopping area.

For information on regions outside Munich, contact the *Fremdenverkehrsverband München-Oberbayern* (Upper Bavarian Regional Tourist Office) at Sonnenstr. 10, near the Karlsplatz (597347).

The Tourist Office produces an official program of events in the city every month, the *Monatsprogramm,* which gives details of all upcoming events. It is available at most hotels, newsstands, and at all tourist offices for DM. 1.30. English tourist information on museums, galleries, castles, and city sights can be obtained around the clock by dialing 239162 (museums and galleries) and 239172 (castles and city sights).

USEFUL ADDRESSES. Consulates. *American Consulate General,* Königinstr. 5–7 (23011). *British Consulate General,* Amalienstr. 62 (394015). *Canadian Consulate,* Maximiliansplatz. 9 (558531).

Currency exchange. There is a 24-hour automatic money changing machine outside the Stadtsparkasse bank at Sparkassenstr. 2 in the Tal area near the Viktualienmarkt, which will convert US dollars, Austrian schillings, Swiss francs, and Italian lire into deutschmarks.

Emergency. *Police,* tel. 110. *Fire department,* tel. 112. *Ambulance,* tel. 19222. *Medical emergencies,* tel. 558661. *Pharmacy emergency service,* tel. 594475.

Lost property. *City lost property office,* Ruppertstr. 19 tel. 233; *main rail station,* tel. 1286664; *post office,* tel. 139552.

Pharmacists. *Ludwigs Apotheke,* Neuhauserstr. 8 (2603021), in the pedestrian zone near the Marienplatz; international pharmacy. *Inter-Apotheke,* at the corner of Luisenstr. and Elisenstr. 5 (main rail station, north exit), tel. 595444, stocks American and British products. Open Mon.–Fri. 8–5.30, Sat. 8–1.

Post offices. *Main post office,* Bahnhofplatz 1, at main rail station; open 24 hours; also money exchange; public telex facilities, daily 7 A.M.–11 P.M. There are also post offices inside the main rail station and at Riem airport.

Travel agents. *American Express,* Promenadeplatz 6 (21990). *Amtliches Bayerisches Reisebüro* (Official Bavarian Travel Office), Promenadeplatz 12; Karlsplatz; Sendlingerstr. 70–71; Arabella Park; etc.; central tel. no. 12040. *Cooks,* Lenbachplatz 3.

TOURS. Organized by the *Munich Sightseeing Tours Company,* the blue buses for sightseeing tours (in German and English) leave all year round from the rail station square, Bahnhofplatz, near Hauptbahnhof (no student reductions). They include:

Short tour (1 hour), daily at 10, 11.30, and 2.30, DM.13. With trip to Olympia Turm (2½ hours), daily at 10 and 2.30, DM.23.

Long tour with visits to Frauenkirche, the Neues Rathaus and Alte Pinakothek (2½ hours), daily (except Mon.) at 10, DM.23. With visits to Schloss Nymphenburg and Amalienburg (2½ hours), daily (except Mon.) at 2.30, DM.23.

"Munich by Night" with visits to three nightspots (approx. 5 hours), Wed.–Sat. at 7.30, including dinner, DM.100.

Further details of all these tours, and many others, are available from the tourist office (tel. 23911) or the tour operator (tel. 1204-248).

EXCURSIONS. Bus excursions to the Alps, into Austria, to the royal palaces and castles of Bavaria, or along the Romantic Road can be booked from the Tourist Office or from the following travel agents: *ABR* (Official Bavarian Travel Office) at the main rail station (tel. 591315 or 59041), *Reiseburo Autobus Oberbayern,* Lenbachplatz 1. (558061), or *"Isaria" Reisen,* Neuhauserstr. 47 (237230). All tours leave from Elisenstr., in front of the Botanischer Garten.

The Upper Bavarian Regional Tourist Office—*Fremdenverkehrsverband München-Oberbayern,* Sonnenstr. 10 (near Karlsplatz), (597347)—provides information and brochures for excursions, roundtrips and accommodation outside Munich.

The S-Bahn can take you quickly to some of the most beautiful places in the countryside around Munich, for example line S6 will take you in half an hour to the lakeside of Starnberger See, and the S4 goes to the depths of the Ebersberger Forest. You can also take a bicycle with you on S-Bahn trains.

SPORTS. The Olympia Park, built for the 1972 Olympics, is the largest sports and recreation center in Europe. For general information about clubs, organizations, events, etc. contact the *Haus des Sports,* Brienner Str. 50 (520151), or the *Städtischen Sportamt,* Neuhauserstr. 26 (2336224).

Golf. There are courses at Strasslach (near Grünwald), (08170450), with 18 holes, and at Thalkirchen, with nine holes, tel. 7231304. You must already be a member of a golf club in your own country to play at either. Green fee is DM.57. Visitors are not admitted at weekends.

Mini-golf courses can be found all over town. Information from the *Bayerischer Bahnengolfverband,* Thomas v. Kempen Weg 12 (754812).

Ice-skating. There are ice rinks at the *Eissportstadion* in the Olympia Park, Spiridon-Louis-Ring 3, and an outdoor rink next to it; *Prinzregenten*

Stadium, Prinzregentenstr. 80; *Eisbahn-West,* Agnes-Bernauer Str. 241; and outdoor skating in winter on the lake in the Englischer Garten and on the Nymphenburg Canal—watch out for danger signs *(Gefahr)* warning of thin ice. Information from *Bayerischer Eissportverband,* Brienner Str. 52 (521336).

Mountain-walking and climbing. Information from the *Deutsche Alpeinverein,* Praterinsel (293086), and from the sports stores *Sport Scheck* (21660) and *Sport Schuster* (237070).

Rowing boats. These can be hired on the Olympiasee lake in the Olympia Park, daily, 10–7 on the southern bank; also on the Kleinhesseloher See in the Englischer Garten, or Hinterbrühler See near the zoo in Thalkirchen.

Sailing and windsurfing. There is sailing and windsurfing on Ammersee and Starnbergersee. Windsurfers should pay attention to restricted areas at bathing beaches. Information on sailing from the *Bayerischer Segler-Verband,* Augustenstr. 46 (5244); on windsurfing from the *Verband der Deutschen Windsurfing Schulen,* Weilheim (0881 5267).

Swimming. In the Isar at Maria-Einsiedel if you are hardy; the river flows from the Alps and the water is frigid. Warmer natural swimming from the beaches of the lakes near Munich, for example Ammersee and Starnbergersee.

Pools: *Cosima Bad* with man-made waves, corner of Englschalkingerstr. and Cosimastr. in Bogenhausen; *Dantebad,* Dantestr. 6, outdoors, heated in cold months; *Florian's Mühle,* Floriansmühlerstr. in Freimann suburb; *Michaelibad,* Heinrich-Wieland-Str. 24; *Olympia-Schwimmhalle,* Olympic grounds; *Volksbad,* Rosenheimerstr. 1.

Nude bathing: on certain days of the week at the city's pools; *Freizeitparadies Isartal;* Feringasee lake in Unterföhring.

Tennis. Indoor and outdoor courts at: Münchner Str. 15 in München-Unterföhring; corner of Drygalski-Allee and Kistlerhofstr. in München-Fürstenried; *Rothof Sportanlage,* Denningerstr., behind the Arabella and Sheraton hotels. In addition there are about 200 outdoor courts all over Munich. Courts can also be booked from *Sport Scheck,* tel. 21660, who have installations all over town.

Prices vary from DM.18–25 an hour, depending on the time of day. Full details from the *Bayerischer Tennis Verband,* Brienner Str. 50 (524420).

PARKS AND GARDENS. Botanischer Garten (Botanical Garden). Menzinger Str. 63, Nymphenburg suburb. Impressive collections of orchids, cacti, cyads, Alpine plants and rhododendrons; 14,000 other varieties. Open air sections open daily 9–5. Hothouses, 9–12 and 1–4.

Englischer Garten (English Garden). One of the largest city parks in Europe, stretching from Prinzregentenstr. northwards for miles along the left bank of the Isar. The brainchild of British-American Benjamin Thompson. Boating lake, four large beer gardens, charming Greek temple—the Monopteros—on top of little hill with fine views of old Munich, plus the famed Chinese pagoda.

Hirschgarten. Large recreation ground in Nymphenburg with wild deer enclosure, playgrounds, beer garden. S-Bahn to Laim.

Hofgarten (Palace Park). Off Odeonsplatz, in city center. Formal garden in French style, with arcades, fountains and small temple. Only a few minutes' walk from main stores.

Luitpold Park. Karl Theodor Str. Schwabing's city park.

Olympia Park. Constructed for 1972 Olympic Games, now one of Europe's largest sports and recreational centers as well as a thriving "village." 275-meter (900-ft.) Olympia-Turm (Olympic Tower) with T.V. mast, observation platform and revolving restaurant (quite expensive). Easily reached by U-Bahn or bus.

Tierpark Hellabrunn (Zoo). South of center in Isar valley. 4,000 animals living in 170 beautiful acres. The only zoo in the world that arranges the animals according to their geographical origins. Bus from Marienplatz.

West Park. Site of 1983 International Horticultural Exhibition (IGA '83). Some 710,000 sq. meters formed to resemble the Lower Alpine landscape of Upper Bavaria, with undulating hills, man-made lakes and valleys, and regional and international flora. Restaurants, cafés, beer-gardens, children's playgrounds, openair theater, concert arena. Admission free. U-Bahn lines U3 and U6 to West Park or Reuland Str.

HISTORIC BUILDINGS AND SITES. Admission to many of the following is free. Admission fees and opening times can be checked with the Tourist Office. For information in English telephone 239175.

Alter Hof. Entrance in Burgstr. First of the Wittelsbach castles, originally forming the northeast corner of the city. Built about 1255 by Ludwig the Stern. Emperor Ludwig the Bavarian also lived here, thus making the castle the first permanent imperial residence. Today the building houses the Munich finance authorities.

Altes Rathaus (Old Town Hall). Burgstr. near Tal. Built 1474 by Jörg Ganghofer who also built the Frauenkirche. The Ballroom was considered one of the most beautiful Gothic halls in Germany. Interior wholly destroyed during World War II, but the exterior was rebuilt according to original plans.

Bayerisches Hauptmünzamt (Bavarian State Mint). Pfisterstr. 4. Built by Wilhelm Egkl in 1563–67, originally for ducal stables and art collection. Classical facade added 1809. Inner courtyard divided into three stories, each with own architectural style.

Maximilianeum. On bank of Isar. Seat of Bavarian State Parliament and Senate, built 1857. Terrace in front is open to visitors, view over city and parks.

Neues Rathaus (New Town Hall). Marienplatz. Completed 1909. Glockenspiel, the largest in Germany, is famous for its clockwork figures of the Munich *Schäffler* (coopers) which dance daily at 11 A.M. In the evening at 9 P.M. the *Münchner Kindl* (little monk) is put to bed by nightwatchmen.

Residenz. Max Joseph Platz 3. Built 16th–19th centuries. Home of generations of the Bavarian House of Wittelsbach, of dukes, princes and kings. Magnificent interior—completely reconstructed after severe World War II bomb damage—forms the *Residenz Museum.*

Schloss Blutenberg. Moated castle on River Würm at Obermenzing, west Munich. Former hunting lodge of Duke Albrecht III who married a barber's daughter from Straubing, Agnes Bernauer. International Children's Book Library. Summer concerts in chapel or Barocksaal hall, or outdoors in monastery gardens a mile south.

Schloss Nymphenburg. About eight km. (five miles) northwest of city center. The building of Nymphenburg Palace was begun in 1664 and went on for 100 years. Beautiful park with pavilions, including *Amalienburg,* a hunting lodge designed by Cuvilliés. The *Marstallmuseum* is a carriage museum which contains Ludwig II's luxurious sleighs; on the first floor is the new Bäumler Collection of Nymphenburg porcelain. Botanical gardens, laid out 1909–14 adjoin the park. The famous porcelain factory is also in the palace grounds.

Schloss Schleissheim. About 19 km. (12 miles) north of Munich, the new palace (Neues Schloss) of Schleissheim contains a renowned Baroque art gallery and a magnificent ballroom famous for its concerts of Baroque music (June–Sept.). 18th-century French style gardens. *Lustheim,* a little garden palace, houses Germany's largest collection of Meissen porcelain.

Viktualienmarkt. Behind Peterskirche. Munich's popular daily food market, complete with beer garden and numerous snack stalls.

CHURCHES. Asamkirche (Church of St. John of Nepomuk, or of the Asam brothers). Sendlingerstr. Designed and built next door to their home by the Asam brothers, 1733, it shows remarkable harmony. A seminal early-Rococo masterpiece.

Burgsaal Kirche. Neuhauserstr. 47. Built 1710 by Viscardi; virtually destroyed in World War II. Ignaz Günther's *Schutzengelgruppe* (guardian angel group) sculpture is worth seeing. In crypt is grave of Rupert Mayer, Munich Jesuit priest persecuted by Nazis for helping Jews.

Frauenkirche (Cathedral and Parish Church of Our Lady). Frauenplatz. Built 1468–88 in late-Gothic style by Jörg Ganghofer, it suffered severe damage in 1944 but has now been largely restored. Original tomb of Emperor Ludwig the Bavarian was undamaged. Its twin towers with onion domes have become Munich's symbol. Take the elevator up the south tower for magnificent view.

Ludwigskirche. Ludwigstr. 22. 19th-century building, with second largest church fresco in the world, painted 1836–40 by Peter Cornelius. Byzantine and early-Renaissance elements of the building are unusual for Munich.

Michaelskirche. Neuhauserstr. 52. In pedestrian zone. The most important Renaissance church in Germany, built 1583–97; badly damaged in World War II and rebuilt. In crypt is tomb of Ludwig II; Eugène de Beauharnais, Napoleon's stepson, is also buried here.

Peterskirche. Just off Marienplatz. Munich's oldest parish church (a fourth St. Peter's was consecrated on the original site in 1368) and a well-known landmark. Climb its tower for a good view of the city.

Theatinerkirche (Church of the Theatines). Odeonsplatz. Former court church of the Bavarian Electors. Begun 1651; facade, however, is by Cuvilliés, 1768. Former monastery buildings on south side.

MUSEUMS AND GALLERIES. Opening times vary, so it's best to check with the Tourist Office or their *Monatsprogramm.* For information in English, call 239174. Most museums and galleries are open Tues. to Sat., 9.30 or 10–4.30; Sun. 10–1; closed Mon. Some open one or two evenings a week, 7–9. Admission charges are usually DM.2–5, with reductions and sometimes free entry for students; all museums are free on Sundays and holidays. There are also numerous temporary art exhibitions held in banks, offices, stores and hotels.

Alte Pinakothek. Barerstr. 27. One of Europe's great picture galleries. European paintings from the 14th to the 18th centuries. Among the chief treasures of this museum are works by Van der Weyden, Memling, Hieronymus Bosch, Holbein, Dürer (including one of the most famous self-portraits), Grünewald, Breughel, a rich group by Rubens, Van Dyck, Frans Hals, Rembrandt, Poussin, Chardin, Boucher, El Greco, Velasquez, Giotto, Botticelli, Leonardo da Vinci, Titian, Raphael, Tintoretto. Not to be missed by any remotely interested in painting.

Antikensammlungen (Museum of Antiquities). Königsplatz 1. Greek, Roman and Etruscan art.

Bayerisches Nationalmuseum (National Museum of Bavaria). Prinzregentenstr. 3. Remarkable collection of medieval art and sculpture, miniature art, arts and crafts, folk art, applied art, etc. Largest collection of early German sculpture in the country, the best tapestries in Germany, a fine group of woodcarvings by Tilman Riemenschneider, 16th-century armor and the unique Krippenschau, Christmas crib collection.

Bayerisches Staatsbibliothek (Bavarian State Library). Ludwigstr. 23. Over 3 million volumes, including 16,000 incunabula and medieval texts such as the Bible of Emperor Otto III, with its Reichenau illuminations and its ivory binding inset with gems.

BMW Museum. Lerchenauer Str. 36. Opposite Olympia Park. Vintage cars and motorcycles displayed using dazzling audio-visual techniques.

Deutsches Jagd- und Fischerei Museum (German Museum of Hunting and Fishing). Neuhauserstr. 53. In former Augustinian church. Trophies, weapons, dioramas.

Deutsches Museum (German Museum of Science and Technology). Museum Island. First-rate scientific museum, with 16th-century alchemists' workshops, excellent mining and historical railroad sections, planetarium, vast aerospace halls. Open Mon., too.

Glyptothek. Königsplatz 3. Ancient Egyptian, Greek and Roman sculpture.

Haus der Kunst. Prinzregentenstr. 1. Antique fairs, art and book exhibitions. Houses *Staatsgalerie für Moderne Kunst* with art and sculpture of the 19th and 20th centuries.

Münchner Stadtmuseum (City Historical Museum). St.-Jakobs-Platz 1. The history of Munich. Also musical instruments, photographs, puppets, fairground exhibits, and more.

Museum für Völkerkunde (Museum of Ethnology). Maximilianstr. 42. Fine collections from the Far East and South America.

Neue Pinakothek. Corner of Barerstr. and Theresienstr. Some of the best of 18th and 19th century art. French Impressionists, German Romantics, plus Goya, Turner, Manet; housed in magnificent new building.

Prähistorische Staatssammlung (State Prehistoric Collection). Lerchenfeldstr. 2. Prehistoric finds from all over Bavaria.

Paleontologische und Geologische Staatssammlung (State Collection of Paleontology and Geology). Richard Wagner Str. 10. Fossils, ancient life forms, 10-million-year-old mammoth.

Residenzmuseum. Max-Joseph-Platz 3. State rooms and princely suites in Renaissance, Rococo and neo-Classical styles. Porcelain and silver. *Schatzkammer* (treasury) with gold and jeweled masterpieces going back ten centuries. Rococo *Altes Residenztheater* (Cuvilliés-Theater). The State

Collection of Egyptian Art *(Staatliche Sammlung Agyptischer Kunst)* is now here, entrance in Hofgartenstr.

Schackgalerie. Prinzregentenstr. 9. Late 19th-century German painting—Böckling, Feuerbach, Schwind.

Staatliche Graphische Sammlung (State Collection of the Graphic Arts). Meiserstr. 10. Drawings and prints from the late Gothic period to the present.

Städtische Galerie im Lenbachhaus (Municipal Gallery). Luisenstr. 33. Works by Lenbach; the *Blaue Reiter* (Blue Rider) school (Kandinsky, Marc, Macke); Paul Klee.

Theatermuseum. Galeriestr. 4a. In the Hofgarten Arcade. 40,000 volume library, portraits of actors, designs for stage sets.

Valentin-Museum. In the tower gate of Isartor. Museum of curiosities and nonsense dedicated to the German comedian.

Villa Stuck. Prinzregentenstr. 60. Restored villa of Franz von Stuck with original frescos, paintings, graphics and documents from the early 1900s.

THEATERS. Munich has scores of theaters and variety show haunts, though most productions will be largely impenetrable if your German is shaky. But we nonetheless list all the better-known theaters, as well as some of the smaller and more progressive spots, as a visit should prove the city's reputation for cultural excitement.

Prices for most are reasonable, but all opera productions—and Munich is one of the great European centers for opera—are very expensive. Moreover, tickets for performances at the Bavarian National Theater (the State Opera House) are well nigh impossible to obtain. However, you could try one of the following agencies: *ABR-Theaterkasse,* am Stachus; *Bauer,* Landschaftstr. 1 (in Rathaus building); *Max Hieber,* Kaufingerstr. 23; *Radio-RIM,* Theatinerstr. 17; and in some bookshops. Most theaters are closed in July and August.

Bayerisches Nationaltheater (State Opera House). Max-Joseph-Platz. Home of the Bavarian State Opera Company. Rebuilt and reopened 1963 following severe bomb damage, and interiors again refurbished in 1987; the auditorium is magnificent with stuccoed ceiling and 180-light chandelier suspended from the dome. Huge underground parking lot with direct access to theater. Tickets from the Opera ticket office, Maximilianstr. 11; open Mon. to Fri. 10–1 and 4–6; Sat., Sun. and holidays 10–1.

Bayerisches Staatsschauspiel/Neues Residenztheater (Bavarian State Theater/New Residence Theater). Max-Joseph-Platz. (2185413). Mainly classical theater. Box office open Mon.–Fri. 10–1 and 3.30–5.30, Sat. 10–12.30; also one hour before performance.

Cuvilliés-Theater/Altes Residenztheater (Old Residence Theater). Max-Joseph-Platz. (221316). Breathtakingly-beautiful Rococo theater designed by court architect Francois Cuvilliés. Molière, Baroque period operas, Richard Strauss. Box office open Mon.–Fri. 10–1 and 3.30–5.30, Sat. 10–12.30; also one hour before performance.

Deutsches Theater. Schwanthaler Str. 13. (593427). Musicals and spectacular shows with international stars. Vast auditorium. Box office open Mon.–Fri. 12–6, Sat. 10–1.30.

Intimes Theater. Künstlerhaus, Lenbachplatz 8. Mainly comedies.

Kammerspiele im Schauspielhaus. Maximilianstr. 26. (23721328). Classical and contemporary plays. Box office open Mon.–Fri. 10–6, weekends and holidays 10–1.

Kleine Komödie. Bayerischer Hof Hotel, Promenade Platz 6 (292810) and at Max II Denkmal, top end of Maximilianstr. (221859). Two small theaters performing popular comedies. Box office, Bayerischen Hoff, open Mon.–Sat. 11–8, Sun. and holidays 3–8. Box office Max II Denkmal, open Mon. 11–7, Tues.–Sat. 11–8, Sun. and holidays 3–8.

Marienkäfer (Ladybird). Georgen, corner Schraudolphstr. 8. Music, poetry, contemporary theater.

Marionettentheater. Blumenstr. 29a. (265712). Puppet theater. Box office open Tues.–Sun. 10–12.

Platzl. Munzstr. 8–9 (23703355). On the tiny square of the same name. Shows with typical Bavarian humor, yodeling and *Schuhplattler*. Shows Sun.–Fri.

Puppentheater. Künstlerhaus, Lenbachplatz 8. Puppet theater.

Scala Theater am Wedekindplatz. Drugstore, Feilitzschstr. 12. Small cozy cabaret theater with bar, for guest appearances and one-man shows.

Schwabinger Brettl. Walter Novak, Occamstr. 11. Modern interpretations of prose and poetry, with musical interludes.

Theater in der Brienner Strasse. Brienner Str. 50. Mainly drama.

Theater "Die Kleine Freiheit" ("Small Freedom"). Maximilianstr. 31. (221123). One of Munich's boulevard theaters, showing Broadway type plays. Box office open Mon.–Sat. from 11, Sun. from 2.

Theater am Gärtnerplatz. Gärtnerplatz 3. Light opera and operettas.

Theater der Jugend. Franz Joseph Str. 47, at Elizabethplatz in Schwabing. (23721365). For children and youngsters. Box office open Tues.–Sat. 1.30–5.30.

Theater am Marstall. Marstallplatz. Mainly drama.

Theater 44. Hohenzollernstr. 20. Avant-garde, experimental theater.

CONCERTS. Munich has several big concert halls, as well as a number of churches in which choral concerts are performed. The four main orchestras are the Munich Philharmonic, the Bavarian State Orchestra, the Bavarian Radio Orchestra and the Symphony Orchestra Kurt Graunke. Choral societies include the famous Bach Choir, the Münchner Motettenchor and the Musica Viva, the latter for contemporary music.

Full details of forthcoming concerts can be obtained from *Vorschau* or *Monatsprogramm* and tickets can be bought from the following: *Otto Bauer, Musikalienhandlung,* in the Rathaus (221757); *Buchhandlung Lehmkuhl,* Leopoldstr. 45 (398042); *Residenz Bücherstube,* Residenzstr. 1 (220868); *Radio-RIM,* Theatinerstr. 17 (44170253); *Hieber Max* Liebefrauenstr. 1 (226571).

Concert Halls

Alabamahalle. Schleissheimerstr. 418. One-time factory. To the north of the city; presents mainly avant-garde works.

Amerika Haus. Karolinerplatz 3.

Bayerischer Rundfunk. Rundfunkplatz 1. (558080). Concert Hall of Bavarian Radio. Box office open Mon.–Fri. 9–12 and 1–5.

Cuvilliés-Theater. Residenz, Max-Joseph-Platz.

Galerie im Lenbachhaus. Luisenstr. 33. (521041). Soloists and chamber music groups.

Gasteig Kulturzentrum. Corner of Rosenheimerstr. and Am Gasteig. (4181614). Open since 1984 and now the city's major concert hall, home of the Munich Philharmonic. A multi-purpose cultural center. Box office open Mon.–Fri. 10.30–2 and 3–6, Sat. 10.30–2.

Herkules Saal in der Residenz. (224641). The big concert hall inside the Residenz (Max-Joseph-Platz). Box office opens one hour before performances.

Hochschule für Musik. Arcisstr. 12. (559101). For soloists and chamber music.

Kongress Saal, Deutsches Museum. Museumsinsel 1 (298430 or 221790). On its island in the middle of the Isar. The second most important concert hall in Munich, and the largest. Box office opens one hour before performances.

Festsaal, Künstlerhaus. Lenbachplatz 8. For recitals and chamber music.

Olympiahalle, (30613577). Pop concerts. Box office open Mon.–Thurs. 8–5, Fri. 8–2.

Schauspielhaus. Maximilianstr. 26.

Sophiensaal. Sophienstr. 6. With a fine organ.

Church Music

The best church music is provided by the choirs of *Michaelskirche* (St. Michael's), Neuhauserstr.; *Matthäuskirche* (St. Matthew's), Sendlinger Tor Platz; and the *Dom Chor* (Cathedral Choir) which sometimes sings in the *Frauenkirche* and sometimes in the *Dreifaltigkeitskirche* (Holy Trinity) in Pacellistr.

Summer Concerts

One of the summer delights of Munich are the many concerts held in palaces and castles in and around the city. Tickets can usually be bought from large travel agents. Among the regular venues are:

Schloss Amerang. Near Wasserburg. Medieval castle about 50 km. (30 miles) southeast of Munich. Concerts of Baroque music and folklore take place in courtyard (covered in bad weather) from late June to mid-August.

Schloss Blutenberg. Moated castle, west of Munich. Concerts in castle or in monastery garden at Würminsel near Marienplatz in Pasing about 1½ km. (one mile) south of the castle. The Schloss Blutenberg organization also arranges concerts of Renaissance music in the French Gardens of Schloss Schwaneck at Pullach on the Isar 16 km. (ten miles) south of Munich. Advance booking: *Theatergemeinde*, Goethestr. 24.

Benediktbeuern. Near Bad Tölz. 1,200-year-old monastery. Concerts of Baroque music or by Tölzer Knabenchor (boys' choir), June–end Aug., in Barocksaal, Basilika (famous double-towered church), or outdoors in cloister courtyard. Tickets for Basilika concerts from *Theaterkasse,* ABR, Stachus-Karlsplatz, Munich, tel. 59815.

Brunnenhof, Residenz. Residenzstr. End of June through Sept. Concerts in courtyard or Herkulessaal in bad weather. Concert Organization, tel. 6091198.

Schloss Herrenchiemsee. Island of Herrenchiemsee. Chamber music in palace ballrooms, 17 May–27 Sept., Sat. at 7.30 and 8.30. Ferryboats from Prien on Chiemsee to the island, last one leaves island 9.50. Bus excursions from Munich offered by American Express and Autobus Bayern, Lenbachplatz 1.

Schloss Nymphenburg. Nymphenburg, West Munich. Summer Music Festival 22 June–13 July in the Steinerner Saal of the palace.

Schloss Schleissheim. Schleissheim, 19 km. (12 miles) north of Munich. Concerts held, June–Sept., in Grosser Barocksaal. International Music Weeks, 1–29 June. Concert Organizer, tel. 6091198.

SHOPPING. Munich has some fascinating shopping streets and pedestrian zones. The main ones are: pedestrian mall from Karlsplatz (Stachus) to Marienplatz; Wein and Theatinerstr., and Diener and Residenzstr.; the pedestrian zone from the Hauptbahnhof, the main station, to Karlsplatz. Other fine shopping streets are Briennerstr., Maximilianstr., the Maxburg block at Pacellistr. and the small streets near the Hofbräuhaus and the pedestrian zone in Sendlingerstr. The largest department stores are *Kaufhof, Karstadt, Hertie,* and *Beck* (of Fifth Avenue fame) at the corner of Diener Str. between the old and new city halls.

Antiques. The expensive and select dealers are to be found around the Viktualienmarkt, in *Antic Haus* at Neuturmstr. 1 near the Hofbräuhaus (50 dealers on three floors), and in side streets in Schwabing— Schellingstr., Amalienstr. and Türkenstr. *Boheme* at Türkenstr. 79 is a tavern selling antiques. *Schloss Haimhausen* out at Schleissheim is a palace full of antiques.

Less expensive are the shops in the Haimhauserstr., Siegestr. and Ursulastr., and *Antiquarius* in the courtyard at Leopoldstr. 61. The antique fleamarket in the Dachauer Str. is fun, with a huge range of items.

Beer steins and pewter. *Ludwig Mory* in the Rathaus am Marienplatz sells particularly beautiful and varied pewter articles and a large selection of beer mugs. *Franz Mayer'sche Hofkunstanstalt,* Seidelstr. 20, has handpainted glass mugs. *Wallach,* Residenzstr. 3 for original beer steins. *Sebastian Weseley,* Rindermarkt 1, for beer steins, glass, wood-carvings and local handicrafts.

Clocks. *Andreas Huber,* Weinstr. 8; *Hauser,* Marienplatz 28, Neuhauserstr. 19.

Chocolates and candy. *Elly Seidl,* Am Kosttor, in street opposite opera house, manufacturer of fine confectionery for over 60 years; *Bonbonniere,* Westenriedstr.

Dirndls and folk dresses. *Dirndl Eck* on Platzl near Hofbräuhaus; *Dirndlstube,* Karlsplatz 8; *Haslinger,* Rosental 10, at the Viktualienmarkt; *Leder-Moser,* Herzogspitalstr. 7 (entrance at Karlstor on Stachus), for leatherwear; *Loden-Frey,* Maffeistr. 7–9, famous for Bavarian fashions; *Wallach,* Residenzstr. 3, for fine and elegant folk costumes and hand-printed cottons. Handicrafts. *Bayerischer Kunstgewerbeverein* (Bavarian Association of Artisans), Pacellistr. 7, for handicrafts with a modern touch; *Weinberger,* Herzogspitalstr. 7 (near the Karlstor).

For typical Bavarian woodcarvings, try: *Karl Storr,* Kaufingerstr. 25; *A. Kaiser,* Rindermarkt 1 (next to the Peterskirche).

For wax candles, try: *Koron,* Mazaristr. 1 (near the Frauenkirche); *Wachszieher am Dom,* Sporerstr. 2 (also near the Frauenkirche).

Porcelain. *Nymphenburger Porzellanmanufaktur,* Nördliches Schloss-rondell 8, Nymphenburg. In grounds of Schloss Nymphenburg, eight km. (five miles) northwest of city center is the famous porcelain factory. Exhibition and sales rooms open Mon. to Fri., 8–12 and 1–5.

RESTAURANTS. Munich has ten times more places to eat than there are days in the year, with specialty restaurants from all parts of the globe, French, Italian and Chinese topping the bill. You will find everything from the only 3-star restaurant in Germany through exotic and elegant gourmet temples, regional specialty eating houses, wholesome family taverns and the cheap, quick snack-bars *(Imbiss)* on the corner.

Among the best known Munich specialties are *Leberkäs,* a meat loaf made from pork and beef, and *Weisswurst,* a small, white, nonsmoked sausage made from veal and various other ingredients; both are eaten warm, with sweet Munich mustard, and as a snack rather than a main meal course and call for copious drafts of beer; tradition has it that the Weisswurst should be eaten only between midnight and noon. Delicious *Brathendl* (chicken from spit) and *Steckerlfisch* (fish grilled on sticks) are served primarily during the Oktoberfest and are intended to work up your beer appetite. Other typical Munich dishes include *Kalbshaxe* (veal shank), *Schweinshaxe* (pork shank), and various types of *Geselchtes* (smoked pork), accompanied by the Bavarian type of *Knödel* (potato or bread dumplings). *Radi* (white or red radishes) are another beloved bite to go with beer.

Although there are numerous restaurants with first-class wine cellars and taverns specializing in wine from certain regions, such as Pfalz or Franken, the "national" drink of Munich is, of course, beer. In the most typical beer halls the minimum you can order is a *Mass,* a "measure" which in this case means a 1-liter mug (a bit over a U.S. quart); elsewhere *ein grosses* (½ liter) or even *ein kleines* (¼ liter) can be had. You order *helles* (light) if you like the regular or *dunkles* (dark) if you prefer a somewhat heavier, sweeter type. You will meet the product of several dozen breweries, but the great names among them have remained the same for several centuries: Löwenbräu, Paulaner-Salvator-Thomasbräu, Hackerbräu, Spatenbräu, Augustinerbräu, and Pschorr Bräu. Weihenstephan beer produced in nearby Freising since 1040 is the oldest brew in Germany. Among the several seasonal types of beer, all of them stronger than the "regular", are: *Wiesenbier,* brewed for Oktoberfest which takes place on the Wiesen (meadows) hence the name; various kinds of *Starkbier* (strong beer) produced during the Lent season, with Latin names, the best known of which is *Salvator; Maibock,* brewed and drunk in May. If none of these should be available and you wish for a strong beer, ask for *Bock* (light or dark). If you prefer wheat beer, order a *Weissbier.*

The following lists of restaurants are only a small selection of Munich's countless eating and drinking establishments. All hotels with restaurants already listed (see *Hotels* above) are not given here unless they are of outstanding quality. Good-value, plain eating can be found in most of the large department stores—*Kaufhof, Karstadt* and *Hertie*—while at the Viktualienmarkt there are *Imbiss-Buden* (snack-bars) serving a variety of tasty snacks.

Lunch is normally served from noon until about 2.30, dinner from 6 P.M. In all cases, you should check opening times and *Ruhetage,* closing days each week.

Expensive

Aubergine. Maximilians Platz 5 (598171). Munich's finest and most expensive restaurant, serving highest quality *nouvelle cuisine.* Small, quiet and elegant. Advanced booking essential. Reservations from 12–1.30 and 6.30–9.30. Allow four hours for your meal. Closed Sun., Mon., Christmas and New Year's, and the first three weeks of Aug. MC

Austern Keller. Stollbergstr. 11 (298787). Large, vaulted cellar-restaurant near opera; for lovers of oysters and scallops (fresh fish flown in daily from the Riviera). Popular, sometimes noisy, reserve well in advance. Closed Mon. and Christmas. AE, DC, MC, V.

Bogenhausener Hof. Ismaninger Str. (985586). Munich's newest elite spot with cuisine to match. Small and very popular—reservations essential.

Boettner's. Theatinerstr. 2 (221210). The oldest of Munich's classy restaurants provides a quiet, gracious contrast to the bustle of the city center outside. Seafood dominates the menu. Reservations essential. AE, DC, MC, V. Closed Sat. for dinner, Sun., and holidays.

Bouillabaisse. Falkenturmstr. 10 (297909). Wide variety of fish specialties as well as fine all-round menu. Cozy, on two floors with wine-cellar tavern. Open to midnight; meeting place for performers from the ballet and opera. Must reserve. Closed Sun., Mon. lunch, and Aug. AE, DC, MC, V.

La Cave. Maximilianstr. 25 (223029). Elegant, exclusive restaurant and bar, open to 2 A.M. Mostly French cuisine, crawfish a specialty. AE, DC, MC.

Chesa Rüegg. Wurzerstr. 18 (297114). Fine Swiss cuisine in chalet-style building near the National Theater. Special theatergoers menu starting at 6 P.M. with cocktails, and continuing after the performance. Swiss wines. AE, DC, V.

Csarda Piroschka. Prinzregentenstr. 1 (295425). In Haus der Kunst. Hungarian food; served to the accompaniment of authentic gypsy orchestras from Budapest. AE, DC, MC.

Dallmayr. Dienerstr. 14 (213500). On first floor of huge, world-famous delicatessen shop. Delicious selections in small rooms. AE, DC.

Le Gourmet. Ligsalzstr. 46 (503597). Next to Messegelände. Particularly comfortable, with antique furnishings. Reservations advised. Closed Sun. and first week in Jan. AE, DC, MC.

Halali. Schonfeldstr. 22, between Königinstr. and Ludwigstr. (285909). Small and pretty hunting-lodge style restaurant numbering among the top Munich addresses for fine Bavarian specialties with international flair. Book well in advance.

Hax'nbauer Stuben. Twin, rustic-style establishment: the larger one at Sparkassenstr. (Münzstr. 2, tel. 221975); the smaller, more exclusive one, with mountain hut interiors, around the corner (at Münzstr. 5, tel. 295309). *Schweinshaxen* and *Kalbshaxen* from the open fire; other Bavarian delicacies. MC, V.

Ile de France. Rosenheimer Str. 32 (4481366). In the Motorama building near the Penta Hotel. Fine, good-value cuisine and first-class service.

Käferschänke. Corner of Prinzregentenstr. and Schumannstr. (41681). Another delicatessen paradise, with large store downstairs, and cellar where they serve everything from truffles to quails' eggs and vintage champagne. Reservations advised. Closed Sat. and holidays. AE, DC, MC.

Königshof. Karlsplatz 25 (558412). Reputedly the best hotel-restaurant in Munich; on first floor with view across the bustling Karlsplatz. International cuisine and excellent service. AE, MC, V.

Maximilian Stube. Maximilianstr. 27 (229044). International cuisine, but accent on Italian. Evening dining to zither accompaniment. AE, DC, MC, V.

La Mer. Schraudolphstr. 24 (2722439). Exclusive fish restaurant of almost exaggerated elegance. Fine conventional cuisine. AE, DC, MC.

Mifune. Ismaningerstr. 136 (987572). In Bogenhausen suburb. Munich's premier Japanese restaurant—traditional style and decor. AE, DC, MC.

La Piazzetta. Oskar von Miller Ring 3 (282990). Large dining restaurant-rosticceria, serving fine food, with one of the longest Italian wine lists in town. Adjoining it is a sophisticated coffee bar open to 6 A.M. with music, snacks, beer garden.

Preysing Keller. Innere Wiener Str. 6 (481015). Elegant, rustic restaurant in vaulted 16th/17th-century cellar. Fine reputation and excellent service. International menu; large impressive wine cellar (German, French, Austrian wines). Reservations essential. Closed Sun., Christmas, and New Year's. No credit cards.

Sabitzer. Reitmoorstr. 21 (298584). Elegant and pricey little place in fashionable old-town quarter of Lehel. *Nouvelle cuisine* with emphasis on exquisite sauces. Menus devised by chef-patron (four courses at lunch, seven at dinner). Wine is expensive; service efficient and discreet. Reservations essential. Closed Sat., Sun., July, and Aug. AE, DC, MC.

Tai Tung. Prinzregentenstr. 60 (471100). In beautiful old Villa Stuck. Munich's oldest (and finest) Chinese restaurant. Good service and friendly atmosphere in stately surroundings. DC, MC.

Tantris. Johann-Fichte-Str. 7 (362061). At northern end of Schwabing in modern building in side street. Pop-art decor but perfect service in one of the best restaurants in Germany, with the largest selection of French food in town (introduced *nouvelle cuisine* to Munich). Reservations essential. Closed Sat. lunch, Sun., Mon., first week in Jan., and 3 weeks in Aug. AE, DC, MC.

El Toula. Sparkassenstr. 5 (292869). Franco-Italian cuisine in elegant surroundings. Personal service and very good wine list. AE, DC, MC, V.

Walliser Stuben. Leopoldstr. 33 (348000). Features Swiss food and wines. AE, DC, MC, V.

Weinhaus Schwarzwälder. Hartmannstr. 8 (227216). Traditional old Munich establishment, still boasting the largest wine list in town. Interesting for its old interiors, otherwise rather over-priced. DC, V.

Zum Bürgerhaus. Pettenkofer Str. 1 (597909). Munich's second-oldest eating establishment in attractively restored Biedermeier house with appropriate decor. French cuisine and Bavarian specialties. Popular, so book. DC, MC.

Moderate

Asia. Einsteinstr. 133 (472124). Good-value Chinese restaurant with lower-priced lunchtime menus. Enormous portions; crowded in evening. DC, MC, V.

Bier Museum. Burgstr. 12 (224315). Between the Alte Hof and Marienplatz. Good-value old Munich restaurant dating from 1252. Wholesome local dishes with a touch of haute cuisine. Oldest vaulted cellar in Munich. AE, MC.

Bistro Terrine. Amalienpassage, corner Türkenstr. (entrance Türkenstr. 84), (281780). Typical French bistro-style restaurant. Reservations advised. Closed Sun. AE, MC.

Braunauer Hof. Frauenstr. 40 (223613). Favorite hotel-restaurant for visitors and locals alike. Building full of local atmosphere. Jovial chef-patron; traditional Bavarian specialties, plus international dishes. Open 11.30–2.30 and 6–10.

La Coquille. Römerstr. 15 (390539). Small, cozy cellar-restaurant in quiet Schwabing street. Specializes in small, delicate suppers for late-night homegoers. Open until midnight. DC, MC.

Datscha. Kaiserstr. 3 (341218). Food from Caucasus, Turkestan and Russian in wooded-hut interiors. Colorful courtyard in summer with open grill. Fiercely moustachioed waiters add to exotic atmosphere. AE, DC, V.

Don Quijote. Biedersteiner Str. 6 (342318). Quaint cellar with corner tables serving Spanish food. Menus from shrimp with garlic to Steak Torero; good Spanish wines. AE, DC, MC, V.

Goldene Stadt. Oberanger 44 (264382). Authentic Bohemian specialties. Reservations advised. Closed Sun. AE, DC, MC.

Hamburger Fischstrbe. Isartorplatz 8 (225420). This no-frills fish restaurant features north German seafood at terrific prices. Reservations advised. AE, DC, MC, V.

Hannen Stube. Prannerstr. 2 (220774). Behind Bayerischer Hof hotel. In addition to Bavarian and international specialties.

Hundskugel. Hotterstr. 18 (264272). Munich's oldest tavern, dating from about 1640. Wholesome, good-value home cooking. DC.

Kasak. Friedrichstr. 1 (391771). The best Greek food in town. Reservations advised. AE, DC, MC, V.

Kay's Bistro. Utzschneiderstr. 1 (260584). The bizarre decor changes weekly, the menu is similarly varied. This is the place for a chic and fun night out. Reservations essential. No credit cards.

K.U.K. Monarchie. Reichenbachstr. 22 (2015671). Near the Gärtner Platz Theater. Evening restaurant with specialties from the far reaches of what was once the Austrian Empire. DC.

Mykonos. Rathausplatz 1 (6414052). In Grünwald. Old-established and much frequented Greek restaurant. DC, MC.

Nürnberger Bratwurstglöckl. Frauenplatz 9 (220385). Nürnberg sausages and charcoal grilled meats in colorful interiors. Reservations advised. No credit cards.

Oma's Kuche. Leopoldstr. 194 (340971). In Holiday Inn hotel. Recent, but full of nostalgia with decor and menu as in grandmother's day. Open all week until 11 P.M.

Ratskeller. Marienplatz 8 (220313). In cellar of Rathaus. A series of more or less modern rooms, some small and inviting, some uncomfortably barn-like, replacing the old, tradition-filled Ratskeller. The food, however, remains good—emphasis on Bavarian specialties—and is served until midnight. Reservations advised. AE, MC, V.

Straubinger Hof. Blumenstr. 5 (2608444). Authentic Munich-Bavarian menu. Good-value, quick service; shady garden; popular so must reserve.

Torggelstuben. Platzl (292022). Antique furnishings on upper floor; rustic and wine decor on ground floor and in cellar wine tavern. Outstanding food; mostly wine drinking in cellar.

Zum Bögner. Tal 72 (226750). Halfway between Rathaus and Isartor gate. Old Munich restaurant. AE, DC, MC, V.

Zum Spöckmeier. Rosenstr. 9 (268088). Famous old Munich restaurant in a new building, with sidewalk tables on the pedestrian mall in summer.

Inexpensive

Berni's Nudelbrett. Peter's Platz 8 (264469). Near pedestrian zone and Rindermarkt. Set meals at various prices. Lots of pasta and pizza.

Bratwurst Glöckl Am Dom. Frauenplatz 9 (220385). Dark, smokey atmospheric old Munich grill-sausage restaurant near the Cathedral. Very traditional.

Gebo's. Frauenstr. 18 (224309). Café-restaurant serving breakfast (English-style if required), snacks and gourmet meals at reasonable prices.

'Grüner Hof. Bayerstr. 35 (595571). Opposite south exit of main rail station, the Hauptbahnhof.

Hundskugel. Hotterstr. 18 (264272). Munich's oldest tavern, dating back to 1640, serves simple Bavarian fare at its best. Try the Spanferkel (roast suckling pig). Reservations advised. No credit cards.

Kanzleirat. Oettingenstr. 36 (220084). Between Englischer Garten and Prinzregenten Str. Balkan specialties, with friendly service and generous portions.

Max-Emanuel-Brauerei. Adalbertstr. 33 (2715158). One of the oldest genuine Bavarian eating houses, with small stage and beer garden. Reservations advised. DC, MC.

Il Mulino. Görresstr. 1 (5233335). Italian spot in Schwabing, with cozy interior; pretty full but you'll probably find a place. Garden.

Murr-Imbiss. Snack bar in all Vincenz-Murr butcher's shops. Good for small, hot meals such as *Leberkäs,* grilled chicken *(Halbes Hendl),* thick soups.

Scheck-Alm. Sendlingerstr. Next door to sports shop of same name. Alpine decor with typical Bavarian snacks as well as more expensive dishes. Breakfast buffet-bar. Ideal lunch spot for shoppers and sightseers.

Wurstküchl. Amalienstr. 87 (281577). World's oldest sausage bar. DC, MC.

In addition there are **McDonald's** at Martin-Luther-Str. 26, Leopoldstr. 17, Augustenstr. 53, Schwanthalerstr. 8 and in many other places in town. **Wienerwald** restaurants can be found at many locations, including Leopoldstr. 44, Ungererstr. 56, Fraunhoferstr. 39 and Odeonsplatz 6. **Wendy's** are at Leopoldstr. 60, Tegernseer Landstr. 44a, Zweibrückenstr. 1 (near Marienplatz), Arnuflstr. 12 (near main station).

Traditional Beer Halls

These establishments, mostly owned by large breweries, are enormous in size. Similarly gargantuan are the mugs of beer, the portions of food, and the waitresses serving them. The liveliest activity is concentrated in the large main hall (in summer usually in a vast garden) where a brass band plays merry folk tunes, although a series of restaurant rooms is often attached to the place. Usually dancing on weekends. Prices are inexpensive to moderate.

Augustiner-Keller. Arnuflstr. 52 (594393). Has Munich's largest and perhaps most attractive beer garden.

Hofbräuhaus. Platzl 9 (221676). The most famous beer hall in the world. Rowdy *Schwemme* (watering place) on the ground floor; first-class restaurant for Bavarian specialties one flight up; large hall with brass band and dancing further up; courtyard garden in summer. Touristy but atmospheric nonetheless.

Löwenbräukeller. Stiglmaierplatz (526021). Similar to the *Hofbräuhaus* with indoor and outdoor sections.

Mathäser Bierstadt (Beer City). Bayerstr. 5 (592896). Near Hauptbahnhof. Don't be put off by exterior. Also owned by Lowenbräu and probably the largest beer hall in the world. Cellar-restaurant features *Weissbier.*

Pschorr-Keller. Theresienhöhe (501088). Near Messegelände (exhibitions grounds). Beer-hall/restaurant which has lost some of its original flavor. Shady beer garden seats 3,500. DC, MC. *Hackerkeller* nearby is similar.

Salvator-Keller. Hochstr. 77 (483274). At the Nockherberg, home of the famous *Starkbier* (strong beer), which is on draft during its lively beer festival Mar./Apr. This beer really knocks you out, so stick to small quantities. Garden.

Beer Restaurants/Cellars

These are usually sponsored, if not owned, by large breweries. They are intended, however, primarily for eating and serve mainly Bavarian fare and the sponsor's beer, although some wine can be had in most of them. Prices range from moderate to inexpensive. Most of them are vast establishments, often occupying several floors.

Augustiner Grossgaststätten. Neuhauserstr. 16 (2604106). Historic beer restaurant.

Franziskaner und Fuchsenstuben. Perusastr. 5 (645548). Not far from Rathaus; an establishment with great tradition, dating back to the early-15th century. *Weisswürst* breakfast, *Leberkäs* for lunch, international and Bavarian specialties in the evening.

Haxnbauer. Munzstr. 2 (221922). The most sophisticated of the beer restaurants, with a greater emphasis on the food. Reservations advised. MC, V.

Schneider's Weisses Bräuhaus. Tal 10 (299875). Favorite haunt of locals, typically Munich.

Spatenhaus. Residenzstr. 12 (227841). Famous for good food and old-fashioned atmosphere. MC.

Welser Küche im Feldherrnkeller. Residenzstr. 27 (296565). Dine as in the Middle Ages. Ten-course banquet with dark beer, Bavarian humor and tradition. Book well in advance. AE, DC, MC.

Zum Pschorr-Bräu. Neuhauserstr. 11 (2603001). Large establishment in pedestrian zone. DC, MC.

Wine Taverns

Munich has a series of genuine wine taverns where the accent is on drinking rather than on eating. In addition to the long lists of bottled wines they usually offer some two dozen types of open wine, sold by the ¼-liter glass, prices ranging according to quality. Long tables call for making acquaintances with your drinking neighbors. Prices are moderate to inexpensive.

Altdeutsche Weinstube. Tattenbachstr. 6 (225268). In Lehel section. Extensive list of German wines, and a good selection of foods to accompany them. Open Fri. until 1 A.M., Sat. until 3. Music.

Bacchus Keller. Innere Wiener Str. 18 (595151). Round the corner from the Gasteig Cultural Center. Open all week. Own garage. International wines.

Hahnhof. Five establishments in Munich, the most popular of which is at Leopoldstr. 32 in Schwabing. Sells wines from its own vineyards in the Pfalz. AE, DC, MC.

Neuner. Herzogspitalerstr. 8 (2603954). Old wine tavern with good food. AE.

Pfälzer Weinprobierstube. Residenzstr. 1 (225628). Highly atmospheric and warren-like; in Residenz. Also specializes in Pfalz wines. No reservations. No credit cards.

St. Georg. Prinzregentenplatz 13 (473038). One of the few wine taverns open until the early hours of the morning.

Weinhaus Neumer. Herzogspitalstr. 8 (2603954). Munich's oldest wine tavern serves good food as well as superior wines. Reservations advised. Closed Sun. AE, DC, MC.

Weinkrüger. Maximilianstr. 21 (229295). Favorite meeting place for opera and theatergoers. Also in Feilitzschstr. 25 in Schwabing, recent, but in old tavern tradition. Wines from all over Germany.

Weinstadl. Burgstr. 5 (221047). Very atmospheric, in what is probably the oldest house in Munich (last rebuilt in 1551).

CAFÉS. Two chains offering good-value coffee and pastries are *Eduscho* and *Tschibo.* Their stand-up coffee shops are cheaper than the cafes with waitress service. Two branches on Rosental, right by the Viktualienmarkt, another in Leopoldstr.

Café Extrablatt. Corner Georgenstr. and Leopoldstr. in Schwabing. New 1982, owned by Munich's most prominent society columnist; the clientele is very much "in." American-style breakfast served until midnight; excellent coffee; good range of beer, wine and light meals in '20s atmosphere. Prices Moderate.

Café Glockenspiel. Marienplatz 28 (top floor). Difficult to find (entrance in the passage next to *Schuh Klein* shoeshop) but offers fine pastries and excellent view of Rathaus and Glockenspiel.

Café Hag. Residenzstr. 26. Munich's oldest pastry shop.

Café Höflinger. Elisabethstr. 19 and Schleissheimerstr. 87. Famous breakfast meeting place for early risers.

Café Luitpold. Brienner Str. 11. Also has grill room and sidewalk tables as well as the ubiquitous pastries. Elegant and pricey, but worth visiting.

Café Wintergarten. Elisabethplatz. Intimate, art-nouveau style; piano. Also a sort of bistro serving snacks outside in summer.

NIGHTLIFE. As you will have realised by now, one of the cheapest forms of entertainment in Munich is an evening in a beer hall (listed above). However, Munich's nightlife has variety, amusement and not a little class—as long as you don't let yourself be talked into visiting one of the clip-joints of the Goethe-, Schwanthaler-, Schiller- and Josephsspitalstr. area or near the *Platzl* variety hall. Some taxi drivers get a pay-off for every guest they deliver to these dubious nightclubs. So choose your nightspot for yourself and keep to the city center and the well-known streets of Schwabing.

Bars, clubs and discos are in general, as everywhere else, expensive, although you can spend an evening in a regular bar without breaking the bank. Keep off spirits and stick to glasses of wine or beer. A Scotch can cost DM.10–12 or more, and a bottle of wine *(Flaschenwein)* from the wine list at least three times as much as in a supermarket. *Offene Wein* or wine in a carafe is cheaper.

If you really don't fancy exploring the night scene alone join one of the conducted "Munich by Night" coach tours, which take in three typical nightspots. These trips leave every Friday and Saturday at 7.30 P.M. from the corner of Prielmayerstr. near the station, and cost about DM.100, including evening meal. Call *Munich Sightseeing Tours* on 5904314 for more information and reservations.

Most bars and clubs are open only until 1 A.M. at the latest. A few are open until 3 A.M., a very few the whole night long. Here is a small selection.

Alter Simpl. Türkenstr. 57. Once a literary café, still frequented by Schwabing arty crowd. Nightly show.

Aquarius. *Holiday Inn* hotel, Leopoldstr. 194, Schwabing. New. Formerly *Yellow Submarine,* still an underwater nightclub built into a steel tank, but now without the 40 sharks.

Bayerischer Hof Nightclub. In the luxury hotel, Promenadeplatz 2–6. Expensive, frequented by the haute monde for dancing to live bands.

Eve's Cabaret. Maximiliansplatz 5. International program of first-class strippers, dancers and good music. Show begins 11 P.M., best after midnight. AE, MC.

Harry's New York Bar. Falkenturmstr. 9. Copy of typical American bar. Good international beers, realistic prices, piano music in cellar. AE.

Intermezzo. Maximiliansplatz 16. Excellent nightspot for cabaret and striptease. Elegant surroundings. 10 P.M.–4 A.M. MC.

Kay's Bistro. Utzschneiderstr. 1 (2603584). *The* meeting place for media personalities, the chic and the blue-bloods. Very expensive.

Lola Montez. Am Platzl 1. (Near Hofbräuhaus.) Non-stop show, primarily striptease. AE, MC.

Maxim. Färbergraben 33 (corner Altheimer Eck). Large bar. Plushy niches for intimate conversation, attractive hostesses, variety show mixed with strip. 9 P.M.–4 A.M. AE, MC.

P-1 Club. Prinzregentenstr., in the Haus der Kunst. The original Munich jet set still meets here, with a smattering of the aristocracy. 9 P.M.–3 A.M. AE, MC.

Rigan Club. Apianstr. 7(3087171). Best show begins at midnight.

St. James' Club. Briennerstr. 10. Cozy bar with somewhat British atmosphere. Very popular with Munich's trendies. Large selection of cocktails in plush surroundings.

Other luxury hotel have nightclubs and dancing, such as **Marco Polo** and **Bavaria** in the *Hilton,* **Vibraphon** in the *Sheraton,* and the **Bayerischer Hof Nightclub** in the hotel of the same name.

Discos

Black-out. Herrnstr. 30. Relatively new disco for the young.

Charly M. Maximiliansplatz 5. Frequented by the high-society of Munich disco freaks. Pricey; selected admission. AE, DC.

Crash. Lindwurmstr. 88 (773272). Well-established disco for youngsters, lively and loud. Admission charge entitles you to a drink.

East Side. Rosenheimer Str. 30. In Motorama building, near *Penta Hotel.* Chic nightclub/disco for up to 600 visitors. Get there early to ensure a seat. Ties obligatory (for men). AE, DC, MC.

Namenlos. Oscar von Miller Ring 25. Perhaps the most popular of all. Crowded dance floor; males outnumber females. AE, DC, MC.

Sugar Shack. Herzogspitalstr. 6. The latest in disco-lighting; very hi-tech and glamorous. Selected admission.

Why Not. Brienner Str. 12. Disco open to anyone and everyone.

Jazz and Rock

Star performances by big names take place mainly in the Circus Krone building, the Olympia Halle and the Alabamahalle. Open-air pop concerts are put on in summer in the Theatron of the Olympic Park, and the Olympic show-jumping arena in Riem.

The following are just a few of the nightspots on the jazz and rock scene which have live bands to listen to or dance to, soloists, or just a good pianist.

Allotria. Türkenstr. 33 (287342). Jazz.

Alte Burg. Bismarckstr. 21 (331452). Open 7 P.M., music from 9 P.M. Jazz.

Arena. Occamstr. 8 (344974). Jazz and rock.

Doktor Flotte. Occamstr. 8. Jazz.

Domicile. Leopoldstr. 19 (399451). One of Munich's best known jazz and rock spots. Regularly changing program of live bands. Open from 9 P.M. Best nights Fri. and Sat.

Fregatte. Sonnenstr. 17. Live bands of international fame. Mixed and slightly older crowd. Reasonable prices. Open to 4 A.M.

Jenny's Place. Georgenstr. 50. Run by a vivacious English performer with a great voice and a warm welcome for U.S. and British visitors. Jazz.

Kaffée Giesing (6934873). Very popular, crowded and "in." Jazz, rock and cabaret.

Kleines Rondell. Luisenstr. 25 (554653). Jazz.

Oklahoma. Schäftlarnstr. 156 (7234327). Out of town, towards Hellabrunn Zoo. Country and Western music with live bands. Changing program.

Schwabinger Podium. Wagnerstr. 1 (399482). Renowned jazz club. Open from 8 P.M.

Waldwirtschaft Grosshesselohe. Georg Kalb Str. 3 (795088). Down by the Isar in Grosshesselohe, summer only. Gasthof in the forest with live Dixieland jazz bands.

ALONG THE ALPS

From Bodensee to Berchtesgaden

The German Alps of Upper Bavaria, or Oberbayern, run the length of the country's southern border, a matter of some 250 km. (155 miles) in all, from Lake Constance, or Bodensee as the Germans know it, in the west to Berchtesgaden on the Austrian border in the east. The area in all comprises nine different regions, and as well as the purely Alpine area stretches northwards to Munich to include the Alpine lowlands around the valleys of the rivers Iller, Lech, Isar and Inn.

In many ways, the multitude of Germany's little Alpine villages, a *Gasthof* seemingly on every corner, zither music and brass bands resounding in every inn, and the low houses strewn in summer with flowers, correspond more nearly than any other single attraction in Bavaria to most people's idea of Germany's largest state. But the Alps also contain winter-sports resorts of unimpeachable sophistication—with prices to match—a clutch of exquisite Rococo churches, such tourist meccas as Lake Constance (Bodensee) and Berchtesgaden, and, perhaps most spectacular of all the man-made delights, Ludwig II's idiosyncratic and extravagant palaces and castles. However, it is the mountains that remain the principal attraction, rearing to 3,050 meters (10,000 ft.) in places and providing excellent vacation areas for lovers of mountain scenery, folklore and, of course, winter sports.

Bodensee

Our exploration of the Alps begins at Bodensee, at the extreme west of the Alpine region on the Swiss-German border in the state of Baden-Württemberg. The lake, through which the Rhine flows, is shaped like some weird crustacean from whose main body—Bodensee itself—two arms project: the Überlingersee in the north, the Untersee in the south. Scattered around its perimeter are wine villages and medieval towns. The largest town on the lake is Konstanz, lying in the fork formed where the lake splits.

To the west of Konstanz in the heart of the Untersee is the little island of Reichenau. It is believed that the island was the site of one of the earliest cultures in the whole of Germany. A Benedictine abbey was founded here in 724, which at the peak of its power boasted no fewer than 1,600 monks and was the seat of one of the country's most famous schools of medieval painting. The abbey was secularized in 1799, but the three churches at Mittelzell, Oberzell and Niederzell provide potent testimonials of its resplendent past.

Konstanz itself lies directly on the Swiss border, where the lake narrows before passing into the Untersee. Unlike most other larger south German cities, Konstanz escaped the devastations of the war almost entirely, not least as a result of its proximity to neutral Switzerland, and the center of the old town is chock full of delightful old buildings. The main sights include the 14th-century Rathaus, or Town Hall, originally the seat of the linen weavers' fair and later named after the Council of Konstanz (1414–18), because the conclave which elected Pope Martin V was held in this building in November 1417; the imposing cathedral, whose construction was started in the 11th century and completed in the 16th, but has additions in many different styles from many different periods up to the mid-19th century; the hotel Insel, once a Dominican Monastery and a hotel since 1875, still preserving the original magnificent cloisters—Count Ferdinand von Zeppelin, the inventor of "Zeppelins", was born here and a memorial to him stands at the boat landing stage nearby; the Renaissance City Hall; Rheintor and Schnetztor tower gates and Pulverturm, "the powder tower," since it was once used as a depot for gunpowder; St. Stephan's Church at the square of Obermarkt surrounded by patrician houses.

Just to the north of Konstanz is the little island of Mainau, located at the southern end of the Überlingersee. It's known as "the little island of flowers," and from spring to fall a staff of 300 ensure that Mainau is thickly carpeted with thousands of flowers: tuilips, narcissi and hyacinths in April and May; irises and lilies in July; dahlias in September; and a great variety of roses from June to the end of September. In addition, there are hothouses of orchids, palms, lemon and orange trees, and rare and old trees in its arboretum. The Baroque palace on the island used to be the summer residence of the Grand Dukes of Baden, and was inherited shortly after World War II by Prince Wilhelm of Sweden from his mother, Queen Victoria of Sweden, a sister of the Grand Duke of Baden. Today it is inhabited by Count Lennart Bernadotte, uncle of Carl Gustav of Sweden, and his family.

Located at the mid-point of the northern shore of the Überlingersee is Überlingen, with its close-set old houses hugging the lakeside. Once an imperial free town, it has preserved many of its towers, defense walls and old patrician homes, such as the Reichlin-Meldegg House, built in 1462, and now containing the local museum. The five-nave Gothic cathedral has a famous Renaissance altar and the Rathaus, also Gothic, is known for its Pfennig Tower and the woodcarved grand hall from 1492. Überlingen, which is also well known for Kneipp (cold water) cures, is referred to locally as the German Nice, in reference to its mild climate, which, of course, it shares with all the lakeside resorts.

A few miles inland from Überlingen in the hills back from the lake is Heiligenberg, boasting a castle containing magnificent works of art, and in which the Renaissance Knights' Hall is particularly striking.

Continuing along the lake shore, you could hardly make a mistake stopping anywhere at random: Birnau, with its Rococo church on the high shore; Unteruhldingen, where there are reconstructions of the homes of the ancient lake dwellers (this is another point from which you can go to Heiligenberg); peaceful Meersburg, a marvelous old town with Germany's oldest inhabited castle (Altes Burg), one of whose towers dates from the 7th century, a wine-growing center boasting several colorful old taverns, and a particularly favored summertime lake resort. The 18th-century former Prince Bishops Baroque Palace is well worth a visit, especially during the international concert season (Jun. to Sept.) when concerts are held in its splendid Hall of Mirrors (Spiegelsaal). A panoramic path along the heights between Meersburg and Hagnau offers another magnificent view of the entire lake and the Austrian and Swiss Alps. From Meersburg, ferryboats cross to Konstanz day and night, thus considerably shortening the journey around the lake if you are in a hurry.

From Meersburg, the next stop along the lake is Friedrichshafen. This is a place that has helped make aeronautic history. It was the birthplace of the Zeppelins, named after Count Zeppelin, their inventor. Their hangars and the plants which built them were here, and it was from here that they started out on their transatlantic flights in the days before disaster ended their career. It was here, too, that the Dornier flying boats were built, and their powers tested over the convenient, wide, calm, landing surface provided by the lake before they took off on their flights to America. It is rather quieter today, the chief traffic being provided by ferryboats, for this is the point from which they leave for the crossing to Romanshorn, in Switzerland.

You will find the lake more attractive if you stop at smaller places than this, the smaller the better. Beyond Friedrichshafen is the charming town of Langenargen with its Montfort Castle; the town clustered along the lake is a favored vacation spot. A little further is another small place, Nonnenhorn. You will enjoy the town square with its chapel and the lakeside walks among the fruit trees and vineyards.

The other little settlements along the lake are equally entrancing— Wasserburg, with its splendid church rising from the peninsula on which it stands, and Bad Schachen, a lakeside spa in a lovely setting.

Lindau is in the lake rather than on it—it's built on an island. It doesn't look quite credible from the shore, floating on the water as if moored by the two narrow bridges which hold it to the land like hawsers, with its towers rising here and there from its trees and houses. It doesn't look quite credible when you get there, either, with its narrow, twisting streets lined with fine old buildings. You should be warned that a lot of people have discovered how attractive Lindau is, and the place gets packed out.

At the lakeward end of the island you can sit and gaze out through the twin pillars of its little harbor (they are not identical twins; one is a lighthouse, the other a statue of a lion) towards the mountains beyond the lake. On a clear day you will be able to see the peaks known as The Three Sisters in neighboring Liechtenstein, the tiny independent principality lying between Switzerland and Austria.

In addition to the pretty little harbor, the main sights in Lindau include the beautifully-frescoed Altes Rathaus (the Old Town Hall), built in 1422 and the scene of the 1492 Imperial Diet held under the Emperor Maximilian; the Cavazzan House, one of the finest burgher houses in the Lake Constance area and home today of a folklore museum and Lindau's notable art collection; the Stadtmuseum, or City Museum; the two principal city churches (one Catholic and one Evangelical) on the same square; the Diebsturm (Thief's Tower) with a section of the old town walls; the nearby Romanesque Peter's Church, reputed to be the oldest on the lake, with frescos by Hans Holbein the Elder (today the church is a war memorial chapel); the many narrow streets lined with romantic old houses.

The Allgäu

Lindau lies just within the Allgäu—or the Westallgäu as it here is, to be more exact—which in all comprises three separate districts, the Westallgäu, Oberallgäu and Ostallgäu, and stretches between Lindau and Füssen, 80 km. (50 miles) to the east. Although a distinct geographical region in itself, the Allgäu nonetheless forms part of Bavarian Swabia—Bayerish Schwaben—one of the local government districts of Bavaria proper.

From Lindau or Friedrichshafen, the principal areas of interest north of Lake Constance are Ravensburg, whose impressive gates and towers date from the time when it was the Swabian stronghold of the Guelphs, and, a few miles north, Weingarten, site of the second largest Baroque church in Germany. It was designed by Moosbrugger and consecrated in 1742; the ceiling frescos are partly the work of the celebrated Cosmas Damian Asam. As is characteristic of many of southern Germany's finest Baroque and Rococo churches, the plain exterior gives little indication of the richness within. Alternatively, head for Wangen, 20 km. (14 miles) northeast of Lindau, for a look at its centuries-old gates and fine medieval streets.

Heading east from Lake Constance soon brings you into the Oberallgäu, known chiefly for its winter sports resorts, though you will also find that many of the towns and villages farther to the north make excellent bases for trips into the mountains. This is true of charming Sonthofen, in the upper Iller Valley, reached from Lindau via the scenic German Alpine Road through two more winter sports centers: Oberstaufen, known especially for its unique Schroth cures based on dieting, and Immenstadt with a 17th-century castle and a Baroque parish church. But Oberstdorf, a little to the south, is the best known winter sports center and Alpine summer resort in the region, lying in a broad valley ringed by lofty peaks. A three-mile-long (5 km.) new cable-car leads up to the 2,250-meter (7,380-ft.) Nebelhorn and its gigantic ski jump. Seven smaller valleys lead up into the

Alpine stillness. Especially recommended is the walk along the Heilbron-
nerweg, reaching the Kempter refuge at 1,830 meters (6,000 ft.).

From Oberstdorf it is also possible to explore Kleinwalsertal (Small
Walser Valley—the Great Walser Valley being on the other side of the
mountain barrier in Vorarlberg)—a mountain fastness of incomparable
beauty and site of the villages of Riezlern, Hirschegg and Mittelberg.
There is a bus from Oberstdorf rail station that runs the length of the 19-
km. (12 mile) valley. Oddly enough, the valley itself is actually in Austria,
but being inaccessible to Austria other than by twisting footpaths has been
integrated economically with Germany for many years now. Take your
passport with you if you intend to explore the area, or you may have difficulties crossing the border. A final curiosity provided by this little section
of the Oberallgäu is found in Unterbalderschwang, 14 km. (9 miles) northwest of Oberstdorf, site of Germany's oldest tree, a double-trunked yew
reputed to be 4,000 years old.

Due north again of Oberstdorf some 32 km. (20 miles) is the capital
of the Allgäu, Kempten. It's also the home of the famous Allgäuer cheese,
first-cousin to Emmentaler and Gruyère. Appropriately, the south German Cheese Exchange (Käsebörse) is located here, while in the numerous
Käskuchä or cheese dairies you can watch master cheese-makers at work,
churning out 70-kilo cheeses by hand. For culture vultures, Kempten's
major attractions are the Allgäu Folklore Museum (Allgäu Heimat Museum) in the Corn House, or Kornhaus, which, in addition to a collection
of ancient coins, charts the city's history from its Roman foundation—the
Romans called the town Cambodunum—through the Middle Ages and
the Renaissance. The building itself is one of the finest of its kind in the
Allgäu and together with the Basilica of St. Laurence—the first significant
Baroque church in south Germany, completed in 1666—and the Residenz
give the Kornshausplatz, in which they stand, a charmingly romantic aspect. Also of note is the Rathaus, the City Hall, built in 1382 but with
a Renaissance staircase and Baroque towers.

Heading north again from Kempten to Memmingen, 14 km. (20 miles)
away, you come to Ottobeuren, site of the largest Baroque church in Germany. It is the church of the Benedictine Abbey here, founded originally
under Charlemagne in 764, though the present Abbey buildings date from
the early-18th century. The massive church itself was largely the work of
Johann Michael Fischer and in the grandeur of its conception and execution is generally considered to represent the climax of German ecclesiastical Baroque architecture. Its highlights include the magnificently detailed
and carved choir stalls and the world-famous organ. But simply to wander
around its lustrous and brilliantly decorated interior is a highlight in itself.

A few miles farther north again is Memmingen, which, once a free imperial city, has preserved five towers and part of its walls. Its Rathaus square
and several narrow streets are lined with gabled, arcaded or half-timbered
houses, while the Church of St. Martin contains fine Gothic choir stalls.
Similarly, the Frauenkirche boasts frescos from the same period. East of
Memmingen and Ottobeuren, among forests and meadows, lies Bad Wör-
ishofen, the principal cold water health resort in Germany, where Father
Sebastian Kneipp invented and started the famous cold water treatments
in the last century. The Kneipp Museum is in the Dominican Convent
and a monument to him stands in the town which, once a little village,

has become an important spa with up-to-date installations and all modern amenities.

The remaining attractions of the Allgäu lie in the Ostallgäu, southeast of Kempten and Memmingen. Coming from Kempten, you cross into the Ostallgäu at Nesselwang, a health resort and popular winter sports center. It lies at the foot of the 1,400-meter (4,600 ft.) Alpspitze, the summit of which is served by a chair lift. 5 km. (3½ miles) farther southeast is Pfronten, the largest vacation resort in the Ostallgäu and famous as a regular venue for the annual World Cup ski competition. A cable car will take you up to the 1,870-meter (4,500 ft.) Breitenberg, while a chair lift goes all the way to the summit of the 1,600-meter (5,250 ft.) Hochalp, from where a series of excellent walks, offering sensational views, are available. Perhaps the most romantic sight in the area, however, is provided by the ruined castle at Falkenstein, 1,030 meters (3,380 ft.) above sea level, and the highest castle ruin in the country. Ludwig II had plans to rebuild the castle, but sadly even he baulked at the immense practical difficulties involved.

From Pfronten, it's no more than 10 km. or so (6 miles) to Füssen, the road skirting along the northern edge of the Weissensee Lake, lying at the end—or beginning—of the Romantic Road, which runs between here and Würzburg in Franconia. Füssen-Bad Faulenbach, to give the town its full name, spa and winter sports resort, is an old mountain town that owes its location to the fact that it was originally the site of a fort guarding a pass through the Alps; but its position might just as easily have been chosen with the idea of giving it perfect scenic surroundings. From a majestic wall of mountains behind the town, the river Lech comes tumbling down to the green plains cradled within the encircling heights, and flows by the ancient stone buildings of the town. Lakes dot the country about Füssen— the Alpsee, the Schwansee, the Bannwaldsee, the Hopfensee, the Weissensee and the lake-river formed by the broadening of the Lech, the Forggensee. The best of the many fine views of Füssen is from a point where the Lech rolls over a long low fall. Beyond it rise the ancient walls of the castle, the churches, and the medieval buildings of the town; beyond them rise the Alps. Wander through the town, and you will find that all the streets are picturesque; but what you should particularly not fail to visit are the castle (Hohes Schloss), once the summer residence of the Prince Bishops of Augsburg; the St. Mangkirche, which has a much admired Romanesque crypt; and Hiebeler's *Totentanz* (The Dance of Death) in St. Anne's Chapel.

The town also makes an excellent base from which to visit the two neighboring castles of Hohenschwangau and Neuschwanstein, and which, no more than a mile apart, can easily be visited together. Hohenschwangau, built between 1832 and 1836 in a Romantic and somewhat fanciful Gothic style by Maximilian II, was the childhood home of Ludwig II and in large part provided Ludwig with the inspiration to build his own fairytale castle, Neuschwanstein, perched on its pinnacle of rock. In almost every respect Neuschwanstein, constructed from 1870 onwards, surpasses Hohenschwangau, being larger, more flamboyant, more dramatic and much more expensive to build. But at the same time it is wholly lacking in any of the domesticity that makes Hohenschwangau a real castle (Ludwig in fact scarcely lived here at all), and has instead a melancholy and strangely unloved quality. Nonetheless, it has enormously lavish interiors and superb views; concerts are held here at the beginning of September.

From the obsessive 19th-century splendor of Hohenschwangau and Neuschwanstein, head north to Steingaden and Rottenbuch, 21 km. (13 miles) and 30 km. (18 miles) respectively north of Füssen for three architectural experiences of a very different kind. Steingaden is the site of an impressive and somewhat incongruous Abbey church, founded originally in the 12th century and retaining its heavy Romanesque exterior but with an 18th-century interior. The Abbey church at Rottenbuch has a similar juxtaposition of contrasting architectural styles. Parts of the interior were remodeled in the 18th century, but significant sections of the original 15th-century Gothic interior were left intact. The third building here, however, presents no such difficulties. This is the little Wieskirche, located mid-way between Steingaden and Rottenbuch. Built by Dominikus Zimmermann between 1746 and 1754, it represents, in tandem with the pilgrimage church at Vierzehnheiligen in North Bavaria, the culminating point of German Rococo ecclesiastical architecture. As at Vierzehnheiligen, the simple interior gives no hint of the glittering treasures within. A complex oval plan is animated by a series of brilliantly colored stuccos, statues and gilt, while an enormous ceiling fresco completes the decoration. The choir and organ loft are especially beautiful.

The final halt in this exploration of the Allgäu is Schongau, situated on the river Lech and fond of calling itself "The Town in Front of the Mountains," not unreasonably perhaps as this is the first point, were you coming from the other direction, where you would see the dramatic backdrop of the Alps looming over the horizon. Schongau today is a quiet rural center, but during the middle ages was a lively staging post on the busy trade route between Augsburg, to the north, and Italy. Its little town center is accordingly crammed with old city walls, towers and historic buildings. In addition, there is a fine church, the Pfarrkirche Mariä Himmelfahrt, or Parish Church of the Blessed Virgin Mary of the Assumption, to give it its full name.

Landsberg and Augsburg

At this point a detour is in order, to Landsberg and, north again, to the ancient city of Augsburg, both on the Romantic Road. Neither are Alpine towns, but both, lying in that part of Bavarian-Swabia just to the north of the Alpine lowlands, have played important roles in the history of Bavaria and the Alpine regions, their folklore and culture.

Landsberg, straddling the river Lech, is perhaps *the* place to visit to see the Rococo wonders of Dominikus Zimmermann, burgomaster of Landsberg (aside, that is, from the Weiskirche). Among the highlights are St. Johann's Church (Johannskirche), dating from 1740–54, and the Ursulinenkirche. More famously, he also built the facade of the Altes Rathaus, the Old Town Hall, the interior of which dates from 1699. Among the town's other attractions are the Bayertor, or Bavarian Tower, one of the most beautiful late-Gothic city gates in Germany, dating from 1425, and the 14th-century Schöner Turm, or Beautiful Tower, by the Town Hall. There's also a City Museum, the Stadtmuseum, in the Mutterturm on the banks of the Lech. Every fifth year the Rüthen Festival in the middle of

July, during which 1,500 children parade in historical costumes, draws hordes of visitors to the town.

From Landsberg, the road crosses the Lechfeld, where the German Emperor Otto the Great inflicted a crushing defeat upon the Magyars in 995, stopping forever their predatory incursions into Germany and contributing to their pacification and final settlement in what is today Hungary. The road then takes you through the Red Gate (Rotes Tor), providing a spectacular introduction to a spectacular city, the greatest city on the Romantic Road, gateway to the Allgäu and the Alps, and the oldest town in Bavaria—Augsburg. This impressive complex of tower, bridge, ramparts, and moat, against whose massive background open-air opera is staged in summer, gives you a foretaste of the architectural riches of a city that also has been accumulating them for 2,000 years. 1985 saw the 2,000th anniversary of the city.

Though in Bavaria, Augsburg is in many other ways more Swabian than Bavarian: the architecture, dialect, and food are all distinctly different from those in the rest of the State. Perhaps this difference is appropriate, given the immensely distinguished history to which the city can lay claim. Founded originally by the Romans, Augsburg grew to prominence in the early Middle Ages, a status it retained at least until the 18th century. By the 10th century, for example, it had become an international center of trade, while in the 15th and 16th centuries it could lay claim to being the richest town in the whole of Europe, whose leading lights were the two families Fugger and Welser—a Welser was subsequently to *own* Venezuela! The Fuggers, comparable to though if anything wealthier than the Medicis in Florence, were perhaps the dominant family, financing wars and pulling the strings that determined the fate of the Holy Roman Empire.

Among other famous sons of the town were both Holbeins and Leopold Mozart, father of the composer (the famous 18th-century piano maker, Stein, was also a native of the city). Elias Holl, the architect who built the Rotes Tor, is buried here. Bertolt Brecht was born in this city in 1898 and his birthplace still exists. The Würzburg Theater presents many of his works.

Augsburg is known also by an important date in German history. In 1555 the Augsburger Religionsfriede (Religious Peace of Augsburg) was ratified in the form of a treaty between the Catholic and Lutheran princes of the Holy Roman Empire, which provided that any member state of the empire might set up either creed as its official religion. Those who refused to conform were guaranteed the right to dispose of their estates and emigrate.

Augsburg is the seat of the oldest social settlement in the world, the Fuggerei, built in 1519 to house indigent but deserving families at a nominal rent and still doing so. The present rent is the same as at the time of its foundation, the equivalent of one Rhenish Florin of those times, or, in today's terms, one mark and 71 pfennigs a year. Augsburg is also important industrially, it has been the biggest textile center in southern Germany for 500 years, it is the birthplace of Rudolf Diesel, inventor of the Diesel engine, and in addition to the Diesel plant, important factories here include those of the Messerschmitt airplane makers and the National Cash Register Company.

A complete list of the sights of Augsburg would fill an entire book. Among the most important are the cathedral, begun in 995, which boasts the oldest stained glass in the world (11th century) and altar paintings by Hans Holbein the Elder; an early 11th-century bronze door, and a series of tombs in the cloister (from the 13th to the 18th century); St. Ulrich, which not only has two towers but is two churches—for as a Protestant *and* Catholic church, it embodied in stone the spirit of the Religious Peace of Augsburg, achieved in 1555; the Maximilianstrasse, considered the finest Renaissance street in Germany; the Perlach tower and the Rathaus beside it, one of the most impressive creations of German Renaissance buildings, by Elias Holl; and in the Schaezler Palais, where the municipal art collections are displayed, is the Festive Hall, opened in 1770 to receive Marie Antoinette, then on her way to Paris from Vienna to become the bride of Louis XVI. In summer candle-lit concerts are held in the Rococo hall.

For contemporary outdoor recreational needs Augsburg has constructed the Rosenaustadion, a thoroughly up-to-date athletic stadium, seating 45,000 spectators and located near the Wertach River, and the world's first canoe-slalom stadium (24,000 spectators), on the Lech River, site of this event in the 1972 Olympics. Also in the southern outskirts of the city in the pleasant Siebentisch woods are the new botanical garden (on the site of the 1985 State Horticultural Show and retaining the original Japanese gardens) plus a fine zoo.

Ammergauer Alps and Werdenfelser Land

Continuing eastward again along the Alps, brings us to the next two regions of Germany's Alps—the Ammergauer Alps and Werdenfelser Land. They contain perhaps the two best-known towns in the entire Bavarian Alps: Oberammergau and Garmisch-Partenkirchen.

Coming from Munich, if you first wish to visit Oberammergau and the Garmisch area and prefer not to use the autobahn, travel through Starnberg on the Starnberger Lake and continue through the old market town of Murnau, located at Staffel Lake with its wooded islets, to either Oberammergau or Garmisch. A scenically more rewarding route to Oberammergau (you must have a car) is from Starnberg through Weilheim to Schongau on the Romantic Road; then through Rottenbuch with its Rococo decorated monastery church and over Echelsbacher Brücke, a single-span bridge above the Ammer River.

Oberammergau is, of course, famous mainly for its Passion Play, performed every ten years in years ending with zero. The next performance is scheduled for 1990, though in 1984 a celebratory 350th-anniversary performance was staged. Even if there is no play the year when you are visiting, you can see the theater in which it is given and the bearded actors carrying on their everyday occupations—many of them carving wood, for Oberammergau is a great woodcarving center, with a school that teaches the craft. The play, which was first given in 1634 in fulfillment of a vow to present it every decade if the Black Plague were ended, requires over 1,000 performers. As they are all natives of Oberammergau, whose population is only 5,000, it is evident that it is very much the focal point of life in the town.

Play year or not, Oberammergau is a rewarding place to visit, with its attractive old houses and its pleasant parish church lying peacefully among broad grassy fields, from which the great rocks of the Alps rise abruptly. From it you can take the bus trip into the Graswangtal Valley, to visit Schloss Linderhof, one of Ludwig II's most fanciful castles. In front is an artificial pond with a gilded statue of Flora and a 31-meter (105-ft.) fountain. The castle itself was built in Rococo style and has a number of ornate suites. In the park King Ludwig II also had constructed an artificial blue grotto in imitation of the one at Capri and a Moorish Kiosk with enameled bronze peacocks.

Oberammergau is also an ideal starting-off point for hiking tours in the surrounding mountains. There are a variety of marked footpaths to choose from, and every year on 24 August anyone can take part in an organized Mountain Hiking Day *(Gebirgswandertag)* called "In King Ludwig's Footsteps" in memory of the "Dream King" of Bavaria. The day ends with a spectacular sight when, at dusk, huge bonfires are set ablaze on the surrounding mountainsides.

Proceeding from Oberammergau or Linderhof to Garmisch the road passes through Ettal, known mainly for its beautiful Benedictine Abbey founded in 1330. Its church was built first in Gothic style and was changed in the early 18th century into a Baroque structure with a large dome whose ceiling was painted by Johann Jakob Zeiller.

An alternative route from Munich to Garmisch-Partenkirchen is southward via Wolfratshausen, the railroad then making straight for Bichl, while the road makes a slight loop to the east to pass near Bad Heilbrunn. From this minor spa, or from Bichl via Bad Heilbrunn, it is a short side trip to a major one, Bad Tölz, delightfully located on the Isar against a background of high mountains. It is an old place (the Romans had a settlement here in the 5th century, named Tollusium) and it remains conscious of tradition. This is local costume country and if you happen to be on hand on November 6, you can take in the Leonhardi Ride, in honor of the patron saint of horses.

Continuing south from Bichl, road and rail alike pass through Benediktbeuern, where there is a 1,200-year-old monastery, whose double-towered church bears the familiar onion domes of this region. At Kochel there is a lovely lake, the railroad ends and train travelers must take to the bus. The road continues through Walchensee, where there is another delightful example of the beautiful lakes that characterize this region, with the mountains rising steeply straight from the water; Wallgau, a pleasant little village of 900 inhabitants, nestled in a small valley cupped by mountains, and Krün, somewhat larger but in a situation much the same, to Garmisch-Partenkirchen.

Garmisch-Partenkirchen

This town is among the world's top winter sports centers, and the largest in Germany. Before World War I, there was only a village here; it took ten hours to reach the peak of the Zugspitz, where, in those days, it was assumed only eccentrics would want to go. Now thousands reach its top every year in minutes by the cable car from the nearby Eibsee.

Garmisch-Partenkirchen lies on comparatively flat ground in the valley of the River Loisach, from which mountains spring to terrifying heights on every side. The giants of the group are the Wank to the east, 1,780 meters (5,840 ft.); the Hausberg and Kreuzeck to the south, 1719 meters (5,640 ft.); nearby the Alpspitze, 2,219 meters (7,285 ft.) and to the southwest, on the Austrian border, Germany's highest mountain, the majestic Zugspitze, 2,963 meters (9,717 ft.). These great peaks, plus Garmisch's famed sunny climate, which made it a health resort before skiing seized upon it, and the fact that snow can be depended upon here from the latter part of November until the middle of May, are the natural factors which account for the popularity of this resort. Man-made attractions have completed its assets.

The Olympic Ski Stadium and Olympic Ice Stadium were built for the winter Olympic Games held here in 1936. The Olympic Ski Stadium has two ski jumps and a slalom course. There is room for 100,000 people, although "only" 30,000 of them can be accommodated in the grandstands. The Olympic Ice Stadium provides nearly an acre of ice surface and its grandstands can take 12,000 spectators. Another rink, with stands for 6,000 persons, is next to the first one.

There are any number of breathtaking excursions from Garmisch. There is a beautiful four-mile walk to Grainau, offering superb views. There are two gorges well worth visiting, the Partnachklamm and the Höllentalklamm. The lovely little Riessersee is a lake on the outskirts of Garmisch, while further away is the Eibsee, with the tremendous rock wall of the Zugspitze rising above it. The Wank is reached from Partenkirchen by small cable cars; the Kreuzeck, Graseck, Eckbauer and Hausberg are also reached by cable car. But for the Zugspitze, the Number One excursion from Garmisch, you have your choice between a Bavarian mountain railway and cable car and a Tyrolean cable car (from Obermoos which can be reached by train and bus from Garmisch), since the Zugspitze marks the Germany/Austria border.

For the full variety of the marvelous scenery, the best idea is to go by one route and return by the other. On the Bayrische Zugspitzbahn you pass the dark-blue Eibsee, framed by deep-green pine forests, and reach Schneefernerhaus through a long tunnel. At this point a broad skiing area spreads out, the highest in Germany, the Zugspitzplatt; if your object is not skiing, but the view, a cable car will take you still higher, to the Summit Station, anchored by cables to the lofty pinnacle on which it stands, from which you can see all the way to the central Alps of Switzerland. You can also reach the peak of Zugspitze directly from Eibsee by cable car.

Garmisch, together with Partenkirchen, however, is not only a sports center and a point of departure for trips and excursions. It is a very attractive town in its own right, with balconies and painted façades on its Alpine-style houses, and with the Baroque parish church and 15th-century Church of St. Martin. Garmisch is also a health resort with a lovely Kurpark staging outdoor summer concerts.

Some 16 km. (10 miles) southeast of Garmisch, in the valley of the Isar, is Mittenwald, one of the most beautiful Alpine towns, with the rugged rocky face of Karwendel rising almost vertically above it. Many colorful houses line the streets, some with magnificent façade paintings, such as the Neunerhaus at Obermarkt. The Baroque church with frescoed tower was originally built in Gothic style. In front of it stands the monument to the violin-maker Mathias Klotz, who in the 17th century introduced his craft to the town, and set Mittenwald on the path to world fame in this field. The Geigenbau- und Heimatmuseum (Museum of Violin-Making and Regional Life) in Ballenhausgasse has good displays illustrating the history of violin-making here. A two-stage lift (first stage chair and second stage gondola) takes you to the 1,390 meter (4,560 ft.) Kranzberg with a magnificent view of the Karwendel and Wetterstein mountain ranges and a cable car takes you close to the top (to about 2,240 meters 7,350 ft.) of Karwendel.

In the vicinity of Mittenwald are several small blue-green lakes such as Lautersee, Ferchensee and Barmsee. A few miles north of Mittenwald are the villages of Krün and Wallgau which you have passed earlier on one of the routes to Garmisch. Another very scenic and less frequented road follows the Isar Valley (toll road for a while) from Wallgau through Fall and the unpretentious climatic resort of Lenggries, completing the round-trip back once again at Bad Tolz.

Between the Loisach, Isar and Inn

East of Bad Tolz and the Isar Valley, in a ring of high mountains lies Tegernsee, one of the most beautiful Bavarian lakes, dotted with sails in summer and spinning ice skaters in winter; its tree-lined shores garland it with flowers in the spring while in the fall they provide a magnificent contrast between the red and golden leaves and the already snow-capped peaks in the background. All the localities on the lake are summer and winter resorts; the most important are Gmund in the north; Tegernsee with the former Benedictine monastery (now ducal castle and parish church), which was founded in 747, on the eastern shore; Bad Wiessee with chloride, iodine, and sulfuric springs and a large spa establishment on the western shore including a modern covered promenade connected with the music pavilion; Rottach-Egern with Walberg Mountain, reached by cable car, at the southern end. Farther south is the idyllic village of Kreuth from where the road continues through Wildbad Kreuth, a tiny spa, and Glashütte to Austria.

Continuing eastward from Tegernsee we come to another lovely lake, the Schliersee, whose main community bears the same name, and less than 11 km. (7 miles) south, high up along a twisty mountain road, is yet another blue gem of the Bavarian Alps, the tiny Spitzingsee, a favorite winter sport and summer hiking resort. About 16 km. (10 miles) southeast of Schliersee is the village of Bayrischzell with a sharply-pointed church spire, another important skiing center and summer resort. Above Bayrischzell to the north is Wendelstein Mountain (1,838 meters, 6,029 ft.) which can be reached via a new cable car. There's also a cogwheel railway that runs up the north side and is the oldest of its kind in Germany. At the top there's a little church, designed in 1888–90 by Max Kleiber, no mean mountaineer himself—he carried the cross for the roof up the mountain on his back—where extravagant alpine weddings take place. And on the very summit stands the tiny St. Wendelin chapel dating from 1718.

The Inn River comes rushing from Austria and flows north under the high bridge of the Munich—Salzburg autobahn, reaching Rosenheim a few miles beyond it. Rosenheim, which has been a market town since 1328, is a busy industrial city. The Old Town has several picturesque old facades, onion-shaped steeples, and arcaded streets, and is separated from the New Town by the 14th-century Mittertor (Middle Gate). About 11 km. (7 miles) west of the city is Bad Aibling with peat and mud baths, one of the nicest Kurparks in Bavaria with a modern concert hall, music pavilion and remodeled Kurhaus, and the oldest and largest flea-market in Bavaria. About 8 km. (5 miles) east of the city is the quiet lake of Simsee, the summer playground for the inhabitants and visitors of Rosenheim. Following the Inn due north of Rosenheim you reach Wasserburg am Inn, a picturesque medieval town, whose riverside waterfronts have given rise to its second name of Kleine Venedig (Little Venice).

Chiemgau

Traveling east from Rosenheim you enter the Chiemgau region of Bavaria and in Prien you find yourself on the shores of the largest lake in Bavaria, the Chiemsee, sometimes called the Bavarian Sea, whose greatest attractions are the two islands, Frauenchiemsee, with a 1,200-year-old convent and minster church, and Herrenchiemsee, where one of the fantastic castles built by Ludwig II stands. On Saturday nights (in summer) the great ballroom is lighted by thousands of candles, with classical chamber groups performing.

In addition to Prien and its lake section of Stock, from where the lake boats take you to Herreninsel and Fraueninsel, a cluster of small and unspoiled towns is strung around Chiemsee. Not much more than 8 km. (5 miles) from the eastern shore of the lake is Traunstein, a market town with a long history, which is presently known primarily as a health resort offering brine and mud baths and cold water Kneipp cures. South from the Chiemsee is the very popular Alpine resort of Reit im Winkl, close to the Austrian border. If you are coming from Prien, there is no direct railway connection, but postal buses leave five times daily for this tranquil vacation spot. As a winter sports center, it has the reputation of receiving the heaviest snowfalls in Bavaria.

From Reit im Winkl proceed on the very scenic section of the German Alpine Road to the pleasant town of Ruhpolding, surrounded by high mountains—there is a cable car on Rauschberg—its houses hugging a small hill crowned by a church.

The Berchtesgadener Land

Continuing south on the Alpine Road, you come to the Berchtesgadener Land, the biggest tourist attraction in the whole of the eastern Bavarian Alps, with its giant rugged mountains and exquisite Alpine lakes.

Striking deep into the heart of the region, you come first to the little village of Ramsau, an excellent base for mountain climbing, the principal peak here being the Hochkalter, towering over the village. A few miles to the east is Hintersee, a small lake surrounded by steep slopes, while south again is the tumultuous torrent that pours down through the Wimbach Gorge, originating in the snowfields separating the Hochkalter from the even higher and wilder peak of the Watzmann at 2,714 meters (6,900 ft.).

The center of the Berchtesgadener Land is of course Berchtesgaden itself, an ancient market town and long the site of an Augustinian Abbey, secularized in the early-19th century. The pretty little town is extremely popular—as a winter sports resort it is second only to Garmisch—and frequently extremely crowded, especially in summer.

The main sight in the town is the Königliche Schloss Berchtesgaden, the Royal Castle, originally the Abbey but taken over by the Wittelsbachs, rulers of Bavaria, in 1810. It is now a museum, many of whose treasures were originally collected by Prince Rupert of Bavaria, who died here in 1955. The 13th-century cloisters and Gothic dormitory plus a number of fine Renaissance rooms provide the principal exhibition spaces for the Prince's collections, which are particularly rich in 15th- and 16th-century German wood-carvings. The adjoining Abbey church, built in the 12th century but with many later additions, is also very beautiful. Berchtesgaden is a wood-carving center, and the Heimatmuseum, the Local Museum, in Schroffenbergallee, has a good collection of carvings from the area.

However, perhaps the most famous sight in Berchtesgaden is the Salzbergwerg, the Salt Mines, source of the town's prosperity since the early-16th century. A visit here is a unique experience. You will be provided with protective clothing—trousers, apron and cap—and a leather "seat" on which you then slide down a 500-meter (1,640-ft.) chute into a labyrinth of tunnels and galleries, their walls shimmering with salt crystals. A boat trip across an underground lake and short film-show, outlining the development of the mines, end the trip. The mines are open all year, but for limited periods only from October to May.

There are a number of excellent excursions from the town, of which perhaps the best is to Königsee, a beautiful fjord-like lake set between almost vertical mountain-walls in the middle of the Berchtesgaden National Park, a nature and wildlife reserve. Electric boats, the only sort allowed on the lake, take you from the little town of Königsee at the head of the lake to the 18th-century chapel of St. Bartholomä, whose clover-leaf shaped dome is the symbol of Berchtesgaden.

Another excellent trip is from Berchtesgaden to Kehlstein, reached by post bus via Obersalzburg—site of Hitler's luxurious mountain retreat—some three miles out of town. From here special buses run up the private road, the highest in the country and built by Hitler in 1937–39, to the Eagle's Nest, some 1,834 meters (6,017 ft.) high and today an inn and restaurant. (It's worth pointing out that despite its name and dramatic location, this was not the site of Hitler's Alpine stronghold). The view from the top, and from the road too, is sensational. An alternative trip is along the Rossfeld Höhenringstrasse, again reached via Obersalzburg, the second-highest road in the country.

The final halt in this exploration of the Berchtesgaden Land is the fashionable spa of Bad Reichenhall, source of the most powerful saline springs in Europe, a few miles north of Berchtesgaden. The town is best-known as a luxurious health resort, and boasts many excellent hotels, practically all of which specialize in health treatments, and in all has the rather discreet atmosphere of many of Germany's more expensive spas, an effect encouraged by the well-tended parks, Botanic garden, casino and concert hall. However, it is also a popular winter-sports resort, and summer and winter a cable runs up to Predigstuhl, from where there is a splendid view of the rocky giants of Berchtesgaden Land. The town also has an interesting Romanesque Cathedral, St. Zeno's, much of which was remodeled in the 16th and 17th centuries. In addition, there is a remarkable Salt Works, the Alte Saline—like Berchtesgaden, Bad Reichenhall was an important salt-producing center—which Ludwig I built in 1834 in an extraordinary medieval manner, the whole as lavish as it is unlikely.

PRACTICAL INFORMATION FOR THE ALPS

TELEPHONES. We have given telephone codes for all the towns and villages in the hotel and restaurant lists that follow. These codes need only be used when calling from outside the town or village concerned.

HOTELS AND RESTAURANTS. With very few exceptions, all hotels and *Gasthäuser* in the Bavarian Alps and lower alpine regions are in local, traditionally styled, low-roofed alpine chalets with wooden balconies and a multi-colored mass of flowers in summer. Standards are generally high. Breakfasts in smaller establishments are simple.

Upper Bavaria offers everything from super-luxurious hotels to the simplest *Gasthof* out in the country, not forgetting the large choice of farmhouse and self-catering accommodations. Garmisch-Partenkirchen and Berchtesgaden head the field in this region, which is bountifully supplied with accommodations in all categories and special spring, fall and, particularly, winter seven-day packages. Although prices are higher here than in other mountain areas, there are still many lesser-known resorts (Inzell, Kreuth) and inexpensive hotels and pensions everywhere, plus a number of beautifully situated mountain hotels. A few of the resort hotels may close for a short period in the fall.

Accommodations in the Allgäu tend to be about ten to 20 percent less than in the Bavarian Alps proper, and the further away from the mountains you are the cheaper it is. Outside the main tourist centres it is even possible to find bed and breakfast for as little as DM.10. There are also special package arrangements, particularly in such places as Balderschwang, Fischen, Kleinwalsertal, Oberstaufen and Scheidegg, as well as in the better-known tourist centers. You can write to any of the regional tourist offices (see below) and ask for their brochure of *Pauschalangebote* (special arrangements), which include stays from between three days and two weeks often combined with sporting activities.

Amerang (Inn Valley). *Gasthof Palm* (M), Wasserburgerstr. 10 (08075–207). With annexe, 30 beds, most rooms with bath. Terrace, swimming pool, and restaurant. *Pension Steinbauer* (M), Forellenweg 8 (08075–211). With quietly located annexe. 100 beds. Indoor pool (closed in summer) as well as an outdoor one. Cycles for hire.

Aschau (Chiemgau). *Pension Alpenblick* (M), Spitzensteinstr. 13, in Sachrang section (08052–360). 23 rooms with bath. Very quiet and picturesque location; indoor pool. *Edeltraud* (M), Narzissenweg 15, in Aschau (08052–552). 15 rooms with bath. Lovely mountain view. *Gasthof Weissbräu* (I), Frasdorferstr. 7 in Aschau (08052–1424). Good-value traditional quest-house, located near the swimming pool.

Augsburg (Bavarian Swabia). *Steigenberger Drei-Mohren* (L), Maximilianstr 40 (0821–510031). 110 rooms with bath, and operating since 1723. One of Germany's historic hotels; former guests include Russian czars and German emperors, as well as Mozart and Goethe. Fine restaurant, terrace cafe, and dance bar. *Fuggerkeller* wine cellar is located in same building (Maximilianstr. 38), serving first-class Franconian wines. AE, DC, MC, V. *Alpenhof* (E), Donauwörther Str. 233, in the northwest suburbs (0821–413051). 136 rooms with bath or shower. Indoor pool, sauna, fitness room, games room, casino, restaurant. A Ringhotel. AE, DC, MC, V. *Dom Hotel* (M), Frauentorstr. 8 (0821–153031). 43 rooms with bath or shower. Very quiet location in the old town near the station. Breakfast only. MC, V. *Holiday Inn* (M), Wittelsbacherpark (0821–577087). 185 rooms with bath. Europe's tallest (35-story) hotel tower. Indoor pool, sauna, solarium. Grill specialties in the top floor Panorama restaurant. AE, DC, MC, V. *Riegele* (M), Viktoriastr. 4, near station (0821–39039). 57 beds. Smaller hotel, good restaurant. AE, V. *Gästehaus Iris* (I), Gartenstr. 4 (0821–510981). 10 rooms, most with shower or bath. Centrally but quietly located near the Dominican Monastery. Breakfast only. AE, DC, MC. *Post* (I), Fuggerstr. 5/7, at Königsplatz (0821–36044). 45 rooms, most with bath or shower. Terrace restaurant. Closed Christmas and New Year's. AE, DC, MC, V.

Restaurants. *Berteles Weinstuben* (E), Philippine-Welser-Str. 4 (0821–3119). Definitely superior tavern. DC, MC. *Die Ecke* (E), Elias-Holl-Platz (0821–510600). Old Augsburg atmosphere for gourmets and wine connoisseurs. Reservations advisable. DC, MC. *Welser Küche* (E), in the old Patrician Stiermann house Maximilianstr. 83 (0821–33930). A rare dining experience: you can enjoy original recipes in 16th-century style (Mon. to Sat. at 8 P.M.; Sun. 7 P.M.), prior telephone arrangements are a must. AE, DC, MC. *Fischertor* (M), Pfärrle 16 (0821–518662). In the narrow side streets of the old town, serving fine Swabian regional specialties. MC, V. *Fuggerei-Stube* (M), Jakoberstr. 26 (0821–30870). Specialty restaurant in the world-famous Fuggerei. Popular among the locals. AE, DC, MC. *Ratskeller* (M), in the Rathaus with *Elias-Holl-Stube* and *Badische Weinstube* (0821–517848). AE, DC, MC. *Zeughausstuben* (I), Zeugplatz (0821–511685). In the historic armory building. Very atmospheric specialty restaurant; beer garden in summer. MC.

Bad Reichenhall (Berchtesgadener Land). *Kurhotel Luisenbad* (E), Ludwigstr. 33 (08651–5011). Traditional and old-established cure-hotel. 84 beds, all rooms with bath, indoor pool, sauna, fitness center, cosmetic studio. Elegant *Luisenbad* restaurant, rustic *Holzstubin* tavern. *Steigenberger's Axelmannstein* (E), Salzburgerstr. 4 (08651–4001). 167 rooms, most with bath. Luxurious hotel in the famous Steigenberger chain. Excellent *Parkrestaurant* with terrace, cocktail bar, own thermal bath. Located in large park with swimming pool; also indoor pool and tennis courts. AE, DC, MC, V. *Bavaria* (M), Am Münster 3 (08651–5016). 173 spacious studio-apartments. Located in a fine private park, quiet, but still only a short walk from the pedestrian zone. Indoor pool, sauna, health facilities, two restaurants. *Bayersicher Hof* (M), Bahnhofsplatz 14 (08651–5084). 64 rooms with bath or shower. On the main station square. Pool on roof terrace, health facilities, café with afternoon music, nightclub and three restaurants. Closed Jan. 5–Feb. 20. AE, DC, MC, V.

Alpenhotel "Fuchs" (M) Nonn 50 (08651-61048). In the Nonn section, above the town, surrounded by forest and meadow. 36 rooms, most with own bath. First-class restaurant. Tennis courts five minutes away. Hotel has its own ski-training slope for novices. Closed Nov. 1–Dec. 22. AE, DC, MC, V. *Tiroler Hof* (M), Tirolerstr. 12 (08651–2055). A Ring Hotel located in the pedestrian zone. 45 rooms with bath or shower. Indoor pool, garden and garages. Colorful, wood-beamed restaurant dating back to 1634. AE, DC, MC, V. *Schlossberghof* (M), Schlossberg 5, in the Marzoll section (08651–3002). 100-bed hotel with apartments, near the ancient Schloss Marzoll castle. Good value. Indoor pool, large restaurant, beer garden and coffee terrace. *Carola* (I), Friedrich-Ebbert-Allee 6 (08651–2629). 20 rooms, 15 with shower. Quietly located two to three minutes from the Kurpark. No restaurant. Closed Nov. 1–Feb. 20. No credit cards.

Bad Tölz (Isar Valley). *Jodquellenhof* (E), on the left bank of the Isar at Ludwigstr. 13–15 (08041–5091). 78 rooms and 3 suites with bath. Three pools, one with thermal iodine water, open March through October. Restaurant with special dietary menu. AE, DC, MC, V. *Hiedl* (M), Ludwigstr. 9 (08041–9774). 28 beds. Cozy, rustic-style hotel-pension with particularly good cooking in its *Bürgerstuben* restaurant. *Kolberbräu* (M), Marktstr. 29 (08041–9158). In the same family since 1600; good restaurant. MC. *Gästehaus Bergblick* (I), Benedikt-Erhard-Str. 6 (08041–3622). 16 rooms, half with bath or shower. Quiet; no restaurant.

Restaurants. *Altes Fährhaus* (M), An der Isarlust 1 (08041–6030). Directly on the banks of the Isar; former ferry boat station. Serves typical Upper Bavarian specialties with a touch of gastronomic élan. *Schwaighofer* (M), Marktstr. 17 (08041–2762). Located in the town center.

Bad Wiessee (Tegernsee). *Kurhotel Lederer am See* (E), Bodenschneidstr. 9 (08022–8291). 190 beds, 90 baths, 3 apartments. Lovely location on lake with own beach and tennis courts. Comfortable restaurant and tavern. DC. *Kurhotel Rex* (E), Münchner Str. 25 (08022–82091). 56 rooms and 2 suites with bath or shower. Park. Closed Nov. 1–Apr. 15. No credit cards. *Terrassenhof* (E), Adrian-Stoop Str. 50 (08022–82761). 86 rooms, all with bath. Pool, café, wine tavern and summer dancing. *Kurheim Wilhelmy* (M), Freihausstr. 15 (08022–81191). In pleasant location, 28 rooms. *Resi von der Post* (M), Zilcherstr. 14 (08022–82788). 30 rooms. Quiet and comfortable, some apartments. *Wiesseer Hof, der Kirchenwirt* (M), Sanktjohanserstr. 46 (08022–82061). Belongs to the Ring hotel group. Rustic restaurant. AE, DC, MC, V. *Haus Börner* (I), Seestr. 24 (08022–8558). 14 rooms, some with bath. Small hotel, but particularly comfortable and with excellent service; no restaurant. Quiet, and pleasant view. *Berggasthof Sonnenbichl* (M) (08022–81365). On the slopes above the town at Sonnenbichlweg 1. Has own ski lift and some rooms.

Restaurant. *Freihaus Brenner* (M), Freihaushohe 4 (08022–82004). Rustic restaurant in an old farm house high above the town. A real local tip; its popularity makes reservations essential in summer—in winter it's often cut off from the town. Hearty Bavarian specialties mixed with international cuisine at more than reasonable prices. MC.

Café-Restaurant: *Bauer in der Au* (M) (08022–81171). At almost 900 meters (3,000 ft) on the mountainside—accessible by foot only on well-marked hiking trails from Weissach—with a 200 year-old covered courtyard. Serves some of the best cakes around. Open until 7.00 P.M.

Balderschwang (Allgäu). *Pension Lässer* (M), Wäldle 8 (08328–1018). 26 rooms, half-board terms only. Fine view. Sauna, solarium and sports room. *Luisenhof* (M) (08328–1054). 42 beds.

Bayrischzell (Schliersee). *Meindelei* (E), Michl.-Meindl-Str. 13 (08023–318). Romantik Hotel located on the south slopes of the Wendelstein in a quiet position. 15 rooms, all with bath. Furnished with old Bavarian peasant furniture and antiques. Restaurant with open fireplace and ceramic tile oven. Small indoor pool. MC, V. *Alpenrose* (M), Schlierseestr. 6 (08023–620). 50 beds, all rooms with bath or shower. Well-known restaurant serving Bavarian specialties, as well as international menu. Some holiday apartments available. *Schönbrunn* (M), Sudelfeldstr. 23 (08023–726). On the road up to Sudelfeld, located in own large park near the Kneipp Center. Fine restaurant and café. MC. *Berghotel Sudelfeld* (I), Unteres Sudelfeld (08023–607). 71 rooms. On the mountain at Sudelfeld, right next to the ski slopes. *Feuriger Tatzelwurm* (I) (08034–8695). Alpine Gasthof. Located at the end of the "Alpine Road," at the famous Tatzelwurm waterfalls. Cozy atmosphere, good restaurant. MC.

Berchtesgaden. In **Markt Berchtesgaden:** *Geiger* (E), Stanggass (08652–5055). 40 rooms, 8 apartments and 3 suites with bath. In quiet location on outskirts; indoor and outdoor pools, fitness room, trout specialties in restaurant, antique furnishings. Closed Nov. AE, DC, V.
Bavaria (M), Sunklergässchen 11 (08652–2620). Most rooms with shower. Cozy atmosphere. Centrally located near the main station, but still with a splendid panoramic view of the Watzmann summit and surrounding mountains. *Grassl* (M), Maximilianstr. 15 (08652–4071). Large rooms but street front can be noisy; breakfast only. AE, DC, MC, V. *Krone* (M), Am Rad 5 (08652–2881). Small and quiet, on the outskirts. *Vier Jahreszeiten* (M), Maximilianstr. 20 (08652–5026). 62 rooms and 3 apartments with bath or shower. Centrally-located; has belonged to the same family since 1876. Indoor pool, sauna, solarium, fitness room. *Hubertusstuben* restaurant serving game specialties. AE, DC, MC, V. *Watzmann* (M), Franziskanerplatz 2 (08652–2055). 37 rooms, half with shower. Very comfortable inn just opposite the church; good value restaurant, own butchery, heated garden-terrace. Closed Nov. 1–Dec. 22. AE, MC, V.
Café Waldluft (I), Bergwekstr. 37 (08652–2328). 55 beds, most with own shower. Peacefully located on the edge of a forest and at the foot of the Obersalzberg peak. Ten minutes from the center. Restaurant and terrace café. *Weiherbach* (I), Weiherbach Weg 6–8 (08652–2333). 22 rooms, most with shower. Ten minutes' walk from the center, five minutes' from the skilift; rustic building, quiet. Closed Nov. 3–Dec. 20. No credit cards.
Restaurants. *Gasthof Neuhaus* (M), Marktplatz 1. AE. *Gasthof Bier-Adam* (I), Marktplatz 22 (08652–2390). Quality Bavarian fare served with style. Closed Wed. in winter. AE, DC, MC, V.
In **Königssee:** *Restaurant-Pension Lichtenfels* (M), Alte Konigseer Str. 15 (08652–4035). Conveniently located between town center and Konigsee with good public transport. Good restaurant. **In Oberau:** *Alpenhotel Denninglehen* (M) (08652–5085) located on the mountainside at about 3,000 ft. Alpine styled building with all modern facilities of a luxury hotel. Restaurant and beauty farm. Reservations advised. Closed Dec. 1–20. No credit cards. In **Obersalzburg:** *Zum Türken* (I), Hintereck 2

(08652–2428). 17 rooms, half with bath or shower. Small mountain hotel in quiet location. Closed Nov. 1–Dec. 20. AE, DC, MC, V. In **Ramsau:** *Alpenhof* (I), Am See 27 (08657–253). Near Hintersee Lake; well-located for walking, angling or pony rides; pleasant terrace garden.

Restaurants. *Haslinger am Luitpoldpark* (M), Kälbersteinerstr. 2 (08652–2605). *Kurhaus* (M), Maximilianstr. 9 (08652–4364). With splendid view from terrace.

Bergen (Chiemsee). *Säulner Hof* (M), ten minutes from the lakeside near the Hochfelln cable car station Saulnerweg 1 (08662–8655). 15 rooms with bath or shower. Very comfortable hotel-restaurant in local style, with excellent food: a combination of regional and *haute cuisine* at reasonable prices. Ideal for both winter and summer vacations. Closed Nov. V.

Bischofswiesen (Berchtesgadener Land). *Brennerbascht* (M), Hauptstr. 46 (08652–7021). 54 beds, some apartments, all with own bath or shower; rustic-style terrace, sunbathing lawn. *Bauernstube* restaurant serving Bavarian and international dishes from own hunting and fishing grounds. *Gästehaus Elvira* (I), Reitweg 25 (08652–2631). 18 beds. Small pension, on a quiet southern slope only 2 km. (1.2 miles) from Berchtesgaden itself. Heated indoor pool.

Chiemsee (Chiemgau). In **Chieming:** *Gasthof Unterwirt* (I), Hauptstr. 32 (08664–551). 20 rooms, 8 with bath. Good restaurant with local specialties, particularly *renke* and trout. Garden. Closed Oct. 21–Nov. 25. No credit cards.

Restaurant. *Gasthof zur Post* (M), Laimgruber Str. 5 (08664–447). Has *Zwergclause restaurant* for late dining.

In **Gstadt:** *Pension Jägerhof* (I), Breitbrunner Str. 5 (08054–242). 30 rooms, 11 with bath or shower. Particularly comfortable hotel-pension. Terrace, sauna, solarium and sports room. Closed Nov.–Mar. AE, DC, MC, V.

In **Ising:** *Hotel Gutsgasthof Zum Goldenen Pflug* (E), Kirchberg 3 (08667–421). All rooms with bath; plus seven apartments. Typically Bavarian rustic hotel with attractively furnished rooms in various period styles, beautifully-located in fields and meadowland. Six different restaurants with Bavarian and Austrian specialties as well as an international menu. Riding school, large stables, own bathing beach on Chiemsee lake, 20 minutes' walk away. Sailing, surfing and golf-course nearby. AE.

In **Prien:** *Sport und Golfhotel* (E), Erlenweg 16 (08051–1001). 40 rooms with rustic furnishings, all with own bath; two apartments. Modern Bavarian-style building; indoor pool, pleasant garden, good restaurant serving game specialties, also a café. A few minutes from a nine-hole golf course. MC. *Gästehaus Drexler-König Ludwig Stuben* (M), Seestr. 95 (08051–4802). 17 rooms, about half with own bath or shower. Right next to the Chiemsee ferry quay. Beer garden and cafe. *Reinhart* (M), Seestr. 117 (08051–1045). 28 rooms, most with own bath or shower. Quietly-located with panoramic view over the lake. Terrace, cafe and restaurant. AE, MC, V. *Gaststätte-Lindenhof* (I), Rathausstr. 24. 17 beds. Simple Gasthof in the town center. Good wholesome food and shady beer garden. *Pension Bartlhof* (I), Seestr. 100 (08051–2807). On the lake.

In **Rimsting:** *Seehof* (M), Schafwaschen 4 (08051–1697). Right on the lakeside with its own mooring jetty and beach; large lakeside café terrace.

In **Seebruck:** *Landgasthaus-Hotel Lambachhof* (M), Lambach 10 (08667–427). 56 beds, most with own bath or shower. Large local-style hotel, outside the town center on the lakeside road at picturesque Malerwinkel. Shady garden surrounded by meadowland. Rustic restaurant with excellent local specialties, including lamb from own farm. *Post* (M), Ludwig-Thomas-Str. 8 (08667–216). 100 beds. On the lake with its own beach. Garden restaurant, bar.

Restaurant. *Malerwinkel,* Lambach 23 (08667–488). Very popular excursion destination. Large hotel-restaurant directly on the lake with a lovely view across to Fraueninsel. Good food, but crowded with poor service in high season.

In **Seeon:** *Pension-Restaurant Gruber Alm* (I), in the Roitham section, Almweg 18 (08624–696). 50 beds. Sauna, solarium. Home-made bread and wine.

Ettal (Ammergauer Alps). *Benediktenhof* (M), Zieglerstr. 1, a little out of town on the way to Oberammergau (08822–4637). 17 rooms, each furnished with Bavarian Baroque or rustic furniture, most with own bath; also one apartment. An original farmstead with plenty of wooden beams and painted walls, over 500 years old. The hotel restaurant (with terrace and café) serves excellent local and international cuisine. *Hotel Ludwig der Bayer* (M), Kaiser Ludwig Platz 10 (08822–6601). 66 rooms, most with own bath, two apartments. Indoor pool, sauna, game rooms, garden, restaurant. Closed Nov. 9–Dec. 20. No credit cards. *Hotel-Gasthof Zur Post,* Kaiser Ludwig Platz 18 (08822–596). Has annexe (M). 18 rooms, 4 apartments, most with bath or shower. Terrace and café. Two good-value restaurants, *Post Stüberl* and the *Gästehaus Restaurant* in the annex at Hauptstr. 15. Closed Nov. 10–Dec. 20. AE, DC, MC, V.

Fischen (Allgäu). *Kur-und-Sport Hotel Sonnenbichl* (E), Sagestr. 19 (08326–1851). In nearby Langenwang. Most rooms with bath or shower. Small indoor pool, tennis. Particularly comfortable with fine view. *Gästehaus Burgmühle* (M), Auf der Insel 4 (08326–7352). All rooms with bath or shower. Garni. *Haus Rosenstock* (M), Berger Weg 14 (08326–1895). All rooms with balcony. *Kur-und-Sporthotel Tanneck* (M), next to the ski lift, a bit outside town and higher up, Maderhalmer Weg 20 (08326–1888). 180 beds, all with bath or shower; apartments. Excellent restaurant and small indoor pool and sauna. *Pension Haus Alpenblick* (I), Maderhalmerweg 10 (08326–337). At about 900 meters (3,000 ft.). Café with homemade pastries.

Fraueninsel (island in Chiemsee). *Hotel Linde* (M) (08054–316). Pleasant garden and restaurant.

Restaurants. *Inselwirt* (M) (08054–630). Also with a garden and well-known for its good food, particularly excellent fish from the lake. *Kloster Café* (I), near the *Inselwirt* and next door to the convent (08054–653). Here you can taste the famous Chiemsee *Klosterlikör,* a liqueur made by the nuns of the 1,200 year-old convent. Full restaurant service as well as café. All these only open in summer.

Friedrichshafen (Bodensee). *Buchhorner Hof* (M), a Ring Hotel, Friedrichstr. 33 (07541–2050). 65 rooms, about half with bath; 2 apartments, 2 suites. Sauna, solarium. A good restaurant with the accent on local fish and game. Closed Dec. 20–Jan. 10. AE, DC, MC, V. In nearby Schnetzenhausen, *Hotel City-Krone* (M), Schanzstr. 7 (07541–22086). For good value comfort. Large, quiet rooms; good location. Indoor pool and restaurant. Closed Dec. 12–Jan. 20. AE, DC, MC, V.

Füssen (Allgäu). *Hirsch* (E), Schulhausstr. 2–4 (08362–6055). Near Augsburger-Tor-Platz. 47 rooms, about half with bath. Authentic rustic furnishings, tavern, restaurant. Closed Nov. 15–Dec. 20. AE, DC, V. *Alpenkurhotel Filser* (M), Säulingerstr. 3 (08362–2068). Hotel and sanatorium. Quiet location with Kneipp water cures. *Kurhotel Wiedemann* (M), in the Bad Faulenbach suburb, Am Anger 3 (08362–37231). Quiet and pleasant, also with Kneipp cures. *Sonne* (M), Reichenstr. 37 (08362–6061). 32 rooms with bath or shower. Cheerful, modern hotel with traditional furnishings, café, disco/nightclub. No restaurant. AE, DC, MC, V. *Sailer's Kur-und-Ferienhotel* (M), Bildhauer Sturm Str. 14 (08362–7089). 40 beds, all rooms with own bath. Indoor pool, sauna, solarium. Located in one of the prettiest parts of town at the foot of the Galgenbichl heights. "Cure hotel" with all the best health facilities. *Seegasthof Weissensee* (M), on the shores of Lake Weissensee (08362–7095). 40 beds, all rooms with bath and lakeview. On its own bathing beach. Good local fish specialties in restaurant.

Restaurants. *Alpen-Schlossle* (M), Alatseestr. 28 (08362–4017). Rustic restaurant on a mountain site. Reservations advised. Closed Tues. and Nov.–mid-Dec. No credit cards. *Pulvertum* (M), in the Kurhaus, Schwedenweg 1 (08362–6078). Fine view from the terrace. MC. *Gasthaus zum Schwanen* (I), Brotmarkt 4 (08362–6174). Good regional cooking with no frills at low prices. Closed Sun. evening, Mon., and Nov. No credit cards.

Garmisch-Partenkirchen (Werdenfelser Land). *Clausing's Posthotel* (E), Marienplatz 12 (08821–58071). 31 rooms, most with bath or shower. A Romantik Hotel. A Baroque chalet with a long tradition and outstanding Bavarian cuisine. Dancing in the evening. AE, DC, MC. *Dorint Sporthotel* (E), Mittenwalder Str. 59 (08821–7060). New 1985. 480 beds, including some apartments; pleasant harmony of elegance and rustic charm. Wide variety of sports facilities and ski school run by German champions Rosie Mittermaier and Christian Neureuther. *Grand-Hotel Sonnenbichl* (E), Burgstr. 97 (08821–7020). 100 rooms, all with own bathroom; some suites available. Opposite the Garmisch golf course in beautifully wooded area. Excellent cuisine, either in the elegant gourmet restaurant or Bavarian specialties in the cozy *Zirbelstube*. Tennis, skating and fishing, as well as golf, nearby. DC, V. *Holiday Inn* (E), Mittenwalderstr. 2 (08821–7561). 117 rooms, all with bath. In Partenkirchen; the resort's largest hotel. *Kurhotel-Bernriederhof* (E), Von-Muller-Str. 12 (08821–71074). Enormous old farmhouse with 41 rooms, all tastefully furnished in regional style with real comfort—especially the marble bathrooms. Health cure facilities, restaurant. Centrally located with a splendid view across to the mountains. Also has vacation apartments. AE, DC, MC, V. *Obermühle (Silence Hotel)* (E), Mühlstr. 22 (08821–7040). 88 rooms, 6 apartments, 4 suites, most with bath. Five minutes from the center, in parkland. *Mühlenstube* rotisserie restaurant with international cuisine and rustic bar serving Bavarian specialties. Indoor pool, sauna, solarium. AE, DC, MC, V. *Partenkirchner Hof* (E), Bahnhofstr. 15 in Partenkirchen (08821–58025). 80 rooms with bath. A charming mix of first-class elegance and cozy Bavarian charm, located near the station. Pool, sauna, beauty farm, as well as 14 delightful apartments in *Wetterstein* annex. Well-regarded *Reindl Grill* restaurant. Closed Nov. 15–Dec. 15 AE, DC, MC, V. *Posthotel Partenkirchen* (E), Ludwigstr. 49 (08821–51067). 90 beds. Original stagecoach post. First-class service, good restaurant and wine tavern with music. AE, DC, MC, V.

Aschenbrenner (M), Loisachstr. 65A (08821–58029). Near the Kurpark. 24 rooms and 1 suite, most with bath. A mixture of modern comfort, *belle époque* furnishings and a noble country house. AE, DC, MC, V. *Buchenhof* (M), Brauhausstr. 3 (08821–52121). Comfortable house with 20 beds, some apartments, all rooms with bath or shower. Small indoor pool, sunbathing lawn, café. *Forsthaus Graseck* (M), Graseck 10 (08821–54006). Situated 900 meters (3,000 ft.) above Garmisch in idyllic surroundings. 74 beds. Indoor pool, restaurant and terrace with panoramic view. Reached by its own cable car. AE, DC, MC. *Garmischer Hof* (M), Bahnhofstr. 53 (08821–51091). 43 rooms with bath or shower. Right in the town center; no restaurant. AE, DC, MC. *Schneefernhaus* (M), on the Zugspitz, reached by cogwheel railway from Garmisch or cable car from Eibsee. 30 beds. The highest hotel in Germany (over 2,650 meters or 8,7000 ft.) with large public rooms and sun terraces. *Wittelsbach* (M), Von Brug Str. 24 (08821–53096). 100 beds, all with bath or shower, most with balcony and panoramic view. Beautifully situated in town center in its own grounds; indoor pool. AE, DC, MC.

Gästehaus Hohenzollern (I), Alpspitzstr. 6 (08821–2950). 19 beds, some with own bath or shower. No restaurant. *Gästehaus Kornmüller* (I), Höllental Str. 36 (08821–3557). 32 rooms, 8 apartments, 4 suites, most with bath. Friendly guesthouse in local style; three minutes by car from town center. AE, MC, V.

Restaurants. *Posthotel Partenkirchen.* (E), Ludwigstr. 49 (08821–2075). Bavarian dishes, Swiss and French regional specialties. Reservations advised. AE, MC, V. *Rotisserie Mühlenstube* (E), Mühlstr. 22 (08821–7040). Fresh salt-water fish thanks to specially built tanks. Reservations advised. AE, DC, MC, V. In addition to the high class restaurants in the main hotels: *Café Bauer* (M), Griesstr. 1 (08821–2109). Local atmosphere and music. *Gasthof Fraundorfer* (M), Ludwigstr. 15 in Partenkirchen (08821–2176). Typical Bavarian tavern with *schuhplattler* dancing, very popular with visitors. Reservations advisable. Some rooms, too. *Heuriger Zum Melber* (M), Ludwigstr. 37 (08821–2055). Rustic surroundings; also has a bowling (skittles) alley and dancing. *Isis Goldener Engel* (M), on Marktplatz (08821–56677). Café, bar, wine-tavern. *Werdenfelser Hof* (M), Ludwigstr. 58 (08821–3621). Opposite the *Drei Mohren* Hotel (see above). Particularly good game specialties. Reservations advised. Closed Thurs. DC, MC. *Stahl's Badstuben* (I), Klammstr. 47 (08821–58700). In the Alpspitz Wellenbad swimming and sports center. Good set menu and self-service. Reservations advised. No credit cards.

Grainau (Werdenfelser Land). *Alpenhof* (M), Alpspitz Str. 22 (08821–8071). 40 rooms. Pool. AE, DC. *Badersee* (M), Am Badersee 5 (08821–8685). On the lake, quiet with noted restaurant; boating. AE, MC.

Grainauer Hof (M), Schmolzstr. 5 (08821–50061). 52 beds, most rooms with own bath. Indoor pool, sauna, solarium. No restaurant. AE, DC, MC. *Post* (M), in the Obergrainau section, Postgasse 10 (08821–8853). 33 rooms and 7 apartments, with bath or shower. Restaurant. Closed Oct. 20–Dec. 20 and Jan. 10–Feb. 1. AE, DC, MC.

Grassau (Chiemgau). *Gasthof zur Post* (M), Kirchplatz 8 (08641–3113). 8 rooms. Cozy inn near the town center. Restaurant with local and international food, also a café. Terrace and outdoor pool. AE, MC. *Pension Gamsei* (I), Wöhrstr. 15 (08641–2749). 12 rooms. Very quietly located with beautiful views of the mountains from the garden. Heated outdoor pool; no restaurant.

Restaurants. *Gasthof Restaurant Fischerstüberl* (M), in nearby Rottau, Hauptstr. 5 (08641–2334). Locally-caught fish specialties; also some rooms. *Sperrer* (M), Ortenburgerstr. 5 (08641–5011). Bavarian fare, magnificent views. Reservations advised. Closed Mon. and Nov. No credit cards.

Herreninsel (island in Chiemsee). **Restaurant.** *Schlosshotel Herrenchiemsee* (M) (08051–1509). Open all year round, next to the castle. First-class restaurant serving fish specialties and home-made cakes and pastries. Also has its own beach. No accommodations.

Hindelang (Allgäu). *Prinz Luitpold* (E), Andreas-Gross-Str. 7 (08324–2011). 190 beds. Quietly-located on the southern slopes with a beautiful view. Bar, tennis court, swimming pool and health cures in the house; good food. Special arrangements for winter and summer packages, and *Alpengasthof Hirsch* (M), Kurzegasse 18 (08324–308). Rustic-style inn with good food. Both in the Bad Oberdorf section. *Alpengasthof Rosen-Stuben* (M), Jörg Lederer Str. 17 (08324–2370). Small, 10 rooms, most with bath. Fine view and restaurant. *Bären* (M), Bärengasse 1 (08324–2001). 47 beds, most rooms with bath or shower. Colorful traditional inn dating from 1812. Quietly-located on the southern edges of town. Rustic restaurant. *Kur und Sporthotel Haus Ingeburg* (M), eight km. (five miles) out of town, in Oberjoch, Am Prinzewald 3 (08324–7111). Bar, tennis court and small indoor pool. *Sonne* (M), in the town proper, Marktstr. 15 (08324–2026). 60 rooms, 46 apartments. Cozy restaurant and dance bar. AE.

Hintersee (Berchtesgadener Land), lakeside section of Ramsau. *Alpenhof Bartels* (I), Am See 27 (08657–253). 34 beds. On the lake in quiet location. Good restaurant with local specialties. *See-Hotel Gamsbock* (I), Am See 75, on the lakeside (08657–279). 34 rooms, all with bath or shower. Only a few minutes from start of the Berchtesgaden National Park, ideal for walking; also private fishing, and boating. Wonderful view, lakeside terrace, restaurant with game specialties from own hunting grounds.

Hohenschwangau (Allgäu). *Lisl und Jägerhaus* (E), Neuschwansteinstr. 1 (08362–81006). 57 rooms. Hunting-manor style building; outdoor pool and restaurant. AE, DC. *Müller* (E), Alpseestr. 14 (08362–81056). 46 rooms and four apartments. Attractive *Kutscherstube* restaurant. AE, DC.

Inzell (Chiemgau). *Dorint-Hotel* (E), Lärchenstr. 5 (08665–6700). 88 rooms, 130 apartments, all with bath or shower, radio, color T.V., telephone and balcony. Five minutes' walk from the town center. Bar, smart restaurants with international menu and Bavarian specialties. v. *Falkenstein* (M), Kreuzfeldsstr. 2 (08665–250). 66 beds, some rooms with own bath, most with shower; four apartments. Restaurant and cozy *Bauernstube*. AE. *Gasthof Schmelz* (M), in the Schmelz section, Schmelzer Str. 132 (08665–834). 35 rooms and apartments with bath or shower; eight holiday flats. Sauna, two solariums, indoor pool, massage and cosmetic treatment. Ponies for hire and winter sports on the doorstep. Restaurant. AE.

Kempten (Allgäu). *Fürstenhof* (E), Rathausplatz 8 (0831–23050). 300 year-old building with period furniture. All rooms with bath, three suites. Near the Town Hall. Fine restaurant serving French cuisine and rustic *Ratskeller* with Allgäuer specialties. AE, DC, MC. v. *Bahnhof Hotel* (M), Mozartstr. 2 (0831–22073). 40 rooms; newly renovated. Near the main station. Restaurant. AE, DC, MC. *Haslacher Hof* (M), Immenstädterstr. 74 (0831–24026). Near the station with view of the mountains. Good value. AE, DC, MC. v. *Peterhof* (M), Salzstr. 1 (0831–25525). A Ring Hotel. 51 rooms, all with own bath. In the town center, well known for good food in its *Peterhof Stüble*. AE, DC, MC. v. *Pension Haus Liesl* (I), Sängerstr. 13 (0831–23879). 20 beds. No restaurant.

Restaurants. *Sir Alexander* (M), Haslacher Berg 2 (0831–28322). Fine gourmet restaurant with international menu. *Café-Restaurant Hummel* (M), Immenstädter Str. 2 (0831–22286). Has own garden and home-made pastries. AE, DC, MC. *Weinhaus Winkel* (M), Fischersteige 9. (0831–22457). Historic wine tavern. Wholesome local specialties and fine international dishes on the menu. Good German wines and beer. DC, MC. *Goldene Traube* (I), Memmingerstr. 7 (0831–22187). Specialty gasthaus-restaurant serving large selection of fish dishes, international and local, as well as good game. Also some rooms. MC.

Kleinwalsertal (Allgäu). Actually in Austria, but it can only be reached by road from Oberstdorf. *Alpenhof Wildental* (E), Höfle 8 (08329–5611). 121 beds, all rooms with bath/shower. A modern I.F.A. hotel in the Mittelberg section. Quiet, sunny location amid fields and hills. Restaurant and bar, indoor pool and other first-class amenities. *Ifen Hotel* (E), Oberseitestr. 6 (08329–5071). In the Hirschegg section, a quiet location at the foot of the Ifen peak (2,000 meters or 6,600 ft.). Modern but in local rustic style. 67 rooms with large balconies, sauna, solarium massage, health facilities and large indoor pool. Fine restaurant with international cuisine. *Walserhof* (E), Walserstr. 11 (08329–5684). All rooms with bath or shower, also some apartments and hotel suites, also in the Hirschegg section. Modern, but in local style. Indoor pool, tennis courts, buffet and grill room, dancing.

Alpenrose (M), Walserstr. 46 (08329–5585). In Mittelberg section. Heated pool. *Alte Krone* (M), Walserstr. 87 (08329–5728). In Mittelberg section. Indoor pool. *Der Berghof* (M), Walserstr. 22 (08329–5445). In Hirschegg section. Traditional establishment with peaceful location and fine view. *Montana* (M), Schwarzwasseralstr. 13 (08329–5361). All rooms with bath or shower. Indoor pool, sauna. *Sporthotel Riezlern* (M), Schwendestr. 9 (08329–6652). 80 two-room apartments, all with bath or shower and some with kitchenette. In Riezlern section. Indoor pool, sauna, horseback riding.

Kochel (Walchensee). *Alpenhotel Schmied von Kochel* (M), Schlehdorfer Str. 6 (08851–216). 34 rooms, all with bath or shower. Bavarian inn with long, low wooden roof and brightly colored painted walls. Zither music every evening in the restaurant. MC, V. *Fischer am See* (M), in the Urfeld section, directly on the Walchensee lake (08851–818). Delightfully-located with a beautiful view. Lakeside terrace and openair pool. Good fish in the *Fischerstüberl* restaurant. *Grauer Bär* (M), Mittenwalder Str. 82 (08851–861). 26 rooms, some with balconies overlooking the lake. Located directly on the banks of the lake. Simple, tasteful hotel in cozy rustic style. Good wholesome local specialties in the restaurant, which has a lakeside terrace garden. AE, MC.

Konstanz (Bodensee). *Steingenberger Insel* (E), Auf der Insel 1 (07531–25011). A former monastery on a small island near the lake shore. 120 rooms, all with bath. Three restaurants and private park overlooking the lake. Own swimming beach. AE, DC, MC, V. *Barbarossa* (M), Obermarkt 8–12 (07531–22021). Historic inn with 100 beds. *Buchner Hof* (M), Buchnerstr. 6 (07531–51035). Neat, friendly and small hotel located in a residential area. 13 rooms, all with own bath. Sauna, solarium; good service but no restaurant. Closed Christmas–Jan. 10. AE. *Dom-Hotel St. Johann* (M), Brückengasse 1 (07531–22750). Built in the 10th century and looking like an old church. Has noted restaurant. *Seeblick* (M), Neuhauser Str. 14 (07531–54018). Second largest hotel with 86 rooms, most with own bath. Relatively simple furnishings, but comfortable. Indoor pool, solarium, sports room and tennis. Restaurant. AE, DC, MC. *Strandhotel Löchnerhaus* (M) (07534–411). 76 beds. On nearby Reichenau Island. Large hotel facing the lake with private swimming facilities. *Schiff am See* (I), in the Staad section, William-Graf-Platz 2 (07531–31041). Fine view. AE, DC, MC, V. *Zur Traube* (I), Fischerstr. 4 (07531–31317). Near the ferry boat landing stages.

Restaurants. *Casino* (E), in the Casino building, Seestr. 21 (07531–63615). Rustic-style, with pleasant terrace overlooking the lake, outstanding cuisine and dance bar. AE, DC. *Siber* (E), Seestr. 25, in Seehotel Siber (07531–63044). Best restaurant in town and among the finest in Germany. Closed second week in Feb. AE, DC.

Konzil (M), Hafenstr. 2, in the old Council Hall building (07531–21221). Has terraces and a lake view. *Zum Nikolai Torkel* (M), Eichhornstr. 83 (07531–64802). Fine cuisine, terrace with a pleasant view. *Zur Linde* (M), Radolfzeller Str. 27 (07531–77036). Also a café and Gasthof with pleasant comfortable rooms. *Engstler* (I), Fischmarkt 1 (07531–23126). At the lake corner of Marktstätte, with a large beer garden. Family restaurant. Game dishes. Closed Jan.–Feb. AE, DC, MC, V. *Terrine* (I), Bodanstr. 17 (07531–23718). For lovers of thick hearty soups; over 100 varieties. Open 11.30 A.M. to 9 P.M.

On the **Island of Mainau**, *Schwedenschenke* (M), (07531–303166). Swedish specialty restaurant inside an enormous wine barrel.

Kreuth (Tegernsee). *Zur Post* (E), Nördliche Hauptstr. 5 (08029–1021). 55 rooms, all with own bath. In the town center, with restaurant. Special weekend arrangements. *Bachmair-Weissach* (M), in the Weissach section, Tegernseer Str. 103 (08029–24081). 53 rooms, all with own bath and balcony; some apartments. Large indoor pool, sauna, solarium and massage, sunbathing lawn. Cozy, rustic wine tavern with first-class Bavarian dishes. **Restaurant.** *Gasthof Café Zum Batznhäusl* (M), Am Kurpark (08029–249). Near the river. Good Bavarian specialties and afternoon coffee and cake.

Landsberg Am Lech. *Goggl* (M), Herkomer Str. 19 (08191–2081). 49 rooms, most with own bath. Restaurant. AE, DC, MC.
Restaurants. *Schmalzbuckl* (M), Neue Bergstr. 7 (08191–47773). Rustic style, atmospheric. *Historisches Wirtshaus Alt Landtsperg* (M), Alte Bergstr. 436 (08191–5838). Historic old inn with fine food. Reservations essential. Closed Wed., Sun. lunch, last 2 weeks in Feb., and Aug. AE, MC.

Langenargen (Bodensee). *Kurhotel Seeterrasse* (E), Obere Seestr. 52 (07543–2350). 80 beds, about half of the rooms with bath. Restaurant with lakeside terrace, heated pool and own beach. *Litz* (M), Obere Seestr. 11 (07543–2212). Rooms with bath and lake view usually higher. Lakeside terrace. *Löwen* (M), Obere Seestr. 4 (07543–3010). *Engel* (M), Marktplatz 3 (07543–2436). DC. *Seemann* (I–M), in town at Obere Seestr. 28 (07543–2579).

Lenggries (Upper Isar Valley). *Brauneckhotel* (M), Münchner Str. 25 (08042–2021). With all the facilities one would expect of an Arabella hotel. Rooms in Bavarian style. Good restaurant serving Bavarian and international specialties. AE, DC, MC, V. *Zum Papyrer* (M), Fleck 5 (08042–2467). 20 double rooms, some without bath in the old building. Located between Lenggries and the Sylvenstein lake. Traditional hotel-restaurant, much frequented by Munich citizens as an excursion trip. Idyllic position, typical Bavarian furnishings and character. First-rate restaurant serving Upper Bavarian specialties, with a good wine list and 11 different brands of beer. *Gästehaus Seemüller* (I), Oberreitrweg 3 (08042–2781). Small, all rooms with a bath or shower. Located in a quiet area at the foot of the Geierstein peak. Indoor pool.

Lindau (Bodensee). *Hotel Bad Schachen* (E), (08382–5011), in the Bad Schachen health resort in the western suburbs. A magnificent castle-like building in its own huge park right on the lakeside. 210 beds and all possible amenities, including beauty farm, tennis, water sports, health cure facilities and acupuncture. Has its own landing stage. AE, DC, MC, V. *Hotel Helvetia* (E), Seepromenade (08382–4002). 60 rooms, 2 apartments, all with bath. On the harbor. Canopied beds, TV, pool, sauna, restaurant, creperie-bistro, bakery. Closed Nov. 15–Feb. AE, DC, MC, V. *Bayerischer Hof* (M), Seepromenade (08382–5055). 172 beds, most with bath. Closed in winter. DC. *Goldenes Lamm* (M), Schafgasse 3 (08382–5732). Oldest and largest inn in Lindau. Restaurant. *Lindauer Hof* (M), Seepromenade (08382–4064). 23 rooms, 17 with shower, 6 with bath; 4 apartments. Stately hotel on the harbor. Indoor pool, sauna, solarium, restaurant. Closed Nov. 15–Mar. 15. AE, MC, V. *Reutemann* (M), Seepromenade (08382–5055). Most rooms with bath. Open all year. DC. *Seegarten* (M), on the Seepromenade (08382–5055). 50 beds. *Zum Stift* (M), Stiftsplatz (08382–4038).

In the market place next to the two churches in the middle of the pedestrian zone. 53 beds. Restaurant with Bavarian and Swabian specialties, as well as a good selection of Bodensee fish.

Restaurants. *Anton Lenz* (E), in nearby Stockenweiler (08388–243). Notable cuisine in country-house setting. Dinner only. *Hoyerberg Schoessle* (E), Hoyerbergstr. 64 (08382–25295). One of the culinary highspots of the Bodensee, with fish and game specialties, 6- and 8-course dinners. Stunning view. Dress is expected. Reservations necessary in summer. Closed Mon. and Feb. AE, DC, MC. *Lieber Augustin* (E), Augustin Arkaden, Ludwigstr. 29 (08382–5055). On the island peninsula, in the arcades. *Spielbank* (E), in the casino building in the city park (08382–5200). Has lakeside terrace. AE, DC, MC. V. *Walliser Stuben* (E), Ludwigstr. 7 (08382–6449). Good value, local style. AE, DC. *Weinstube Frey* (M), Maximilianstr. 15 (08382–5278). Old wine tavern dating from 1560. *Gasthaus Zum Sunfzen* (I), Maximilianstr. 1 (08382–5865). Former patricians' inn, now a local favorite with good regional specialties. Reservations accepted. Closed Feb. AE, DC, MC, V. *Schlechterbräu* (I), In der Grub (08382–5842). Large beer restaurant. Good sausages and Bavarian specialties. Reservations accepted. Closed end–Feb. and mid-Nov. No credit cards.

MEERSBURG (Bodensee). *Rothmund am See* (M), Uferpromenade 11 (07532–6054). 21 rooms, 3 apartments, 4 suites, all with shower. On the lake front. Perfect for families. Outdoor pool with garden. Closed Nov.–Mar. AE. *Strandhotel Wilder Mann* (M), also on lake front (07532–9011). Outdoor and indoor glassed-in terrace restaurant and café with music and dancing; closed in winter. *Terrassen-Hotel Weisshaar* (M), Stefan-Lochnerstr. 24 (07532–9006). On the hill above the lake, marvelous views. *Zum Bären* (I), Marktplatz 11 (07532–6044). 16 rooms with shower. Atmospheric old inn in center of Old Town. Beautiful restaurant/wine bar. Closed mid-Nov.–mid-Mar. No credit cards.

Restaurants. *Burgkeller* (M) (07532–6028). With garden and musical entertainment. *Winzerstube zum Becher* (M), Höllgasse 4 (07532–9009). Next to the Neuen Schloss; oldest wine tavern on Lake Konstanz, very atmospheric. *Ratskeller* (I), the vaulted Town Hall cellar (07532–9004). AE. *Vinothek Winzerstube* (I), Winzergasse 4 (07532–7510). Well-known and atmospheric wine tavern. *Winzertrinkstube* (I), Steigstr. 33 (07532–6484). Ample portions of Schwabish food. Terrace. Reservations accepted. Closed Dec.–Feb. No credit cards.

MITTENWALD (Werdenfelser Land). *Post* (E), Obermarkt 9 (08823–1094). 90 rooms, 10 apartments, 4 suites, most with bath. Three restaurants, garden café, indoor pool, health cure facilities. No credit cards. *Wetterstein* (E), Dekan-Karl-Platz 1 (08823–5058). Indoor pool, health cure facilities, restaurant, bar and café. AE, DC, MC, V. *Wipfelder* (M), Riedkopfstr. 2 (08823 1057). 15 rooms, most with own bath. Riverside terrace. Breakfast only, but 100 meters away has separate first-class *Arnspitze* restaurant at Innsbrucker Str. 68 (08823 2425). *Hotel Rieger* (M), Dekan-Karl-Platz 28 (08823–5071). 46 rooms with bath or shower. Rustic hotel of great charm, with indoor pool, health-cure facilities, sauna, restaurant. Closed Nov.-3rd week of Dec. AE, DC, MC, V.

Alpenhotel Erdt (M), Albert-Schott-Str. 7 (08823–2001). Good food. DC, MC, V. *Gästehaus Franziska* (M), Innsbruckerstr. 24 (08823–5051). Garni.

Comfortable, with garden and good view. AE, DC, MC. *Jagdhaus Drachenburg* (M), Elmauer Weg 20 (08823–1249). View over the town; game specialties in restaurant. AE, MC.

Restaurant. *Alpenrose* (M), Obermarkt 1 (08823–5055). Hearty Bavarian fare, excellent venison dishes in the fall. Reservations advised.

About three km. (two miles) west of Mittenwald is *Sporthotel Lautersee* (E), Am Lautersee 1 (08823–1017). 50 beds. Near the lake of the same name. About five km. (three miles) north is *Tonihof* (M), Brunnenthal 3 (08823–5031). In lovely quiet location, indoor pool.

Murnau (Ammergauer Alps). *Alpenhof* (E), Ramsachsstr. 8 (08841–1045). 52 rooms, all with own bath and tastefully spacious; also some apartments. Near the end of the Munich–Garmisch autobahn and a short distance from Stafelsee. Heated pool, bar; first-class service. Restaurant *Alpenhof* (E) serves typical old Bavarian dishes and nouvelle cuisine. Regina Hotel (E), Seidlpark 2 (08841–2011). 60 rooms and 2 suites, with bath or shower. Quiet location with impressive view of the surrounding mountains from rooms on the south side. All first-class amenities including indoor pool, sauna, health cure facilities, sports room. Restaurant and café. AE, DC, MC. *Pension St. Leonhard* (I), Dorfstr. 3 (08841–1253). In the suburb of Froschhausen, on the lake of the same name. 19 rooms, some with bath. Nearby beach.

Nesselwang (Allgäu). *Bären* (M), Hauptstr. 3 (08361–3255). 25 beds. In the town center. Cozy, established, brewery-Gasthof. Good restaurant with Alpine specialties. DC, MC. *Brauerei-Gasthof-Post* (M), Hauptstr. 25 (08361–238). All rooms with bath or shower. Traditional Gasthof in Allgäu style. Local specialty restaurant, zither music once a week. Beer from their own brewery. *Kur und Sporthotel Alpspitz* (M), Badeseeweg 10 (08361–255). Comfortable rooms with own bath or shower. Health cure facilities. Good restaurant, bar, sun terrace, sports room, swimming pool across the road. AE. *Sportheim Böck* (I), on Alpspitz (1,500 meters or 4,900 ft.) (08361–3111). 30 beds in rustic-style rooms. Wonderful position above town; panoramic restaurant with good cooking. It can only be reached by cable car, followed by a two-minute walk. Baggage delivered separately. Hang-gliding instruction.

Nussdorf (Inn Valley). *Gästehaus Binder* (M), Hochriesweg 7 (08034–2919). 32 beds, all rooms with own bath. Quiet, atmospheric guest house. Terrace, sauna, solarium. No restaurant.

Oberammergau (Werdenfelser Land). *Alois Lang* (E), St. Lukasstr. 15 (08822–4141). 44 rooms with bath or shower. Sauna, solarium, cozy restaurant and bar. AE, DC, MC, V. *Böld* (E), König Ludwigstr. 10 (08822–520). Ring Hotel. 62 rooms, most with bath or shower. Panoramic views, bar, terrace and restaurant. AE, DC, MC, V. *Alte Post* (M), Dorfstr. 19 (08822–6691). Magnificent facade, garden and pleasant Ludwig-Thomas-Stube. AE, MC. *Friedenshöhe* (M), König Ludwigstr. 31 (08822–598). Small, all rooms with bath or shower. AE, MC, V. *Turmwirt* (M), Ettaler Str. 2 (08822–4291). 22 rooms with bath. Hotel band presents regular Bavarian folk evenings. Restaurant. Closed Jan. 10–Jan. 30. AE, DC, MC, V. *Wittelsbach* (M), Dorfstr. 21 (08822–4545). 100 beds. Beer tavern.

AE, DC, MC, V. *Wolf* (M), Dorfstr. 1 (08822–6971). 31 rooms with bath. Bavarian atmosphere. Outdoor pool, sauna, solarium, restaurant. AE, DC, MC, V. *Ambronia* (I), Ettaler Str. 5 (08822–532). 54 beds. Garden restaurant. AE, MC. *Gasthof zur Rose* (I), Dedlerstr. 9 (08822–4706). 29 rooms, most with bath. Lovely view. Restaurant. Closed Nov.–Dec. 15. AE, DC, MC, V. All these hotels offer special 6-day packages from May to Oct.; contact local tourist offices.

Oberstaufen (Allgäu). *Allgäu Sonne* (E), Am Stiessberg 1 (08386–7020). On the hillside with panoramic view. All modern comforts and health cure facilities in rustic surroundings. *Alpina* (E), Am Kurpark (08386–1661). Period furniture in the public rooms; indoor pool. *Löwen* (E), Kirchplatz 8 (08386–2042). Near the church. Colorful chalet-style building. Good restaurant. *Rosenalp* (M), Am Lohacker 5 (08386–7060). All rooms with bath or shower. *Traube* (M), (08325–451). Ring Hotel in nearby Thalkirchdorf. AE, DC, MC, V.

Oberstdorf (Allgäu). *Kurhotel Adula* (E), in Jauchen outskirts, In der Leite 6 (08322–7090). 130 beds, all rooms with bath and balcony. Indoor pool, cure facilities, rustic bar and restaurant. *Parkhotel Frank* (E), Sachsenweg 11 (08322–5555). One of the town's most comfortable hotels. AE, MC. *Alpenhof* (M), Zweistapfenweg 6 (08322–3095). 45 beds, built in Allgäu country style; indoor and heated outdoor pools. AE. *Filser* (M), Freibergstr. 15 (08322–1020). 150 beds. Excellent restaurant, indoor pool, cure facilities. *Wiese* (M), Stillachstr. 4A (08322–3030). Beautiful view; quiet and with a cozy atmosphere. Breakfast only. *Wittelsbacher Hof* (M), Prinzenstr. 24 (08322–1018). 115 beds, many rooms with bath. Noted restaurant, bar, heated pool (closed Apr. and May, Oct. to mid-Dec.).

Nine km. (5 miles) south of town in the Stillachtal valley is *Alpengasthof Pension Birgsau* (I), (08322–4036). Very quiet location, bus connection into town, all rooms with bath or shower. Short distance from Felhornbahn cable-car station, and ideal as a starting-out point for summer walking or winter cross-country skiing. Good food.

Pfronten (Allgäu). *Bavaria* (E), Kienbergstr. 62 (08363–5004). In the Dorf section. Luxurious; good view, convenient for hiking or skiing. *Flora* (M), Auf der Geigerhalde 43 (08363–5071). Quietly located in own grounds, in Weissbach; large terrace and sunbathing lawn. Fine view of the mountains from all rooms. AE, DC, MC, V. *Post* (M), Kemptener Str. 14 (08363–5032). 27 rooms, all those in the main building with own bath; some rooms in a connecting annex, where it is quieter and the mountain view better. Quaint, rustic-style restaurant. AE, DC, V. *Schlossanger-Alp* (M), in the Obermeilingen section, Schlossanger 1 (08363–381). 15 rooms, most with own bath, and 16 apartments. Indoor pool, sauna, solarium and cross-country skiing on the doorstep. Restaurant specializing in health foods. AE, DC, MC, V. *Haus Achtal* (I), in the Dorf district, Brentenjochstr. 4 (08363–8329). 16 rooms and one apartment. Indoor pool, sauna, solarium. No restaurant. *Pension Pfronter Blick* (I), Burgweg 25, in the Meilingen section (08363–8568). Very quiet location; rooms in rustic style, cozy lounge with open fireplace. Ski instructor in house.

Reit Im Winkl (Chiemgau). *Steinbacher Hof* (E), Steinbachweg 10, in the Blindau section (08640–8410). All rooms with bath. On hillside, with a ski lift. Quiet and luxurious with a fine view. Indoor pool. *Unterwirt* (E), Kirchplatz 2 (08640–8811). 69 rooms, most with bath. Pool, bar and restaurant. Open year-round. *Pension Sonnenblick* (M), Dorfstr. 49 (08640–8261). Indoor pool. *Post* (M), Kirchplatz 7 (08640–1024). Garden and sun terrace. *Alpengasthof Augustiner* (I) Klammweg 2 (08640–8235). 25 beds. At Winklmoosalm (1,158 meters or 3,800 ft.) about 11 km. (seven miles) southeast of Reit im Winkl; with restaurant.

Restaurant. *Kupferkanne* (I), Weitseestr. 18 (08640–1450). Good country fare with some interesting Austrian specialties. Reservations advised. Closed Sat. and Nov. DC, MC.

Rottach Egern (Tegernsee). *Bachmair am See* (E) Seestr. 47 (08022–2720). First class international complex on lakefront with 400 beds in its eight buildings; all rooms and apartments with bath. Seven restaurants, particularly good is the *Barthlmä-Stuben* for atmosphere. Dancing and entertainment in nightclub. Indoor and heated outdoor pools; also well known for its beauty farm. AE, DC. *Seehotel Überfahrt* (E), Uberfahrtstr. 7, also on lakefront (08022–26001). Nearly as large with indoor pool, lakeside terrace, nightclub. AE, DC, MC. *Bachmair-Weissach* (M), at Weissach, Tegernseestr. 103 (08022–24081). 35 rooms. Excellent Bavarian specialties in attractive restaurant. AE, DC, MC. *Hotel Jaedicke* (M), Aribostr. 17–23 (08022–2780). 45 rooms, individually decorated and offering the highest standard of comfort, but accommodations are mostly in large self-contained apartments with balcony or terrace; hotel service is optional. Set in its own beautiful park. Cozy café with superb home-made pastries, but no restaurant. AE, MC. *Wallberghotel* (I), at the top of the Wallberg cable car (08022–6800).

Restaurant. *La Cuisine* (E), Südliche Hauptstr. 2 (08022–24764). On the first floor of a shopping arcade in the town center. Splendid décor and first-class French cuisine and extensive wine list. Among the best restaurants on Tegernsee lake. AE, DC, MC, V. *Café-Restaurant Alpenwildpark* (M), at cable car departure station (08022–5832). With sun terrace.

Ruhpolding (Chiemgau). *Steinbach* (E), Maiergschwendterstr. 10 (08663–1644). Ruhpolding's largest hotel with 167 beds with bath or shower, balcony or terrace. Many rooms with hand-painted rustic furniture. Self-service breakfast buffet, *Pils* tavern and fine food in the *Hobelspan* restaurant. *Zur Post* (E), Hauptstr. 35 (08663–1035). 100 beds, most with bath. 650 year-old Gasthof, tastefully furnished in traditional style. Heated indoor pool, sauna, solarium, terrace. First-class restaurant and dancing every evening.

Ruhpoldinger Hof (M), Hauptstr. 30 (08663–1212). 76 beds, most rooms with bath or shower. Central position. Indoor pool with underwater massage. First-class food, particularly from own trout farm. Dancing. AE, DC, MC. *Sporthotel am Westernberg* (M), Am Wundergraben 4 (08663–1674). A Ring Hotel. 70 beds. On hillside with panoramic view. Indoor pool, thermal baths, sauna and fitness center and restaurant. AE, DC, MC, V.

Haus Heidelberg (I), Brettreichweg 4 (08663–9215). Particularly quiet and comfortable. *Hotel-Garni Alpina* (I), Niederfeldstr. 11 (08663–9905). Elegant, rustic. No restaurant.

Scheidegg (Allgäu). *Kurhotel Scheidegg (Silence Hotel)* (E), Kurstr. 18 (08381–3041). All rooms and apartments with bath and balcony. Beautiful view of the Alps. Indoor pool, tennis, ice-skating, Kneipp water cures. Restaurant, bar. Pension terms only. DC, MC. *Gästehaus Allgäu* (M), Am Brunnenbühl 11 (08381–5250). 14 rooms, all with own bath; one holiday flat. Quiet with a fine view. *Gästehaus Bergblick* (I), Am Brunnenbühl 12 (08381–7291). 14 rooms. Small and quiet with good view. No restaurant.

Schliersee (Schliersee). *Schliersee Hotel Arabella* (E), Kirchbichlweg 18 (08026–4086). 130 luxurious rooms, apartments and holiday flats, all with balconies or terraces. Indoor pool, sauna, solarium, cure facilities, bowling, rustic-style *St. Sixtus Stube* restaurant and cozy wine and beer taverns with open fireplaces. DC. *Hotel Reiter* (M), Risseckstr. 8 (08026–6010). 29 rooms, most with bath or shower; two apartments. Quietly-located (Silence Hotel) on hillside above the lake, with fine views of the lake and mountains. Indoor pool, sun terrace, cozy bar with open fireplace. *Schlierseer Hof-am See* (M) Seestr. 21 (08026–4071). 80 beds. Lakeside terrace, own lake facilities. AE, MC. *Haus Vogelsang* (I), Waldschmidtstr. 5 (08026–7308). 24 beds. Breakfast buffet, sauna, terrace. *Postgasthof-Café St. Bernhard* (I), Seeweg 1 (08026–71011). Terrace and lake swimming. V.

In the *Spitzingsee* section, high above Schliersee on the mountain lake of the same name: *Spitzingsee Hotel* (E), Spitzingstr. 5 (08026–7081). 84 rooms. A luxurious Arabella hotel right on the lakeside with a fine panorama of the surrounding mountains and forest. Two restaurants. AE, DC, MC, V.

Restaurant. *Ratskeller* (I), Rathausstr. 1a (08026–4786). A place to meet the locals. Wholesome Bavarian food. Closed Mon. and last 3 weeks in Nov. and Feb. No credit cards.

Schönau (Berchtesgadener Land). *Alpenhof* (E), Richard Voss Str. 30 (08652–6020). 80 beds, all rooms with own bath. First-class cure-hotel in the middle of the Alpine National Park. Indoor pool, sauna. *Stoll's Alpina* (E), Ulmenweg 14–16 (08652–5091). Two hotel buildings and some apartments in their own park. Indoor and outdoor heated pools, sauna. Fine rustic restaurant serving Bavarian and international specialties. *Zechmeisterlehen* (M), Wahlstr. 35 (08652–3897). 55 beds, most rooms with bath, seven apartments. Stands amidst its own meadowland, ideal for winter and summer sports. Indoor pool, restaurant. Generous breakfast buffet.

Schongau (Ammergauer Alps). *Alte Post* (M), Marienplatz 19 (08861–8058). In the town center with café and restaurant. *Holl* (M), Altenstädter Str. 39 (08861–7292). 50 beds, all rooms with own bath; one apartment and one holiday flat. Quiet location with a fine view. Restaurant serves fresh and imaginative fish dishes. AE, DC, MC, V.

Sonthofen (Allgäu). *Der Allgäu Stern* (E), Auf der Staiger Alp (08321–4012). 870 beds, 150 apartments. On the heights above the town with a wonderful view, set in its own park. Kingly establishment with every imaginable facility, including health cures. Three restaurants and nightclub entertainment. AE, DC, MC, V. *Sonnenalp* (E), outside and above the town at Ofterschwang (08321–720). 222 rooms and apartments. Cure hotel and paradise for sportsmen and women: 26 different sports to indulge in, including riding, golf, tennis, swimming and skiing. Three first-class restaurants; beer cellars and bars. Has one of the best breakfast buffets in Germany. Fine view. *Allgäuer Berghof* (M), also in Ofterschwang (08321–4061). 69 rooms, most with own bath. At 1,300 meters (4,200 ft.), it can be reached from Sonthofen and Bihlerdorf by a private toll road. Indoor pool, sauna, solarium, tennis, health cure facilities. Isolated location with a panoramic view.

Starnbergersee (Ammergauer Alps). In **Starnberg** itself— *Bayerischer Hof* (M), in front of the station (08151–12133). Has a garden restaurant, café and tennis. AE, DC, MC. *Seehof* (M), Bahnhofsplatz 4 (08151–6001). Has good *Ristorante Romagna* Italian restaurant, a lakefront café and a dance bar. AE, V. *Tutzinger Hof* (M), Tutzinger Hof Platz (08151–3081). 65 beds, all rooms with own bath. Terrace and restaurant noted for its Bavarian specialties. AE, DC, MC, V.

Restaurant. *Seerestaurant Undosa* (M), in Starnberg, right on the lakeside (08151–12144). Garden restaurant. Openair dancing in summer on Sunday afternoons. AE, MC.

In **Berg**—*Strandhotel Schloss Berg* (M), right on the lake. Seestr. 17 (08151–50021). 40 beds, ten baths. Grill specialties in the restaurant. Bar, tennis, lake swimming, ferry landing-stage.

In **Feldafing**—*Golf-Hotel Kaiserin Elisabeth* (M), Tutzingerstr. 2–6 (08157–1013). 125 beds. On golf course in lovely country surroundings. Outdoor dining terrace, bar, tennis, riding and swimming facilities. Schroth cures. Departure point for excursions by colorful old stagecoach. AE, DC, MC, V.

In **Tutzing**—*Hotel-Restaurant Café am See* (M), Marienstr. 16 (08158–490). 45 beds, including apartments, some self-catering. Good restaurant serving freshly caught fish. Lakeside.

Restaurant. *Forsthaus Ilkahöhe* (M), auf der Ilka-Höhe (08158–8242), with a superb view from the terrace or upstairs veranda. Excellent cuisine in typically Bavarian surroundings. Off the road to Weilheim.

Tegernsee (Tegernsee). *Bastenhaus am See* (E), Hauptstr. 71 (08022–3080). 36 beds. In the main street, but with a lakeside garden. Good food, particularly local fish. Own beach. *Haus Bayern* (E), Neureutherstr. 23 (08022–1820). On the slopes above the lake, in its own park. Indoor pool, sauna, fitness room, bowling. Restaurant with a terrace café. AE, DC, MC. *Fischerstüberl am See* (M), Seestr. 51 (08022–4672). In one of the most beautiful locations in the Schlossbucht Bay. A few minutes' walk from an outdoor pool; large sunbathing terrace. Well-known for the good food in its restaurant, particularly fish. *Luitpold* (M), Hauptstr. 42 (08022–4681). Also on the lakefront, all rooms have a view over the lake, balcony and bath or shower. Indoor pool and rustic restaurant. DC. *Seehotel zur Post* (M), Seestr. 3 (08022–3951). On the lakefront, all rooms with bath. Good terrace restaurant and café. AE, DC, MC.

Restaurants. *Weinstub'n "Zum Brendl"* (M), Hauptstr. 8 (08022–

4502). Cozy cellar-tavern with local and international dishes. Music until 1 A.M. *Berggasthof Lieberhof* (I), Neureutherstr. 52 (08022–4163). Quiet location above the lake. Small, colorful tavern. *Herzogliches Bräustuberl (I), Schlossplatz 1 (08022–4141). Former monastery, now a popular brewery-restaurant. Beer brewed on the premises. Good views. No credit cards.*

Traunstein (Chiemgau). *Parkhotel Traunsteinerhof* (M), Bahnhofstr. 11 (0861–69041). 62 rooms, most with own bath. Restaurant. AE, DC.

Restaurant. *Brauereigasthof Schnitzlbaumer* (M), Stadtplatz 13 (0861–4534). In the center of the market square. In addition to the traditional Bavarian dishes on the menu, a wide variety of international gourmet dishes are served, including fish from Chiemsee.

Überlingen (Bodensee). *Parkhotel St. Leonhard* (M), Obere-St.-Leonhard-Str. 83 (07551–8080). 158 rooms, 2 suites, all with bath or shower. Quietly located (Silence Hotel) on the slopes above the lake, with a lovely view from the sun terrace. Own park with a wild game reserve. Modern rooms, indoor pool, tennis courts and billiard room. Restaurant serving international and Swabian specialties. AE. *Ochsen* (M), Munsterstr. 48 (07551–4067). Excellent location for sailing; good facilities. AE, DC, MC, V. *Gasthof Engel* (I), Hafenstr. 1 (07551–63412). Wine tavern.

Restaurant. *Romantik Hotel Hecht* (M), Munsterstr. 8 (07551–63333). Has a fine restaurant in the 200-year-old *Weinstube.* Good value specialty is the eight-course meal. Reservations necessary. Closed Mon. and Feb. AE, DC, MC, V.

Wasserburg (Bodensee). *Schloss Wasserburg* (E), Hauptstr. 5 (08382–5692). 14 rooms, most with bath or shower. Hotel in 8th-century castle on an island peninsula; panoramic view, terrace, pool on the lakeside, restaurant. *Pfälzer Hof* (M), Hauptstr. 83 (08382–6511). Small, 13 rooms; garden restaurant. *Haus des Gastes* (I), Hauptstr. 12 (08382–24848). Pleasant Gasthof-restaurant with seven rooms, all with own bath or shower. Fine terrace view.

Wasserburg Am Inn (Inn Valley). *Fletzinger* (M), Fletzingergasse 1 (08071–8010). 30 rooms, about half with own bath. Restaurant. AE, DC, MC. *Paulaner Stuben* (I), Marienplatz 9 (08071–3903). 19 rooms, most with own bath or shower. Fine view from the terrace. Restaurant. AE.

Wendelstein (Schliersee). *Berghotel Wendelstein* (I), near the top of the 1,800-meter (6,000-ft.) mountain of Wendelstein. The oldest mountain hotel in the Bavarian Alps, built in 1833. 60 beds. Restaurant, bar, café. Rather crowded in summer.

CAMPING AND YOUTH HOSTELS. Camping. Campsites are plentiful throughout the region, most of them well equipped and picturesquely located with a large number also open throughout the winter. General information and free brochures may be obtained from the Camping Section of the *ADAC Auto Club,* Camping Referat, Hauptverwaltung, Baumgartnerstr. 53, 8000 München 70 (089–76761) or from the respective regional and local tourist offices:

For Munich and Upper Bavaria: *Fremdenverkehrsverein Oberbayern,* Sonnenstr. 10, 8000 München 2. For Lake Constance region: *Fremden-verkehrsverband Bodensee-Oberschwaben,* Schützenstr. 8, 7750 Konstanz (ask for brochure "Camping Baden-Wurttemberg"). For Berchtesgadener Land, write to: *Kurdirektion, Berchtesgadener Land,* Königsseer Str. 2, 8240 Berchtesgaden.

Youth Hostels. For general information on youth hostels in the region, inquire at the headquarters of the Bavarian. Section of the German Youth Hostel Association in Munich: *Landesverband des Deutschen Jugendher-bergswerkes,* Mauerkircherstr. 5, 8000 Munchen 80 (089–987451).

MOUNTAIN HUTS. There are many mountain huts and hostelries dot-ted all over the alpine region offering simple accommodation, with or with-out breakfast, for hikers and climbers. These *Berghütten* generally belong to the German Alpine Association (Deutsche Alpenverein) and are run by a landlord or innkeeper. For those huts which are not run by anyone and provide overnight accommodation only, keys must usually be picked up from an address in the nearest town or village, and returned afterwards. The local tourist offices can provide lists of available mountain hut accom-modation, or, if you already belong to an alpine club of some kind, you can obtain a list of huts open to members of the German Alpine Associa-tion only. (See *Facts at Your Fingertips,* Addresses).

TOURIST INFORMATION. There are two regional tourist offices for the whole area: the *Fremdenverkehrs verein Allgäu Bayerisch-Schwaben,* Fuggerstr. 9, D-8900 Augsburg (0821–33335) and the *FVV Bodensee-Oberschwaben,* 8 Schützenstr. 7750, Konstanz (07531–22232) cover the Allgäu and Bodensee areas. In addition the *FVV München-Oberbayern,* Sonnenstr. 10, 8000 München 2, (089–597347) covers the whole of south-ern Bavaria and the Bavarian Alps. A selection of local tourist offices (some providing an accommodations booking service) is as follows:

Augsburg, *Verkehrsverein,* Bahnhofstr. 7, 8900 Augsburg (0821–502070). **Bad Reichenhall,** *Kur-und-Verkehrsverein,* im Hauptbah-nhof-Nebenbau, 8230 Bad Reichenhall (08651–3003). **Bad Tölz,** *Kurverw-altung,* Ludwigstr. 11, 8170 Bad Tölz (08041–70071). **Bayrischzell,** *Kuramt,* Kirchplatz 2, 8163 Bayrischzell (08023–648). **Berchtesgaden,** *Kurdirektion,* Königsseer Str. 2, 8240 Berchtesgaden, (08652–5011). **Gar-misch-Partenkirchen,** *Verkehrsamt der Kurverwaltung,* Bahnhofstr. 34, 8100 Garmisch-Partenkirchen (08821–18022). **Lindau,** *Verkehrsverein am Hauptbahnhof* (at main station), 8990 Lindau, (08382–5022). **Mittenwald,** *Kurverwaltung,* Dammkarstr. 3, 8102 Mittenwald (08823–1051). **Oberam-mergau,** *Verkehrsamt,* Eugen-Papst-Str. 9a, 8103 Oberammergau (08822–4921). **Prien am Chiemsee,** *Kurverwaltung,* Am Bahnhof 8210 Prien (08051–3031). **Reit-im-Winkl,** *Verkehrsamt,* Rathausplatz 1, 8216 Reit-im-Winkl (08640–8207). **Rottach-Egern,** *Kuramt,* Nördliche Haupt-str. 9, 8183 Rottach-Egern (08022–671341). **Wasserburg,** *Verkehrsverein,* im Rathaus, 8090 Wasserburg am Inn (08071–3061).

HOW TO GET AROUND. By air. The main airport for the region is, understandably, Munich, from where buses transfer you to the main rail-way station for connections to the rest of the region. If you are travelling with a package tour, the transfer buses will be at the airport to meet you and drive you to your holiday destination. Stuttgart is a connecting airport for the Friedrichshafen Delta airline serving the Bodensee, and there is also a direct express rail route from Zurich (Kloten) Airport to Lindau.

By train. Munich once again is the big rail center for southern Germany, with the main FD (Fern-Express) and Inter-City express lines running to Lindau, Kufstein (and on to Innsbruck) and through to Salzburg and Vienna. Four of the FD Express Trains, the *Berchtesgaden, Königsee, Chiemgau* and *Wörthersee,* connect the Rhine and Ruhr areas of northern Germany and Hamburg and Hanover respectively with the Berchtesgadener Land, as well as Inter City routes from Hamburg, Bremen, Dortmund, Hanover and Münster, and the new express (D-Zug) connection from Karlsruhe, in addition to the existing direct express lines from Kassel and Trier. Augsburg is the main rail terminus for the Allgäu.

By bus. Augsburg and Munich are both main stops on the Europabus Romantic Road and other long-distance bus routes. The network of Bahn- and Postbuses (German Railways and German Post buses) is particularly far-reaching and connects all those resorts to which there are no, or only inconvenient, rail services. In Garmisch Partenkirchen, for example, there is a regular nostalgic post bus service throughout the summer months between the rail station and Badersee lake. In addition, private coach companies organize excursion tours from almost every town and these day trips are very good value for sightseeing. Inquire at local tourist offices and travel agents, such as the *ABR* (official Bavarian Travel Agent).

A good number of popular winter sports resorts have shuttle bus services to take skiers to and from the ski lifts. Also, in some places (such as Ruhpolding), buses connect the various outlying pensions with the town or resort center, free of charge for guests possessing a *Gästekarte* or *Kurkarte* pass (available from the Tourist Office for a small fee). Inquire at the Tourist Offices for "Pendelbusverkehr." There are also reductions on various trains and buses.

By bike. Cycling in the Alps is not quite as mad as it sounds; or, at any rate, cycling in the Alpine lowlands along the valleys of the rivers Isar, Mangfall, Loisach, Inn and Lech, and around lake Chiemsee and the east Allgäu. Many of these areas are both reasonably flat and, bizarre as it may at first seem, ideal for cycling, with good roads and a positive surfeit of magnificent scenery; plus plenty of strategically placed inns and gasthofs where you can quench your thirst and still your appetite. (There are even specialized cyclists' inns known as "Radler Einkehr," easily recognized by the bicycles propped up outside and the sportily-clad Bavarians inside or in the beer garden quaffing *Radler,* a mixture of beer and lemonade much favored by the experienced Alpine cyclist). One exceptionally pretty route is the 31-km. (19-mile) cycling path connecting the resorts of Reit im Wirkl, Ruhpolding, and Inzell, which goes through some of the beautiful scenery of the region's nature park.

The Bavarian Regional Tourist Office in Munich (see *Tourist Information* above) produces a good brochure detailing cycling routes and organizations in Upper Bavaria. While the Ammersee and Lech Tourist Office (Von Kühlmann Str. 15, 8910 Landsberg/Lech) also produces a brochure detailing 11 different cycling routes, all starting from an S-Bahn station and all taking in at least one bathing spot and one gasthof en route. The regional tourist office for the Bodensee area lists local resorts—52 in all—with bikes for hire.

As ever, bicycles can be hired from many rail stations and Tourist Offices.

Mountain railways and cable cars. Mountain railways, cable cars, chairlifts or cogwheel railways (*Seilbahn, Sessellift, Zahnradbahn*) serve practically all the major mountains in the Alps, affording easy access to vantage points with panoramic views, and high-altitude walking routes in summer, and of course skiing in winter. The Zugspitz at Garmisch-Partenkirchen (at almost 3,000 meters or 10,000 ft. Germany's highest mountain) is served by both a cogwheel railway from the Zugspitz Railroad Station, and a spectacular cable car from Eibsee. Both are rather expensive. The cogwheel railway departs from Zugspitz Station—connecting with main line trains—and travels via Grainau and Eibsee, costing a pricey DM.45 return (in winter 42 in conjunction with a ski-pass) through a tunnel, right to the summit of the Zugspitz. The journey takes just under an hour.

The other giant peaks in the same group—the Alpspitz (7,284 ft.), the Wank (5,840 ft.), the Hausberg and Kreuzeck (5,420 ft.)—are served by a further five cable cars: the *Osterfelderbahn,* up to the 6,150-ft. Osterfelderkopf on the Alpspitz; the *Wankbahn,* from the center of Partenkirchen up to 5,340 ft. on the Wank; the *Hausbergbahn,* up to 4,044 ft.; the *Kreuzeckbahn,* up to 4,041 ft.; the *Eckbauerbahn,* from the cable-car station next to the Olympic Stadium to the panoramic and sundrenched Eckbauer peak, 3,678 ft.

Other important mountain railways in the region are at: Aschau, Kampenwandbahn, 4,500 ft.; Bad Reichenhall, Predigstuhlbahn, 4,840 ft.; Bad Tölz, Blombergbahn, 3,650 ft.; Bayerischzell, Wendelsteinbahn, 5,170 ft.; Berchtesgaden, Jennerbahn, 5,400 ft.; and Obersalzbergbahn 3,060 ft.; Kleinwalsertal, Kanzelwandbahn, 6,000 ft.; Lenggries, Brauneckbahn, 4,650 ft.; Mittenwald, Karwendelbahn, 6,730 ft.; Oberammergau, Laberbergbahn, 5,040 ft.; Oberstdorf, Nebelhornbahn, 5,800 ft. and Fellhornbahn, 4,500 ft.; Pfronten, Breitenbergbahn, 4,500 ft.; Rottach-Egern, Wallbergbahn, 4,850 ft.; Ruhpolding, Rauschbergbahn, 4,900 ft.; Samerberg, Hochriesbahn, 4,650 ft.; Schliersee, Schliersbergbahn, 3,180 ft.; Schwangau, Tegelbergbahn, 5,160 ft.; Spitzingsee, Taubensteinbahn, 4,840 ft.

By car. The main autobahn routes into the Alpine region are the A7 from the northwest (Ulm and Kempsten); from the northeast the A95 (E6) via Munich; from the west via Lake Konstanz, the A96; and from the south the E533 from Innsbruck—the last two of these are still incomplete with long stretches of regular highway, the most important of which is the Lindau to Munich stretch, the B12 or B18.

One road of particular scenic interest is the Deutsche Alpenstrasse (German Alpine Road), which runs all the way from Lindau on the Bodensee to Berchtesgaden. It passes some of the most beautiful mountain scenery in Europe, but as it is still incomplete, some detours into the lowlands are necessary. Another scenic route that begins (or ends!) in this region is the Romantische Strasse (Romantic Road) running from Fussen, near the Royal Castles, north to Würzburg. Other scenic routes running through the Allgäu are: the Oberschwäbische Barockstrasse (of architectural interest); the Schwäbische Dichter Strasse (for lovers of poets and poetry); and the Schwäbische Bader Strasse (thermal spa tour).

Or you can take the B20 road—the Blaue Route (Blue Route)—which follows the valleys of the Inn and the Salzach east of Munich and takes

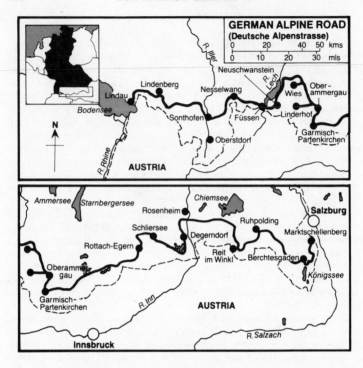

in some beautifully tranquil and unspoilt scenery such as the Waginger See and Abtsdorfer See, two little-known bathing lakes, the warmest in Upper Bavaria and a paradise for family excursions.

From Wasserburg on the River Inn to Traunstein on Chiemsee lake and on to Berchtesgaden is the southermost stretch of the long Deutsche Ferienstrasse (German Holiday Road) which runs the length of West Germany from Kiel on the Baltic coast to the Alps. The B304, 305 and 306 take in such towns as Amerang with its famous castle, Seebruck, Prien and Chieming on Chiemsee lake, the Chiemgau mountains, on through Inzell, Weissach, Schneizelreuth, Unterjettenberg and the Raumsau with its idyllic alpine scenery and past the magnificent Watzmann peak to its destination in Berchtesgaden.

It should be noted that some mountain roads in the Alps are toll-roads, usually forest roads, for which you must pay a fee at the start of the particular stretch where you see the sign *Maut*.

By boat. Try a trip on the Bodensee with the German-Austrian-Swiss Weisse Flotte (White Fleet) which has been ferrying passengers on Lake Constance for 120 years. There is a Bodensee Pass available for about DM.70, and valid for 15 days, on 7 of which free trips on all ferryboats and regular cruise ships, and on the remaining 8 days, a reduction of 50%. On all 15 days you are entitled to reduced fares on all excursion trips in the area, as well as local rail, bus and mountain railway services.

There are also good car-ferry services across the lake linking Germany, Austria and Switzerland.

Inquiries about cruises on Lake Chiemsee ("the Bavarian Sea") can be made at *Chiemsee Schiffahrt,* L. Fessler, Seestr. 108, 8210 Prien (08051–1510). Steamer services are also available on the Ammersee, Starnberger, Königsee and Tegernsee. Information from local tourist offices or the German railways.

Rowing boats, pedal, sail and electric boats may be hired at all of these large lakes. One of the main attractions of Fünf Seen Land (Five Lakes Land), as the lakes Ammersee, Wörthsee, Wesslingersee, Pilsensee and Starnbergersee southwest of Munich are known, is the hire of rowboats rented out by fishermen for about DM.6 an hour. Motorboats would cost between DM. 15 and 20 an hour.

SPORTS. There is pretty well every sport imaginable available in this region—something for everyone. Summer sporting activities include swimming, surfing, sailing, hiking, cycling, riding, mountain-climbing, hang-gliding or just plain sunbathing. Then there is the vast spectrum of winter sports activities: skiing, tobogganing, ice-skating, curling, sleigh-riding or just après-ski for the less sport-minded. The following is just a small selection of what sports you can take part in and where, but for more details inquire at the regional and local tourist offices (see *Tourist Information* and *Useful Addresses*). The Allgäu tourist association, for example, offer interesting sports packages as combination holidays, in particular at Fischen, Füssen, Lindau, Nesselwang and Oberstaufen.

Swimming. You can swim in all lakes. Modern indoor pools can be found in Garmisch-Partenkirchen (*Alpspitz Wellenbad,* with waves, is one of the finest swimming-pools and fitness centers in Europe), in Berchtesgaden, Bad Reichenhall (salt water), Bad Tölz (*Alpamare* with waves and fitness center), Oberammergau (Wollenberg, with waves) in Inzell and Kochel (*Trimini* fitness center), and the beautifully situated lake establishments near Füssen.

Sailing and Windsurfing. On all principal lakes. There are sailing and windsurfing schools at Füssen, Immenstadt, Nesselwang, Isny and Lindau in the Allgäu; on Chiemsee at Bernau, Chieming, Gstadt, Prien, Seebrück, Übersee and Waging am See; and on Tegernsee, Starnbergersee and Ammersee. One of the best lakes for windsurfing is the *Walchensee,* because of its good air currents, and on the same lake there is a recently opened diving school at Einsiedel for exploring the depths of the crystal clear waters on a sort of Alpine underwater safari. Information from the Kurverwaltung (Cure Offices) in Mittenwald.

Water-skiing. Possible at Immenstadt and Lindau on the Bodensee and on some parts of Starnberger and Ammersee. Best for **kayaking** are the Isar from Bad Tölz through Munich-Landshut to the Danube near Deggendorf; the Inn from the Austrian border at Kufstein through Rosenheim, Wasserburg, Neu-Otting and along the German-Austrian border to Passau (easy) and at Schleching near Reit im Winkl in turbulent mountain waters.

The Lech River is also good for kayaking; it is very scenic from Füssen to Schongau and difficult in some spots; from Schongau to Landsberg it goes through artificial lakes and dams (nine portages), and from Landsberg to Augsburg it is easy.

Tennis. There are courts in all spas and resorts, some indoor and open year-round. **Golf** courses can be found in Garmisch, Berchtesgaden, Bad

Tölz, Augsburg, Chiemsee, Bad Wiessee, Feldafing on Starnberger Lake, Wörthsee and Lindau, Ottobeuren and Bad Waldsee in the Allgäu. There are American-run golf courses at Gmund on the Tegernsee and at Obersalzburg, Berchtesgaden (9 holes, 3,300 feet up, with a distracting view of the Watzmann range). The latter is open for play from May through October; tel. 08652–2100 for information. A spectacular 18-hole course is located at Bad Wiessee, high above the Tegernsee; tel. 08022–8769.

Bowling. Many resort hotels have their own bowling alleys (usually English-style skittles; rarely 10 pin). The *Hotel Bayerischer Hof* in Bad Reichenhall (08651–5084) organizes skittle weeks from March to June. The DM.535 cost includes half-pension, unlimited skittling, and two competitions with prizes.

Horseback riding. There are schools and facilities in many areas, including Amerang, Aschau and Chieming around Chiemsee Lake, at Ruhpolding, Tittmoning and Traunstein in the Chiemgauer Land, in Berchtesgaden and Oberstdorf in the Allgau and in Augsburg. Prices for an hour or more's ride out are expensive, and if you are really keen on horseback riding as a holiday pastime it is better value to book one of the all-inclusive holiday-sport-packages, where the price includes bed and breakfast and riding lessons. The tourist office of the Allgäu has some attractive offers.

Hang-gliding. See the Alps from above. If hang-gliding's your thing, tel. 08822–520 or 08822–4470 in Oberammergau.

Fishing. Good in almost all the streams and lakes but you must have a permit, usually available from the tourist office or from the local gamekeeper. Once again, you can book all-inclusive angling holidays through the various tourist offices, where permit formalities are taken care of for you. The holiday region of East Allgäu between the River Lech and the Bodensee has some of the best stocked fishing waters. Such Allgäu towns as Immenstadt and Fischen offer seven-day packages for anglers for as little as DM.212, including bed and breakfast, a four-day angling permit and other extras. Inquire from the *Verkehrsamt Immenstadt,* Marienplatz 3, 8970 Immenstadt, *Verkehrsamt Fischen,* 8975 Fischen i. Allgäu, or for general information from the *Fremdenverkehrsband Allgäu Bayerisch Schwaben* (see *Tourist Information*).

Bicycling. Most local rail stations have bikes to rent at DM.10 per day; half that if you have a valid train ticket. Many local sports shops also have limited numbers of bikes for rent: Try *Sport Eich,* Fendtgasse 5, Oberammergau, and *Sport Bittner,* Andreas-Fendt-Ring 1, Bischofswiesen, near Berchtesgaden. The Bavarian regional tourist office in Munich (see Tourist Information) issues a regularly updated booklet on recommended cycling routes. A particularly striking route runs between the resorts of Reit im Winkl, Ruhpolding, and Inzell, and is 32 kilometers (19 miles) long. Bikes can be rented from the rail station at Ruhpolding.

Hiking and Mountain Walking. As indigenous a pastime to the Alps as the lederhosen-clad locals who participate almost every Sunday. Depending on your level of fitness, and your clothing and equipment, there are virtually unlimited possibilities for hiking and mountain walking tours. It would not be possible for us to name all the centers with starting points for Alpine walking tours here. Every local tourist office can supply you with a hiking-map (*Wanderkarte*) of the area, with suggestions for mountain tours according to the degree of difficulty you want to attempt. Every excursion by foot into the mountains should be undertaken with care and in accordance with a few simple rules: take note of weather-forecasts, advice and warnings from the locals and mountain guides. Never start a mountain tour without wearing sturdy, warm and heavy-soled (with a good tread) shoes and taking some kind of waterproof clothing with you. Mountain weather is very changeable. Before setting off, always leave details of your destination with someone in your resort, so that in case of accident, the Mountain Rescue Squad (*Bergwacht*) can search in the right area. Also, in summer and winter, check the daily avalanche report (*Lawinenbericht*) displayed in every winter sports center, usually at the ski-lift station or tourist office.

Hiking trails are well marked—in mountainous regions usually in red or blue—and usually lead to a panoramic viewpoint. Hiking round-trips are organized by most of the larger tourist centers. These can either be individual day trips along suggested routes, organized hikes with guide, or inclusive arrangements lasting two or more days with bed and breakfast accommodation.

Full information about all forms of mountain walking and hiking can be obtained from the *Deutsche Alpenverein* (German Alpine Association) at Praterinsel 5, 8000 Munchen 22 (089–293086). They can also issue you with lists of mountain huts, guides, routes, etc. Naturally, members of the Association are given preferential treatment, and quite often fill up the mountain lodges in advance.

Mountain Climbing. The Bavarian Alps are the most important climbing region in Germany. An efficiently-run net of mountain lodges provides direct access to rock faces and mountain guides are available at all important points of departure; Garmisch-Partenkirchen has a school (Bergsteigerschule Zugspitze) as does the Berchtesgadener Land in Straub. The principal valley bases are: Garmisch and Grainau for the Wetterstein group, which includes Zugspitze; Mittenwald and Krün for the Karwendel group; Rottach-Egern, Wildbad Kreuth, and Bayrischzell for the German offshoots of the Mangfall group, most of which is in Austria; Berchtesgaden, Ramsau, and Bad Reichenhall for the Berchtesgaden Alps; Hindelang and Oberstdorf for the Allgäu mountains. Rock-scaling tours in the Bavarian Alps, and thousands of easy hiking paths.

Mountain-climbing guides: Bayrischzell, inquire at Gustl Müller sports shop; Berchtesgaden, Hellmuth Schuster, Locksteinstr. 5. Heinz Zembsch, Burgergraben 11, 8244 Strub. Garmisch-Partenkirchen, (inquire at Deutschen Alpenverein, Bahnhofstr. 13), several in Grainau; Mittenwald, consult board showing names in Bahnhofstrasse; Bad Reichenhall, inquire at Sport-Noack, Innsbrucker Strasse 5; Oberstdorf at Bergsport Oberstdorf, Hauptstr. 6; Hindelang at Bergfuhrerburo at the Kurverwaltung (Cure Direction), tel. 08324–2061.

WINTER SPORTS. The Bavarian Alps constitute the principal winter sports region of southeastern Germany and of Germany as a whole. The skiing season lasts in the valley areas from December to early March, above 1,500 meters (5,000 ft.) until late April, and above 2,000 meters (6,500 ft.) from November until late May.

For cross-country skiing *(Langlauf)* all the main centers offer long stretches of prepared ski tracks or *Loipen,* through beautiful winter scenery. If you're a Nordic skier, match your speed against Bavaria's best in Oberammergau's annual King Ludwig race, the first weekend in February. The town also hosts events over distances of six kilometers (four miles) and 15 kilometers (nine miles) every Wednesday during the winter season.

Special winter sports trains run in the winter season between Munich and the principal skiing centers at reduced rates. The roads leading to various of the winter resorts have recently been improved considerably. There are even well equipped winter camping sites at Berchtesgaden, Königsee, Ruhpolding, Reit im Winkl and Mittenwald-Krün, as well as at Aschau, Ramsau, Sachrang, Seeshaupt, Königsdorf and Kreuth.

When deciding upon an area in which to ski, first consult the respective tourist office about the different prices and arrangements for ski-passes and season tickets. There is often quite a price difference between day tickets and two or seven-day passes. If you intend to stay a week or more in the same resort, these passes often include vouchers for indoor pools, saunas and car parking.

EAST BAVARIA

Germany's Last Frontier

In parts wild and rocky, in others fertile and productive, bordered by Czechoslovakia to the east and Austria to the south, East Bavaria is one of Germany's last frontiers, a land well off the beaten track, as rich in scenery as it is in history. It extends north as far as the Fichtelgebirge mountains east of Bayreuth and west as far as Ingolstadt, due north of Munich. But its most interesting areas are concentrated in its southeastern corner around Regensburg and along the Danube to Passau on the Austrian border; and between the Danube and the Czechoslovak border in and around the Bayerischer Wald, the Bavarian Forest, the largest unbroken stretch of forest in Central Europe.

Exploring East Bavaria

Regensburg is the principal city of East Bavaria and the fourth largest in Bavaria. It is the best point of departure for the exploration of this region. If you are coming from Munich, you may also like to stop off in Landshut on the way, although this route is a bit longer than the direct one.

Landshut is an interesting old city with gabled houses of the 14th and 15th centuries lining its central squarelike streets of Altstadt and Neustadt, and Dreifaltigkeit Square. It has been the seat of government of Lower Bavaria since 1839. The impressive Gothic Church of St. Martin, built in the early-15th century, has a richly carved portal, superb and very high interior vaulting, the high altar from 1424, and a 133-meter (436-foot) brick church tower supposed to be the highest in the world. Stadt-Residenz (City Residence Palace), once inhabited by the Dukes of Bavaria, contains Renaissance, Baroque and neo-Classical sections, and in addition contains a very fine painting gallery and several museum collections in addition to the period-decorated suites of the 16th and 18th centuries. Landshut is dominated by Burg Trausnitz, a powerful castle-fortress on the hill above it, with the 13th-century double chapel and Wittelsbach Tower, and with such interior details in the main building as the "Fools' Staircase," so called because it is decorated with scenes from Italian comedy.

The city has many other interesting buildings, such as the Rococo church of Seligenthal Abbey, but Landshut is just as renowned for its recollection of the very good times it once had at a wedding. That event took place in 1475, when Prince George, the son of the reigning Duke, married the Polish Princess Hadwiga. The feasters consumed 333 oxen, 275 hogs, 40 calves and 12,000 geese, with, it must be assumed, a few side dishes as well, and something to wash it all down. Landshut has never forgotten that celebration, and every three years it enacts the Princely Wedding all over again, with most of the population turning out in medieval costume.

Ancient Regensburg

Much bigger and older than Landshut, Regensburg was originally a Celtic town, taken over by the Romans about 2,000 years ago. Next to the Celtic settlement, to which the name Radasbona was given, the Romans built a military fortress town and called it Castra Regina. When the Bavarian tribes migrated to this area in the early 6th century, they occupied it, made it the seat of their dukes, and apparently on the basis of the Latin name, called it Regensburg. Later the city became the capital of the Carolingian monarchs and in the middle ages developed into a commercial center. Later it became a free imperial city and for some 150 years was the site of the Imperial Diet. An important archeological find was made at the end of 1982, when workmen in the Niedermünster Church in Regensburg stumbled across the remains of what must have been the house altar of the Roman Emperor Commodus, dating back to between 180 and 190 B.C. A 50–60 cm.-high stone plinth buried in clay beneath the church bears an inscription stating that the pillar was the altar for incense offerings to the house god of Commodus. The site is now open to the public as a museum.

To get a general view of Regensburg, walk to the far end of the Steinerne Brücke, the Stone Bridge. This early 12th-century structure was an engineering miracle for its time and is the oldest bridge in Germany. Penetrating into the city, keeping straight ahead from the bridge, you will come to the square where the magnificent St. Peter's Cathedral stands. It was built in its present form between the 13th and 15th centuries and rates among the finest examples of the German Gothic ecclesiastical architecture. In addition to works of art (the Gothic sculptures deserve special note), it has preserved some of the 14th-century stained-glass windows and its treasury contains valuable items from the late middle ages. For the next four or five years, unfortunately, the interior, the nave in particular, has been turned into a building site, while necessary renovation and restoration are carried out. The building of a Bishops' Crypt is also planned. For the duration of this work, large sections of the cathedral will be closed to the public, and church functions and concerts drastically reduced. The Cathedral's famous Regensburger Domspatzen (Regensburg boys' choir) can meanwhile be heard every Sunday in the nearby Niedermünster Church. The cathedral is connected by an arcaded courtyard with the early Romanesque St. Stephan's Church and the late Romanesque All Saints Chapel. Across the cathedral square is the 13th-century St. Ulrich's Church.

At the nearby Alter Kornmarkt is the Romanesque Alte Kapelle (Old Chapel), of which the earlier parts date from about 1000 and which was the church of the ducal castle that stood here in the Middle Ages. This is also the area where the Roman fortress was located and in a narrow street between the cathedral and the Danube you can still see the Porta Praetoria, constructed in 179, which was one of its gates. The continuation of the same narrow street towards the west is called Goliath Strasse because the Goliath House is located here, which in turn received its name from the giant 16th-century fresco.

Several other old patrician houses and narrow streets give this section of the city a truly medieval appearance; particularly interesting examples are the 13th-century Baumburger Turm on Watmarkt and the 9-story Goldener Turm in Wahlen Strasse, both built in the form of towers. Goliath Strasse ends at Kohlenmarkt and Rathaus Square, with the Old Town Hall built in 1350. Its star exhibit is the Reichstagssaal (Imperial Diet Hall), where the Diet sat, but it also boasts dungeons, instruments of torture, and some fine, richly medieval rooms.

Continuing in the same westerly direction and crossing the Haidplatz, which was a tournament field in the middle ages, you come to the twin squares of Arnulfsplatz and Bismarckplatz, separated by the city theater. At the Jakobstrasse corner is Schottenkirche St. Jakob, a 12th-century Romanesque church built by Scottish and Irish monks, particularly known for its north portal, on which Christian and pagan sculptural motifs are curiously intermixed. Not far from it, in Beraiterweg, is Dominikanerkirche, a noted 13th-century Gothic basilica, with some murals of the 14th and 15th centuries.

One other particularly important sight in Regensburg is the palace of the Princes of Thurn and Taxis, their residence since 1748, set in a pleasant park not far from the railroad station. This was originally the Abbey of St. Emmeram, and the adjoining St. Emmeram's Church, a Romanesque basilica parts of which go back to the 8th century (St. Emmeram's tomb, over which it is built, is even earlier, since he was buried there in 652), is one of the most interesting of this group of buildings.

Excursions from Regensburg

There are two particularly notable excursions (which can be made by boat if you like) from Regensburg. One is southwest along the Danube to Kelheim, an old town formerly belonging to the Wittelsbach family and located where the Altmuhl flows into the Danube. Its two principal sights are the Befreiungshalle, an impressive rotunda commemorating the wars of Liberation against Napoleon, and the Benedictine monastery of Weltenburg, which was founded shortly after the year 600, where there is a splendid Baroque church built in the early 18th century by the Asam brothers and containing a magnificent figure of St. George on horseback above the altar. In good summer weather, this can be made a delightful trip by walking from the Befreiungshalle to the monastery, which will take you about an hour, by a lovely clearly-marked forest path which takes you past the pre-Roman ramparts, and returning to Kelheim by motorboat, through a spectacular piece of the Danube Valley, known as the Donaudurchbruch, where the river narrows as it forces its way between limestone cliffs which run up to some 122 meters (400 feet). Every year on the first Saturday in July at Kelheim there is a spectacular illumination of the gorge known as "Flammende Donau" (Danube in Flames).

The other classic excursion from Regensburg is along the Danube in the opposite direction, to the east, and takes you to Donaustauf, where there is a remarkable view from the ruins of the Romanesque castle of the Bishops of Regensburg, and from Walhalla, the Hall of Fame, a somewhat incongruous neo-Classical temple designed by the architect Leo von Klenze spurred on by King Ludwig I, and containing marble busts and memorial plaques of some 200 famous Germans.

Proceeding farther downstream along the Danube, we enter the pleasant town of Straubing, also a Celtic and a Roman settlement, whose chief landmark is the 16th-century city tower crowned by several pinnacles. Straubing lies in the middle of a particularly fertile plain stretching between the mountains of the Bayerischer Wald north of Regensburg southwards to the hilly region of lower Bavaria around Passau. As far back as historical records go, this region has been famous for its agriculture and cattle rearing and became the granary center of Bavaria. Every year in mid-August the traditional Gäuboden (Fertile land) Folksfest takes place, the second largest folklore festival in Bavaria after the Oktoberfest, when the town of Straubing celebrates with folklore processions, music and country fare from its rich "Gäuboden." The town's Gäuboden Museum is also worth a visit with its prehistoric collection, including the world-famous Römischen Schatzfund (Roman Treasure Trove) excavated in 1950 and comprising golden masks, armor, harnesses and bronze figures.

Straubing is also the city of Agnes Bernauer, accused of sorcery in the year 1435 by Duke Ernst of Bavaria, who could see no other reason to explain why his son had married her, and so had her thrown into the Danube. Her tombstone is in the graveyard of the 12th-century Peterskirche; every four years Straubing gives summer performances in the Ducal Palace of Friedrich Hebbel's tragedy which recounts the story of Agnes Bernauer. The next performance will be in July 1989.

Still farther down the Danube is Deggendorf, another ancient town, founded around 750, which has also preserved its 14th-century city tower. The 16th-century Rathaus (Town Hall) stands alone in the center of the wide Luitpoldplatz square. Also of interest in the town is the Heimatmuseum (Local Museum), in Oberen Stadtplatz, with a rich collection of ecclesiastical art, local handicrafts, clocks, weapons and paintings. The prehistoric section illustrates the history of the early inhabitants of the Danube Valley.

Deggendorf is known as the "Gateway to the Bayerischer Wald," whose hills rise immediately to the north. In the vicinity of Deggendorf are several interesting excursion spots. The Kloster Metten is a Benedictine abbey dating back to the 8th century. The present church was built in 1720 with a sumptuous Baroque interior and magnificent wood carvings. It contains a valuable library. Not far from Metten is the Schloss Egg, a 12th-century castle, and a little further down the Danube is another Benedictine abbey at Niederalteich and the Baroque and Rococo Altenmarkt monastery church, with interiors by the Asam brothers. Another city tower, this time dating from the Renaissance, can be seen in Vilshofen, also an old town on the Danube. From here to Passau, about 24 km. (15 miles) away, the road on the left bank of the river is very scenic but before visiting that city we shall explore the area north of the Danube.

Oberpfalz and Bayerischer Wald

About 72 km. (45 miles) north of Regensburg is Amberg which refers to itself as "the Rothenburg of Oberpfalz" because, like that famed town on the Romantic Road, it has preserved its old walls, with their sentry walk and their four gates. In addition, there are many buildings of interest—the 15th-century Gothic St. Martin's Church, the unusual 14th-century Gothic St. George's Church, and the 17th–18th-century Baroque Mariahilf pilgrimage church on the outskirts; the 13th–14th-century castle of the Counts Palatine, with its fine Gothic chapel and 15th-century glass, and the 17th-century Elector's Palace; the 14th–16th-century Gothic Rathaus and the 17th-century building of the Knights of Malta.

Near Amberg, at Hirschau there are huge hill-like piles of white kaolin sand—Monte Kaolino—where skiing can be practised in summer. This is a porcelain-making area and kaolin is used for porcelain paste.

On to Weiden, in the valley of the River Naab and the cultural and commercial center of the northern Oberpfalz, with its four-yearly Music Festival, next to be held in April 1988. We then proceed southeast, following the Ostmark Road along the Oberpfälzer Wald and through the Bayerischer Wald, the largest stretch of unbroken mountainous forestland in Germany, with the first German National Park, covering over 777 square km. (300 square miles) of idyllic wildlife reserve.

Shortly after Weiden you come to Leuchtenberg Castle ruins on a wooded hill, easily reached from the road and worth walking up for the view from its top. A little beyond it, the road connecting Nürnberg with Prague takes you to the idyllic village of Waidhaus near the Czech border. From Waidhaus a very scenic road—though in poor condition—runs through Oberpfälzer Wald near the Czech border, passing through Schönsee and Tiefenbach to the small 1,000-year-old town of Waldmünchen, on Perlsee Lake, which can be reached more directly from Rötz on the parallel Ostmark Road. A net of rewarding hiking paths surrounds Waldmünchen which, however, is better known for its annual Trenck-the-Pandour Pageant in July and August, named in memory of the terrible occupation it endured in the 18th century at the hands of Baron Trenck and his wild Croatian pandours (mounted constabulary).

Dragons and Castles

Furth im Wald, some 16 km. (ten miles) southeast of Waldmünchen, has been a border town since the middle ages, for crossing into Czechoslovakia. It is noted for its "Drachenstich," the "Dragon-Sticking" pageant which takes place on the second and third Sunday in August every year.

A most realistic dragon is done to death in the streets of the town, and there is a procession with costumed groups, horses, musicians and decorated floats. Places of interest in the town include the Heimatmuseum (Local Museum), inside the city wall's tower, and the Pfarrkirche (Parish Church). The best way to reach Furth im Wald from Ostmark Road is via Cham, idyllically located on the Regen River. In Charlemagne's day, Cham was the commercial and cultural as well as geographical focal point of the region. Today it is still the commercial and transit center of the upper Bavarian Forest. There is an impressive city gate on the bridge over the Regen with distinctive, ochre-colored twin towers. This gate, the Biertor (Beer Gate) or Burgtor, is the town's symbol, and dates back to the 13th century. Also worth seeing are the late Gothic-style City Hall, the 13th-century St. Jacob's Church and the former Gasthof Krone, an old lodging house of knights and princes.

We are now in the Bayerischer Wald, along the Czech border, one of the most densely-forested areas of the country. The Regen flows into the Danube at Regensburg. In the section of the Bayerischer Wald between the Regen and Danube are many old castles and quiet villages offering simple vacations. Farther along the Ostmark Road is Viechtach, an unpretentious summer and winter resort, and the town of Regen with the nearby Pfahl ridge of natural rocky towers and the ruins of Weissenstein Castle.

The Regen River that flows through the town of Regen is actually the Black Regen and joins the White Regen—which passes through the folk-costume-conscious village of Kötzting—shortly below the Höllensteinsee into the Regen River proper. The Black and the White Regen form a giant pair of pincers that include in their grip Arber, the highest mountain of the Bayerischer Wald (1,458 meters, 4,780 ft.), whose top can be reached by a chair lift and you can drive up to the lower station. This is a skiing and hiking area with several pleasant winter and summer resorts dotted around the mountain, such as Bayerisch-Eisenstein, Lam, Grosse and Kleine Arbersee. Bodenmais is another of these resorts, with a museum of precious stones, minerals and fossils from all over the world, and geological specimens from the region, together with articles from the silver- and bronze-mining days of Bodenmais in the 18th and 19th centuries. There is also an abandoned ore mine shaft nearby, which can be visited on guided tours.

Passau

The old city of Passau lies on land which narrows to a point as the Inn and the Danube come together on either side of it (the little Ilz, dwarfed by the other two, enters modestly from one side, opposite the point) and on the two flanking banks across from the city, on both rivers, rise wooded heights. Its old buildings lining the waterfront, the varying levels of the streets rising to the hill in the center of the old city, and picturesque architectural details such as the archways joining one house with another all combine to make it a thoroughly delightful city—Humboldt called it one of the seven most beautiful cities in the world.

It is the 15th-century St. Stephan's Cathedral that dominates Passau, situated as it is on the highest point in the town. It is of rather unusual appearance, with an octagonal dome built over the point where the transept and nave roofs cross, as well as the more conventional two towers of the west façade. In it is the largest church organ in the world—17,000 pipes, 208 stops—which you may hear played at noon every day during the summer, with an additional recital at 6 P.M. in July and August. On the choir side of the cathedral is the Residenzplatz, surrounded by fine old patrician houses, a testimonial to the wealth of Passau in the past centuries. On Residenzplatz also stands the Baroque 18th-century New Residence Palace of the Prince-Bishops (hence the name of the square),with beautiful staircase, hall and Rococo interiors. Passau—which in Roman times was called Castra Batava and was a Roman military town—has been the seat of a bishop since 739. At that time the bishopric was set up mainly for the support of the missionary activities in the eastern territories. Later Prince-Bishops ruled Passau for many centuries. From summer 1987 a new Cathedral and Diocesan Museum can be visited in the "Hofsaal" and library of the Residence.

Among other outstanding buildings in the central section of the town are: the Gothic Rathaus on Landeplatz near the Danube with two large halls containing murals that depict the scenes of Nibelungen sagas; nearby in the 11th-century house Hotel Wilder Mann, the fascinating Glass Museum, exhibiting over 10,000 superb pieces of 19th and 20th-century glass from Bavaria, Bohemia and Austria; the Old Residence of Prince-Bishops, now Law Courts, in Zengergasse; the former Niedernburg Abbey (now a girls' school) with Holy Cross Church, founded in the 8th century as a convent, rebuilt in Baroque style—in the church is the grave of Abbess Gisela, the sister of Emperor Heinrich II and the widow of St. Stephen, the first Hungarian King (the cathedral is named after him). Across the Inn River, on a hill with a fine view of the city, is Mariahilf pilgrimage church.

You cross the Danube by the Luitpoldbrücke for the second most important building of Passau, the Veste Oberhaus, also on a dominating position on the heights. This is a great fortress, started in the early 13th century by the Prince-Bishops, and continually added to for the next seven and a half centuries.

Excavations in 1974 on the south bank of the Inn River revealed the long-sought Roman town of Boiotro, where St. Severin was known to have lived in the 5th century, when he undertook the Christianization of the Germanic tribes. Although the archeological work is not completed, to date they have unearthed the remains of the Roman fortress, with walls four meters broad, five defense towers, and a well, which is still full and fresh.

There are many excurisons which start from Passau. One would be a visit to the 11th-century Schloss Neuberg, about 11 km. (seven miles) south on the River Inn. The castle is built on a cliff high above the river, and, as a border fortress, was frequently the object of feuds between the Wittelsbachs and the Habsburgs. On the ground floor it houses the charming little St. Georgs Kapelle, dating back to the 14th century. Buses belonging to German Railways (Bahnbus) take in parts of the Bayerischer Wald, such as the regular service to Bayrisch Eisenstein in the National Park, and Dreisessel on the Arber mountain. You can also take a motorboat at the Rathausplatz or the Inn Promenade for a river ride.

In fact a boat trip on the Danube is a must for any visitor to Passau. Fast, comfortable cruise steamers of the Danube Steamship Company with first-class restaurants, sun decks and cabins on board leave the Rathausplatz daily for excursions to Regensburg, the Austrian Danube Valley, an afternoon's "Three Rivers Tour" (*Dreiflusserrundfahrt*) around Passau on the Danube, Inn and Ilz or directly to Vienna from where passenger steamers of Austrian, Hungarian, Czech or Russian shipping lines offer exciting tours of the Danube ports in five different countries on the way to the Black Sea.

PRACTICAL INFORMATION FOR EAST BAVARIA

TELEPHONES. We have given telephone codes for all the towns and villages in the hotel and restaurant lists that follow. These codes need only be used when calling from outside the town or village concerned.

HOTELS AND RESTAURANTS. There are many unpretentious, but nonetheless charming, summer and winter resorts. Accommodations are for the most part in the lower price categories, especially in the low season or April/May and Sept./Oct. Hotels remain open all year round, and most of them have restaurants. There are also a great many inexpensive bungalow villages and vacation apartments and houses available, particularly in connection with the increasingly popular farmhouse holiday program for family accommodation—*Ferien auf dem Bauernhof.*

Abensberg. *Klosterhotel Biburg* (M), Eberhardplatz 1 (09443–1427). In the old monastery in the town of Biburg; period furnishings, own brewery.

Aicha Vorm Wald. *Aichacher Hof* (I), (08544–283). *Gasthaus zur Linde* (I), Hofmarktstr. 20 (08544–283).

Altötting. *"Zur Post"* (M), Kapellplatz 2 (08671–5040). Renowned tavern dating back to 1280. 92 rooms. Contains *Jägerstuberl* tavern and *Postkeller* cellar-bar and Baroque banqueting hall. DC, MC, V. *Schex* (M), Kapuzinerstr. 11–13 (08671–4021). 55 rooms, half with own bath. Restaurant and garden. Quiet location, but still in easy reach of the center. DC. *Plankl* (I), Schlotthamerstr. 4 (08671–6522). 65 rooms in two modern inns next door to each other.

Amberg. *Bahnhof–Hotel* (M), Batteriegasse 2 (09621–12178). Near station, with garden. *Brunner* (M), Batteriegasse 3 (09621–23944). Breakfast only. DC. *Goldenes Lamm* (M), Rathausstr. 6 (09621–21041). In pedestrian zone. DC.
Restaurants. *Casino Altdeutsche Stube* (M), Schrannenplatz 8 (09621–22664). AE, DC, MC. *Churpfälzer Stuben* (M), Obere Nabburger Str. 28 (09621–12218).

Bayerisch-Eisenstein. *Berggasthof Brennes* (M), Brennes 14 (09925–256). On Arber. 33 rooms with bath, solarium, restaurant, terrace with excellent view. Closed Nov.–mid.-Dec. and Mar.–Apr. AE, DC, MC, V. *Waldspitze* (M), Hauptstr. 4 (09925–308). 50 rooms and 100 apartments with bath. Indoor pool, sauna, steam room, games room, restaurant. No credit cards. *Pension am Regen* (I), Anton-Pech-Weg 21, (09925–464). 16 rooms and 6 apartments with bath, indoor pool, sauna; quiet and comfortable small hotel. Closed mid-Mar.–mid-May and mid-Oct.–mid-Dec. MC.

Bierhütte. *Romantik Hotel Bierhütte* (M), (08558–315). Located high up on the borders of the Bavarian Forest, in building dating back to 1545, and centrally-located for visits to Passau and the Danube Valley. Bohemian decor and antique furniture; excellent cuisine and wines. AE, DC, V.

Bischofsmais. Near Regen in Bayerischer Wald. *Wastlsäge* (M), Lina-Muller-Weg 3 (09920–170). 86 rooms, 5 apartments with bath or shower. In a beautiful, isolated location. Good cross-country skiing and walking trails. Indoor pool, sauna, solarium, masseur, tennis, games room, cozy restaurant, bar. AE, DC, MC, V. *Pension Berghof-Plenk* (I), Oberdorf 18 (09920–442). 17 rooms with bath or shower. No credit cards.

Bodenmais. *Atlas Hotel Sonnenhof* (M), Rechensöldenweg 8 (09924–7710). All rooms with shower. Apartments, 2 restaurants, tavern-bar, nightclub and cure treatment. AE, DC, MC, V. *Silence-Hotel-Andrea* (M), Hölzlweg 10, Am Sonnenhang (09924–386). First class, most rooms with shower; on edge of forest. A few apartments. MC. *Zum Hofbräuhaus* (M), Marktplatz 5 (09924–7021). Indoor pool, sauna, 2 apartments. *Fürstenbauer* (I), Kötztinger Str. 34 (09924–7091). 21 rooms, 1 apartment, all with bath or shower; five minutes from center. Breakfast buffet. AE, DC, MC.

Cham. *Hotel–Restaurant Ratskeller* (M), Kirchplatz (09971–1441). 11 rooms, with bath or shower. Good restaurant. AE, DC, MC. *Randsbergerhof* (M), Randsberger-Hof-Str. 15, near Grasselturm (09971–1266). 65 rooms, modern. Lovely garden cafe, weekend dancing and good restaurant. AE, DC, MC. *Gästeheim am Stadtpark* (I), Tilsiter Str. 3 (09971–2253). Breakfast only. *Gasthof Pension Steif* (I), (09461–235). In nearby Obertraubenbach, a farmhouse pension. *Hotel Sonnenhof* (I), Am Fuchsbühl 14 (09975–30398). In Schlondorf, on edge of forest. Restaurant and cafe; bicycles for hire.

Restaurant. *Burgerstuben* (I), Furtherstr. 11 (09971–1707). In the city hall, an authentic Bavarian dining experience. Reservations advised on weekends. DC.

Deggendorf. *Central Hotel* (E), Östliche Stadtgraben 30 (0991–6011). Modern, centrally-located hotel with indoor pool, sauna and fitness center. Restaurant with Bavarian and international food. AE, DC, MC, V. *Schlosshotel Egg* (E), 8351 Schloss Egg (09905–289). 19 rooms with bath. Atmospheric rooms in a castle and adjoining guesthouse, 3 miles outside of town. Excellent restaurant. AE, DC, MC, V. *Berggasthof Rusel* (I), 8351 Schaufling, on B-11 road north (09920–316). 35 rooms, 20 with bath. Mountainside inn, hiking trails, ski lift, nearby golf course, restaurant. Closed Nov. AE, DC, MC, V.

Restaurant. *Ratskellar* (M), Oberer Stadtplatz 1 (0991–6737). In the town hall. Good Bavarian menu. Closed Fri. MC. *Zum Burgwit* (I), Deggendorfer Str. 7 (0991–32236). In Natternberg section. Cozy, typical Bavarian hotel-restaurant. 18 rooms. *Zum Grafenwirt* (I), Bahnhofstr. 7 (0991–8729). Filling Bavarian dishes and Danube fish. Reservations advised on weekends. Closed Tues. and late-May–early June. AE, DC, MC.

Falkenfels. About 19 km. (12 miles) north of Straubing in the Bavarian Forest. *Burghotel Falkenfels* (M), Burgstr. 8 (09961–6385). Originally medieval castle-fortress, first mentioned in 1100. Heated outdoor pool, fishing, good food.

Furth Im Wald. *Hohenbogen* (M), Bahnhofstr. 25 (09973–1509). 23 rooms, restaurant and cafe with dancing. Special diet meals. DC. *Bayerwald* (I), Bahnhofstr. 21 (09973–1888). All rooms with shower, garden, breakfast only. *Gastehaus Kolbeck* (I), Wutzmühlstr. 1 (09973–1868). Restaurant closed Fri.

Grafenau. *Parkhotel am Kurpark* (M), Freyungerstr. 51 (08552–2444). 50 rooms with bath. Cozy, rustic interior. Indoor pool, sauna, solarium, restaurant. AE, DC, MC, V *Säumerhof* (M), Steinberg 32 (08552–2401). Small, quiet and comfortable. First class restaurant. *Steigenberger Sonnenhof* (M), Sonnenstr. 12 (08552–2033). 196 rooms with bath or shower. Indoor pool, sauna, solarium, indoor/outdoor tennis courts, mini-golf, restaurant. AE, DC, MC, V.

Kelheim. *Ehrnthaller* (Ring Hotel) (M), Donaustr. 22 (09441–3333). 67 rooms, most with own bath. AE, MC, V. *Aukoferbräu* (I), Alleestr. 27 (09441–1460). 54 rooms, about half with own bath, terrace and restaurant. AE.

Kellberg. Near Thyrau. *Pfälzer Weinstube* (M), Kurpromenade 11 (08501–1315). Quietly-located with beautiful view. 26 rooms, terrace, sauna, solarium, tennis court and restaurant. DC.

Lalling. Resort in the Bavarian Forest national park, in a particularly favorable climatic area known as the "Lallinger Winkel." *Thula Sporthotel* (M), (09904–323). 17 rooms, all with own bath, 1 apartment. Quiet and scenically located, with indoor pool, sauna and tennis courts. Cafe and restaurant.

Landshut. *Romantik Hotel Fürstenhof* (E), Steinhamerstr. 3 (0871–82025). Modern hotel in a former "art nouveau" house; very tastefully furnished with every comfort. Attractive old Bavarian country-styled *Herzogstuberl* restaurant with small but good selection of dishes. AE, DC, MC. V. *Goldene Sonne* (M), Neustadt. 520 (0871–23087). Garden restaurant. *Hotel-Garni Bergterrasse* (I), Ger.-Hauptman-Str. 1. (0871–89190). Small and quiet. No restaurant. *Peterhof* (I), Niedermayerstr. 15 (0871–50113). 11 beds.

Restaurants. *Klausenberg* (M), (0871–41477). On the hill of the same name, with fine view of city from its terrace. *Bergcafe* (M), (08702–2285). Located in Niederaichach; hard to find, but has excellent food and view. DC.

Passau. *Passauer Wolf* (E), Rindermarkt 6/8 (0851–34046). 43 rooms. In the heart of the old town on the waterfront. First class restaurant. AE, DC, MC, V. *Wilder Mann* (E), Am Rathausplatz (0851–35071). 60 rooms with bath. Class and comfort in this 11th-century patrician house, furnished with antiques. Indoor pool in the vaulted cellars. First-class restaurant. AE, DC, MC, V. *Schloss Ort* (M), am Dreiflusseck (0851–34072). At the confluence of the rivers Danube, Inn and Ilz. The hotel is a 13th-century castle, converted to a hotel at the turn of the century. 58 rooms, all with own bath or shower, restaurant, sun terrace and garden, directly next to the river promenade and ferryboat pier. No credit cards. *Zum Laubenwirt* (M), Am Dreiflusseck, Ort 14 (0851–33453). Also on the point where the three rivers join. Small, with good terrace restaurant. AE, DC, MC, V.

Restaurants. *Blauer Bock* (M), Fritz–Schäffer–Promenade (0851–34637). Waterfront terrace, music. *Heilig Geist Stifts-Schänke* (M), Heilig Geist Gasse 4 (0851–2607). Founded in 1358; garden, good wines. Reservations advised. Closed Wed. and Jan. 6–30. AE, DC, MC. *Gasthof Andorfer* (I), Rennweg 2 (0851–51372). One of the finest wheat beers in lower Bavaria is brewed here. Fine views and a few rooms. No credit cards. *Ratskeller* (I), Rathausplatz (0851–34686). In the Rathaus, with terrace on the Square.

Regen. *Pension Panorama* (M), Johannesfeldstr. 27 (09921–2356). 17 rooms, all with own bath; indoor pool. *Wieshof* (I), Poschetsriederstr. 2 (09921–4312). 15 rooms, with bath, pool, bowling, restaurant. No credit cards. *Burggasthof Weissenstein* (I), Haus No. 32 (09921–2259). In suburb of same name. Located directly beneath the castle. 15 rooms, with bath, fine view and restaurant. Closed Nov. No credit cards.

Regensburg. *Avia* (E), Frankensstr. 1 (0941–4300). 95 rooms, garden, good restaurant, bar. Situated in the suburbs across the river; good value. AE, DC, MC, V. *Kaiserhof am Dom* (E), Kramergasse 10 (0941–54027). Just west of the Cathedral. All rooms with shower, half with own bath. Separate *Taverne* restaurant (M). AE, MC. *Park Hotel Maximilian* (E), Maxstr. 28 (0941–51042). 52 rooms, all with own bath, very comfortable. Elegant, first-class establishment. Rustic *Jägerstube* restaurant. AE, DC, MC, V. *Münchner Hof* (M), Tändlergasse 9 (0941–58262). 65 rooms, almost all with own bath/shower. Located in the heart of the Old Town, near the pedestrian zone. Good restaurant. AE, DC, MC. *St. Georg* (Ring Hotel) (M), Karl Stieler Str. 8 (0941–97066). Located halfway between the autobahn and the city center. All rooms with bath or shower; restaurant, beer tavern and open fireplace, terrace. AE, DC, MC, V. *Weidenhof* (M), Maximilianstr. 23 (0941–53031). 50 rooms, some with own shower. Three minutes' walk from the main station. Standard comfort. Breakfast only. AE, DC, MC. *Peterhof* (I), Fröhliche Türkenstr. 12 (0941–57514). Modern, with good-value restaurant.

Restaurants. *Historisches Eck Zur Stritzelbäckern* (E), Watmarkt 6 (0941–52966). *Alte Munz* (M), Fischmarkt 7 (0941–54886). Historical tavern serving local specialties. *Leerer Beutel* (M), Bertholdstr. 9 (0941–58997). Next to the Minoriten Church. *Zum Krebs* (M), Krebsgasse 6 (0941–55803). Small and atmospheric, in the old town. Reservations advisable. *Historische Wurstkuche* (I), Weisse-Lamm-Gasse 3 (0941–59098). Next to the Steinernen Brücke (Stone Bridge). *Kneitinger*

Garten (I), Müllerstr. 1 (0941–86124). Typical old beer tavern with lots of dark wood and nostalgic wall decorations. Plenty of good-value, tasty Bavarian specialties.

Inexpensive beer restaurants. *Brandl-Bräu-Gaststätte,* Ostengasse 16 (0941–51487). *Hofbräuhaus,* Rathaus Platz (0941–51280). *Spitalgarten,* Katharinenplatz 1 (0941–52300). Serving beer since 1300.

Wine taverns. *Alt Regensburger Weinkeller,* Fischgassl 4 (0941–54747). Well-known wine tavern/restaurant. AE, MC. *Bastei,* Hinter der Grieb 5–7 (0941–51463). Rustic tavern with open fireplace. *Zum Steidlwirt,* Am Ölberg 13 (0941–52618).

St. Englmar. *Aparthotel Predigstuhl* (M), (09965–81). 400 self-catering apartments, also hotel rooms. AE, DC, V. *Berghotel Maibrunn* (M), in Maibrunn section (09965–292). 22 rooms and indoor pool. *Kurhotel Gut Schmelmerhof* (M), Rettenbach (09965–517). Rustic decor, all rooms with bath or shower. Restaurant, indoor and outdoor pools, sauna. *Kur-und Sporthotel* (M), (09965–312). On the Predigstuhl. Especially equipped for tennis and riding holidays. AE, DC, MC.

Straubing. *Heimer* (M), Schlesische Str. 131 (09421–61091). Small, all rooms with bath or shower. AE, DC, MC, V. *Motel Lermer* (M), Landshuterstr. 55 (09421–3485). Small, all rooms with bath or shower. DC, MC, V. *Seethaler* (M), Theresienplatz 25 (09421–12022). Bavarian cooking. All rooms with bath or shower.

Vilshofen. *Parkhotel* (M), Furtgasse 2 (08541–8037). 31 beds; garden restaurant. DC, MC. *Bayerischer Hof* (I), 8358 Vilshofen (08541–5065). 31 rooms, half with bath or shower. Comfortable, park-like setting, with beer garden and restaurant. Closed Dec. 27–Jan. 10. MC.

Waldmünchen. *Post* (I), Marktplatz 9 (09972–1416). DC. *Schmidbräu* (I), Marktplatz 5 (09972–1349). With annexe and local specialty restaurant. DC. *Pension Gruber* (I), Herzogau 19 (09972–1439). Located in Herzogau, four km. southeast of town, in a quiet position near the forest.

Weiden. *Europa* (M), Frauenrichterstr. 173 (0961–25051). All rooms with shower. AE, DC, MC. *Hotel am Tor* (M), Hinterm Wall 24 (0961–5014). 33 rooms, all with bath; quiet and romantic; in the old town next to the city gate. Rustic *Turmkeller* bar and *Turmstuberl* restaurant. AE, DC, MC. *Stadtkrug* (M), Wolframstr. 5 (0961–32025). 52 rooms, all with own bath. Restaurant with garden. AE, DC, MC, V.

Restaurant. *Zum Heindlwirt* (M), Pfarrplatz 2 (0961–44705). Also some rooms.

Zwiesel. *Kurhotel Sonnenberg* (M), Augunstinerstr. 9 (09922–2031). 19 rooms with bath or shower, 1 apartment. Comfortable, quiet, modern hotel with fine view. Indoor pool, sauna, solarium, fitness room, restaurant. No credit cards. *Linde* (M), Lindenweg 9 (09922–1661). Located outside the town on the south slopes of the Hennenkobels peak above Zwiesel, in the Rabenstein section. Directly on the edge of the forest. Modern hotel with rustic interiors. 74 beds, all rooms with own bath, balcony and panoramic view over the town and Bavarian Forest. Indoor pool, sun terrace and fine restaurant with Bavarian and international specialties. *Waldbahn* (M), Bahnhofsplatz 2 (09922–3001). 28 rooms with bath or shower. Opposite the station, with a beautiful garden and good-value restaurant. Closed Nov. No credit cards.

Restaurants. *Gasthof Deutscher Rhein* (M), Am Stadtplatz (09922–1651). Rustic restaurant serving Bavarian and Bohemian dishes. Live music on Tues., Wed., and Sat. Reservations advised. DC. *Braustuberl* (I), Regenerstr. 9 (09922–1409). Sample the beers of one of the oldest and best breweries in the Bavarian Forest. Basic Bavarian fare. No credit cards.

YOUTH HOSTELS. Youth hostels are well distributed throughout the whole region. For a complete list of addresses and telephone numbers write to the Regional Tourist office. See below for address.

CAMPING. East Bavaria offers a wide selection of campsites for tents and caravan trailers, including camping on farms. For a full list, also including separate lists of sites especially run for young people, write to the Regional Tourist Office in Regensburg for their informative brochure *Camping*.

MOUNTAIN HUTS. A full list of addresses of self-catering huts can be obtained from the Regional Tourist Office in Regensburg. (See *Tourist Information*). Other huts open to the public, and serving meals include: **Bayerisch Eisenstein.** Arberschutzhaus (09925–242). **Bischofsmais.** Landshuter Haus in Unterbreitenau (09920–255). **Ludwigsthal.** Falkensteinschutzhaus (09925–313). **Sankt Oswald.** Lusenschutzhaus (08553–1212). In summer reserve beds in advance.

TOURIST INFORMATION. The main regional tourist office for East Bavaria is the *Fremdenverkehrsverband Ostbayern,* Landshuter Str. 13, 8400 **Regensburg** (0941–57186). The region around the southern Bavarian Forest (Bayerischer Wald) between the Rivers Danube and Inn is covered by the *Fremdenverkehrsgemeinschaft Passauerland,* Domplatz 11, 8390 **Passau** (0851–3971) and for the nature park region of the upper Bavarian Forest around Cham, write to *Gemeindeverwaltung, Verkehrsamt Landkreis Cham,* Postfach 154, 8490 **Cham** (09971–781).

Information about Bavarian Forest National Park is available from *Nationalparkverwaltung,* 8352 Grafenau (08552–2077), or *Direktion für Tourismus,* 8393 Freyung (08551–4455).

Information about the southern Bavarian Forest is available from *Fremdenverkehrsgemeinschaft Passauer Land,* Domplatz 11, 8390 Passau (0851–3971). For holiday centers in the Bavarian Forest, write *Ferienzentrum Bayerwald,* Gottsdorf, 8391 Untergriesbach (08593–444).

The following are area tourist offices. When writing to them, address your letters to the *Verkehrsamt.*

Bayerisch Eisenstein. Schulbergstr. 8371 Bayerisch-Eisenstein (09925–327). **Bodenmais,** Bergknappenstr. 10, 8373 Bodenmais (09924–214). **Cham,** Rosenstr. 1, 8491 Cham (09971–4933). **Deggendorf,** Oberer Stadtplatz 4, 8360 Deggendorf (0991–380169). **Freyung,** Rathausweg 1, 8393 Freyung (08551–4455). **Fürth-im-Wald,** Schlossplatz 1, 8492 Fürth-im-Wald (09973–3813). **Grafenau,** Rathaus, 8352 Grafenau

(08552–2085). **Kelheim,** Neues Rathaus, 8420 Kelheim (09441–3012). **Lalling,** Verkehrsamt "Lallinger Winkel", 8351 Lalling (09904–374). **Landshut,** Altstadt 315, 8300 Landshut (0871–23031).

Passau, *Tourist Information,* Am Rathausplatz, 8390 Passau (0851–33421). **Regen,** Stadtplatz 1, 8370 Regen, (09921–2929). **Regensburg,** Altes Rathaus, 8400 Regensburg (0941–5072141). **St. Englmar,** Rathausstr. 6, St. Englmar (09965–221). **Straubing,** Rathaus, Theresienplatz, 8440 Straubing (09421–16307). **Tittling,** Marktplatz 10, 8391 Tittling (08504–2666). **Viechtach,** Rathaus, 8374 Viechtach (09942–1622). **Vilshofen,** Rathaus, Stadtplatz 29, 8358 Vilshofen (08541–8022). **Waldkirchen,** Hauzenberger Str. 1, 8392 Waldkirchen (08581–665). **Zwiesel,** im Rathaus, 8372 Zwiesel (09922–1308).

HOW TO GET AROUND. By car. The region is quiet and generally empty. However, the Autobahn A3 (Frankfurt–Nürnberg–Regensburg–Passau) is open all the way, linking Germany's southeastern city directly with the cities of the north such as Hamburg, Hannover, Dortmund, Köln and West Berlin. The scenic holiday route, *Ostmark Strasse,* from Bayreuth to Passau (roads B22 and B85) traverses the Oberpfälzer and Bavarian forests from northeast to southwest.

By train. The whole region is well-served with rail connections, the main rail stations being Regensburg, Landshut and Passau on the Frankfurt–Vienna, Oostende–Nürnberg–Passau–Linz–Vienna and Munich–Berlin lines. To these, many smaller towns are linked by rail and post buses.

There are five through trains daily to Passau from Munich, calling at Landshut, Dingolfing, Landau, Plattling, Osterhofen, Wilshofen and Passau, and two daily on the Munich–Passau–Bayerisch Eisenstein express route, which continues from Passau via Deggendorf into the Bavarian Forest, terminating at Bayerisch Eisenstein.

By bicycle. There is delightful cycling countryside in and around the Bavarian Forest, the National Park, the Oberpfälzer Wald and in the river valleys. The Regional Tourist Office for East Bavaria, *Fremdenverkehrsverband Ostbayern,* Landshuter Str. 13, 8400 Regensburg, publishes the cycling brochure *Radeln in Ostbayern* (Cycling in East Bavaria), describing the most suitable areas, suggested routes, places with bicycles for hire, cycle tracks, and interesting sights en route.

By bus. The whole of East Bavaria is covered with a dense network of bus routes. Timetables of municipal bus lines are available from railway stations or the local tourist offices, although bus connections into the Bavarian Forest are not particularly good. However, from Passau there are several regular services of the German Railway buses to places of interest in the Bavarian Forest and surroundings. These buses, connecting with trains, are usually listed in rail timetables; further information is available from the bus terminus in front of the main rail station in Passau (0851–501357).

Furthermore, all major towns throughout the region possess bus companies offering organized trips and day-excursions into the surrounding countryside, including into Austria and Czechoslovakia, for which the tour organizer takes care of the necessary visa formalities.

By boat. Throughout the summer months (May to Sept.) regular motorboat services operate between Regensburg and Passau calling at Straubing,

Deggendorf and Vilshofen. The return journey can also be by rail from
Passau's main station. Information and timetables from *Donauschiffahrts-
gesellschaft Wurm & Koch,* Bräugasse 8, 8390 Passau (0851–2065 or
2066).

Numerous other boat excursions by various shipping lines include trips
to the romantic Wachau wine growing region of Lower Austria; day or
week-end trips to Linz in Austria; cruises from Regensburg into the valley
of the Altmühl to visit the beautiful castle Schloss Prunn; evening dance-
cruises from Passau. In addition, there are passenger steamers to Vienna
and the Black Sea run by Austrian, Hungarian and Russian shipping lines,
which all call in at Passau, or the new, super *Donauprinzessin* belonging
to the Deilmann Line of Germany which operates a luxury cruise from
Passau to Budapest and back every Saturday.

There are also various shorter round-trips to places of interest, departing from Kelheim, Regensburg, Straubing or Passau, and inter-town ferry
services all along the Danube. The tourist offices supply information about
the various private shipping companies operating ferry services and boat
trips.

SPORTS. Hiking tops the list of pastimes in East Bavaria (see below
for more details) but in addition there is **swimming** in the Ilz and Danube
rivers and in many outdoor and indoor pools, such as in Regensburg
(*Westbad,* Messerschmittstr. 4) or in Passau (*Schwimmbad "Bschütt,"* an
openair pool near the Ilz bridge, and the *Hallenbad Passau* in Neuburger-
str.). There is also bathing in the lakes of Pocking and Hartkirchen near
Passau. **Water sports,** including **motorboat hire** (from Regensburg) and
water-skiing, forbidden on many other lakes, are allowed on the Danube
near Obernzell; **rowing** and **canoeing** on the Altmuhl. **Sailing** and **windsurfing** on the lakes of Perisee near Waldmünchen, Badesee at Eging, Ranna-
see near Wegscheid and the Höllensteinsee near Viechtach. There is a
squash court in Pocking, south of Passau; **golf courses** at Regensburg,
Furth-im-Wald, Eggenfelden, Schmidmühlen (which offers combined
package deals with instruction), Schwarzenfeld, Lallinger Winkel, and
Waldkirchen in the Bavarian Forest. **Tennis courts** can be found in most
towns.

There is **horseback riding** in 46 resorts throughout the Bavarian Forest.
In most of the riding stables, covered waggons and carriages can also be
hired. The cost of hourly riding instruction ranges from DM.7 to DM.16,
and carriages and waggons about DM.20 for up to four passengers.

Fishing is generally good in the rivers of the Bavarian Forest and the
Oberpfalz, particularly for trout. A specialty of the area is *Huch* (huck),
a large and savage river salmon, caught in the Danube and its tributaries,
as well as eel and sheathfish. Day permits must be purchased, and vary
from about DM.7 to DM.10. Lists of places issuing permits can be obtained from the local tourist offices, the town hall or from the booklet published by the Regional Tourist Office for East Bavaria in Regensburg, entitled *Angeln in Ostbayern.*

HIKING. Hiking is a favourite pastime in East Bavaria, especially
around Waldmünchen in the Oberpfälzer Wald and the Arber mountain
area. You can follow the historic Pandurensteig trail, one of the most beautiful hiking paths in Germany, which stretches from Waldmünchen to

Passau for 150 km. along the ridge in the center of the Bavarian Forest National Park. The trail can be hiked in stages, with 10 overnight stays in the *Wandern ohne Gepäck* (Hiking without Luggage) program where accommodation and transfer of luggage is arranged in advance from Gasthof to Gasthof. Contact the regional Tourist Office in Regensburg for information and reservations. Sturdy mountain walkers and those in search of real wildness will find the mountains of the Bavarian Forest southeast of the Arber along the Czech border and their approaches particularly challenging. There are also several mountain lodges here belonging to the Bavarian Forest Trust where you can stay overnight. Some also offer meals. It's advisable to telephone in advance in the high season as dormitories quickly get filled. (See below).

The whole of the Bavarian Forest contains a dense network of hiking trails, all well-marked with a numbering system. A word of warning, however: take great care when walking in the areas near the Czech border not to cross over the border itself, marked with red and white poles.

For less strenuous walking and in less rugged surroundings, try the four nature parks of the Oberpfälzer Wald.

Three resorts of the Bavarian Forest—Kellberg, Hauzenberg and Büchelberg—have joined forces to offer a good-value hiking holiday called *Wandern mit Tapetenwechsel* ("Hiking with a Change of Scene"). The all-in package includes 14 days' hiking, bed and breakfast, guided hiking tour, luggage transportation for around DM.450. Information from the *Verkehrsamt Kellberg,* 8391 Thyrnau (08501–320).

WINTER SPORTS. Next to the Black Forest East Bavaria is the most important winter sports region in Germany outside the Alps. There are still excellently prepared facilities for both downhill and crosscountry skiing. In addition to long stretches of marked crosscountry *(Langlauf)* tracks, ski-lifts, floodlit pistes, etc., there are facilities for skating, curling and tobogganing. The best winter sports centers are in the Bayerischer Wald, where the skiing season lasts from December until early March. World Cup downhill ski championships take place on the Arber mountain in January and February, as well as international crosscountry competitions. The main winter sports regions are: Arber-Osser-Falkenstein (includes towns of Bayer, Eisenstein, Bodenmais, Zwiesel, etc.); Rachel-Lusen (includes Frauenau and Grafenau); Freyung-Mitterfirmiansreut (includes Freyung); St. Englmar-PröllerPredigstuhl (includes St. Englmar and Viechtach); Gibacht-Voithenberg-Hoher Bogen (includes Furth-im-Wald, Grafenwiesen and Waldmünchen). Details of resorts offering winter sports facilities in East Bavaria are available in the booklet *Winter Information fur Ostbayern-Urlauber* issued by the Regional Tourist Office. Look too for special winter packages *Pauschalangebote,* also available from the tourist office.

Christkindlmarkt.

FRANCONIA

Medieval Glories and Rococo

Franconia, or Franken, is the northernmost region of the state of Bavaria and comprises Upper, Middle and "Swiss" Franconia. Its western edge includes most of the northern section of the Romantic Road and, in the Spessart hills, reaches a point only 32 km. (20 miles) from Frankfurt. Its northern border runs along the frontier of East Germany. In the east it extends to the Upper Palatinate, the Oberpfalz, while to the south it extends to the Danube and Lower Bavaria.

Franconia contains some of the most lovely and tradition-laden areas of all Germany. It is a land of exquisite and intricate medieval cities; of magnificent Baroque and Rococo palaces built by pleasure-loving, art-loving Prince-Bishops; of brooding hilltop castles and stately Gothic cathedrals; and of rich vineyards whose golden grapes mature to be pressed into pale, dry wines. Here the Minnesingers created Germany's lyric poetry in the early Middle Ages, and the Mastersingers later sang to the beat of their craftsmen's tools.

We also cover the peaceful Altmühl Valley and the Franconian Forest (Frankenwald) running along the East German border in this chapter.

Exploring Franconia

The most direct route from Frankfurt to Würzburg, the chief city of Unter-Franken (Lower Franconia), passes through Aschaffenburg, only

40 km. (25 miles) southeast of Frankfurt and still on the Main but already within the borders of the state of Bavaria.

Aschaffenburg is an important cultural and trade center endowed with some outstanding buildings in delightful parks and surrounded by lovely countryside. The most notable is the 800-year-old monastery church of St. Peter and Alexander; its main treasures are a Romanesque cloister with superbly graceful arches, and a fine painting by the early Renaissance master, Matthias Grünewald, of the dead Christ. Aschaffenburg in fact calls itself "the city of Grünewald"; and though the artist was born in Würzburg he lived for several years in Aschaffenburg where he also collaborated on the construction of the imposing Renaissance Johannisburg Castle which dominates the view of the city from the Main side with its fortress-like bulk and its four turrets. A curious structure is the Pompejanum, an imitation of the Castor and Pollux house in Pompeii, built by Ludwig I of Bavaria. Visitors will appreciate the quaint alleyways and half-timbered houses of Aschaffenburg's old town—and, in contrast, the vast new covered shopping center, City Galerie, with its 40,000 sq. meters of fully air-conditioned shopping arcades—as well as its beautiful parks—Schönbusch with its small neo-Classical palace mirrored in the tranquil waters before it, and Schöntal, about three km. (two miles) outside, whose pond reflects the ruins of an old cloister church.

Aschaffenburg is the capital of and gateway to Spessart, a region of un-dulating hills, mostly covered by forests, many of them old oak forests, with a number of atmospheric small towns and villages hidden among them. Mespelbrunn is noted for its Renaissance moated castle while Rohr-brunn, approximately in the center of the region on the main route between Aschaffenburg and Würzburg, has an interesting hunting castle and many hiking paths, for Spessart is a walker's paradise.

If you continue due south, following the Main, you reach the most wester-ly corner of Franconia, the area known as Mainischer Odenwald and the next stop is Miltenberg, on the river Main. Its market square with the 16th-century fountain offers one of the most beautiful half-timbered pic-tures in Germany while several medieval tower-gates still watch the ap-proaches to the city. In 1987 the city celebrated its 750th anniversary. Across the river from Miltenberg are the green forested hills of Spessart.

Only a few kilometers south of Miltenberg is Amorbach, founded by Benedictine monks in 734. The abbey church is Baroque and contains the biggest Baroque organ in Europe; the parish church here is Rococo. West of Amorbach is the heart of the Odenwald region in the state of Hesse.

Proceeding along the main route again from Aschaffenburg through Spessart we meet the Main again near Marktheidenfeld. At this spot you either cross the river, continuing straight to Würzburg, or follow the lon-ger but much more interesting road along the right bank. This route passes through a series of picturesque small towns: Hafenlohr, where regional rustic pottery is made; Rothenfels, with its medieval castle; Gemünden, where the Sinn and Saale rivers flow into the Main; Karlstadt, with 13th-century walls and gates, the ruins of an even older castle across the river, and an exquisite 15th-century Town Hall.

Just a few kilometers before reaching Würzburg is the Baroque Veitschöchheim Castle, with Rococo adornments and a beautiful, formal park; this was the former summer residence of the prince-bishops of Würz-burg.

Würzburg

The prehistoric finds in the immediate vicinity of Würzburg have shown that this area was already inhabited 120,000 years ago. A chain of fragmented pottery leads us to the Celts who for several centuries lived at the foot of Marienberg and built a fort on the top of the same hill (on the site of the present castle). Germanic tribes settled on the present city site at the beginning of the Christian Era, but became christianized much later when Kilian, the Irish missionary—called the Apostle of the Franks—came to this area together with his companions Kolonat and Totnan. Their efforts eventually bore fruit, but not until all three of them had been put to death. In spite of this early opposition the city was made a bishopric as early as 742 and it was only half a century later that the Würzburg bishops acquired secular power as well; as prince-bishops, they ruled the city for 1,000 years.

Kilian, who was canonized after his martyrdom, is buried in a crypt over which the Baroque Neumünster Church was later erected. The nearby monumental cathedral is also named after him; though essentially Romanesque, it has many later additions. Neumünster was once an abbey church (Stiftskirche) and in the former cloister courtyard—today the site is called Lusamgärtlein—the canons were buried, and among them, by special imperial order, Walther von der Vogelweide, the famous Minnesinger, who spent his last days in this monastery and died in 1230. Other outstanding churches in the city are the Gothic Marienkapelle (St. Mary's Chapel) on the market square and the half-Romanesque and half-Gothic St. Burkard's, named after the first bishop of Würzburg and located at the foot of the vineyards rising to Marienberg Fortress.

The fortress (Festung) is one of the main attractions of Würzburg. Not only is it a majestic sight when seen from the pleasant promenade on the right riverbank or from the 15th-century Old Main Bridge, but it also offers a splendid view over the city from its terrace garden. You can walk up from the Old Main Bridge (Alte Mainbrücke), or drive up by a roundabout way, first following route No. 27 (marking the beginning of the Romantic Road) to the heights south of the river, and then taking the narrow Oberer Burgweg, the street leading through several gates of the fortress to one of the main courtyards. From this courtyard a gate leads into the castle proper; here stands the former arsenal, today housing the Mainfränkisches Museum. Of outstanding artistic interest in the museum is the section devoted to the sculptor Tilman Riemenschneider, where some of his best works in wood and stone are displayed; Riemenschneider was born in the Harz region but spent most of his life in Würzburg, where he became a city councillor and mayor, and where he was imprisoned for a brief period in 1525 for having sided with the peasants in the great peasant rebellion of the same year.

In the interior castle courtyard stands the round Marienkirche, one of the oldest churches in Germany (built in 706), looking more like a fortified tower than a church. Nearby is the 104-meter (341-foot) well that provided the fortress with water, and a tower called Sonnenturm, where the treasury and the archives were kept and in whose dungeon Riemenschneider was imprisoned. The castle suffered severe bomb damage towards the end of the last war and while the exteriors have been repaired and rebuilt, the precious interior furnishings were almost totally lost.

The prince-bishops lived in the fortress until the 18th century, when they moved into the splendid castle-palace (Residenz) in the city, built by the famed Baroque architect Balthasar Neumann. The 300th anniversary of Neumann's birth was celebrated in 1987. Although the greater part of the Residenz was burned out during the same air raid which set the Marienberg fortress and the rest of the city ablaze, its facade, the most beautiful halls, and above all the unique Grand Staircase miraculously escaped serious damage. The Grand Staircase, with the huge ceiling painting by Tiepolo of *The Four Continents,* is one of the most sensational Rococo interiors in Europe, while the Kaisersaal (Emperor's Hall), where the Mozart Festival concerts are performed in summer by the light of thousands of candles, and the Hofkirche (Court Church), in the southeast corner of the palace, are considered among the best specimens of early Rococo in Germany. Both have further frescos by Tiepolo. Intricate wrought-iron gates, 18th-century masterpieces by Oegg, lead into the adjoining palace garden.

Rococo is everywhere in Würzburg: in the original Julius Hospital Pharmacy; on the facade of the Haus zum Falken on the market square, once a proud patrician dwelling; on the figures of Rokokobrunnen and Vierröhrenbrunnen, two fountains near the Rathaus which, however, is much older; in the interior decorations of Käppele pilgrimage church, on a hill next to Marienberg, though the building itself, again by Neumann, is Baroque.

Bocksbeutel Road

Franconian wine is, in fact, almost as famous for the *Bocksbeutel,* the dumpy green flagon it comes in, as for any other attribute. Not surprisingly, the best wine-tasting route here is known as the Bocksbeutel Road. Between May and October about 100 wine festivals take place in the wine-growing towns and villages en route. The "heart" of this road is shaped by a huge southward bend of the Main. It begins a bit northwest of Würzburg and ends, following the river, at Zeil am Main, a few villages north of Escherndorf. This is a tiny village with a big reputation among wine drinkers, for it is here that the Escherndorfer Lump (The Rascal of Escherndorf) gushes from the wine pressses into the barrels and bocksbeutels and matures into "The Rascal."

The medieval watchtowers of two ancient towns stand guard at the lower point of the Bocksbeutel heart: Ochsenfurt, with its Gothic Rathaus and Glockenspiel, and Markbreit. On the right bank of the Main, north of Markbreit, is Kitzingen, a center of the wine trade, whose curiosity is a medieval tower with a leaning spire; it is located on the direct route from Würzburg to Nürnberg. Farther up the river is Dettelbach, a small town founded in 515, still enclosed by 15th-century walls with 36 towers.

Iphofen, an authentic medieval town, and nearby Rödelsee are important wine-growing centers. Volkach's principal sights include the 16th-century Rathaus, the Baroque Schelfenhaus, and the *Rosary Madonna* by Riemenschneider in the pilgrimage church on the nearby Kirchberg. All three of these towns are situated on the edge of Steigerwald, a region of low hills reaching to Bamberg.

Approximately in its center, on the direct Würzburg to Bamberg road, stands the 13th-century monastery church of Ebrach, one of the best examples of early German Gothic (with interior additions from later periods), and the adjoining Baroque monastery with five courtyards and some fine interiors. Follow a side road at the western edge of Steigerwald for Schloss Weissenstein near Pommersfelden, about 19 km. (12 miles) south of Bamberg, built in the early 18th century by the Bamberg architect Johann Diezenhofer with the assistance of Lukas von Hildebrandt, the famous Austrian architect. This splendid castle, with a spectacular grand staircase, a series of richly-decorated halls, and a gallery of paintings, rivals the finest Baroque castle-palaces of southeastern Germany.

Instead of crossing the Steigerwald, we can proceed northward to Schweinfurt. Its finest buildings are the 16th-century Town Hall and the Protestant Johanniskirche. A few kilometers to the southwest is the Baroque Werneck Castle, while the northbound road leads to the Franconian spa region at the foot of the Rhön hills.

Bad Kissingen is the leading spa of this area and a one-time favorite of Bismarck. It has several thermal and mineral springs, lovely parks, 16th-century Altes Rathaus, a Baroque Neues Rathaus, a large Kurhaus (Regentenbau) with several halls and with arcades connecting it with the mineral water outlets in Brunnenhalle, and with Wandelhalle, a huge promenade lobby. Bad Kissingen also offers some very unusual attractions: a giant ten-meter-square chess-board with meter-high figures, installed by the spa management for the benefit of the guests who wish to exercise their brains and their muscles at the same time; and a 9-seat bright yellow stagecoach, drawn by four white horses, with blue-liveried coachmen, running daily from early May through October between Bad Kissingen and the eight-km.-distant (five miles) Bad Bocklet, operated by the German Federal Post and still transporting mail as well as passengers, the only regular service of this kind still existing in Germany.

On the market square in Bad Kissingen you will see a bust of Peter Heil, who in 1643 devised an ingenious defense stratagem while the town was beleaguered by hostile forces during the Thirty Years War: he advised his fellow town defenders, who had run out of ammunition, to hurl beehives from the city walls upon the attackers, and the latter fled in panic.

To the north lie Bad Neustadt, in a lovely location on the Saale River, with the nearby Salzburg fortress, one of the largest in Germany, and Bad Brückenau, surrounded by woods in the dreamy Sinn Valley with the border of Hesse just beyond it. For beautiful views of the surrounding region drive up the scenic roads to Wasserkuppe, the highest summit in Rhön and one of the main German gliding centers, or to Kreuzberg, which is almost as high and on whose top stand the three crosses of the Crucifixion.

Resuming our upstream journey along the Main from Schweinfurt, we pass through Hassfurt, a medieval town that has retained its old gate towers and its 15th-century Gothic Ritterkapelle (Knight's Chapel) with 240 coats of arms of Franconian noble families. North of Hassfurt are the wooded hills of Hassberge, with numerous castles, quiet, unspoiled villages, rushing streams, and hundreds of pleasant and easy hiking paths.

Bamberg

The Regnitz River, which joins the Main just a few kilometers below Bamberg, flows through the city in two arms. Its left arm cuts through the heart of the city and was once the border between the Bishop's Town on its left bank and the Burgher's Town on its right bank. This accounts for the fact that the Altes Rathaus, which had to administer both halves of the city, is picturesquely located in the middle of a bridge that connects them, like a stone ship.

The foremost sight in Bamberg, as well as one of the main architectural and artistic attractions in Germany, is the famous cathedral, whose four spires rise above the city and whose mighty two-choir Romanesque building dominates the Bishop's Town. Half-hourly organ concerts are held every Saturday at noon throughout the summer, and from time to time choral concerts take place with the Cathedral choir and the famous Bamberg Symphony Orchestra. The contruction was started by Emperor Heinrich the Holy in 1003 and the consecration took place on Heinrich's birthday in 1012. During the ensuing two centuries it was enlarged and partially rebuilt, acquiring Gothic additions. The exquisitely-figured Adam's Portal, St. Mary's Portal, and Prince's Portal lead into the interior with its numerous artistic treasures including the noble equestrian statue known throughout the world as the Bamberg Rider, chiseled in stone around 1230 by an unknown master and interpreted as the personification of medieval German knighthood; the sculptures of the Visitation group and the nearby Smiling Angel; two elegant early Gothic female figures representing "Church" and "Synagogue"; the limestone tomb of Emperor Heinrich and his wife Kunigunde (both canonized after death) carved by Riemenschneider; St. Mary's or Christmas Altar, carved in wood by Viet Stoss; the 14th-century choir stalls. In the west choir of the church is the grave of Pope Clement II, a former Bishop of Bamberg and the only pope buried in Germany, while the cathedral treasury contains some of his ecclesiastical garments as well as clothing of Emperor Heinrich and Empress Kunigunde.

Near the cathedral stands the beautiful Old Residence (Alte Hofhaltung) of the Bamberg prince-bishops, now housing a regional historical museum, built in German Renaissance style except for the half-timbered wing in the inner courtyard, which is from the 15th century and which was once part of the now defunct fortress. On the other side of the cathedral square is the Baroque New Residence (Neue Residenz), built by Dienzenhofer with a representative picture collection. The rear of the palace encloses a lovely rose garden, which offers an excellent view of another majestic ecclesiastic edifice, topping the highest hill in the city: the former Benedictine abbey, site of the church of St. Michael's, built originally in the Romanesque period but remodeled in the 17th century.

In the narrow, romantic streets between the cathedral hill and the left arm of the Regnitz River, many old houses recapture days gone by. Perhaps the finest among them are the two patrician houses, once owned by Böttinger, an influential and wealthy citizen of Bamberg, and built upon his orders: the Böttingerhaus in Judengasse and Concordia Palace right on the river.

Crossing the left arm of the river through the Old Town Hall—for one of the two bridges that support it passes through it—the waterfront presents a unique view: a row of colorful old fishermen's houses called Klein Venedig (Little Venice). St. Martin's Church in the center of the Burgher's Town is another outstanding Baroque building. The State Library next to it has among its thousands of books, manuscripts, and incunabula works by Dürer and Cranch, a 5th-century manuscript by Roman historian Livy, the Alcuin Bible from the early 9th century, and the prayer books of Emperor Heinrich the Holy and his wife Kunigunde.

On Schillerplatz, across from the city theater, stands Hoffmann-Haus, today a museum, from 1809–13 the residence of writer E. T. A. Hoffmann, who was also the composer, musical director and scene painter in the Bamberg city theater, and whom Offenbach made the main character in his *Tales of Hoffmann.*

To the Sources of the Main

At Bamberg we entered Ober-Franken (Upper Franconia). Proceeding north along the Main valley, we come to Staffelstein, an old town with an exquisite half-timbered Rathaus, situated beneath the Staffelberg from whose top there is an extraordinary view of the Main valley. Nearby are two gems of ecclesiastical architecture, both with very rich interiors. One is the pilgrimage church of Vierzehnheiligen, the finest Rococo church in northern Bavaria built by Balthasar Neumann; its name means "fourteen saints" and it is built on the spot where, in 1445 and 1446, a young shepherd had visions of 14 *Nothelfer* (saints who help people in times of need); they are represented in a ceiling fresco. The church is generally considered to represent the high point of German Rococo architecture and decoration, and many may find it the high point of a visit here. The other one is the former Benedictine Abbey of Banz, dating from 1071 and later rebuilt several times; its Baroque abbey church and the main monastery building are the works of the Bamberg master, Dienzenhofer, and another monastery wing is by Neumann. Not far away is Lichtenfels, center of German basket-making, with a basket-weaving school, old town gates and a castle.

Situated in the valley of the Itz, Coburg was for several centuries the seat of the family of Saxe-Coburg-Gotha, a kind of royal stud farm which provided consorts to almost every royal house of Europe; one of them was Prince Albert, the consort of Queen Victoria, herself descended from the same family, and you can visit his birthplace at Schloss Rosenau. A statue of Prince Albert stands in Coburg market square, flanked by the Renaissance Stadthaus and the Rathaus, first erected in the 16th century and later rebuilt, but preserving the original Renaissance Great Hall. But the finest Renaissance building in the city is Gymnasium Casimirianum, built in 1605 and named after its founder, Duke Johann Casimir of Coburg. Opposite is the Protestant Morizkirche, with two uneven towers and with portal stone sculptures from 1420. Schloss Ehrenburg was the ducal town palace and its 17th- to 19th-century apartments and chapel are open to the public.

High above the town you will see the massive walls of a fortress, from whose interior rise the roofs of the buildings it surrounds. This is the Veste, over 900 years old and one of the largest fortified strongholds in Germany, shut in by a triple line of ramparts. The approach to it has been beautified by the creation of a park that begins at the town below and extends all the way up the slope to the castle. Stop halfway up and visit the Natural History Museum (one of the largest bird collections in Europe, more than 8,000 specimens). The fortress, too, houses a museum. Its apartments contain a wealth of period furniture, porcelain, silver, and its art collections include works by both Cranachs, Dürer and Rembrandt.

Before leaving Route 2203 for Schloss Rosenau, stop at the Goebel factory in Rödental to see the manufacture of the enormously popular Hummel figures and the porcelain museum.

Among the several castles on the outskirts of Coburg is Schloss Rosenau, the summer residence of the dukes and birthplace of Prince Albert. Neustadt, a town devoted to the manufacture of dolls, has a museum with 1,000 dolls in folk costumes and a toy show portraying fairy tales. Another curiosity of Neustadt is the goat bleat announcing the noon hour from the Rathaus; this recorded "baa baa" is sounded in memory of a medieval tailor who saved the town from a siege by sewing himself into a goat skin and frolicking on the ramparts to convince the enemy that the defenders had plenty of food. In the vicinity is medieval Kronach with picturesque old streets and buildings, the powerful fortress of Rosenberg that was never captured, and the house where the painter Lucas Cranach the Elder was born. Kronach is a good center from which to explore the thickly-forested hills of Frankenwald, harboring at its northern end the summer resort of Ludwigsstadt, with the 1,000-year-old Lauenstein Castle nearby.

Kulmbach is famous for the production of excellent beer. Its Luitpold Museum contains, among other exhibits, a collection of 32 pieces of fine goldsmiths' work of the late 16th and early 17th centuries, which was hidden so effectively during the Thirty Years' War that it was not found again until three centuries later, in 1912. The town is dominated by the Plassenburg Fortress, with a beautiful arcaded Renaissance courtyard and a series of dioramas containing over 300,000 tin figures representing all sorts of scenes from mammoth hunting to famous battles.

Just below Kulmbach, the White Main, on whose banks the town is located, and the Red Main flow together forming the beginning of the Main proper. The Red Main comes from the northeastern edge of Fränkische Schweiz (Franconian "Switzerland") and passes through Bayreuth.

Traveling up the White Main from Kulmbach, you come to its source in the Fichtelgebirge, a range of granite mountains and plateaus covered with conifers, and an increasingly popular summer and winter vacation area. Coming from the west you enter them at Bad Berneck, a health resort. Approximately in the center of the Fichtelgebirge are lovely Fichtel Lake and the winter sports center of Ober-Warmensteinach. In the vicinity is the old town of Wunsiedel, with the nearby Luisenburg, the name given to an amazing pile of huge rocks near the top of a hill; their position is so intricate that the marked path leading through them is a veritable labyrinth, and it takes two hours of twisting and turning to cover its mile and a half. The great rock pile provides a fine background for the Luisenburg festival of drama that is held here every summer.

North of Wunsiedel are Selb, the porcelain manufacturing city, and Hof, a textile and brewing center. A specialty of Fichtelgebirge is glass blowing and decorating. The town of Bischofsgrün, the highest climatic resort in these mountains, has the longest ski lift in Europe and an 800-year-old glassmaking tradition, while there are glass factories in many other places.

Wagner's City

Bayreuth is known throughout the world as the city where the yearly Wagner Festival is given in the theater designed by Richard Wagner himself for the presentation of his operas under ideal conditions. Today it is impossible to move two steps in Bayreuth without being reminded of Wagner. The shops are packed with souvenirs, the streets are named after his family and characters from his operas. You should be warned that prices of nearly everything rise by 100% during the Festival.

However, Bayreuth was an important center of arts and music even before Wagner opened his theater in 1876. The Margraves of Bayreuth had been longtime sponsors of the arts, particularly during the mid-18th century. When Wilhelmine, the favorite sister of Frederick the Great, married into the Bayreuth ruling family, she and her husband made the city a center of art and music, and during their lifetime the finest buildings of Bayreuth were built. At the command of Margravine Wilhelmine, the famous Baroque Margrave's Opera House was built, where Wilhelmine herself often acted. Today the Franconian Festival Week, featuring Baroque music, is staged in it every year in late spring.

Wagner designed his Festspielhaus (Festival Theater) primarily to achieve perfect acoustics for his operas: for this reason the seats have no upholstering, a cloth is suspended in a horizontal position about 25 feet below the ceiling, and the orchestra pit is almost completely covered by a wooden boarding. This last innovation ensures that a balance is kept between the orchestral sound and the singers, a balance that very few other opera houses can provide. The stage is very high and very deep and has an excellent lighting system. The building cost vast amounts of money and Wagner never had sufficient financial means to give the theater a fancy finish, explaining the spartan look.

Richard Wagner and his wife Cosima, the daughter of the composer Franz Liszt, lived in Haus Wahnfried and are buried in the garden behind it. The house is now a museum. Liszt also spent his closing years in a nearby villa, where he died three years after Wagner; he is buried in the city cemetery.

A section of the New Castle, once the residence of the Margraves and now a museum, includes the State Gallery of Painting, City Museum, and a regional collection of natural history. Other museums include the Hean-Paul Museum, dedicated to the poet Jean-Paul Friedrich Richter; the City Museum (Stadtmuseum); the fascinating Typewriter Museum (Museum Historischer Schreibmaschinen); and the German Freemasons' Museum (Deutsche Freimaurermuseum) in the Hofgarten.

You should not fail to visit Eremitage, a Rococo-style park with two pleasure castles and elaborate fountains, also built and formerly owned by the Margraves about five km. (three miles) outside the city.

Fränkische Schweiz

Southwest of Bayreuth, inside the triangle formed by the roads connecting Bayreuth–Nürnberg–Bamberg–Bayreuth, is Fränkische Schweiz (Swiss Franconia), a group of romantic, narrow valleys and hills, with strange stone formations protruding here and there out of steep, wooded flanks. The name is a misnomer since, except for its idyllic, pastoral character, the area has little in common with Switzerland. Medival castles stand guard on many cliffs, whose interiors harbor some 40 caves rich in stalactites and stalagmites, where many fossils and bones of prehistoric animals have been found. The best starting points for an exploration of Fränkische Schweiz are the towns of Hollfeld in the north, Forchheim in the west, Gräfenberg in the south and Pegnitz in the east.

The Wiesent River flows south from Hollfeld through quaint villages to Behringersmühle, where it turns west and is joined by two other streams: the Alisbach, coming from Rabenstein Castle (near the stalactite cave of Sophienhöhle), and the Püttlach passing through the town of Pottenstein, dominated by a 10th-century castle, with the famous Teufelshöhle, or Devil's Cave nearby (open to the public, as are all the other caves mentioned, and easily reached from Pegnitz on the Bayreuth–Nürnberg autobahn). In the town proper is the parish church of St. Bartholomew, with its enormous high altar and priceless wood-carvings. Across the river is the climatic health resort of Gössweinstein, with a Baroque pilgrimage church designed by Neumann and an impressive castle atop the hill above it that is well worth the short but steep drive up, also for the view. About four km. east is 15th-century Gaillenreuth Castle in whose neighborhood is the Gaillenreuther Zoolithenhöhle, a cavern where prehistoric human remains were found next to those of Ice Age animals. At Streitberg, flanked by the ruins of two castles, are the underground stalactite treasures of Binghöhle.

Forchheim is a bustling textile center whose history dates back to 805. Note the half-timbered Rathaus square, 17th-century Nürnberg Gate, remains of old walls, 14th-century castle (now museum), and Gothic parish church with Baroque onion-shaped spire. If you wish to see the colorful regional folk dress, visit the nearby village of Effeltrich on a church holiday, and particularly at Easter.

You enter Mittel-Franken (Middle Franconia) at the university town of Erlangen, which consists of two parts: the Old Town and the New Town. The latter was built by Margrave Christian Ernst of Bayreuth in a grid pattern around his castle-palace for Huguenot refugees from France, who found haven here towards the end of the 17th century. Among the eminent sons of Erlangen was Simon Ohm, famed German discoverer of the electrical unit named after him.

Nürnberg

The principal city of Franconia and second only to Munich in Bavaria, Nürnberg was a great imperial city dating back at least to the year 1040. Nürnberg owed its supremacy to a number of factors: its position at the crossroads of many important trade routes in medieval Europe, the genius of its citizens, and the favor of the emperors—Charles IV in the Golden Bull of 1356, a medieval constitution of the Holy Roman Empire of the German Nation transforming it from a centralized monarchy into an aristocratic federation, ruled that every emperor should convoke his first diet in Nürnberg.

Nürnbergers were renowned for their intellect and their skill at handicrafts. Its citizens included the Minnesingers—among them Tannhäuser, who was neither an invention of German sagas nor of Richard Wagner,

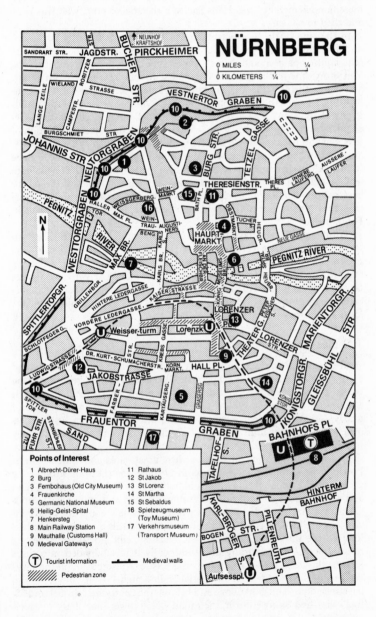

NÜRNBERG

0 MILES ¼

0 KILOMETERS ¼

SANDRART STR. JAGDSTR. PIRCKHEIMER STR.

↑NEUNHOF KRAFTSHOF

LANGE ZEILE
WIELAND
STRASSE
RORITZER STR.
BUCHER STR.
CAMPESTR.
BURGSCHMIET STR.

JOHANNIS STR.
NEUTORGRABEN

VESTNERTOR GRABEN

PEGNITZ

WESTORGRABEN

HALLER TOR
WEISSGERBER
MAX PL.

N

RIVER
MAX BR.

SPITTLERTORGR.

SCHLOTFEGER G.

LUDWIGSTRASSE

SPITTLER TOR

FUHR STR.
STEINBÜHL
STR.

SAND

FRAUENTOR GRABEN

GRILLENBGR.
HINTERE LEDERGASSE
VORDERE LEDERGASSE

Weisser-turm

DR. KURT SCHUMACHERSTR.

JAKOBSTRASSE

KAISER-STRASSE

KARLS BR.
KARLS STR.

WEIN-MARKT

THERESIENSTR.

RATH PL.

WEIN-TRAU-BENG

AUGUSTINERS
HAUPT-MARKT

BURG STR.
TETZEL GASSE

THERES PL.
INNERE LAUFER
AUSSERE LAUFER

DESTMARKT
TUCHER STR.
HEUGBR.
NEUE GASSE

PEGNITZ RIVER

KÖNIG MUSEUMS BR.

Lorenzk

LORENZER PL.

KREBS GASSE
KORN MARKT
KARTÄUSERG.
FARBER STR.
GRASERG

HALL PL.

THEATER G.
PETER VISCHER STR.

LORENZER STR.

HELBG

MARIENTORGR.

GLEISSBÜHL STR.

KÖNIGSTORGR.

KÖNIGS TOR

BAHNHOFS PL.

HINTERM BAHNHOF

TAFELHOF STR.

KARL-BRÖGER STR.

BOGEN STR.
PILLENREUTH STR.

Aufsesspl.

Points of Interest

1 Albrecht-Dürer-Haus
2 Burg
3 Fembohaus (Old City Museum)
4 Frauenkirche
5 Germanic National Museum
6 Heilig-Geist-Spital
7 Henkersteg
8 Main Railway Station
9 Mauthalle (Customs Hall)
10 Medieval Gateways

11 Rathaus
12 St Jakob
13 St Lorenz
14 St Martha
15 St Sebaldus
16 Spielzeugmuseum
   (Toy Museum)
17 Verkehrsmuseum
   (Transport Museum)

Ⓣ Tourist information

Pedestrian zone

Medieval walls

but who lived for a while in Nürnberg in the 13th century—and even more importantly the Mastersingers, whose center was Nürnberg and whose most famous member was Hans Sachs, a shoemaker-poet, who was born and died in the city.

In the field of the arts Nürnberg can boast that it was the birthplace of: Albrecht Dürer, probably Germany's greatest painter; Michael Wolgemut, another painter, and Dürer's master; one of the greatest woodcarvers, Veit Stoss; one of the greatest German sculptors in stone, Adam Kraft; and one of the greatest workers in brass, Peter Vischer—the last particularly fitting, since the development of brass founding was one of this prolific city's inventions. The first pocket watch, the gunlock, gun casting, mechanical toys, (the Toy Museum—Spielzeugmuseum—has a collection of toys from all over the world and from all periods of history), the clarinet, are some of the other Nürnberg inventions. The first geographical globe (now in the Germanic Museum) was also made here by Martin Behaim in 1490–92, just before Columbus, using the nautical tables of the Nürnberg astronomer Regiomontanus, discovered the New World. The German Inventors Exposition is held here every September and a toy fair in February.

Nürnberg does not have the elegant, aristocratic air of many German provincial cities that were the seat of princes and bishops. It has always been a democratic place, ruled by the genius of its citizens and reflecting in its streets and comfortable houses their ideas of how to live. Food figures largely here, and you will find many budget restaurants and beer halls specializing in *bratwürst,* Nürnberg grilled sausages. Have a nibble on the local gingerbread, too.

Exploring Nürnberg

Although wartime air raids almost totally wiped out the genuinely and extraordinarily medieval Nürnberg, intelligent and faithful reconstruction has to a large extent restored the city's medieval character. Nürnberg is a double city, whose two halves are separated by the Pegnitz River. For nearly 150 years the parts led a separate life. Each was enclosed by its own walls, and not until the end of the first quarter of the 14th century were they united in a single strong defensive unit, still almost intact, with their double walls, their moats and their great gates and watch towers. Possibly the number one attraction in Nürnberg is the walk around the walls, and the floodlighting of the old buildings, which you must not miss and which occurs daily during the summer season and during the famous Christmas Market period as well as when the frequent congresses and conventions are held. A good place to begin and end this circuit is the castle-fortress, the Burg. It sprawls along a sandstone cliff, dominating the city from above. Architecturally and historically it is subdivided into three groups: the 12th–16th-century Imperial Castle (Kaiserburg), on the western part of the rock, with the Imperial Hall, Knights' Hall, suites, the Renaissance double chapel (above and below), the courtyard, 50-meter (165-foot) well, and Sinnwellturm, the round watch tower that offers an excellent view of the city. In the center, the remains of the earliest Burgrave's Castle (Burggrafenburg), with the pentagonal tower and the bailiff's house; the Kaiserstallung (Imperial Stables) in the eastern part of the fortress, with several rows of dormer windows on its high roof, built as a granary in the 15th century, rebuilt after the last war and converted into a youth hostel, connected with the pentagonal tower of the middle section of the Burg.

Below the western part of the fortress is a picturesque small square with the Tiergärtner Gate and Albrecht-Dürer-Haus, a fine example of an old Nürnberg burgher's house with original interiors and a collection of originals and copies of works by Albrecht Dürer, who lived in this house from 1509 until his death in 1528. Opposite the house lies the Alstadthof square, with historical brewery cellars, taverns, souvenir shops, folk theater and an atmosphere of "Old Nürnberg." Following the Burgstrasse downhill, we come first to Dürer Square with a monument to the painter and then to St. Sebaldus Church (now Protestant) built in the 13th century, whose style represents the transition from late Romanesque to Gothic. It contains the famous Sebaldusgrab, a masterpiece in brass created by Peter Vischer and his sons; resting curiously on the shells of snails this shrine supports a silver coffin with relics of St. Sebaldus and is ornamented with scores of realistic figures, including those of the Apostles and the artist himself. Among other artistic treasures in the interior of the church are several works by Veit Stoss and on the exterior side of the east choir is a sculptured tomb by Adam Kraft.

Opposite the church on one side is the parish house, with a magnificent Gothic bay window, and on the other side is the Rathaus, with underground dungeons hewn out of rock around 1340. In the court square of the Rathaus stands the Gänsemännchenbrunnen (Gooseman's Fountain) with a figure of a 16th-century peasant taking two geese to market, cast in bronze by Pankraz Labenwolff about 1550. Nearby in Theresienstrasse is a monument to the navigator Martin Behaim and in the Burgstrasse is the Fembohaus, a dignified patrician dwelling from the Renaissance period, presently housing the Old City Museum.

The Hauptmarkt

Between the Rathaus and the Pegnitz River is the main square (Hauptmarkt), a vast pedestrian zone with the 18-meter (60-foot), spire-like Gothic Schöner Brunnen fountain ornamented with 40 statues, and the 14th-century redstone Frauenkirche. The Frauenkirche contains the Tucher-Altar, a fine example of 15th-century Nürnberg painting, and statuary by Kraft. Under the little tower facing the main square is the Männleinlaufen, a clock dating from 1509, that performs every noon and represents Emperor Charles IV receiving homage from the seven Electors. The traditional Christkindlmarkt for Christmas tree decorations and toys is held on the main square in front of the church every December.

Near the Frauenkirche, bridging one arm of the river that forms an island here, is the picturesque Holy Ghost Hospital (Heilig-Geist-Spital), founded in 1331, with several wooden-galleried inner courtyards, among them the Crucifixion Court with the group by Adam Kraft. On the square in front of it is the Hans Sachs Monument. A few bridges downstream is a romantic sight that should not be missed: the Henkersteg (Hangman's Bridge) leading to the 14th-century Water Tower (also called Hangman's Tower) which is connected with the late Gothic, half-timbered Weinstadel (Wine Storehouse), originally built as a hospital and now containing a students' hostel.

St. Lorenz Church

Proceeding from the main square over the Museum Bridge, we come to the Gothic church of St. Lorenz, the most beautiful in Nürnberg. The building was started in the 13th century, finished in the 15th, severely damaged during the last war and rebuilt with the generous help of Rush Kress of New York, whose ancestors emigrated from this area to America in 1752. Its Rosette window is one of the most famous in Germany, and it possesses two other particularly prized works of art, the *Angelic Salutation* by Veit Stoss, carved in wood and suspended from the vaulting, and the Tabernacle by Adam Kraft, chiseled from stone and including a portrait of the artist himself. The restoration of the church was possible only because the pillar with the Tabernacle remained standing after the air raids, supporting part of the choir superstructure.

Outside the church is Tugendbrunnen (Fountain of Virtue), with the jets of water springing occasionally from the breasts of the dignified female figure representing six virtues, and topped by a statue representing Justice. Opposite the church and the fountain is the Gothic, tower-like Nassau House, a patrician city dwelling whose cellar and lower floors originate from the 13th century. About halfway between the St. Lorenz Church and the powerful Königstor is the dormer-windowed Mauthalle (Customs Hall), first built as a granary around 1500. Near Königstor is a reconstructed medieval craftsmen's courtyard known as the Handwerkerhof, where you can watch the blacksmiths, potters, bakers, silversmiths, and even coin minters at work in summer. Nearby is the 14th-century St. Martha Church where the Mastersingers had their singing school from 1578 to 1620.

Not far from the Mauthalle is the Kornmarkt, the former grain market square, where the main entrance to the Germanic National Museum is located. This museum is unique in Germany and its exhibits represent the development of the art and culture of all German lands from the earliest times until the 19th century. Its several buildings include the 600-year-old former Carthusian monastery and church.

Proceeding west from Kornmarkt we come to the reconstructed Gothic St. Jakob's Church and to Ludwigstrasse with the White Tower, also rebuilt, and beyond it the fountain with a bronze figure of Peter Henlein, the pocket-watch inventor. South of the Kornmarkt on Lessingstrasse is the German Transport Museum (Verkehrsmuseum). Germany's first train traveled from Nürnberg to Fürth on 7 December 1835 and to mark the 150th anniversary in 1985 German Railways put on a program of Nostalgic Train excursions which, it is hoped, will be repeated in the following years.

At the other end of Ludwigstrasse are the Spittlertor and the Fürther Gates and beyond them the Fürther Strasse takes us to Fürth, eight km. (five miles) away and virtually an extension of Nürnberg.

In the northern outskirts of Nürnberg are Neunhof, with a moated castle, open on summer weekends as a hunting museum, and Kraftshof with a fortified 16th-century church, destroyed during the last war and restored mainly through the great financial help of the same Rush Kress who contributed to the rebuilding of St. Lorenz Church; his ancestors had founded the church in Kraftshof.

Between Nürnberg and the Danube

East of Nürnberg are medieval Altdorf (once a university town), setting for the yearly Wallenstein-Festspiel in late July with performances of scenes of daily life during the Thirty Years War; Lauf, with an interesting moated castle; and Hersbruck, with old gates, the Shepherds' Museum, and a collection of 50,000 hand-painted lead soldiers.

Southwest of Nürnberg, on the Castle Road, is Heilsbronn with the Gothic Minster, once a Cistercian abbey church, furnished with many works of art but with particularly fine Gothic altars and stained-glass windows. Beyond Heilsbronn is Ansbach, founded over 1,200 years ago and now known as the city of Franconian Rococo. The splendid Margrave's Palace, built in Italian Baroque style and with sumptuous Rococo interiors, is the best preserved 18th-century castle-palace in Franconia, with the single exception of the Residenz in Würzburg.

Turning off the Castle Road we first come to the medieval walled town of Wolframs-Eschenbach, birthplace of famed Minnesinger Wolfram von Eschenbach, the author of *Parzival.* Then we proceed to Gunzenhausen, with medieval towers; Ellingen, with the impressive castle-palace of the Teutonic Knights; Weissenburg, another medieval walled town whose Ellinger Gate is particularly admired and which also has the remains of a Roman fort; and to the nearby 16th-century fortress of Wülzburg, where deer are kept in the dry moat.

South of Weissenburg is Treuchtlingen in the narrow, green Altmühl Valley, whose most romantic scenery extends from here to Kelheim. Its most interesting town is Eichstätt, situated some 24 km. (15 miles) west of the Nürnberg–Munich autobahn. A bishopric for 1,200 years, its many fine buildings include the Baroque Residenz, and the cathedral, with Romanesque towers, a mostly Gothic interior, and a Baroque façade. On an elevation near the city is the massive Willibaldsburg fortress. In the limestone quarries in and around nearby Solnhofen are found some of the best and most interesting bird and fish fossils in Europe, among them *archaeopteryx lithographica,* which, when first found in 1861, caused quite a stir in scientific circles since it was the first example of a transition from reptile to bird. Today it is in the British Museum in London, but five further specimens found in the Altmühl Valley—including the so-called "Eichstätt Specimen" found in Solnhofen in 1951 and perhaps the best specimen of its kind—can be seen in the recently opened Jura Museum in the Bishops' Residence on Willibaldsburg.

At the old fortress town of Ingolstadt we meet the Danube (known in German as the Donau). Among Ingolstadt's many fine buildings note the Gothic Liebfrauenmünster (Basilica of Our Lady), with a magnificent Renaissance-style stained-glass window; the Rococo Maria Victoria Church built by the Asam brothers, a marvel of intricate decoration, including a large ceiling painting; the 13th-century Herzogkasten, the only remaining building of the Old Castle; the New Castle, with late-Gothic interiors, and today the Bavarian Army Museum. A good portion of the 14th- to 15th-century city walls has been preserved, together with over 40 towers and gates, among them notably the elaborate 14th-century tower-gate known as the Kreuztor. Also well worth seeing are the St. Moritz and Minoriten Churches.

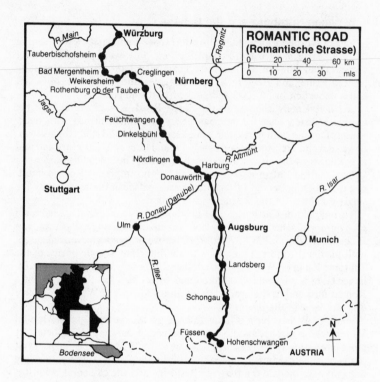

The Romantic Road

Following the Danube westwards from Ingolstadt via Neuburg, we reach Donauwörth, at the confluence of the rivers Danube and Wörnitz and at the intersection of the regions of Franconia, Swabia and Bavaria, to the north and south of which is the Romantic Road, Germany's most famous scenic route, running from Füssen on the Austrian border in the Allgäu to Würzburg. This is a progression through a continuous pageant of history, art and architecture. Accept the ready-packaged journey of around 420 km. (260 miles), providing the concentrated essence of picturesque Germany.

We shall now follow the road northwards as it passes along the western edges of Franconia to Rothenburg ob der Tauber. Starting at Donauwörth, we are once again in a medieval bridge-town, and a well-preserved one, with the old town walls still running along the banks of its second river, the Wörnitz; the quaint Färbertörle gate, the Baroque Holy Cross Church, and the regional parish church, with its medieval frescos, should be visited.

The Romantic Road follows the Wörnitz on Route B25, and crossing over into Swabia, comes to the small town of Harburg, with its stone bridge spanning the water. Above it on a hill is Harburg Castle, a powerful 13th-century fortress. The well-preserved walls harbored collections of such richness that a new museum was opened to display the art treasures of the castle to better advantage. Among them are works by Riemenschneider, Romanesque ivory carvings, a fine collection of Gobelin tapestries and a huge library.

Back again in Franconia, we reach Nördlingen, which is called "the living medieval city,"—at night you will hear the watchman's call echoing through the narrow streets as it has for centuries. The city's holidays hark back to medieval times too. The Staben festival, held in May at the old bastion, goes back several centuries; the Anno 1643 pageant commemorates the town's time of troubles at that date; and the Scarlet Derby (Scharlachrennen) is Germany's oldest. The openair stage provides an appropriate setting for these performances, which accord perfectly with the solid ancient walls that encircle the old town, with the fine patrician houses of this former Imperial Free City, with the medieval shops and homes, with St. George's Church and its 90-meter (300-foot) tower (familiarly referred to as "Daniel"), with the Church of the Savior and its 13th-century frescos, with the Rathaus (14th century) and with the Kürschnerhaus, the oldest fair building in Germany. There is also a fascinating Museum of Medieval Crime and Punishment (Kriminalmuseum) and, in complete contrast, the Doll and Toy Museum (Puppen und Spielzeug Museum), Germany's largest private toy museum, temporarily housed at Sigmundstr. 220.

Proceeding north we enter Dinkelsbühl, another old imperial free city. In July, Dinkelsbühl holds its Kinderzeche (Children's Tribute), with sword dances, guild dances, and an historical play in memory of the salvation of the city during the Thirty Years' War. To that event we owe the fact that once again we have here a medieval city preserved intact, its walls still standing, complete with moat, bastions, gates and towers.

At Feuchtwangen, the monastery church, with its row of arches, serves as a background for openair plays on warm summer evenings. If you stop for them, don't miss the excellent Heimatmuseum collection of folk crafts.

Rothenburg-ob-der-Tauber, which was also an imperial free city, is today the best preserved example of a medieval town in Germany. Here again we have a walled city, with sentry walk, towers and gates intact, a fairy-tale city whose old fountains are alive with scarlet geraniums. It is here we encounter the River Tauber and its peaceful valley.

At Whitsuntide, and again in September, Rothenburg holds a festival centered about a play given in the Rathaus, *Der Meistertrunk,* which you can translate "The Master Drink" or "The Mighty Draught", performed to commemorate the drinking feat that saved the town from destruction in 1631. The enemy commander who conquered the town first ordered it to be destroyed; he than offered to save it on condition that one of the town councillors empty with a single draught a 3-liter mug of wine (over three U.S. quarts). The old mayor, Nusch, succeeded in draining the sizeable container and the town was saved. During the summer, shepherd dances (*Schafertanz*) and Hans Sachs comic plays are performed. You can also see *Der Meistertrunk* clock play every day at 11, 12, 1 and 2 o'clock on a house near the Rathaus. At Christmas there is a particularly attractive *Christkindl* Market.

There is plenty to see in Rothenburg outside of festival time, too—particularly the masterly carving of the Holy Blood altar in the west choir of the St. Jakobskirche, executed by Tilman Riemenschneider of Würzburg, whose work is encountered throughout the Tauber Valley. The impressive Gothic church contains a famous winged High Altar painted by Hans Herlin in 1466 and beautiful stained-glass windows. Visit also the Imperial City Museum (Reichstadtmuseum) of art and handicrafts in the 700 year-old former Dominican Convent.

From Rotherburg, the Romantic Road leaves Franconia and enters Baden Württemberg, passing through the towns of Creglingen, Weikersheim, Rottingen, Bad Mergentheim and Tauberbischofsheim to return to Franconia again at its starting point, Würzburg.

PRACTICAL INFORMATION FOR FRANCONIA

TELEPHONES. We have given telephone codes for all the towns and villages in the hotel and restaurant lists that follow. These codes need only be used when calling from outside the town or village concerned.

HOTELS AND RESTAURANTS. There are many good-value, charming, summer and winter resorts in this area, and the lesser-known resorts of the northeast offer some of the best-value accommodations in Germany. Hotels tend to remain open all year round and most of them have restaurants. There are also good possibilities for holiday apartments and bungalows, as well as holidays on the farm *(Urlaub auf dem Bauernhof)*. Contact regional or local tourist offices (see below for addresses) for details.

Abenberg. (Near Roth.) *Burg Hotel Abenburg* (M), Burgstr. 16 (09178–217). 24 beds. Large restaurant, cellar wine-tavern, pool, garden terrace. A peaceful castle-hotel with a panoramic view. DC.

Ansbach. *Am Drechselgarten* (M), Am Drechselgarten 1 (0981–89020). All rooms with bath or shower. Terrace-café with fine view, wine-tavern and nightclub. AE, DC, MC, V.

Aschaffenburg. *Romantik Hotel Post* (E), Goldbacherstr. 19 (06021–21333). Situated in the center of town, but quiet, and most rooms airconditioned. Excellent restaurant; indoor pool, sauna and solarium. AE, DC, MC, V. *Aschaffenburger Hof* (M), Frohsinnstr. 11 (06021–21441). 130 beds, and annexe. Two minutes' from the station. AE, DC, MC, V. *Wilder Mann* (M), Löherstr. 51 (06021–21555). 80 beds. Delicious Main fish and Franken wine in its wood-paneled *Stuben*. AC, DC, MC, V.

Restaurant. *Schlossweinstuben* (E), Schlossplatz (06021–12440). Wine tavern at Johannisburg Castle with view of Main valley. AE.

Auerbach. *Romantik Hotel Goldener Löwe* (E), Unterer Markt 9 (09643–1765). 47 beds, most rooms with own bath or shower. Dates back over 800 years; authentic-looking furnishings and good hearty food. AE, DC, MC.

Bad Brückenau. *Dorint Kurhotel* (E), Heinrich von Bibra Str. 13 (09741–850). 220 beds, all rooms with bath. Located in the Cure Park.

Luxurious. *Schlosshotel Fürstenhof* (E), Heinrich-v.-Bibra Str. 16 (09741–5071). 44 rooms, all with bath; café-restaurant with beautiful period furniture. A castle hotel in its own beautiful park, the former summer residence of Ludwig I. *Gasthof zum Stern* (M), Alstadt 6 (09741–789). Atmospheric old inn with restaurant. AE, DC, MC. *Zur Mühle* (M), Ernst-Putz-Str. 17 (09741–5061). 14 rooms all with bath; terrace café. MC.

Bad Kissingen. *Das Ballinghaus* (E), Martin Luther Str. 3 (0971–1234). 70 rooms; indoor pool, thermal baths. MC, V. *Dorint Hotel* (E), Frühlingstr. 1 (0971–3050). 94 rooms, all with bath. Restaurant. AE, DC, MC, V. *Steigenberger "Kurhaushotel"* (E), Kurhausstr. (0971–80410). 83 rooms, all with bath; cure facilities, rustic-antique *Kissinger Stüble* bar and garden terrace. Luxurious. AE, DC, MC, V. *Diana* (M), Bismarckstr. 40 (0971–4061). 75 rooms, most with bath; indoor pool. *Motel Fürst Bismarck* (M), Euerdorfer Str. 4–6 (0971–1277). Café, indoor pool. AE, DC, MC. *Am Ballinghain* (I), Kissinger Str. 129 (0971–2763). In Reiterwiesen section. Quiet. MC.

Restaurants. *Casino Restaurant "Le Jeton"* (E), at the Luitpold Park (0971–4081). Evening meals only. *Ratskeller* (E), Spitalgasse 1 (0971–2550). In the Rathaus; music and dancing in the evening. *Bratwürstglöckle* (M), Grabengasse 6 (0971–4406). Franconian sausages, ten kinds of beer. *Weinhaus Schubert* (M), Kirchgasse 2 (0971–2624). Cosy restaurant with old Franconian atmosphere. Fresh baked bread and Franconian regional dishes. Good local wines. AE, DC, MC.

Bamberg. *Gastehaus Steinmuhle* (E), Obere Muhlebrucke 5–7 (0951–54074). Historic millhouse dating back to 1855, converted in 1984 to comfortable hotel with elegant interiors. Good *Bottingerhaus* restaurant. AE, MC, DC. *Alte Post* (M), Heiliggrabstr. 1 (0951–27848). 75 beds, most rooms with bath or shower. Located near the station. V. *Altenburglick* (M), Panzerleite 59 (0951–54023). Near Altenburg castle; no restaurant. *Barock-Hotel-am-Dom* (M), Vorderer Bach 4 (0951–54031). Located by the cathedral. Historic, elegant, baroque town house with 19 rooms. Fully modernized; no restaurant. AE, DC, MC. *Bamberger Hof-Bellevue* (M), Schönleinsplatz 4 (0951–22216). 70 beds. First-class, right in the town center. AE, DC, MC, V. *Romantik Hotel Weinhaus-Messerschmitt* (M), Lange Str. 41 (0951–27866). 17 beds; old wine from 1832, good food and wines, game and fish specialties. AE, DC, V. *Roter Ochse* (I), Untere Königstrasse 13–15 (0951–21573). 86 beds; on the banks of the Main river.

Restaurants. *Böttingerhaus* (E), Judenstr. 14 (0951–54074). On the first floor of a Baroque house, in beautifully-restored rooms; elegant French cuisine. DC. *Michel's Küche* (M), Markusstr. 13 (0951–26199). On opposite side of Pegnitz to Old Town. First-class food. *Weierich* (M), Lugbank 5 (0951–54004). Traditional tavern-restaurant with dining rooms in various old Franconian styles; wide variety of Bamberg beers including *Rauchbier*. MC. *Schenkerla* (I), Dominikanerstr. 6 (0951–56060). Old-style tavern in 15th-century house, serving *Rauchbier*.

Bayreuth. *Bayerischer Hof* (E), Bahnhofstr. 14 (0921–22081). 98 beds. With roof-garden restaurant. AE, DC, MC. *Am Hofgarten* (M), Lisztstr. 6 (0921–69006). 18 rooms, about half with own bath; sauna, solarium, terrace, no restaurant. *Goldener Anker* (M), Opernstr. 2–6 (0921–65500). 27

rooms, most with own bath; no restaurant. Near the opera house. *Goldener Hirsch* (M), Bahnhofstr. 13 (0921–23046). 38 rooms, most with own bath; restaurant. Near the station. MC. *Königshof* (M), Bahnhofstr. 23 (0921–24094). Formerly the "Reichsadler." Right opposite the station, with restaurant. AE, DC, MC. *Schlosshotel Thiergarten* (M), Obertheirgartnerstr. 36 (09209–1314). In Wolfsbach suburb. A castle full of history and atmosphere. Elegant restaurant with Franconian/French cuisine. AE, DC, MC, V. *Zum Edlen Hirsch* (I), Richard Wagner Str. 77 (0921–64120). 93 beds, about half of the rooms with own bath or shower. AE, MC.

Restaurants. *Annecy* (M), Gabelsberger Str. 11 (0921 26279). High quality French restaurant. *Brückenschenke* (M), Schulstr. 5 (0921–21442). Small, gourmet restaurant in two rooms tucked away behind a bistro; magnificent cold buffet. *Eule* (M), Kirchgasse 8 (0921–64346). Atmospheric, calls itself an artists' tavern. MC. *Metropol* (M), Josephsplatz 8 (0921–69662). With view over city, with café and grill, dancing. MC.

Coburg. *Blankenburg* (M), Rosenauer Str. 30 (09561–75005). With café-terrace; fine *Kräutergarten* restaurant. *Goldener Anker* (M), Rosengasse 14 (09561–95027). Near the Market Square; indoor pool and roof terrace. *Goldene Traube* (M), Viktoriabrunnen 2 (09561–9833). Near the market. Cozy restaurant and bar. AE, DC, MC. *Schloss Neuhof* (M), Neuhofer Str. 10 (09563–2051). A reasonable castle-hotel, with mostly modern rooms, and restaurant in the Knights' Hall. V. *Stadt Coburg* (M), Lossaustr. 12 (09561–7781). Pleasant hotel near the main station. 75 beds, all rooms with bath. Atmospheric restaurant. *Wald-Pension* (M), Gersbach (09561–30755). With 250-year-old wine cellar, and riding and fishing.

Restaurants. *Rittersteichstuben* (M), Hahnweg 1 (09561–92441). Evenings only except Sundays. *Ratskeller* (M), Markt 1 (09561–92400). In the Rathaus. Franconian specialties. *Schaller* (M), Ketschendorfer Str. 22 (09561–25074). Located in hotel "Coburger Tor." Serves a mixture of new and traditional dishes; the lunch menu includes regional specialties while in the evening *nouvelle cuisine* is offered. Pleasant decor and good service.

Wine taverns. *Burgschänke* (M), (09561–75153). In the Veste Coburg. Franconian specialty restaurant, also café. *Künstlerklause* (I), Theaterplatz 4a (09561–75261). *Lorely* (I), Herrngasse 14 (09561–92470). Coburg specialties.

Dinkelsbühl. *Blauer Hecht* (M), Schweinmarkt 1 (09851–811). 28 rooms, 1 apartment, 1 suite, all with bath or shower. A Ring Hotel in a renovated brewery-gasthof. Modern rooms; variety of regional and international dishes served in the restaurant. Closed Jan. AE, DC, MC, V. *Deutsches Haus* (M), Weinmarkt 3 (09851–2346). Half-timbered house built in 1440. All bedrooms fully modernized. Delightful local specialties in its restaurant. AE, DC, MC, V. *Eisenkrug* (M), Dr. Martin Luther Str. (09851–3429). 11 rooms, all with bath/shower; very central. Fine restaurant (closed in winter). AE, DC, MC. *Goldene Kanne* (M), Segringerstr. 8 (09851–6011). Near train station. Popular wine tavern and fine local food. AE, DC, MC, V.

Feuchtwangen. *Romantik Hotel Greifen-Post* (E), Marktplatz 8 (09852–2002). 41 rooms, 2 apartments, 1 suite, with bath. Indoor pool, sauna, solarium, restaurant serving Franconian specialties. Dates back to 1588. AE, DC, MC, V.

Hammelburg. (Near Bad Kissingen.) *Schloss Saaleck* (M), (09732–2020). Castle-hotel on a hill above town, colorful restaurant with own wines; very quiet.

Ingolstadt. *Holiday Inn* (E), Goethestr. 153 (0841–2281). 125 rooms, all with bath, radio and TV; modern. Situated near the autobahn exit, with grill restaurant, attractive tavern and pool. AE, DC, MC, V. *Rappensberger* (M), Harderstr. 3 (0841–3140). 170 beds; indoor pool; particularly comfortable. AE, DC, MC. *Bavaria* (I), Feldkirchner Str.67 (0841–56001). Quiet, café, indoor pool. AE.

Restaurants. *Bastei* (E), Schlosslände 1. With terrace and fine cuisine. DC, MC. *Schumann-Stuben* (M), Schumannstr. 21. Courtyard dining in summer.

Ludwigsstadt. *Burg Lauenstein* (I), (09263–256). 40 beds. Castle-hotel in Lauenstein section, reached by road No. 85 from Kronach. One of the best-preserved medieval castles, with rooms furnished in period style; romantic restaurant.

Miltenberg. *Riesen* (M), Hauptstr. 97 (09371–3644). Historic half-timbered inn dating from the Middle Ages, reputed to be the oldest hostelry in Germany. No restaurant. 50 different Franconian wines in adjoining restaurant. DC. *Rose* (M), Hauptstr. 280 (09371–2001). Centuries-old guild house of river boatmen and fishermen, overlooking the Main. AE, DC, MC, V. *Brauerei Keller* (I), Hauptstr. 66–70 (09371–3077). Good restaurant with large wine list. AE, MC, V.

Nördlingen. *Sonne* (M), Marktplatz 3 (09081–5067). Next to the Rathaus; dates from 1477. Wine tavern. Closed Dec. 26–mid-Jan. AE, MC. *Schützenhof* (M), Kaiserwiese 2 (09081–3940). 15 rooms with bath. Fine local specialties and fresh fish in the restaurant. Closed first half of Aug. AE, DC, MC, V. *Zum Engel* (I), Wemdinger Str. 4 (09081–3167). Quiet, brewery-gasthof. 15 beds. Good-value restaurant.

Restaurants. *Meyer's Keller* (M), Marienhohe 8 (09081–4493). Fine cuisine, beer garden and panoramic view. Reservations advised. Closed Mon. No credit cards.

Nürnberg. *Am Sterntor* (E), Tafelhofstr. 8 (0911–23581). 120 rooms; in quiet location near station and shops. AE, DC, MC, V. *Atrium Hotel* (E), Münchener Str. 25 (0911–47480). In the suburb of Luitpoldhain in the Meistersingerhalle park. Large, modern hotel conveniently sited for concerts and trade fairs. First-class *Rotisserie Medoc* restaurant. Indoor pool. AE, DC, MC, V. *Carlton* (E), Eilgutstr. 13–15 (0911–200333). 175 beds, rooms with radio and TV; excellent restaurant, dancing in night bar. Garden-terrace. AE, DC, MC, V. *Grand-Hotel (Penta)* (E), Bahnhofstr. 1–3 (0911–203621). 200 beds, some suites; excellent cuisine in restaurant, bar, café, 60-car garage. Luxurious. AE, DC, MC, V. *Maritim* (E), Frauentorgraben 11–13 (0911–23630). 520 beds, all modern facilities. Fine *"Die Auster"* restaurant and *Nürnberger Stuben* tavern. AE, DC, MC, V.

Am Hauptmarkt Kröll (M), Hauptmarkt 6–8 (0911–227113). Very centrally-located, though no restaurant; small but modern. *Cristal* (M), Willibaldstr. 7 (0911–564005). Excellent service, noteworthy breakfast. No restaurant. AE, DC, MC, V. *Burghotel* (M), Lammgasse 3 (0911–204414). Centrally located comfortable hotel-garni. Rustic interiors, pool, sauna, bar. Ask for accommodation in *Grosses Haus* to avoid the not-so-conveniently located annexe. AE, DC, MC, V. *Deutscher Hof* (M), Frauentorgraben 29 (0911–203821). 80 beds; near the German National Museum, cozy *Holzkistl* restaurant and wine cellar-bar. AE, DC, MC. *Blaue Traube* (I), Johannesgasse 22 (0911–22958). 26 beds. AE, DC, MC, V. *Pension Christl* (I), Laufamholzstr. 216c (0911–501249). 23 beds, some rooms with own bath; terrace, no restaurant, quiet.

Restaurants. *Essigbrätlein* (E), Weinmarkt 3 (0911–225131). Oldest eating-house in town, dating back to 1550. Very atmospheric, fine *haute cuisine.* AE, DC, MC, V. *Goldenes Posthorn* (E), Glöckleinsgasse 2 (0911–225153). At the St. Sebaldus Church, founded in 1498, once frequented by Albrecht Dürer and Hans Sachs. AE, DC, MC. *Nassauer Keller* (E), Karolinenstr. 2 (0911–225967). The deep 13th-century cellar of the Nassau House; good wines, music. DC. *Romantik Restaurant Rottner* (E), Winterstr. 15 (0911–612032), in Grossreuth suburb. Cozy restaurant in a beautiful old, half-timbered house. Excellent food including fresh game. DC, MC, V. *Schwarzer Adler* (E), Kraftshofer Haupstr. 166 (0911–305858). In Kraftshof suburb. Dates back to 1752. Fine haute cuisine in rustic-elegant surroundings. Also beer garden serving local dishes. DC, MC.

Heilig-Geist Spital (M), Spitalgasse 12 (0911–221761). Heavy wooden furnishings and over 100 wines from all over Germany. DC, MC. *Zum Sudhaus* (M), Bergstr. 20 (0911–204314). Traditional rustic inn. Reservations essential. MC, V. *Bratwürst Friedl* (I), Hallplatz 21 (0911–221360). Tavern serving Nürnberg sausages. *Bratwurstglocklein im Handwerkerhof* (I), Am Königstor (0911–227625). Local color at the craftsmen's courtyard.

Beer restaurants. *Gaststätte Kaiserburg,* Obere Krämergasse 20 (0911–221216). Beer from the wood; regular musical events. *Mautkeller,* Hallplatz 2 (0911–224773). Music at weekends.

Cafés and pastries. *Atlantik,* Karolinenstr. 43/II. *Berger Kroll,* Hauptmarkt 6, on the second floor. With large terrace and unique view of the main square area. *Café-Confiserie Neef,* Winklerstr. 29. Excellent pastries.

Pegnitz. *Pflaums Posthotel* (Ring Hotel) (E), Nürnbergerstr. 14 (09241–7250). Pretty, half-timbered Franconian building, housing a traditional hotel. The restaurant numbers among the best in Franconia. AE, DC, MC, V.

Rothenburg Ob Der Tauber. *Burg Hotel* (E), Taubertal, Klostergasse 1 (09861–5037). 15 rooms, 8 suites, all with bath. Tranquil rooms overlooking the river. No restaurant. AE, DC, MC, V. *Prinzenhotel* (E), An der Hofstatt 3 (09861–6051). Formerly Hotel Stadt Rothenburg. 47 rooms, most with bath. Located within walking distance of ancient town wall and center. *Romantik Hotel Markustrum* (E), Rodergasse 1 (09861–2370). 26 rooms, most with bath. Excellent family hotel with good restaurant (fresh trout specialties). Closed Jan. 10–Mar. 18. AE, DC, MC. *Eisenhut* (E), Herrengasse 3–5 (09861–2041). 82 rooms, 3 suites, all with bath or shower. Three medieval houses in exquisite antique style, excellent cuisine and wine. Strongly recommended. Closed Jan.–Feb. AE, DC, MC, V. *Goldener Hirsch* (E), Untere Schmiedgasse 16 (09861–2051). 80 rooms, most with bath or shower. Historical patrician house, filled with antiques; fine dining on the Blue Terrace with outstanding view of town. Closed mid-Dec.–Jan. AE, DC, MC, V. *Adam* (M), Burggasse 29 (09861–2364). 13 rooms, 12 with bath or shower. Charming rooms and gardens. Closed Nov.–Easter. No credit cards. *Roter Hahn* (M), Obere Schmiedgasse 21 (09861–5088). With ancient half-timbered balcony-corridors in the back. AE, MC, V.

Restaurants. *Baumeisterhaus* (M), Obere Schmiedgasse 3, Marktplatz (09861–3404). Perhaps the most attractive building in town, built in the 16th century; good food and wines and period furnishings. Reservations advised. AE, DC, MC, V.

Volkach. *Romantik Hotel "Zur Schwane"*, Hauptstr. 12 (09381–515). 40 beds. Has been an inn since 1404. Comfortable building, and fine restaurant serving Franconian specialties and wines from own vineyard. DC, MC, V.

Weissenburg. *Romantik Hotel "Rose"* (E), Rosenstr. 6 (09141–2096). 50 beds. Inn dating back to 1625; Baroque breakfast room, elegant gourmet restaurant, and Ratskeller serving Franken and Baden-Württemburg wines. AE, DC, MC, V.

Wirsberg. *Romantik Hotel "Post"*, Marktplatz 11 (09227–861). 90 beds, about half rooms with own bath. Roman-style indoor swimming pool, sauna, solarium, some luxury suites; good restaurant. Health facilities. AE, DC, MC, V.

Wunsiedel. *Kronprinz von Bayern* (M), Maximilianstr. 27 (09232–3509). With noted restaurant. AE, V. *Berggasthof Waldlust* (M), (09232–2103). A pleasant inn with garden and glassed-in terrace, on Luisenburg hill.

Würzburg. *Rebstock* (E), Neubaustr. 7 (0931–30930). All rooms with bath or shower; neo-Baroque building with good facilities, and gourmet restaurant serving Franconian specialties with the flair of *nouvelle cuisine.* Also a colorful wine tavern. AE, DC, MC, V. *Wittelsbacher Höh* (Ring Hotel) (E), Hexenbruchweg 10 (0931–42085). 53 rooms, all with own bath; five apartments. Located high above the city with a panoramic view across to the Marienfeste fortress. Rustic decor, sauna, solarium, garden-restaurant. AE, DC, MC, V. *Russ* (M), Wolfhartsgasse 1 (0931–50016). With good restaurant (trout specialties); garage. *Schloss Steinburg* (M), Auf dem Steinburg (0931–93061). Sited on the famous vineyard hill in Unterdürrbach; outdoor pool, terrace and dancing at weekends. AE, DC, MC, V. *Walfisch* (M), Am Pleidenturm 5 (0931–50055). Front rooms with view of river and fortress. V. *Gasthof Stadt Mainz* (I), Semmelstr. 39 (0931–53155). With good restaurant serving Franconian dishes, fine wines and *Rauchbier.* *Luitpoldbrücke* (I), Pleichertorstr. 26 (0931–50244). Near Luitpold bridge. AE, MC, V.

Restaurants. *Burggaststätten* (M), Marienburg Fortress (0931–47012). With terrace, fine view and a candlelit tower room. *Ratskeller* (M), Langgasse 1 (Beim Grafeneckart), (0931–13021). Franconian and international dishes, fine wines and beer; with *Ratsbierstuben* beer tavern. *Schiffbäuerin* (M), Katzengasse 7 (0931–42487). Specializing in local fish, including *Meerfischli. Schnabel* (M), Haugerpfarrgasse 10 (0931–53314). Freshwater fish from glass tank, and good meat dishes.

Taverns. All the following serve wines from their own vineyards, and all fall within M–I price categories. *Bürgerspital zum Heiligen Geist,* Theaterstr. 19 (0931–13861). A visit here is a must; the old tavern had several levels, hidden corners and leather-aproned waiters. DC, MC. *Hofkellerei Weinstuben,* Residenz Platz 1 (0931–54670). In a rebuilt annexe of the Residenz Palace; rambling, with garden. *Juliusspital,* Juliuspromenade 19 (0931–54080). Similar to the "Bürgerspital" and just as famous; Franconian dishes served. *Weinhaus zum Stachel* (M), Gressengasse 1 (0931–52770). Atmospheric, with particularly good food and Franconian wines.

CAMPING AND YOUTH HOSTELS. The whole region has numerous campsites, many delightfully located on riverbanks. All offer various sporting activities. Details can be obtained from the German National Tourist Office, regional and local Tourist Offices and from the German Camping Club. Sites become crowded in summer, so it's worth booking in advance.

A full list of all Youth Hostels in Franconia is available from the German Youth Hostel Association, Bülowstr. 26, 4930 Detmold, and from local and regional Tourist Offices. There is a particularly attractive hostel in Dinkelsbühl.

TOURIST INFORMATION. Ansbach, Rathaus, Martin-Luther Platz 1, Ansbach (0981–51243). **Bamberg,** Hauptwachstr. 16 (0951–26401), after office hours, contact Hotel Straub, Ludwigstr. 31 (0951–25838) for accommodations service. **Bayreuth,** Luitpoldplatz 9, Bayreuth (0921–22015). **Coburg,** Herrngasse 4/Markt, Postfach 666 (9561–95071). **Dinkelsbühl,** Verkehrsamt, Marktplatz, 8804 Dinkelsbühl (09851–90240). **Eichstätt,** Domplatz 18, Eichstätt (08421–7977). **Erlangen,** Rathausplatz, Erlangen (09131–25074). **Miltenberg,** Städtisches Verkehrsbüro, Engelplatz (im Rathaus), 8760 Miltenberg (09371–67272). **Nördlingen,** Städtisches Verkehrsamt, Marktplatz 2, 8860 Nördlingen (09081–4380). **Nürnberg,** Postfach 4248, Nürnberg (0911–23360), also information service in the main hall of the railway station and at the Hauptmarkt. **Rothenburg-ob-der-Tauber,** Marktplatz 2 (09861–40492). **Würzburg,** Pavillon vor dem Hauptbahnhof, Würzburg (0931–37436).

In addition there are a number of regional Tourist Offices for the area. The main office for **Franconia** is the *Fremdenverkehrsverband Franken,* Am Plärrer 14, 8500 Nürnberg 80 (0911–264202). There are also regional offices as follows: **Altmühltal,** Tourist Information Naturpark Altmühltal, Landratsamt, Residenzplatz 1, 8078 Eichstätt (08421–70238). **Fichtelgebirge,** Tourist Information Fichtelbirge, Bayreuther Str. 4, 8591 Fichtelberg (09272–6255). **Fränkische Schweiz,** Tourismus-Zentrale Fränkische Schweiz, Oberes Tor 1, 8553 Ebermannstadt (09194–8101). **Frankenwald,** Amtsgerichtsstrasse 21, 8640 Kronach (09261–748). **Romantische Strasse,** Tourist Information Land an der Romantischen Strasse, Kreisverkehrsamt, Crailsheimerstr. 1, 8800 Ansbach (0981–68232). **Spessart-Main-Odenwald,** Tourist Information Spessart-Main-Odenwald, Promendenweg 11, 8751 Heigenbrücken (06020–1694). **Steigerwald,** Tourist Information Steigerwald, Rathaus, 8602 Ebrach (09553–217).

HOW TO GET AROUND. By air. The main international airports are Nürnberg, Frankfurt and Munich, from where trains connect into the whole region. From Frankfurt there are regular flights between the Rhein-Main airport, Bayreuth and Hof.

By car. The region is served by four major Autobahn routes: the A7 from Hamburg, the A3 from Köln and Frankfurt, the A81 from Stuttgart, the A6 from Heilbronn, and the A9, Munich–Berlin. The most famous scenic route in the area is the Romantic Road (see pp. 32 and 190), but just as interesting is the eastern section of the *Burgenstrasse* (Castle Road) running west to east from Heidleberg to Nürnberg and the *Bocksbeutel Strasse* (or Franconian Wine Road) which follows the course of the Main from Zeil am Main along the wine-growing slopes of the river valley to Aschaffenburg, as well as the *Deutsche Ferien Strasse* (German Holiday Road), that runs from the Baltic to the Alps and crosses the region from northwest to southeast.

By train. The major rail centers are Würzburg and Nürnberg, both of which lie at the center of a series of major rail lines on the Inter-City network, such as the Stuttgart–Hof and Munich–Berlin routes, connecting with all parts of Germany. Good train services to many parts of the region are available from both cities.

There are also weekend packages and rail rover tickets available for Franconia. Details from regional and local Tourist Offices, or from main rail stations.

By bus. The Europabus route 190/190A runs along the Romantic Road from Würzburg to Füssen from June to September, via Frankfurt, Augsburg and Munich, and from March to November from Wiesbaden to Füssen. Route 189 runs along the Burgenstrasse from Mannheim in Baden-Württemberg along the Neckar Valley to Rothenburg ob der Tauber, from where buses of the German Railways continue the journey to Nürnberg, and the Romantic Road bus interconnects for Füssen. Local bus services inter-connect with rail stations throughout the region.

By bicycle. Bicycle hire is extremely popular in Franconia, and the tourist authorities have made great efforts to attract cyclists. The terrain of the Altmühltal valley is particularly suitable for cycling and the Tourist Information center of Eichstätt (Residenzplatz 1) issues leaflets with different suggestions for cycling tours and includes a list of addresses for hiring bicycles. You can hire bicycles in almost all main towns, or at major railway stations. There are a series of brochures detailing cycle tracks in the region (both in towns and in the country). The regional tourist office in Nürnberg will provide information about bicycle hire and cycling in the region.

By boat. A total of 15 different lines operate cruises from April to October through the region. Contact the Fremdenverkehrsverband Franken, Am Plärrer 14, Nürnberg, and ask for details of their *Weisse Flotte* cruises.

EXCURSIONS. The most popular excursion in the area is along the Romantische Strasse, the Romantic Road, the most famous scenic route in Germany. It is closely followed by the Burgenstrasse, the Castle Road, which also crosses part of Franconia. The tourist office in Nürnberg orga-

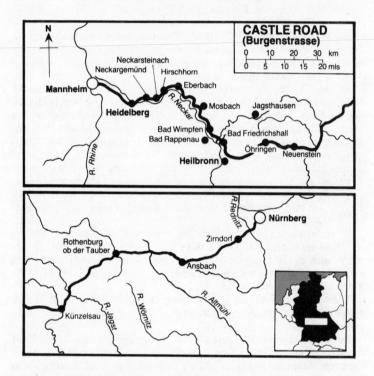

nizes bus tours following both roads to 1,000-year-old Rothenburg-ob-der-Tauber or Dinkelsbühl.

Other popular excursions include those to vineyards and to the many historic towns and villages of the area. Contact the local tourist office for details.

There are also regular boat excursions on the Main from Würzburg and Miltenberg, or on the Main-Danube Canal starting from Nürnberg. You can obtain timetables and information about cruises from the tourist offices in Würzburg and Miltenberg.

The *Fränkische Personen Schiffahrt* (FPS) company in Würzburg operate 9-, 11- or 13-day cruises on the Main and the Main-Danube Canal, among them the longest river cruise in the country, which takes in six different rivers and the Main-Danube Canal between Esslingen and Passau and covers 912 kms. FPS cruises also link up the Franconian waterways with the Rhine and Neckar. The cruises begin in Mainz with a stopover in Heidelberg, Ladenburg, Bad Wimpfen, Marbach and Esslingen. Information from the FPS. You can also join the cruise on the way and cruise the stretches, Aschaffenburg–Mainz; Aschaffenburg–Nürnberg; Mainz–Nürnberg; Aschaffenburg–Passau on the Main, Pegnitz and Main-Danube Canal as well as take bus excursions into the surrounding countryside from various points along the river (into the Altmühl Valley for example, Steigerwald or Swiss Franconia). There are also guided city tours (Aschaffenburg, Würzburg, Nürnberg, etc.), as well as new Study Cruises *(Studienfahrt)* for lovers of art and architecture. For full details about the cruises available, departure dates and accommodations, contact *Fränkische Personen Schiffahrt,* Kranenkai 1, 8799 Würzburg (0931–55356).

SPORTS. Sporting activities of all kinds are available here. Write regional Tourist Offices, or contact the German National Tourist Office, and ask for their *Unterhaltsamer Urlaub in Franken* brochures for the sport(s) you're interested in.

The most popular sports here are walking, riding, climbing and potholing, plus all manner of water sports (swimming pools, indoor and outdoor, are found in all major towns and cities, such as the modern Thermal Pool and Fitness Center in Rodach near Coburg), particularly in the newly created holiday region *Fränkische Seenland* (Franconian Lakeland), comprising man-made Atlmühlsee, Brombachsee and Rothsee, all located between Allersberg, Pleinfeld and Gunzenhausen, the latter acting as the main tourist center of the region with a brand new open-air thermal pool and activity center, *Juramar.* The project is still under construction, but the holiday facilities on all lakes except the Brombachsee are open; you can also swim in the many forest lakes. Similarly, tennis courts, including some indoor courts, are plentiful. Anglers are well-provided for, too. The lakes and rivers are well-stocked with trout, carp and pike; permits can be obtained from local Tourist Offices (small fee).

Hang-gliding and Gliding. Hang-gliding enthusiasts can take part in a 14-day training course in Stadtsteinach in the Frankenwald forest hills. Contact the Tourist Office, Badstr. 5, 8652 Stadtsteinach (09225–774). The strong air currents of the Rhön and Spessart regions are ideal for gliding, and you can participate in round-trip flights by contacting the Regional Tourist Office of the Spessart, Promenadenweg 11, 8776 Heigenbrücken, or the local tourist offices of Aschaffenburg, Marktheidenfeld, Miltenberg, Mömlingen.

Walking tours. The vast stretches of forest and numerous nature parks make much of North Bavaria and Franconia an ideal destination for walking holidays, a fact that the Germans have not been slow to exploit. In Franconia alone, there are over 40,000 km. (25,000 miles) of hiking trails, the greatest concentration (5,000 km.—3,125 miles) being in the Altmühltal Nature Park, Germany's largest nature park, and in the Frankenwald Forest. There are also marked trails (2,500 km.—1,560 miles) in the Fichtelgebirge mountains; and in Swiss Franconia, and in and around Coburg—including the romantic valleys of the Upper Main and Rodach that border on the foothills of the vast Thüringer Forest of East Germany. Between 28 July and 1 August 1988 Bamberg will host the German National Hiking Days and up to 25,000 are expected to participate in a hiking rally.

Well-orgnaized *Wanderen Ohne Gepäck* schemes, where your luggage is sent ahead every day to your next destination, are available for many areas. Other specialty walking tours include fossil hunting in the lime stone quarries around Solnhofen and Eichstätt in the Altmühltal. Details of all walking tours are available from local and regional Tourist Offices and the German National Tourist Office.

WINTER SPORTS. There are three well-established winter sports centers in Northern Bavaria: the Fichtelgebirge mountains; the Frankenwald Forest; and the Rhön mountains, including the Spessart. In all there are 70 chair and drag lifts serving the region, and one of the longest cable railways in Europe, the Ochsenkopfbahn in the Fichtelgebirge. In addition to the good downhill skiing, there is a vast network of well-prepared cross country tracks, plus tobogganing, curling, skating, horse-riding, and even winter hang-gliding. Conditions are generally good, and though the season is by no means as long as in the Alps (December to mid-March only), the low prices make this an area well-worth considering for a budget winter sports vacation.

Details from local and regional Tourist Offices, and from the German National Tourist Office.

Swiss Franconia also offers winter sports possibilities when snowfalls are heavy enough. For information (in German) about snow and winter sports in N. Bavaria you can call throughout the winter months: 09772–212 (for the Rhön), 09276–435 (Fichtelgebirge), and 09265–1919 (Frankenwald).

SOUTHWEST GERMANY

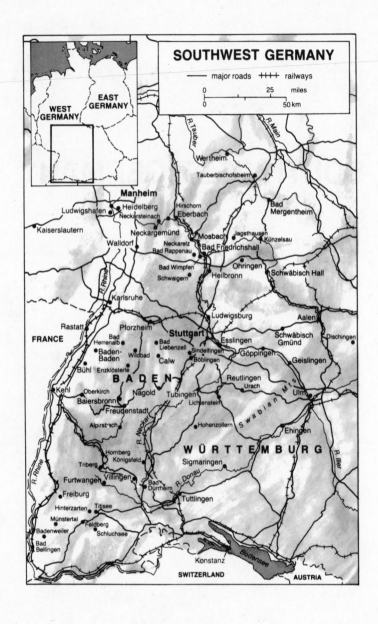

SOUTHWEST GERMANY

— major roads ┼┼┼┼ railways

0   25   miles
0   50 km

WEST GERMANY

EAST GERMANY

R. Tauber

R. Main

Wertheim

Tauberbischofsheim

Manheim

Ludwigshafen
Heidelberg
Hirschorn
Neckarsteinach
Eberbach
Bad Mergentheim

Kaiserslautern

Neckargemünd
Mosbach
Jagsthausen
Künzelsau

Walldorf
Neckarelz
Bad Friedrichshall
Bad Rappenau

Bad Wimpfen
Öhringen
Schwäbisch Hall
Schwaigern
Heilbronn

R. Rhine

Karlsruhe

Ludwigsburg
Aalen

Rastatt
Pforzheim
Stuttgart
Schwäbisch Gmünd
Dischingen

FRANCE
Bad Herrenalb
Bad Liebenzell
Esslingen

Baden-Baden
Wildbad
Sindelfingen
Göppingen
Geislingen
Böblingen

Bühl
Enzklösterle
Calw

B A D E N
Reutlingen
Urach
Ulm

Kehl
Oberkirch
Nagold
Tübingen

Baiersbronn
Lichtenstein
Swabian Mts

Freudenstadt
Hohenzollern
Ehingen

Alpirsbach

R. Neckar

W Ü R T T E M B U R G
R. Iller

Hornberg
Königsfeld
Sigmaringen

Triberg
Villingen
R. Donau

Furtwangen
Bad Dürrheim
Tuttlingen

Freiburg

Hinterzarten
Titisee

Münstertal
Feldberg

Badenweiler
Schluchsee

Bad Bellingen

R. Rhine

Konstanz
Bodensee

SWITZERLAND
AUSTRIA

STUTTGART AND THE
SWABIAN MOUNTAINS

Land of Gushing Rivers

Stuttgart, one of Germany's largest and most important industrial centers, lies towards the southwest of the country, north of the Black Forest and east of the Rhine. An ancient city that traces its origins back to the 10th century, it is also a great center of book publishing, as well as the site of the largest mineral water spring in western Europe. An hour or so by car from Stuttgart, either to the south or east, is the great mass of the Swabian Alps, the Schwäbische Alb, a mountain chain 200 km. (125 miles) long and 40 km. (25 miles) wide, running northeast from a point due south of Stuttgart towards Franconia. It offers an unforgettable mixture of scenery: high ridges and peaks, towering cliffs and deep ravines side by side with delightful valleys of meadowland, lightly-forested lands laced with springs and streams, and rich, open, agricultural areas.

Stuttgart

Stuttgart, as we say, traces its origins back to the 10th century when the Alemannic Duke Liutolf set up here his *Stutengarten,* a "stud garden" or stud farm, hence the horse in the Stuttgart coat-of-arms. It took a while—and a coincidence—before Stuttgart came of age. In 1311 the Counts of the nearby "Wirtenberg" saw their castle destroyed by the not very neighborly citizens of Esslingen and decided to move their seat to Stuttgart. When its rulers were promoted to Dukes in 1495, Stuttgart became the capital of the Duchy of Württemberg and in 1806, in the same manner, capital of the Kingdom of Württemberg.

Its history is reflected in the city's old buildings, restored after severe damage during the last war. The Altes Schloss, originally a 13th-century moated castle, was enlarged and remodeled for the Dukes of Württemberg in the 16th century in Renaissance style. Today it houses the Landesmuseum. Its splendidly arcaded courtyard once served as the ground for tournaments of armored knights. Next to the Old Castle, across the Schiller Square, stands the Gothic Stiftskirche (collegiate church), exactly reconstructed after the last war. Today it is the parish church of the Old Town but it has been called Stiftskirche since the time when the Counts of Württemberg moved to Stuttgart and brought along their canons as well as their dead ancestors; the canons were then installed and the ancestors re-buried in this church.

Schillerplatz, whose other sides are framed by the Prinzenbau (once the residence of the Crown Princes) and Alte Kanzlei (formerly the royal chancellery), is presided over by the Schiller statue and offers a lively, colorful picture on Tuesdays, Thursdays and Saturdays when it becomes the flower and vegetable market; in December it holds the traditional Stuttgart Christmas Market, well worth a visit. Beyond the Stiftskirche you can see the tall clock tower of the modern, postwar Rathaus, where a Glockenspiel plays different folksongs several times a day and even performs concert programs during the summer. Not far away, on Leonhardsplatz, is the late-Gothic Leonhard Church constructed by Aberlin Jörg, the court architect of the Württemberg rulers in the 15th century. In the narrow streets south of the City Hall are a few Old Town houses which survived the last war, and the graceful wrought-iron Hans-im-Glück Fountain in the Geiss Strasse.

Neues Schloss

On the north side of Altes Schloss is the Baroque Neues Schloss, a vast palace which served as the residence for the Kings of Württemberg. It was painstakingly restored after World War II and its state rooms with marble walls, frescos, crystal chandeliers and Empire furniture are now used by the government of Baden-Württemberg for glittering receptions. Neues Schloss faces the great park-like Schloss Square, with a 60-meter (200-ft.) granite column monument from 1846 commemorating the rule of King Wilhelm I of Württemberg, and flanked on the opposite side by the neoclassic Königsbau building along Königstrasse, the main business artery of Stuttgart.

To the north of Neues Schloss is the beginning of the large Schlossgarten park. Here is the lovely Theater Lake with the cupola-crowned Kunstgebäude (house of art) on one side, while the other side is lined with the glass and cubic Landtag (state parliament), the turn-of-the-century Grosses Haus (opera house) and the ultramodern, hexagonal Kleines Haus (drama and comedy). This might well be the goal for any visitor to Stuttgart interested in the performing arts, for the state companies are internationally famous, and especially the ballet company. In fact, Stuttgart serves as the ideal example of state-subsidized theater. Most provincial centers in Germany have resident drama, opera and ballet companies with enviable standards, but the Stuttgart Ballet Company has reached a position of eminence on the world scene that would make a visit to their home town worthwhile to see one of their performances alone.

Even before the war Stuttgart was known for its advanced designs in contemporary building and such great architects as Ludwig Mies van der Rohe, Walter Gropius, Le Corbusier and Hans Scharoun, among many others, collaborated on the construction of the famous Weissenhof colony of apartment houses. War destruction brought the necessity of reconstruction and with it the realization of the most advanced architectural plans, encouraged by the city fathers. In addition to the Landtag and Kleines Haus mentioned earlier, some of the newest, most outstanding examples of contemporary architecture include: the asymmetrical and wavy-lined Liederhalle by Rolf Gutbrod and Adolf Abel, with superior acoustics in its three concert halls (guided tours on certain weekdays); the twin skyscrapers and the library of the Technical University; the 215-meter (700-ft.) television tower designed by Dr. Fritz Leonhardt and the first of its kind in the world located on the Bopser hill and revealing a fine panoramic view from its observation platform.

The Garden City

In view of all its industry and 20th-century building, one might expect Stuttgart to be, like too many modern cities, a prison of steel and cement. Actually, it is a garden city. Only 25 percent of its area is built over; 50 percent consists of parks, vineyards, orchards, gardens, meadows and fields, while 25 percent is covered by woods. In the suburbs you can still see genuine farmhouses with cattle in the pastures, and the vineyards reach almost downtown. The finest laid-out park on the heights is Killesberg and you can also enjoy an exceptional view of the city from such vantage points as the Zeppelin-Aussichtsplatte on Zeppelin Strasse in the northwest, Eugenplatz and Haussmann Strasse above the Schlossgarten to the east, from the upper sections of Alte Weinsteige to the south and Hasenbergsteige in the southwest area.

On the right bank of the Neckar is the suburb of Untertürkheim, the home of Daimler-Benz, oldest automobile factory in the world, which produces Mercedes cars and exports half of its yearly production to practically every country in the world. The impressive automobile museum belonging to the factory is now housed in a new building, while in Bad Cannstatt, located next door to the northwest, you can visit the original workshop of Gottlieb Daimler at Taubenheim Strasse 13.

Stuttgart is not thought of as a spa, but in its Bad Cannstatt and Berg sections it has 18 mineral springs and is Europe's second biggest (after Budapest) source of mineral water. Some of the springs feed the three mineral water swimpools and the extensive cure facilities. It is also not usually thought of as a wine and fruit center but Stuttgart is one of the biggest wine-producing communes in Germany, possessing some 1,100 acres of vineyards actually inside the city limits, and the biggest orchard community in Germany with eight million fruit trees growing within a 32-km. (20-mile) radius from the city center. Better known is the leading role of Stuttgart in the field of publishing: about 200 publishers are established here (among them such veterans as Cotta, the original publisher of Goethe and

Schiller, and Württembergische Bibelanstalt, the oldest and still the biggest bible publisher in Germany), along with 160 printing establishments and 300 bookbinderies.

The suburb of Bad Cannstatt is a spa in its own right with a neo-Classical Kursaal in a lovely Kurpark. It is best known, however, for the lively Cannstatt Folk Festival, a 16-day yearly event in late September and early October, which was celebrated for the first time in 1818 in thanksgiving for a good crop after years of poor harvests and famine. 1988 will see a particularly spectacular parade marking the 170th anniversary of the festival. Still retaining its basic agricultural character, it is staged on the Cannstatter Wiesen (Cannstatt Meadows) along the right bank of the Neckar and its salient points are the great parade on the first Sunday, with Swabians from all the Swabian areas participating, and great fireworks displays.

At Ludwigsburg, just north of Stuttgart, everything centers about the castle-palace. The Ludwigsburger Schloss, inspired by Versailles, is the largest Baroque palace in Germany, with a fine park, its own theater, a Baroque and a Rococo chapel, and a huge barrel in its cellars. It also has one of Germany's finest collections of Baroque art. April to October it is the background for illuminations and firework displays. Ludwigsburg, noted also for its summer concerts and garden show, is another point from which to visit the Maulbronn Monastery, as well as nearby Marbach, birthplace of the great German poet, Schiller.

The Swabian Mountains

The gateway to the Swabian Mountains (Schwäbische Alb) is generally considered the former Imperial town of Reutlingen, due south of Stuttgart. However, Aalen, located in the eastern section of the mountains, makes a generally more convenient starting point for an exploration of the area. From Aalen, we describe a tour along the eastern and southern slopes of the chain, returning along the northwestern side. You can turn off this route into the heights at more or less any point and the result will be much the same. You will find beautiful mountain country, little towns and villages with half-timbered steep-roofed gables, dignified old churches and castles more or less anywhere.

Aalen is easily reached from Stuttgart on a recently opened stretch of autobahn and fast highway (the B29) which runs due east via Waiblingen following the Rems Valley. The next town of importance on the way is Schwäbisch Gmünd, a former free imperial town and the oldest remaining city from the period of the Hohenstaufen emperors (Stauferzeit). Until a few decades ago it was primarily a goldsmith and jewelry-making center, though today its importance is mainly industrial. It has a fine Gothic cathedral (Heilig Kruez Münster) with exquisite portals and stained glass windows, and the unusual Romanesque-style Church of St. John (Johanniskirche) with a richly decorated facade. Just north lies Lorch, in the center of the Rems Valley, with the ruins of an early 12th-century abbey in the woods above town, of which the 11th-century abbey church remains intact. Southeast of Schwäbisch Gmünd, near the town of Weiler, is the Hornberg, a high plateau which affords a good view over hilly Swabia. Another impressive vantage point is found at Hohenstaufen, south of Schwäbisch Gmünd on the road to Göppingen (site of an interesting Renaissance castle). Hohenstaufen lies at the foot of the Hohenstaufen Mountain, on the peak of which are the rather scanty remains of the fortress of the same name, seat of the family of Hohenstaufen emperors, the most important dynasty from the 11th to the 13th century.

Continuing eastwards following the River Rems you will reach Aalen, another former free imperial town with both an old and new Town Hall, and many venerable houses. From here you might want to take a side trip to the southeast to see the grandiose Baroque abbey church at Neresheim and the nearby Katzenstein Castle. South of Aalen on the Swabian Mountain Road is Heidenheim, dominated by the Hellenstein Castle. A few kilometers southeast is Giengen, home of the famous Steiff toy animals. A bust of President Theodore Roosevelt was unveiled here in 1958 to celebrate the 100th anniversary of his birth, for it was in Giengen, in 1903, that the original Teddy Bear was made and named after him.

Ulm, on the Danube, possesses one of the most beautiful cathedrals in Germany, a 14th-century Gothic structure whose 160-meter (528-foot) tower is the highest church tower in the world. Inside the cathedral are some wonderfully-carved choir stalls by Jörg Syrlin, a 15th-century master, which are as spectacular in their way as the cathedral is as a whole. The old city walls, with their gates and towers, the old town houses, the picturesque fishermen's and craftsmen's quarter (Schiefes Haus) along the River Blau, an arm of the Danube, the Rathaus, and the museums, particularly the unique German Bread Museum, are also worth seeing. Ulm is also noted as the birthplace of Albert Einstein.

The Hochschule für Gestaltung (School of Design) is situated at Ulm. It is the successor to the famous Dessauer Bauhaus, which originated the movement to integrate the arts into commercial and industrial fields. It also created a new form of modern design and architecture.

At Ulm one of the first attempts at flying was made as long ago as 1811 by Albrecht Ludwig Berblinger, known to posterity as the "Flying Tailor of Ulm." The poor but proud tailor devised some sort of homemade wings that fastened over each arm, and announced that he would make a flight over the Danube in honor of a state visit to Ulm by the King of Württemberg. Watched by some 10,000 onlookers, Berblinger leaped from the town wall with his weird-looking wings and plummeted like a stone into the Danube. His wife later sold the wings to an umbrella maker who used the silk for parasols.

As a major road and rail junction, Ulm is a good starting point for explorations south to the Allgäu region, or southwest into the Swabian Mountains; excursions can be arranged by the Ulm Tourist Office.

Stalactites and Scholars

Southwestward of Ulm lies Blaubeuren, with more of Syrlin's superb carvings in the Benedictine monastery, and Zwiefalten, with the Benedictine church, one of the best examples of late Baroque in South Germany. In the vicinity is the Friedrichshöhle, an interesting cave. South is Riedlingen in the upper Danube Valley, with 14th-century frescos in St. George's Church, picturesquely built over the river.

Following the Danube upstream you come to Sigmaringen with the impressive castle of the Princes of Hohenzollern, housing a very fine museum and gallery of paintings; Hausen, with Werenwag Castle on top of a rocky hill and two more castles in the vicinity; Beuron, with the famous Benedictine abbey which has fostered arts and choral singing since 1077 and whose present church is a fine example of the Baroque; the small industrial town of Tuttlingen amid beautiful woods, with Honberg castle ruins and a fine view from the top of the nearby Witthoh (854 meters/2800 feet).

From Tuttlingen you cross the southwestern end of the Schwäbische Alb to Rottweil, passing through the summer and winter resort of Spaichingen at the foot of the Dreifaltigkeitsberg, known particularly as a gliding center. Rottweil on the Neckar, once a free imperial town, has preserved several of its medieval gates, towers, walls, patrician houses and churches, and has recently restored its "Roman Baths," built between A.D. 110 and 130. Traveling downstream along the Neckar you reach Tübingen through Balingen with an old Zollern castle with water tower and Hechingen which has preserved some of its fortifications and two castles.

Six km. (four miles) south of Hechingen, on a high elevation, is Hohenzollern Castle, the original family seat of the Hohenzollerns, the royal and later imperial house of Germany, and a magnificent structure with many artistic treasures. This is a castle straight from medieval legend, worth seeing for itself and for the tremendous view from the battlements.

East of Hechingen, along the Schwäbische Albstrasse, you come to a speleologist's heaven. For there are some 70 fantastic stalactite caverns inside these mountains, particularly at Erpfingen, where the Karlshöhle and Bärenhöhle are located, and near Lichtenstein Castle (worth visiting for its own sake) where the Nebelhöhle, a complex labyrinth of caves, is to be found. At the foot of Lichtenstein Castle, which stands on a 230-meter (760-foot) cliff above the valley, is the pleasant little town and summer vacation spot of Honau.

Further northeast on the Swabian Mountain Road in a deep valley is Urach, a climatic spa resort with a half-timbered main square and some notable waterfalls about three km. (two miles) away from where, traveling northwestwards along part of yet another scenic route traversing the region—the Schwäbische Dichter Strasse (Swabian Poets' Road)—you reach Reutlingen. Here the road leads westwards to yet another of the former imperial free towns along the Neckar—Tübingen—a famous university town as well. Thiis fact accounts for the large number of eminent intellectuals who have lived here—the poet Hölderlin, the philosophers Hegel and Friedrich von Schelling. The university, founded in 1477, is one of the oldest educational institutions in Europe. Melanchthon, the famous theologian and author, and Johannes Kepler, Germany's well-known astronomer, both studied here. It possesses many fine buildings—the Gothic Collegiate Church, the massive Pfalzgrafen Castle, the old houses clustered around the market square, including the 15th-century Rathaus, the late Gothic Stiftskirche, and the 16th-century Alte Aula, part of the old university, with its students' prison. It is a pleasant place to spend a few days, and one where admirers of Neckar Valley scenery can take their choice of the river in two moods—upstream from Tübingen it is turbulent and rapid; downstream from the same point it becomes calmer and flows sedately around great sweeping curves on its way to the Rhine.

PRACTICAL INFORMATION FOR STUTTGART

TELEPHONES. The telephone code for Stuttgart is 0711. To call any number in this chapter, unless otherwise specified, this prefix must be used. Within the city, no prefix is required.

HOTELS. The city has some 200 hotels ranging from the luxurious to simple but adequate and clean rooms in small guest houses; be warned that prices are among the highest in Germany. It is advisable to reserve in advance, particularly in the better establishments. The tourist offices also offer an accommodations service. (2228–236 and 2228–237).

Deluxe

Am Schlossgarten. Schillerstr. 23 (299911). 125 rooms. In the large Schlossgarten near the main railway station; smart restaurant and Swabian-style tavern, two-floor café with terrace; good bar. AE, DC, MC, V.

Airport-Hotel-Movenpick. Randstr. (79070). 160 beds, all rooms with own bath. At the airport; restaurant. Modern. AE, DC, MC, V.

Europe. Siemesstr. 26–28 in the Feuerbach suburb (815091). Close to the Fair Grounds, about 5 km. (3 miles) from the main rail station. 252 beds, all rooms with bath/shower. Restaurant. AE, DC, MC, V.

Graf Zeppelin. Arnulf-Klett Platz 7 (299881). A Steigenberger hotel. 280 rooms, and airconditioned. Opposite the main station; 3 top restaurants offering Swabian specialties and décor, American bar, nightclub, indoor pool, garage. Extremely expensive. AE, DC, MC, V.

Holiday Inn. Schwertstr. 65 (07031–81088). 10 km. (6 miles) southwest of Stuttgart in Sindelfingen, near the autobahn. With fine restaurant. DC, V.

Novotel. Korntalerstr. 207 (801065). In Stammheim. 234 beds, pool.

Park Hotel. Villastr. 21 (280161). 100 beds, 50 baths; in the Berg section, quiet location, good food. Fine *Villa Berg* restaurant. AE, DC, MC, V.

Royal. Sophienstr. 35 (625050). 90 rooms; in the center but quiet location. An elegant restaurant with fine cuisine; bar; TV in most rooms. AE, DC, MC.

Stuttgart International. Plieninger Str. 100 (72021). 160 rooms; situated at Möhringen, about halfway between airport and city near the Degerloch autobahn exit; indoor pool, sauna, 4 restaurants, bar, café, nightclub and, in summer, a Viennese-style garden café. AE, DC, MC, V.

Waldhotel Schatten. Gewand Schatten 2 (681051). In the suburb of Vaigingen-Büsnau 15 minutes from city center. Holiday atmosphere in noble country manor style. Individually furnished rooms, all with bath; Swabian specialties served in the restaurant. DC.

Expensive.

Azenberg. Seestr. 116 (221051). Quiet location, indoor pool and sauna. No restaurant. AE, DC, MC, V.

Buchenhof. Hasenbergsteige 90 (652018). On the heights with a beautiful view of the city. No restaurant. AE, MC.

Espenlaub. Charlottenstr. 27 (240022). 23 rooms, most with shower. Very centrally located. Clean, simple and pleasant. No restaurant. v.

Inter-City Hotel. Arnulf-Klett-Str. 2 (299801). 135 beds; located within the main railway station, with restaurant. AE, DC, V.

Ketterer. Marienstr. 3 (294151). In city center on a pedestrian mall. 100 beds, all rooms with bath/shower; good restaurant. AE, DC, MC, V.

Kötzle. Eschenauer Str. 27 (872013). 14 rooms, all doubles with bath or shower. In the northern suburb of Rot. Can be reached with U-Bahn to Zuffenhausen, Schozacher Strasse. No restaurant.

Kronen Hotel. Kronenstr. 48 (299661). 88 rooms, most with own bath; very comfortable, pleasant hotel near the city; particularly good breakfasts. No restaurant. AE, DC, MC, V.

Rotenberg Hotel. Stettener Str. 87 (331293). In the Untertürkheim-Rotenberg suburb, in vineyards. No restaurant. DC.

Ruff. Friedhofstr. 21 (250161). East of the main station. All rooms with own bath; indoor pool and restaurant. AE, DC, MC, V.

Moderate

Mack. Kriegerstr. 5–7 (291927). Near main rail station. Half of rooms with shower/bath; no restaurant.

Pflieger. Kriegerstr. 9–11 (221878). Half of rooms with own shower/bath. Restaurant and wine tavern.

Rieker. Friedrichsstr. 3 (221311). Opposite the station; modern. All rooms with bath or shower. AE, MC.

Wartburg Hospiz. Lange Str. 49 (20450). Fairly centrally located. All rooms with bath or shower. Restaurant. AE, DC, MC, V.

Inexpensive

Fremd Gambrinus. Möhringer Landstr. 26 (731767). Some rooms with own bath; in the suburb of Vaihingen. Near the U-Bahn station Vaihingen-Schillerplatz. Restaurant.

Köhler. Neckarstr. 209 (2622004). On the edge of the Schlossgarten.

Krämer's Burgerstuben. Gablenberger Hauptstr. 4 (465481). Simple gasthof in Gablenberg suburb.

Camping

The privately owned **Campingplatz Stuttgart** (556696) is on the Neckardamm, at the edge of the Cannstatter Wasen meadows, where the famous folk festival is held each autumn. Completely renovated in 1986. Open April to end September.

Youth Hostels

Stuttgarter Jugendherberge. Haussmannstr. 27 (241583). Entrance in Werastr., corner Kernerstr., about 15 minutes' walk from the main station. Reopened after extensive refurbishment.

HOW TO GET AROUND. From the airport. The international airport of Stuttgart is located 13 km. (eight miles) south of the city near Echterdingen. Bus line "A" connects daily between the main station, the City Air Terminal (at the corner of Kronenstr. and Lautenschlagerstr.), and the airport. Departures from the station every 20–30 minutes between 5.25

A.M. and 10.55 P.M. Departure from the City Air Terminal five minutes later. In the opposite direction, buses leave the airport every 20–30 minutes between 6.25 A.M. and 11.35 P.M.

Taxis can be found at the main station, the City Air Terminal and the airport.

City transportation. An efficient streetcar and bus network (VVS) connects all the important points in the city and the suburbs. The central bus station is on the east side (Cannstatter Strasse) of the main railway station. The new S-Bahn now has several lines in operation; the main station is located under the main railway station square.

Visitors to Stuttgart should buy a 24-hour ticket. This costs DM.7.50 (children DM.3.20), and is valid on all public transport within the city environs, including the cogwheel railway from Marienplatz to Degerloch and the cable-car at Südheimer Platz. Or you can purchase multiple-ride tickets, also valid for all forms of public transport, from almost all bus and tram stops and at the U- and S-Bahn stations.

Free maps of the transport network and instructcions in English as to how to buy and cancel tickets are available from the "i-Punkt" information in the Klett Passage at the Hauptbahnhof.

From the central bus station most buses of the Stuttgart Public Transport System (VVS) depart, also German Railways (DB) and private buses.

Taxis can be reserved from the *Taxi-Auto-Zentrale* by dialing 566061.

TOURIST INFORMATION. The principal tourist office—"Touristik Zentrum i-Punkt" (recognizable by the "i" sign)—is in the Klett Passage at the main station. They provide information about the city, sell copies of the monthly calendar of events *Monatsspiegel,* have an accommodations service and sell tickets for city sightseeing tours, nightclub tours, theaters, concerts and sporting events. The main office is: *Verkehrsamt der Landeshauptstadt Stuttgart,* Lautenschlagerstr. 3, Postfach 870, 7000 Stuttgart 1 (2228240). Open Mon. to Sat. 8.30 A.M.–10 P.M., Sun. 11 A.M.–8 P.M. An informative guide to the city in both German and English is published by the *Trade Fair Association,* Messe und Kongress-Gesellschaft, Am Kochenhof 16, 7000 Stuttgart 1.

USEFUL ADDRESSES. Car rental. *Avis,* Katharinenstr. 18, and at the airport (7901–504). *Europcar,* Charlottenstr. 42 (247389). *Herz,* Hohenstaufenstr. 18 (643044), also at the airport.

Consulates. *United States,* Urbanstr. 7 (210221). *Great Britain,* Kriegsbergstr. 28 (293216).

Emergencies. Police (89901). Ambulance (280211).

Lost and found. *City Lost Property Office,* (Fundbüro) Eberhardsstr. 61a (216–2016). *German Railways Lost Property Office,* Wolframstr. 19 (2092–5468). *Stuttgart Public Transport Lost Property Office,* Filderstr. 47 (2505–3360).

Post Offices. *Main Post Office,* Bolzstr. 3, alongside the Königsbau, main hall of central station, both open till 11.00 P.M. weekdays.

Travel agents. *American Express,* Lautenschlagerstr. 3. *Hapag-Lloyd,* Königstr. 21. *Wagons Lits/Cook,* Königstr. 45.

TOURS. City sightseeing tours are arranged by the "i-Punkt" tourist service. Two- or three-hour bus tours with guide depart daily from outside the Hindeburg building opposite the main station. Timetable and tickets from the tourist office at the main station. There is also, year round, an evening tour—"Stuttgarter Nächte"—on Wed., Thurs. and Fri. from 7.30 P.M. to 1.30 A.M. For details and reservations, again contact the "i-Punkt."

Boat tours. From the end of March to the end of October, the *Neckar Personen Schiffahrt* (NPS) operates a series of different cruises on the Neckar, from the pier opposite the main entrance to the Wilhelma Zoo in Bad Cannstatt. For details write to the *Neckar Personen Schiffahrt,* Schiffsanlegestelle Wilhelma, 7000 Stuttgart 50 (541073), or contact the tourist office.

EXCURSIONS. A large number of excursions into the areas surrounding the city can be made from Stuttgart. The Neckar Valley, the idyllic wine villages of the Remstal Valley to the east, the Black Forest, and of course the Swabian Mountains themselves, are all within easy reach of the city. A large number of organized bus tours are available—ask at the tourist information office for details. Alternatively, you can reach many places on public transport. Again, ask at the tourist office. All bus tours depart from the bus depot at the main rail station (Hauptbahnhof).

In addition there are some excellent walking tours in areas around the city. Perhaps the best is the *Stuttgarter Rundwanderweg,* which follows the heights around Stuttgart. The whole route is well-marked, and many places en route are connected to the city by public transport. Maps from the tourist office.

There are also several walking tours through the vineyards, with signs en route giving information about wine cultivation. Similar informative hiking routes run through the forests for lovers of animal and bird life. Ask at the tourist office for information about *Weinlehrpfad* and *Waldlehrpfad.*

SPORTS. Stuttgart has many sports facilities available. The largest stadium is the Neckar Stadium in Bad Cannstatt which can accommodate 75,000 spectators. Soccer games and track and field competitions take place there.

The second largest and most impressive sports and special events hall is the new *Hans-Martin-Schleyer Halle,* in the Mercedesstrasse, one of the most modern in Germany.

Tickets for all sporting events are available from the Advanced Booking Office *(Vorverkauf)* in the Kartenhäusle at the Kleinen Schlossplatz, Mon. to Fri. 8.30 A.M.–6.30 P.M., Sat. 8.30 A.M.–1.30 P.M. (295583). Tickets are also available directly from the ticket offices of the relevant stadiums. For more details of all Stuttgart's sporting events and facilities, ask at the "i-Punkt" for the brochure "Spiel und Sport in Stuttgart."

Golf. The local courses are The Solitude Club at Monsheim on Engelberg, and Neckertal between Kornwestheim and Aldingen. (For details contact Stuttgarter Golfclub, Böblinger Strasse 72).

Horseback riding. The Neckar Stadium also has a section for riding tournaments. For saddle horses and riding instructors contact Reitverein, Am Kräherwald 101, or Reitschule Hölzel in Möhringen.

Rowing and sailing. Boats can be rented on the Neckar bank in Bad Cannstatt between Gaisburger and König-Karls-Brücke.

Skating. Ice skating at Königsträssel in Degerloch, and the ice skating center in Reutlingen, Rommelsbacher Str. 55, from mid-Sept. to the end of Mar. From May through Aug. the rinks are converted for roller skating enthusiasts.

Swimming. There is a choice between mineral and regular water pools. Among several mineral water pools: Mineralbad, Leuze, König-Karls-Brücke; Mineralbad Berg, Neckarstr. 260; Mineralbad Breuninger, on roof of Breuninger Kaufhaus; Mineralbad Cannstatt, Sulzerrainstr. 4. Numerous outdoor pools include one on Killesberg.

Tennis. Stuttgart has 19 tennis courts, and other courts are available at tennis clubs spread around the city. There is a tennis school at Sonnenberg.

PARKS AND GARDENS. There are numerous parks and open areas all over the city—in fact Stuttgart is known as Germany's "Greenest City." **Hohenheim Botanischer Garten.** Botanical Gardens in the grounds of Schlosshohenheim.

Höhenpark Killesberg. On the heights in the north of the city. Has narrow-gauge railway and chairlift.

Rosensteinpark. English-style park laid out in 1823. Borders directly on to the Unteren Schlossgarten park and stretches as far as the Löwentor gate.

Schlossgartenanlagen. The most well-known of the city parks. Former royal gardens belonging to the King's Palace, laid out in 1805–1818. Site of the German Horticultural Shows of 1961 and 1977. Begins in the city center at the Neues Schloss palace and runs almost four km. (two miles) to the banks of the Neckar where it adjoins Rosenstein Park.

Silberburganlage und Karlshöhe. In the west of the city with fine view from the terraces; cafeteria.

HISTORIC BUILDINGS AND SITES. Altes Schloss (Old Palace). am Schlossplatz, Schillerplatz and Karlsplatz. Built in 1320 as a moated castle (the Karlsplatz wing); other wings from 1553–70. Houses the Regional Museum.

Alte Kanzlei (Old Chancellory). am Schillerplatz, built 1541–43, extended 1566 and rebuilt in 1952.

Fernsehturm (Television Tower). Built in 1954–56, 217-meter (700-foot) high tower with observation platform and restaurant. Modern symbol of Stuttgart.

Neues Schloss (New Palace). am Schlossplatz, built 1746–1807, and renovated in 1958–64. Reception rooms of the state government; Ministries of Finance and Culture in the side wings.

Schellenturm. Weberstr. 72. Last remaining tower of the old city walls and ramparts. Built 1564 and so named since 1811 because of the "Schellenwerkern" or prisoners working chained together with hand- and foot-irons called "Schellen."

Schloss Rosenstein (Rosenstein Palace). In Bad Cannstatt, above the Neckar. Built as regal country residence in 1824; renovated in 1950–60 as Regional Museum of Natural History.

Schloss Solitude (Solitude Palace). Located in the forest west of the city. Built 1763–67 by von Weyhing, and vastly renovated. Daily guided tours.

Wilhelma. Neckartalstr. in Bad Cannstatt, summer residence of Wilhelm I. Built in Moorish style in 1842–53 by Ludwig Zanth. Today houses the zoo and botanical gardens in its park, and is Stuttgart's most visited place of interest.

CHURCHES. Hospitalkirche. Hospitalstrasse/Büchsenstr. Built
1471–93 by Aberlin Jörg; the tower in 1729. A beautiful crucifixion group in the Choir by Hans Seyffer dating from 1501.
Leonhardskirche (St. Leonhard's Church). Hauptstätter Str. on Leonhardsplatz. Built by Aberlin Jörg in 1463–66.
Stiftskirche (Collegiate Church). am Schillerplatz, built on the site of a Roman Basilica by Hänslin and Aberlin Jörg in 1433–1531 in late-Gothic style. The West Tower is 58 meters (190 feet) high.
Veitskapelle (St. Veit's Chapel). In the Neckar town of Mühlhausen. Most important piece of Gothic architecture in Stuttgart. Built 1380–85 by members of the Prague Bauhütte and Court art school.

MUSEUMS. Most of Stuttgart's museums have free admission. Almost
all are closed on Mondays. Information about special exhibitions and opening hours can be found in the monthly calendar of events *Monatsspiegel,* available from the tourist office.
Bibelmuseum (Bible Museum). Balingerstr. 31 in Möhringen (720030). 3,000 bibles in many languages and from over four centuries, including the Luther Bible of 1545 with wood-carved covers.
Daimler-Benz-Museum. In Mercedes-Benz Works in Untertürkheim (special bus D from the bus station) (172578). Huge vehicle collection includes the first motorcycle constructed by Daimler and Maybach, the first motorboat, the first aircraft engine and the first cars by Benz and Daimler.
Deutsche Spielkartenmuseum (German Playing Card Museum). Schönbuchstr. 32 (798–6335). In Leinfelden-Echterdingen suburb. Impressive collection of playing cards from all over the world.
Galerie der Stadt Stuttgart (City Art Gallery). In Kunstgebäude on Schlossplatz (295566). 19th- and 20th-century paintings by artists from the State of Baden-Württemberg. Periodic exhibitions organized by the *Württembergischer Kunstverein* in the halls on the other side of the same building.
Lindenmuseum. Hegelplatz 1 (2050–3222). One of the largest ethnological museums in Germany; Peruvian masks to Javanese figures.
Museum für Naturkunde (Natural History Museum). Located in Rosenstein Palace (541071). Interesting exhibition on animals from various lands.
Planetarium. Mittlerer Schlossgarten. Founded in 1928 and rebuilt after total destruction during the war. One of the most modern of its kind in the world. Fascinating electronic "time machine" and aerospace section.
Staatsgalerie (Regional Art Gallery). Konrad Adenauer Str. 32 (212–5050). Comprising the Alte Staatsgalerie (Old Gallery), with an outstanding collection of paintings from the Middle Ages to the 19th century, including Holbein, Rembrandt, and Tintoretto, as well as the ultramodern Neue Galerie designed by English architect James Stirling, with an equally compelling collection of modern works, including masterpieces by Renoir, Monet, Cézanne, Modigliani. Also one of the most important and largest Picasso collections in Germany.

Stadtisches Lapidarium. Mörikestr. 24, in a garden. Antiquities, statues, gravestones, architecturally interesting remains of old buildings.
Württembergisches Landesmuseum In Altes Schloss (Old Castle). History, culture and art in Württemberg and other Swabian lands from the Stone Age to the turn of the century.

THEATERS. Stuttgart has a rich year-round theatrical and concert program, of international standard. Tickets for concerts, ballet, theater and other performances can be bought in advance from Touristikzentrum "i-Punkt", Klett Passage (299411); Kartenhäusle, Kleiner Schlossplatz (295583); Musik Mayer, Bad Cannstatt (561730). Notable theaters include:

Altes Schauspielhaus, Kleine Königstr. (225505). Classical and modern plays.
Komödie im Marquardt. Bolzstr. 4 (291484). Boulevard theater on the Schlossplatz.
Renitenztheater. Königstr. 17 (297075). Political-literary-satirical cabaret.
Stuttgarter Marionettentheater (now called *Puppen & Figuren Theater*). Eberhardtstr. 61A (6872973).
Theater der Altstadt. Charlottenplatz, lower floor (244342). From classical to repertory performances.
Theater im Westen. Rotebühlstr. 89, at Feuersee lake (623154). Performances in different styles, including poetry readings and cabaret.
Variete Theater Killesberg (Summer Theater at Killesberg Park). International variety from 1 May to 31 Oct. Tickets, tel. 251197.
Württembergische Staatstheater (State Theater). Oberer Schlossgarten (20321). For ticket reservations tel. 203–2444. Comprises the "Grosses Haus" (literally "big house") for opera and ballet; the "Kleines Haus" ("little house") for plays as well as the internationally acclaimed Stuttgart Ballet Company; and the Neues Kammertheater housed in the Staatsgalerie, for workshop theater.

MUSIC. Stuttgart is an important musical center with a State Academy of Music, and five renowned orchestras: *Württemberg State Orchestra, Stuttgart Philharmonic Orchestra, Symphonic Orchestra* of the South German Radio, the *Paul-Gerhardt-Chamber-Orchestra,* and the *Stuttgart Chamber Orchestra* which has toured North and South America and Japan in addition to Western Europe. Most outstanding among many choirs are the *Stuttgart Philharmonic Choir* and *Hymnus-Chorknaben,* a boys' choir.

Concerts are given mainly in the Beethoven Hall, Mozart Hall and Silcher Hall of the ultramodern *Liederhalle,* in *Gustav-Siegle-Haus,* and in the halls of *Süddeutscher Rundfunk* and of the *Hochschule für Musik.* Newly opened in 1988 is the *Forum am Schlosspark* cultural center, theater, and concert hall out at Ludwigsburg. Church concerts are scheduled mainly in Stiftskirche and Markuskirche. Outdoor serenade concerts are performed during summer in Hospitalhof and Paul-Gerhardt-Hof and light music on summer weekends in Killesberg Park, on Schlossplatz and in the Kurpark of Bad Cannstatt. Tickets for concerts only can be purchased from *Südwestdeutsche Konzert-direktion,* Charlottenplatz 17 (290349); open Mon. to Fri. 10–6.

SHOPPING. The Königstrasse between the main station (Hauptbahnhof) and the Wilhelmsbau, for the most part a pedestrian zone, is the main shopping street. From this central area a network of smaller side streets branch off. In particular Calwer Str., with the Calwer Passage Arcade and the Klett Passage Arcade, underneath the main station square, are worth investigating.

A most luxurious department store, unique in its kind in Germany and comparable to stores such as Bloomingdale's or Harrods, is *Breuninger* on Marktplatz.

Every Saturday a flea market is held on the Karlsplatz square next to the Altes Schloss.

RESTAURANTS. In Württemberg, in and around Stuttgart, a specialty is *Spätzle*, flour and egg noodles cooked in water, with infinite variations. You'll have it in soup, with liver, with ham or sauerkraut, *Spätzle* fried richly brown, with roast meat or mushrooms. In the same neighborhood you'll find a local version of the *Schlachtplatte:* it's made of sauerkraut, *Spätzle*, mashed peas, liver sausage, and bits of boiled pork. Typical also is the *Maultasche*, a sort of extra-large ravioli filled with a delightful mixture of sausage stuffing, ham, meat, spinach, onion and herbs. It is served either in strong, clear beef broth, or *gschmalzt*, that is, with melted butter and fried onions.

Also, taste their *Saiten*—juicy sausage served with lentils and *Spätzle*, and a wonderful soup of thin slices of potatoes, beef and *Spätzle*.

Württemberg, and for that matter the city of Stuttgart itself, produces very good white wines, a fact little known outside of Germany. When in the Stuttgart area try the *Untertürkheimer, Cannstatter, Uhlbacher* or *Rotenberger*.

Expensive

Alte Post. Friedrichstr. 43 (293079). Olde-inn decor, and noted for regional and international cuisine. DC, MC.

Alter Simpl. Hohenheimer Str. 64 (240821). Atmospheric old restaurant with long tradition of fine food. Reservations essential.

Baron de la Mouette (in the Mövenpick Rotisserie). Kleiner Schlossplatz 11, (220034). Downstairs is a cozy, rustic half-timbered room. First-class fish specialties, prime steaks, and Swiss food. AE, DC, MC, V.

China Garden. Königstr. 17 (223866). First-class Chinese food. AE, DC, MC, V.

L'Entrecote. Marktstr. (2198–736). Entrance on Karlstr. Mainly French; but exquisite cuisine.

Graf Zeppelin. Arnulf Klett Platz 7 (299881). In Hotel Graf Zeppelin. Fine international cuisine, good service, in the famous grillroom of this noble hotel. AE, DC, MC, V.

Lamm. Mühlstr. 24 (853615). In the old town suburb of Feuerbach. Well-known restaurant; fine cuisine and tasteful furnishings.

Öxle's-Lowen. Veitstr. 2 (532226). In Mühlhausen suburb. Small, elegant restaurant with select menu of top French cuisine. Good wines and service. AE, MC.

Schwyzer Eck. Neckarstr. 246 (265890). Fine Swiss cooking. AE, DC, MC, V.

Moderate

Börse. Heustr. 1 (292698). Good-valve and first-class Swabian food in cozy surroundings.

Breuninger Selection. Marktstr. 3 (21981). Exquisite dining corner in the department store of the same name. Small selection, but always seasonal and fresh. Wonderful desserts, pastries, and teas. Also an inexpensive cafeteria with daily specials in the same store.

Come Prima. Steinstr. 3 (243422). Stuttgart's best Italian restaurant; modern and elegant. AE, DC, MC, V.

La Concha. Dobelstr. 2 (241851). Spanish food.

Fernsehturm Restaurantbetriebe. Jahnstr. 120, in Degerloch (246104). Enjoy the panorama and the cooking in the "crow's nest" restaurant almost 150 meters (500 feet) up the 200-meter (700-feet) television tower on Bopser Hill in the outskirts. AE, V.

Maredo. Friedrichstr. 35 (296674). Argentinian steak-house. AE, DC, MC.

Schwarze Schaf. Böblingerstr. 57 (604248). Very cozy, "family" atmosphere, and home-style cooking with a fine touch. Good local wines. Live music.

Wine Taverns

All of the following offer good local wines from Stuttgart and vicinity, which are among the best in Württemburg. They also all fall within the moderate and inexpensive price categories.

A special attraction for wine lovers takes place annually for ten merry days beginning on the last Friday in August at the Stuttgart "Wine Village." About 350 Baden and Württemberg wines, choice Swabian specialties, and other culinary delicacies are served to visitors seated in the covered stalls on Marktplatz, Schillerplatz, and in the Kirchstrasse.

Archè. Bärenstr. 2 (245759). Located between the market and the Rathaus. Old Stuttgart wine-tavern; good, wholesome local specialties.

Bäckar-Metzger. Aachener Str. 20 (544108). Over 100 years old. Good-value food, old Swabian recipes.

Bäckerschmiede. Schurwaldstr. 44 (466035). Another old Swabian tavern.

Eulenspiegel. Bärenstr. 3 (242380). Cosy wine-tavern with carved fountain. Frequented by tourists of all nationalities, especially Americans. In addition to wines, good beer also served.

Kiste. Kanalstr. 2 (244002) Located between Charlottenplatz and Rosenstr. The city's best known and most popular wine tavern. Very atmospheric.

Weinstube Hasen. Innsbrucker Str. 5 (322070). In the wine-growing section of Uhlbach, a 19th-century house, and wine tavern for over 70 years. Today an elegant wine-restaurant.

Weinstube Paule's. Augsburger Str. 643 (321471). In the suburb of Obertürkheim. A tavern for almost 100 years. Hearty Swabian specialties and extra touches such as *Zwiebelkuchen* (onion tart) in fall, and Swabian Advent cookies at Christmas.

"Besenwirtschaften"

A peculiarity to Stuttgart, and a very popular and charming one, are the so-called "Besenwirtschaften" (literally, "Broom taverns") in Vintners' houses, recognized by the broom sign hanging over the door. In these establishments, only open during the winter and early spring, the vintners have their own new wines on sale for several weeks. For full information about addresses and periods of opening, consult the Stuttgart monthly calendar of events *Monatsspiegel.*

CAFÉS. Am Schlossgarten. In hotel of the same name. Large café overlooking the park.

Greiner. Opposite the main station in the Hindeburg building. Music on Thursdays from 3.30 P.M. Good pastries; also serves food.

Königsbau. Am Schlossplatz. Near the palace.

Reinsburg. Paulinenstr. 38, corner Marienstr. Mainly for pastries.

Schweickhardt, Marktstr. 24 in Bad Cannstatt; also at König-Karl Str. 37.

Sommer. Charlottenplatz 17. Quiet, Viennese-style café.

NIGHTLIFE. The night time tempo in Stuttgart is surprisingly fast. Jazz in particular is very popular. *Monatsspiegel* carries full details of all upcoming performances. In addition the Tourist Office organizes jazz concerts every Sunday from 6–10 P.M. in the Music Garden of the "Cure Park" in Bad Cannstatt.

Stuttgart also boasts a full complement of discos, mostly in the city center. Most stay open till 2 A.M., some till later. Again, *Monatsspiegel* gives full details.

Bars

Intercity-Bar. In Hotel Intercity at the main station.

Old Ascot. Königstr. 5 (295333).

Parkhotel. Villastr. 21. Noble cocktail bar, in the hotel.

Pianino-Piano Bar. Köngistr. 47 (291118). City's only piano bar. Outside terrace in summer. Snacks.

Rob-Roy Pub. Kleiner Schlossplatz 11 (220034). Small and snug, with newly created cocktails daily. Private art exhibits.

Steigenberger Hotel Graf Zeppelin. Arnulf Klett Platz. Elegant bar, in first-class hotel.

Tiffany. Schulstr. 10 (292627).

Treffpunkt Bar. In Flughafen (Airport) hotel.

Clubs

Most feature striptease of one variety or another.

Champain. Hirschstr. 16 (225967). Open until 4 A.M.

Evergreen. Kronprinzstr. 6 (291233). Open until 4 A.M.

Exselsior. Königstr. 54A (296773). Open until 5 A.M.

Imperial. Rathauspassage 7 (244328). Open until 5 A.M.

Moulin Rouge. Königstr. 58 (294707).

Discos

Bierdorf Königshof. Königstrasse 18 (290855). Open until 3 A.M. on Friday and Saturday.

Boa. Tübingerstr. 12–16, entrance Krumme Str. (223113).

Coupe. Friedrichstr. 31 (294849). Open until 4 A.M.

Perkins Park. Stresemannstr. (252062). In Killesberg section. Largest among the discos.

Tanzpalast. Rotebühlplatz 4, entrance Kronprinzstr. (224412). Open from 9 P.M. to 5 A.M.

Jazz and Rock

The following are a few of the jazzclubs on offer, most open from 7.30 or 8 P.M. until midnight or shortly after:

At-Podium City. Königstr. 51. Entrance in Hirschstr. with performances by international guests.

Dixieland Hall. In the Ketter-Keller cellar-bar, Marienstr. 3.

Jazzclub im Bruddler. Schlossstr. 28.

Laboratorium. Wagemburgstr. 147. Folk and blues; guest concerts.

Longhorn Club. On the Wangen Industrial Estate, the largest country and western club this side of the Atlantic.

PRACTICAL INFORMATION FOR
THE SWABIAN MOUNTAINS

TELEPHONES. We have given telephone codes for all the towns and villages in the hotel and restaurant lists that follow. These codes need only be used when calling from outside the town or village concerned.

HOTELS AND RESTAURANTS. You will find quality accommodations often at below-the-usual prices. Regional specialties include *Spätzle, Maultaschen, Schlachtplatte* and *Saiten,* already mentioned under "Stuttgart". Another specialty of the Swabian country is the *Käseflädle,* a sort of pancake made with rich Allgäu cheese or fried separately and folded over the cheese. Try all the soups: *Flädle-Suppe, Riebele-Suppe, Brisle-Suppe,* and *Klössle-Suppe.*

As well as the hotels listed below, there are farmhouse holidays available, which are very popular in the region. For a list of addresses, or to make reservations in guesthouses, private pensions and holiday apartments on the farm, contact the regional tourist offices (see below for addresses).

Aalen. *Kälber* (M), Behringstr. 26 (07361–8444). In Unterkochen, about four km. out. A member of the Ring-Hotel group, with the expected comforts. 20 rooms, all with own bath, 2 apartments; fine view. AE, DC, MC, V.

Bad Urach. *Graf Eberhard* (E), Bei den Thermen 2 (07125–1711). Right at the thermal baths. All rooms with bath; restaurant and café. AE, DC, MC. *Am Berg* (M), Ulmer Str. 12–14 (07125–1714). 50 beds; good food, terrace. A little above town with view. AE, DC, MC. *Vier Jahreszeiten-Frank* (M), Stuttgarter Str. 5 (07125–1696).

Böblingen. *Novotel* (E), Otto-Lilienthal Str. (07031–23071). 178 rooms, all with bath. Located in the suburb of Hulb. Indoor pool and restaurant. v. *Böblinger Haus* (M), Keilbergstr. 2 (07031–227044). 26 rooms, all with bath or shower; terrace and restaurant (closed Sat. and Christmas, and three weeks in the summer).

Burg Hohenzollern. Near Hechingen. **Restaurant.** *Burg Schenke* (E), (07471–2345). Situated in this magnificent castle, the restaurant has several sections: *Berliner Stube* with large windows overlooking the valley, the wood-paneled *Zollerklause,* and large outdoor terrace on the ramparts.

Gammertingen. *Romantic Hotel Post* (M), Sigmaringer Str. 4 (07574–877). Country house style hotel with 60 beds, most with bath; garden, solarium and café. Fine *Posthalterei* restaurant with particularly good-value menu. AE, DC, MC, V.

Göppingen. *Hohenstaufen* (M), a Ring Hotel. Freihofstr. 64 (07161–70077), with annex (Gästehaus) opposite. 40 rooms and 1 apartment. Good-value restaurant. AE, DC, MC, V.

Kernen. *Romantik Hotel Zum Ochsen* (M), Stetten, Kirchstr. 15 (07151–42015). In the valley of the Rems, northeast of Stuttgart. Attractively renovated hotel in a colorful inn. Good starting out point for exploring the hills and valleys of the region. 49 beds, rooms with bath or shower; good, very popular restaurant. AE, MC, V.

Langenau-Rammingen. *Romantik Hotel Landgasthof Adler* (E), Riegesstr. 15 (07345–7041). Just a short distance from the autobahn exit Ulm-Echingen though in completely quiet surroundings. 12 rooms, first-class cuisine. Offers special short-stay packages including rambling, cycling, and golfing. AE, DC, MC,

Lichtenstein. In the Honau section, near Reutlingen. *Adler* (E), Heerstr. 26 (07129–2370). DC, MC. *Alb-Hütte Traifelberg* (M), in Traifelberg near Lichtenstein Castle, quiet location with garden, good restaurant. 23 rooms. *Forellenhof Rössle* (M), Heerstr. 20 (07129–4001). With good restaurant.

Ludwigsburg. *Schlosshotel Monrepos* (E), (07141–3020). About four km. north, a castle hotel. 83 rooms, all with bath; located in a lovely park; noted restaurant with Swabian specialties and large wine list; pool. AE, DC, MC, V. *Heim* (M), Schillerstr. 19 (07141–26144). At the railroad station. No restaurant. AE, DC, MC, V. *Schiller Hospiz* (M), Gartenstr. 17 (07141–23463). Modern. AE.

Restaurants. *Alte Sonne* (E), Kirche 3, am Marktplatz (07141–25231). In hotel of the same name. AE, DC, MC, V. *Ratskeller* (M), Wilhelmstr. 13

(07141–26719). With garden. AE, DC, MC, V. *Post-Cantz* (I), Eberhardstr. 6 (07141–23563). AE, DC, MC, V.

Niederstotzingen. *Schloss Hotel Oberstotzingen* (E), Stettener Str. 37, between Langenau and Heidenheim (07325–6014). Early 17th-century Renaissance castle, recently renovated. 14 rooms, 2 holiday apartments. Riding available. Excellent *Vogelherd* restaurant. DC, MC, V.

Reutlingen. *Achalm* (Silence Hotel) (E), auf der Achalm (07121–17011). 17 beds, most rooms with shower or bath; newly-built on the heights above town, with magnificent view over the Swabian Mountains (balconies in all rooms). Very good restaurant with lamb specialties and terrace. AE, DC, MC. *Ernst* (E), am Leonhardsplatz (07121–44081). 120 beds, most rooms with bath; terrace café, bar and the fine *Kompa's* restaurant. AE, DC, MC, V. *Reutlinger Hof* (M), Kaiserstr. 33 (07121–17075). 55 beds, most rooms with bath or shower; heated indoor pool; no restaurant. AE. *Württemberger Hof* (M), Kaiserstr. 3 (07121–17056). 72 beds, most rooms with bath or shower. Fully-renovated establishment with rustic-furnished restaurant. The hotel is the starting point for the "Hiking without Luggage" ("Wandern ohne Gepäck") tour of the mountain foothills around Reutlingen, organized by the local tourist office. AE, DC, MC.

There are also several inexpensive *Gasthöfe.*

Restaurants. *Fürstenhof* (E), Kaiserpassage 5 (07121–3180). Gourmet restaurant in the luxurious Hotel Fürstenhof. Also a bistro, café, beer and wine tavern with beer garden, and a second restaurant. V. *Stadt Reutlingen* (E), Karlstr. 55 (07121–42391). AE, DC, MC. *Alte Mühle* (M), Frankonenweg 8 (07121–38786). Wine restaurant. *Ratskeller* (M), Marktplatz 22 (07121–38490). In the Rathaus. AE, DC, MC, V.

Saulgau *Hotels Kleber-Post* (E) Hauptstr. 100 (07581–3051). A Ring Hotel in the middle of the Swabian Mountains located within easy reach of the Bodensee, the Danube Valley and the pretty villages of Upper Swabia, which has been in the same family hands for over 300 years. 35 rooms, about half with bath. Restaurant renowned for its excellent cooking from locally grown produce and fine wines. AE, DC, MC, V.

Schwäbisch Gmünd. *Bahnhofshotel* (M), Bahnhofstr. 12 (07171–2039). 20 rooms, also fine restaurant; at the station. AE, DC, MC. *Pelikan* (M), Freudental 24–26 (07171–69098). Quiet, small, with good restaurant, has a large annexe. AE, DC, MC, V.

Restaurant. *Postillion* (E), Königsturmstr. 35 (07171–61584). Well-known all over Germany for first-class cuisine. Small, select menu full of variety. AE, DC, MC.

Sigmaringen. *Fürstenhof* (M), Zeppelinstr. 14 (07571–3076). 32 rooms, all with bath, 3 apartments, restaurant. MC. *Gästehaus Schmautz* (M), Im Mückentäle 33 (07571–51554). 14 rooms; quietly located with a fine view. A little outside town on the left side of the Danube.

Tübingen. *Krone* (E), Uhlandstr. 1 (07071–31036). 51 rooms, most with own bath, 3 apartments; colorful first-class restaurant and *Uhlandstube* wine tavern. AE, DC, MC, V. *Barbarina* (M), Wilhelmstr. 94

(07071–26048). 36 beds, most rooms with bath, 1 apartment. AE. *Hospiz* (M), Neckarhalde 2 (07071–26002). 50 rooms, most with bath. AE, DC, MC, V. *Hotel am Schloss* (M), Burgsteige 18 (07071–21077). 80 beds; near the castle; no restaurant. AE, DC, MC, V. *Gasthof Ritter* (I), Am Stadtgraben 25 (07071–22502). 10 beds.

Restaurants. *Alpirsbacher Schindelstube* (M), Brunnenstr. 9 (07071–212226). Swabian specialties. *Hölderlinturm* (M), Bursagasse 4B (07071–21227). Swabian specialties. *Museum* (M), Wilhelmstr. 3 (07071–22828). Large café-restaurant. AE, DC, MC, V. *Ratskeller* (M), Haaggasse 4 (07071–21391). In the cellar vaults beneath the Rathaus. *Waldhorn* (M), Schönbuchstr. 49 (07071–61270). In the suburb of Bebenhausen. Reservations essential; fine food and good value.

Wine Taverns. *Bierkeller La Cave* (I–M), Kirchgasse 6 (07071–27571). *Forelle* (I–M), Kronenstr. 8 (07071–22938). Also a good restaurant specializing in fresh trout and game. *Zur Alten Weinstube Göhner* (I–M), Schmidtorstr. 5. Good-value Swabian specialties.

Ulm. *Intercity Hotel* (M), Bahnhorsplatz 1 (0731–61221). 110 rooms, most with own bath. At the main station; two restaurants. AE, DC, MC, V. *Mövenpick Hotel Neu Ulm* (E), Silcherstr. 40 (0731–80110). In Neu-Ulm. Large, built in 1980 as Germany's first of this chain; on the banks of the Danube. Good restaurant, café and club bar. AE, DC, MC, V. *Neutor Hospiz* (M), Neuer Graben 23 (0731–15160). 92 rooms, all with bath. AE, DC, MC, V. *Stern* (M), Sterngasse 17 (0731–63091). With annexe. 55 rooms, most with own bath; sauna, restaurant. AE, DC, MC, V. *Ulmer Spatz* (M), Münsterplatz 27 (0731–68081). Opposite the cathedral. 45 rooms, most with bath; restaurant, terrace and garden. AE, MC.

Restaurants. *Pflugmerzler* (E), Pfluggasse 6 (0731–68061). Wine tavern well-known for its good food. *Forelle* (M), Fischergasse 25 (0731–63924). Well-known for fish specialties and international cuisine. Located in an old, fisherman's house; small terrace on the Blau river. DC, MC. *Herrenkeller* (M), Herrenkellergasse 4 (0731–65513). Good wholesome home cooking and Swabian specialties. *Höhehgaststätte Oberberghof* (M), Ober Eselberg, about five km. (three miles) northwest, with view from terrace.

CAMPING AND YOUTH HOSTELS. There are a total of 84 campsites and many youth hostels in the region of the Neckar Valley and Swabia. For a full list of sites with details of size, prices, facilities and telephone numbers, write the regional tourist office for Neckarland-Schwaben for their free brochure *Camping in Baden Württemberg.*

TOURIST INFORMATION. The main regional tourist offices are the *Gebietsgemeinschaft Schwäbische Alb, Verkehrsverein,* An der Neckarbrücke, Postfach 2623, 7400 Tübingen (07071–35011), and *Fremdenverkehrsverband Neckarland-Schwaben,* Wolhausstr. 14, 7100 Heilbronn (07131–629061).

There are also local tourist offices at the following places: **Aalen,** Städt. Verkenrsamt, Postfach 1740, Neues Rathaus, 7080 Aalen (07361–500301); **Böblingen,** Verkehrsamt der Stadt Böblingen, Informationspavillon vor der Kongresshalle, Tübinger Str. 14, 7030 Böblingen (07031–23011); **Dischingen,** Fremdenverkehrsamt, 7925 Dischingen (07327–721 or 722); **Ehingen,** Stadtverwaltung or Ehingen Reisebüro (travel agent), Bahnhofstr. 17, 7930 Ehingen (07391–5030); **Esslingen,** Kultur und Freizeitamt/Stadtinformation, Marktplatz 16, 7300 Esslingen (0711–3512441); **Geislingen,** Städt. Kulturamt, Hauptstr. 19, 7340 Geislingen an der Steige (07331–24266); **Göppingen,** Stadt. Verkehrsamt, Marktplatz. 2, 7320 Göppingen (07161–65292); **Lichtenstein,** Bürgermeisteramt, Postfach 5, 7414 Lichtenstein (07129–4071); **Lorch,** Städt. Verkehrsamt, Markt 5, 7073 Lorch (07172–6022); **Reutlingen,** Verkehrsamt, Listplatz 1, 7410 Reutlingen (07121–303622); **Schwäbisch Gmünd,** Fremdenverkehrsverein Schwäb. Gmund, Johannisplatz 3, Prediger Passage, 7070 Schwäbisch Gmünd (07171–603415); **Sigmaringen,** Städt. Verkehrsamt, 7480 Sigmaringen (07571–106121); **Sindelfingen,** Städt. Verkehrsamt, Pavillon am Rathaus, Postfach 180, 7032 Sindelfingen (07031–6101325); **Tübingen,** Verkehrsverein, an der Neckarbrücke, 7400 Tübingen (07071–35011); **Tuttlingen,** Verkehrsamt, Rathaus, 7200 Tuttlingen (07462–340); **Ulm,** Verkehrsbüro, Münsterplatz 51, 7900 Ulm (0731–64161); **Bad Urach,** Städt. Kurverwaltung, Bei den Thermen 4, Postfach 1206, 7432 Bad Urach (07125–1761).

HOW TO GET AROUND. By train. Fast intercity trains from all parts of Germany connect at Stuttgart, Ulm/Neu-Ulm and Tübingen main railway stations (Hauptbahnhof). A good network of local train services connect the towns and villages on the perimeter of the Swabian Mountains, and from Tübingen there is a north–south route across the center of the region via Hechingen to Sigmaringen in the south. There are embarkation stations for the motorail (*Autoreisezig*) at Kornwestheim near Stuttgart and at Lorräch.

By bus. The usual German Railways buses (Bahnbüsse) connect with outlying towns and villages not on the main rail routes. The Europabus routes T84 (Stuttgart–Donaueschingen–Titsee–Basel) and T78 (Reutlingen–Tübingen–Rottenburg–Freudenstadt–Strasbourg) also traverse the region, as do long-distance buses between Stuttgart, Reutlingen, Sigmaringen, Meersburg, and Tubingen, Reutlingen, Bad Urach, Munsingen, Ehingen/Donau, and Lindau.

By bicycle. Bicycles and touring maps are available from most tourist offices. Bicycles can also be rented at most main rail stations.

EXCURSIONS. City sightseeing tours are organized by the tourist offices in most main cities and towns. They also arrange full-day and half-day excursions out to local places of interest. If you wish to plan your own excursions, these are the most important towns to include: Ellwangen on the Jagst River; Göppingen, the town of the Hohenstaufen emperors; Heidenheim with its openair theater, recreation park and game reserve of Schloss Hellenstein; Rottenburg, an old Roman town; Geislingen an der Steige, with the steepest stretch of railroad in Germany and beautiful old half-timbered houses; Aalen with its beautiful old town and museums; Reutlingen with its city gates and battlements; Tübingen, the oldest university town in Germany (1477) and old town on the banks of the Neckar; and, of course, Ulm, with the highest church tower in the world. From Ulm you can embark on round-trip boating expeditions along the Danube, departing from the Metzgerturm Pier.

For those touring by car, there are also various scenic routes around the region. The Schwäbische Weinstrasse (Swabian Wine Road) is the most well-known scenic route of Baden Württemberg, running from Schloss Horneck near Gundelsheim north of Heilbronn, southwards along the course of the Neckar to Stuttgart and then to its destination in Esslingen. Information from *Fremdenverkehrsverband Neckarland-Schwaben,* Charlottenplatz 17, 7000 Stuttgart.

The Schwäbische Dichter Strasse (Swabian Poet's Road) traverses the heart of Baden Württemberg, from Bad Mergentheim in the north to Meersburg on Lake Constance in the south. The tour combines literary tit-bits with some beautiful excursion countryside. Information from *Fremdenverkehrsverband Neckarland-Schwaben,* Wollhausstr. 14, 7100 Heilbronn.

The Strasse der Staufer (Staufer Road) is around 130 km. (80 miles), touching on almost all of the important places that are connected with the history, art, culture and political life of the Hohenstaufen emperors in their homeland. Information from *Fremdenverkehrsgemeinschaft Stauferland,* im Städt. Verkehrsamt, 7320 Göppingen.

SPORTS. Fishing. Licences can be obtained in Adelberg, Böblingen, Ehingen, Ellwangen, Ludwigsburg, Möhringen, Nürtingen, Sigmaringen, Tuttlingen and Ulm. A full list is available from the Regional Tourist Office.

Gliding and Hang-gliding. Very popular owing to the suitable terrain of the Swabian Mountains. There is particularly good hang-gliding country around Hohenstaufen, while gliding schools and airfields abound. Full information from *Drachenflieger Club Stuttgart,* c/o Peter Rieger, Reinhardtstr. 43, D-7441 Wolfschlugen (07381–711) for hang-gliding possibilities; for gliding information contact the local tourist offices.

Golf. Courses at Hechingen and Göppingen.

Hiking. A specialty of this region. For full details of hiking possibilities and suggested routes, as well as lists of farmhouse accommodations on hiking trails, contact the *Schwäbische Albverein,* an der Neckarbrücke, 7400 Tübingen (tel. 07071–35011), or the *Verkehrsverein Reutlingen Albvorland,* Listplatz 1, 7410 Reutlingen (07121–37600) for walking in the central areas of the mountain region, or the *Rundwanderweg Schwäbische Alb,* Aachtalstr. 5, 7902 Blaubeuren-Weiler (07344–7675) for the southern routes.

Horseback riding. Widely practiced and saddle horses, often with instructors if desired, are available at Bad Urach, Balingen, Ehingen, Esslingen, Göppingen, Ludwigsburg, Marbach on Lauter (state stud farm), Reutlingen, Rottweil, Tübingen, Tuttlingen, Ulm, Schwäbisch Gmünd and elsewhere.

Kayaking. On the Danube from Beuron to Ulm (137 km./85 miles) through a very attractive landscape but somewhat strenuous for paddling. Information at Beuron, at the Danube Bridge (07466–324).

Rowing and sailing are practiced on the Neckar, the Jagst at Ellwangen, the Danube, the gravel pits around Niederstotzingen (also wind surfing), and the lakes around Rosenberg.

Swimming. For swimming you have a choice of mineral and regular water pools. There are indoor baths in most of the larger towns throughout the region. In addition, there are bathing beaches on many of the man-made bathing lakes, gravel pits and rivers, a list of which is available from the Regional Tourist Office in Heilbronn. One of the most attractive is the Ebnisee Lake at Welzheim on a tributary of the Rems.

WINTER SPORTS. There is a steadily increasing number of ski resorts in the Swabian Mountains and, to a lesser extent, in the Swabian Forest. The terrain is more rolling than the Alps and perhaps not as dramatic, but it nevertheless offers good skiing possibilities, and throughout this area there is an unusually large number of ski jumps, as well as prepared cross-country tracks *(loipen)* and floodlit pistes.

NECKARLAND

Land of Rivers and Mountains

The valley of the Neckar runs through a vast area of southwest Germany known as Neckarland-Schwaben (part of the state of Baden-Württemberg), stretching from the Danube valley in the southwest to the Rhine plateau in the northwest. Apart from the Neckar itself, the area incorporates the dramatic Tauber, Jagst and Kocher rivers, as well as parts of the Swabian mountains (Schwäbische Alb) in its southwest corner and the Swabian Forest (Schwäbischer Wald) to the east.

An excellent way to explore the area is to follow the Burgenstrasse, the Castle Road, in all some 300 km. (190 miles) long, from Mannheim, where the Neckar joins the Rhine, to Nürnberg in Franconia. In this chapter we shall follow the section between Mannheim and Heilbronn, and then the areas east—along the Tauber—and west—between the Rhine and the Neckar—of that route.

Mannheim

Mannheim today is a great industrial center and its river port the second largest in Europe; it is an important rail junction and the meeting point of several autobahns. The city was developed in the early 18th century by the Electors of the Palatinate. The streets were laid out on a gridiron pattern within a roughly oval frame, lying between the Rhine and the Neckar, with the streets parallel to the two rivers lettered (from the Rhine to the Neckar) A to K for the west half, L to U for the east half. The cross streets are numbered, with the numbers running from the center outwards in both directions, and each block thus has a different name—so if your hotel's address is given as B 2, you know that it is in the second block from the Rhine and the second block to the west of the center.

The Residenzschloss, the Electors' Palace, built 1720–60, is one of the largest Baroque buildings in Europe. It is now occupied by the University. The main staircase, the library and chapel are of particular interest. Mannheim's Jesuitenkirche (Jesuit Church) with its ornate facade and exquisite wrought-iron gate is an outstanding example of the Baroque style. Also notable are the twin buildings of the Altes Rathaus (Old Town Hall) and Untere Pfarrkirche (Lower Parish Church) on Marktplatz. A well-known feature of the city is the Wasserturm, or Water Tower, near which is the Kunsthalle, in Moltkestrasse, housing a representative collection of 19th- and 20th-century art. Worth seeing are the house occupied from 1782 by Dalberg, first manager of the National Theater, and the theater itself—rebuilt in 1957 after destruction during World War II.

It was at Mannheim that the first bicycle was constructed, by Baron von Drais in 1817, and the first automobile by Benz in 1885. You can discover more about local history and culture in the Reiss Museum, at C5, which also has a fine collection of Frankenthal porcelain.

Heidelberg

About 18 km. (11 miles) away is Heidelberg, where the Electors had their main residence for five centuries before moving to Mannheim. The massive tree-girt castle ruins rising above the old town, with its graceful bridge across the Neckar, give Heidelberg a delightfully romantic appearance, highlighted by the nightly floodlighting of the castle on certain evenings in summer, when grand firework displays, during the open-air theater festival from July through September, recall the destruction of the castle by Louis XIV in 1693. The spectacle is particularly enjoyable from on board one of the Neckar passenger boats. The castle can be reached by foot, car or cable railway. Built over several centuries in Gothic and Renaissance styles, enough remains to make it well worth your while to join a guided tour. The Deutsches Apothekenmuseum (Pharmaceutical Museum) and the Grosses Fass—the enormous wine barrel associated with the court jester Perkeo—can be visited separately. Concerts are held in the courtyard in summer. The grounds are open all day free of charge and there are fine views of the town from the terraces. For further views take the cable railway (Bergbahn) to Molkenkur, or to Königstuhl at the top (566 meters, 1,860 feet).

After being sacked and burned by the French at the end of the 17th century, the town was rebuilt in Baroque style but on its medieval and Renaissance foundations, the old street pattern being kept. Thus Heidelberg has a charming, higgledy-piggledy air and provides the visitor with numerous unexpected vistas. Important buildings which survived the fire are the late Gothic Heiliggeistkirche (Holy Ghost Church) and opposite it the Haus Zum Ritter with its fine Renaissance front (1592) in Hauptstrasse.

Heidelberg University, founded in 1386 by Elector Ruprecht I, is the oldest in Germany. Near the 18th-century building on Universitätsplatz is the new building added in 1930–32 with the aid of funds collected in the United States by J.G. Schurman, one-time American Ambassador to Germany and a former student at Heidelberg. Nearby in Augustiner-strasse is the Studentenkarzer, the Students' Jail, with interesting graffiti dating from many centuries. The University Library (Universitätsbibliothek, in Plöck) has a permanent exhibition which includes a facsimile of the *Manesse Codex,* a fine early-14th-century illuminated manuscript of medieval poetry. The Kurpfälzisches Museum (Palatinate Museum, at Hauptstrasse) is in the Palais Morass, built 1712 by Breunig, the architect of the Old University. Notable exhibits are: the Twelve Apostles Altar (completed 1509) by Tilman Riemenschneider, the great woodcarver of Würzburg; paintings and drawings of the Romantic period, many of Heidelberg; and a replica of the prehistoric jaw of Heidelberg Man.

To see Heidelberg from across the Neckar, cross the Old Bridge (Alte Brücke, built 1788), turn left and go a little way down Neuenheimer Landstrasse to the Schlangenweg, a narrow path ascending to the Philosophenweg (Philosophers' Way). Turn left toward the Bismarck monument, or go right toward the Hölderlin memorial for a longer walk through the forest, returning to the town via Hirschgasse.

The Neckar Valley

Following the road along the north bank of the Neckar, where the valley forms a gorge between high wooded hills, Neckargemünd is the next place of interest, rising calmly on the south bank with its church steeple dominating the old houses. Beyond is Neckarsteinach, with four castles, while across the river is the walled fortress of Dilsberg, one of the finest in the region, surrounded on three sides by the river. Further up-river is Hirschhorn, where the knights of Hirschhorn built their fortress in 1200. Its remains, as well as the town walls and Carmelite church, are impressive.

The next major place of interest is Eberbach, a spa town at the narrowest point of the Neckar valley. It dates back to 1196 and lies in the nature park of Neckartal-Odenwald, one of the many beautiful regions of the Odenwald Forest that stretches north into the state of Hesse and towards the river Main. From Eberbach, with its buildings clustered thickly about the bridge over the Neckar, the route continues on to Stolzeneck, whose castle, Burg Stolzeneck, rises proudly on the forested left bank of the Neckar, and Zwingenberg, where there's another castle, on the right bank, possibly the most impressive and best preserved on the whole Burgenstrasse.

The countryside around Neckarelz now begins to change character, with forests giving way to meadows and orchards. The remains of an ancient Roman settlement, the Villa Rustica, are here as well as many charming old buildings and churches. A short distance inland from Neckarelz is Mosbach, whose recorded history can be traced back to 736; a wonderful town with whole streets of half-timbered houses. Moving on, Neckarzimmern is the site of Schloss Hornberg, the castle where Götz von Berlichingen, the outlaw knight with the iron hand and hero of Goethe's play of the same name, spent the last years of his life. Across the river are the castles of Guttenberg and Ehrenburg. Schloss Guttenberg in particular is worth visiting and has a famous restaurant.

Bad Friedrichshall is a small spa town located at the junction of the Neckar and the Kocher. Just before Bad Friedrichshall another river, the

Jagst, still relatively unpolluted, joins the Neckar. It's worth following it to Jagsthausen, where there are three castles, all of which belong to the Berlichingen family. It was in the oldest that Götz von Berlichingen was born, in Götzenburg, today boasting carefully laid out gardens and grounds.

Back on the Neckar you come next to Bad Wimpfen on the south bank. It is an old imperial free town, with a tight cluster of old houses, and the remains of the 12th-century castle (Kaiserpfalz).

This brings us to Heilbronn, another imperial town, today a flourishing community and the largest wine center of the Neckar Valley. There are many interesting buildings here, some restored to their former glory and the best dating from Heilbronn's days of splendor in the 16th century. The tower of the Kilianskirche (St. Kilian's Church) represents one of the earliest appearances in Germany of Renaissance architecture: the tower was started in 1513, though other parts of the church date back to the 13th century. Other historic buildings include the Götzenturm (1392) named after the iron-handed knight; the Bollwerksturm, a 14th-century tower (Götz slept here); the Gothic Rathaus, with 16th-century Renaissance additions; the Käthchenhaus, a patrician dwelling from Heilbronn's most flourishing period; and the Baroque tower, the Hafenmarktturm. The town museum, with exhibits of local history and culture, is housed in the Deutschordenshof, a former settlement of the Order of Teutonic Knights, in Eichgasse. The Natural History Museum (Naturhistorisches Museum) is in Kramstrasse.

The Tauber Valley

The Tauber Valley is the most easterly region of Neckarland, bordering the Bavarian state of Franconia. The valley of the Tauber is 120 km. (65 miles) long and runs between Wertheim and Rothenburg-ob-der-Tauber. Its peaceful, idyllic scenery, forests and vineyards and mild climate make it popular among tourists and have given rise to the affectionate nickname, the "Liebliche" (lovable) Tauber Valley.

The Tauber flows into the Main at Wertheim, a town which acquired city rights in 1306. Here the slender Kittstein Tower rises beside the Tauber like a gun-barrel standing on end, while on the heights beyond is the massive castle (Kurmainzisches Schloss) of the Counts of Wertheim. Narrow streets in the old town are lined with splendid old houses, while the market square is framed by half-timbered architecture.

From Wertheim we come to Tauberbischofsheim with its round watchtower, once part of a mighty fortress, and a number of half-timbered houses and Baroque courtyards. The parish church contains a fine side altar, the work of Riemenschneider or one of his pupils.

Following the Tauber southeast past Lauda-Königshofen, also boasting historic half-timbered houses as well as the largest water-wheel in southern Germany, we pass on to the foremost health resort of the region, Bad Mergentheim.

From 1525 to 1809, Bad Mergentheim was a center of the Teutonic Knights, and their castle is still the great sight of the old city on the south bank of the Tauber, where high-roofed buildings of the Middle Ages confront you at every turn. When Napoleon dissolved the Order, it appeared that Mergentheim, however interesting it might remain as a museum, was doomed to fade away so far as active contemporary life was concerned. Then a shepherd, Franz Gehrig, grazing his sheep on the north bank of the river in 1826 discovered mineral springs. A new Mergentheim, baptized Bad Mergentheim, rose across the stream from the old town. The springs turned out to be four in number, each slightly different in its chemical composition, with the Albert Spring producing the strongest sodium sulphate and bitter salt-waters in Europe. Excavations disclosed that the springs had been in use in the early Bronze and late Iron Age, and had then apparently silted up and become lost until their lucky rediscovery gave to the town a new lease of life. One of Bad Mergentheim's modern attractions is the Wildpark, a huge nature park with game reserve and aviary.

If you stop at Bad Mergentheim, you should not fail to visit the village church of Stuppach, a few kilometers to the south, to see one of the most famous pictures one of the most famous painters of Germany—*The Virgin with the Infant Christ* by Matthias Grünewald (1519).

Still following the Tauber upstream, turn east toward Weikersheim, the site of the oldest residence of the Princes of Hohenlohe, set in its own Baroque garden. You can enjoy a glass of wine in the castle cellars with great casks in the background.

As you draw closer to Franconia you reach Creglingen, where the Tauber leaves Baden-Württemberg. In the Herrgottskirche (Chapel of Our Lord) Riemenschneider's intricate altar, illustrating the *Assumption of the Virgin,* the Marienaltar, can be seen. Creglingen also has the ruins of the castle-fortress Burg Brauneck.

The Swabian Forest

Now for a short circular tour of the Swabian Forest (Schwäbischer Wald) and Hohenlohe, an area delineated approximately by the Rems, middle Neckar, lower Jagst, and upper Kocher rivers. This is a lovely region worth visiting for its natural beauty, its castles, and its unspoiled old towns. From Heilbronn continue along the Burgenstrasse (Castle Road), through Weinsberg, harboring castle ruins; Öhringen, with the 15th-century abbey church; Künzelsau and its half-timbered houses; to Langenburg, with its castle.

Here turn south to Schwäbisch Hall, the most picturesque town of the entire region. Visit it for its half-timbered houses, two romantic wooden bridges spanning the river, 15th-century parish church atop a broad 18th-century staircase, Baroque Town Hall (Rathaus), open to visitors, the castle ruins of Limburg and Keckenburg, the nearby powerful abbey-fortress of Comburg (Grosskomburg), and the Keckenburg Museum of local history in a medieval town mansion. From Schwäbisch Hall you can proceed south to Gaildorf, with an interesting castle and Rathaus, then west to Murrhardt, for its Romanesque Walterich Chapel and Carl-Schweizer-Museum, and then return via Mainhardt, where remains of a Roman fort can be seen, to Heilbronn and to Heidelberg.

West of Heidelberg is Schwetzingen, site of the 18th-century summer residence of the Palatine Electors, with its famous Rococo theater, set in a magnificent formal park. Schwetzingen is also well-known for asparagus, which can be bought in May and June from roadside stalls or eaten in local restaurants. There is an annual festival in May in the palace and grounds.

Wiesloch, the wine center at the southern end of the Bergstrasse, has an interesting local museum. The next stop should be at Bruchsal to see its magnificent Baroque palace. Destroyed during World War II but now fully restored, it was partly designed by Balthasar Neumann.

You are now in a famous wine-growing area between the Neckar and the Rhine, the Kraichgau, with a wealth of vineyards, half-timbered houses, inns and wine-tasting taverns. Before joining the central part of the Schwäbische Weinstrasse you may like to visit Bretten and Maulbronn. Bretten has many early 16th-century buildings, unchanged since Melanchthon, scholar, religious reformer and friend of Luther, lived here. Maulbronn's monastery demonstrates how early-Romanesque architecture developed into late-Gothic; a well-preserved medieval monastery, it is not difficult to imagine what it was like in its heyday.

Karlsruhe

One of Germany's major cities, Karlsruhe is a busy industrial center and a major rail nexus as well as an important inland harbor, although the city proper is not quite on the Rhine, but somewhat east of it. It is also an important brewery town, where half a dozen leading brands of beer are made.

Karlsruhe (founded around 1715) is a comparatively late German city and its pattern, more original than the gridiron plan of Mannheim, is in the shape of a fan. This arrangement was due to the Margrave Karl Wilhelm, who conceived the idea in 1715, when he began building a new palace for himself here. The completion of his design took place 66 years later under Grand Duke of Baden Karl Friedrich by architect Friedrich Weinbrenner, a native of Karlsruhe.

The handle of the fan is provided by the palace, whose two wings, leaving its central portion at obtuse angles, started the side of the fan, while long rows of impressive buildings housing the Margrave's ministries continued the outer edges to the point where they were joined by a third curving line of structures which constituted its top. In spite of the changes wrought by time, this basic plan is still traceable, and there is virtually no change at all in what lies to the other side of the fan and the palace—the palace park and beyond that an extensive wooded area which also presents a fanlike aspect, because of the long avenues radiating outward like the spokes of a wheel of which the castle is the hub, while two concentric half-circle avenues with the palace as their center complete the pattern.

In 1806 Karlsruhe became the capital of the Grand Duchy of Baden. The predominant architectural style of the city is neo-Classical, much of it designed by Weinbrenner in the late-18th and early-19th centuries. Marktplatz, the 19th-century center of the town, has an interesting pyramid monument flanked by Weinbrenner's Town Hall and his Protestant City Church (Stadtkirche). Badly bombed during World War II, enough remains of Karlsruhe's important buildings to retain the general impression, which is that of a monumental city of imposing structures in a setting of noble parks and avenues. It is an appropriate home for Supreme Constitutional Court of the Federal Republic, established here in 1951 in the former Prinz-Max-Palais.

An outstanding modern building is the multi-purpose Schwarzwaldhalle (Black Forest Hall), used for concerts, congresses, grand balls and the like. The Staatliche Kunsthalle (Fine Arts Museum), in Hans Thoma Strasse, has paintings from the Middle Ages to the present, including works by Grünewald, Rembrandt, Holbein, and many Impressionists. It also houses the children's museum, the Kindermuseum. In the former Grand Ducal Palace is the Badisches Landesmuseum (Baden Provincial Museum), with collections of prehistory, Greek, Roman and early Germanic art, as well as a good sculpture collection. The extensive and pleasant Stadtgarten (City Park) includes a zoo and a botanical garden, with Japanese and Rose Gardens.

PRACTICAL INFORMATION FOR
THE NECKARLAND

TELEPHONES. We have given telephone codes for all the towns and villages in the hotel and restaurant lists that follow. These codes need only be used when calling from outside the town or village concerned.

HOTELS AND RESTAURANTS. Other than in Mannheim, Heidelberg and Karlsruhe, prices in the charming old towns and castle-studded hills of this area are generally 10–20% lower than in similar areas along the Rhine. Accommodations are plentiful and farm holidays are popular.

There are numerous all-in package deals, including hobby holidays and gastronomical tours, *Romance and Relaxation* in the countryside and *Wandern Ohne Gepäck* (hiking without luggage). Details from *Fremdenverkehrsverband Neckarland-Schwaben,* Wollhausstr. 14, 7100 Heilbronn, or your travel agent.

Bad Friedrichshall. *Schloss Lehen* (M), Hauptstr. 2 (07136–4044). 23 rooms. Garni. Castle built 1553, large park. DC, V. *Gasthof Schöne Aussicht* (I), Deutschordenstr. 2 (07136–6057). 16 rooms.

Bad Mergentheim. *Kurhotel-Viktoria* (E), Poststr. 2 (07931–5930). 100 rooms, most with bath and balcony. Restaurants, atrium, roof terrace; heated pool. Wines served from own vineyard. AE, DC, MC, V. *Garni am Markt* (M), Hans-Heinrich-Ehrler-Platz 40 (07931–6101). 32 rooms. AE, DC, MC. *Park Hotel* (M), Lotha Daiker Str. 6 (07931–56100). 116 rooms, indoor pool; two restaurants and wine cellar tavern. *Irmgard* (I), Wachbacherstr. 6 (07931–2369). No restaurant. *Petershof* (I), Wachbacherstr. 14 (07931–2336). With restaurant. *Tauberblick* (I), Edelfingerstr. 21a (07931–8161). No restaurant, but half- or full-board available on request.

Bad Rappenau. *Schlosshotel Heinsheim* (E), 07264–1045. 40 rooms. Castle hotel at Heinsheim. Lovely park, swimming pool, top restaurant with own wine.

Bad Wimpfen. *Blauer Turm* (M), Burgviertel 5 (07063–225). 23 rooms, all with bath. Very atmospheric, and quiet location; lovely terrace. *Pension Neckarblick* (I), Erich-Saifer-Str. 48 (07063–8548).

Eberbach. *Hotel-Pension Hohencafé-Neckarblick* (M), at Breitenstein (06271–2489). Very quiet with fine view, pool, restaurant; just outside town on hill. DC, V. *Krone-Post* (M), Hauptstr. 1 (06271–2013). 48 rooms. Splendid view from terrace; restaurant. AE, DC, MC, V.

Heidelberg. *Crest* (E), Pleikartsförsterstr. 101 (06221–71021). 113 rooms. At Kirchheim, three km. (two miles) out, near autobahn. DC, MC, V. *Der Europäische Hof* (E), Friedrich-Ebert-Anlage 1 (06221–27101). 125 rooms; some apartments. Perhaps the most comfortable in town; very fine restaurant *Kurfürstenstube.* AE, DC, MC. V. *Hirschgasse* (E), Hirschgasse 3 (06221–49921). 42 rooms, all with bath or shower. Quiet, historic inn dating from 1472, a few minutes from old town. Restaurant *Gaudeamus Igitur* of "Student Prince" fame has high-quality cuisine. DC, MC, V. *Parkhotel Atlantic* (E), Schloss-Wolfsbrunnen-Weg 23 (06221–24545). 23 rooms, some with magnificent view of Neckar. Elegant, cozy; no restaurant. AE, MC, V. *Prinzhotel* (E), Neuenheimer Landstr. 5 (06221–40320). 46 rooms, all with bath. Overlooking the Neckar and Old Heidelberg. Original building in Art Deco style, completely renovated to former elegance, with all modern facilities. Fine Italian restaurant and piano bar. AE, DC, MC, V. *Romantik-Hotel Zum Ritter* (E), Hauptstr. 178 (06221–24272). 36 rooms, all with bath or shower. Built 1592; with magnificent Renaissance facade; the only large building to survive the destruction of the town by the French in 1693. Delightfully furnished. Restaurant and rustic tavern; regional and international cuisine. AE, DC, MC, V. *Neckar* (M), Bismarckstr. 19 (06221–23260). 32 rooms, all with bath or shower. No restaurant. AE, MC, V. *Parkhotel Haarlass* (M), In der Neckarhelle 162 (06221–45021). At Ziegelhausen, three km. (two miles) east, on river. 170 beds. Fine terrace restaurant and café. DC.

Restaurants. *Kurpfälzische Weinstube* (E), Hauptstr. 97 (06221–24050). Atmospheric wine restaurant in Kurpfälzische museum. MC, V. *Molkenkur* (E), Klingenteichstr. 31 (06221–10894). Half-way up the Königstuhl at cable railway (Bergbahn) stop; magnificent view; terrace. MC. *Perkeo* (E), Hauptstr. 75 (06221–160613). Fine, traditional food since 1701. AE, DC, MC, V. *Weinstube Schloss-Heidelberg* (E), in the castle (06221–20081). Atmospheric wine restaurant. MC. *Zur Herrenmühle* (E), Hauptstr. 239 (06221–12909). 17th-century inn serving *haute cuisine.* AE, DC, MC, V. *Altdeutsche Weinstube* (M), Hauptstr. 224 (06221–24138). Atmospheric wine tavern. *Königstuhl* (M), 06221–21607. At top of cable railway; fine view. MC. *Schinderhannes* (M), Theaterstr. 2 (06221–24405). Grill specialties. *Sole d'Oro* (I), Hauptstr. 172 (06221–21480). Italian food.

Historic student taverns. *Knösel,* Haspelgasse (06221–23445). Dates back to 1863. *Roter Ochsen,* Hauptstr. 217 (06221–20977). Dates back to 1703. *Schnitzelbank,* Bauamtsgasse 7 (06221–21189). In side street next to Kurpfälzisches Museum. *Schnookeloch,* Haspelgasse 8 (06221–22733). Dates back to 1407. *Zum Sepp'l,* Hauptstr. 213 (06221–23085). Dates back to 1634.

Cafés. *Knösel,* Haspelgasse (06221–22345). *Schafheutle,* Hauptstr. 94 (06221–21316). With garden. *Scheu,* Hauptstr. 137 (06221–21103).

Heilbronn. *Götz* (E), Moltkestr. 52 (07131–18001). 86 rooms, all with bath. Central. v. *Insel* (E), Friedrich-Ebert-Brücke (07131–6300). 120 rooms, most with bath. On island in the Neckar. Pool, sauna; good restaurant, café terrace; bar open until 3 A.M. AE, DC, MC, v. *Burkhardt* (Ring Hotel) (M), Lohtorstr. 7 (07131–62240). Centrally located near the city hall. 55 rooms, all with bath. Good quality restaurant, with local atmosphere and regional specialties, yet gourmet cuisine. DC, MC, v. *City* (M), Allee 40 (07131–83958). 18 rooms; on 14th floor of Shoppinghaus; no restaurant, but good breakfasts. AE, MC, v. *Beck* (I), Bahnhofstr. 31 (07131–81589). 44 beds; café.

Restaurants. *Wirtshaus zum Götzenturm* (E), Allerheiligenstr. 1 (07131–80534). By Götzenturm (Götz Tower); old and atmospheric; good local specialties and *haute cuisine*. *Harmonie* (M), Allee 28 (07131–86890). With lovely garden terrace. *Ratskeller* (M), Marktplatz 7 (07131–84628). Excellent wine tavern in Rathaus; wholesome regional specialties. Garden.

Hirschhorn. *Schloss Hotel* (M), auf Burg Hirschhorn (06272–1373). 19 rooms. Modernized castle–hotel with much medieval atmosphere; reasonable restaurant with superb view from terrace over the Neckar. *Forelle* (I), Langenthalerstr. 2 (06272–2272). With terrace. DC.

Jagsthausen. *Burghotel Götzenburg* (M), 07943–2222. 14 rooms. Medieval castle, in park, and birthplace of famous knight Götz von Berlichingen; still owned by Berlichingen family. Excellent food and wine. Open Apr. through Oct. AE, DC, MC, v. *Zur Krone* (I), Brückenstr. 1 (07943–2397). 10 rooms. In town; very simple.

Karlsruhe. *Eden* (E), Bahnhofstr. 17 (0721–28718). 68 rooms, all with bath or shower. AE, DC, MC, v. *Erbprinz* (E), Rheinstr. 1, Ettlingen (07243–12071). 75 rooms, all with bath; some apartments and suites. Pleasantly furnished. Eight km. (five miles) south of Karlsruhe. Garden terrace; has one of Germany's top restaurants. AE, DC, MC. *Kaiserhof* (E), Am Marktplatz (0721–26616). 40 rooms, most with bath. Central; good restaurant. AE, DC, MC, v. *Mövenpick Parkhotel* (E), Ettlinger Str. 23 (0721–37270). 130 rooms, all with bath or shower. Good restaurant on 10th floor with grill specialties and view over city; wine tavern, café. AE, DC, MC, v. *Ramada Renaissance* (E), Mendelssohnplatz (0721–37170). Opened 1984, formerly Hilton International. 432 beds, some apartments. First-class modern comfort; bars, restaurant, wine tavern. AE, DC, MC, v. *Schlosshotel* (E), Bahnhofplatz 2 (0721–3540). 96 rooms, all with bath. Renovated and restored in early 1900s style; first-class comfort; two fine restaurants *La Residence* and *Schwarzwaldstube*. AE, DC, MC, v. *Greif* (M), Ebert Str. 17 (0721–33001). 87 rooms. 7-foot beds for 6-footers available on request. AE, MC, v. *Erbprinzenhof* (M), Erbprinzenstr. 26 (0721–23890). 59 rooms. No restaurant. *Kübler* (M), Bismarckstr. 39 (0721–22611). 85 rooms. No restaurant. AE, MC. *Maison Suisse* (M), Hildebrandstr. 24 (0721–406048). 15 rooms. AE, DC, MC, v.

Restaurants. *Schloss Augustenburg* (E), Kirchstr. 20 (0721–48555). Hotel-restaurant with international gourmet menu. Building dates back to 10th-century; birthplace of the Margrave Karl Wilhelm von Baden, the city's founder. v. *Künstlerkneipe zur Krone* (M), Pfarrstr. 18 (0721–

572247). In Daxlanden suburb. Old wine tavern, in the same family since 1859. Garden, excellent wines, first-rate food. *Oberländer Weinstube* (M), Akademiestr. 7 (0721–25066). Karlsruhe's oldest wine tavern; regional dishes and French cuisine. AE, DC, MC, V. *O'Henry's Spezialitäten Restaurant* (M), Breite Str. 24 (0721–385551). Small; seafood specialties. AE, DC, MC, V. *Unter den Linden* (M), Kaiserallee 71 (0721–849185). Regional and international dishes; fish and game specialties. AE, DC, MC, V. *Goldenes Kreuz* (I), Karlstr. 21a (0721–22054). Popular local inn with large menu; quick service; open all day until midnight.

Beer and wine bars. *Badische Weinstube,* in the Botanical Garden (0721–661867). Local atmosphere and good local specialties. *Bierakademie,* Douglasstr. 10 (0721–27302). Seven different sorts of beer from the barrel; Baden specialties; jazz on Sun. mornings. *Harmonie,* Kaiserstr. 57 (0721–374209). The "in" music and beer tavern with weekly performances by well-known musicians and other artistes. Two set menus daily, plus *à la carte* menu and salad buffet. *Pfälzer Weinstube,* Wilhelmstr. 17 (0721–607838). Rustic interiors.

Mannheim. It is advisable to book in advance for March, May and September, which are busy tourist and congress periods. *Augusta* (E), Augusta-Anlage 43 (0621–418001). 110 rooms, most with bath. Central, comfortable; good restaurant and *Badische Weinklause* tavern. AE, DC, MC, V. *Holiday Inn-Mannheim City Center* (E), Kurfürstenarkade 6 (0621–10710). 146 rooms. Centrally located with own shopping center. Superior facilities; indoor pool, good restaurant. AE, DC, MC. *Maritim Park* (E), Friedrichsplatz 2–4 (0621–45071). Completely renovated to original elegance with superior facilities. 200 rooms, most with bath, three apartments. Restaurant with international cuisine and rustic wine tavern serving local specialties. Indoor pool. *Novotel* (E), Auf dem Friedensplatz (0621–417001). 180 rooms; pool. On city edge at Heidelberg autobahn. AE, DC, MC, V. *Steigenberger Hotel Mannheimer Hof* (E), Augusta-Anlage 4–8 (0621–45021). 200 rooms, most with bath. Central; smart restaurant, bar, colorful *Holzkistl* tavern. AE, DC, MC, V. *Holländer Hof* (M), U1, 11–12 (0621–16095). 32 rooms, all with shower. No restaurant. AE, DC, MC, V. *Inter-City* (M), Bahnhofsplatz 15 (0621–22925). 47 rooms, all with bath or shower; two restaurants at main rail station. AE, MC, V. *Mack* (M), Mozartstr. 14 (0621–23888). 76 rooms, half with bath or shower. Central; no restaurant. AE, DC, MC, V. *Wartburg* (M), F4, 4–11 (0621–28991). 163 rooms, most with bath or shower. Near Rathaus; with restaurant. AE, DC, MC, V.

Restaurants. *Blass* (E), Friedrichsplatz 12 (0621–13031). Considered Mannheim's best restaurant. Elegant interior; first-class cuisine and wines. *L'Epi d'Or* (E), H7 3 (0621–14397). High-class French cuisine. AE, DC, MC, V. *Alte Münz* (M), P7, 1 (0621–28262). Regional specialties; dancing. Adjoins onto Münz Chalet, with American-style bar and cocktail lounge. MC, V. *Amicitia* (M), Paul Martin Ufer 3 (0621–411155). Café-restaurant on the Neckar with row-boats for hire. Senior citizens' dancing. *Rosengarten* (M), Friedrichsplatz 7a (0621–443007). In the Congress Hall; grill and international specialties. AE. *Skyline* (M), (0621–443007). Rotating restaurant on the TV tower. International and regional specialties.

Beer and wine restaurants. *Eichbaum-Stammhaus* (M), P5, 9 (0621–21294). Beer tavern with grill specialties. *Goldene Gans* (M), Tattersallstr. 19 (0621–22353). Mannheim's best-known and oldest wine tavern; grill and Palatinate specialties. *Habereckl-Braustübl* (M), Q4, 15 (0621–26112). International grill and game specialties. MC. *Henninger's Gutsschänke* (M), T6, 28–29 (0621–14912). Half-timbered rustic wine tavern in side street opposite theater; home-made sausages. *Parkbräu* (M), Hauptstr. 114, Seckenheim (0621–471855). Three km. (two miles) from center. Meeting place of Mannheim's artists and and other high flyers.

　　Cafés. *Das Vollwert-Restaurant-Café* (M), N7, 12–13. Large salad bar and café with decidedly *haute* vegetarian dishes. *Kiemle,* Plankenhof-Passage; Mannheim specialties. *Rhein-Café,* Schwarzwaldstr. 38. With terrace overlooking Rhine. Also (I) restaurant and a few (I) beds. *Schuler,* Luisenpark; with music and dancing.

　　Mosbach. *Zum Radschuh* (M), Sulzbacher Str. 2 (06261–2280). 19 rooms, some with bath. *Zum Lamm* (M), Hauptstr. 59 (06261–12021). 87 rooms. Half-timbered building. DC, V. *Goldener Hirsch* (I), Hauptstr. 13 (06261–2307).

　　Neckarelz. *Schloss-hotel Hochhausen* (M), in nearby Hassmersheim (06261–3142). 20 beds. Original medieval castle rebuilt in Baroque style in 1752; owned by Counts of Helmstatt. Good restaurant with Baden wines. AE. *Schloss Neuburg* (M), in nearby Obrigheim (06261–7330). Castle-hotel with particularly good restaurant and lots of atmosphere. DC.

　　Neckargemünd. *Hotel Zum Ritter* (M), Neckarstr. 40 (06223–7035). 41 rooms. Historic inn dating from 1579. Garden with 200-year-old lilac tree and colorful restaurant serving top food—including *Rittermahl* (Knight's meal) (order in advance). Terrace; dancing on summer evenings. AE, MC, V.

　　Neckarmühlbach. (Near Hassmersheim.) *Burg Guttenberg* (E), 06266–228. Castle tavern offering own wine and Swabian specialties. Open Mar. through Oct.

　　Neckarsteinach. *Vierburgeneck* (M), Heiterswiesenweg 11 (06229–542). With riverside terrace, garden restaurant and café. *Zum Schiff* (M), Neckargemünder Str. 2 (06229–324). Most rooms with bath; riverside terrace.

　　Neckarzimmern. *Burghotel Hornberg* (M), 06261–4064. 27 rooms. Medieval castle dating from 1040. Beautiful view; café *Im Alten Marstall* and spit-roasts in the large terrace-restaurant *Götzengrill,* own wines. V.

　　Öhringen. *Schlosshotel Friedrichsruhe und Waldhotel* (L), 07941–7078. At Friedrichsruhe, six km. (four miles) north in elevated location at edge of magnificent forests. 23 rooms in castle proper and 40 in the *Waldhotel.* Owned by the Princes of Hohenlohe-Öhringen; outstanding food, own wines; small heated pool, golf course. DC, MC, V.

　　Schwäbisch Hall. *Goldener Adler* (M), Marktplatz 11 (0791–6168). Half-timbered building, an inn since 1586. AE, DC, MC, V. *Ratskeller* (M), Marktplatz 12 (0791–6181). 64 rooms; restaurant. AE, MC, V. *Ringhotel Ho-*

henlohe (M), Am Weilertor 14 (0791–75890). 96 rooms. Magnificent view of the old town from its riverside rooms, restaurant and roof-garden café. DC, MC, V.

Cafés. *Ableitner,* Bahnhofstr. 5. *Hammel,* Schulstr. 1.

Schwaigern. About 15 km. (nine miles) west of Heilbronn. *Zum Alten Rentamt,* Schlossstr. 6 (07138–5258). Restaurant and wine tavern. A few (M) beds in period-furnished rooms. Former administrative seat of the Counts of Neipperg, who still oversee its restaurant.

Walldorf. About 15 km. (ten miles) south of Heidelberg. *Holiday Inn* (E), Roter Str. (06227–360). 130 rooms, all with bath and airconditioning. Indoor and outdoor pools; sauna, solarium; tennis. AE, DC, MC, V. *Vorfelder* (E), Bahnhofstr. 28 (06227–2085). 35 rooms, all with bath or shower; restaurant. Excellent. AE, DC, MC, V.

Weikersheim. *Hotel Laurentius,* Marktplatz 5 (07934–7007). Historic building in the Tauber Valley on the Romantic Road, located next to the palace of the Princes of Hohenlohe. Interiors attractively modernized; 12 rooms, about half with bath. Vaulted cellar-restaurant with good food and pleasant outdoor cafe. AE, DC, MC, V.

Wertheim. *Schweizer Stuben* (E), Geiselbrunnweg 11, in Bettingen section (09342–4351). Small hotel in regional style; tennis courts. Well-known for its *Schweizer Stuben* restaurant, one of the finest in Germany. AE, DC, MC.

CAMPING AND YOUTH HOSTELS. Campsites are numerous in the Neckarland. For a full list of addresses write to: *Fremdenverkehrsverband Neckarland-Schwaben,* Wollhausstrasse 14, 7100 Heilbronn, and ask for the brochure *Camping in Baden Württemberg.* A full list of youth hostels is available from the German Youth Hostel Association (DJH)—see *Facts at Your Fingertips.* Or contact local and regional tourist offices.

TOURIST INFORMATION. The main regional tourist office for all areas of Neckarland-Schwaben is: **Heilbronn,** *Fremdenverkehrsverband Neckarland-Schwaben,* Wollhausstr. 14, 7100 Heilbronn (07131–629061). Other regional offices are: **Heilbronn,** *Gebietsgemeinschaft Neckar-Hohenlohe-Schwäbischer Wald,* Städt. Verkehrsamt, Rathaus, 7100 Heilbronn (07131–562270). **Künzelsau,** *Fremdenverkehrsgemeinschaft Hohenlohe,* Landratsamt, 7118 Künzelsau (07907–2055). **Tauberbischofsheim,** *Gebietsgemeinschaft Liebliches Taubertal,* Landratsamt, Gartenstr. 1, 6972 Tauberbischofsheim (09341–821).

Other local tourist offices are located at: **Heidelberg,** *Tourist Information am Hauptbahnhof,* 6900 Heidelberg (06221–21341). **Heilbronn,** *Verkehrsamt,* Rathaus, 7100 Heilbronn (07131–562270). **Hirschhorn,** *Verkehrsamt,* Alleeweg 2, 6932 Hirschhorn (Neckar), (06272–1742). **Mannheim,** *Verkehrsverein,* Verkehrspavillon, Bahnhofsplatz 1, Postfach 2560, 6800 Mannheim (0621–101011). **Mosbach,** *Gebietsgemeinschaft Neckartal-Odenwald,* Landratsamt Neckar-Odenwald Kreis, Renzstr. 7, 6940 Mosbach. **Neckargemünd,** *Verkehrsamt,* Hauptstr. 56, 6903 Neckargemünd (06223–3553).

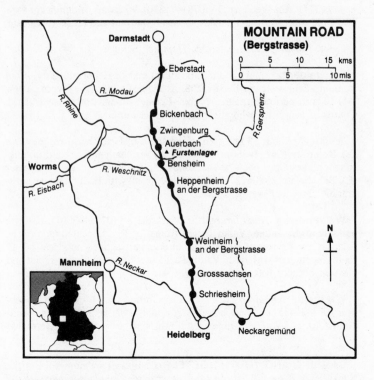

MOUNTAIN ROAD (Bergstrasse)

Darmstadt

Eberstadt

R. Modau

Bickenbach

Zwingenburg

Auerbach

▲ *Furstenlager*

Bensheim

Worms

R. Weschnitz

Heppenheim an der Bergstrasse

R. Eisbach

Weinheim an der Bergstrasse

Mannheim

Grosssachsen

R. Neckar

Schriesheim

Heidelberg

Neckargemünd

R. Rhine

R. Gersprenz

N

HOW TO GET AROUND. By train. Mannheim, at the confluence of the Rhine and Neckar, has the area's major rail station, and is indeed Germany's main rail junction. However, Heidelberg, Heilbronn, Karlsruhe and Stuttgart are also well-served by trains, both German and international, with good connections to smaller places in Neckarland-Schwaben. A map of the rail network is available from the regional tourist office in Heilbronn.

By bus. The German post buses link the smaller towns with all railroad points. In addition, Europabus No. 189 runs the whole stretch of the Burgenstrasse (Castle Road), from Mannheim to Rothenburg ob der Tauber, connecting with the Romantic Road line (EB 190) for Füssen (calling at Augsburg and Munich), as well as for Nürnberg. The route operates from May to the end of Septmber, in both directions; tickets and further information from all DER Travel Bureaus or from *Deutsche Touring,* 6000 Frankfurt am Main 90. Europabus No. 190, the Romantic Road Route, passes through the Tauber valley towns on its way to Rothenburg.

By car. The Neckar valley has a number of superb scenic routes, well maintained and marked. The principal routes here are: the Bergstrasse (Mountain Road) running parallel to the Rhine along the western edge of the Odenwald; the Nibelungenstrasse (Nibelung Road) beginning at Worms on the Rhine and continuing across the Odenwald from Bensheim to Michelstadt and beyond; the Burgenstrasse (Castle Road) running from

Mannheim to Nürnberg via Heidelberg, Heilbronn and Rothenburg; the Schwäbische Weinstrasse (Swabian Wine Road), which takes in all the wine producing towns and villages from Bad Mergentheim in the Tauber valley southwest across the middle and lower Neckar to the upper Neckar valley, ending at Metzingen. The Wine Road is an all-embracing route and a separate vacation in itself, but smaller sections of it make interesting day tours, using Stuttgart and Heilbronn as starting points.

By boat. A river trip is perhaps the finest way to enjoy the magnificent Neckar scenery. Services are varied and excellent. There are half or full-day trips from Heilbronn and Heidelberg, including, for example, a round trip to Neckarsteinach. At Heidelberg the *Weisse Flotte* steamers of the *Rhein-Neckar-Fahrgastschiffahrt* (RNF) departing from the Kongresshaus Stadthalle go either upstream past historic towns and castles, or downstream to the Rhine and the cathedral cities of Speyer and Worms. Details from any travel agent in Heidelberg or telephone 06221–20181 or in Heilbronn from *Stumpf Schiffahrt,* Friedrich-Ebert-Brücke, tel. 0731–85430.

There is a new cruise along the Neckar from Heidelberg to Stuttgart on Germany's first hotel barge, the 10-passenger *Lys* run by the U.S. cruise company *Floating through Europe.* Departures scheduled June 9 through October 27.

By bike. Maps and route plans are available from regional tourist offices. An excellent, specially marked route is the Odenwald Runde (Odenwald Forest Circuit), running from Mosbach northeast to Elztal Rittersbach, Limbach and Mudau in the very middle of the Odenwald forest, returning to Mosbach via Neckarelz; details from Fremdenverkehrsgemeinschaft Stromberg, Rathaus, 7137 Sternenfels. Organized bike tours through the Neckar Valley vineyards (with luggage transfer by accompanying bus) are arranged through the regional tourist office for Baden-Württemburg.

A list of towns with bicycle hire facilities is available from the Regional tourist office in their catalogue *Hobby & Freizeit A-Z.*

EXCURSIONS. Mannheim's tourist office offers a large selection of tours, including a bus excursion along the Burgenstrasse, daily from July to September, departing at 7.15 A.M. and returning at about 8.45 P.M. The Mannheim monthly program gives details. Heidelberg is also a good starting point for bus excursions. Heilbronn's tourist office also arranges trips, including one to Tripsdrill, a popular and original recreation park. Contact tourist offices for further details.

SPORTS. For further information about sporting and recreational activities contact regional and local tourist offices. The Fremdenverkehrsverband Neckarland-Schwaben publishes a brochure *Hobby & Freizeit A-Z* listing sporting activities in the region with useful addresses and telephone numbers.

Boating. Rowboats, pedal and paddle boats can be hired at many places on the Neckar and Tauber rivers such as at Heilbronn (Götzenturmbrücke) on the Neckar, in the Swabian Forest region near Schwäbisch Hall, as well as on the Waldsee at Murrhardt-Fornsbach and the Tiefer See at Maulbronn. Motor-boats are available at Bad Friedrichshall, Bad

Wimpfen, Eberach, Hirschhorn, Mannheim, Neckarsteinach, and Wertheim.

Fishing. Information about permits and hire of equipment may be had from tourist offices. The Jagst, Kocher and Tauber are fished for trout, pike, carp and eel, and the Neckar also has mullet.

Golf. Heidelberg at the Golfclub Heidelberg, Lobenfeld (tel. 06226–40490).

Horseback riding. Facilities exist in all larger towns and riding is a popular sport throughout the Neckar valley and Tauber valley areas. For riding lessons in Heidelberg telephone 06221–2749.

Swimming. While not prohibited in the Neckar, the amount of river traffic means that the water is not inviting for bathing; the Jagst and Kocher are more suitable. However, there are many indoor and outdoor pools in most of the larger towns, as well as bathing in artificial lakes, the natural bathing lakes of the lake plateau (Seenplatte) in the Swabian Forest, oxbow lakes and openair pools alongside the river.

Walking. The Neckar and Tauber valleys are a walker's dream, with almost endless hiking and walking tracks, many of them marked. The Bergstrasse-Odenwald and Neckar Valley-Odenwald wild life parks (Naturparks) provide the best and most dramatic terrain for hiking, but really there is almost no limit to what you can do here. Facilities are well organized and many package tours are available, including a number where your luggage is sent ahead to your destination every day; these tours are known as *Wandern Ohne Gepäck*. Details are available from the Neckarland-Schwaben Tourist Office or from Fremdenverkehrsgemeinschaft Fränkischer Odenwald, Abt. Kinbacher Str. 1, 6967 Buchen.

Gliding facilities, with instructors, exist in the region at Mannheim, Mosbach, Schwäbisch-Hall and Niederstetten, and there is a **hang-gliding** (Drachenfliegen) school at Münsingen in nearby Wernau (Kirchheimerstr. 82). There are golf courses at Mannheim, Heidelberg, Eberbach and Östringen. **Kayaking** enthusiasts can try the Neckar from Stuttgart to Heidelberg—160 km. or 100 miles on a slow current, taking six days. There are **tennis** courts in most larger towns, notably Mannheim.

WINE TASTING. Finally, a word or two about one of the greatest delights of the Neckarland. Throughout the region, wine tasting and the more erudite, indeed positively scientific, pastime of wine seminars (good German essential) are organized by an immense variety of vineyards, vintners' associations and Tourist Offices. Along the Schwäbische Weinstrasse (Swabian Wine Road) from Bad Mergentheim to Metzingen, practically every village has a wine-tasting cellar which you can visit at almost any time of day. Remember, however, that Germany has very strict drinking and driving regulations.

At Heilbronn, for example, the wine cellar of the *Genossenschaftskellerei Heilbronn-Erlenbach-Weinsberg* can be visited (07131–10027), and the Heilbronn Autumn Wine Festival takes place in mid-September. At Neckarsulm there is an informative walking trail around the vineyards and a wine cellar to be visited (07132–6319). Further information, addresses and telephone numbers are in the *Die Schwäbische Weinstrasse* brochure, available free of charge from the Fremdenverkehrsverband Neckarland-Schwaben.

THE BLACK FOREST

Stronghold of Folklore

The Black Forest, or Schwarzwald, is one of those magic names that evoke for everyone a vague feeling of romance. If it conjures up for you a somewhat sinister image, a formidable wilderness of twisted growth below and matted foliage above, through which the sun never pierces, you are quite wrong. The Black Forest isn't black in that sense. It isn't even forest in that sense. In fact, it's not easy to find much in the way of underbrush in this region. The dark evergreens that help to give the forest its name rise from soil so free of tangle that you would be excused for wondering whether landscape gardeners are not responsible for keeping it so neat and clean.

Nor does the forest extend unbroken. Conifers clothe the slopes of the mountains, which are not overpowering, though they do have their moments of pride—in the north the Hornisgrinde (1,160 meters, 3,806 feet), in the central section the Kandel (1,242 meters, 4,075 feet), in the south the Belchen (1,414 meters, 4,639 feet) and its neighbor, the region's highest, the Feldberg (1,493 meters, 4,898 feet). But the valleys are green with open fields. Your chief impression of the region will be picturesqueness—a much abused word, but one that describes the farmhouses, with their high-pitched thatched roofs, and the farm people, who still wear the regional costumes, not only on Sundays or on holidays, but often weekdays as well.

Exploring the Black Forest

The Black Forest lies along the east bank of the Rhine, running north from the Swiss frontier as far as Karlsruhe. It is divided into three regions: Northern - (Nörddicher Schwarzwald), Mid - (Mittlerer Schwarzwald), and Southern - (Südlicher). Beginning in the north and heading southward from Karlsruhe will take you through its suburb of Ettlingen, an interesting old town dating from the Roman period, which has preserved many of the buildings of its past in their pleasant location in the Alb Valley. Further up towards the end of the same valley is Bad Herrenalb, a reputed climatic resort in an exquisitely tranquil green spot surrounded by waves of forested ridges. The first inhabitants of Bad Herrenalb were Cistercian monks and the ruins (Klosterruine) of their abbey and church, founded 1149, survive. Also worth visiting is a 700-year-old saw mill (Plötzsäge-mühle) with intact water wheel and an openair museum (Freilicht-museum) in the Zeiflensberg section. Southeast from here, most easily reached from Pforzheim, is the well-known spa Wildbad in the Enz Valley, with a mountain railway to Sommerberg, the charming resort of Enzklösterle, and Bad Liebenzell in the Nagold Valley, with nearby Burg Liebenzell, a castle dating back to 1220, now an international youth forum. At the western edge of the Black Forest is Rastatt, a sizable town built around a large Baroque palace, Schloss Rastatt, which houses the West German Military Museum (Wehrgeschichtliches Museum). Between Rastatt and Baden-Baden lies the splendid Baroque Schloss Favorite. Built in 1711 by the Bohemian master-builder Rohrer for the Margravin Sybilla Augusta, widow of "Türkenlouis" Margrave Ludwig Wilhelm von Baden, as her summer residence, it has sumptuous interiors, a collection of Delft-ware, and a delightful garden. Guided tours are from March to October, with concerts in summer.

Fashionable Baden-Baden

In an age of informality, Baden-Baden continues to operate as in the 19th-century days of its glory, when the very wealthy and the very noble considered that they owed it to themselves never to miss the season at this noted spa. It is, in the evening, a soft-music-and-champagne-in-a-silver-bucket sort of place and in the daytime a horseback-riding-in-the-bridlepaths haunt—for that matter, you can go riding in a coach and pair if you feel like it.

If all this makes Baden-Baden sound somewhat like an anachronism, banish the thought. The town has long since moved confidently into the modern age, with modern facilities nicely balancing the Belle Epoque splendors. In tune with the times "anti-stress" cures are already offered, a sure sign that Baden-Baden is moving into the '80s. Its fame originally stemmed from the natural springs here. The Romans started using them first (you can see the remains of their bathing establishment, and they are still going strong. There are radioactive, chloride, and hot springs, whose waters one may drink, lie in, combine with soil for mud baths, or inhale.

The time to come to Baden-Baden is definitely the summer. August is the big month, and its last week the big week. The attraction is the horse-racing at Iffezheim, which, back in the 19th century, used to attract such giants of the literary world as Victor Hugo and Turgenev. The sights are conveniently grouped in three clusters, the largest being the bathing establishments—the massive Friedrichsbad and the Landesbad, the state hospital. The Friedrichsbad, old on the outside but with the latest equipment inside, is well supplemented by the ultra-modern Carcalla-Therme thermal pool and fitness complex. Under the Römerplatz are the ruins of the Roman baths. Three ecclesiastical buildings are tucked in among the baths—the Kloster; the Stiftskirche; and the Spitalkirche, which houses Baden-Baden's most notable art object, a 15th-century crucifix by Nikolaus von Leyden. Across from these buildings is the New Castle, or Neues Schloss, with its fine gardens: originally a 14th-century fortress, it was rebuilt as a Renaissance palace and was until 1918 the summer residence of the Grand Dukes of Baden. It now houses the Zähringer Museum of local history and art. The Old Castle (Altes Schloss) can be reached by following the Altschlossweg from the New Castle; you will be rewarded by a panoramic view of the city and Rhine plateau from the tower. Built during the 11th to 15th centuries, the Old Castle was Burg Hohenbaden, seat of the Margraves of Baden; it was destroyed by fire in the late 16th century.

A pedestrian mall leisurely brings you to the second group of buildings clustered around the Kurhaus (Casino) on the banks of the Oos, the lively little stream that flows so pleasantly through the heart of town. The Trinkhalle, where you drink the waters, stands behind the Kurhaus, and on the other side are the Municipal Theater and the Art Museum. Across the river are the new Haus des Kurgastes, "House of the Spa Guest," with the ultra-modern Kongresshaus.

The third point of interest is farther along the Oos, where the swimming pool is located. There are tennis courts on one side of the stream here and on the other side a varied collection of churches—the Evangelical Church, the English Church and the Russian Church.

One of the most traditional attractions is the 1913-built Merkur Hill Cable Railway. Reopened in 1979, new fast cabins take only minutes to reach the observation platform at the summit from where there is a superb view of the surrounding countryside.

Just out of town to the south is Yburg, a former knights' castle, destroyed in the 1525 peasants' revolt but rebuilt by the Margrave Georg Friedrich. Here you can enjoy magnificent views over the Rhine plain, and there is a restaurant. On the other side of town, just beyond the Hohenbaden ruins is Ebersteinburg, a knights' castle dating from the 13th century. Rebuilt in the 19th century for the Margraves of Baden, it is now a wine growing estate with a restaurant and panoramic views over the Murg valley.

The Black Forest Scenic Roads

Baden-Baden is the starting point of the Black Forest High Road (Schwarzwald-Hochstrasse) that runs through a succession of charming little resorts, all of which share the same delightful natural settings—Bühlerhöhe, Plättig, Sand, Unterstmatt, Mummelsee (near that high peak already mentioned, the Hornisgrinde), Ruherstein, Allerheiligen (monastery ruins and the Bütten waterfalls), Oppenau, Bad Peterstal and Bad Griesbach, Kniebis and Freudenstadt.

Two other scenic drives, parallel to the High Road, run through the northern half of the Black Forest in a north–south direction. The one to the east is the Black Forest Low Road (Schwarzwald-Tälerstrasse), beginning at Rastatt and continuing through Gernsbach (interesting St. Jacob's Church and three castles in the vicinity); Forbach, with an old wooden bridge and a notable parish church; and Baiersbronn (Sankenbach waterfalls in the vicinity) to Freudenstadt. The one to the west is the Baden Wine Road (Badische Weinstrasse), starting in Baden-Baden and proceeding through the picturesque wine villages on the slopes of the Black Forest to Offenburg, once a free imperial town, and to Gengenbach in the Kinzig Valley, from where you can continue either to Triberg or to Freiburg.

Freudenstadt was founded in 1599 by the Duke of Württemberg to house the local silver miners. The residents are still mining silver, but not from the earth. It comes from tourists now, who seem to provide richer pickings. Freudenstadt's Number One claim to distinction is that it enjoys more hours of sunshine during the year than any other German resort. It lies in beautiful country, so the great sport here is walking, and there are approximately 160 kilometers (100 miles) of well-tended paths in the vicinity for that purpose. There is also good fishing and hunting. If you get bored with nature, wander about the lovely town square's Renaissance arches and good shops.

Continuing southward, you pass through Alpirsbach, another climatic health resort with a fine Romanesque monastery church (Klosterkirche); Schiltach, where there is a pleasant marketplace; Wolfach (the castle and the town gate are to be noted, as is the glass-blowing factory, Glashütte, which can be visited); Gutachtal, for local color (you'll see regional costumes worn and impressive peasant houses; and may visit the Freilicht Museum, an openair museum of rural life); Hornberg, where there is a castle; and thus come to Triberg, a highly popular health resort. The town has an excellent museum (Triberger Schwarzwaldmuseum) charting the cultural and economic history of the Black Forest, with an interesting collection of clocks, handcrafts, folk costumes, and blown-glass articles. Take the path from the Gutach bridge through the Kurpark to the waterfalls (Wasserfälle) which are perhaps the most beautiful in Germany, the water dropping some 163 meters (535 feet) in seven steps. Triberg is also a good central point for excursions through the area, especially to some of the peaks in the region.

You are now deep in cuckoo-clock country. To prove it, there is at Furtwangen a really remarkable historical clock collection (Uhrenmuseum). East of Furtwangen and southeast of Triberg we come through the climatic and cold water (Kneipp) resort of Villingen, a 1,000-year-old town with a 12th-century church, site of the largest and most famous Black Forest carnival (Fasching) processions lasting from the Sunday before Shrove Tuesday until the early hours of Ash Wednesday; Schwenningen, in whose vicinity the Neckar has its source; Bad Dürrheim with its chloride brine baths; and finally to Donaueschingen. The palace at Donaueschingen has an important museum (Fürstenbergisches Museum, Karlsplatz) with works by German old masters and many fine medieval manuscripts. The palace is set in a park where you can watch the birth of the Danube, which, formed by underground sources that surface here and by the river Brigach, flows almost 2,900 kilometers (1,800 miles) to the Black Sea. Donaueschingen lies on the main road connecting Bodensee with Freiburg.

Freiburg—Capital of the Black Forest

The largest city of this region and its capital, Freiburg im Breisgau is the gateway to the southernmost part of the Black Forest, where its mountains are highest (Freiburg itself is backed by a wall of them). It was badly damaged in the war, but was fortunate in that its most spectacular buildings, such as the cathedral and the Kaufhaus, escaped. Those that were destroyed have been mostly replaced by new structures, which for all their modernity are inspired by motifs borrowed from the medieval houses about them.

The view of the city from the surrounding hills is dominated by the cathedral, whose roof rises as high as many of the steeples of the other churches of the town, while its own lacework steeple soars still higher—to 112 meters (370 feet). Among its eight bells is a five-ton bell, cast in the 13th century and called Hosanna, or in popular version, Susanne.

Freiburg's cathedral was started about 1200 and finished some three centuries later; its steeple has been called the most beautiful tower of Christianity's finest period. The 13th- to 16th-century stained glass windows are remarkably good (some have been removed to the Augustiner Museum for protection), the main altar painting is by Hans Baldung Grien and dates from between 1512–16. There are also several woodcarvings by Hans Wydyz; a painting by Lukas Cranach the Elder in the sacristy; an altar painting by Holbein the Younger in one of the choir chapels; Gobelin tapestries; and many other treasures.

The rest of the square (a pedestrian zone) in which the cathedral stands is also interesting. On its south side is one of the most fascinating buildings in the town, the Kaufhaus, in front of which, if you pick the right time, you may watch the colorful openair market. It could hardly have a more picturesque background. Four great arches at the base of the Kaufhaus curve over the sidewalk; at the next level, four statues of Habsburg monarchs stand against the wall between cunningly-shaped windows; above, the steep roof rises so sharply that its height seems to equal that of all the building beneath it, and from its slope, tiny windows peer out of gables like eyes half-covered by sleepy eyelids. And at the two corners, standing above the outermost columns of the arches, as though balanced on a single stilt, are two pulpit-like excrescences wearing high conical pointed hats. As though this were not enough for one square, it also contains the Wenzinger Palace, a gem of 18th-century architecture housing the City Museum of local history.

A good many other sights might be mentioned in Freiburg, but we will restrict ourselves to two other squares. One is the Rathaus square, in which you will see the City Hall, made by joining together two 16th-century patrician houses, complete with Renaissance gables and oriels. Of the latter, the southern one, built in 1545 carries a much admired bas-relief, *The Maiden and the Unicorn*. Chimes ring at noon from the City Hall tower. The 13th-century church of St. Martin stands opposite the façade of the old City Hall; if you wish to see it at its best, come at night, when the Gothic cloisters are lighted. The other square you should not miss is Oberlinden, for its medieval burgher houses, one of the oldest inns in Germany, Zum Roten Bären (the Red Bear), and towering above the square's end the 13th-century Swabian Gate.

You might also visit the university, founded in 1457, one of the most important in Germany, whose buildings are conveniently located in the heart of the city. Freiburg is the cultural as well as the commercial center of this region (with no less than six museums with important collections), and the university is at once part of the cause and part of the result of this circumstance. American visitors to Freiburg should pause to pay their respects to Martin Waldseemüller's birthplace—for they owe their name to him. It was this geographer who for the first time put upon a map the word America.

Excursions from Freiburg

The nearest excursion takes you in 45 minutes from the city itself up to the top of the 1,284-meter (4,200-foot) Schauinsland Mountain by streetcar, bus, and cable car. You can also drive up on a dramatic mountain road, which is also used for car races. If you are driving, you can carry on from Schauinsland to the summer and winter resorts of Todtnauberg and Todtnau, as well as to Feldberg and Titisee. Another pleasant trip is to a small spa north of Freiburg, Glottertal, the home town of the Black Forest Girls' Choir whose broadcasts have made it famous all over Germany.

You might also go west to the Kaiserstuhl, a height near the banks of the Rhine, which stands as a sort of advance guard of the Black Forest mountains, for at Freiburg the wall ends abruptly, and the level plain of the Rhine succeeds it. This is famous wine country, and the towns in the Kaiserstuhl region—you might select Ihringen as typical—are devoted to the cultivation of the grape.

Just beyond Ihringen, on the Rhine and on the French border, is Breisach, whose St. Stephen's Cathedral is worth the trip. It is a massive 14th-century structure perched above the river. Its high altar and frescos are particularly interesting. Breisach also encloses remains from Roman times and old city gates, among the latter notably the Rheintor. The views from Breisach are quite stunning, and you will easily see why its position made it highly sought-after by warring factions.

Traveling east from Freiburg, the main road traverses the Höllental (Hell Valley), a wild and rocky gorge, and leads to the lovely resort town of Hinterzarten, the highest point on the Freiburg–Donaueschingen road and about 800 years old. Some buildings date back to the 12th century, the Oswaldkirche (St. Oswald's Church), for example, to 1146. About five kilometers (three miles) away lies Titisee, a rare jewel among lakes, set in a mighty forest; the only settlement on the lake, also called Titisee, was built primarily for summer vacationists and winter sports enthusiasts. There are more than 100 kilometers (60 miles) of signposted walks around the village.

Titisee, like Todtnau, is a good base from which to visit Feldberg, the highest mountain of the Black Forest. Halfway between Titisee and Todtnau (about 11 kilometers, seven miles, from each) lies the highest point on this road, the Feldbergsattel. From here it is an easy walk to the summit of Feldberg, and a most rewarding one, for the mountain flora is abundant and fascinating. Skiers flock here in winter.

A few miles south of Titisee is Schluchsee, another beautiful lake in a green setting; this is, however, an artificial lake and at its lower end you can observe the mighty dam holding back its waters. It, too, is a popular summer vacation spot.

On the Upper Rhine

South of Schluchsee is St. Blasien, possessing a magnificently decorated church with a mighty dome that seems incongruous in these surroundings. It is in fact the legacy of a former Benedictine abbey. From St. Blasien there is an interesing little circular swing into the extreme southwestern tip of Germany, delineated by the upper Rhine, which flows in an east–west direction as far as Basel where it makes a right angle continuing north. This is chiefly a scenic trip. It will take us through the picturesque mountain valley town of Bernau; Schönau, from which one may ascend the 1,414-meter (4,639-foot) Belchen; Badenweiler, which claims to have been a spa for at least 1,900 years and has the best preserved Roman baths north of the Alps, built by the Emperor Vespasian in the first century A.D.; Müllheim to the west, if you don't mind retracing your route to Badenweiler afterwards, for the sake of visiting the Markgräflerland wine country of which this town is the center (southward from Müllheim the road will land you in Basel, Switzerland); back on our main loop, Kandern, a resort famous for its bakery specialties; Lörrach, the site of Rötteln Castle, only a few miles from Basel; and then either through Schopfheim or through the historic town of Säckingen (almost as much Swiss as German) and the Wehra Valley to Todtmoos, a climatic health resort with a famous pilgrimage church, and thus back to St. Blasien.

The road continues southward through the Albtal, a deep rocky valley, where it is necessary to dodge continuously in and out of tunnels hewn through the rock. At Albbruck we reach the Rhine, whose left bank is in Switzerland, and then turn east to Waldshut, another storybook town, with a tower straddling one of its streets. We pass through Tiengen, with its old castle and suddenly, in front of us, is Switzerland again.

PRACTICAL INFORMATION FOR
THE BLACK FOREST

TELEPHONES. We have given telephone codes for all the towns and villages in the hotel and restaurant lists that follow. These codes need only be used when calling from outside the town or village concerned.

HOTELS AND RESTAURANTS. Accommodations here are varied and plentiful, with something for every pocket, from simple rooms in private pensions or on the farm (a brochure entitled *Urlaub auf dem Bauernhof* is available from Postbox 5443 in 7800 Freiburg), through rustic gasthofs or inns with heaps of local color, to luxury suites in first-class hotels, beauty farms and luxury health-cure establishments. In this small, southwestern corner of Germany even the simplest gasthaus is likely to offer a good meal, while dining in the grander hotels is memorably highclass. Bed and breakfast stays at a farm can be had for as little as DM.15

to DM.20, while the average price for overnight accommodations outside the major resorts ranges between DM.22 and DM.35; in fashionable centers double this amount or more. Self-catering holiday apartments are also frequently available in most resorts and cost from around DM.22 to DM.60 a day.

Baden-Baden and Freiburg are particularly well off for accommodations in all categories. In summer Schluchsee and Titisee are apt to be crowded, so it is best to reserve well ahead. Note that some hotels, particularly those in spa resorts, close for a period in winter, so check when booking.

For a list of good-value private accommodation, of which there is plenty throughout the region, write to the tourist office in Freiburg asking for the brochure *Urlaub zu Kleinen Preisen* (literally "Holidays at small prices").

Bad Bellingen. Thermal resort. *Paracelsus* (M), Akazienweg 1 (07635–1018). 22 rooms. Quiet. *Quellenhof* (M), Im Mittelgrund 1 (07635–1072). 23 rooms; heated pool. No restaurant. *Gasthof Schwanen* (I), Rheinstr. 50 (07635–1314). 14 rooms. Asparagus specialties and own wine in excellent restaurant.

Bad Dürrheim. *Kur- und Sporthotel Hänslehof* (M), Hofstr. 13 (07726–8034). 126 rooms. Rustic-style decor, sauna, indoor pool, tennis; fine *Hänslehof* restaurant. AE, DC, MC, V. *Salinensee* (M), Am Salinensee 1 (07726–8022). 20 rooms. Quiet location on lake; good restaurant and terrace. *Krone* (I), Friedrichstr. 22 (07726–334). Small; good restaurant.

Baden-Baden. *Badischer Hof* (E), Langestr. 47 (07221–22827). 150 rooms. Thermal water in rooms with bath. A Steigenberger hotel in 17th-century former monastery building. AE, DC, MC, V. *Brenner's Parkhotel* (E), Schillerstr. 6 (07221–3530). 109 rooms. Internationally famed luxury hotel. Garden terrace opening on to park; indoor pool; elegant bar; superb cuisine. *Der Kleine Prinz* (E), Lichtentaler Str. 36 (07221–3464). 20 beds. The city's prettiest hotel. No restaurant. AE, DC, MC. *Der Selighof* (E), Fremersbergstr. 125 (07221–2171). One of the most beautifully situated hotels in Baden-Baden, right next to golf course. 200 beds, all rooms with bath or shower. Pool and sauna. Restaurant and wine tavern. AE. *Holiday-Inn Sporthotel Baden-Baden* (E), Falkenstr. 2 (07221–33011). 121 rooms; apartments. Modern and comfortable, with sports and beauty farm. International cuisine in *Galerie* restaurant; wine tavern and whiskey bar. AE, DC, MC, V.

Greiner (M), Lichtentaler Allee 88 (07221–71135). 33 rooms; charming and good value. No restaurant. *Holland* (M), Sofienstr. 14 (07221–25595). 60 rooms; indoor pool, garden terrace. No restaurant. *Müller* (M), Lange Str. 34 (07221–23211). 26 rooms, some apartments. No restaurant. *Tanneck* (M), Werderstr. 14 (07221–23035). 30 beds, over half rooms with bath or shower. Quiet location above Kurhaus and casino at the Kurpark. V. *Tannenhof* (M), Hans-Bredow Str. 20 (07221–271181). 24 rooms, most with bath. Fine view. Bar serving good Baden wines; small restaurant.

Adler (I), Oosers Hauptstr. 1 (07221–61858). In suburb of Oos, family hotel near station with good bus connections to town center. AE, DC, MC, V. *Am Markt* (I), Marktplatz 18 (07221–22747). 27 rooms. Attractive; good restaurant. AE, DC, MC, V. *Gasthaus-Hotel zum Felsen* (I), Geroldsauer Str.

43 (07221–71641). 9 rooms, most with shower. Cozy hotel, good restaurant. In Lichtental section.

Restaurants. In addition to those in the main hotels (all of which are expensive and generally very good), try one of the following: *Mirabell-im-Kurhaus* (E), Kaiserallee 1 (07221–22717). In spa establishment, with terrace, wine tavern and dance-bar. AE, DC, MC, V. *Stahlbad* (E), Augustaplatz (07221–24569). Superb cuisine in pleasant surroundings. AE, DC, MC, V. *Merkurius* (M), Klosterbergstr. 2 (07223–5474). A little out of town in Varnhalt, in former country house. First-class food; fine view from terrace; some rooms. Closed Sun., Mon., and Tues. evenings. AE, DC, MC. *Zum Alde Gott* (M), Weinstr. 10 (07223–5513). Neuweier section; fine food. Closed Thurs. and Fri. lunch. AE, DC, MC, V.

Café. *Café-König* (M), Lichtentaler Str. 12 (07221–23573). Good pastries.

Badenweiler. *Eckerlin* (E), Römerstr. 2 (07632–5061). 37 rooms. Pleasant location; indoor and outdoor pools. *Parkhotel* (E), Ernst-Eisenlohr Str. 6 (07632–710). 85 rooms, also a few apartments. Quiet location with pleasant view; thermal baths. Fine grill and other specialties in *Parkstüble* restaurant. *Römerbad* (E), Schlossplatz 1 (07632–700). 111 rooms. Luxurious, with thermal baths in house, thermal-water outdoor and indoor pools; excellent restaurant, bar. V. *Schwarzmatt* (E), Schwarzmattstr. (07632–6042). 45 rooms, 12 apartments, all rooms with bath. Indoor pool, solarium. Quiet, in pleasant location. *Romantik-Hotel Sonne* (E), Moltkestr. 4 (07632–5053). 40 rooms; some holiday apartments with all comforts and hotel service. Dates back to 1620; exquisite cuisine in colorful *Altdeutsche Weinstube*. AE, DC, MC, V. *Post* (M), Sofienstr. 1 (07632–5051). 55 rooms, some in annex; indoor pool; attractive and quiet with good food. MC. *Berghotel Hochblauen* (I), 07632–388. 15 rooms. On summit of Hochblauen mountain. Pleasant; half-board only.

Bad Herrenalb. *Mönch's Post-Hotel* (E), Dobelstr. 2 (07083–2002). 50 rooms. Heated pool, hunting and fishing. Fine cuisine in renowned old tavern *Klosterschänke*. AE, DC. *Parkhotel Adrion* (E), Oswald-Zobel-Str. 11 (07083–3041). 70 rooms. Quiet and in scenic location. *Kull* (M), Bernsteinweg 3 (07083–2088). 37 rooms; indoor pool. AE, MC. *Landhaus Jäger* (M), Birkenwaldstr. 7 (07083–1666). 14 rooms; quiet; indoor pool. *Waldhotel Sonnenblick* (I), Im Wiesengrund 2 (07083–2749). Modern chalet-style pension on the edge of the hamlet of Gaistal. 125 rooms, most with bath. No restaurant, but good breakfast and cold evening snacks. Peaceful and friendly.

Bad Liebenzell. *Kronen* (M), Badweg 7 (07052–2081). 60 rooms, all with bath or shower. Noted restaurant (try their ten-year-old *Kirschwasser*). *Ochsen* (M), Karlstr. 12 (07052–2074). 48 rooms, all with bath or shower in the annex. Good restaurant. AE. *Waldhotel* (M), Hölderlinstr. 1 (07052–2095). 28 rooms; comfortable. No restaurant.

Baiersbronn. Health and winter sports resort seven km. (4½ miles) north of Freudenstadt. *Kurhotel Mitteltal* (E), Gärtenbühlweg 14 (07442–471). 65 rooms, all with bath; 36 apartments. In the Mitteltal section; luxurious establishment with various sports facilities. Excellent res-

taurants *Bareiss* (E) and rustic *Kaminstube* (M) with regional cuisine. *Kur-
und Sporthotel Traube* (E), Tonbachstr. 237 (07442–4920). 182 rooms, all
with bath. Luxurious hotel in the Tonbach section. Indoor pool, sauna,
sports room, tennis. Renowned French restaurant *Schwarzwaldstube* (E),
and hotel restaurant *Köhlerstube*, both atmospheric with good-value *à la
carte* menus. AE, DC.

Bühl. *Schloss-Kurhotel-Bühlerhöhe* (E), 07226–50. 70 rooms. Beautiful
location about 20 km. (12 miles) south of Baden-Baden along the Schwarzwald-Hochstrasse, and about the same distance east of Bühl. Health cures,
indoor pool, park. Good restaurant, wine tavern and cocktail bar. *Grüne
Bettlad* (M), Blumenstr. 4 (07223–24238). 8 rooms. Atmospheric inn with
good food. *Plättig* (M), 07226–226. 66 rooms. Scenic location on Schwarzwald-Hochstrasse, in Bühlertal. Indoor pool; excellent restaurant and bar.
AE, MC, V. Also along the same road in the Bühlertal at Sand, *Kurhaus Sand*
(M), 07626–222. 33 rooms, half with bath; once a favorite of Queen Wil-
helmina of the Netherlands. Quiet, with restaurant.
    Restaurant. *Burg Windeck* (E), Kappelwindeckstr. 104 (07223–23671).
Partially restored castle-fortress with top-notch restaurant and view. AE,
DC, MC.

Enzklösterle. *Waldhorn-Post* (E), Wildbaderstr. 1 (07085–711). 48
rooms. In same family since 1766. Sauna, tennis; restaurant with fine game
specialties from own estate. AE, DC, V. *Enztalhotel* (M), Freudenstädter Str.
67 (07085–611). 51 rooms, 2 apartments. Quiet location; indoor pool.
Hetschelhof (M), Hetschelhofweg 1 (07085–273). 18 rooms, half with bath.
Quiet location; (Silence Hotel); terrace, restaurant, cafe. DC.

Ettlingen. *Hotel Erbprinz.* (E) Rheinstr. 1 (07243–12071). Over 200
year-old building recently fully renovated to provide modern comfort
without the loss of atmosphere. 50 rooms with bath or shower. Elegant
and cosy restaurant with best of traditional German cooking. AE, DC, MC.

Feldberg. *Dorint-Hotel-Feldberger Hof* (E), Am Seebuck 12, in the
town itself (07676–311). 70 rooms, also some apartments. Indoor pool,
sauna, ski school and lifts. AE, DC, MC, V. *Berghotel Behabühl* (M), Talstr.
10 (07655–305). 14 rooms, all with bath or shower. In the Bärental section
in the direction of Titisee. Quiet location with fine view from terrace. *Waldeck* (I), Windfällstr. 19 (07655–364). 20 rooms, all with bath. In the
Altglashütten section. Restaurant with garden. *Höhengasthof Grüner
Baum* (I), 07655–234. 23 rooms, most with bath; with annex. Quiet, in
Neuglashütten, in the direction of Schluchsee. *Seehof* (I), am Windfällw-
eiher (07655–255). 11 rooms, all with bath. In Altglashütten. Terrace and
restaurant.

Freiburg. *Colombi* (E), Rotteckring 16 (0761–31415). 80 rooms with
balconies, many with bath. Excellent *Falken Stube* restaurant; bar, wine
tavern. AE, DC, MC, V. *Novotel* (E), Am Karlsplatz (0761–31295). 112 rooms,
all with bath. Modern; restaurant, bar. AE, DC, MC, V. *Panorama-
Jägerhäusle* (E), Winterer Str. 89 (0761–551011). 86 rooms. In Herden
suburb. Primarily for weight-reducing cures; indoor pool, sauna. AE, DC,

MC, V. *Victoria* (E), Eisenbahnstr. 54 (0761–31881). 40 rooms. Very comfortable; good restaurant. AE, DC, MC, V.

Barbara (M), Poststr. 4 (0761–26060). 20 rooms; quiet. No restaurant. *Rappen* (M), Münsterplatz 13 (0761–31353). 19 rooms. Of recent vintage, with traditional Black Forest furniture in reception rooms. Restaurant. AE, DC, MC. *Zum Roten Bären* (M), Oberlinden 12 (0761–36969). 33 rooms. Ring Hotel. Reputed to be Germany's oldest inn, dating from 1311. Atmospheric restaurant with Black Forest specialties. AE, DC, MC, V. *Schwarzwälder Hof* (I), Herrenstr. 43 (0761–32386). 62 beds. With delightful Weinstube. V. *Stephanie* (I), Poststr. 3 (0761–33566). 39 beds. Quiet; no restaurant.

Restaurants. Restaurants in Freiburg have a habit of changing names and hands, even of closing; however, in addition to the above hotel restaurants, try the following: *Kühler Krug* (E), Torplatz 1 (0761–29103). In Günterstal district; very fine; also a few rooms. AE. *Oberkirch's Weinstuben* (E), Münsterplatz 22 (0761–31011). Near Kaufhaus. Attractive, with own wines; also (M) hotel. *Greiffenegg-Schlössle* (M), 0761–32728. On Schlossberg, with magnificent views. AE, DC, MC, V. *Ratskeller* (M), Münsterplatz (0761–37530). In the restored Kornhaus (1498). Closed Sun. AE, MC, V. *Wappen von Freiburg* (M), (0761–403840). On the Lorettoberg, with fine view. DC. *Weinstube Karcher* (M), Eisenbahnstr. 43 (0761–22773). Wine tavern. *Zur Trotte* (M), Fischerau 28 (0761–30777). Wine tavern.

Freudenstadt. *Kurhotel Eden* (E), Am Golfplatz (07441–7037). 86 rooms, all with bath or shower. Sauna, pool, water treatments, golf. Terrace, bar, restaurant. Quiet location outside town. AE, DC, MC, V. *Steigenberger* (E), Karl-von-Hahn-Str. 129 (07441–81071). 145 rooms, all with bath or shower. Sauna, riding, tennis; two restaurants. AE, DC, MC, V. *Kurhotel Sonne am Kurpark* (E), Turnhallestr. 63 (07441–6044). A Ring Hotel. 48 rooms, most with bath or shower. Sauna, riding, golf. AE, DC, MC, V.

Bären (M), Langestr. 33 (07441–2729). 15 rooms with bath or shower. Good restaurant. DC. *Langenwaldsee* (M), Strassburgerstr. 99 (07441–2234). 34 rooms, most with bath or shower. New, country-house style hotel, on edge of town in attractive location; pools; restaurant, cafe. *Luz-Posthotel* (M), Stuttgarter Str. 5 (07441–2421). 45 rooms, all with bath or shower. Terrace, restaurant. *Württemberg Hof* (M), Lauterbadstr. 10 (07441–6047). 28 rooms, some with bath or shower; rooms are small. Indoor pool, sauna, riding; restaurant. AE, DC, MC.

Zur Stadt (I), Lossburger Str. 19 (07441–2719). Pension with 16 rooms, some with bath or shower. Quiet location; no restaurant.

Restaurants. *Bärenschlössle* (M), Christophstal (07441–7850). AE. *Ratskeller* (M), Marktplatz 8 (07441–2693). Colorful. V.

Hinterzarten. *Parkhotel Adler* (E), Adlerplatz 3 (07652–711). 76 rooms, all with bath. Owned by the same family since 1446. Wood paneling and antique furnishings; dancing, indoor pool, tennis; good cuisine. Located in own park. AE, DC, MC, V. *Kesslermühle* (M), Erlenbrucker Str. 45 (07652–1290). 31 rooms, all with bath. Quiet location; indoor pool, sauna, solarium. *Sassenhof* (M), Adlerweg 17 (07652–1515). 24 rooms. Pleasant; indoor pool; no restaurant. *Weisses Rössle* (M), Freiburgerstr. 38 (07652–1411). 67 rooms. Renowned for comfort; park location; indoor pool, tennis; attractive restaurant. AE, MC, V.

Hornberg. *Adler* (M), Hauptstr. 66 (07833–367). 24 beds, half rooms with bath. Restaurant. AE, DC, MC. *Schloss Hornburg* (M), Auf dem Schlossberg 1 (07833–6841). 31 rooms, most with bath; terrace with fine view; café and restaurant. AE, DC, MC, V.

Kehl. On the Rhine, connected by bridge with Strasbourg. *Astoria* (M), Bahnhofstr. 4 (07851–3066). 30 rooms, most with bath. AE, DC, MC, V. *Europa* (M), Strassburger Str. 9 (07851–2795). 100 beds, most rooms with bath. Recently renovated. V.

Restaurant. *Traube* (M), Grossherzog-Friedrich-Str. 18 (07851–2241). French cuisine; also a few beds. AE, DC, MC.

Königsfeld. *Schwarzwald-Hotel* (M), (07725–7091). 56 rooms, half with bath. Some 13 km. (eight miles) north of Villingen. Villa-like; fine eating in the colorful *Fässle* restaurant, noted for trout dishes. AE, DC, MC, V.

Mummelsee. *Berghotel Mummelsee* (I), 07842–1088. 25 rooms. Quiet location on the Schwarzwald-Hochstrasse near the high peak of Hornisgrinde; postal address is Seebach. V.

Münstertal. *Romantik-Hotel Spielweg* (M), Spielweg 61, in Obermünsterthal (07636–618). 36 rooms, all with bath or shower. Beautiful old inn with charming and atmospheric rooms. First-class restaurant serving regional specialties; has the reputation of being the best Gasthof in the area. AE, V.

Nagold. *Hotel Post Gästehaus* (M), Bahnhofstr. 3–4 (07452–4048). Recently built guesthouse combining modern architecture with antique interiors. No restaurant. 24 rooms, all with bath. AE, DC, MC, V.

Restaurant. *Romantik-Restaurant Alte Post* (M), Bahnhofstr. 2 (07452–4221). Historic inn dating from 1696, with food a mixture of local specialties and *nouvelle cuisine.* The King of Württemberg was among restaurant guests; trout and apple cake are specialties. Closed Sat. lunch and 2 weeks in Jan. AE, DC, MC, V.

Oberkirch. *Romantik-Hotel Obere Linde* (M), Hauptstr. 25–27 (07802–3038). 46 rooms, most with bath or shower. Dating back to 1659, one of the most beautiful half-timbered houses in the area, linked by wood bridge to annex. Excellent restaurant. AE, DC, MC, V.

Pforzheim. *City Hotel* (E), Bahnhofstr. 8 (07231–3811). Near the station. 27 beds, half the rooms with bath; no restaurant. AE, DC, MC, V. *Gute Hoffnung* (E), Dillsteiner Str. 9–11 (07231–22011). 26 rooms, some with bath. Fine restaurant serving regional delicacies and *nouvelle cuisine* in French countryhouse atmosphere. *Ruf* (E), Am Schlossberg (07231–16011). 90 rooms. Opposite the station in the city center, but still quiet. DC, MC, V. *Monch's Schlosshotel* (M), Lindenstr. 2 (07231–16051). Bar and *bijou* restaurant. AE, DC, MC, V. *Schwarzwaldhotel* (M), Schlossgatterweg 7 (07231–32818). 50 beds.

Restaurants. *Hoheneck* (E), Huchenfelderstr. 70 (07231–71633). Out of town in the direction of Bad Liebenzell. Excellent cuisine and atmospheric surroundings. AE, DC. *Goldener Adler* (M), Leopold Platz (07231–15081). MC. *Ketters Bräustüble* (I), Jahnstr. 10 (07231–21732).

Schluchsee. *Hetzel-Hotel Hochschwarzwald* (E), Am Riesenbühl (07656–70326). 212 rooms. New and luxurious; Kneipp cures as well as every imaginable facility. AE, DC, MC, V. *Parkhotel Flora* (M), Sonnhalde 22 (07656–452). 26 rooms, all with bath or shower and balcony; indoor pool. *Schiff* (M), Am Kirchplatz (07656–252). 32 rooms; indoor pool. *Wochners-Hotel Sternen* (M), Dresselbacherstr. 1 (07656–251). 43 rooms; local-style restaurant. *Blasiwälder Hof* (M), 07656–276. In the Blasiwald section; quiet, near the forest.

Titisee. *Schwarzwald-Hotel-am-See* (E), Seestr. 12 (07651–8111). 86 rooms. Indoor pool, private beach, tennis, terraces overlooking the lake; excellent food. AE, MC, V. *Kurhotel Brugger* (M), Strandbadstr. 14 (07651–8010). 67 rooms; own beach and lakeside terrace. AE, DC, MC, V. *Romantik-Hotel Adler-Post* (M), Hauptstr. 16 (07651–5066). 32 rooms. In Neustadt suburb. 400-year-old coaching inn with atmospheric restaurants *Posthalterei* and *Rotisserie Postillion*. AE, DC, MC, V. *Seehotel Wiesler* (M), Strandbadstr. 5 (07651–8330). 20 rooms, all with bath or shower; indoor pool. AE, V. *Seestern* (I), Jägerstr. 1 (07651–8417). 15 beds, all rooms with bath or shower. Private pension with café.

Triberg. *Romantik-Hotel Parkhotel Wehrle* (M), Marktplatz (07722–86020). 56 rooms. Known since 1608 as the "Golden Ox," lying between Triberg market place and its own park, in which are a guest house and park villa, heated openair pool, indoor pool, sauna, solarium, etc. Excellent food; extra charge for breakfast. AE, DC, MC, V. *Hotel-Cafe Adler* (M), Hauptstr. 52 (07722–4574). 21 rooms. AE, MC, V. *Burghof* (I), Schulstr. 8b (07722–4395). Quiet location, most rooms with bath; no restaurant.

Villingen. *Parkhotel* (M), Brigachstr. 8 (07721–22011). 18 rooms, all with bath. *Gasthof Bären* (I), Bickenstr. 19 (07721–55541). 43 rooms. AE, MC, V.

Wildbad. *Badhotel* (E), Kurplatz (07081–1760). 128 beds, 60 rooms with bath. Thermal baths; arcaded inner court; new 1984. AE, MC. *Sommerberg* (E), (07081–1740). 98 rooms, all with bath and balcony offering fine view. On Sommerberg (cable railway). In modern semi-circular form; luxurious, with Black Forest-style decor. Indoor pool, tennis; terrace cafe. Fine *Jägerstüble* restaurant. *Bergfrieden* (M), Bätznerstr. 78 (07081–2594). 53 rooms. *Hospiz Deutscher Hof* (M), Konig-Karl-Str. 17 (07081–2766). Hillside location near the mountain railway station. 48 beds; cozy restaurant. *Waldesruh* annex at Panoramastr. 15. *Kurhotel-Post* (M), Kurplatz 2 (07081–1611). 69 rooms. Over 60 years of tradition. Indoor pool; restaurant and terrace-café. Annex at Uhlandstr. 40. AE, MC.

CAMPING AND YOUTH HOSTELS. There are more than 85 campsites in the Black Forest. Some of the nicest in the north are at Bad Herrenalb, Bad Wildbad, Alpirsbach, Schömberg, Enzklösterle, Bad Liebenzell and Calw, while the south has more than 40 excellent sites. For a full list write to: *LFVV Baden-Württemberg,* Postfach 304, 7000 Stuttgart

(0711–481045), asking for their brochure *Camping in Baden-Württemberg*, or inquire at the German Camping Club's advice offices in Freiburg, Gugel-Werke, Starkenstr. 15. A list of youth hostels in the region is available from the *German Youth Hostel Association (DJH)*, *Landesverband Baden*, Weinweg 43, 7500 Karlsruhe, or *DJH Landesverband Schwaben*, Urachstr. 37, 7000 Stuttgart 1.

FARMHOUSE VACATIONS. Holidays on farms are offered, some on working farms with animals. Accommodations vary. Write for the brochure *Farm Holidays in Baden-Württemberg* to *Verein zur Förderung des Urlaubs auf dem Bauernhof*, Postfach 5443, 7800 Freiburg (0761–274012).

TOURIST INFORMATION. The regional tourist office for the state of Baden-Württemberg is: *LFVV Baden-Württemberg*, 23 Bussenstr., 7000 Stuttgart (0711–481045). For the Black Forest in general and the southern part in particular: *FVV Schwarzwald*, 45 Bertoldstr., 7800 Freiburg (0761–31317). For the northern part: *Schwarzwald Information*, Marktplatz 1, 7530 Pforzheim (07231–302140).

A selection of local tourist offices follows. **Baden-Baden,** Kurverwaltung, Augustaplatz 8, 7570 Baden-Baden (07221–275200). **Badenweiler,** Kurverwaltung, Ernst-Eisenlohr-Str. 4, 7847 Badenweiler (07632–72110). **Bad Herrenalb,** Kurverwaltung, 7506 Bad Herrenalb (07083–7933). **Bad Liebenzell,** Kurverwaltung, Kurhausdamm 4, 7263 Bad Liebenzell (07052–2015). **Feldberg,** Kurverwaltung im Ortsteil Altglashütten, Kirchgasse 1, 7821 Feldberg (07655–1092). **Freiburg,** Verkehrsamt, Rotteckring 14, 7800 Freiburg im Breisgau (0761–2163289). **Freudenstadt,** Kurverwaltung, Lauterbadstr. 5, 7290 Freudenstadt (07441–6074). **Pforzheim,** Stadtinformation, Rathaus, Marktplatz 1, 7530 Pforzheim (07321–392190). **Schluchsee,** Kurverwaltung, Fischbacher Str., 7826 Schluchsee (07656–301). **Titisee-Neustadt,** Kurverwaltung, in Titisee, 7820 Titisee-Neustadt (07651–8101). **Triberg,** Kurverwaltung im Kurhaus, Luisenstr. 10, 7740 Triberg (07722–81230). **Wildbad,** Verkehrsamt, König-Karl-Str. 7, 7547 Wildbad (07081–10281).

HOW TO GET AROUND. By air. The main international airports serving the Black Forest are Stuttgart and Frankfurt. From Stuttgart there is a regular bus service every 30 minutes to Pforzheim, and Saarbrücken. But there are also express train services from Frankfurt's Rhine-Main airport into the region. The southern Black Forest is also accessible from Basel, and from Strasbourg and Mulhouse (Mülhausen) in Alsace.

By train. For travelers by rail a direct line to Basel follows the Rhine, passing through Dortmund, Darmstadt, Karlsruhe, Baden-Baden, Offenburg, and Freiburg. The Rhein Express from Holland and InterCity trains use this route.

Karlsruhe and Pforzheim are good points from which to start a trip through the Black Forest from north to south. The main rail routes serving the region are Karlsruhe–Rastatt; Stuttgart–Eutingen; Konstanz–Horb (both with connections to Freudenstadt); and Offenburg–Hausach. Many of the smaller towns and villages are linked by train, and regular bus services (Bahnbusse) complete the network.

By bus. Long-distance bus services connect Freiburg with Mulhouse on the French border, and with Schramberg (German Railways, DB, Long-Distance Route no. 1066); Tübingen with Freudenstadt and Baden-Baden (German Touring Route T77); Freudenstadt with Strasbourg and Reutlingen in the Swabian Mountains (Touring Route T78); and Stuttgart with Donaueschingen, Titisee, Feldberg, Todtnau, Lörrach and Basel (T84).

Rail- and postbuses (Bahnbusse and Postbusse) complement the rail network, going across country, linking for example Nagold with Freudenstadt and Stuttgart, and running regularly from such stations as Baden-Baden, Bad Herrenalb, Bühl, Calw, Freudenstadt, Nagold and Wildbad to smaller towns and resorts in the hinterland. Reduced fares (Schwarzwald Bus Pass) are available for holders of cure passes.

By car. This is splendid holiday motoring country—the only thing against it being that so many other people think so. Like the English Lake District it is no place for anyone in a hurry. Flanked in the west by the A5 and in the east by the A81, it is crossed laterally by two main roads, Nos. B28 and B31, which take all the serious traffic.

The Black Forest also has a number of delightful scenic routes. The Schwarzwald-Hochstrasse (Black Forest High Road) was created over 50 years ago and is the most well-known, as well as the most beautiful. Running between Baden-Baden and Freudenstadt, the road (designated the B500) follows old mountain passes. Information may be had from *Schwarzwald Hochstrasse,* 7580 Bühl, or from the tourist offices in Baden-Baden and Freudenstadt.

The Schwarzwald-Bäderstrasse (Black Forest Spas Road) follows a circular course of 200 kilometers (125 miles) through the mountainous northern Black Forest between Pforzheim and Freudenstadt, taking in such well-known health resorts as Bad Liebenzell, Wildbad, Bad Herrenalb and Baden-Baden. Information and maps from *Schwarzwald-Bäderstrasse,* Stadtinformation, Marktplatz 1, 7530 Pforzheim.

The Schwarzwald-Tälerstrasse (Black Forest Valleys Road, or the B462) snakes its way through the wild romantic valleys of the Rivers Murg and Kinzig, from Rastatt to Schenkenburg via Alpirsbach: from Schloss Favorite to Schloss Eberstein, to the gigantic damm of the Schwarzenbachsee reservoir, past the ruins of Kloster Reichenbach, across the Schwarzwald-Hochstrasse at Freudenstadt, to Kloster Alpirsbach, ending at Schenkenburg. Information from *Schwarzwaldinformation,* Marktplatz 1, 7530 Pforzheim.

The Schwarzwald-Panoramastrasse (Black Forest Panorama Road), created only in 1983, takes in the stretch of idyllic country from Waldkirch to Hinterzarten, ascending the Kandel peak and passing through the towns of St. Peter with its 18th-century monastery and St. Märgen with its twin-towered abbey. Still relatively little-known, the route affords wide-sweeping views over the Black Forest heights, across into the Rhine valley and beyond to the Vosges and the Alps. Walkers, cyclists and bus travelers can enjoy the route, too.

By boat. Steamers and cruises operate on the Rhine from Basel (on the Swiss side), via Karlsruhe, Mannheim and the Rhineland, to Rotterdam and Amsterdam. These are run by the KD German Rhine Line and Botel Cruises. The tourist office in Kehl (Hauptstrasse 53, tel. 07851–88226) also provides information about river trips on the Rhine from Kehl to Strasburg.

In addition, boats can be hired on the Black Forest lakes of Waldsee, Schluchsee, and Titisee, the latter having regular round-trip cruises by motor-boat.

By bike. "Cycling without Luggage" tours are available. A particularly strenuous tour in this scheme—for individuals or groups—is that of 12 Black Forest mountain passes. For ordinary mortals, however, most main resorts have numerous cycle tracks marked according to degree of difficulty. Cycles can be hired in many holiday resorts. Inquire at the local tourist offices for addresses of rental firms—in many cases they will include the railway station—as well as for maps, route plans and information about group tours. Or write in advance to the regional tourist offices in Freiburg and Pforzheim.

EXCURSIONS. The Black Forest, located in the southwest of Germany, makes an excellent base for excursions not only into the nearby resorts of southern Baden-Württemburg—the Swabian Forest and Mountains, Lake Constance (Bodensee), or Stuttgart, capital of the state—but also into France, Switzerland and even Austria. A day trip is all that's needed to visit the French Vosges Mountains or Alsace (for which Kehl is the best starting-out point), or Basel in Switzerland, and Bregenz and the Vorarlberg in Austria. The DER travel agencies in Badenweiler and Freiburg, for example, have a "Three Countries Tour," covering France, Switzerland and Austria; similarly, local and regional tourist offices can arrange trips to one or all countries.

SPORTS. Regional and local tourist offices will help with information about sporting and recreational activities. Ask about packages too: for example, Baden-Baden offers tennis, golf and riding holiday packages.

Angling. The rivers and lakes of the northern Black Forest offer good angling, particularly for trout. Inquire at the local tourist offices about licenses. Bad Liebenzell, for example, offers a special angler's package in summer for seven days bed and breakfast and angling license to fish for trout, grayling, eel, and whitefish in the Rive Nagold for between DM.220 and DM.510.

Gliding. Particularly good thermal currents make Baden-Baden ideal for gliding. The Aero Club gives instruction. Freiburg's Aero Club offers air-tours over the city and the Black Forest, and there is gliding and flying in light aircraft at Calw-Hirsau, Freudenstadt, Dornstetten, Haiterbach, Kappel, Müllheim, Nagold, Rastatt and Wildberg.

Golf. Baden-Baden, Badenweiler, Donaueschingen, Herrenalb, Freiburg, and Freudenstadt have courses.

Hang-gliding. There is a world-famous hang-gliding (*Drachenfliegen*) school at Loffenau. Baiersbronn and Bernau also have schools.

Horseback riding. There are schools at Baden-Baden, Freiburg and Freudenstadt (new riding hall); horses can also be hired in Badenweiler, Villingen and many other places. Inquire at the tourist office.

Horseracing. Well-known horse races take place at Baden-Baden on the Iffezheim track, which has been in operation since 1858. The most important yearly events are the International Race Week and the Great Week of Baden-Baden, the latter always in the last week of August.

Sailing. Sailing, windsurfing and rowing are practised on the lakes of Titisee and Schluchsee. There is a sailing school at Schluchsee.

Swimming. Baden-Baden has a swimming stadium with five pools in addition to its gigantic new Carcalla-Therme thermal pool and fitness complex. Nearby Gaggenau has four openair pools and one stadium. Freiburg has several outdoor swimming places in addition to indoor pools. Freudenstadt has its new *Panorama Bad* indoor and outdoor pool and fitness center. Badenweiler, which has an outdoor thermal swimming pool also has a monumental marble indoor pool. Wildbad has a newly renovated thermal pool, Eberhardsbad, open in summer and closed by sliding glass doors in winter, as well as a heated outdoor pool in the forest at Calmbach. Bad Liebenzell has a large indoor thermal pool. All resorts and larger towns have outdoor pools, and there is swimming in the lakes of Titisee and Schluchsee.

Tennis. There are courts in all resorts and larger towns. Important international tennis tournaments are scheduled every year in Baden-Baden.

Walking. The Black Forest is ideal walking country: the grandeur of its scenery, its low, rolling mountains and forest trails make it perhaps Germany's best region for walking. Three principal trails cross the region in a north–south direction: the Westweg (West Trail), marked by a red diamond, from Pforzheim to Basel, total length about 270 kilometers (170 miles); the Mittelweg (Middle Trail), marked by a white stem in a red diamond, from Pforzheim to Waldshut, total length about 225 kilmeters (140 miles); and the Ostweg (East Trail), marked by a black and red diamond, from Pforzheim to Schaffhausen, about 212 kilometers (133 miles). Pforzheim tourist office will provide information and also details of a package to help you on your way.

With hundreds of miles of trails, possibilities are limitless. Each resort issues hiking maps and can provide guides if desired. There are many tours and packages to choose from, and *Wandern Ohne Gepäck* (hiking without luggage), a scheme which originated from a group of Black Forest hoteliers, is on offer, with week-long tours priced at between DM.430 and DM.640 per person according to type of accommodations required.

Winter sports. For economy skiing vacations, this area is tops, offering many inexpensive to moderate accommodations, including bungalows and vacation apartments. Skiing up to 700 meters (2,300 feet) lasts from Christmas until the end of February; up to 1,000 meters (3,300 feet), from early December until mid-March; above 1,000 meters (3,300 feet), two or three weeks longer. Ski tours are possible everywhere up to the highest elevations of the Black Forest (over 1,500 meters or 4,900 feet). For downhill skiers the Todtnau region and Hinterzarten around the Feldberg, the highest peak in the Black Forest, offers some challenging terrain. But the winter sport for which the Black Forest is best suited is undoubtedly cross-country skiing, for which it is, with the exception of Scandinavia, the outstanding European destination. There are literally hundreds of miles of well-marked and prepared ski-tracks (*Loipen*), in particular around Baden-Baden, Bad Herrenalb, Bad Liebenzell, Dobel, Freudenstadt, Gernsbach-Kaltenbronn, Kniebis, Lossburg, Oberreichenbach, and Waldach. The longest and most demanding of all the Black Forest trails is the 60-mile trek from Schonach, near Triberg, to the village of Multen on the eastern slope of Mount Belchen. Packages are available which allow you to spread the route over several days, skiing from village to village and spending a night in gasthaus of choice en route; your luggage will be transferred by car to the next destination when you set off in the morning. Information on such tours can be had from *Arbeitsgemeinschaft Skifernwanderwege*, 7745 Schonach (07722–6033) for the middle and southern regions, and *Gebietsgemeinschaft Nördlicher Schwarzwald*, Marktplatz 1, 7530 Pforzheim (07221–17929) for the northern region.

A brochure detailing over 100 winter sports centers throughout the region and the facilities available in each is supplied by the regional tourist office in Freiburg. In addition, there is a new brochure issued by the *Verkehrsgemeinschaft Hochschwarzwald*, Goethestr. 7, 7820 Titisee-Neustadt, for DM.6, giving information for cross-country skiers on over 80 marked trails in the region.

WINE TASTING. Baden wine can be said to be one of the Black Forest's natural resources: the best wines come from the Kaiserstuhl near Freiburg and from Ortenau in the north. Another delightful experience for wine lovers would be a trip along the Badische Weinstrasse (Baden Wine Road) which runs the whole length of the wine-growing area, through the sunny western borders of the Black Forest, all the way from Baden-Baden to Basel. Try to visit the Kaiserstuhl, an extinct volcano with an astonishingly mild climate, and sample, for instance, a *'71 Ihringen Winkelberg* from the town of Ihringen. Details of organized wine-tasting and trips to vineyards (including a four-day walk through the wine-growing countryside around Baden-Baden) can be obtained from the *Kultur und Verkehrsamt*, Gärtnerstr. 6, 7600 Offenburg, and from local tourist offices, such as that of Kehl.

Private wine tasting can be arranged on the vineyard estate of Count Wolf Metternich in the little town of Durbach, or close by with Germany's biggest private winegrower, the Markgraf of Baden-Wurttemberg at Schloss Staufenberg. Call the tourist office in Durback at 0781–42153.

CENTRAL GERMANY

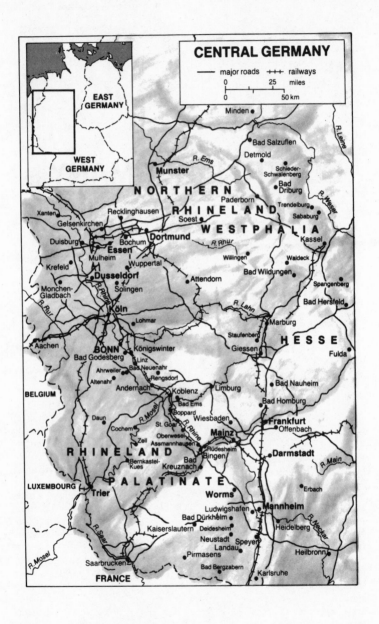

CENTRAL GERMANY

— major roads +++ railways

0   25   miles
0   50 km

EAST GERMANY

WEST GERMANY

Minden

Bad Salzuflen

Detmold

R. Ems

Münster

Schieder-Schwalenberg

Bad Driburg

NORTHERN

RHINELAND

Paderborn

Trendelburg

R. Weser

Xanten

Recklinghausen

Soest

Sababurg

WESTPHALIA

Gelsenkirchen

Kassel

Duisburg

Bochum

Dortmund

R. Ruhr

Essen

Willingen

Waldeck

Krefeld

Mulheim

Wuppertal

Bad Wildungen

Monchen-Gladbach

Dusseldorf

Attendorn

Spangenberg

Solingen

Bad Hersfeld

R. Rhine

Köln

R. Lahn

Aachen

Lohmar

Marburg

BONN

Königswinter

Staufenberg

HESSE

Bad Godesberg

Linz

Giessen

Fulda

Ahrweiler

Bad Neuenahr

Altenahr

Rengsdorf

Andernach

Koblenz

Limburg

Bad Nauheim

Daun

R. Mosel

Bad Ems

Bad Homburg

Cochem

Boppard

Wiesbaden

Frankfurt

St. Goar

R. Rhine

Offenbach

Zell

Oberwesel

Mainz

Assmannshausen

Rüdesheim

Darmstadt

RHINELAND

Bernkastel-Kues

Bingen

R. Main

Bad Kreuznach

Erbach

PALATINATE

Worms

LUXEMBOURG

Trier

Mannheim

Ludwigshafen

Heidelberg

R. Neckar

Bad Dürkheim

Kaiserslautern

Deidesheim

R. Saar

Neustadt

Speyer

Heilbronn

Pirmasens

Landau

Saarbrucken

Bad Bergzabern

Karlsruhe

R. Mosel

FRANCE

BELGIUM

St Ursula

THE RHINELAND-PALATINATE

A River of Wine

It is above Köln that the Rhine becomes most like its popular image, and it is from this point southward that the tourist who has no time for a longer voyage should try a leisurely cruise in the comfortable, efficiently-operated river steamers which ply up and down, making frequent stops, so that you can fit the boat ride into any itinerary you may have planned along the river.

As you mount the stream, it winds between lovely hills, some of which are thickly wooded, while others rise, step on step, in a terraced pattern of the vineyards which produce the fruity golden wines of the Rhine. Massive stone castles, or the ruins of castles, crown almost every hill. Attractive villages lie scattered along the shore.

Above Koblenz, the Rhine swings around a sharp curve at St. Goar, forced out of a more direct path by a sheer mountain of rock to whose sides only sparse vegetation has been able to cling. You can readily understand how, in an age when river boats were less powerful, strong winds and tricky currents could dash them against this forbidding crag. Legend turned this dangerous rock into either a scaly hideous monster or, even less likely, a beautiful siren who lured boatmen to death by bewitching them with song; for this is the Lorelei: a massive chunk of mountain, the triumph of geology over legend. Or is it? Even today, the river boats have to tack from one side of the narrow gorge to the other, and pleasure boats put on the recorded Lorelei song in which everybody who knows it joins, until the danger is passed.

Farther south, the river takes a major curve eastward, by Rüdesheim, the center of Rhine wine-growing on the right bank and, on the left, by Bingen, where the river Nahe joins the Rhine.

Exploring the Rhineland-Palatinate

Traveling on the Rhine south from Bonn and Bad Godesberg, the first landmark which greets you in the state of Rhineland-Pfalz is Rolandsbogen (Roland's Arch), the only remains of the castle of Knight Roland, destroyed in 1475. It stands on the slope of the Roddersberg. This peak is an inactive volcano, for the Eifel region which separates the Rhineland-Palatinate from Nordrhein-Westfalen, below this point is an ancient volcanic region of which the Roddersberg is the northernmost peak—a fact that accounts for the prevalence of hot springs in this country. A little further upstream and across the river on the right bank is the pleasant summer resort of Unkel, framed by vineyards. Southward on the left bank Remagen, a small town of Roman origin, lies near the confluence of the Ahr and the Rhine.

This could be the starting point for a westerly swing from the Rhine, with Trier as its main objective. The first stop would be Bad Neuenahr, an internationally-known spa with the largest gambling casino in Germany. This was for six years the place Beethoven chose for his summer vacation, staying with a private family in a house that is now known locally as the Beethovenhaus.

Passing up the lovely valley of the Ahr, pinched tightly between hills with terraced vineyards rising up their slopes and producing most of the German red wine, you reach medieval Ahrweiler with massive tower gates and Altenahr, where stand the ruins of the castle of the 12th-century Archbishop of Köln, Konrad von Hochstaden, who was responsible for the building of Köln Cathedral. The Ahrgau Museum here with Roman finds, uniforms, ecclesiastical books and sculptures, and the family history of the Counts of Ahr, is worth visiting. Next comes Adenau. Here you are at the Nürburgring, a world famous track over which international car and motorcycle races are held yearly. If you drive through here when there are no races scheduled, you can try the course yourself—170 curves in 27 km. (17 miles), in the shade of the Hohe Acht, the highest point in the Eifel (747 meters/2,450 feet).

Daun is a climatic resort with a mineral water source, in whose vicinity there are three crater lakes, or *Maare* (for you are now in really ex-volcanic territory); from there take a side road through Manderscheid (castle ruins; excursion to Mosenberg, the best preserved former volcanic hill in Eifel, with four craters) to the 12th-century Abbey Himmerod, rebuilt in Baroque style. A little farther to the west is Kyllburg, a small resort town picturesquely located above the Kyll River, with a 13th-century watch tower and 14th-century church.

Trier and the Mosel Valley

The oldest city in Germany, Trier is also one of the most interesting. Situated between the points where the Saar and the Ruwer flow into the Mosel, the city is a museum of the European history of which it was for so long an important part—for Trier was the Rome of the north, the point from which western Europe was governed by the Roman emperors who made it their northern capital—Constantine, Valentinian and Gradianus all had residences here in the 4th century. Later the Archbishop of Trier was one of the three ecclesiastical princes of the realm (the other two were the Archbishops of Mainz and Cologne) and was made one of the seven Electors of the Empire by the Golden Bull of 1356.

Just how old Trier is no one really knows, but in 1984 the town celebrated its 2,000th anniversary. The historical date given for the official founding of the city by the Emperor Augustus was 15 B.C. But though the Romans chose to regard this as the official starting date, there must have been something there already for Julius Caesar to conquer in 58 B.C. It is indeed known that there was a Celtic settlement dating from about 400 B.C., of a tribe known as the Treveri, but they did not give their name to the city— on the contrary. For legend, going back more than 2,000 years, ascribes the founding of Trier to Assyrian Prince Trebeta, who gave it his name, in 2053 B.C. Traces of human occupation have been found going back to about the year 2500 B.C.

From the time of the Romans onwards, the city has preserved monuments of all its periods. Rome left behind a bridge across the Mosel; two bathing establishments (the Barbara baths, dating from about A.D. 150, the Imperial Baths, from about 300) now in ruins; an amphitheater built about A.D. 100; the Basilica, which was the palace of the Roman Emperors; and the Porta Nigra, the pride of Trier. The Porta Nigra is a massive structure, once the northern gate to the Roman Empire. Now fully restored, it is open to the public. Climbing up on to the Petrisberg, a short distance away, you get an impressive view of the city.

From the Middle Ages the city has preserved its impressive churches; the Romanesque cathedral (with later-style additions) whose oldest part dates from the 4th century; Liebfrauenkirche, next to the cathedral and forming one group of buildings with it, is one of the oldest Gothic churches in Germany; the imposing and uniquely designed St. Matthew Church, Romanesque but with additions from later periods, a very well-known pilgrimage church because in a golden shrine in the choir it houses the earthly remains of St. Matthias, who should not be confused with the writer of St. Matthew's Gospel. The cathedral has a rich treasury, including a seamless cloak that Christ is believed to have worn; called the "Holy Robe," it is supposed to have been given as a present to the Bishop of Trier, in the 4th century, by the mother of Constantine the Great, and she is said to have brought it personally from Palestine. This relic is very rarely displayed to the public. Of more recent vintage, is the Baroque St. Paulinus Church, one of the finest examples of this style in Rhineland.

The town has several museums. The Rheinische Landesmuseum has prehistoric exhibits and Roman and early medieval art (see especially the 4th-century Roman glass); the Bischöfliches Museum (Episcopal Museum) contains exhibits from the time of Constantine; the Städtl. Museum (City Museum) is housed in the Simeon monastery building next to the Porta Nigra and contains valuable medieval sculptures and the municipal art collection with works from Gothic to the present day; the Schatzkammer der Stadtbibliothek (City Library Treasury) contains remarkable illuminated manuscripts (see particularly the jewel-set binding of the Ada manuscript and the Egbert Codex, painted in 980 in the monastery school of Reichenau); and the Karl-Marx-Haus, birthplace of the founder of communism.

Nor does Trier live only in the past, it is the commercial center for wine grown along the banks of the three rivers converging in this area, known among the wine merchants and connoisseurs as the Mosel-Saar-Ruwer wine region. Foremost examples of German wine cultivation are the old cellars of the Hohe Domkirche, the Priesterseminar, the Bischöfliches Konvikt, and the Vereinigte Hospizien with cross-shaped vaults, artistically carved tuns, and old tankards. Altogether almost 8 million gallons of wine can be stored in the subterranean cellars extending under the buildings and streets of the city. The Trier tourist office arranges conducted tours of the cellars with wine tasting included.

Upstream from Trier, in the Saar Valley, is Saarburg, metropolis of the Saar wine trade, surrounded by some fine vineyards. It rings, picturesquely, a steep hill crowned, with the ruins of a castle; the Burg Saarburg is one of the oldest hill-fortresses in West Germany, first mentioned in 964. It was the favorite residence of the Archbishops of Trier in the 14th century and blown up by the French in 1705. Particularly impressive is the ruin of a Romanesque towerhouse with tower added at a later date. The "Burg" is accessible by cable-car. The town also offers the spectacle of the 19-meter (63-ft.) Leuk waterfall; and if you are curious about how bells are cast, you might visit the local foundry and watch the craftsmen at work.

One way back to the Rhine from either Saarburg or Trier would be the excellent Hunsrück mountain road, leading through thick woods over a high plateau, and disclosing from its curves a view of the Mosel Valley to the north and the Nahe Valley to the south. It begins at Niederzerf, a village east of Saarburg or south of Trier (the better approach), and ends at Koblenz. Another even newer and faster road beginning at Schweich near Trier takes you to Koblenz.

But if you only have enough time to make this trip in one direction, it is more rewarding to return to the Rhine via the lovely Mosel Valley. This route takes us through Pfalzel, a small town with an old Romanesque church and once the residence of Merovingian kings, and through the renowned wine villages of Trittenheim and Piesport to Bernkastel, the best known of them all.

Bernkastel, with its suburb of Kues across the river, is a colorful town with half-timbered houses, steep vineyard slopes, crowned by Landshut Castle, and a romantic story-book Rathaus square. The 15th-century scientist-philosopher Nicolaus Cusanus, "Nikolaus von Kues," was born here; and in the Middle Ages a Prince Bishop of Trier lay seriously ill at his castle overlooking Bernkastel—the Burg Landshut—and his physicians could seemingly do no more to help him. However, one of the bishop's wine-growing tenants, hearing of his master's illness, brought him some wine from one of his best vineyards. A few sips, then a whole glass, and finally a bottle or two are said to have effected a cure; whereupon the Prince Bishop blessed the elixir and decreed that the vineyard should be named "Doktor." Hence, Bernkasteler Doktor, an excellent white wine. The Mosel Wine Museum is part of the center for the preservation of Riesling wine. Every year in the first week of September the Middle Mosel Wine Festival is held.

From here on, if you are a wine drinker, you will recognize the name of almost every town and village: Grach, Wehlen, Zeltingen, Ürzig, Kröv are some of them. In all there are 12,000 wine-producing concerns along the Mosel and its tributaries the Sauer, Saar and Ruwer. Traben-Trarbach is the center of the wine trade in the middle Mosel Valley. On the bow of the river here, is the Festung Mont Royal, a masterpiece of fortress architecture, built by Ludwig 14th around 1687. The mighty fortress possessed in addition to an army fort, armory and storehouses, a whole town with church and city hall. In 1690, 14 regiments were stationed here with 8,450 men. Razed to the ground in 1698, the ruins were excavated in the 1920s. Guided tours can be arranged through the Mittelmosel Museum in Traben-Trarbach.

Near Traben-Trarbach in the Kautenbach Valley is the beautifully situated Bad Wildstein, a thermal spa with warm springs. Farther down the Mosel River is Zell, another renowned wine-growing town famous for its wine "Zeller Schwarzer Katz," with the former castle of the Elector of Trier. Not far from Zell is Alf, at the foot of Marienburg and Arras castles.

From here you can slip up a side valley to the northwest to Bad Bertrich, a tiny spa known since Roman times, and it is referred to as "the mild Karlsbad" because its waters, the only warm sulphate of soda springs in Germany, are almost the same as those of the Czech town of Karlovy Vary, formerly Karlsbad.

The way back to the Rhine continues through Bullay, an important point for train and bus connections into the Mosel and Rhine valleys and starting point for excursions into the Eifel. On to Cochem, a lovely town on the Mosel, whose vineyards rise in a checkerboard of terraces to the splendid castle above; the Reichsburg (Imperial Fortress) has parts that date back to the 11th century, although it was destroyed in 1689 and rebuilt in the 19th century. The splendid interiors can be seen on guided tours between March and December.

The next town is Moselkern, from where there are less than five km. (three miles) to the romantic Eltz Castle, one of the finest in Germany. The original complex of four separate residences was built between the 12th and 17th centuries, and has been preserved in all its glory. The Mosel flows into the Rhine at Koblenz.

Across the Rhine from Remagen, where we had left the Rhine for our trip west to the Eifel Mountains, Trier, and the Mosel Valley, is the old town of Linz with half-timbered houses and remains of town walls. South of Remagen, on the left bank, are Bad Niederbreisig with thermal springs and the Rheineck Castle in the vicinity, which can be reached by a chair lift; Brohl, near the largest of the crater lakes of the Eifel, the beautiful Laachersee, on whose shores stand the 11th-century Maria Laach Abbey and the abbey church, the latter a surpassingly satisfying Romanesque structure dating from the 12th century; and the walled town of Andernach with its Round Tower, the 13th-century Liebfrauen Church which has an exquisitely arcaded façade, and an ancient crane which was in use until 1911. Maria Laach Abbey can also be visited from Andernach, by a road a little beyond the fork for Maria Laach that takes us also to the medieval town of Mayen, with 13th-century walls and castle, that today house the Eifelmuseum of local history, folklore and tradition. Just outside town is the Schloss Bürresheim, founded in the 12th century, and held to be one of the most important examples of German castle architecture. Over the centuries the building has been transformed from a castle to a palace with fine interiors. It is open to visitors.

Koblenz and the Middle Rhine

Located at a geographical nexus known as "the corner of Germany," Koblenz is the heart of the middle Rhine region. Rivers and mountains both converge here. Koblenz stands where the Mosel runs into the Rhine, and just south the Lahn enters it from the opposite side. Three mountain ridges intersect at Koblenz. West of the Rhine are the Eifel Mountains north of the Mosel, and the Hunsrück ridge south of it. East of the Rhine the undulating plateaus of Westerwald hide among their forests many small and quiet climatic resorts and towns, such as Rengsdorf, Flammersfeld, Marienburg, Westerburg and many others. Koblenz is the gateway to the most romantic section of the Rhine. Here the Rhine has cut deeply between the heights on either side. Little wine villages line the shores and castles (or ruins) stand on every hill. If what you prefer is a quiet vacation, pick any of the riverside towns here.

Koblenz is the cultural, administrative and business center of the middle Rhine area. Its position at the confluence of two rivers bustling with steamers, barges, tugs and every other kind of river boat makes it also one of the most important traffic points on the Rhine. Through the construction of a series of locks and dams the Mosel has become navigable all the way to Luxembourg and France. A bridge across the Rhine and a new autobahn link connect Koblenz directly with the autobahn net of Germany.

Koblenz was founded by the Romans and its history goes back 2,000 years. The city suffered severely from air raids during the last war (85 percent of the buildings destroyed) but some of the most architecturally valuable buildings partially remained and have been reconstructed. The most interesting churches include the 9th-century Romanesque basilica of St. Kastor, the 12th-century Romanesque Liebfrauenkirche with a Gothic choir, and the 11th-century St. Florin's, erected on Roman foundations. Alte Burg (Old Castle) originates from the 13th century and now houses the City Library, while next to it the Balduin Bridge across the Mosel is about a hundred years younger. The Rathaus (1700), formerly a Jesuit college, is Baroque, whereas the large and monumental Schloss, the former palace of the Prince Electors, is neo-Classical. Outstanding among the examples of contemporary architecture is the ultramodern Rhein-Mosel-Halle containing several halls for theatrical performances, concerts, conventions, congresses, balls and other events. The lovely promenade along the Rhine extends from the outdoor water stage where operettas and concerts are performed during summer to the point where the Mosel flows into the Rhine, called Deutsches Eck (the corner of Germany) because it was here that the German Order of Knights (Deutscher Orden) established its first post on German soil in 1216.

Across the Rhine the powerful Ehrenbreitstein Fortress towers above the city; it can be reached by chair lift, and houses the Rheinmuseum and the municipal collection of technical instruments and equipment from bygone days. Each year, on the second Saturday in August, you can witness a magnificent firework display, *Der Rhein in Flammen,* from the fortress battlements.

Koblenz also has the Mittelrhein-Museum (Middle Rhine Museum), with collections of ancient history and art from the Middle Ages to the present; the Rheinmuseum, with exhibits on Rhine shipping and natural history; and a museum of Beethoven memorabilia.

Just east of Koblenz is the internationally known spa of Bad Ems, which was for 20 years (1867–87) the spot Kaiser Wilhelm chose for his yearly cure. Pleasantly laid out along both banks of the Lahn River, Bad Ems provides all the amenities of a modern spa, including its newly-opened casino. Further up the Lahn Valley is Nassau, a climatic health resort with the ancestral castle of the house of Orange-Nassau, the reigning dynasty in Holland.

From Koblenz upstream the principal settlements are:

Oberlahnstein, east bank: at the confluence of Lahn River with Rhine with some of the old fortifications preserved; above it is Lahneck Castle with a pentagonal tower and beautiful view over Lahn Valley.

Braubach, east bank: St. Barbara Church dates from 1300; above it is the magnificent Marksburg, the best-preserved medieval castle on the Rhine with outstanding interiors, particularly the Knights' Hall.

Boppard, west bank: a wine-producing town, located on a wide bend of the Rhine, along which are three km. (two miles) of pleasure grounds. There is also a fine municipal forest.

St. Goar, west bank: founded in 570 by Irish monk St. Goar; above it the remains of the Rheinfels Fortress, once the strongest on the Rhine.

St. Goarshausen, east bank: above it Burg Katz (Cat Castle) an impressive castle-fortress, built in 1371 by Count Wilhelm II von Katzenelnbogen, hence its name. Further downstream is Burg Maus (Mouse Castle). Its nickname was allegedly given by the owner of Burg Katz, out of spite.

Lorelei, east bank: if you haven't viewed it from the river steamer, the next best view is from the road on the west bank of the river. You can drive up the Lorelei by a back road, and enjoy the view of the Rhine from its top.

Oberwesel, west bank: a small town surrounded by vineyards, much frequented by those interested in architecture (Schönburg Castle on the hill, below the medieval walls and towers, Our Lady's Church, St. Martin's Church, St. Werner's Chapel) and nature (Rhineside promenade, excursions into the Hunsrück hills). The town also has an interesting Postcard Museum and a Wine Market in September.

Kaub, east bank: here, in the middle of the river, on an island, stands a small but famous castle, the Pfalz. This was a toll house, where in medieval times boats using the river had to pay tribute. Above the town is Gutenfels Castle-Fortress which was garrisoned as late as 1806, now also an exquisite, tiny, castle hotel which serves an enormous breakfast.

Bacharach, west bank: a particularly beautiful town. Above it is Stahleck Castle with its unique youth hostel. And there are half-a-dozen other castles on this bank before getting to Bingen, where the Rhine makes a big turn from a roughly south–north course to an east–west one. On the right bank are Rüdesheim and other vineyard towns of Rheingau, all part of Hesse.

Bingen, on the other side of the Rhine, at the confluence of Nahe and Rhine, is an important river port, and its principal attractions are the Klopp Castle, which serves as the city's emblem and was built on the site of Roman remains; the Mäuseturm (Mouse Tower) on a tiny island in the river, which dates back to the 13th century and until 1974 served as a signal tower for Rhine shipping; and St. Rochus Chapel on a nearby hill.

Around this church the 300-year-old Rochus Festival is held at the end of August commemorating the saving of the town from the Black Death. St. Rochus was the protector against pestilence, and the chapel erected to him at that time has become an important pilgrimage goal.

Pfalz (The Palatinate)

From Bingen you can proceed straight to Mainz, the capital of the state of Rhineland-Palatinate, where with another turn the Rhine again resumes its south–north course. But in order to make a tour of the Pfalz section of this hyphenated state, turn at Bingen up the Nahe River.

Bad Kreuznach, a good-sized radium spa, also grows wine, and is locally called the "town of roses and nightingales," both of which are to be found in abundance in its well-kept parks. The most picturesque of its relics of the past are the 15th-century houses built on its bridge. One of its historic houses is reputed to have been the home of Dr. Faust. The Karl-Geib-Museum contains Roman finds, including well-preserved floor mosaics. Bad Münster am Stein, another spa, is dwarfed by the tremendous towering crag of the Rheingrafenstein that rises above it. A short distance from here is Ebernburg with its castle, where Franz von Sickingen, the aristocratic propagator of Reformation, was born; the castle has an interesting Knights' Hall, museum, and historic inn. The double town of Idar-Oberstein is dominated by the ruins of two castles and by a unique "rock church" built in 1482 halfway up the cliff; but the town is even better known for agate grinding and for the manufacture of other precious and semi-precious jewelry; there is a permanent exhibition of jewelry in the Gewerbehalle, the hall of the local business organization.

South of Bad Kreuznach is Donnersberg, the highest mountain in Pfalz, in whose eastern approaches lies Kirchheimbolanden, a town founded in Carolingian times, with a few wall towers and two gates preserved from the Middle Ages. There is also a 17th-century castle, Schloss Kirchheimbolanden, built on the site of a 14th-century fortress. In the castle church is a famous organ built in 1745, on which Mozart is said to have played. Travelling southeastwards you will reach Bockenheim, located at one end of the Deutsche Weinstrasse (German Wine Road) which runs to the French border at Schweigen-Rechtenbach. From here the road is lined with vineyards and the towns of wine growers, the most important among which are (north to south): Bad Dürkeim, the largest wine-growing commune in Germany, and also a notable spa with a lovely park and casino; Wachenheim, with old patrician houses and Gothic parish church; Deidesheim and its medieval main square; Neustadt, the wine-trade center of the area, and site of the German Wine Harvest Festival during the first week of October with the Gothic Stiftskirche, interesting Rathaus, and nearby Hambacher Schloss, also called Maxburg, with a fine view and at Hassloch, Germany's largest holiday park, including a magnificent giant model railway; Maikammer, with half-timbered houses; Rhodt unter Rietburg, where you can find the world's oldest productive vineyard, and Edenkoben, with the largest wooden-cask cellar; Leinsweiler, also with half-timbered houses and the Neukastel Castle ruins.

Not far away from Landau, with it lovely parks, and Annweiler, with the imposing Trifels Castle-Fortress that belonged to the early German emperors. Farther south on the Wine Road are Bergzabern, with its Renaissance Schloss, and Schweigen, with a "Wine Gate" marking the other end of the Wine Road, and the French border beyond.

To continue the tour of Pfalz, return to Bergzabern and from there take the extremely scenic road through Wasgau to the small town of Dahn. Wasgau is the name of the southernmost section of Pfalz, with romantic, unspoiled scenery, castle-forts built on sharp cliffs, unusual rock formations, trout streams, and hundreds of hiking paths. Bergzabern and Dahn are the main points for the exploration of this area. Near Dahn are the interesting Altdahn Castle ruins as well as many strange rock formations.

At Hinterweidenthal, join the main road coming from Landau and leading to the cities of Pirmasens and Zweibrücken, and to Saarland. Pirmasens is the center of German shoe manufacturing with a fascinating Shoe Museum in the Rathaus, while Zweibrücken is known particularly for horse breeding and for its extraordinary Rose Garden with 70,000 rose bushes; there are also the ruins of the Residenz Palace, Alexander Church, Schloss Zweibrücken (the largest secular Baroque building in the Palatinate, now the seat of the Palatinate High Court), and the historic Zum Hirsch inn, the oldest house in the city (built around 1600).

Kaiserslautern is the district capital. Founded by Emperor Barbarossa, it is an important industrial center, and its chief sights include the 13th-century Abbey Church, St. Martin's Church from the same period, the ruins of Emperor Barbarossa's castle and a Museum of Historic Folklore; a few kilometers southwest of the city is Lake Gelterswoog.

In order to explore the little-visited, scenically beautiful area to the north of Kaiserslautern, take the road through Wolfstein to the Glan Valley and end at Idar-Oberstein. The main road for Saarland also leads through Kaiserslautern, in a westerly direction. To the east, it leads across the green landscape of Pfälzer Wald (Palatine Forest), Germany's largest nature reserve with thousands of well-constructed and well-signposted footpaths, back to Neustadt on the Wine Road, and from there to Speyer.

From Speyer to Mainz

Speyer is believed to have originated some 3,000 years ago as an early Celtic settlement; traces of Celtic tribes dating back to the 2nd century B.C. have been discovered. It is also one of the old cities of the Holy Roman Empire, and in its cathedral, the largest Romanesque church in Europe, begun in 1030 by Conrad II, no less than eight emperors are buried. Conrad II's grandson, Heinrich IV, left from here in 1076 on his long walk of repentance to Canossa, now in northern Italy, to seek forgiveness and the blessing of the Pope who had excommunicated him. There is also an important Protestant Memorial Church, the 18th-century Trinity Church, remains of the city walls and Altpörtel, an imposing tower-gate from 1230. The Historisches Museum der Pfalz (Palatine Historical Museum) has fine collections of prehistoric and Roman relics and medieval art. It also includes a very interesting Wine Museum with priceless articles, such as a sealed glass case containing the world's oldest (from A.D. 300) wine preserved in liquid state.

Descending the Rhine from Speyer, you come to a pair of cities facing each other across the stream. Ludwigshafen, on the west bank, and Mannheim, on the east bank, are actually twin cities. But while the first is in the Rhineland-Palatinate, the latter belongs to Baden-Württemberg. Ludwigshafen is the center of the German chemical industry and one of its biggest river ports.

Worms has played an important part in the history of Europe. Its early beginnings are reflected in the fine historic collections of the Municipal Museum with objects from 3000 B.C., and in Hagen's Monument on the bank of the Rhine showing this mythical hero of ancient German sagas throwing the famous Nibelungen hoard into the river; and it is from Worms that the Nibelungs were supposed to strike towards the east, hence the "Nibelungen Road" begins here. The remains of medieval walls remind us of later times when the Imperial Diet sat here, when the Emperor and the Pope in 1122 reached agreement about the roles of spiritual and secular power, beginning a new era in the political development of Europe, and when the edict of Worms in 1521 condemned Martin Luther. Worms has since then become two-thirds Protestant and has erected an impressive Reformation Monument, reputed to be the greatest in the world. But the city is presently best known for its magnificent 12th-century cathedral (Dom St. Peter), whose exteriors are in the purest Romanesque style to be found in Germany. Heylshof Museum contains 15th–19th century art and outstanding exhibits of porcelain and glass painting. The Gothic Liebfrauenkirche in the middle of vineyards has given the name to Liebfraumilch, the famous white wine. Schloss Herrnsheim was built in 1460 as a moated castle. The round-tower has been preserved but the rest was burned to the ground in the 17th century and was later rebuilt in neo-Classical style. It is now owned by the city and houses valuable furniture and tapestries. You can either continue directly northwards to Mainz, following the Rhine along the eastern flanks of the Palatinate, or take the western route through the middle of Rhine-Hesse via Alzey, the center of a wine-growing region.

Mainz is the capital of Rhineland-Palatinate. A bridge across the Rhine connects it with the suburb of Kastel and from here there are only about 13 km. (eight miles) to Wiesbaden. Mainz is an ancient city, whose imposing Romanesque cathedral is a thousand years old. Its interior contains perhaps the finest collection of works of art of any German cathedral. Note the Rococo choir stalls, the Gothic cloister colonnade, and the Diocesan Museum with its famous medieval sculpture that includes works by the unknown Master of Naumburg. Mainz was the seat of a Prince Elector, and the birthplace (1397) of Johannes Gutenberg, inventor of movable type, who died here in 1468.

Although ancient Mainz, which celebrated its 2000th anniversary in 1962, lost most of its old buildings during World War II, some have now been reconstructed including the Renaissance Palace of the Prince Electors with the Roman-Germanic Museum; the former Elector's Stables which now contain the Museum of Antiquity and the City Art Gallery; portions of the former Clarissen Convent (presently the Natural History Museum); and the Renaissance-style "Römischer Kaiser" with a modern annex—both housing the Gutenberg Museum with such rare works as the the Book of Hours of Charles the Bold.

Other sights include: The Gutenberg Monument on Gutenberg Square; the citadel with Drusus Monument; the Church of St. Stephan on the Stephansburg with six unique stained-glass windows by Marc Chagall, the last completed in 1981; the Burg Windeck, a splendid example of a well-preserved medieval moated hill castle-fortress; the market square fountain;

the lovely promenade along the Rhine; the old houses in the Kirschgarten; the university named for Gutenberg; and the busy river harbor. The colorful market is held Tuesdays, Fridays and Saturdays from 7 A.M. to 1 P.M.

Mainz is at its liveliest at Mardi Gras, when it holds a famous festival, and during the August–September Wine Market, for the city plays a leading role in the German wine trade. It is also a good point from which to take a boat for a trip on the Rhine—or for that matter on the Main, which joins the Rhine here, to Frankfurt.

Saarland

Following an agreement between Germany and France, the Saar, or Saarland, was politically reunited with Germany in 1957. Economic reintegration followed in 1959, the German Mark was reintroduced as the currency of Saarland, and this entirely German-speaking province, long disputed by France and Germany, took its place among the other provinces of West Germany.

The capital of Saarland, Saarbrücken, is best reached from Frankfurt via Mannheim and Kaiserslautern, or via Mainz and Kaiserslautern. Saarland is usually associated with the coal and iron industry of which it is an important center; less well known is the fact that its countryside offers lovely rural landscape, and that certain sections of the winding Saar River are of outstanding natural beauty. One-third of Saarland is covered by forests and more than one-half of it is cultivated land. Industry is concentrated in the southern part of the province where Saarbrücken is located.

Saarbrücken is not only the business but also the cultural center of this state. There is a university whose modern buildings are quietly located in a suburban forest; opera, operetta, ballet, and drama are performed in the city theater; and there is also a symphony orchestra. The principal sights include: the Baroque Elector's Palace and gardens; the Protestant Ludwigskirche also in Baroque style and built by Stengel, who came here from Fulda, developed his own version of Baroque, and became the master builder in this area; the Gothic Abbey Church of St. Arnual, located in the city district of the same name; the Saarland Museum, with displays on regional history, culture and art, porcelain and furniture; and the Rathaus.

Since Saarland is small, all the points of interest can easily be reached from Saarbrücken. The road along the Saar River, through the industrial centers of Völkingen and Saarlouis, offers particularly beautiful, unspoiled landscape after Merzig (St. Peter's Church) through the picturesque Mettlach ("Alter Turm" from the year 987, the remains of the old abbey) and continues to Saarburg and Trier.

At Orscholz the Saar flows in a magnificent horseshoe bend. A few kilometers west is the village of Nennig, with its vineyards and Roman villa boasting an extraordinarily well preserved Roman mosaic.

Starting out north of Saarbrücken, you can make a round trip through: Lebach, with a castle, 1,000-year-old oak tree, and Gothic church; Tholey, with the 13th-century Benedictine Abbey; the climatic resort of Nonnweiler in the mountains of Schwarzwalder Hochwald, with nearby Hunnenring, a huge fortification from Celtic times; St. Wendel, with the Gothic Wendlinus Church; the medieval Ottweiler; and the industrial town of Neunkirchen.

PRACTICAL INFORMATION FOR
THE RHINELAND-PALATINATE

TELEPHONES. We have given telephone codes for all the towns and villages in the hotel and restaurant lists that follow. These codes need only be used when calling from outside the town or village concerned.

HOTELS AND RESTAURANTS. Accommodations in this area are plentiful. It is wise to make advance reservations during the spring and summer; otherwise consult the local tourist offices. Hotels in the Rhine and Mosel Valleys are more expensive than in the Palatinate and the Saarland. Naturally, in the most popular tourist centers such as Koblenz, Cochem, Bernkastel-Kues, Trier, Bad Kreuznach, Mainz and Bad Durkheim, you can generally expect higher prices. Alternatively, there are plenty of good-value inexpensive accommodations in the wine villages of the Palatinate along the German Wine Road. A moderate Gasthof may only cost around DM.60 per night for two, including bath or shower and breakfast. Private accommodations are even less expensive, such as on the numerous vintners' estates where you will often see the "Zimmer Frei" (Rooms) sign. A full list of accommodations is available from the Regional Tourist Office for the Rhineland-Palatinate in Koblenz.

Altenahr. *Hotel Lochmühle* (E), Bundesstr. 62, in nearby Mayschoss (02643–1345). 70 rooms, all with own bath, 2 apartments. Located among vineyards, on the road B 267. Indoor pool, sauna, solarium, and excellent restaurant serving own wines. v. *Zum Schwarzen Kreuz* (M), Brückenstr. 7 (02643–1534). 18 rooms, most with own bath. An historic house with its own vineyard and rustic restaurant. MC.

Andernach. *Parkhotel* (E), Konrad Adenauer Allee 33 (02632–44051). Modern; 28 rooms all with bath. Restaurant and café-terrace with fine view. AE, MC, V. *Altenhofen* (M), Steinweg 30 (02632–4447). Located between the market square and the Marienkirche church. Dates back to 1667, fully renovated with antique furnishings and modern comforts. AE, DC, V.

Bad Bergzabern. *Apart-Hotel Pfalzblick* (M), Mozartstr. 17 (06343–2929). Apartments and cure facilities. Also full or half board available. DC. *Parkhotel* (M), Kurtalstr. 83 (06343–2415). 45 large rooms. Nostalgic setting in the forest; indoor pool, sauna, restaurant, own trout farm. DC, MC. *Hotel-Pension Seeblick* (M), Kurtalstr. 71 (06343–2539). 57 rooms. View over lake; thermal pool, terrace. *Petronella* (M), Kurtalstr. 47 (06343–1075). Newly built near the Cure Park, with all modern facilities. MC. *Waldrestaurant-Pension St. Germanshof* (I), Hauptstr. 10 (06394–1455). 21 beds. Located in Bobenthal suburb about 11 km. (seven miles) south, near German-French border in village of same name. Very quiet, garden, fishing, hunting and very good-value menu. Restaurant closed in summer on Mon. evenings and Tues.

Restaurants. *Landgasthof Schlossberg Keller* (M), Im Bienengarten 22 (06343–1582). In the Pleisweiler suburb among vineyards. Reputed for its fine food; own wines. *Wilder Mann* (M), Weinstr. 19 (06343–1500). Excellent French cuisine, good wine list and rustic atmosphere. DC.

Cafés. *Herzog* (I), Marktstr. 48. *Weinstube Boch* (I), Weinstr. 17. *Weinstube Koch* (I), Am Plätzl.

Bad Breisig. *Zur Mühle* (M), Koblenzer Str. 15 (02633–9142). Quietly located on banks of the Rhine. Fine views; 39 rooms, about half with own bath. Indoor pool and good-value restaurant. *Zum Weissen Ross* (M), Zehnerstr. 19 (02633–9135). Known primarily for its outstanding cuisine. AE, DC, MC.

Restaurant. *Künstlerklause,* Waldstr. 2 (02633–95255).

Bad Dürkheim. On the wine road. *Dorint Hotel* (E), Kurbrunnenstr. 30–32 (06322–6010). 200 beds, all rooms with bath. Restaurant, bakery, café-bar and nightclub. AE, DC, MC, V. *Kurparkhotel* (M), Schlossplatz 1–4 (06322–7970). 109 rooms, about one third with own bath; indoor pool, sauna, solarium, fitness room, Kneipp cures. Good restaurant, wine tavern and bar. The casino is in the same building. AE, DC, MC, V.

Restaurants. *Dürkheimer Riesenfass* (M), (06322–2143). Near the Würstmarkt (Sausage Fair). The famous tavern inside a huge beer barrel. Wines from all over the region and Palatinate specialties; popular tourist attraction. *Käsburo* (M), (06322–8694). In the Seebach section. Historic wine tavern with international cuisine. Also some rooms. *Zum Winzer* (M), Kaiserlauterer Str. 12 (06322–2171). Traditional German and Palatinate specialties. Summer-house with terrace.

Bad Ems. *M.C.I. Hotel Staatliches Kurhaus* (E), Römerstr. 1–3 (02603–3016). 160 beds. At the cure center on the Lahn promenade. Riverside café-terrace and good restaurant. AE, DC, MC, V. *Park Hotel* (E), Malbergstr. 7 (02603–2058). 50 beds, all rooms with own bath; terrace with fine view, restaurant. AE, DC, MC. *Guttenberg* (M), Mainzer Str. 5 (02603–4084). 75 beds, 13 rooms with own bath, no restaurant. DC. *Russischer Hof* (M), Römerstr. 23 (02603–2344). 35 beds, most rooms with bath or shower. Located at the cure park. Czar Nicholas II stayed here. Separate restaurant. DC, V. *Altes Weinhaus* (I), Silberausstr. 18 (02603–4960). Wine tavern. *Goldenes Fass* (I), Römerstr. 7 (02603–2232). 21 beds. Opposite the Kursaal. With good-value restaurant.

Restaurants. *Alt Ems* (M), Marktstr. 14 (02603–12345). Local-style with regional cooking. Dancing at weekends. *Berghotel-Café Wintersberg* (M), Braubacherstr. (02603–4282). About 3 km. from town in the forest, with panoramic view over the surrounding countryside. Good coffee and pastries, also small snacks in local style. Also has 12 rooms.

Bad Kreuznach. *Steigenberger Kurhaus* (E), Kurhausstr. 28 (0671–2061). 200 beds; 2 restaurants, café, wine tavern. AE, DC, MC, V. *Tourotel Caravelle* (E), Im Oranienpark (0671–2495). 180 beds, all rooms with bath; openair pool, sauna. AE, DC, MC, V. *Michel Mort* (M), Eiermarkt 9 (0671–2388). Quietly located hotel—no restaurant—near the historic egg market. Cozy, atmospheric interiors, particularly the beer-pub. 36

beds, all rooms with bath. *M-Hotel* (I), Wilhelmstr. 54 (0671–33624). 26 rooms, about half with own bath. No restaurant. AE, DC.

Restaurant. *Die Kauzenburg* (M), Auf dem Kauzenburg (0671–25461). In old castle ruins up on the heights. AE, DC, MC, V.

Bad Neuenahr-Ahrweiler. *Giffels Hotel Goldener Anker* (E), Mittelstr. 14 (02641–8040). A Ring Hotel. 93 rooms, all with own bath, 3 apartments; sauna, solarium, sport room. Attractive garden. AE, DC, MC, V. *Steigenberger Kurhotel* (E), Kurgartenstr. 1 (02641–2291). 240 rooms; themal baths in house and fine *Pfeffermühle* restaurant. Located in spa park. AE, DC, MC, V. *Pfäffle* (M), Lindenstr. 7 (02641–24235). 48 rooms, all with own bath, 1 apartment; terrace. DC, MC. *Zum Stern* (M), Markt 9 (02641–34738). 15 rooms, some with own bath; simple and clean. Historic building, the oldest hostelry in the Ahr Valley. Rustic restaurant.

Restaurants. *Gourmet* (E), Im Teufenbach (02641–34198). In a rural setting surrounded by vineyards. Serves a delicate combination of "nouvelle cuisine" and regional specialties. AE, DC. *Ratskeller* (E), Casinostr. 8 (02641–25466). Rustic appearance, fine cuisine. Closed Tues. and Wed. until 7 P.M. DC. *Romantik Restaurant St. Peter* (E), Walporzheimerstr. 134 (02641–389911). In Walporzheim suburb. A wine estate since 1246. Very atmospheric, fine food; serves wines from own *Sekt* cellar. AE, DC, MC, V.

Bernkastel-Kues. *Burg Landshut* (M), Gestade 11, in Bernkastel (06531–3019). 61 beds, most rooms with own bath, some with balcony. Fine restaurant with music on summer evenings. AE, DC, MC, V. Closed Dec. 15–27. *Drei Könige* (M), Bahnhofstr. 1 (06531–2035). In Kues section, on the riverside. AE, MC. *Mosel Hotel* (M), Uferallee 3 (06531–8527). 15 rooms. In the suburb of Wehlen, five km. (three miles) from the center. Quietly located, rustic-styled, directly on the riverside promenade. Terrace restaurant with view over the river. All in Bernkastel: *Älteste Weinstube* (I), Kallenfelsstr. 25–27 (06531–4064). 21 beds, all rooms with bath or shower. Half-timbered 18th-century building; sauna, whirlpool, bowling, beergarden, good restaurant. AE, DC, V. *Haus Behrens* (I), Schanzstr. 9 (06531–6088). With large sun terraces. MC. *Zur Post* (I), Gestade 17 (06531–2022). 39 rooms with bath or shower. Closed Jan. AE, DC, MC, V.

Restaurants. *Hubertusklause* (M), Cusanusstr. 26 (06531–8045). Combination of fine old German cuisine and wholesome cooking. MC. *Ratskeller,* in Rathaus, with music. AE, DC, MC. *Pfeffermühle* (I), Schwanenstr. 9 (06531–8590). Grill. *Graacher Tor* (M), Graacher Str. 3 (06531–2204). In Bernkastel.

Bingen. On the Rhine. *Germaniablick* (M), Mainzer Str. 142 (06721–14773). 18 rooms, most with own bath. Terrace with river view. AE, DC, MC, V. *Starkenburger Hof* (M), Rheinkai 1–2 (06721–14341). 30 rooms, most with bath. Facing the river. AE, DC, MC, V.

About eight km. (five miles) down the river, above Trechtinghausen, the 11th-century castle *Reichenstein* (06721–6101) is now a 12-room hotel (E) with a Knight's Room and converted horse stable restaurant; concerts in the crystal-chandeliered festivity hall. V.

Boppard. On the Rhine. *Klostergut Jakobsberg* (E), (06742–3061). 39 rooms. Castle-hotel. Riding, indoor pool, wild game park, restaurant, and even a wedding chapel. AE, DC, MC, V. *Bellevue* (M), Rheinallee 41 (06742–1020). 88 rooms; pool, sauna, tennis and good restaurant. AE, DC, MC, V. *Motel am Ebertor* (M), Heerstr. (06742–2081). 48 rooms with shower. AE, DC, MC, V.

Cochem. In Mosel Valley. *Alte Thorschenke* (M), Brückenstr. 3 (02671–7059). Historic inn dating from 1332; wine tavern, hunting and own vineyard. AE, DC, MC, V. *Brixiade* (M), Uferstr. 13 (02671–3015). Fine view over the Mosel and Cochem from the terrace restaurant. Can be noisy. AE. *Germania* (M), Moselpromenade 1 (02671–261). A Ring Hotel. 31 rooms; bar terrace; eel specialties. AE, DC, MC, V.

Daun. *Kurfürstliches Amtshaus* (M), Auf der Burgberg (06592–3031). Up on the hill with panoramic view, pool, fine restaurant. Quiet. AE, DC, MC, V.

Deidesheim. On the Wine Road. *Haardt* (M), Weinstr. 11 (06326–6056). 84 rooms with bath or shower; thermal treatment, pool, wine-tasting cellar. AE, DC, MC. *Hatterer's Hotel zum Reichsrat* (M), Weinstr. 12 (06326–6011). 80 rooms; wine tavern. AE, DC, MC. *Romantik Hotel Deidesheimer Hof* (M), Am Marktplatz (06326–1811). 49 beds, most rooms with own bath/shower; very comfortably furnished, lovely reception rooms and first class cuisine. Rich in tradition. AE, DC, MC, V. *Gastehaus Hebinger* (I), Bahnhofstr. 21 (06326–387). Small pension with garden and room terrace, own wines. No restaurant.
Restaurant. *Zur Kanne,* Weinstr. 31 (06326–396). 12th-century house with own vineyard; French cuisine. AE, DC, MC.

Kaiserslautern. *Dorint Hotel Pfälzerwald* (E), St. Quentin-Ring 1 (0631–28071). 226 beds, all rooms with bath; pool; solarium and fitness center. Restaurant, beer and wine-tavern; garden terrace. AE, DC, MC, V. *Pfälzer Hof* (M), Fruchthallstr. 15 (0631–61922). AE, MC. *Bonk* (I), Riesenstr. 13 (0631–65023). 31 rooms, all with bath. Garni.
Restaurant. *Weinrestaurant Haus Hexenbäcker* (E), Muhlstr. 1, Am Fackelrondell (0631–72920).

Koblenz. *Continental-Palzerhoff* (E). Bahnhofplatz 1 (0261–33073). Modern hotel near the main rail station and Koblenz's fashionable old quarter. Elegantly furnished in Bauhaus-era style. All rooms with bath or shower; pool, sauna, restaurant, bar. AE, DC, MC, V. *Scandic Crown* (E), Julius-Wegeler-Str. 6 (0261–1360). On the Rhine Promenade. 170 rooms, all with bath. Modern. 2 restaurants and garden-terrace. AE, DC, MC, V. *Diehl* (M), Am Pfaffendorfer Tor 10 (0261–72010). 120 beds. On Ehrenbreitstein bank. AE, DC, MC, V. *Hohenstaufen* (M), Emil Schuller Str. 41–43 (0261–37081). 68 rooms with bath or shower; also near the rail station. AE, DC, MC, V. *Kleiner Riesen* (M), Kaiserin Augusta Anlage 18 (0261–32077). 22 rooms; facing the Rhine on the city bank, beautiful setting and commendable service. AE, DC, MC, V. *Haus Morjan* (I), Rheinzollstr. 14 (0261–34187). 57 beds, most rooms with bath or shower. V. Facing the landing stages for Rhine and Mosel boats. AE, DC, MC, V. *Jan Van Werth* (I), Van Werth Str. 9 (0261–36500). 10 rooms, no restaurant. Closed in

April and at Christmas. *Union-Victoria* (I), Altlöhrter 16 (0261–33003). 70 rooms. AE, DC, MC, V.

Restaurants. *Balkan Restaurant* (M), Hohenzollern Str. 116 (0261–34924). In the small Christo Bajew hotel. *Rhein-Mosel-Halle* (M), Julius-Wegeler-Str. (0261–36542). In the building of the same name. *Ratsstuben* (M), Am Plan 9 (0261–38834). In the pedestrian zone, with terrace and skittles.

Wine Taverns. *Weinhaus Hubertus* (M), Florinsmarkt 6 (0261–31177). Hunting atmosphere, an inn since 1689. *Binding Fass* (I), Lohrstr. 96 (0261–36320).

Weindorf (Wine Village). Built on the occasion of the 1925 German Wine Exhibition and located by the Rheinbrücke bridge about ten minutes' walk from the main station. It is a precise model of a vintners' village. The village square is enclosed by a real vineyard and surrounded by half-timbered houses representing the noble German wine areas. There are four taverns, open all year round from 11 A.M. till midnight (except in November).

Linz. On the Rhine. *Burg Ockenfels* (M), Burgstr. (02644–2071). 23 rooms. Castle hotel, magnificent views over the Rhine and Ahr rivers, gardens, riding. AE, DC, MC, V. *Weinstock* (M), Linzhausenstr. 38 (02644–2459). 38 rooms, pleasant terrace. Passenger ship landing-stage. AE, DC, MC, V.

Ludwigshafen. On the Rhine. *Excelsior* (E), Lorientalallee 16 (0621–519201). 160 rooms; good restaurant, sauna, pool. Near the main station. AE, DC, MC, V. *Ramada* (E), Pasadenallee 4 (0621–519301). 204 rooms; good restaurant, sauna, pool. Near the main station. AE, DC, MC, V. *Viktoria* (M), Bahnhofstr. 1B (0621–515088). 100 beds. AE, DC, MC, V. *Park-Pension Speichermann* (I), Luitpoldstr. 150 (0621–694521). 32 beds.

Restaurants. *Goldener Weinberg* (M), in the Hotel Excelsior building (0621–519413). Closed Fri. evening until Sat. midday. *Pfalzbau,* Berliner Str. 30 (0621–519165). AE, DC, MC. *Ratsstuben,* Bahnhofstr. 13 (0621–516399). AE, DC, MC.

Mainz. *Bristol* (E), Friedrich Ebert Str. 20 (06131–8060). 57 rooms with own bath. In the Weisenau section near the Weisenauer Rhine bridge. AE, DC, MC, V. *Favorite Park Hotel* (E), Karl-Weiser-Str. 1 (06131–82091). At the Stadtpark, with splendid view from the garden-terrace. 42 rooms, all with bath. With Hotel restaurant (M), *Bierkutsche* tavern (I) (06131–81416), and *Stadtparkrestaurant Favorite* (M) (06131–82730). *Hilton International Mainz* (E), Rheinstr. 68 (06131–2450). 240 rooms in the original building plus a further 195 in the newer section. Through its linking corridors with the Rheingoldhalle, it now represents one of the largest conference centers in Europe, while at the same time being a highly comfortable five-star hotel. Panoramic *Rheingrill* restaurant; wine tavern, two bars and a bistro. AE, DC, MC, V. A PLM-Etap Hotel. *Mainzer Hof* (E), Kaiserstr. 98 (06131–233771). 72 rooms, with all comforts. On the Rhine promenade; restaurant with panoramic view on the top floor. AE, DC, MC, V. *Novotel* (E), in Bretzenheim section, Essenheiner Str. 200 (06131–361054). 242 beds, all with bath. Pool, restaurant. AE, DC, MC, V. *Am Hechenberg* (M), Am Schinnergraben 82 (06131–507001). Most rooms with own bath. Situated in Hechtsheim suburb between the town and the airport; sauna and fitness room. AE, DC, MC. *Am Römerwall* (M), Römerwall 53 (06131–232135). Located in the town's green-belt near the University Clinic. 62 beds, about half with own bath or shower. *Hammer* (M), Bahnhofsplatz 6 (06131–611061). 60 beds, most rooms with own bath. No restaurant. At the station. AE, DC, MC, V.

Restaurants. *Drei Lilien* (E), Ballplatz 2 (06131–225068). Elegant with antique furnishings and fine "nouvelle cuisine." AE, DC, MC, V. *Walderdorff* (E), Karmeliterplatz 4 (06131–222515). Highly recommended, with good value *table d'hôte* menu. AE, DC, MC, V. *Man-Wah* (M), Am Brand 42 (06131–231669). Most popular Chinese restaurant in town. One minute's walk from Rheingoldhalle. AE, DC, MC, V. *Rats und Zunftstuben Heilig Geist* (M), Rentengasse 2 (06131–225757). Building in part dates back to Roman times. Modern building in vaulted Gothic style with antique furnishings and rustic atmosphere. Good, wholesome cooking. Very popular so reservations essential. AE, DC, MC.

Old Mainz Wine Taverns. *Alt Deutsche Weinstube,* Liebfrauenplatz 7 (06131–234057). Also good hearty food. *Hottum,* Grebenstr. 3 (06131–223370). Simple tavern in a side street near the cathedral. Small snacks. *Zum Beichstuhl,* Kapuzinerstr. 30 (06131–233120). Easily overlooked, but one of the most attractive and historic taverns in town. "Handkäs" and "Spundekäs" served.

Oberwesel. On the Rhine. *Schönburg* (M), (06744–7027). Castle hotel above town. Only a few rooms, all with bath; first-class restaurant. Very romantic. AE, MC, V. *Römerkrug* (M), Marktplatz 1 (06744–8176). On the Market Place.

Rengsdorf. Climatic resort in Westwald. *Obere-Mühle* (M), an der Strasse nach Hardert (02634–2229). 50 beds; terrace-restaurant and park. *Zur Linde* (M), Westerwaldstr. 35 (02634–2155). 80 beds. AE, DC, MC. *Rengsdorfer Hof* (M), Westerwaldstr. 26 (02634–2213). 46 beds.

Saarbrücken. *Am Triller* (E), Trillerweg 57 (0681–580000). Modern; 130 rooms, some apartments. AE, DC, MC, V. *Etap Kongress Hotel* (E), Hafenstr. 8 (0681–30691). 300 beds, most rooms with bath or shower. Centrally-located, with pool, sauna, solarium. AE, DC, MC, V. *Novotel* (E), Zinzingerstr. 9 (0681–58630). 99 rooms, all with bath and air-conditioning; located near the Paris–Mannheim autobahn, but quiet. AE, DC, MC, V. *Meran* (M), Mainzer Str. 69 (0681–65381). Centrally-located, comfortable. AE, DC, MC, V.

Restaurants. *E. Welsch* (E), Breite Str. 12 (0681–49311). In the Tivoli Haus; rustic elegance, cuisine with a personal touch. AE, DC. *Handelshof* (E), Wilhelm-Heinrich-Str. 17 (0681–56920). Dated back to 1740. Alsace specialties and good wines in period surroundings. DC. *Gasthaus Horch* (M), Mainzer Str. 2 (0681–34415). An inn since 1792, furnished in local style. *Zum Stiefel* (M), Am Stiefel 2 (0681–31246). One of the oldest and most attractive inns in town with over 280 years of service as a hostelry. Hearty regional specialties; beer garden serving locally-brewed Saarland beer. Next door, *Hauck-Weinstuben,* notable wine tavern with fine Saarland wines and specialties.

St. Goar. *Berghotel Auf der Loreley,* Auf der Loreley (06771–2676). On the famous rock, on the other side of the river at St. Goarhausen. Has fine views and a restaurant. AE, DC, MC. *Schlosshotel-Burg Rheinfels* (E), Schlossberg 47 (06741–2071). 46 rooms. At the castle ruins; superb views, heated pool, sauna, terrace, gourmet restaurant. Can be crowded and noisy at weekends. AE, DC, MC, V. *Pohl's Rhein Hotel Adler* (M), (06771–2613). 73 rooms with bath or shower. Turn-of-the-century hotel perched on the edge of the Rhine, with good views of castles. Garden, terrace, pool, solarium, restaurant. AE, DC, MC, V. Closed Nov.–Feb. *Herrmannsmuhle* (I), Forstbachstr. 46 (06771–7317). Some rooms with showers. Chalet-style hotel at the foot of the slopes with vineyards; an ideal spot to set off for a country walk. Restaurant. No credit cards.

Speyer. *Goldener Engel* (M), Gilgenstr. 27 (06232–76732). Evening meals served in *Zum alten Engel* tavern. AE, DC, MC. *Kurpfalz* (M), Mühlturmstr. 5 (06232–24168). No restaurant. *Luxhof* (M), (06205–3581). A small country hotel, across the Rhine, near bridge, in Hockenheim suburb.
Restaurant. *Backmulde* (E), Karmeliterstr. 11 (06232–71577). Fine, good-value cuisine.

Traben-Trarbach. Restaurant. *Altes Gasthaus Moseltor* (M), Moselstr. 1 (06541–6551). On the right bank of the Mosel. Praiseworthy cuisine and good-value menus. Wine tastings from local vineyards on Sat. at 3.30 P.M. Reservations must be made by Fri. evening. Some rooms. AE, DC, MC, V.

Trier. *Dorint Porta Nigra* (E), Porta Nigra Platz 1 (0651–27010). 67 rooms, with bath; restaurants, 350-car underground garage. AE, DC, MC, V. *Europa Parkhotel-Mövenpick* (E), Kaiserstr. 29 (0651–71950). 170 beds; garden terrace. AE, DC, MC, V. *Scandic Crown Hotel* (E), Zurmaiener Str. 164 (0651–23091). Two minutes' walk from the station; top-grade facilities, heated indoor pool. AE, DC, MC, V. *Petrisburg* (M), Sickingenstr. 11 (0651–41181). 18 rooms, no restaurant; on the hill of the same name. *Deutscher Hof* (I), Südallee 25 (0651–46021). 90 rooms. *Rebenhof* (I), Wasserbilliger Str. 34 (0651–85932). 16 rooms; restaurant. In the Zewen suburb.
Restaurants. *Pfeffermühle* (E), Zurlaubener Ufer 76 (0651–26133). Near the cable-car station. The best restaurant in town, serving light, fine "nouvelle cuisine" with a particularly good selection of fish dishes. Good Moselle wine list. Reservations advisable. MC, DC. *Steipe Ratskeller* (M), Hauptmarkt 14 (0651–75052). In the cellar beneath the Gothic town hall. Various dining rooms on different levels, also café with terrace. AE. *Zum Domstein* (M), Hauptmarkt 5 (0651–74490). Several small taverns and courtyards and has 170 wines from its old Roman wine cellar. Wine tasting from DM.4 per person. Regional dishes. AE, DC, MC, V. *Krokodil* (I), Böhmerstr. 10 (0651–73107).

Wintrich. *Weinstube St. Michael* (M), Moselweinstr. 4 (06534–233). Small inn on wine-grower's estate with good (I) restaurant serving local specialties.

Worms. *Nibelungen Hotel* (E), Martinsgasse 16 (06241–6977). 96 beds, all rooms with own bath; restaurant. AE, MC. *Dom Hotel* (M), Obermarkt

10 (06241–6913). 60 rooms, all with bath or shower; restaurant. AE, DC, MC. *Hüttl* (I), Peterstr. 5–7 (06241–87874). 40 beds. Opposite city hall. Delightful breakfasts; cosy. *Kriemhilde* (I), Hofgasse 2–4 (06241–6278). Apartment to let; restaurant with garden terrace. AE, DC, MC.

Restaurant. *Rotisserie Dubs* (E), Kirchstr. 6 (06242–2023). Located about 10 km. (six miles) north of town in the direction of Mainz. Rustic surroundings and first-class regional food. Excellent wines.

Zell. *Schloss Zell* (M), Schlossstr. 8 (06542–4084). 12 rooms, period furnishings, honeymooner's guest room in one of the towers. Dates from 1220. "Zeller Schwarze Katz," the well known Mosel wine, comes from its vineyards. Avoid weekends if possible. AE, DC, V.

CAMPING AND YOUTH HOSTELS. There is an abundance of campsites throughout the region, and the countryside of river valleys, lakes and forestland makes excellent camping terrain. A complete catalogue of all sites can be obtained from the Regional Tourist Office at Koblenz.

There are also Youth Hostels to be found in all the main centers of the region, and again a full list can be obtained from the Regional Tourist Office.

TOURIST INFORMATION. The Regional Tourist Office is *Fremdenverkehrsverband Rheinland-Pfalz*, Postfach 1420, 5400 **Koblenz.** There is also a regional office for the whole of the Südliche Deutsche Weinstrasse (Southern German Wine Road) at *Weinstrasse Zentrale für Tourismus*, Postfach 2124, 6740 **Landau.**

Other tourist offices are as follows: **Bad Dürkheim**, *Verkehrsamt*, Mannheimstr. 24, am Bahnhofplatz, 6702 Bad Dürkheim (06322–793275). **Bad Kreuznach**, *Kurverwaltung*, Postfach 649, Kurhausstr. 23, 6550 Bad Kreuznach (0671–92325), also kiosk at the main station. **Bad Ems**, *Kur- und Verkehrsverein*, Lahnstr. 90, 5427 Bad Ems (02603–4488). **Bad Neuenahr-Ahrweiler**, *Kur- und Verkehrsverein*, Hauptstr. 60, 5488 Bad Neuenahr-Ahrweiler (02641–2278). **Bernkastel-Kues**, *Tourist Information*, Gestade 5, 5550 Bernkastel-Kues (06531–4023). **Deidesheim**, *Verkehrsamt im Rathaus*, Marktplatz, 6705 Deidesheim (06326–1921). **Kaiserslautern**, *Fremdenverkehrsamt im Rathaus*, 6750 Kaiserslautern (0631–852316). **Koblenz**, *Verkehrsamt*, (in the pavilion opposite the main station) 5400 Koblenz (0261–31304). **Landau**, *Verkehrsamt*, Marktstr. 50, 6740 Landau (06341–13301). **Ludwigshafen**, *Verkehrsverein*, Pavillon am Hauptbahnhof (at main station), 6700 Ludwigshafen (0621–512035). **Mainz**, *Verkehrsverein*, Bahnhofstr. 15, 6500 Mainz (06131–233741). **Neustadt**, *Verkehrsamt*, Exterstr. 4, 6730 Neustadt an der Weinstrasse (06321–855329). **Pirmasens**, *Verkehrsamt*, Dankelsbachstr. 19, 6780 Pirmasens (06331–84444). **Saarbrücken**, *Verkehrsamt*, Pavillon, Trierer Str., 6600 Saarbrücken (0681–36515). **Speyer**, *Verkehrsamt*, Maximilianstr. 11, 6720 Speyer (06232–14395). **Trier**, *Tourist Information, an der Porta Nigra*, 5500 Trier (0651–48071). **Worms**, *Verkehrsverein*, Neumarkt 14, 6520 Worms (06241–25045).

HOW TO GET AROUND. By air. Frankfurt International Airport is connected by InterCity express trains with Koblenz directly from the airport building, providing a fast service into the Rhineland and the Mosel

Valley. Mainz is connected directly by S-Bahn (30 mins) as well as by autobahn (27 km). There are also rail connections to the region from the airports of Köln-Bonn and Düsseldorf.

Saarbrücken in the region of Saar also has an international airport with
flights to and from London, Manchester, Berlin, Düsseldorf and Frankfurt.

By train. The main railroad centers of the region are Koblenz, Mainz,
Mannheim, Ludwigshafen, Kaiserslautern and Karlsruhe, all lying in a
more or less north–south line. Then there are fast train connections to
Neustadt an der Weinstrasse and further west to Trier on the Mosel. Bullay is the most important interconnecting rail station for the Mosel and
Rhine valleys. Mannheim is probably the most convenient starting point
for rail connections into the Palatinate. There is also a railway route following the whole length of the German Wine Road, with a large junction
at Neustadt, connecting the Landau–Neustadt, Neustadt–Ludwigshafen
and Mainz–Ludwigshafen routes.

By bus. The Europa Bus route Frankfurt–Saarbrücken–Paris (EB185)
runs through Mannheim and Kaiserslautern, from where bus routes connect to all parts of the region. In addition, the parallel Deutsche Touring
(German Touring) express bus line (T91S), from Frankfurt to Barcelona,
calls at Mainz, Bad Kreuznach, Idar-Oberstein and Trier, all of which
have connecting bus services. There is also a special Wine-Road bus service *(Weinstrassenverkehr)* from Neustadt-an-der-Weinstrasse (departures
from the main station square every hour) to Edenkoben and Landau.
From Landau the *Weinstrassenbahnbus* (German Railways bus) takes
over and runs twice daily (10 A.M. and 1.15 P.M.) from the bus park (stop
no. 7) at the main station to Weissenburg at the end of the Wine Road,
via Bad Bergzabern. Information and timetables from the tourist office
or bus station in Neustadt (06323–2810) or the information office of the
German Railways in Landau (06341–20966). German Railways "Bahnbus" service, *Mosel-Talbahn,* operates along the Mosel valley from Bullay
to Trier, calling at all main resorts en route.

By car. Koblenz is a one-hour drive from Köln airport. Rental cars are
available at all airports. Scenically the best part of the Rhine is from Koblenz to Mainz. There is a road on both banks of the river, the larger being
on the west, near which there is also an autobahn, the A 61. In spite of
this, the river roads are crowded, one sees very little of the river and the
little villages along it have difficulty in accommodating the tourists who
flood them. The only satisfactory way to see the river is to go along it by
boat, taking your car with you. But get off at Bingen and drive up the
Nahe River, or follow the enchanting Weinstrasse which ends near the
French border.

In addition, there are 13 specially-designed scenic routes criss-crossing
the region and taking in all the diversity of landscape the Rhineland-
Palatinate has to offer, from the volcanic Eifel in the north to the wine-
growing Palatinate and Saarland in the south. The most famous of all,
and with the exception of only the Romantic Road, perhaps the most well-
known route in Germany, is the Deutsche Weinstrasse (German Wine
Road). Stretching from Bockenheim near Worms to the French border,
it meanders through the main wine-growing areas of the Palatinate, via
the center of wine production, Neustadt-an-der-Weinstrasse, the 13th-
century fortress town of Landau, on to the small spa town of Bad Bergzab-

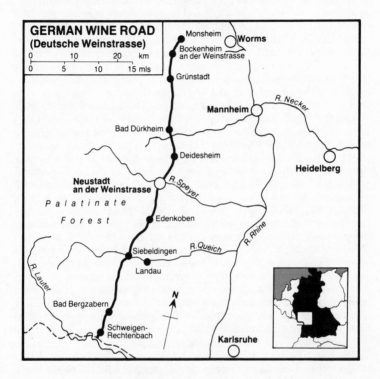

GERMAN WINE ROAD
(Deutsche Weinstrasse)

ern, to Schweigen-Rechtenbach, the official end (or beginning, as the case may be) of the Wine Road.

The Nahe and Ahr Valleys also boast two scenic routes, the Ahr Rotweinstrasse and the Nahe Weinstrasse (the Ahr Red Wine Route and the Nahe Wine Route). The Ahr Rotweinstrasse runs from Sinzig along the course of the river Ahr through Bad Neuenahr to Altenahr, with the ruins of the fortress built in 1100 by the Counts of Ahr and the 18th-century Schloss Kreuzberg, towering above the town on rugged cliffs.

The Nahe Weinstrasse follows a circular route along the Nahe, starting at Bingenbrück where the Nahe flows into the Rhine, and continuing in a southwest, northeast direction through Bad Kreuznach, Norheim, Odernheim, Merxheim, Bockenau, Sponheim with its famous castle, Burg Sponheim, and back to the Rhine via the wine towns of Wallhausen, Hergesheim, Genheim, Burg Layen and Dorsheim.

The Mosel Valley also has its own wine road. Starting from Koblenz it follows the river via Kobern-Gondorf, with the oldest half-timbered house in Germany, Moselkern with the famous Burg Elz castle, Cochem with its beautiful market square and chairlift up to the Reichsburg, and the well-known resorts of Zell, Traben-Trarbach, Bernkastel-Kues, on to the oldest wine village in Germany, Neumagen-Dhron, and thence to the Roman city of Trier. The route ends at Perl on the French border and gives you plenty of opportunity for sampling the delicious Mosel wines.

In the Eifel you can tour the Deutsche Wildstrasse (German Wild Animal Road), which starts at Daun and passes through beautiful parkland with protected herds of deer and wild boar, and, in the Kasselberg nature-park near Gerolstein, wolf and eagle enclosures. It continues through the Eifel towns of Prüm, Schönecken, Wiersdorf, the mountain-deer park of Gondorf, with a grizzly bear enclosure, returning to its starting point via Grosslittgen, the health resort of Manderscheid, Gillenfeld and the volcanic lakes of Schalkenmehren and Gemünden.

There are two other routes worth noting. The Rheingoldstrasse from Rhens to Rheindiebach on the opposite side of the river to the Lorely Valley, and following the townships of the legend of Siegfried and the treasure of the Nibelungs, the Rheingold. The treasure is supposedly buried in the Rhine under the Lorely rock, and its golden reflection is said to appear from time to time at sunset over the hills along this part of the Rhine.

The last route we shall describe here is the Deutsche Edelsteinstrasse (German Gem Road), between the Nahe River and the Hunsrück Hills. This is a tour interesting for geologists, mineral hunters and anyone interested in semi- and precious stones. Starting at Fischbach, with its medieval copper mine, the route branches out in a variety of directions such as to Niederwörresbach, with its mineral exhibition, Kirschweiler, site of a fountain made out of mountain crystals. Sensweiler with its openair geological museum, Schauren, with a precious-stone exhibition and Idar-Oberstein, home of the German Precious Gem Museum and center of the industry with the German Diamond and Precious Gem Exchange. For full details of all 13 scenic routes and route-plans write to the regional tourist office for the Rhineland-Palatinate in Koblenz, asking for their *Entdeckungsrouten* and *Happy Touring* brochures.

By boat. Between mid-April and the end of October, the Köln-Düsseldorfer Steamship Company, or KD, operate a fleet of motor-boats, steamers, paddle-steamers and a hydrofoil on the Rhine between Mainz and Düsseldorf, the Main as far as Frankfurt and, from mid-May, also on the Mosel from Koblenz to Cochem and to Trier. Trips from Trier to Pfalzel leave every hour-and-a-half, and you can stop for an unlimited amount of time in Pfalzel.

The KD operate a variety of different excursions taking in various landmarks, and the passenger can disembark at will, re-boarding another steamer or motor-cruiser later on with the same ticket. There is a combined German Railways/KD rail/ship package for a short cruise on the Mosel between Koblenz and Trier, including rail ticket to the point of embarkation (Koblenz) and return from Trier, plus accommodation on board, excursions, wine-tasting, etc. Available from May to October, the tour can be booked (at least one month in advance) through any DER travel agent or directly from German Railways.

In addition to the regular routes, the KD also organize an assortment of special cruises and packages with music, dancing, wine-tasting and children's parties, as well as combined 1- and 2-day trips, some including excursions on land with overnight hotel accommodation. Reservations in advance are recommended for all special excursion trips, and most of these take place in the summer months. For boat trips upstream inquire at *KD.,* 5000 Köln 1, Frankenwerft 15 (0221–20881); downstream from 6500 Mainz, Am Rathaus (06131–24511). Price reductions are given on return tickets, and groups; children up to 14 years half-fare, toddlers free.

The Hebel-Line of Boppard have an attractive program of Lorely Valley cruises from March to November, with day excursions to Koblenz, Rüdesheim and Bad Ems, and evening "Nightboats" with music and dancing. Information from *Philipp Hebel,* 5407 Boppard (06742–2420).

Similarly, the Bingen-Rüdesheimer shipping line at Bingen—Rheinkai 10, 6530 Bingen, (06722–2972)—operate various regular tours on the Rhine between Rüdesheim and St. Goarshausen, also with evening dance-cruises and a car-ferry service running between Bingen and Rüdesheim from May to October.

The KD also operate on the Mosel from mid-May to mid-October with a daily regular service from Trier to Bernkastel, Beilstein, Cochem, Koblenz and back, leaving daily at 9.15 A.M. and returning at 7.50 P.M., with a two-hour stopover in Bernkastel-Kues. Information from the KD agency in Bernkastel (06531–6618) or Trier tourist information (0651–75440).

By bike. Almost every large town and important holiday resort in the region has bicycle hire facilities. You can hire bicycles at some railway stations (*Fahrrad am Bahnhof*) and return them to any other on your route. Inquire from the local tourist offices.

In addition there are numerous all-inclusive 2–14-day bicycling tours on marked routes arranged through the tourist offices in the Eifel-Hunsrück-Mosel region. And there are many more such touring suggestions in the brochure issued by the Regional Tourist Office in Koblenz and entitled *Rheinland-Pfalz, Hobby Spezial.*

EXCURSIONS. Apart from the many river trips available (see above), there are numerous day excursions organized by the various local bus companies and some tourist offices.

The tourist offices of Koblenz, Mainz and Trier offer guided tours of their cities, with English-speaking guides, as well as bus excursions into the surrounding countryside and river trips.

SPORTS. Horseback riding is very popular in this area with riding schools and horses to hire in many centers. For full lists of stables, schools, farm accommodations, etc. write to the Palatinate Regional tourist office in Koblenz.

Golf courses in Bad Ems, Bad Neuenahr, Gisingen near Saarlouis and Hillesheim (9-hole); and golf tournaments at Bad Ems. There are **tennis** courts in all spas and larger towns and international tennis meets are held in Trier.

Swimming pools, both indoor and outdoor, abound. Thermal pools in Niederbreisig (indoor and outdoor), Hönningen and Bodendorf. The numerous rivers afford opportunities for **kayaking** along long stretches of unspoiled scenery. The Mosel between Trier and Koblenz (120 miles, moderately swift current, requires about a week) is scenically one of the finest. Also on the river Wied in the Westerwald and **canoeing** on the Saar in Saarbrucken, Saarlouis and Merzig.

The principal **winter sports** centers are in the Eifel and include Nürburg-Hohe Acht (2 ski lifts, 2 ski jumps), 4 prepared cross-country skiing tours, including a double track around the Nürburgring when sufficient snowfall permits, Hollerath (ski school, ski lift, ski jump), Adenau, Daun, Hellenthal and Monschau. Skiing also in Westerwald and Hunsrück.

Fishing in Mosel, Saar, Ahr Lahn, and Rhine, especially for trout, pike, perch, carp and eel. Permits and information from regional tourist offices.

Walking. The Pfälzer Wald (Palatinate Forest) is a great walking area, with a huge network of signposted trails: Dahn in the Wasgau holiday region in the southwest has 250 km. (155 miles) of marked footpaths with wayside benches; Hauenstein, an officially registered health resort in the Palatinate Forest Nature Park, has 200 km. (124 miles) with conducted walks arranged by the tourist office; Idar-Obenstein, Eppenbrunn, and Deidesheim are also some towns well worth visiting who also arrange conducted walks through the Palatinate Forest. In the Saarland a well-marked 235 km. round-trip hiking trail encircles the state.

The Eifel and the Ahr Valley regions boast over 1,000 km. (620 miles) of local marked hiking trails with resting places, refuge huts and panoramic viewpoints. There are a variety of different marked circular hiking tours in the various different landscapes. Full details of tours available from the local tourist offices of Bad Breisig, Remagen, Sinzig, Altenahr and Niederzissen.

The "Hiking without Luggage" scheme as well as 2–3 day hiking holidays are popular: from Cochem in the Mosel Valley you can join a Mosel Wine Walking Tour lasting seven days and organized by the tourist association, where your luggage is sent on ahead by car. Information from Tourist Office, Cochem Holiday Region, P.O. Box 1550, Endertplatz, 5590 Cochem (02671–3971).

WINE TASTING. There are vineyards and vintners' estates galore throughout the Rhineland-Palatinate. Wine-tasting tours can be arranged through several of the local tourist offices or, sometimes even the hotel concierges in the wine-growing towns can be of help. Visitors are welcome to call in whenever they see the sign "Weinprobe."

THE NORTHERN RHINELAND

The Realm of Charlemagne

The A, B, C and D of Northern Rhineland cities are Aachen, Bonn, Cologne (Köln), and Düsseldorf. To these we might add an E for Essen, Ruhr industrial center and the largest city of the region. But cities alone represent only a small part of the regional story, which boasts as well a wealth of art treasures, historical interest, and natural beauty.

Exploring Essen

Essen is the center of the Ruhr and the largest city in the region, known the world over as the capital of the powerful Krupp industrial concern. It boasts the tallest and largest Town Hall (Rathaus) in West Germany, over 90 meters (300 feet) high and completed in 1979. With its modern business buildings, busy streets, underground railway, and immense industrial plants in the outskirts, Essen does not at first glance appear to have much relation to old Germany or to the legendary country of the Rhine. But its cathedral (Münsterkirche) dates from 852, while the abbey at Werden (Abteikirche Werden), some eight km. (five miles) south of the city center, dates back to the 8th century. The treasury of the cathedral (Münsterschatz, in Burgplatz) is famous for its valuable and unique examples of Romanesque goldsmiths' art, including three crosses of the Abbess Mathilde, numerous reliquaries, and the Gold Madonna dating from around 1000. Two other churches are worth visiting: the 11th-century Marktkirche (Market Church), scene of the Reformation in Essen in 1563, located in the center; and the Luciuskirche (St. Lucius Church) in Werden, the oldest German parish church, and founded in 995. Essen's *Alte Synagogue* was built as a copy of the Temple of David in Jerusalem between 1911–13. Since 1980 it has been a memorial center to all victims of violence with a permanent exhibition dedicated to persecution and resistance in and around Essen during the years of Nazi terror. The 13th-century castle, Schloss Borbeck, in a large forest-park in a northwestern suburb, was formerly the residence of the princess-abbesses of Essen.

Another Essen treasure house is the modern Folkwang Museum, with its excellent collection of 19th- and 20th-century art. It's located in Bismarckstrasse. The art of the poster may be appreciated at the Deutsche Plakat Museum (German Poster Museum) in Steeler Strasse, with examples from many countries from the 19th-century onwards. The museum of local and natural history—Ruhrland-und Heimatmuseum—is located in the southwestern suburb of Rüttenscheid, in Witteringstr. Also in Rüttenscheid is the Grugapark and Botanischer Garten. Laid out for the international horticultural show of 1929, Grugapark not only has a fine botanical garden and tropical hothouses, but is a popular recreation area with aquarium, terrarium, mini-railway and sports facilities. The Grugahalle, an undistinguished modern building, is the scene of cultural and sporting activities and conventions. Other notable examples of modern architecture are the Städtischer Saalbau, where concerts and congresses are held, many buildings on the Huyssenallee and Freiheit square, and the Bauzentrum. The latter has an exhibition devoted to the building industry, while the Haus Industrieform, on Kennedyplatz, has a permanent display of industrial design.

Essen's summer playground for sailing, swimming and boating is Baldeneysee, a lake situated in the southern suburbs. Presiding over the lake, in Bredeney suburb, is the Villa Hügel, former residence of the Krupp family. Built in 1870, since 1953 it has been made available by them for concerts and exhibitions. Among other items of interest in the villa are the Flemish tapestries and the Krupp collection of the history of German industry. The large park is also open to the public.

Essen and music, particularly choir music, are as well mated as Krupp and steel. There are around 100 choirs, of which nine are more than 100 years old, and many choir festivals are held to display their internationally-known talent. One choral rarity is the famous Johannes-Damascenus-Chor, which sings Eastern Orthodox liturgy in the original Church Slavic. Further evidence of Essen's love of music are its several orchestras, the most famous being its Philharmonic, and the Folkwang School of Music, Theater and Dance. From October through December, Essen bursts out in full glory during the Weeks of Light, an annual event in which the shopping center is illuminated with a hundred thousand electric bulbs.

Mülheim, Duisburg and Oberhausen

Mülheim an der Ruhr 10 km. (six miles) to the west of Essen is a large city on both banks of the Ruhr river which has managed to keep its industry (served by a river port) in a section entirely separate from the rest of the town. The town itself comprises both a modern quarter and some old buildings, particularly in the outskirts, that escaped the bomb damage that leveled others—notably Schloss Broich, parts of which date from A.D. 1000 and one of the strongest fortresses on the Lower Rhine, and the Zisterzien-serinnenkloster at Saarn, a Romanesque church dating from 1214. Almost completely destroyed in World War II, the 11th-century Petrikirche (St. Peter's Church), Mülheim's symbol, has been lovingly rebuilt. Around the Petrikirche in the Altstadt (Old Town) are many half-timbered houses, notably the Tersteegenhaus, offering a glimpse of 18th-century life in the house of the preacher and church song-writer Gerhard Tersteegen.

The suburbs straggle along both river banks: this peculiarity has led to the laying out of long avenues linking different sections of the associated Mülheims, and you can easily get into the surrounding countryside. If you like taking river trips, steamers leave from the attractive Wasserbahnhof (Water Station) on the lock island in the Ruhr. Mülheim also has its own private spa in Solbad Raffelberg, with a lovely Kurpark.

Duisburg, a city at the junction of the Ruhr and the Rhine, is probably the largest inland port in Europe, and a visit to its river harbor is well worth while. In its Gothic Salvatorkirche you may see the gravestone of Gerhard Mercator, the famous Renaissance map maker, after whom a concert and congress hall has been named (Mercatorhalle). The Lehm-bruck Museum in Düsseldorferstrasse houses the works of local sculptor Wilhelm Lehmbruck (1881–1919), as well as recent additions of other modern sculpture and post-Expressionist German painters. Duisburg also has a zoo with a dolphinarium and whale aquarium (am Kaiserberg) and outdoor sports' facilities at the Sechs-Seen-Platte (Six Lakes Plateau), the Mattlerbusch leisure park, and at the Wedau sports complex.

Just north of Duisburg is Oberhausen, a modern industrial city of coal, iron and steel, where the first iron works in the Ruhr (the St. Anthony Iron Works) were founded more than 200 years ago and thus known as "the cradle of the Ruhr industry." The main attraction is Schloss Ober-hausen, housing the Municipal Gallery with modern art and an unusual collection of 20th-century glass. There is also an interesting modern stained glass window in the 14th-century Holtener Church; and the 16th-century Vondern Castle, a small red brick structure typical of this area, in the Osterfeld part of the city. In contrast to these, stands the modern Stadthalle, with stages and halls for theater, concerts and congresses.

From Blast Furnaces to Windmills

From Oberhausen it is possible to take off on a little circular tour of the northwestern corner of the Rhineland—Niederrhein, or Lower Rhine—through the former Hanseatic strongholds of Wesel, Rees and Emmerich, on the right bank of the Rhine, where the scenery evokes Hol-land rather than Germany. Here the hills fade away, the Rhine becomes broader, the river is busy with boats and barges crossing the nearby Dutch frontier and the landscape is peppered with little old redbrick towns and windmills.

Crossing to the left bank, you arrive in the old city of Kleve, associated in legend with Lohengrin, whose Schwanenburg Castle, once seat of the Dukes of Kleve, stands on a cliff over the Rhine. This was the home of Anne of Cleves, fourth wife of Henry VIII. The town museum at Haus Koekkoek is also worth a visit.

Swinging back to the south, we come first to Kalkar, where you must not fail to see the beautifully carved altars of the Nikolaikirche, St. Nicholas's Church. The Mary Magdalene alone justifies this whole detour. On to Xanten, whose well-preserved examples of medieval architecture include the impressive remains of the 14th- and 15th-century fortifications, with the massive Klever Tor city gate (1393) and the Gothic Cathedral of St. Viktor (Dom), begun in the 12th century and which has a beautiful cloister. The cathedral treasure is in the Dom Museum.

Once a Roman garrison, Xanten has excavated the original Roman amphitheater and drama and comedies from classical and modern playwrights are performed here during the summer. The Roman reconstruction is in what is now an archeological park and is reached on the B57 between Moers and Kleve. They even serve Roman food here! Continuing through Kevelaer, whose Gnadenkapelle (Chapel of Graces) is a pilgrimage center, you reach Krefeld.

Capital of silk and velvet making (along with nearby Ürdingen), Krefeld is also the center of the clothing industry. There is a textile museum in the Textile Engineers' School at Ürdingen, while Krefeld's Kaiser Wilhelm Museum at Karlsplatz 35 has Italian Renaissance art as well as regional arts and cultural history in the Lower Rhineland Countryside Museum (Landschaftsmuseum des Niederrheins). Krefeld also owes its prosperity to heavy industry, with iron and steel works, and the principal agricultural center in this area, with important agricultural experimental institutes. While you are in Krefeld, you could make a trip to Wasserburg Linn, a moated castle with a fascinating archeological and folklore museum.

Turn west for Süchteln, with an interesting Heimat Museum in the 18th-century house known as Jakobsgut, the Romanesque St. Clemens Church and sand quarries of value to the steel and iron industry. The nearby city of Viersen is known primarily as the cultural center of this border area, with an unusually large number of concerts and stage presentations by important international and German ensembles, and spectators coming also from neighboring Holland. The tall Gothic St. Remigius Church, the symbol of Viersen, presides over the parks, gardens and tree islands of this quiet town, surrounded by unspoiled countryside. Immediately south is Mönchengladbach, a busy textile center, which not only manufactures cloth and maintains technical schools on textile production, but is also an important producer of textile machinery. The town possesses many notable buildings, among them the 13th-century cathedral (Münster), the former Benedictine Abbey of Neuwerk (Klosterkirche Neuwerk, built in the 11th and 12th centuries) and the Baroque Rathaus. The Abteiberg Museum has a collection of 20th-century art. Mönchengladbach is proud of its reputation as the German capital of male chorus singing.

Two small streams, the Schwalm and the Nette, with their lakes, provide a pleasant natural background for picturesque water mills and moated castles. Nearby Rheydt has a moated Renaissance castle, Schloss Rheydt, housing the Städtisches Museum (city museum) of Renaissance and Baroque art and the new City Arts Center (Stadthalle) with opera house, theater and two concert halls.

Returning to the Rhine you reach Neuss, one of the oldest German towns, dating back more than 2,000 years and probably a thriving settlement during the Stone Age. A Roman garrison and town here was known as Novaesium and recent discoveries have unearthed early Christian graves and relics and an early Christian chapel under the cathedral, the

Quirinusdom (1209), whose round dome (1741) and square tower are landmarks of Neuss. In 1956 an early 4th-century baptismal cellar of the Cybele cult, at that time a great rival to Christianity, was discovered, the only such cellar, except for one in Ostia near Rome, which has been found within the boundaries of the former Roman Empire. The Obertor, a massive medieval gate, and the adjoining Clemens-Sels-Museum, should not be missed. Visit also the Dreikönigenkirche with interesting stained glass windows, and the old town houses, including the historic inn Em Schwatte Päd. The modern St. Konradkirche has an unusual stained glass window-wall. A short jump across the Rhine is Düsseldorf.

Tour of Bergisch Land

From Düsseldorf, the most direct route for the exploration of the Rhine Valley would be straight south to Köln. But for the more leisurely traveler, there is an opportunity here for a circular swing through the territory east of the Rhine. The key to this area, known as Bergisch Land, is Velbert, the center of the German lock industry since the 16th century and the home of the German Museum for Locks and Keys (Deutsches Schloss- und Beschlägemuseum), in the Rathaus at Thomasstrasse 1. This amazing collection includes 4,000 examples from all over the world and from the earliest times (such as an Assyrian wooden lock from 5000 B.C.) to the latest devices of the modern age.

Wuppertal is a city with several dams in its vicinity, among them the oldest in Germany; and one of its sights is an elevated railway, invented by a Wuppertal engineer and built in 1900, that hangs suspended from an overhead rail. Always a patron of the arts, Wuppertal has a fine collection of paintings from the 17th to 19th centuries in its Städtisches Museum and modern art in its Studio für Neue Kunst section. The Clock Museum, with a Glockenspiel, displays a long line of historic time-measuring devices, beginning with an Egyptian water clock dating from around 1400 B.C. A beautifully landscaped zoo contains several thousand exotic animals and it blossoms in the spring with innumerable flowers. Among the many examples of modern architecture is Stadtbad Johannisberg, an elegant glass structure, in a park, which houses several swimming pools.

Proceeding south from Wuppertal, the chief city of the Bergisch Land, we continue through Remscheid, the German center for the manufacture of machine tools, with a tool museum (Deutsches Werkzeug Museum) in Cleffstrasse. Its Heimatmuseum, presenting the history, economy and culture of the region, is a beautiful example of the patrician houses of this region. Röntgen, the discoverer of X-rays, was born here and in the suburb of Lennep, in Schwelmer Strasse, is a museum devoted to him and his discovery.

Sited high above the Wupper is one of the biggest fortresses in West Germany, Schloss Burg, once the castle of the Counts of Berg and now home of the Bergisches Museum, devoted to their former territory. Solingen is a city of workshops famous for flatware. Swords have been made here since the 14th century and the craftsmanship of Solingen's swordsmiths and cutlers is celebrated in the Deutsches Klingenmuseum (Blade Museum), in Wuppertaler Strasse, in the suburb of Gräfrath. Typical of the town are roomy, two-story houses with slate roofs, white windowsills and green shutters. *Kotten,* or knife-grinders' workshops are to be seen, and there are old workshops along the Wupper, some of them half-timbered. The Wupper is spanned by Germany's highest railway bridge, the Müngstener Brücke.

From Solingen you can follow the eastern edge of Bergisch Land, moving from ploughed fields to slowly rising, thickly forested hills. You come first to Wipperfürth, not far from the Neye Dam; there are several other dams farther east and north, as well as the artificial lakes created by them. This is also an area of underground caves, spreading from here in an easterly direction through the rest of Bergisch Land and through Sauerland. Two caves of note are Aggertal Cave near Ründeroth, and a stalactite cavern, near Wiehl. Also nearby is Marienhagen, one of the best-preserved medieval villages in the whole area: a wealth of half-timbered houses and a small Gothic church known as the Bunte Kirche (Church of Colors), which has valuable Gothic frescos and carved doors.

From Ründeroth a very scenic stretch of road takes us to Gummersbach and the nearby Aggertal Dam and artificial lake. From here we may proceed directly south through Denklingen and Waldbröl to reach the Sieg valley, and stop off in Siegburg, whose 11th-century Benedictine Abbey on Michaelsberg commands a magnificent view over the surrounding hills. The Servatiuskirche has a famous Romanesque treasury, with masterpieces of the goldsmiths' art. Siegburg was a well-known pottery center in the Middle Ages, as the collection of pottery and ceramics in the Heimat Museum shows. Don't miss the pillory on the Market Square and the historic 15th-century Weinhaus "Auf der Arken." Also visit the building which now houses the Magistrate's Court, birthplace of composer Engelbert Humperdinck.

Continuing north we come to Bensberg, with its old castle and the Baroque palace of the Counts of Berg. Some 13 km. (eight miles) northwest is the Altenberg Dom, also known as the Bergischer Dom, built on the site of a 12th-century Cistercian monastery. The present church (1255–1379), surrounded by forest, is the most important ecclesiastical Gothic building in the Bergisch Land and the west window is the largest church window in Germany.

Leverkusen, virtually a suburb of Köln, has a new city center and "Forum" cultural center worth seeing. It also offers the 120-meter (400 feet) high Bayer skyscraper, the Bayer plant with a Japanese garden, besides a host of modern structures. A little outside is Schloss Morsbroich which houses the city museum and changing art exhibitions. Across the Rhine stands Köln.

Aachen—Charlemagne's City

About 15 km. (nine miles) south of Köln is Brühl, where the Baroque castle of Augustusberg, with a famous stairway by Balthasar Neumann, is set in magnificent gardens. Here, too, is Phantasialand, a 60-acre leisure park, with bob-sled runs, monorail and boat trips.

West of Cologne, a bit more than an hour's drive via the autobahn, is Aachen, founded in 795. Aachen—or if you use the French name for it, Aix-la-Chapelle—is also known as Bad Aachen, and is a noted spa, with the hottest springs in northwest Europe.

The French name refers to the early 9th-century Imperial Chapel, once a part of the imperial palace and later enlarged into the present cathedral

(Kaiserdom) whose importance was due to the fact that Aachen was Charlemagne's capital. Between 936 and 1531, 32 of the Holy Roman Emperors of the German nation were crowned in the cathedral whose most admired central section, the Carolingian-style Oktogon, was built around 800 by Charlemagne. From 1349, the coronation dinners were held in the Reichssaal of the Gothic Rathaus, built in the 14th century on the foundations of the former Carolingian palace; two towers, however, Granusturm and Marktturm, have remained from the Carolingian times. The marble throne of Charlemagne may still be seen in the upper section of the cathedral and his remains lie in the richly-ornamented and sculptured Karlsschrein, located on the main altar. The choir has enormous stained glass windows and presents a brilliant spectacle.

Another great treasure, located on the altar of the St. Nicholas Chapel, is the Shrine of Mary, an intricately and richly sculptured gold and silver reliquary, finished in 1237, designed to hold the four holy relics of the city. The cathedral treasury, the Domschatzkammer, is the most outstanding north of the Alps. Here you can see a host of other jeweled objects, many of gold and silver, such as the bust of Charlemagne, dating from 1350 and containing part of his skull; the 10th-century Lothar Cross; the Bible of Charlemagne from about 800; the Bible of Otto III from about 1000.

Other principal sights include the city gates, Marschiertor and Ponttor; two fountain statues, the "Chicken Thief" on the Hühnermarkt (Chicken Market Square), and Marktbrunnen with Charlemagne's statue on the Rathaus square; the 14th-century Gothic City Hall (Rathaus), considered one of the most beautiful in Germany; the Suermondt Museum, Wilhelmstrasse 18, for 15th–17th century Dutch, Flemish and German painting and medieval woodcarvings; the Sammlung Ludwig, a collection of modern art at Komphausbadstr. 19; and the Couven Museum in Haus Monheim, Hühnermarkt 17, for Rococo and Biedermeier furnishings. The Museum Burg Frankenberg, in a 13th-century castle on Bismarckstrasse, east of the main rail station, contains collections relating to the history and culture of Aachen. Aachen has an International Press Museum, the Internationales Zeitungsmuseum at Pontstrasse 13, a unique collection of newspapers from all over the world, housed in the oldest (1495) burgher's house in Aachen. For further old-world atmosphere, wander through the old Körbergäschen; for spa atmosphere and water the Kurhaus and Kurgarten, and Elisenbrunnen. For those looking for a different kind of excitement, Aachen has a modern casino.

Markets in Aachen are a great attraction: they include good craft and art, a flea market, flowers, and sometimes a peddlers' market with the sellers in traditional costumes and traveling players to entertain.

Northeast of Aachen is the old town of Jülich, once the granary of the Holy Roman Empire. The 13th-century Witches' Tower (Hexenturm) and the 16th-century Citadel are worth a visit.

At Aachen you are at the beginning of the Eifel mountain region, which extends south of this point, west of the Rhine. Journeying southwards we come immediately to Monschau, squeezed into the narrow rocky valley of the Ruhr. Local sports enthusiasts enjoy going over a dam on the river in a "canoe slalom." Narrow steep-roofed, half-timbered houses, in particular the Rote Haus housing the local museum, often perched on stone foundations rising three or four stories from the river in apparently perilous equilibrium, line both shores. Monschau looks just as it did in the 18th century.

Penetrating deeper into the Nord Eifel, we pass through the Hürtgen forest; by the Castle (Burg) of Nideggen; on to the climatic resort of Gemünd, where the Urft and Olef flow together, where you are in the Eifel lake district and where you can see the Rur Dam (Rurtalsperre), about six km. (four miles) from Gemünd; through Steinfeld, with its monastery and the Eifel Cathedral; through Schleiden, a resort in forested mountains whose Gothic church has famous stained glass windows and the 14th-century King's Organ and where there is also a 12th-century palace, to Blankenheim, above which towers a castle, another climatic station at the source of the Ahr River; and then, swinging northward on the return loop, to Bad Münstereifel.

This town, with its medieval city walls, towers and gates well preserved, boasts a Romanesque Stiftskirche with crypt from Carolingian times; old patrician houses (half-timbered and gabled), such as Windeck-Haus; one of the few Romanesque houses north of the Alps at Langenhecke No. 6 and a few Gothic houses, among them the Rathaus.

Bonn, the Capital

The history of Bonn, capital of the German Federal Republic since 1949 and gateway to the romantic Rhine Valley, stretches back for 2,000 years. 1989 will mark the city's 2,000th anniversary, with a large program of special cultural events planned. Under the name of *Castra Bonnensia* it was an important link in the Roman defense line along the Rhine. In A.D. 253 two Roman soldiers, Cassius and Florentius, were put to death because of their Christian beliefs. One of the first Christian shrines arose over their graves, the place where the cathedral (Münster) stands today, with its fine 12th-century Romanesque cloister and spire.

In the 13th century the powerful Prince Electors of Cologne moved to Bonn and built up the city as a worthy capital of their domain. In the 18th century they erected two palaces: the Kurfürstliches Schloss with its fine Hofgarten and ornate gate, the Koblenzer Tor—completed in 1725 in a late Baroque manner, and today accommodating the university—and the Poppelsdorfer Schloss, built 1715–1740. The palaces are linked by Poppelsdorfer Allee and neither is open to the public, though the Botanical Gardens in the grounds of Poppelsdorfer Schloss can be visited. The Electors also built the City Hall on Market Place (Rathaus, am Markt), in 1738.

The regional museum, Rheinisches Landesmuseum, in Colmanstrasse, presents the history and culture of this area of the Rhineland, with relics including the skull of Neanderthal Man. The City Art Collection, Städtisches Kunstmuseum, in Rathausgasse, has German painting from the 18th century on, with works by Rhineland expressionists, including August Macke. Bonn also has an important zoological museum, the Alexander König Museum in Adenauerallee.

Beethoven's birthplace is at Bonngasse 20, now a museum with pictures and documents, an ear trumpet or two, and his last grand piano. Nearby is the Gothic Church of St. Remigius. An annual Beethoven festival is held in the modern Beethovenhalle by the Rhine. An attractive promenade extends along the Rhine from the Alter Zoll, a mighty bastion overlooking the river, to the Bundeshaus, the German Federal Parliament building (originally a teachers' training college, built in 1933). Near the Bundeshaus are the building for the Members of Parliament (completed 1969) and the Federal Chancellery (1976). For another pleasant view of Bonn, visit the Venusberg.

South of Bonn is Bad Godesberg, one of Germany's oldest spas. This is the site of the Godesburg, a watch tower 32 meters (105 feet) high. It was built in 1210 and, amazingly, in 1583 the hill on which it stands was blown up but the tower itself survived, and now has a restaurant and hotel attached. Bad Godesberg's 18th-century Redoute Kurhaus is today the center of diplomatic social activities in Germany. Across the Rhine at Königswinter are the Siebengebirge (Seven Mountains), a natural preserve of forested hills, magnificent views over the Rhine and the Eifel mountains, very good wine (the famous Dragon's Blood), and steeped in legend.

The top of Drachenfels (Dragon's Crag), the most famous of the seven with the ruins of a former fortress of the Archbishops of Köln, can be reached via easy footpaths and a cogwheel railroad (the first and oldest in Germany—built in 1883). Concerts are held here throughout the summer. Earlier the Siebengebirge were noted for their quarries, which provided stone for most of the surrounding castles and churches, including Köln Cathedral, but since being declared a national park in 1889, the quarries are no longer worked. The name Königswinter derives from the Latin *Vinitorium (Vintra)* meaning King's Vineyards, a name in existence since the 14th century and acknowledging the fact that many of the vineyards were in the possession of the kings of Germany.

From this romantic vantage point leave the Northern Rhineland to continue upstream to the Rhineland-Palatinate.

PRACTICAL INFORMATION FOR
THE NORTHERN RHINELAND

TELEPHONES. We have given telephone codes for all the towns and villages in the hotel and restaurant lists that follow. These codes need only be used when calling from outside the town or village concerned.

HOTELS AND RESTAURANTS. The whole of the Northern Rhineland is well provided with hotels and restaurants in all categories, though in larger cities prices are generally rather higher than elsewhere. It's advisable to make reservations in advance (again, especially true of the cities), though tourist offices can also help with accommodations if you do get stuck.

Aachen (Aix-La-Chapelle). *Aquis-Grana-City-Hotel* (E), Büchel 32 (0241–4430). 90 rooms, all with bath, 3 apartments. New, central, and near cathedral and shopping areas. Indoor pool, thermal treatments, restaurant. AE, DC, MC, V. *Steigenberger Hotel Quellenhof* (E), Monheimsallee 52 (0241–152081). 200 rooms, most with bath. Luxurious establishment at the Kurpark. Indoor pool, thermal treatments, restaurant. AE, DC, MC, V. *Novotel* (E), Am Europaplatz (0241–164091). 119 rooms, all with bath.

Indoor pool; restaurant. AE, DC, MC, V. *Schloss-Hotel Friesenrath* (E), Pannekoogweg 46 (02408–5048). Beautiful country mansion and awe-inspiring garden. Limited number of rooms, with bath. Restaurant, bar. Reservations necessary. *Hotel Garni Lousberg* (M), Saarstrasse 108 (0241–20031-2). 25 rooms, most with shower. Small, pleasant hotel near the tower. No restaurant. *Romantik Hotel Altes Brauhaus Burgkeller* (M), Klatterstr. 8–12 (02402–27272) and its modern annexe nearby *Parkhotel Hammerberg,* Hammerberg 11 (02402–20031), in the suburb of Stolberg 11 km. (7 miles) from the city center. Restored brewery with 30 rooms, most with bath; garni; fine old rustic restaurant. 21 rooms, all with bath, in new building with indoor pool, sauna, tennis. AE, DC, MC, V. *Brüls am Dom* (I), Hühnermarkt 2 (0241–31704). 11 rooms, most with bath or shower. Very central, no restaurant.

Restaurants. Aachen enjoys the privilege of having more restaurants per head than any other West German city. *La Bécasse* (E), Hanbrucher Str. 1 (0241–74444). DC, MC, V. *Gala* (E), Monheimsallee 44 (0241–153013). Highly recommended. DC, MC, V. *St. Benedikt* (E), Benediktusplatz 12 (02408–2888). In the Kornelimünster section. *Schloss Friesenrath* (E), Pannekogweg 46 (02408–5048). MC.

Belvedere (M), 0241–35676. Tower restaurant on Lousberg, offering a magnificent view of the city. DC, MC. *Comeback Steak House* (M), Alesianergraben 2 (0241–34505). International steak specialties. No credit cards. *Elisenbrunnen* (M), Friedrich-Wilhelm-Platz 13 (0241–29772). Noted for fine cuisine, with garden and café terrace. AE, DC, MC, V. *Ratskeller* (M), Am Markt (0241–35001). One of the most interesting and historic eating and drinking taverns in this part of Germany. AE, DC, MC, V.

Os Oche (I), Alexanderstr. 109 (0241–36670). Typical Aachen beer tavern, famous for its stews. DC, V. *Zum Schiffgen* (I), Hühnermarkt 23 (0241–33529). Worth trying. AE, DC, MC, V.

Bad Godesberg. *Rheinhotel Dreesen* (E), Rheinstr. 45–49 (0228–82020). A Ring Hotel. 90 rooms, some in lower price ranges. With restaurant. AE, DC, MC, V. *Godesberg-Hotel* (M), Auf dem Godesberg 5 (0228–316071). 14 rooms, one apartment. Comfortable; modern annex to the medieval Godesberg Castle ruins; with restaurant. AE, MC, V. *Drachenfels* (M), Siegfriedstr. 28 (0228–343067). 20 rooms, all with bath. Quiet, on the river in Mehlem; no restaurant. AE, DC, MC. *Insel* (M), Theaterplatz 5 (0228–364082). 70 rooms with bath or shower. Restaurant. AE, DC, MC, V. *Parkhotel* (M), Am Kurpark 1 (0228–363081). Hotel garni, but restaurant attached. MC. *Rheinland* (M), Rheinallee 17 (0228–353087). Quiet; good restaurant. AE, DC, MC, V. *Schaumberger Hof* (M), Am Schaumberger Hof 10 (0228–364095). 34 rooms. At Plittersdorf on the river; garden; restaurant. AE, MC. *Zum Adler* (M), Koblenzerstr. 60 (0228–364071). 40 rooms. Tradition-filled, furnished with antiques. No restaurant. AE, DC, MC, V.

Restaurants. *Korkeiche* (E), in Lannesdorf suburb, Lyngsbergstr. 104 (0228–347897). Beautifully preserved, half-timbered house with rustic atmosphere and good-quality food. *La Redoute/Claire Fontaine* (E), Kurfürstenallee 1 (0228–364041). Opposite the Redoutenpark. Fine, good-value haute cuisine. Closed Sat. and Sun. *Da Roberto* (M), Gotenstr. 126 (0228–373775). Trattoria atmosphere, excellent Italian cooking. MC. *Maternus* (M), Löbestr. 3 (0228–362851). MC.

Bonn. Advance reservations recommended for all tours. *Bristol* (E), Prinz-Albert-Str. 2 (0228–26980). 120 rooms, all with bath or shower. Very comfortable; swimming pool, sauna; first-class cuisine. AE, DC, MC, V. *Godesburg Hotel* (E), Bonn-Bad Godesberg (0228–316071). Historic hotel with beautiful view of the Rhine and the Seven Hills. Popular restaurant with interesting selection of wines. *Königshof* (E), Adenauerallee 9 (0228–26010). 139 rooms, all with bath or shower. Excellent cuisine and wine cellar. AE, DC, MC, V. *Schlosspark-Hotel* (E), Venusbergweg 27 (0228–217036). 67 rooms, all with bath or shower. Very quiet location; indoor pool, sauna; restaurant. AE, DC, MC, V. *Steigenberger* (E), Am Bundeskanzler Platz (0228–20191). 160 rooms, all with bath; eight apartments. Indoor pool. Two restaurants, on 18th floor: *Ambassador* (E) and *Atrium* (M). AE, DC, MC. *Bergischer Hof* (M), Münsterplatz 23 (0228–633441). 28 rooms. Restaurant. *Haus Daufenbach* (M), Brudergasse 6 (0228–637944). Rustic exterior and homey atmosphere. Comfortable rooms, most with bath, but no showers. No credit cards. *Haus Hofgarten* (M), Fritz-Tillmann-Str. 7 (0228–223482). 15 rooms. No restaurant. *Hohenzollernplatz* (M), Plittersdorfer Str. 56 (0228–362177). Most rooms with bath or shower. Charming turn-of-the-century hotel. Sauna. No restaurant. *Muskewitz* (M), Dechenstr. 5 (0228–632045). 31 beds. No restaurant. DC, MC, V. *Novotel* (M), Pascalstr. (0228–52010). 142 rooms, all with bath or shower. In the Hardtberg section; restaurant. AE, DC, MC, V. *Rheinland* (M), Berliner Freiheit 11 (0228–658096). 32 rooms, all with bath or shower. Near the Kennedy-brücke; no restaurant. *Savoy* (M), Berliner Freiheit 17 (0228–651356). 39 beds. Near Kennedy-brücke; no restaurant. AE, DE, MC, V. *Sternhotel* (M), Markt 8 (0228–654455). 65 rooms, all with bath or shower. No restaurant. AE, DC, MC, V.

Restaurants. *Grand Italia* (E), Bischofsplatz 1 (0228–638333). Outstanding Italian cuisine. AE, DC, MC, V. *Le Marron* (E), Provinzialstr. 35 (0228–253261). In the Lengsdorf section. AE, DC, MC. *Beethovenhalle* (M), Fritz-Schröder-Ufer (0228–633348). The concert hall restaurant, with view of river. AE, V. *Im Stiefel* (M), Bonngasse 30 (0228–634806). Excellent cuisine and relaxed ambience, just a few doors down from Beethoven's birthplace. V. Closed Sun. *Jacobs* (M), Friedrichstr. 18 (0228–637353). Colorful tavern with excellent wine cellar. *Petit Poisson* (M), Wilhelmstr. 23a (0228–633883). Exquisite bistro which boasts a superb wine list. AE, DC, MC. *Weinpavillon Rheinland-Pfalz* (M), Charles-Gaulle-Str. (0228–235249). This large, lovely wine restaurant serves good local specialties and fresh bread from the restaurant's own bakery. Reservations necessary after 6 P.M. *Zum Kapellchen* (M), Brüdergasse 12 (0228–651052). Colorful wine tavern with fine cuisine. Reservations recommended. AE, DC, MC, V. Closed Sun.

Duisburg. *Novotel* (E), Landfermannstr. 20 (0203–300030). 324 beds, all rooms with bath; indoor pool, sauna. *Töpferstube* restaurant. *Steigenberger Hotel Duisburger Hof* (E), Neckarstr. 2 (0203–331021). 128 rooms with bath or shower. Bar, café with music, restaurant. AE, DC, MC, V. *Am Stadion* (M), Kalkweg 26 (0203–724024). 27 beds. No restaurant. *Haus Reinhard* (M), Fuldastr. 31 (0203–331316). 16 rooms, all with bath. Comfortable; no restaurant. *Mercator* (M), Mercatorstr. 92 (0203–20983). 17 beds; no restaurant. *Rheingarten* (M), Königstr. 78 (02136–5001). 28 rooms, all with bath. In Homburg suburb; restaurant. AE, DC, MC, V.

Restaurants. *Postkutsche* (M), Amtsgerichtsstr. 20 (0203–82342). In nearby Ruhrort. MC. *Rotisserie Laterne* (M), Mülheimer Str. 38 (0203–21298). AE.

Essen. *Arosa* (E), Rüttenscheider Str. 149 (0201–72280). 70 rooms, all but two with bath, all airconditioned. In the Rüttenscheid section; bar, two restaurants. AE, DC, MC, V. *Scandic Crown Hotel Bredeney* (E), Theodor-Althoff-Str. 5 (0201–7690). 314 rooms, all with bath. Spacious, located in Bredeney section near autobahn to Düsseldorf; three good restaurants. AE, DC, MC, V. *Essener Hof* (E), Teichstr. 2 (0201–20901). 130 rooms; restaurant. AE, DC, MC, V. *Handelshof* (E), Am Hauptbahnhof (0201–17080). 200 rooms, all with bath. At the main rail station. *Mövenpick* restaurant, bistro, bar and nightclub. AE, DC, MC, V. *Romantik-Hotel Résidence* (E), Auf der Forst 1 (02054–8911). 18 rooms, most with bath. In Kettwig, about 11 km. (seven miles) southwest. Riding; terrace, garden, restaurant. AE, DC, MC, V. *Schloss Hugenpoet* (E), August-Thyssen-Str. 51 (02054–6054). A Castle-Hotel. 21 rooms, most with bath. In Kettwig; riding, tennis, hunting, fishing; outstanding restaurant. AE, DC, MC, V. *Sheraton* (E), Huyssenallee 55 (0201–20951). 207 rooms, all with bath and air-conditioning. Its *Restaurant am Park* overlooks the city gardens. AE, DC, MC, V.

Luise (M), Dreilindenstr. 96 (0201–239253). 29 rooms; tastefully furnished; no restaurant. AE. *Parkhaus Hügel* (M), Freiherr-vom-Stein-Str. 209 (0201–471091). 12 rooms, 3 with bath. On the lakeside of Baldeneysee. Restaurant. AE. *Schmachtenbergshof* (M), Schmachtenbergstr. 157 (02054–8933). 27 rooms, most with bath. In Kettwig; Gasthaus since 1726. MC. *Touring,* Frankenstr. 379 (0201–42982). 52 rooms, half with bath. Motel in quiet location in Bredeney section; no restaurant. AE. *Heihoff* (I), Essener Str. 36 (0201–211183). 17 rooms, most with bath. In Stoppenberg; restaurant.

Restaurants. *Ange d'Or* (E), Ruhrtalstr. 326 (02054–2307). Excellent; in Kettwig, 11 km. (seven miles) southwest of city center. Evenings only. *La Buvette* (E), An den Altenburg 30 (0201–408048). In Werden section. AE. *Kockshusen* (M), Pilgrimsteig 51 (0201–471721). 17th-century house in Schellenberg Forest, in Rellinghausen suburb. AE, DC, MC. *Schwarze Lene* (M), Baldeney 38 (0201–442351). Overlooks Baldeneysee lake. DC, MC. *Zum halben Hahn* (M), Kennedyplatz 5 (0201–236855). In city center. Downstairs, good-value daily menu with regional specialties; upstairs, international specialty restaurant. *Mathäser-keller* (I), in *Hotel Handelshof,* at main station, with music. AE, DC, MC.

Königswinter. Across the river from Bad Godesberg. *Günnewig Rheinhotel* (E), Rheinallee 9 (02223–24051). Modern hotel right on the banks of the Rhine. 110 beds, all rooms with bath. Indoor pool, sauna, restaurant and café. *Rheingold* (M), Drachenfelsstr. 36 (02223–23048). 50 rooms, most with bath; two apartments. Terrace café. AE, DC, MC, V.

Restaurants. *Schlemmerstuben Kante-Eck* (E), Kantering 1 (02223–22524). High quality and good value cuisine. V. *Weinhaus Winzerhäuschen* (I), Drachenfelstr. 100 (02223–21469). On footpath up to the Drachenfels. Quaint, half-timbered house with attractive garden and Rhine-terrace.

Krefeld. *Parkhotel Krefelder Hof* (E), Ürdinger Str. 245 (02151–5840). 139 rooms, all with bath; nine apartments. Excellent, with quiet but central location; very good food in restaurant *L'Escargot* (E). AE, DC, MC, V. *Bayerischer Hof* (M), Hansastr. 105 (02151–37067). 16 rooms, all with bath. Restaurant. AE, DC, MC, V. *Dahmen* (M), Schönwasserstr. 12 (02151–590296). 52 rooms. Noisy and central and with panoramic view; no restaurant. AE, DC, MC, V. *Haus Uhlen* (I), on corner of Nordwall and Steinstr. (02151–772114). 12 rooms, most with bath; no restaurant. AE, V.

Restaurants. *La Capannina* (E), Uerdingstr. 552 (02151–591461). Fine Italian specialties; book ahead. AE, DC, MC. *Le Crocodile* (E), Uerdinger Str. 336 (02151–500110). Small and elegant with first-class food and personal service. AE, MC. *Gasthof Korff zum Königshof* (E), Kölner Str. 256 (02152–311789). AE, DC. *Aquilon* (M), Ostwall 199 (02151–800207). DC, MC, V. *Seidenweberhaus* (M), Theaterplatz 1 (02151–21094). AE, DC, MC, V. *Von Bekerath-Stuben* (M), Uerdinger Str. 42 (02151–64716). AE, DC, MC.

Lindlar. *Schloss Georghausen* (M), Hommerich (02207–2561). 10 km. southwest of Lindlar at Georghausen. Castle-hotel with 18-hole golf course. 15 rooms, some with bath. Riding. Fine, atmospheric restaurant.

Lohmar. East of Köln, autobahn exit at Siegburg. Nearby *Schloss Auel* (E), (02206–2041). 21 rooms with bath; two apartments. Dates back to 1391. Antiques, indoor pool, riding, trout fishing; helicopter pad; good restaurant *Rôtisserie St. George.* AE, DC, MC.

Mönchengladbach. *Holiday Inn* (E), am Geroplatz (02161–31131). 200 rooms, all with bath; indoor pool, sauna; local specialties in restaurant. AE, DC, MC, V. *Dorint* (M), Hohenzollernstr. 5 (02161–86060). 102 rooms, all with bath; some suites. Good restaurant. AE, DC, MC, V. *Maros* (M), Hindenburgstr. 175 (02161–13071). 16 rooms. Handy to the main rail station; restaurant. MC.

Restaurants. *Chopelin* (E), Weiherstr. 51 (02206–12540). Highly recommended, good value. *Schloss Rheydt* (M), Schloss Str. (02166–20102). Renaissance castle in the suburb of Rheydt; also has a few rooms. *La Pampa* (M), Berliner Platz 11 (02206–16017). Charcoal-grilled steaks.

Mülheim An Der Ruhr. *Noy* (E), Schloss Strasse 28 (0208–44671). 65 rooms, most with bath. Smart restaurant. AE, DC, MC, V. *Handelshof* (M), Friedrichstr. 15 (0208–35003).

Restaurants. *Am Kamin* (E), Striepensweg 62 (0208–760036). Nouvelle cuisine. AE, DC, MC. *Fuente* (E), Gracht 209 (0208–431853). High-class French cuisine. AE. *Becker Eichbaum* (M), Obere Saarlandstr. 5 (0208–34093). Cozy. *Mintarder Wasserbahnhof* (M), August-Thyssen-Str. 129 (02054–7272). In Mintard suburb. With view of river. AE, DC, MC, V.

Solingen. *Historisches Hotel In der Strassen* (M), Wermelskirchener Str. 12 (02122–44011). In the Burg-on-the-Wupper section, near the castle. Dates from 1673. 27 rooms, all with bath. Atmospheric restaurant. MC, V. *Turmhotel* (M), Kölner Str. 99 (02122–13050). 43 rooms, all with bath; no restaurant. AE, DC, MC, V.

Wassenberg. *Burg Wassenberg* (M), Kirchstr. 17 (02432–4044). Castle hotel north of Aachen on Dutch border. 21 rooms, all with bath. Fine restaurant. AE, DC, MC, V.

Wuppertal. The city consists of two main districts: Elberfeld to the west, and Barmen to the east. *Golfhotel Juliana* (E), Mollenkötten 195 (0202–64750). In the Ober-Barmen section. 69 rooms, all with bath. Also some less expensive rooms. Indoor pool, sauna. Two good restaurants: *Oktogon* (E) and *Bergische Stube* (M). AE, DC, MC, V. *Kaiserhof* (E), Döppersberg 50 (0202–459081). At railroad station in Elberfeld. A PLM Hotel. 126 rooms, most with bath. Some less expensive rooms. Sauna; two good restaurants: *Orangerie* (M) and *Pfeffer und Salz* (M). AE, DC, MC, V. *Zur Post* (M), Poststr. 4 (0202–450131). In Elberfeld. 54 rooms, most with bath; no restaurant. AE, DC, MC, V. *Nüller Hof* (I), Nüllerstr. 98 (0202–761306). In Elberfeld. 26 beds, most with bath.

Restaurants. *Palette-Röderhaus* (M), Sedanstr. 68 (0202–506281). With adjoining art gallery; in Barmen. AE, DC, MC. *Ratskeller* (M), Neumarkt 10 (0202–446292). In Elberfeld. AE, DC, MC. *Schloss Lüntenbeck* (M), 0202–743751. In the Sonnborn section; atmospheric surroundings. DC. *Windlichter,* in Varrebeck section, two restaurants together: *Gourmet in Windlicht* (E), good value, and *Tribüne im Windlicht* (M), both at Deutscher Ring 40 (0202–710220). Both closed Tues. and Sat. midday.

Xanten. A short distance outside the city walls is the castle *Burg Winnenthal* (M), 02802–3037. 34 rooms, all with bath. The oldest moated castle in Germany. Inside is a modern hotel-restaurant run with flair. AE, DC, MC, V.

CAMPING AND YOUTH HOSTELS. For a list of campsites write to: *Landesverkehrsverband Rheinland,* Bad Godesberg, Postfach 200861, 5300 Bonn 2; or telephone the Camping Department of ADAC in Köln on 0221–382051. A full list of youth hostels is available from the German Youth Hostel Association (DJH)—see *Facts at Your Fingertips* section— or direct from the Regional Tourist Office for the Rhineland.

FARMHOUSE VACATIONS. Inexpensive holidays are available through the *Urlaub auf dem Bauernhof/Ferien auf dem Land* scheme, often on farms with animals and riding instruction. Details from the regional tourist office in Bad Godesberg.

TOURIST INFORMATION. The regional tourist office for the Northern Rhineland is: *LVV Rheinland,* Rheinallee 69, Bad Godesberg, 5300 Bonn 2 (0228–362921).

Aachen, Kur- und Verkehrsamt, Markt 39, 5100 Aachen (0241–33491); **Bad Godesberg,** Tourist Information, Moltkestr. 66, 5300 Bonn-Bad Godesberg (0228–356040); **Bonn,** Tourist Information, 2 Münsterstr. 20, 5300 Bonn (0228–773466); **Duisburg,** Stadt-informationen, 1 Königstr. 53, 4100 Duisburg (0203–2904); **Essen,** Verkehrsverein, 1 Freiheit (at the main rail station, south entrance), 4300 Essen (0201–235472), including accommodations service; **Königswinter,** Verkehrsamt, Drachenfelsstr. 7, 5330 Königswinter (02223–21048); **Krefeld,** Verkehrsverein, Seidenweberhaus, Theaterplatz, 4150 Krefeld (02151–29290); **Mönchengladbach,**

Verkehrsverein, am Hauptbahnhof (at the main rail station), 4050 Mönchengladbach (02161–22001); **Mülheim an der Ruhr,** Verkehrsverein, im Rathaus, 4330 Mülheim (0208–4559016); **Solingen,** Presse- und Informationsamt, Potsdamer Str. 41, 5650 Solingen (02122–2902333); **Lohmar,** Gemeindeverwaltung, Bachstr. 12, 5204 Lohmar (02246–15145); **Wuppertal,** Informationszentrum, Wuppertal-Elberfeld, 1 Döppersberg (0202–5632180), and Presse- und Informationsamt, Wuppertal-Barmen, Rathaus, 5600 Wuppertal (0202–5636367); **Xanten,** Verkehrsamt, Rathaus, 4232 Xanten (02801–37238).

HOW TO GET AROUND. By air. Düsseldorf is the main international airport for the region, with direct flights from New York, Miami, Toronto, Montreal and Vancouver, and from 38 European airports. The S-Bahn goes to the main rail station at Dusseldorf, and buses also go direct to the city center, Essen and Krefeld. Köln international airport serves Bonn, with direct rail and bus connections. Frankfurt Rhine/Main airport is linked to the Rhineland by domestic flights and Lufthansa's *Airport Express*—see *Facts at Your Fingertips,* page 27.

By train. The whole region is well served by Intercity and Express trains. The Ruhr cities, and Aachen, Köln and Bonn are linked by a useful hourly IC network as well as Euro-City expresses. Long-distance expresses (FD) link Dortmund, Essen, Düsseldorf, Köln and Bonn with southern Germany: the "Wörthersee Express" goes to Munich, the "Donau Kurier" to Passau, the "Bodensee Express" to Konstanz, the "Allgäu Express" to Obersdorf, the "Chiemgau Express" to the Chiemsee region, and the "Königsee and Berchtesgadener Land Expresses" to Berchtesgaden.

Fast S-Bahn trains connect Düsseldorf, Mülheim, Essen, Oberhausen, Langenfeld and Solingen. Wuppertal has a unique suspension railway (*Schwebebahn*), built 1900, and Königswinter has Germany's oldest mountain railway, running up to the Drachenfels cliffs. Regional public transport information from *Verkehrsverbund Rhein-Ruhr,* Postfach 103052, 4650 Gelsenkirchen.

By bus. Europabus (line EB 169, although at time of writing temporarily out of service), operate services from Antwerp to Mönchengladbach; from London to Köln, Bonn and Frankfurt (EB 163). Other long distance buses of German Touring connect Düsseldorf, Köln and Frankfurt with the towns of the Ruhr.

There is a German railways bus service (*Bahnbus*) from Essen, via Wuppertal and Solingen to Bad Marienberg (1049, Bergisch Land-Westerwald line).

By car. The Northern Rhineland is a very busy area for road traffic with serveral major autobahns meeting here—the A3 following the Rhine and the A4 and A2 crossing it. Try the minor roads and the car ferries across the Rhine. The ferries are (from north to south): Orsoy to Walsum; Düsseldorf-Kaiserworth to Langst-Kirst (near Meerbusch), Neuss-Uedesheim to Düsseldorf-Himmelgeist, Dormagen-Zons to Düsseldorf-Urdenach, and Köln-Langel to Monnheim and Königswinter to Mehlem-Bad Godesberg.

By boat. The K-D German Rhine line has a regular steamer service between Köln, Bonn, Bingen and Mainz. Their address in Bonn is: Brassertufer, Bonn 1 (tel. 0228—632134). In addition, there are many opportunities for pleasure cruises on the Rhine and waterways of the Northern Rhineland. For cruises and motor-boat trips on the Rhine contact the following companies for details: *Personenschiffahrt Königswinter,* 02223–21818; *Personenschiffahrt Siebengebirge,* Rheinallee 59, 5300 Bonn-Bad Godesberg (0228–345969); *Bonn Passenger Cruiser Company,* Brassert Ufer, Am Alten Zoll, 5300 Bonn 1 (02223–26565)—also has cruises on old paddle steamer *MS "River Lady."*

There are passenger ferries across the Rhine (north to south): Grieth and Grietherort (near Kleve); Rheinkamp and Duisburg; Neuss and Düsseldorf; Dormagen-Zons and Düsseldorf-Benrath; Dormagen and Monnheim; Köln and Leverkusen; Köln-Niehl and Köln-Stammheim; Wesseling and Lulsdorf.

Rursee-Schiffahrt Schwammenauel, 5169 Heimbach 2 (02446–479) runs cruises on the connecting lakes of the Rursee reservoir. For information on cruises on and from Baldeneysee in Essen contact *Essener Verkehrs AG,* Rüttenscheid, Zweigerstr. 34 (0201–7997–421).

By bike. Bicycles can be hired at most rail stations in large towns as well as from private firms: local tourist offices will provide addresses. For full information about package tours for cyclists contact the regional office in Bad Godesberg.

The flat area near the Dutch border—the Niederrhein area—is good cycling country, and the Mönchengladbach tourist office organizes tours. There are marked cycle tracks in the nature parks of Schwalm-Nette on the Dutch border, Kottenforst-Ville west of Bonn, and in the Nordeifel Naturpark; also around the following excursion centers: Odenthal for the Bergisch Land; Königswinter (Siebengebirge); Wegberg and Schermbeck (Niederrhein), Heimbach and Stolberg (Northern Eifel); Simmerath (Rursee).

SPORTS. More exact information about sporting activities in the Northern Rhineland may be obtained from local tourist offices. The regional tourist office in Bad Godesberg has detailed information on boating, fishing, golf, horseback riding, skiing, swimming and tennis: *Reiseführer Niederrhein/Ruhrland* and *Reiseführer Bergisches Land und Siebengebirge,* free of charge.

Fishing. You can fish for a wide variety of fish in the region's many lakes, reservoirs and rivers and on fish farms. Licenses and permission must always be obtained.

Golf. There are courses at Aachen, Bergisch Gladbach, Duisburg (9-hole), Essen, Krefeld, Lindlar, Mönchengladbach, Wuppertal and other places, with annual tournaments at Duisburg, Krefeld and Wuppertal.

Hiking. There are many marked trails for hikers along the Rhine and Ruhr valleys, in the Bergisch Land, and in the nature parks and forests of the Northern Rhineland. Wuppertal, Essen, Solingen, Bonn and Aachen have particularly interesting trail networks around them. Information from the tourist office for the Upper Bergisches Land, Moltkestr. 34 in 5270 Gummersbach.

Horseback riding. Opportunities are good for all ages and abilities, particularly in the Eifel, but Aachen is the equestrian center of the region, and indeed the horseriding and racing mecca of Germany. Top riders of all nations meet for the International Horse Show at the Soer stadium in July as well as the German Grand Prix and the Nations Cup. Many establishments are equipped with indoor schools as well as facilities for jumping, trekking, etc. Riding is particularly good in and around Bergisch Gladbach, Essen, Gummersbach, and Solingen, and Königswinter and Wachtberg in the Eifel.

Sailing and windsurfing. Baldeneysee, the lake at Essen, is the main center for sailing, as well as rowing, and the site of several regattas each year. Sailing is also popular on the lower Rhine. Watersports are popular on the lakes and reservoirs of the Bergisches Land. In the Eifel there is good sailing and sail-boarding in the Kyll Valley, on the Rurstausee reservoir, the Laacher See, Bitburger reservoir, the Vynen recreation center at Xanten, and on the Eifelmaaren, or volcanic lakes, such as Pulvermaar and Schalkenmehrener Maar. Small boats of all kinds, including motor boats, can be hired at many river- and lakesides.

Swimming. Essen has 18 indoor and outdoor heated pools as well as Baldeney lake. All main cities have indoor (Hallenbäder) and outdoor (Freibäder) pools, including Königswinter, with its new recreation and fitness center.

Tennis. All large towns have courts, notably Aachen, Bonn, Duisburg, Essen, Kleve and Mönchengladbach.

Winter sports. The main skiing centers are Hellenthal-Hollerath, Udenbreth, Monschau, Kalterherberg, Höfen, Blankenheim and Gemünd, all in the Eifel. Artificial ice skating rinks are in Essen and Krefeld.

KÖLN AND DÜSSELDORF

Great Cities on the Rhine

The two most important centers of culture, trade and industry on the Rhine are historic Köln and Düsseldorf, less than 56 km. (35 miles) apart. They are both cities with a rich history and an even richer present. We are devoting a chapter to them, since a comparison is easily made on the spot and will provide many glimpses into the way that Germany has brought her history into contemporary focus.

KÖLN

Köln, or Cologne, with a population of about a million, is the largest city in the Rhineland, and the fourth largest—after Berlin, Hamburg and Munich—in Germany. Known throughout the world for its scented waters, Eau de Cologne, first produced over a century ago, the city is today a major commercial center. Many visitors come for one of the numerous trade fairs, rather than as mere tourists; on the Deutzer side of the Rhine are two massive congress centers with over a quarter of a million square meters of exhibition hall space, where over 20 international events are held yearly.

But the city is also a great cultural center: the University, founded in 1388, and numerous technical colleges, the large number of theaters, con-

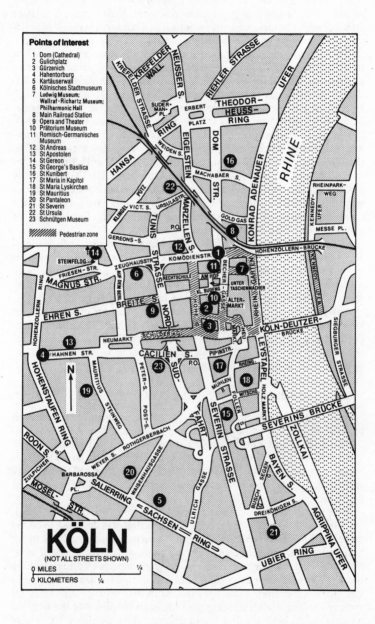

Points of Interest

1 Dom (Cathedral)
2 Gulichplatz
3 Gürzenich
4 Hahentorburg
5 Kartäuserwall
6 Kölnisches Stadtmuseum
7 Ludwig Museum;
  Wallraf-Richartz Museum;
  Philharmonic Hall
8 Main Railroad Station
9 Opera and Theater
10 Prätorium Museum
11 Romisch-Germanisches
  Museum
12 St Andreas
13 St Apostolen
14 St Gereon
15 St George's Basilica
16 St Kunibert
17 St Maria in Kapitol
18 St Maria Lyskirchen
19 St Mauritius
20 St Pantaleon
21 St Severin
22 St Ursula
23 Schnütgen Museum

///// Pedestrian zone

KÖLN
(NOT ALL STREETS SHOWN)

0 MILES   1/4
0 KILOMETERS   1/4

cert halls, the headquarters of the West German Radio and the impressive range of museums, all bear witness to the rich intellectual life of the city—as well as to the depth of its financial resources. Köln's greatest heritage comes from its history, which is embodied in a remarkable range of buildings, dating as far back as the Romans.

The Celts had already occupied the site, but the Romans were the first to circle it with walls, and there are many relics of their adventurous civil engineering. The Rhine was as far as the Romans penetrated into Germany, and Köln's name reflects its status in the Empire. It means "colony," an outpost, and the Romans were able to hold it for more than 400 years, before being ousted by the Franks and other Germanic tribes.

During the Roman period, some 20,000 people lived in Köln. Flourishing trade increased this number over the following centuries—35,000 in the 13th century, 800,000 by the beginning of World War II. But the number had dropped to only 40,000 when the Allies arrived in 1945. Now only half the population is locally born and one in ten is not even German. Despite this, the local dialect and many local traditions have survived in the older neighborhoods, in the traditional Millowitsch Theater and, of course, in the Köln Carnival.

Many famous people have lived here: Marie de Medici, wife of Henri IV of France, who died here in exile in 1642; Peter Paul Reubens, who spent his childhood here in the 1570s; the physicist G.S. Ohm, whose name was given to the electrical unit; and Konrad Adenauer, a Lord Mayor who went on to become the first post-War Chancellor of Germany.

Although the city's historical heritage is vast, there are magnificent new structures to match the aging grace of earlier buildings: the Gerling Versicherung, the ultra-modern Opera House, the new Chamber of Commerce, the gigantic, circular Philharmonic Hall and whole streets like Schildergasse, as well as many pedestrian precincts.

Exploring Köln

At the heart of the ancient city of Köln stands the magnificent cathedral, or Dom, of St. Peter and St. Mary. Largely untouched by the devastating bombing of the last war, its soaring stone spires, carved like lace, are a symbol of the city's proud spirit. They are surrounded by post-war structures—like the glass-walled Central Station next door—but these only serve to accentuate the cathedral's Gothic splendor. Two suggested tours of the city start and end here.

Built mainly between 1248 and the middle of the 16th century, though completed only in the 19th century, the cathedral was designed to be the largest in Europe. From the outside, it is a mass of buttresses and flying buttresses; inside, there are finely carved choir stalls, tombstones of archbishops, religious paintings and stained-glass windows of breathtaking beauty. The high altar dates from 1322 and the golden, jeweled shrine to the Three Kings from 1220. Excavations in the crypt have revealed all sorts of exciting finds, including many Roman remains and the tomb of a young knight in armor. It is worth climbing the spire nearly 100 meters (328 feet) from the ground for a suberb view of Köln and the distant mountains. The first, and longer, tour takes you south as far as the towers of St. Severin, on the western side of the Rhine.

South of the Cathedral

You might like to start with the Römisch-Germanisches Museum (Roman-Germanic Museum) on the south side of the cathedral terrace. Opened in 1974, it contains the famous Dionysus mosaic, as well as a collection of Roman tombstones, glass, coins and jewelry. A portable cassette guide is available.

South of the museum, at the corner of Am Hof and Unter Taschenmacher is the Saaleck House, dating from the 15th century. The whole street once looked as grand, but now it is rather dull, so pass on down Taschenmacher to Kleine Budengasse, where the new City Hall stands. Underneath it is the Prätorium Museum, which contains a 1st-century A.D. excavation of walls once part of the house of the Roman Viceroy.

Retracing your steps, walk south along Burgerstrasse to the Altermarkt (Old Market), once the throbbing center of the old city. Here a weekly market is held every Friday from 8 A.M. to 6 P.M. Most of the buildings were destroyed in the war, but the twin houses "Zur Bretzel" and "Zum Dorn," numbers 20–22, have retained their original 16th-century style. With the completion of the gigantic Rhine Tunnel between the Hohenzollern and Deutzer bridges, the traffic which once streamed across this beautiful square has been absorbed underground. Pedestrians can now stroll undisturbed from the Hohe Strasse, a famous shopping mall, past the Rathaus and Gürzenich, down into the Altermarkt, and right up to the Rhine itself. The right bank of the Rhine has now been enhanced by the extension of the Rheinpark with a stretch of parkland between the Hohenzollern and Deutz bridges. The Rheingarten is landscaped, and now contains the new building for the Wallraf-Richartz/Museum Ludwig as the centerpoint of the new Rhine Bank Museum complex, and the vast Philharmonic Concert Hall.

Just southwest of the market-place is the old City Hall (Rathaus), an impressive ensemble of buildings from several different periods: look out for the 14th-century Hansa Hall, the 15th-century tower with a tuneful peal of bells, and the 16th-century entrance hall, a fine example of Renaissance architecture. Outside stands the famous sculpture of the Apes of Palestrina, dating from the 3rd century.

Southwest again is Gulichplatz, where you can see the remains of a 12th-century synagogue, with its ritual bath or Mikwe. Outside it stands the Carnival Fountain, designed by Grasegger early this century. This is a pretty little square and one of the first producers of Eau-de-Cologne, Johann Farina, had his factory here.

One block further south is the Gürzenich, built as a place for dancing and other festivities in the 15th century. It is still used for this purpose when Köln holds its carnival in February. During its reconstruction after the war, it was extended by a modern section as far as the ruins of St. Albans opposite. These ruins are all that remain of a 10th-century Gothic church and its 14th-century tower, and are now kept as a memorial for the city's victims of the war. It contains Matare's copy of the touching *Sorrowing Parents* by the German sculptress Käthe Kollwitz. Oddly enough, there is another fine sculpture of mourning in the church of St. Maria in the Kapitol, a 12th-century building in Pipinstrasse, just southwest of the Heu Market (Hay Market). Called *The Sorrowful Women*, it was created by Gerhard Marcks in the 1940s, and now stands in the south-west cloister of the church. The building itself, particularly well preserved inside, has a fine crypt and splendidly intricate "leaf" doors, from the 12th century.

Returning towards the river and heading south, you come to the Rhein-gasse, which contains the Industrial Arts Museum—in the last remaining Romanesque house in Köln, Oberstolzen Haus, built in 1225. Just south, along Holzmarkt, by the river, is St. Maria Lyskirchen, a small church for sailors, from the same period: inside are some important 13th-century frescos, 15th-century stained glass and a beautiful 14th-century Blessed Virgin.

Now leave the river, and take Witschgasse through to the Waidmarkt, where St. George's Basilica stands, the only Romanesque building of its kind left in the Rhineland. Outside stands the Hermann-Joseph Fountain, dating from the turn of the last century. From this square, Severinstrasse leads straight south, a typical old city thoroughfare. The Balchem House at number 15, with its gables and bay windows is characteristic of the 17th-century architecture that once filled the street.

Several blocks down is one of the city's oldest and greatest churches, St. Severin, built on the site of early pagan and Christian graves. Severin was Bishop of Köln in the 5th century and his shrine, in the upper church, contains exquisitely carved stalls. There is also a 13th-century Madonna in chalk, and many wall hangings worth seeing. The church marked the southern limit of the old city and marks the limit of this part of the tour.

The southwest wall of the medieval city still stands at one or two spots, and the best place to see them is at Kartäuserwall, just north of the busy Sachsen-Ring. (All the roads whose names end in "Ring" follow the course of the old walls.) From here it is only a stone's throw to the remark-able Church of St. Pantaleon off Waisenhaus Gasse. The west wing is particularly curious. It was the gift of Archbishop Bruno, brother of Otto the Great, and both Bruno and Otto's step-daughter, Queen Theophanu, were buried here. A marble sarcophagus commemorates the queen, among other more ancient figures.

Northwest, along Mauritius-Stein Weg, you come to the ruins of the 19th-century Gothic church of St. Mauritius, now restored in a modern style by the architect Fritz Schaller. Inside is a 15th-century crucifix. If you continue northwest, you come to the western city gate, the Hahnentor-burg, but you can equally well continue north along Mauritius-stein Weg to the church of St. Aposteln, at the west end of the Neumarkt (New Market). Here you are once again on the edge of the inner city. If you walk along Cäcilianstrasse, you come to some of the city's finest museums, notably the Art Gallery, the Art Union and the Schnütgen Museum of Church Art, attached to the Church of St. Cäcilian (Cecilia), one of the most richly endowed in Germany. If you are interested in religious art, set aside several hours to visit them properly.

From this point you can return to the cathedral by way of Hohe Strasse, where, on the north side of the terrace, there are some attractive traditional coffeehouses. This is now a pedestrian precinct and a good spot for shopping and reasonably priced restaurants.

North of the Cathedral

Komödien Strasse runs west from the cathedral terrace, and a few steps along it you can see the charming St. Andreas (St. Andrew) church, dating from the 13th century. Inside is a Roman sarcophagus and, in the crypt, the remains of Albertus Magnus—a medieval philosopher and bishop, who figures largely in the history of the occult. Two blocks south, and in great contrast to this early stone building, is the massive, modern West German Radio Station on the Rechtschule.

Returning to Komödien Strasse, and passing a round tower which remains from the Roman city wall, continue on to the Zeughaus Strasse. On the left is the original city arsenal, built on the remains of the Roman wall, which houses the Kölnisches Stadtmuseum (Köln City Museum): the collection of weapons, documents, armour, paintings and furniture here is well worth a visit. A little further on, across Auf dem Berlich, the corner tower of the Roman wall still stands, with its ornamentation of colored tiles.

Now turn north, along Steinfeldergasse, to one of the most impressive buildings remaining from medieval times, the twin-towered church of St. Gereon. The nucleus is 4th-century, and dedicated to the early Christian martyrs called the Theban Legion, some of whom are buried in the crypt, which, with the nave and the decagon (in between the two towers), was added later. In the choir there is a lovely carved sacristy door. The church has other interesting carvings, an Aubusson tapestry and early frescos.

Following Klingel Putz, turn right along Ursula Strasse, where, just before the road passes under the railway, you will find the magnificent tower of St. Ursula's Church, which contains the marble grave of the saint. A peculiarity inside is the gold closet (Treasury) which contains some valuable relics and liturgical vessels.

Eigelstein leads you north to Ebertplatz, where the northern exit from the medieval city was. The remains of the 13th-century gate still stand there. From here you can stroll through the gardens of the Theodor-Heuss-Ring to the river, before returning south again. There is a famous restaurant here called The Bastei, built on the plinth of a fortress tower and offering a fine view over the Rhine.

On your return southward, you will pass the Church of St. Kunibert, built between 1215 and 1247, the last Romanesque church in Köln with traces of the Gothic already evident. The choir windows are exceptional, and the altar paintings and wall tabernacle are worth seeing. Afterwards, turn right along Machabäer Strasse, past the 18th-century Ursuline church on your right, to the Nord-Süd-Fahrt, a busy main street which takes you quickly back to the cathedral again.

DÜSSELDORF

One of the greatest cities in this most industrialized region of Germany, Düsseldorf is also the capital of the State of Northern Rhineland-Westphalia. In 1988 the city celebrates its 700th anniversary and there will be a variety of events to mark the occasion, including a large exhibition of lead-glazed earthenware—the handicraft specialty of Northern Rhineland-Westphalia. The exhibition will also run parallel in Duisberg, Krefeld and Neuss. It is an important cultural center, one whose eminence in this field is not new. The artist, Peter Cornelius, and the poet, Heinrich Heine, were born here. Johannes Brahms, Robert Schumann, and Goethe lived here. The city is reputed today to present some of the finest theatrical performances in all Germany and a film distributing center has sprung up here, as well as another German venture that lies halfway between art and trade—graphic design. Its excellent Academy of Fine Arts has helped attract many artists, and the Robert Schumann Conservatory has encouraged musical talent. Rich collections from the fields of art, literature and science are housed in many museums.

When you walk on the streets of Düsseldorf, particularly on the main Königsallee, little boys may turn cartwheels in front of you; they are called Radschläger and will expect you to give them a few pfennigs as a reward. It is an old tradition going back to the wedding of Elector Johann Wilhelm, Düsseldorf's beloved ruler in the 17th century, when during the great procession a wheel of the wedding coach became loose and a ten-year-old boy saved the situation by attaching himself to the wheel, gripping the hub, and "cartwheeling" with it to the end of the parade, at which point Johann Wilhelm rewarded him with a golden ducat. The little Radschläger come mostly from a nearby school in the Old Town where there is a competition every year, with the winner receiving a savings book from the Lord Mayor.

"Jan Wellem," as Johann Wilhelm II, Elector of Palatinate, was affectionately called by Düsseldorfers, greatly contributed to the cultural development of Düsseldorf and the grateful citizens erected an equestrian statue of him in 1711, five years before his death. It stands next to the 16th-century City Hall, rebuilt after the war. Here we are in the center of the Old Town between the Oberkasseler bridge and the Rheinkaie bridge and flanked by the Hofgarten, with its two landmarks overlooking the Rhine: the twisted spire of the Gothic St. Lambertus Church and the round Castle Tower, the only remainder of the 13th-century city castle. In the shadow of the Tower are the postwar Cartwheelers' Fountain, and the dock for Rhine excursion steamers. The three-naved St. Lambertus contains a remarkable late Gothic tabernacle, the Renaissance tomb of the 16th-century Duke Wilhelm the Rich, the bronze door by the German sculptor Edward Mataré and a rich treasury. In addition to St. Lambertus there are several other churches, notably the Neanderkirche and St. Andreas with the sarcophagus of "Jan Wellem," and a glockenspiel in the picturesque Wibbel street.

On the southern edge of the Old Town the 24-story Mannesmann Building, a slender tower of glass and steel, soars above the Rhine and on the other side is mirrored in the Spee Graben, one of the many small lakes which, together with the parks, keep the city air fresh. Farther down the east bank from the Mannesmann Building is the city's highest building, the Rheinturm (Rhine Tower) telecommunications tower. From the observation platform at 234 meters (506 feet), there is a splendid view over the city and, in fine weather, to the hills of Bergisch Land in the east and Köln Cathedral in the south.

The heart of Düsseldorf is Königsallee, nicknamed "Kö," an 84-meter-(275 feet) wide boulevard dating from the early 19th century and split in the middle by a many-bridged waterway and lined on one side with café terraces and some of the most elegant stores in Germany. At one end is Graf Adolf Square with a botanical garden and not far from it the Schwanenspiegel (Swans' Pond) and the old Landtag (State Legislature). The new Parliament building should now be completed, at the Berger Harbor on the Rhine. At the other, northern, end, past the Cornelius Square fountain, the expanded Hofgarten area begins with more swans, statues (including one by Maillol, commemorating Heine), the Baroque Jägerhof Castle, another castle called appropriately Malkasten ("Paintbox"—the seat of the local artists' association), and the neo-Classical Ratinger Tor entrance. Above it all rules the 26-story Thyssen building.

Congress, conventions, trade fairs and other business gatherings follow each other practically throughout the year and play an important role in Düsseldorf's tradition. The first trade exhibition was staged here in 1811 and its most prominent visitor was Napoleon. The well-equipped exhibition grounds, located on the northern edge of Hofgarten, extend from the right bank of the Rhine to Fischerstrasse and contain several halls, particularly the ultramodern Messehalle. A pleasant walk along the river banks will take you from the exhibition grounds through the Rheinpark to the Theodor Heuss Bridge (three more bridges span the river within the city limits, including the newly-opened architectural masterpiece of a railway bridge) and the yacht harbor. The Rheinpark has been extended along a newly landscaped stretch of waterfront, providing a green area from the Bäkkerstrasse to the farthest pierhead of the Customs and Excise harbor with new moorings. Farther downstream is Nordpark with fountains, flower gardens, including the famous Japanese gardens, and sculptures.

In fact gardens and lakes characterize much of the town and 1987 saw Düsseldorf hosting the Federal Garden Show. From the Nordpark you walk through a green belt as far as the Trade Fair complex while in southern Düsseldorf, peace and relaxation can be found at the Castle Benrath, a marvellous late-Baroque chateau, with 157 acres of parkland and lakes.

A university was opened in Düsseldorf in 1965. Today it has 13,000 students. In the grounds of the University is the Botanical Garden.

PRACTICAL INFORMATION FOR KÖLN

TELEPHONES. The telephone code for Köln is 0221. To call any number in this section, unless otherwise specified, this prefix must be used. Within the city no prefix is required.

HOTELS. Hotel prices in Köln are a little above the German average. Beware of the spring and autumn fair periods, when hotels are generally booked up. Many hotels offer special reduced prices during holidays, quieter periods and at weekends. An accommodations service is available at the Tourist Office, across the square from the main portal of the cathedral, and is open daily (see *Tourist Information*).

Expensive

Am Augustinerplatz. Hohe Str. 30 (236717). 57 rooms, all with bath. No restaurant. AE, DC, MC, V.

Ascot. Hohenzollernring 95 (521076). 52 beds. New 1985, modern, centrally located. Fitness center; bistro. AE, DC, MC, V.

Consul. Belforstr. 9 (77210). 125 rooms and 5 suites, all with bath. Sauna, indoor swimming pool, restaurant, lounge, bar. AE, DC, MC, V.

Crest Hotel Köln. Dürener Str. 287 (463001). 155 rooms, all with bath or shower. In Lindenthal section, on a lake. Two restaurants, bar. AE, DC, MC, V.

Dom-Hotel. Domkloster 2A (20240). 133 rooms, most with bath, but vary considerably. Restaurant of note, outdoor café with view of the cathedral. AE, DC, MC, V.

Excelsior Hotel Ernst. Domplatz, Trankgasse 1 (2701). 126 rooms all with bath. Sauna, fine grill room. AE, DC, MC, V.

Holiday Inn. Waldstr. 255 (02203–5610). 113 rooms all with bath. Sauna, swimming pool. AE, DC, MC, V.

Hyatt Regency. Kennedy Ufer 2a (8281234). Due to open April '88. First-class luxury. AE, DC, MC, V.

Inter-Continental-Köln. Helenenstr. 14 (2280). 560 beds, all rooms with bath. Restaurant, three bars (one on heated rooftop), indoor pool. AE, DC, MC, V.

Leonet. Rubenstr. 33 (236016). 78 rooms all with bath. Swimming pool, sauna. AE, DC, MC, V.

Novotel. Horbeller Str. 1, corner of Dürener and Horbeller Str. (02234–5140). In suburb of Marsdorf. 280 beds, all rooms with bath. Pool, sportsroom, café and restaurant.

Ramada Renaissance. Magnusstr. 20 (20340). Near main station. 240 rooms, 6 suites; fitness center, 2 restaurants and bar. AE, DC, MC, V.

Regent. Melatengürtel 15 (54991). 188 rooms all with bath. Swimming pool, sauna. AE, DC, MC, V.

Terminal-Porz. Theodor-Heuss-Str. 78 (02101–300021). In Porz section. 120 beds, all rooms with bath. Sauna, solarium, sportsroom, restaurant. AE, DC, MC, V.

Moderate

"An der Tennishalle" Schmitte. Grossrotterweg 1 (02233–22777). In Hochkirchen section. 26 beds, restaurant, tennis courts. AE, DC, MC.

Falderhof. Falderstr. 29 (02236–64244). In Sürth section. 15 beds. No restaurant. AE, DC, MC.

Intercity-Hotel IBIS Köln. Bahnhofsvorplatz, im Hauptbahnhof (132051). 66 rooms all with bath or shower. At the station with view of the cathedral.

Landhaus Gut Keuchof. Braugasse 14 (02234–76033). In Lövenich suburb. Quiet. 20 rooms, all with bath. Restaurant. AE, MC.

Spiegel. Hermann-Löns-Str. 122, in Porz section (02203–61046). 19 rooms all with bath. MC.

Inexpensive

Alstadt. Salzgasse 7 (234187). Central. 28 rooms, some with bath. No restaurant. AE, DC, MC, V.

Drei Könige. Marzellenstr. 58 (132088). 33 rooms, 8 with bath. MC.

Camping

Campingplatz Berger. Uferstr. 53A. In Köln-Rodenkirchen. Open all year.

Campingplatz Waldbad. Peter-Baum-Weg. In Köln-Dünnwald. Open all year round.

Municipal Family Campsite. Weidenweg. In Köln-Poll. Open May 1 through Oct. 10.

Youth Camping Site. Alfred-Schutte-Allee. Also in Köln-Poll. Open July 1 through Sept. 15.

Youth Hostels

Köln-Deutz. Siegesstr. (814711).

Youth Guest House (Jugendgästehaus). An der Schanz 15 (767081). In Köln-Riehl.

HOW TO GET AROUND. From the airport. The city center can be reached from the International Airport Köln/Bonn in 15 minutes via the autobahn. Bus 170 departs from in front of the main airport building for the Bus Terminus behind platform 4A of the Main Rail Station. Buses leave from here for the airport every 20 minutes from 7 A.M. with an earlier bus at 6 A.M. The bus also stops at the station of Köln-Deutz. The trip lasts about 20 minutes and costs DM.5.50 single, DM.8 return.

The airport is also connected with the airports of Düsseldorf and Frankfurt by the Lufthansa Airport Express train.

By car. 10 motorways run into Köln, which is the only city in Europe around which a truly unbroken motorway ring road runs, keeping the through traffic clear of the city center. Before entering the center it is advisable to leave your car in one of the 28 multistory car parks (addresses from the Tourist Office).

By train. Inter-City, Euro-City and Fern Express (FD) train routes intersect at Köln, six IC trains leaving every hour (including one directly to Frankfurt airport). There are good connections to the rest of the Rhineland, the Ruhr, Westphalia and the south. Köln's main rail station is easily accessible to most of the city's major sights.

City transportation. The Köln public transport system (K.V.B.) consists of an integrated network of buses, subways (S-Bahn) and streetcars. The streetcar network extends far out into the suburbs and surrounding areas. You can reach some of the most attractive excursion areas in and around Köln within 15 to 35 minutes. A new central bus station is now at Breslauer Platz.

You can purchase single or multiple tickets, or 24-hour tickets for all forms of city transport costing DM.6.00. There is also a combined city ticket for Köln and Bonn valid for 24 hours which costs DM.15.00. Information about all forms of public transport, tickets etc from the K.V.B. information (547 4471) or the tourist office.

By boat. Köln boasts five harbors on the Rhine. Various passenger and ferryboat companies run regular ferry services, cruises and excursions on the Rhine. KD tours depart daily (March to Sept.) on the hour from 10.30

A.M. to 2.15 P.M. from the KD pier (tel. 20881); Rhein-Mosel passenger ships (March to Oct.), tel. 121600; and Colonia Steamboats (May to Sept.), tel. 211325, leave every 45 minutes from 10 A.M. to 4 P.M. The tourist office will provide full information. Advance bookings from the landing-stages at Deutzer and Hohenzollernbrücke bridges, and on the Rhine promenade in the old town at Frankenwerft.

By taxi. Taxi stands are at the main railway station and in all the more important squares; if you get stuck call 2882.

The Rhine Cable-Car. One station is on the left bank of the Rhine, near the entrance to the zoo in Riehler Str. The other is on the right bank near the Zoobrücke bridge in the Rheinpark. It operates from Easter to the end of Oct. from 10–7.

TOURIST INFORMATION. The tourist office is *Verkehrsamt der Stadt Köln,* Unter Fettenhennen 19, am Dom, 5000 Köln 1 (221 3345). Open weekdays 8 A.M. to 9 P.M.; Sundays and holidays from 9.30 A.M. to 7 P.M. They produce a monthly program of events, the *Monatsvorschau,* and numerous other interesting brochures about the city, such as *Zu Fuss durch Köln* (Through Köln on Foot). They run an accommodations service, open daily 8 A.M.–10.30 P.M., Sun. and holidays 9 A.M.–10.30 P.M. (during winter from 2 P.M.). For advance bookings tel. 221 3311 or 221 3345 for immediate bookings.

Information about public transport is also available from the tourist office or from the Köln Transport Service (K.V.B.) tel. 547 3333.

USEFUL ADDRESSES. American Express, Burgmauer 14 (235613). **British Council.** Hahnenstr. 6 (236677). **Car rental.** *Hertz,* tel. 515084 (city) and 02203–402501 (airport); *Avis,* Clemenstr. 25–27, tel. 234333 and 02203–402343 (airport); *Europcar,* tel. 02203–402304 (airport). **Money exchange.** Regular banking hours until 5 P.M., Fri. until 6.30 P.M.; closed Sat. and Sun. The exchange office inside the main station is open daily 7 A.M.–11 P.M., Sun. 8 A.M.–11 P.M. **Police,** tel. 110. **Pharmacy,** tel. 11500. **Medical emergencies,** tel. 720772. **Emergencies,** Arztnotruf, tel. 02203–51111.

TOURS. Regular city sightseeing tours take place 5 times a day from May to October. Tours are organized by the Küppers Bus Company (tel. 171173) and depart from Burgmauer alongside the Tourist Office. From May to the end of September you can also join a guided city tour on foot, departing from the Tourist Office. From July to the end of August there is an evening tour every Friday and Saturday at 8 P.M., including a trip on the Rhine or a visit to the open-air dance floor *"Tanzbrunnen"* and a supper of cold meats and sausages with "Kölsch" beer.

EXCURSIONS. Trips out into the surrounding countryside can be made by bus and boat. Various companies operate in conjunction with the tourist office, through whom reservations can be made. German Railways and the steamers of the K.D. Rhine Shipping Company (tel. 20881) also run to places of scenic, historical or architectural interest nearby. Their newest offer is a 2-day mini-cruise to or from Frankfurt, or a one-day trip from Frankfurt to Köln. The "Rheinpfeil" hydrofoil takes you from Köln to Mainz in just 4 hours. Information from the tourist office.

The city public transport is also useful for reaching excursion destinations. Some of the favorite spots within easy reach of the city center are the famous Köln Zoo in the suburb of Riehl, with the Botanical Gardens nearby; the Rhine Park, which in summer can be reached by U-Bahn to the zoo, then a cable-car across the Rhine; the Wildgehege Wild Animal Park; the Königsforst forest; the Bruck Wild Animal Park; the "Groov" lake in Zündorf; the Rhine promenade and yacht harbor at Rodenkirchen; the Decksteiner Weiher lake in the Beethoven Park; and the Stadtwald forest animal park. A full list of all these excursion spots and details of the streetcar or subway routes you must take are in a booklet issued by the tourist office at the cathedral, entitled *Kölner Bummel Tips.*

SPORTS. Köln is richly endowed with parks, equipped for sports activities of all kinds, with one tremendous sports center, the Müngersdorfer Stadion on the Aachenerstrasse, with pool, football field, tennis courts, running track, bridle paths, etc. Open May–Sept. **Tennis** at Brücker Sportpark, Oberberbruchweg 6 (tel. 843072); AM Vorgebirgstor (tel. 365134); City-Sport, Rhöndorferstr. 10 (tel. 411092), also **squash.**

A **swimming** pool in summer, **ice hockey** rink in winter, is the Eis- und Schwimmstadion, in Lentstrasse. Indoor swimming pools in Deutz and Ehrenfeld districts, as well as the Agrippa-Hallenbad near Neumarkt in the center.

Golf courses at Refrath (18 holes) and Marienburg (9 holes); **horseracing** at Weidenpesch. For information about sports, dates of sporting events, inquire: Sportamt der Stadt Köln, Aachenerstrasse, Stadion, D5000 Köln 41 (49831).

CHURCHES. In addition to its famous cathedral, Köln boasts 12 Romanesque churches, all of which suffered considerable damage during the war. Reconstruction has continuously been in progress, and by 1982 over DM.250 million had been invested. 1985 was proclaimed the Year of the Romanesque Churches with the goal of having more or less completed reconstruction and restoration work by that time, 40 years after the end of the war.

St. Andreas. Houses the tomb of St. Albertus Magnus and was built in the 10th century as a collegiate church.

St. Aposteln. Built in 1201. Still to be restored to its original colors.

St. Cäcilien. Collegiate church dating back to the 12th century. Houses the Schnütgen Museum collection of sacred art.

St. Georg. Originally 11th-century, now restored to its 12th-century state.

St. Gereon. Extremely interesting architecture from the early 13th century. The foundations date back to the 4th century.

St. Kunibert. Consecrated in 1247. Restoration of parts that were completely destroyed did not begin until 1981.

St. Maria im Kapitol. Built on the foundations of the Roman Capitoline temple in the 11th century. Has one of the largest crypts in Germany and particularly interesting Renaissance rood screen (1523) and 11th-century carved wooden door.

St. Maria in Lyskirchen. Three-aisled galleried basilica dating back to 1210. Its greatest treasures are the paintings in the vaults, also from the 13th century.

Gross St. Martin. The imposing central tower is a landmark in the city. During restoration work the foundations of Roman sports facilities and warehouses were discovered, as well as remains of previous church buildings. These will be open to the public at a later date.

St. Pantaleon. Former Benedictine abbey. Single-aisled 10th-century church, transformed into a three-aisled basilica in about 1150. Gothic vaulting added in 1620 was not restored after the war.

St. Severin. Built on a graveyard. Consecrated in 1237, but some parts predate this.

St. Ursula. Known also as the "Church of the Virgins." Built in the 12th century as a three-aisled galleried basilica, with an imposing west wing.

Dom. Köln cathedral is perhaps the most dramatic Gothic building in the world. It took 632 years to complete, from 1248 to 1880. It contains many art treasures, the most important being: the Gero cross (dating from around A.D. 975), the West's oldest scuplture; the shrine of the Three Kings (1180–1225), an outstanding example of goldsmith's work from the Rhine-Maas area; and the *Dombild* polyptych (around 1450), by Stephan Lochner, a masterpiece of the Köln School of Painting. The High Altar, dating from 1322, is covered by a single 4.5 meter-long slab of black marble and surrounded by arcades of snow-white figures. The choir-stalls, carved out of oak around 1310, can seat 104 people and are the largest in Germany.

MUSEUMS. The *Kölner Museumpass,* costing DM.6, is available at all museum ticket offices and allows three days' free entry to all state museums. Municipal museums are open Tues.–Sun. from 10 A.M. to 5 P.M. Private collections have their own opening times and there are also additional and late night opening times for the major museums. Consult the *"Monatsvorschau"* or ask at the tourist office.

Erzischöfliches Diözesan Museum. Roncalliplatz 2. Ecclesiastical art, lithography, illuminated manuscripts and books.

Kölnisches Stadtmuseum (City Museum). Zeughaussstr. 1–3. History of the city, housed in the 17th-century Zeughaus (armoury).

Kölnisch-Wasser-Museum (Eau de Cologne Museum). Obenmarspforten 21. The history of the production of the world-famous toilet water.

Kunstgewerbemuseum (Arts and Crafts Museum). An der Rechtschule. Arts and crafts from medieval times to the present, including pottery and a comprehensive collection of German enamelling (faience).

Rautenstrauch-Joest-Museum. Ubierring 45. An exceptional ethnological museum with collections from Africa, Polynesia, and Indonesia.

Römisch-Germanisches Museum (Roman-Germanic Museum). Roncalliplatz 4. One of the most famous museums in Germany. Prehistoric artefacts, relics of Roman Köln, with valuable glass, ceramics, jewelry. Also located here is the **Dionysos Mosaic,** left where it was discovered during renovation work at the end of the war. The mosaic is 58 square meters and is composed of 11 million individual stones, making up 31 pictures in all.

Schnütgen Museum. In St. Cecilia's Church near Neumarkt. Ecclesiastical art from early Middle Ages to Baroque.

Wallraf-Richartz-Museum/Museum Ludwig. Bischofsgartenstr. 1, Rheingarten. The largest gallery in the Rhineland, relocated in 1986 in a new building between the cathedral and the river. The Wallraf-Richartz collection is particularly famous for its Dutch and Flemish paintings, old and modern German, some French Impressionist works and an excellent modern exhibit; while the Museum Ludwig concentrates on 20th-century work, including that of Picasso and Andy Warhol. The new building also houses the **Kunst Bibliothek.**

THEATERS AND CONCERTS. For opera and ballet: *Oper der Stadt Köln,* Opernplatz, one of the world's most modern opera buildings. For drama and comedy: *Schauspielhaus,* next to the opera. *Theater am Dom,* Kölner Ladenstadt, Glöckengasse, mostly for modern plays; *Der Keller,* Kleingedankstr. 6, experimental type; *Volkstheater Millowitsch,* Aachener Strasse 5, folk plays in local dialect; *Kefka,* corner Albertus and Magnus Str., the only pure pantomime theater in western Europe; *Senftöpchen,* Brügelmannhaus, Neugasse 2–4. Internationally-famed cabaret; *Stadtische Puppenspiele,* Eisenmarkt, a famous marionette theater.

The city's new Philharmonic Hall holds some 150 events a year, including concerts by the city's main orchestras, the *Gürzenich* and *WDR* (West German Broadcasting Company), choral works, operettas and special "Philharmonic" nights, pop and jazz events.

Information about theater events, box office for advanced bookings, etc. from: *Theaterkasse am Neumarkt* (214232) in the subway; *Theaterkasse im Kaufhof* department store (216692); *Theaterkasse am Rudolfplatz* (246945); *Theaterkasse am Ebertplatz* (737000).

RESTAURANTS. Restaurants range from top German and international dishes and old vintage selections to the spicy river boatman's fare washed down with *Kölsch,* as the light local beer is called, in one of the *Kolsche Weetschafte* (local taverns) or beer gardens.

Expensive

Chez Alex. Mühlengasse 1 (230560). For the gourmet. Reservations advised. AE, DC, MC.

Die Bastei. Konrad-Adenauer-Ufer (122825). View of the Rhine. AE, DC, MC.

Franz Kellers Restaurant. Aachener Str. 21 (251022). With adjoining bistro, *Keller's Keller.* One of the top establishments in town. Reservations necessary. DC, MC.

Goldener Pflug. Olpener Str. 421 (895509). Eight km. out of town in Mehrheim suburb. Luxurious interior and fine cuisine. No credit cards.

La Poele d'Or. Komödienstr. 50–52 (134100). One of the best-known establishments in town. Nouvelle cuisine, French dishes. Reservations essential. AE, DC, MC.

Rino Casati. Ebertplatz 3 (721108). Excellent Italian dishes and wine. Reservations advised. AE, DC, MC, V.

Weinhaus im Waldfisch. Salzgasse 13 (219575). This restaurant is tucked away between the Heumarkt and the river. Can be less expensive if you choose carefully. Get a table downstairs: upstairs is hot and crowded. AE, DC, MC, V.

Moderate

Auberge de la Charrue d'Or. Habsburgerring 18 (217610). Well-placed to be a good half-way stop on your walking tour.

Colon, corner Breitestr. and Neue Langgasse. Köln's biggest beer restaurant with 18 bars and pubs under one roof. Favorite tourist attraction. Disco.

Colonius. Innere Kanalstr. 100 (522061). Rotating restaurant at top of television tower.

Dionysos-Restaurant. Roncallipl. 2 (219402). Next to the Roman museum. AE, DC, MC.

La Lavallier. Am Hof 20 (233891). Opposite the south entrance of the cathedral. AE, DC, MC, V.

Maxwell. Pfeilstr. 25–27 (241624). Good food and great place for people-watching. Reservations advised. DC, MC.

Sigi's Bistro. Kleiner Griechenmarkt 23 (214512). Reasonable spot. DC, MC.

Inexpensive

Typical Old Town taverns with inexpensive restaurants include:

Alt Koln, Trankgasse 7–9 (137474). Traditional brewery-tavern with garden.

Brauhaus Sion, Unter Taschenmacher 5–7 (214203). *Kölsches* beer and good food.

Cölner Hofbräu P.J. Früh, Am Hof 12–14 (236616). The classic Köln "local", opposite the cathedral. Wholesome local dishes.

Haus Töller, Weyerstr. 96 (214086).

Päffgen, Friesenstr. 64 (135461). Tiny beer garden.

Zur Malzmühle, Heumarkt 6 (210117). On edge of old town with rustic interior and typical Köln *köbes,* or waiters, in their dark-blue-and-white traditional dress. Variety of different dishes.

The most famous café is **Reichard am Dom,** Unter Fettenhennen 11 (233891). Faces the cathedral, with an outdoor terrace. No credit cards.

NIGHTLIFE. Most of these are located in the following areas: the area around the Intercontinental: Friesenstrasse, Friesenwall, Hildeboldplatz and near Hohenzollernring: Maastrichterstrasse (between Hohe Str. and City Hall).

For sound evening entertainment, pubs, bars and discos try the Altstadt area between Alter Markt and Frankenwerft:

Apropo. im Dau 17 (311292). Quiet, elegant and exclusive atmosphere. Disco bar.

Ballroom. Hohenstaufenring 25 (247714). Dance hall in converted cinema. Nostalgic "forties" American bar décor. Occasional performances by live jazz bands.

Papa Joe's Biersalon "Klimperkasten." Alter Markt 50 (216759). Live music with no entrance fee.

Papa Joe's Jazz Local "Em Streckstrump." Buttermarkt 37 (217950).

Subway. Aachener Str. 82 (517969). Offering a mixture of disco and live jazz.

Tanzbrunnen. Rheinparkweg (2213368). Open-air theater and dance floor in the Rhine Park. Open May–Sept. with performances by international stars, pop groups and orchestras.

PRACTICAL INFORMATION FOR DÜSSELDORF

TELEPHONES. The telephone code for Düsseldorf is 0211. To call any number in this section, unless otherwise specified, this prefix must be used. Within the city, no prefix is required.

HOTELS. As befits the richest city in the Federal Republic, Düsseldorf has outstandingly good hotels. Prices here are a bit higher than elsewhere but some hotels offer special rates during quieter periods. There are over 10,000 beds in the city, and within a radius of 30 km. (19 miles) the figure rises to over 40,000 with plenty of cheaper accommodations in private pensions and inns.

Deluxe

Holiday Inn. Graf-Adolf-Pl. 10 (38730). 177 rooms with bath, TV, mini-bar. Near fashion boutiques. Indoor pool, sauna, solarium, good restaurants. AE, DC, MC, V.

Inter-Continental. Karl-Arnold-Pl. 5 (45530). Near the airport. 580 beds, all rooms with bath. Roof restaurant and bar with fine view; also, fitness center, heated pool and golf course, as well as Lufthansa check-in desk in foyer. AE, DC, MC, V.

Nikko. Immermannstr. 41 (8661). City's most modern luxury hotel owned by Japanese Airlines. Very expensive. Has *Benkay* Japanese specialty restaurant. Pool, sauna, solarium, lounge, bar. AE, DC, MC, V.

Steigenberger Parkhotel. Corneliuspl. 1 (8651). 160 rooms with bath. View of the Hofgarten park and elegant, modern interiors behind the old-world facade. AE, DC, MC, V.

Expensive

Breidenbacher Hof. Heinrich Heine Allee 36 (13030). Located between the old town and the modern buildings around the Kunsthalle. One of the top hotels in Germany, combining old-style tradition with modern luxury. Particularly elegant breakfast room and fine "Grill royal" restaurant. AE, DC, MC, V.

Central Hotel. Luisenstr. 42 (379001). 130 beds, all rooms with bath. No restaurant. AE, DC, MC, V.

Excelsior. Kapellstr. 1 (486006). In Pempelfort section. 64 rooms and 7 apartments, all with own bath. Very comfortable hotel. No restaurant.

Graf Adolf. Stresemannpl. 1 (360591). 130 beds. No restaurant. Parking nearby. AE, DC, MC, V.

Hilton. Georg-Glock-Str. 20 (43770). Near the airport. 750 beds, all rooms with bath. Luxury amenities. Nightclub. AE, DC, MC, V.

Ramada. Am Seestern 16 (591047). 222 rooms with bath. Good sports facilities. Restaurant. Across the river in Oberkassel sector. AE, DC, MC, V.

Savoy. Oststr. 128 (360336). 130 rooms with bath. Indoor pool, sauna, solarium, sports' room. Restaurant and cafe. AE, DC, MC, V.

Uebachs. Leopoldstr. 5 (360566). 110 beds, most rooms with bath. Restaurant. AE, DC, MC, V.

Moderate

Astor. Kurfürstenstr. 23 (360661). 36 beds, all rooms with bath. No restaurant. Near the main station. AE, MC.

Bahn-Hotel. Karlstr. 74 (360471). 66 beds. No restaurant. AE, DC, MC.

City. Bismarkstr. 73 (365023). 80 beds. No restaurant. AE, DC, MC, V.

Flughafen Hotel. Flughafen Halle 4 (421 6309). 35 beds, all rooms with bath. Right at the airport. No restaurant. V.

Germania. Freiligrathstr. 21 (494078). 35 beds. Near the main station. No restaurant. AE, DC, MC.

Ibis, Konrad-Adenauer-Platz 14 (16720). Modern, plain and efficient. 250 beds. No restaurant.

Nizza. Ackerstr. 8 (360823). 50 beds. No restaurant. AE, DC, MC.

Rheinpark. Bankstr. 13 (499186). 29 rooms. In the north of the town. No restaurant.

Stadt München. Pionierstr. 6 (375080). 45 rooms. Modern, quiet, central. No restaurant. AE, DC, MC, V.

Wurms. Scheurenstr. 23 (375001). 30 rooms. No restaurant. AE, DC, MC, V.

Camping

Camp Unterbacher See. Düsseldorf-Unterbach (899 2038). Recreation area on the north bank of the Unterbach Lake. Swimming, boating, surfing and sailing school. Open Easter through Sept. 15.

Düsseldorf-Lörick in Oberlörick. (591401). On the Rhine. Swimming and boating facilities. Open Apr. through Oct.

Youth Hostel

Düsseldorf Youth Hostel. Düsseldorfer Str. 1 (574041). 80 beds. Easy to reach from city center.

HOW TO GET AROUND. From the airport. There is an S-Bahn commuter train from the airport every 20 minutes going to the Central Railway Station; the trip takes 13 minutes. In addition, there are up to 30 trains a day running between the airport and various towns of the Rhine and Ruhr. Buses (no. 727) also take passengers into Düsseldorf. A taxi ride to the center costs about DM.17.00. Düsseldorf Airport is also linked by Lufthansa's Airport Express with Köln, Bonn and Frankfurt.

City transportation. The city and suburbs are well-served by streetcars (Strassenbahn), buses and suburban (S-Bahn) railway. The whole network is inter-connecting and belongs to the V.R.R. or Verkehrsverbund Rhein-Ruhr (Rhine-Ruhr Transport Authority). The underground is being extended into this network and is scheduled to be in full operation by 1988, with a vast, new U-Bahn station at Heinrich Heine Allee, with underground shopping center and pedestrian subways between Wilhelm Mark Haus and the Opera. Fares are uniform for all transport and tourists are recommended to purchase a 24-hour visitors' ticket, valid on all municipal urban transport services, i.e. buses, trams, S-Bahn and local and fast trains of the German Railways, for all locations within the price category 2 (see the *Tarifzonen* maps displayed at bus and streetcar stops and subway stations). It can be obtained from all ticket booths and offices, from bus and tram drivers and from V.R.R. ticket automats. With this pass you can take up to two children under the age of 14 with you free of charge. However, the ticket must first be cancelled in one of the automatic endorsing machines to be found at railway stations and on buses and trams. Ticket costs DM.8. For information contact either the Information Office of the Rheinische Bahngesellschaft (575058) or, for information in English, the Rheintourist Office (350505).

By boat. There are K.D. landing stages all along the Rhine promenade, as well as those of local passenger ship companies. The fleet of the city public transport association *Rheinbahn,* run regular services between Kaiserwerth to the north and Benrath to the south of town. There is also a hydrofoil service between Mainz and Düsseldorf. For information phone K.D. on 20880.

By taxi. Phone 33333 day and night. Call the same number and your car will be driven wherever you want, at a 20% higher tariff.

TOURIST INFORMATION. Information is available from the *Werbe- und Wirtschaftsförderungsamt* (City Office for Tourism and Business Promotion), Muhlenstr. 29, 4000 Düsseldorf 30 (899–3827). Open Mon. to Fri. 8–5, Sat. 8–1; closed Sun. Information on the city, sightseeing tours, theater tickets, special arrangements, from *Verkehrsverein der Stadt Düsseldorf,* Konrad-Adenauer-Platz 12 (350505). Open Mon to Sat. 8–11, Sun. and holidays 4–10. Hotel accommodations and booking service can be found in the booking hall of the Central Railway Station.

USEFUL ADDRESSES. Car rental. *Inter-Rent,* Charlottenstr. 50 and at airport; *Hertz,* Immermannstr. 48 and airport; *Avis,* Berliner Allee 32, Am Hauptbahnhof, at the Hilton and airport.

Consulates. *United States,* Cecilienallee 5 (490081); *Canada,* Immermannstr. 3 (353471); *Great Britain,* Georg-Glock Str. 14, Nordstern Haus, (43740).

Emergencies. *Police,* tel. 110. *Pharmacy,* tel. 1141. *Medical emergencies,* tel. 597070.

Motorists. *ADAC* (General German Automobile Club), Kaiser Wertherstr. 207; *AvD* (Automobile Club of Germany), Heinrichstr. 155.

Flight information. Tel. 421223.

Travel agency. *Reisebüro Janen,* Konrad-Adenauer-Platz (1606630).

TOURS. Daily bus tours from 15th Apr. through 15th Oct. For the rest of the year there are tours on Saturdays only. Departures at 2.30 P.M. from the bus stop opposite the Central Railway Station. The tour includes a boat trip on the Rhine and a visit to the Rhine Tower. Special tours and bilingual guides can also be arranged. Parties can also be taken on conducted tours by tram with buffet car; contact the Verkehrsverein (tourist office) (350505).

EXCURSIONS. Schloss Benrath, the most beautiful Rococo castle in Northern Rhineland contained in a large park. The western wing houses the local natural history museum. Reached by streetcars 1 and 18.

Grafenberg and Aaper Woods. Very pleasant walks. In Grafenberg Wood is the horserace track and a natural game park with red and fallow deer, roe and wild boar. Several restaurants deep in the woods. Streetcars 3, 9 and 12.

Kaiserswerth. North of the city on the Rhine, reached by streetcars 11 and D and in summer also by river boat. Ruins of the palace built by Emperor Barbarossa. Suitbertus Cathedral dating from 1000 with 13th-century works of the Cologne Goldsmiths' School and with the shrine containing the mortal remains of Suitbertus, the Anglo-Saxon missionary active in this area around 700. Baroque gabled houses.

Neanderthal. Famed as the place where the remains of a Glacial Age man, since then called Neanderthal Man, were found in 1856. The museum shows the life of the glacial period, Neanderthal Man is reconstructed in the place where he was discovered, and there is a reserve stocked with animals of the glacial era: bison, wild horses and wild cattle. About 16 km. (ten miles) from Düsseldorf, bus 43 from the main station.

Zons, the only medieval town on Lower Rhine, a bit upstream from Düsseldorf, with fully preserved walls, gates and towers. Bus line 2242/18 or river boat during summer. Nearby at **Knechtsteden** is the Premonstratensian Cloister with a pure Romanesque church.

SPORTS. The largest sports center is the Rhine stadium in Stockum near the Nordpark with 18 **tennis** courts and a **swimming** pool. Outdoor pools: Freie Schwimmer, Flinger Broich; Strandbad Lörick; Strandbad Unterbacher See. Indoor pools: Kettwiger Str. 50; Münsterstr. 13, in Derendorf; Benrath; Oberkassel; Unterrath; Gerresheim.

For **horseback riding** contact Reitinstitut Rumstich, Jägerhofstr. 10, Düsseldorfer Reiter und Rennverein e.V., Wagnerstr. 26, or Reitinstitut Schmitt, Am Dammsteg 99, and in the Aaper Forest. **Horseracing** at Grafenberg; annual international events include the Grand Prix of Northern Rhineland-Westphalia (July) and the Grand Prix of Industry and Commerce (Oct.).

Golf at the Düsseldorfer Club in Ratingen, the Land und Golf Club in Hubbelrath, or at the only public course in Germany, the *Volksgolf-platz,* an der Lausward. **Yachting** and **motor boating** on the Rhine, contact the yacht harbor administration at Rotterdamer Strasse 30. **Sailing** and **windsurfing** on the Unterbacher See. Two **ice skating** rinks are at Brehmstr. 27.

PARKS AND GARDENS. Düsseldorf is a garden city with parks, some of which were laid out as long ago as 1767. From Graf-Adolf-Platz to the Kö. (Königin Str.), through the Hofgarten as far as the old trade-fair hall, then on through the Nordpark (paying a visit to the Japanese gardens) you can walk continuously through a green belt as far as the new trade fair complex.

Opened in early 1986 is the Aqua-Zoo—a futuristic construction in the Nordpark housing aquariums, terrariums and displays on natural history.

HISTORIC BUILDINGS AND SITES. Altstadt (Old Town). The quarter is not only famed for its restaurants, but for the many significant historic monuments to be found there. A delightful place to explore.

Alter Schloss Turm (Old Castle Tower). Remains of a 13th-century castle burnt down in 1872. Now houses a navigation museum.

Kaiserwerth, Ruine der Barbarossa Pfalz. 12th-century ruins of Emperor Barbarossa's imperial palace, north of town on the way to Duisburg.

Rathaus (City Hall). On Rathausufer on the Rhine. The oldest part dates back to 1573.

Rheinturm (Telecommunications Tower). The highest building in Düsseldorf and the best overall vantage point. Located on the banks of the Rhine, next to the new State Parliament Building. Revolving restaurant on the top floor. Superb views of the city and over into Holland. Open 10 A.M.–11 P.M. Use of the lift costs DM.4.

Schloss Dyck. Southwest of town near Norf. Ancestral home in lake setting (moated castle), built 1656–63. Collection of weapons and park with exotic trees.

CHURCHES. St. Andreas. Andreas Str. Founded in 1629, former court church containing mausoleum of the Electors of the Palatinate, and of Johann Wilhelm II (Jan Wellem).

St. Lambertus. Lambertus Str. Constructed in the 13th century, on the Rhine. Contains the tomb of William the Rich; late Gothic tabernacle; treasury vault.

MUSEUMS AND GALLERIES. Goethe Museum. Jägerhofstr. 1. In the Hofgarten. Contains more than 30,000 manuscripts, first editions, paintings, sculptures and medals; all relating the masterly German man of letters.

Heinrich Heine Institüt, Bilkerstr. 14. A center for specialist information and literature dedicated to the memory of the great Düsseldorf-born poet.

Hetjens Museum (German Ceramic Museum). Palais Nesselrode, Schulstr. 4. A remarkable exhibition of ceramics dating from the Stone Age to the present.

Kunstmuseum (Municipal Art Gallery). In its new building at Ehrenhof 5. A particularly fine collection of Medieval, Baroque and contemporary sculpture, arts and crafts, and of 16th- and 20th-century paintings (among them Rubens' *Venus and Adonis*). Particularly famous for its glass collection, one of the largest in the world, crowned by a splendid and unique collection of Art Nouveau exhibits, now on permanent display in the *Tonhalle* on the banks of the Rhine at Tonhalleufer.

Kunstsammlung Nordrhein-Westfalen (North Rhine Westphalian Art Collection). Relocated in a new building at Grabbenplatz 5. State collection containing 20th-century art. Of particular note is the Paul Klee collection.

Stadt museum (City Museum). Bäckerstr. 7–9. Local history and culture.

Städtische Kunsthalle. Grabbeplatz 4. Exhibitions staged by the Artists' Association of Rhineland and Westphalia.

THEATERS AND CONCERTS. There are more than 20 theaters in Düsseldorf, offering a great variety of performances, from opera to puppets. Advance bookings are recommended. Tickets can be bought from the Tourist Office in Konrad-Adenauer-Pl. except for opera tickets which must be bought from the opera house.

For opera, operetta and ballet: *Deutsche Oper am Rhein,* Heinrich-Heine-Allee 16-a. For drama and comedy: *Schauspielhaus,* Gustaf-Gründgens Platz; *Kammerspiele,* Jahnstr. 3. Spectacular puppet shows at *Rheinisches Marionettentheater,* Bilkerstr. 14.

Ice revues, Broadway spectaculars and musicals in the *Philips-Halle,* Sieburger Str. 15 (tel. 8997744).

Literary cabaret (you have to understand German very well); *Das Kom(m)ödchen,* Hunsrückenstr. 12-b, in the Kuntshalle.

Marionettes: *Theater Rheinischer Marionetten,* Bilkerstr. 7.

The best concert orchestras are *Düsseldorf Symphony Orchestra* and *Düsseldorf City Orchestra.* Concerts are given mainly in the *Robert-Schumann-Saal,* and in the modern *Tonhalle,* opened in 1978 in the former Planetarium building on the edge of the Hofgarten and one of Germany's most beautiful concert halls, where none of the seats is far away from the podium and the acoustics superb.

SHOPPING. Düsseldorf has the reputation of being West Germany's most elegant shopping mecca. It owes this reputation first and foremost to the Königsallee, known locally as the "Kö," with its arcades and shopping centers. There are numerous exclusive fashion shops, plus furs, leather, jewelry, antiques and books.

The Schadow Strasse is good for quick and easy shopping, and has numerous shoe shops. There are wide pavements and seats in green areas.

For boutiques the Old Town is the best place. The streets are crammed with pubs and restaurants, and offer a wide range of little shops.

All three shopping areas are easily accessible on foot.

RESTAURANTS. The Altstadt (Old Town) is good for plain food at reasonable prices (*haxe,* shin of pork; *sauerbraten,* stewed marinated beef; *reibekuchen,* potato fritters; *halwe hahn,* cheese on a rye roll; or grilled *bratwürst*), with Düsseldorfer Altbier. If you prefer haute cuisine, try one of the countless international eating places with international prices.

Expensive

Fischer-Stuben-Mulfinger. Rotterdamer Str. 15 (432612). Located in the Golzheim section. Accent on fish dishes.

Im Schiffchen. Kaiserwerther Markt 9 (401050). Nouvelle cuisine at its finest. We recommend the set, six-course menu for DM.100. AE, DC, MC, V.

Les Continents, Karl-Arnold-Platz 5, in Hotel Intercontinental (45530). Elegant, with cozy *Café de la Paix.*

M & F (Müllers & Fest). Königsallee 12–16 (326001). Cooks prepare each order individually. Outdoor terrace.

Ristorante Savini Di Carlo. Stromstr. 47 (393931). Stylish restaurant serving Italian nouvelle cuisine. Good wine selection. Reservations necessary. AE, DC, MC.

Robert's Restaurant. Oberkasseler Str. 100 (575672). Known internationally. Expensive, but recommended.

Schneider-Wibbel-Stuben. Schneider-Wibbel-Gasse (80000). In the Altstadt. Specializes in steak, lobster, fish and original Pilsener beer. AE, DC, MC.

Weinhaus Tante Anna. Andreasstr. 2 (131163). One of the most historic local inns, dating from the 17th century. Fine variety of food and wine. AE, DC, MC, V.

Moderate

Da Spiegel. Bolkerstr. 22 (329081). A very original restaurant in the old part of town, it offers chess tournaments and musical attractions. No credit cards.

Delikatessa. Heinrich Heine Allee 1, in Carsch-Haus department store. Recently opened and one of the most popular places to eat—standing up. A collection of 22 food-and-drink shops in the basement of the store.

Goldenen Ring. Burgolatz 21 (700–0370). Quaint restaurant where local painters display their work. Simple, regional dishes. No credit cards.

Heinrich Heine Stuben. Bolkerstr. 50 (132314). In the Altstadt, opposite the poet's birthplace. Excellent venison in season. AE, DC, MC, V.

Meuser. Alt Niederkassel 75 (51272) in Niederkassel suburb. Famous for its traditional Düsseldorf specialty, *Speckpfannkuchen,* or pancakes filled with bacon.

Top 180. Stromstr. 20 (84858). Rotating restaurant at the top of the Rhein tower. Good service and wine selection. AE, DC, MC, V.

Inexpensive

A number of inexpensive taverns serve *Obergäriger,* a dry, dark, very still and aged beer, along with typical local dishes fortified by the famous sharp Düsseldorf mustard, in a lively atmosphere created by fast-joking natives.

Im Füchschen. Ratinger Str. 28 (84062).

Zum Schiffchen. Hafenstr. 5 (132421).

Zum Schlüssel. Bolkerstr. 43 (326155).

Zum Uerige. Berger Str. 1 (84455). One of four small independent brewers of *Altbier.*

Cafés

Bittner. Königsallee 44 (80421). Pleasant sidewalk terrace. Several branches.

Bierhof. Oststr. 128 (360336). Glittering café in Savoy Hotel, known for over 100 years for its excellent pastries.

König. Königsallee 36 (upstairs). Good observation point for the "Kö".

NIGHTLIFE. The Altstadt is the heart of Dusseldorf's nightlife. There are organized nightclub tours available, which include drinks in a bar, supper and a visit to one or two nightspots with cabaret show. For lists of night spots, ask for the *Düsseldorfer Gästeführer* brochure, available in most hotels or from the tourist office.

Club 1001, in Hilton Hotel.

Etoile. Parkhotel, Corneliusplatz 1 (8651). For dancing in elegant surroundings, with supper.

Fatty's Atelier. Hunsrückerstr. 13. Special character. Artists' haunt with food and drinks until 3 A.M.

Palette. Hotel Breidenbacher Hof, Heinrich-Heine-Allee 36 (8601). Dancing and supper. Very chic.

Rheinterrasse. Exhibition grounds. Outdoor dancing, overlooking the river. Brass band program.

Sam's. In a modern arcade between the Königsallee and Heinrich Heine Allee. Popular with locals.

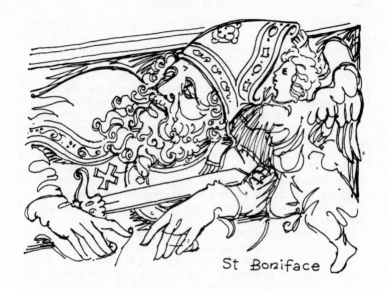

St Boniface

HESSE—SPA COUNTRY

The Land of Healing Springs

This is a region of wooded uplands and peaceful river valleys, of half-timbered houses and fairy-tale castles, of medieval towns and modern commercial cities, and of vast nature parks which cover one quarter of the state. It is a land bubbling with mineral springs, whose health-giving waters were valued even in Roman times. And today a score of famous watering places cluster along Hesse's chain of spas, while some of the best white wines in the world grow in its southwest corner, in the Rheingau. Also in the same corner are the forested Taunus hills. South of Frankfurt the fruit-scented Bergstrasse hill road takes you to the forest of Odenwald and to southern Germany beyond.

Darmstadt and Odenwald

Our exploration of Hesse begins at Darmstadt, a little to the south of Frankfurt. Darmstadt is a town with a long cultural history, and its picturesque artists' colony—founded in 1899 by the last Grand Duke Ernst Ludwig and located in the neighborhood of the Wedding Tower and the Russian Chapel—is still the center of much intellectual activity. It is the site of the annual Darmstädter Gespräche, gatherings of prominent philosophers, artists and scientists for discussions on contemporary issues, open to the public, lasting a week and combined with art exhibits.

In addition to the old artists' colony houses and other buildings on Mathildenhöhe (there is also an artists' colony on Rosenhöhe), the main points of interest are in downtown Darmstadt: the market square with the reconstructed Renaissance Rathaus, the Residence Palace and the White Tower, the Ludwig Column on Luisenplatz; the parish church and the remainder of the 14th-century city walls.

Four km. (two miles) east of the town center, and set in a park, is the Jagdschloss Kranichstein—the former royal hunting lodge built 1571–79, today a stylish hotel. It houses the Jagdmuseum (Hunting Museum). Also of interest is the Schloss (Palace), built from a 14th-century moated-castle, with a crowned tower housing Glockenspiel chimes. Here, too, is the Schlossmuseum, containing state coaches, paintings, furniture, royal tableware, and uniforms. Other museums are the Hessisches Landesmuseum (Regional Museum) with an excellent natural history collection, objects from prehistoric and Roman times, medieval artefacts, paintings by old Dutch and German masters; and the Porzellanmuseum (Porcelain Museum) in the Prinz-Georg-Palais, with valuable 18th- and 19th-century china and porcelain.

After Darmstadt, you are in the rolling hill country of the Odenwald—Odin's wood, named after the king of the gods of Teutonic mythology. Along its west slope runs the Bergstrasse—the Mountain Road, though it does not appear particularly mountainous, as the slope upward from the Rhine to the Odenwald is gentle. The peculiarity of the Bergstrasse is its freak climate. Fruit trees bloom here earlier than anywhere else in Germany, sometimes in March, for the Bergstrasse shares with Frankfurt a much milder climate than the rest of the nation, so not only is this great country for fruit, vegetables and asparagus, but it even grows tobacco. It is wine country too, as you will see for yourself as vineyard succeeds vineyard through Seeheim, Jugenheim, Bensheim and Heppenheim, the last two with especially beautiful half-timbered houses. In September Bensheim is the site of the picturesque and lively Bergstrasse Wine Festival. West of Bensheim is Lorsch with the Carolingian Kings' Hall, built in 774 and once part of a monastery.

Odenwald proper can be explored by two routes soaked in romantic sagas and memories of the past and appropriately named the Nibelungenstrasse and the Siegfriedstrasse. According to legend Siegfried was mortally wounded by Hagen's spear at a well in today's Gras-Ellenbach, reached via the Siegfried road from Heppenheim. The Nibelung Road, only a few kilometers to the north, crosses the Odenwald in a west–east direction: from Bensheim, passing Mount Melibokus, through Lindenfels, a delightful climatic resort from which you can wander through fields and forests, to Michelstadt with its half-timbered 15th-century Rathaus standing on wooden pillars and the Einhardbasilica built in 827 and of considerable architectural significance.

Less than three km. (two miles) south of Michelstadt is Erbach with various historic buildings, ranging from the 12th-century watch tower to the Baroque palace of the Counts of Erbach-Erbach, housing an outstanding collection of medieval armor and the Deutsches Elfenbeinmuseum (German Ivory Museum), a unique collection of carved ivories. The Gräfliche Sammlungen museum contains antique sculptures from Italy, early firearms, and hunting trophies.

From here you might return to Darmstadt via Bad König (north of Michelstadt), with its ferrous waters and remainders of the Roman "Limes," the Roman Empire's fortified frontier with Germany; Neustadt, dominated by the impressive Breuberg castle-fortress; Grosse-Umstadt, an island of vineyards in Odenwald; and tiny Hering with the ancient Otzberg fort above it.

Taunus and Its Spas

Less than 19 km. (12 miles) from Frankfurt is Bad Homburg, one of Germany's loveliest spas. Its springs were known to the Romans, and the town has long since been famous as a spa, particularly at the end of the 19th century, when it was visited by, among others, the Prince of Wales, later Edward VII. In addition the town has played an important role in the development of gambling. It was at Homburg that the French Blanc brothers opened their first casino in 1841, some 25 years before they moved on to found the casino in Monte Carlo. Its fame as a gaming center caused Dostoevsky to use it as a background for his novel, *The Gambler.* The town also gave its name to the Homburg hat.

One of the greatest attractions of Bad Homburg is the beautiful Kurpark. The most popular spring it contains is the highly saline Elisabethbrunnen. Two of the park's features are a Siamese temple and a Russian chapel, mementos of two of Bad Homburg's distinguished visitors, King Chulalongkorn of Siam and Czar Nicholas II. There is also the enormous Taunus Theme thermal bathing and fitness center, newly re-opened after being devastated by fire in 1984. Among its attractions are a Japanese garden, six Finnish saunas and its own cinema.

The chief sights of Bad Homburg are the 17th-century Schloss, the former residence of the Landgraves of Hesse-Homburg, whose state apartments are well worth visiting. The garden around the Schloss is famous for its two great cedars of Lebanon, now almost 150 years old. The Weisser Turm, a 12th-century tower that remains from the castle's earliest form, gives a good view of the town.

A unique attraction of Bad Homburg is seven km. (four miles) away, at Saalburg. Here you can see the best preserved Roman fort of the 550-km.- (342-mile-) long Limes, the northwestern border of the Roman Empire and part of the wall of fortifications which the Romans built from the Rhine to the Danube. The earliest part of this fort is 2nd century and the Romans held it until the latter part of the 3rd century. The Roman structures were not only excavated when they were discovered, they were rebuilt, with the result that it is possible today to envisage the life of a Roman garrison outpost settlement by inspecting Saalburg, just as you can understand Roman civilian life by visiting Pompeii. In addition to the fortification proper, you may see the administrative quarters, the granary (now a museum containing more than 30,000 relics of Roman times), the wells, armories, front and rear camps, the parade ground with its catapults, the houses, shops, baths, and temples of the village that sprang up around the fort during its long existence as a military center.

Bad Homburg lies on the "international promenade of spas" which stretches across Hesse from Wiesbaden near the Rhine to Bad Sooden-Allendorf at the East German border east of Kassel. At the northern tip of Taunus is Bad Nauheim, whose naturally warm carbonic acid springs are particularly beneficial in disorders of the heart and blood circulation. The beautifully-treed Kurpark contains a small lake, many flower beds, a golf course, tennis courts, a relaxing Kurhaus and a heart research institute in addition to cure installations.

Other state-recognized spas in the Taunus are: Camberg, an historic town on the western foothills of the Hochtaunus and known as the "Goldener Grund"; Königstein im Taunus, at the foot of the Grosser Feldberg peak and the ruins of the mighty Burg Königstein fortress; Schlangenbad, in a forested valley on the southern slopes of the Lower Taunus; and Bad Soden am Taunus on the southern slopes of the Hochtaunus near Frankfurt, boasting 30 warm saline springs and the internationally renowned Burgberg Inhalation Center.

Wiesbaden, Queen of Spas

On the shortest route Wiesbaden is only half-an-hour's ride west of Frankfurt, but taking a road closer to the Main river you first come to the village of Hochheim, submerged in vine leaves. Its fine Rhine wines, called Hochheimer, were so much in favor in England that all Rhine wines to this day are referred to as "hock," an abbreviated and anglicized version of Hochheimer.

One of the world's leading spas, Wiesbaden has long enjoyed international renown. Even if it had not been for the healing qualities of its hot saline springs, particularly good for rheumatism, Wiesbaden was bound to attract visitors, for the natural beauty of its situation is combined with accessibility from big cities. It is the gateway to the Rheingau, one of the loveliest stretches of the Rhine Valley, and the place where the best wine grapes grow. Every year at the beginning of August the Rheingau Wine Week is celebrated in the town. It lies next to the autobahn, near Frankfurt and across the Rhine from Mainz, the capital of Rhineland-Palatinate. The city itself is set back from the river; its suburb of Biebrich fronts on to it. Here the river steamers stop and the Schloss Biebrich, the Baroque castle of the Dukes of Nassau, extends its imposing facade along the shore. Its buildings were completed between 1700 and 1744, and it has a fine English-style park. An international riding tournament takes place here every year at Whitsun. Wiesbaden is noted not only for its fine parks, especially the Kurpark, but also for the beauty of the walks in its neighborhood.

Amid these ideal surroundings, activity goes on about the pillars of the famous Brunnenkolonnade (Fountain Colonnade) and Theater-kolonnade (Theater Colonnade), mostly in the Hessian State Theater and the neo-Classical Kurhaus. World-renowned artists appear in operas and concerts, plays are given not only in German but occasionally also in French or English, and the International May Festival presents opera companies, ballet groups and theatrical troupes from many countries. And at all seasons, the roulette wheels spin and the baccarat shoe circulates in the Kurhaus Casino.

Wiesbaden is also the capital of the State of Hesse, whose Landtag (state parliament) sits in the former city palace of the Dukes of Nassau on Schlossplatz. Not far away at the Kaiser Friedrich Baths is the oldest structure in the city, a Roman Arch dating from A.D. 300, while one of the newest, the airy and glass-walled Rhein-Main-Halle exhibition and convention hall is in the vicinity of the main station. On the Neroberg elevation in the northern outskirts, reached by the oldest mountain railway in Germany, constructed in 1888, is another building connected with the

Nassau family: the Greek-Orthodox Chapel, built over a century ago as a memorial church for a romantic Russian-born Duchess of Nassau who died young. Nearby is the Opelbad open-air swimming pool with a panoramic view of the city. The Museum Wiesbaden (City Museum) contains a noted gallery of modern painting, antiquities, prehistoric and Roman finds, and a natural history collection.

From Rheingau to Lahn Valley

West of Wiesbaden the steep and sunny river slopes of the Rheingau hills are covered with vineyards, whose grapes give some of the best and most famous white wines in the world. Half-timbered and gabled wine producing villages, with many castles about them, are strung along the right bank of the Rhine.

The best known and the most popular is Rüdesheim, chief center of this most intensively cultivated part of the Rhine wine region. Its importance will be obvious if you visit one of the wine cellars where the great casks have elaborately and lovingly-carved heads, attend the September wine festival, or visit the Rheingau- und Weinmuseum (Museum of Wine History) in the old Brömserburg Castle. The museum contains wine-presses, drinking-vessels and collections dating from prehistoric times to the present day. Conducted tours through wine cellars, to the Asbach Uralt distillery and the wine factories can be made upon request at the local tourist office. Stop off too at the old Drosselgasse, a small street lined with wine taverns. It is here that the Mechanisches Musikkabinet im Historischen Brömershof (Mechanical Music Collection) is to be found, with its musical boxes, early gramophones and hurdy-gurdies. But Rüdesheim has other attractions than its wine (and brandy, for that is made here too, as well as Sekt, the German version of champagne). Few Rhine towns are richer in beautiful old houses, whose half-timbered walls are enriched by quaintly-shaped gables and turrets. And in addition to Brömserburg, which is the lower castle, there are Boosenburg, the upper castle, and soaring above the Rhine on a nearby hill, the mighty towers of the ruins of Ehrenfels; all three castles are from the 13th century.

Above Rüdesheim, on the elevation of Niederwald, stands a colossal statue erected in the 19th century to commemorate German unification. You can reach it from Rüdesheim by aerial cable-car, by a short motor road, or by lovely walks through vineyards and forests. Your reward will be a splendid view over this section of the Rhine.

Niederwald can be reached by a chair lift from the town of Assmannshausen, which has one of the most beautiful locations on the entire river. On the heights is the old hunting-lodge Niederwald Castle, belonging to the former Prince-Bishops of Mainz. Assmannshausen is also a small spa and red wine is produced here, unusual for the Rhine. Further down the river is Lorch with the Renaissance Hilchenhaus. Near the Niederwald monument is a falconry with a breeding and training center for eagles and a variety of birds of prey, which can be visited throughout the year, weather permitting.

From Lorch a scenic road through the narrow Wisper Valley leads away from the Rhine and wine to the Rheingau's quiet, forested heights, alive with game, and to Bad Schwalbach, an important spa with ferrous waters, which can be reached faster by a direct route from Wiesbaden. At Idstein, with its round Hexenturm (Witches' Tower), we are in the northern approaches of the Taunus. Further north in the Ems Valley is Camberg, with 14th-century walls and gates and with Kneipp cold water cure installations.

The Ems flows into the Lahn a little above Limburg, whose seven-spired Cathedral of St. George, built in 1235, seemingly grows out of the cliff on which it stands and represents perhaps the best example of the transition from the Romanesque to the Gothic in Germany. It contains murals and other artistic treasures from the same period, while its majestic exterior can be best observed from the Lahn tower-gate bridge, constructed in 1315. Other main points of interest include a two-wing Gothic castle, two other churches which are even older than the cathedral, and many half-timbered houses including the oldest one in Germany (1296).

The romantic Lahn Valley is lined by many towns clustered under medieval castles. Some of the most remarkable sights upstream from Limburg include the powerful 12th-century fortress at Runkel, the Renaissance residential castle at Weilburg with rich furnishings, and the Braunfels castle-fortress, high up above the river, towered and turreted, with colossal walls, courtyards and four gateway tunnels. Wetzlar, at the confluence of the Lahn and Dill rivers, is a cathedral town and the place where Goethe sustained his hopeless love for Charlotte, the result of which was his novel, *Werther.*

North of the old university town of Giessen, after passing the 12th-century Staufenburg Castle, we come to Marburg, our last and, in some ways, most interesting stop on the Lahn River. Marburg is the home of the country's oldest Protestant University (it was founded in 1527). Its library, the largest in Germany, is a jewel of Gothic architecture. The 13th-century St. Elisabethkirche is one of the purest examples of Gothic in Europe; it was erected over the grave of St. Elisabeth, a Landgravine of nearby Thuringia and champion of the poor. Of particular interest among its many artistic treasures are the shrine of St. Elisabeth, the Landgrave's choir and the stained glass windows. The State of Hesse was founded in Marburg in 1256 and soon afterwards the ruling Landgraves constructed the massive, early Gothic castle, still standing on the hill above the town and reached either by a steep climb through the terraced streets, lined with half-timbered houses, or by driving up a narrow road. The effort will be well repaid by the sight of the castle's interiors, particularly the splendid Knights' Hall, a stroll in its park (summer performances on the outdoor stage) and the fine view of the town and the surrounding countryside. Other chief sights of Marburg are the old university building with the university church, the 16th-century town hall (its Trumpet of Justice is blown every hour) and the 14th-century Marienkirche.

About 96 km. (60 miles) through the vast forests of Burgwald and Kellerwald, where stag, roe deer and wild boar roam, separate Marburg from Kassel, the principal city of Northern Hesse. First you come to Frankenberg whose landmark is the half-timbered Rathaus from 1509, playfully roofed with ten little spires. Bad Wildungen in Kellerwald, a noted spa, has picturesque town streets and a beautiful Kurpark with trees and flowers transplanted from all over the world. The 1,000-year-old Fritzlar has preserved 18 of its wall towers, the town hall is among the oldest in Germany and the 16-altar Romanesque cathedral was originally founded by St. Boniface in 732. The Eder river is dammed some 32 km. (20 miles) above Fritzlar, forming the 27-km.- (17-mile-) long artificial lake of Endersee, the meeting point of fishing and boating enthusiasts and presided over by the Waldeck Castle, best reached from Bad Wildungen.

Upper Hesse to Kassel

Before visiting Kassel we shall travel through Upper Hesse, a region east of Marburg, Giessen and Bad Nauheim (the last two actually in Upper Hesse). In this land, as well as in the nearby section of northern Hesse, old folk dress and folklore customs have survived. Some of the best preserved folk dress can be seen at Alsfeld, a historic town southeast of Marburg; folklore performances are staged here on the medieval market square in the shadows of the 16th-century Rathaus (Town Hall), Weinhaus (Wine House), Hochzeitshaus (Bridal House) and the even older Walpurgis Church.

Another center of folk dress further southeast is Schlitz, a town with four castles. Schotten, located in the Vogelsberg mountains in the middle of Upper Hesse, has a famous Gothic wing altar in the Liebfrauenkirche but it is even better known for its mountain road race course.

West of Vogelsberg is Fulda, on the river of the same name, where a monastery was founded in the 8th century by Sturmius, a pupil of the Anglo-Saxon St. Boniface whose body lies in the impressive early 18th-century cathedral, with its twin towers and central dome. The whole city is an object lesson in Baroque architecture, none of it more involved than the intricate figures of the "Flora Vase," which stands outside the Orangery. The museum of Schloss Adolphseck, on the outskirts, contains a notable collection of ancient sculpture, porcelain, and glassware. The cathedral treasure includes Boniface and Sturmius reliquaries, episcopal staff of Boniface, and specimens of medieval sacred art. In contrast to the prevailing Baroque style, the Carolingian St. Michael's Church has preserved its original form since A.D. 820.

East of Fulda are the Rhön mountains, the home of glider pilots and the source of the Fulda River. To the north in the Fulda Valley is Bad Hersfeld, a minor spa with the 1,200-year-old ruins of a monastery where plays are staged during summer. From here you can drive to Kassel directly on the autobahn. If you want to loaf through the picturesque small towns on the way, take one of the two main roads east of the autobahn. One will lead you downstream to the peaceful castle in Rotemburg and the half-timbered Melsungen. The other route will take you into Eschwege which also has many half-timbered houses, often enriched with wood carvings, while its castle has a fountain about which many legends have been spun; and to still another spa, Bad Sooden-Allendorf, a medieval town with brine baths. This is a good starting point for hikes to the region of the Hoher Meissner, a mountain in Grimm's fairy-tale country, for this was the abode of Lady Holle, who made snow on the earth by emptying her featherbeds from this height. These regions, along with Bad Sooden-Allendorf, are weekend playgrounds for Kassel.

Kassel, on the Fulda River, is the principal city in northern Hesse and makes a very good base for visiting the country round about. It is a big industrial center, producing such heavy manufactures as railroad rolling stock and locomotives, but it also has considerable attractions for visitors. One of the most important is the Staatliche Kunstsammlungen (Provincial

Art Collection) housed in Schloss Wilhelmshöhe. This is in the beautiful Bergpark Wilhelmshöhe in the western outskirts of the city at Schöne Aussicht. The collection is one of Germany's very finest and has notable works by Rembrandt, Rubens, Hals, Jordaens, Van Dyck, Dürer, Altdorfer, Cranach, Baldung Grien, and others. The Neue Galerie has works by European artists from 1750 to the present day, but it also includes the world-famous Apollo of Kassel, a perfect Roman copy of a statue by the 5th-century B.C. Greek Phidias. The international Documenta art exhibitions take place in Museum Fridericianum on Friedrichs-Platz every four years.

The Brüder Grimm Museum contains manuscripts, illustrations and mementoes of the world-famous fairytale writers, Jacob and Wilhelm Grimm, who lived in Kassel from 1798 to 1830. In 1985 the town celebrated the bicentenary of the brothers Grimm.

In the same building as the Hessische Landesmuseum (Hessian State Museum) is the Deutsche Tapetenmuseum (German Wallpaper Museum). This is perhaps the only museum of its kind in the world and has wallpapers that date back to the 16th century.

Kassel is also known as the city of parks. In the southern section of the city the Schönfeld Park contains a castle and the Botanical Garden. Spread along the left bank of the Fulda, the Karls-Aue with waterways, a lake, the Siebenbergen flower island, the Orangery and other attractions, reaches to the Rathaus and the State Theater in the center of the city. But the most outstanding is the Bergpark Wilhelmshöhe with fountains, pyramids, temples, Löwenburg Castle and a colossal monument of Hercules, the symbol of Kassel. The neo-Classical Schloss Wilhelmshöhe forms the gate to this "park on the hill," as it is commonly known.

About 13 km. (eight miles) to the north is the Rococo Schloss Wilhelmstal with rich interiors. Several more castles can be seen north of Kassel, mainly along and near the route 83, which takes you to the Weser Hills area of Lower Saxony. The most famous among them is the romantic Schloss Sababurg, the legendary castle in the middle of the 1,000-year-old forest of Rheinhardswald. In Arolsen, west of Kassel, is the Baroque palace of the Counts of Waldeck. From there it is only a few kilometers to Westphalia.

PRACTICAL INFORMATION FOR HESSE

TELEPHONES. We have given telephone codes for all the towns and villages in the hotel and restaurant lists that follow. These codes need only be used when calling from outside the town or village concerned.

HOTELS AND RESTAURANTS. The main cities and resorts all have a first-class selection of hotels and restaurants, with a high degree of comfort as befitting former Imperial and Royal "holiday" and "spa" centers. The selection of Romantic and Castle Hotels is also wide, as well as large establishments of international renown such as Novotel.

In the many small climatic health resorts and outlying villages there is a good choice of accommodations in simple inns and pensions, and the number of holiday apartments and houses is steadily on the increase. A particular role in Hessen's accommodations scene is played by the good-value *Ferien auf dem Bauernhof* (holidays on the farm) scheme, and a brochure entitled *Wir machen Ihnen den Hof,* available from the Regional Tourist Office, lists hundreds.

Assmannshausen. Suburb of Rüdesheim. *Anker* (M), Rheinuferstr. 7 (06722–2912). With Rhine-terrace and own vineyard. *Krone* (M), Rheinuferstr. 10 (06722–2036). 136 beds, 30 rooms with bath. An inn since the 16th century. Excellent cuisine; visit the cellars where the produce of its own vineyard is kept. Pool. Some single rooms lower in price but avoid rear rooms facing railway. Closed Nov. through mid-March. MC. *Schön* (M), Rheinuferstr. 3 (06722–2225). *Winzerschänke* (I), Rheingasse 1 (06722–2315). 13 rooms; fine view.

Restaurant. *Ewige Lampe* (M), Niederwaldstr. 14 (06722–2417). Old and atmospheric restaurant; now also offers some modernized rooms.

Bad Hersfeld. *Parkhotel Rose* (M), Am Kurpark 9 (06621–15656). 35 rooms. Restaurant. AE, DC, MC, V. *Romantik Hotel Zum Stern* (M), Linggplatz 11 (06621–72007). Once belonged to the Benedictine monastery and dates back to 1411. Indoor pool, restaurant. AE, DC, MC, V. *Vorderburg* (I), An der Vorderburg 1 (06642–5041). 28 rooms. In nearby Schlitz near A6, quietly-located in a cluster of historic buildings. Good restaurant.

Bad Homburg. *Maritim Kurhaus Hotel* (E), Ludwigstr. (06172–28051). Luxurious, 148 rooms, all with bath. Indoor pool. Restaurant. AE, DC, MC, V. *Geheimrat Trapp* (M), Kaiser-Friedrich-Promenade 55 (06172–26047). 55 rooms, all with bath. Comfortable hotel with fine restaurant serving *nouvelle cuisine.* AE, DC, MC. *Haus Daheim* (I), Elizabethenstr. 42 (06172–20098). 21 rooms, most with bath. AE, DC, MC, V.

Restaurants. *Table* (E), Kaiser-Friedrich-Promenade 85 (06172–24425). High quality food in atmospheric surroundings. DC, MC. *Saalburg* (M), Am Roemerkastell 2 (06175–1007). Dine like the ancient Romans. AE, DC, MC, V.

Four km. south at Friedrichsdorf is one of the top restaurants in the country, *Sänger's Restaurant—Weisser Turm,* Hugenottenstr. 121 (06172–72020) serving topnotch *nouvelle cuisine.* Reservations advisable. Also has 8 rooms.

Bad Nauheim. *Parkhotel am Kurhaus* (E), Im Nördlicher Park 16 (06032–3030). Modern furnishings. DC, MC, V. *Blumes Hotel am Kurhaus* (M), Auguste Viktoria Str. 3 (06032–2072). 18 rooms, most with bath. MC.

Restaurants. *Gaudesberger* (M), Hauptstr. 6 (06032–2508). Cozy with good food; several rooms. AE, DC, MC, V. *Theater Restaurant* (M), Kurpark (06032–3030), in the new Concert Hall and Theater building. Art Nouveau style; fine food and wines.

Bad Wildungen. *Staatliches Badehotel* (E), Dr.-Marc-Str. 4 (05621–860). 74 rooms. In the Kurpark. DC, MC. *Am Golfplatz* (M), Talquellenweg 17 (05621–2092). 22 rooms. *Schwarze* (I), Brunnenallee 42 (05621–4064). 26 rooms, most with bath. Café.

Restaurant. *La Camargue* (M), Brunnenallee 12 (05621–2323).

Darmstadt. *Maritim* (E), Rheinstr. 105 (06151–80041). 80 rooms. Near the station. DC, MC, V. *Schlosshotel und Park Restaurant Jagdschloss Kranichstein* (E), Kranichsteiner Str. 261 (06151–76001). 20 beds, most rooms with bath or shower. A 16th-century hunting castle, six km. (four miles) distant from town; period furnishings and a restaurant specializing in game dishes. *Weinmichel* (M), Schleiermacherstr. 10 (06151–26822). A Ring Hotel. 73 rooms, all with bath or shower. Good-value restaurant and colorful wine tavern.

Restaurant. *Zum Goldenen Anker* (M), Landgraf-Georg-Str. 25 (06151–20825). Brewery restaurant over 300 years old; several different rooms.

Eltville-Erbach. *Hotel Schloss Reinhartshausen* (E), Hauptstr. 35 (06123–4081). 40 rooms. A Ring Hotel. On the banks of the Rhine between Wiesbaden and Rüdesheim, a former imperial palace extensively modernized, in large park; good restaurant and wine tasting. AE.

Fulda. *Maritim Am Schlossgarten* (E), Pauluspromenade 2 (0661–2820). 226 beds, all doubles with bath, indoor pool and fine *Orangerie* restaurant. *Hotel Bachmühle* (M), Künzeller Str. 133 (0661–77800). 19 rooms, all with bath. AE, MC, V. *Hotel Hessischer Hof* (I), Nikolausstr. 22 (0661–72289). 30 rooms, half with bath. Near the station. *Hotel Zum Hirsch* (I), Löherstr. 36 (0661–70082). 19 rooms, only 3 with bath.

Restaurants. *Alte Post am Dom* (M), Wilhelmstr. 2 (0661–72373). At the cathedral. *Dachsbau Grill, Bistro and Wine Tavern* (M), Pfandhausstr. 7 (0661–74030). The oldest wine tavern in town. *Felsenkeller* (M), Leipziger Str. 12 (0661–72784). Brewery restaurant with several atmospheric rooms, garden terrace. DC, MC, V.

Giessen. *Steingarten* (E), Hein-Heckroth-Str. 20 (0641–38990). 84 rooms, all with bath. Indoor pool, restaurant. AE, DC, MC, V. *Hotel Am Ludwigplatz* (M), Ludwigsplatz 8 (0641–33082). 48 rooms, most with bath. Pleasant restaurant. AE, DC, MC, V. *Motel an der Lahn* (I), Lahnstr. 21 (0641–73516). No restaurant.

Restaurant. *Schloss Keller* (M), Am Bradplatz 2 (0641–38306). Elegant, in vaulted cellar of Altes Schloss. *Kloster Schiffenberg* (M). Atmospheric restaurant set in former monastery. Local specialties. Beer garden. Some rooms.

Kassel. *Holiday Inn* (E), Heiligenröder Str. 61 (0561–52151). 155 beds. 16 km. (ten miles) out of town at Autobahn exit Kassel-east. Indoor pool, solarium, sauna, bar. AE, DC, MC, V. *Dorint Hotel Reiss* (M), Werner-Hilpert-Str. 24 (0561–78830). 102 rooms, most with bath or shower. Atmospheric wine tavern. AE, DC, MC, V. *Excelsior* (M), Erzbergerstr. 2 (0561–102984). All rooms with shower. Excellent restaurant. AE, DC, MC, V. *Park Hotel Hessenland* (M), Obere Königstr. 2 (0561–14974). 171 rooms. At the Rathaus, with pleasant roof terrace, dance-bar. AE, DC, MC. *Schlosshotel Wilhelmshöhe* (M), im Schlosspark 2 (0561–30880). 60 rooms with bath. Pleasant setting; modern. DC, MC, V. *Hotel Am Rathaus* (I), Wilhelms-Str. 29 (0561–13768).

Restaurants. *Landhaus Meister* (M), Fuldatalstr. 140 (0561–875050). MC. *Ratskeller* (M), Obere Königstr. 8 (0561–15928). DC, MC.

Limburg. *Schlosshotel Weilburg* (E), Langgasse 25 (06471–39096). In Weilburg, on the road to Wetzlar. 42 rooms and 8 apartments, all with bath. An elegant, Baroque-style castle-hotel, with good view, indoor pool, sauna, restaurant. *Martin* (M), Holzheimerstr. 2 (06431–41001). 30 rooms, most with bath. MC. *Zimmermann* (M), Blumenröder Str. 1 (06431–42030). 27 rooms, all with bath; 10 apartments. Particularly comfortable and quiet. Restaurant for evening meals only. AE, DC, MC, V. *Dom Hotel* (M), Grabenstr. 57 (06431–24077). 64 rooms. Very comfortable and quiet. AE, DC, MC, V. *Huss* (M), Bahnhofplatz 3 (06431–25087). 48 rooms, most with bath. On quiet square. AE, DC, MC.

Restaurants. *St. Georgsstube* (M), Hospitalstr. 4 (06431–26027). DC, MC, V. *Alt Staffel* (M), Koblenzer Str. 56 (06431–2000). Steak, fish and game specialties. Also 14 rooms (I) all with bath.

Marburg. *Waldecker Hof* (M), Bahnhofstr. 23 (06421–63011). 41 rooms, most with bath. AE, DC, MC, V. *Dammühle* (I), Dammühlenstr. 1, Wehrshausen (06421–31007). Hotel-restaurant a little out of town, on the Lahn. An old millhouse, with garden terrace and excellent food. DC, MC.

Restaurants. *Hosteria del Castello* (M), Markt 19 (06421–25884). AE *Zur Krone* (I), Markt 11. Local color, on the main old square; closed Thurs.

Rüdesheim. *Jagdschloss Niederwald* (M), Auf dem Niederwald 1 (06722–1004). 44 rooms, all with bath. Above the town, the former hunting castle of the Prince-Bishops of Mainz. AE. *Rheinstein* (M), Rheinstr. 20 (06722–2004). 43 rooms, most with bath. On the river with fine view. AE, DC, MC, V. *Traube-Aumüller* (I), Rheinstr. 6 (06722–3038). 200 beds, all rooms with bath. AE, DC, MC, V. *Felsenkeller* (I), Oberstr. 39 (06722–2094). 77 rooms, most with bath. V.

Restaurants. One of Germany's top attractions is the unbelievable double row of Weinhäuser in the Drosselgasse. This is *the* place for merry wine-drinking in the musical comedy tradition. Open daily March–Nov. from 12 noon until late at night. The *Drosselhof* (AE, DC, MC, V), *Bei Hannelore* (AE, V) and *Winzerkeller* (AE, MC, V) are the leaders. For good food in quieter surroundings try *Altes Haus* (M), Lorcher Str. 8 (06722–2051). Historic, half-timbered house dating back to 1578. Also some rooms. MC, V.

Sababurg. *Burghotel Sababurg* (M), (05678–1052). 15 rooms. The legendary castle of the Sleeping Beauty, situated about 16 km. (ten miles) from Hofgeismar north of Kassel. With restaurant.

Spangenberg. *Jagdschloss Spangenberg* (E), (05663–866). 27 rooms, all with bath. In a 13th-century castle above the village on the Fulda river, with fine view and restaurant; very quiet.

Staufenberg. *Burg Staufenberg* (I), Burggasse 10 (06406–3012). 25 beds. Restaurant, park, panoramic view. AE.

Trendelburg. *Burghotel Trendelburg* (M), (05675–1021). 23 rooms, all with bath. Near Hofgeismar (north of Kassel). Castle dating from 13th century, some rooms in the round corner tower. Dining indoors by candlelight, outdoors on the ramparts. Try "Trout Poacher's Art" served on hot brick. AE, DC.

Waldeck. *Burghotel Schloss Waldeck* (M), Am Edersee (05623–5324). 25 beds. Above Eder Lake. Originally built 1120, walls and towers date from 16th–17th centuries. Beautiful view and location.

Wiesbaden. *Nassauer Hof* (L), Kaiser-Friedrich-Pl. 3 (06121–1330). 159 rooms, all with bath; 13 apartments. Smart restaurants, bar, thermal baths and treatment, 80-car garage. AE, DC, MC, V. *Schwarzer Bock* (E), Kranzpl. 12 (06121–3821). 160 rooms, all with bath; 21 apartments. A hostelry since 1486, completely modernized, most rooms with period furniture; outstanding cuisine in restaurant, roof garden with view; indoor thermal pool, baths and treatment in the house. AE, DC, MC, V. *Bären* (M), Bärenstr. 3 (06121–301021). 56 rooms, most with bath. Thermal baths. AE, DC, MC, V. *Central* (M), Bahnhofstr. 65 (06121–372001). 58 rooms, half with bath. AE, DC, MC. *Hansa-Hotel* (M), Bahnhofstr. 23 (06121–39955). 79 rooms, most with bath. Near railway station. AE, DC, MC, V. *Albany* (M), Kappelenstr. 2 (06121–521051). 20 rooms, most with bath. No restaurant. AE, DC, MC, V.

Restaurants. *Die Ente vom Lehel* (E), Kaiser-Friedrich-Platz 3, in Hotel Nassauer Hof (06121–133666). A genuine gourmet temple, open from 6 to 11 P.M. Reservations essential. AE, DC, MC, V. *Lanterna* (E), Westendstr. 3 (06121–402522). First-class Italian food. AE, DC, MC, V. *Le Gourmet* (E), Bahnhofstr. 42 (06121–301654). Fine French cuisine. AE, DC, MC, V. *Cattle Baron* (M), Büdingen Str. 4 (06121–302306). An American steak-house. AE, DC, MC. *Mövenpick* (M), Sonnenberger Str. 2 (06121–524005). AE, DC, MC, V. *Weihenstephan* (M), Armenruhstr. 6 (06121–61134). In Biebrich section. Bavarian-style home-cooking; excellent value. *Bobbeschänkelche* (I), Röderstr. 39 (06121–527959). Historical beer and wine tavern. Also, *Burger King,* Kirchgasse, 58, *Churrasco Steak House,* Markstr. 10 and *McDonald's,* at Friedrichstr. 55 and Kirchgasse 64.

Wine Taverns. With local color. *Alte Krone* (M), Sonnenbergerstr. 82 (06121–563947). Historic vaulted cellar. Fine food. *Burg Sonnenberg* (M), Am Schlossberg 20 (06121–541409). Specializes in game and Rhine wine. DC, MC.

CAMPING AND YOUTH HOSTELS. There is a large number of campsites in the region and 50 Youth Hostels, some of them romantically located. Details from local tourist offices or from Hessian Regional Office.

TOURIST INFORMATION. The Regional Tourist Office is *Hessische Fremdenverkehrsverband,* Abraham-Lincoln-Str. 38–42, 6200 **Wiesbaden** (06121–774352). There is also an office in **Kassel,** Entenanger 8 (0561–8273). Local Tourist Offices as follows: **Assmannshausen,** see *Verkehrsamt* **Rüdesheim. Bad Hersfeld,** *Städtisches Verkehrsbüro,* Am Markt 1, 6430 Bad Hersfeld (06621–201274). **Bad Homburg,** *Verkehrsamt im Kurhaus,* Louisenstrasse, 6380 Bad Homberg (06172–12130). **Bad Nauheim,** *Verkehrsverein,* Pavillon in der Parkstrasse, 6350 Bad Nauheim (06032–2120), for room accommodations service, and *Verkehrsamt,* Lugwigstr. 20–22 (06032–3441), for general tourist information. **Bad Wildungen,** *Kurverwaltung,* Langemarckstr. 2, 3590 Bad Wildungen

(05621–6054). **Darmstadt,** *Verkehrsamt,* Luisenplatz 5, 6100 Darmstadt (06151–132780), and *Tourist Information* at the main railway station (06151–132782). **Fulda,** *Städtisches Verkehrsbüro,* Schlossstr. 1, 6400 Fulda (0661–102346). **Giessen,** *Verkehrsamt,* Berliner Platz 2, 6300 Giessen 1 (0641–3062489). **Kassel,** *Tourist Information Hauptbahnhof,* 3500 Kassel (0561–13443) at the main railway station, and *Tourist Information,* Königsplatz, 3500 Kassel (0561–17159). **Limburg,** *Städt. Fremdenverkehrsamt,* Hospitalsstr. 2, 6250 Limburg (06431–203222). **Marburg,** *Verkehrsamt,* Neue Kasseler Str. 1, 3550 Marburg an der Lahn (06421–201249). **Offenbach,** *Städtisches Verkehrsbüro,* Offenbach Information, Am Stadthof, Frankfurter Str. 35, 6050 Offenbach am Main (069–80652946). **Rüdesheim,** *Städtisches Verkehrsamt,* Rheinstr. 16, 6220 Rüdesheim (06722–2962). **Spangenberg,** *Verkehrsamt,* Kirchplatz 4, 3509 Spangenberg (05663–7297). **Trendelburg,** *Verkehrsamt, im Rathaus,* 3526 Trendelburg (05675–1024). **Waldeck,** *Verkehrsamt der Stadt Waldeck,* Rathaus, 3544 Waldeck (05623–5302). **Wiesbaden,** *Verkehrsbüro,* Rheinstr. 15 Wiesbaden (06121–312847).

HOW TO GET AROUND. By air. The International Rhein-Main airport at Frankfurt is the air center for the region. Frankfurt airport is linked by S-Bahn to the two city center rail stations (Hauptbahnhof and Hauptwache), from where further lines connect to Wiesbaden (S1, S14), Darmstadt (S12), Hanau (S7 and S8), Bad Homburg (S5), Kronberg (S4) and Bad Soden (S3). In addition, there are InterCity rail connections into the rest of the region.

By rail. All rail routes in the region lead to Frankfurt, one of the most important rail junctions in the whole of Germany. There are InterCity and Euro-City connections to Frankfurt, Bad Homburg, Fulda, Giessen, Darmstadt, Kassel and Wiesbaden, and regular trains to Alsfeld, Bad Hersfeld, Bad Karlshafen, Büdingen, Hanau, Limburg, Marburg, Offenbach, Rüdesheim, Rüsselsheim and Wetzlar; the long-distance line from Hamburg to southern Germany traverses Hesse on its eastern flanks through Bebra and Fulda. The most important inter-Hessian rail connection connects Frankfurt via Giessen and Marburg with Kassel.

By bus. Frankfurt is naturally a focal point for long distance buses from all parts of Germany and Europe. The main routes intersecting here are: EB 163 and 165 from Oostende via Brussels and Köln; T43 from Amsterdam; EB 185 from Paris via Saarbrücken; T91B, Berlin–Barcelona; T86 Helsinki–Stockholm Travemünde–Hamburg–Frankfurt.

Kassel is included in the Europabus and Long Distance Touring routes EB183 (Helsinki–Zagreb); T91H (Hamburg–Hannover–Frankfurt–Barcelona); T96A (Hamburg–Athens); T96B (Bremen–Bielefeld–München–Istanbul). Wiesbaden lies on routes T81 (Frankfurt–Trier); EB180 (The Romantic Road); T97F (Frankfurt–Zagreb); and T98F (Frankfurt–Belgrade). Local bus companies and the Post and Bahn buses operate all over the region: timetables are available from the tourist offices of main bus stations.

By boat. Hesse's navigable waterways are the Rhine, Main, Weser, Fulda and Neckar. The most important harbors are the Rhine ports of Gustavsburg and Gernsheim, as well as the Main ports of Frankfurt, Hanau and Offenbach. Pleasure cruisers and regular river ferry services of the Bingen-Rüdesheimer company depart from the quays in Rüdesheim and Assmannshausen. Information from *Bingen-Rüdesheimer Fähr- und Schiffahrtsgesellschaft,* Rheinkai 10, 6530 Bingen (06721–14140) or, in Rüdesheim, (06722–2972).

Steamers of the KD Weisse Flotte depart every day for places up- and downstream from Wiesbaden-Biebrich.

Trips on the Fulda can be made from Kassel with the Oberweser Ship Co., or from Schlagd-Altmarkt, and on the Lahn from Limburg.

By car. The most important autobahn routes in Germany cross the state of Hesse at some point: the A7/A5 (Hamburg–Frankfurt–Basle); A3 (Köln–Frankfurt–Wurzberg–Munich); A45 (Ruhr–Giessen–Hanau) and A44 (Ruhr–Kassel). The Deutsche Ferienstrasse, the longest scenic route in Germany, enters Hesse in the northeast at Witzenhausen and takes the traveler through areas of cherry trees, forests, lakes, picturesque old towns, castles, and of course, spas, before leaving the area at Frammersbach. Information from Verein Deutsche Ferienstrasse Alpen-Ostsee, Parkstr. 6, 3588 Homberg. And there is the Deutsche Marchenstrasse (German Fairytale Road) running from Hanau to Bremen. This route is full of the romance and history of the lives and works of the brothers Grimm, passing castles, palaces and museums.

The Bäderstrasse (Spa Road) crosses central Hesse, taking in the rolling countryside of the Rhein-Taunus Nature Park and its spa towns. Information from Kommunale Arbeitsgemeinschaft "Bäderstrasse," Rathausstr. 9, 6209 Heidenrod 2.

The Bergstrasse (Mountain Road) follows what was originally a Roman road. It was named because the route led through the slightly higher-lying townships which escaped flooding when the Rhine annually burst its banks, causing the population to take up residence on the ridgeland. The major attraction, however, is the unusually mild climate of the Bergstrasse region and the proliferation of blossoming fruit-trees in early spring through to May—the best times of the year for a visit. The Nibelungen Strasse, on the other hand, and the Siegfried Strasse, which run from the Rhine Valley to the heights of the Odenwald, are very much steeped in history, following the Roman "limes," the Roman fortified frontier with Germany. Information for the Bergstrasse from *Fremdenverkehrsamt Berg-Strasse Odenwald,* Landratsamt, Gräffstr. 5, 6148 Heppenheim, and for the Nibelungen Strasse and Siegfried Strasse, from *Vekehrs- und Heimatverein,* 6148 Heppenheim.

The Hochtaunus Strasse is a round-trip of about 100 km. (62 miles) from Bad Homburg around the Upper Taunus towns and villages of Oberursel, Schmitten, Weilrod, Waldems and Camberg, to its literal highspot, the Grosse Feldberg peak. Information from *Gesellschaft Hochtaunusstrasse, Landratsamt,* Louisensstr. 86, 6380 Bad Homburg.

The Rheingau-Riesling Route is another German wine road, following the vineyards of the exclusive Rheingau-Riesling wines. The main route is about 100 km. (62 miles) long, but there is an alternative route, exactly following the course of the Rhine, which is only half the distance. The vineyard scenery is interspersed with churches, monasteries and castles, not to mention the inviting wine-tasting cellars. Information from *Hessischer Fremdenverkehrsverband,* Abraham-Lincoln-Str. 38, 6200 Wiesbaden.

EXCURSIONS. City sightseeing tours can be arranged in most of the larger towns, usually with English guides. Ask at local tourist offices for details. There are also various excursions into the areas around each of the towns. Again the tourist offices will make suggestions or provide details of bus or train tours. These day outings take in picturesque villages, castles, nature parks, and special events, such as theater festivals. A novelty of Rüdesheim is an excursion through the vineyards by the *Winzerexpress,* a mini-train departing daily in summer from the Oberstrasse.

NATURE PARKS. Over 40% of the region is forested, and there are a total of 60 nature reserves, and 524 protected areas of countryside. There are nine National Parks, the largest being the Naturpark Bergstrasse-Odenwald which stretches across to Bavaria in the east and Baden-Württemberg in the south. The others are Naturpark Hochtaunus; Naturpark Hessischer Spessart; Naturpark Rhein-Taunus; Naturpark Habichtswald; Naturpark Meissner-Kaufunger Wald; Naturpark Hoher Vogelsberg; Naturpark Hessische Rhön; and Naturpark Diemelsee. There are well-marked hiking trails, parking lots, and tourist and sports facilities in all parks.

SPORTS. **Tennis** courts and swimming abound. **Golf** links at Kronberg, Kassel, Bad Homburg, Bad Nauheim, Bad Wildungen and Hanau. Wiesbaden has an 8-hole course (Chausseehaus) and an 18-hole (Dotzheim-Nerotal). Many facilities for **horseback riding** especially at Landgut Ebental, Rüdesheim, on Shetland, Bosnian and Haflinger ponies. Wiesbaden has two stables, Bad Homburg three; riding and jumping meet at the Biebrich Palace park at Whitsun. Picturesque **cycling** routes through the Taunus are detailed in a brochure from the Hochtaunus Tourist Office, Louisenstr. 86, Bad Homburg.

Sailing and **rowing** on the artificial Eder Lake and on the Rhine in Rheingau. **Water-skiing** and **canoeing** on the Main at Hanau. **Kayaking** on the rivers Eder, Fulda, Weser and Diemel, and especially scenic and not difficult on the Lahn from Marburg to the Rhine (177 km./110 miles, slow current, about a week). Other water sports on the Weser at Bad Karlshafen. **Gliding** and **hang-gliding** at Fulda (Aero-Club Rhön), Dornberg near Kassel, and around Giessen.

Swimming. All the main towns have indoor and outdoor pools. The largest swimming and fitness centers are the *Taunus Therme* in Bad Homburg and the *Kurhessen Therme* in Kassel.

Hunting especially in northern Hesse, mostly for stag, roe deer and wild boar. **Fishing** in Eder Lake, around Waldeck and in Eder and Lahn rivers, primarily for pike, salmon, trout, eel, perch and tench. Permits for both these sports to be obtained in advance.

Skiing on Taunus (Grosser Feldberg), Rhön, Hoher Vogelsberg, Meissner and Waldeckisches Upland, where the main center is Willingen (3 ski lifts, 2 ski jumps, ski school); medium to easy terrains, particularly recommended for beginners and cross-country skiers.

Walking and hiking. The northern part of Hesse has abundant forest and woodland with short walks through the woods and along *naturpfad* (nature trails) or *Trimm-Dich* (keep-fit) paths, such as in the Vogelsberg Nature Park. The southern part of Hesse is also good walking country, particularly in the Odenwald Nature Park, which has over 90 marked hiking round-trips on over 4,000 km. (2,480 miles) of trails. A special feature of the Odenwald as of many of the Nature Parks in Hesse, are the circular hiking tours which lead off from numerous parking lots, enabling you to drive to the area of choice and then set off on your walk. You can walk on your own, without luggage, through the Bergstrasse-Odenwald nature reserve under the *Wandern Ohne Gepäck* arrangement which includes bed and breakfast en route. Information available from *Touristikbüro Bergstrasse/Odenwald,* Postfach 3131, 6140 Bensheim–Auerbach.

The tourist offices in most of the larger towns have lists available, describing local walking routes of varying degrees of difficulty. The Hochtaunus, Hesse's largest nature park, also has many hiking routes. For full details, plus an annotated hiking map, write to the Hochtaunuskreis, Kreisverwaltung, Louisenstr. 86, 6380 Bad Homburg, or inquire at the Bad Homburg tourist office.

CASTLED WESTPHALIA

The Forge of Germany

Westphalia consists approximately of that territory lying between the rivers Weser, to the east, and Rhine, to the west, the whole located northwest of the city of Kassel. It contains both some of the most lovely country in Germany, and some of the most heavily industrialized. The area is perhaps best known for ham, supremely good here due to the superabundance of oak forests whose acorns provide the perfect raw material for pigs to convert into magnificent ham and bacon. Münsterland, in the northwest of Westphalia, a region dotted with superb castles, and the hilly Teutoburger Wald and Lippisches Bergland north of it, are the principal farming areas. Yet between the rivers Lippe and Ruhr—a name synonymous with heavy industry the world over—much of Germany's most important industrial concerns are concentrated.

Exploring Westphalia

However, our exploration of Westphalia begins in the southernmost tip of the province, the Sauerland, the "land of a thousand hills": something of a misnomer, as it consists of a succession of green plateaus and deep valleys. Nonetheless, it offers a great contrast to the smoking chimneys of the Ruhr, less than two hours' drive away. Its thick forests embrace some of the quietest vacation spots in all Germany, many of its rivers have been dammed into artificial lakes, its undersoil is hollowed by huge stalactite caves and its small towns trace their history into the early Middle Ages.

Entering Sauerland west of Kassel you first come to Brilon, a winter and summer resort with the nearby Diemel artificial lake. Less than 32 km. (20 miles) south of Brilon is the village of Winterberg, the leading winter sports center in Westphalia, located on the slopes of Kahler Asten whose 842 meters (2,760 feet) make it the highest mountain in Westphalia. On the other side of Kahler Asten, tiny Alt-Astenberg, the highest village in northwestern Germany, is also well known to skiers. In the spa town of Bad Berleburg, in the vicinity, you may visit the 18th-century castle belonging to the Princes of Sayn-Wittgenstein, the facade of which is coated with cut stones, many of them semi-precious, encrusted in the wall.

Further south is Siegen, the center of Siegerland, birthplace of Peter Paul Rubens, whose parents lived here as refugees, and the former residence of the Princes of Nassau-Orange, whose bodies rest in their crypt in the Lower Castle. The Upper Castle contains works by Rubens, along with a 2,000-year-old iron melting furnace. Less than 64 km. (40 miles) south of Siegen you can reach Limburg in Hesse and the Frankfurt–Köln autobahn. North of Siegen is Attendorn with its Sauerland Cathedral and several lakes in the middle of the Ebbegebirge Nature Park, Schnellenberg Castle and the huge Atta stalactite cave in the vicinity; Altena with its castle overlooking the Lenne river; and the old streets, towers, and fortifications of Arnsberg, called "the pearl of Sauerland." East of Arnsberg lies Meschede, with a Carolingian crypt in the parish church and the Henne Dam nearby, from where the circular tour of the Sauerland leads back to Brilon.

Teutoburg Forest

Paderborn, the gate to the Teutoburger Wald, or Forest, can best be reached from Kassel via Warburg in the Diemel valley, or from the autobahn A44, Kassel–Dortmund, exit Wünnenberg–Haaren. Warburg, a small town, once a member of the Hanseatic League, has preserved some of its medieval fortifications, houses and churches. Paderborn is a city with a long history; here Charlemagne met Pope Leo III in 799 and Paderborn has been a bishopric since 805. The first cathedral was built by Charlemagne in the 8th century, but the present monumental structure with the famous Paradiespforte (Paradise Portal) dates from the 11th–13th centuries with numerous tombs of the Bishops and Prince-Bishops of Paderborn in the cloisters. Other main sights include the Renaissance Rathaus, dating from 1613–16; half-timbered houses from about the same period; the Diözesanmuseum (Diocesan Museum) containing medieval ecclesiastical art, including the *Imad Madonna* from about 1060; the Museum der Kaiserpfalz (Museum of the Imperial Palace), at the cathedral, a reconstructed 11th-century palatial complex, with exhibits of the archeological finds, including ceramics and tools from the Stone Age to the 19th century, glass, metal, coins, jewelry and Carolingian murals; and the Museum für Stadtgeschichte (City History Museum) with prehistoric and early historical finds from Paderborn and southeast Westphalia—frescos, paintings, wood-carvings, sketches, old tools and implements, and coins.

Nearby to the east is Bad Driburg, an elegant spa set among thickly wooded parks, where you can see the ruined Saxon fortress of Burg Iburg, and Burg Dringenberg, the former summer residence of the Prince-Bishops of Paderborn.

The road north from Paderborn takes you to the Teutoburg Forest. Passing through the spas of Bad Lippspringe and Bad Meinberg, we come to Detmold, in the region known as Lippe. Detmold has a picturesque old town center and is a good starting point for trips into the rolling country of the Lippisches Land and the Ravensberger Land, filled with traces of centuries of habitation running all the way back to prehistoric times—which accounts for the wealth of Stone Age, Bronze Age and Iron Age relics in the Lippisches Landesmuseum of Detmold. There is also the Westfälisches Freilicht Museum, an openair museum containing 65 historical buildings in period settings, and the sumptuous renaissance Residenzschloss royal palace, a former moated castle, seat of the Counts and Princes of Lippe since the 16th century. In the vicinity, near the town of Horn (about 11 km./seven miles from Detmold), are the famous Extern Stones, carrying an early Romanesque bas-relief of the Descent from the Cross, while in Berlebeck, only 15 minutes' bus ride away, is Europe's largest eagle and birds of prey observation station (*Greifvogelwarte*) with over 85 different species. Even closer to Detmold (six km./four miles), high on a mountain, is the colossal monument to Arminius, or Hermann, the hero of early German history, who defeated the Romans in this area in A.D. 9 and drove them from Germany. From the monument there is also an excellent view over the surrounding region; nearby are the walls of an old Germanic fort. Both these localities are only a few kilometers from each other and are within easy reach from Paderborn (about 26 km./16 miles). Also near Detmold are several small towns, such as Lemgo, Blomberg, Schwalenberg, which have preserved their medieval aspect.

The road continues through Bielefeld, whose industrial nature is symbolized by the pipe-smoking figure of the Linenweaver's Fountain, and with Sparrenberg Castle, as well as with several interesting buildings in the old town section; then to Halle, with its steep-roofed, half-timbered old houses and the Tatenhausen water castle. From Halle you can either continue in the same direction through the scenic Teutoburger Wald and then descend west to Münster, or you can cut across a tongue of Lower Saxony perhaps visiting Osnabrück. Embarking on the latter course you come close to the northern border of Westphalia at Lübbecke—with its fine 16th-century town hall, its 14th-century St. Andrew's church and other old buildings—and at Minden. An unusual spectacle in this old Hanseatic city is one stream crossing another on a bridge.

From Minden you can pay a visit to one of the chief sights of the region, a natural geological exhibit—the Westphalian Gap (Porta Westfalica), through which the Weser, in prehistoric times, broke through the mountain barrier northward, leaving to this day the traces of this revolution of nature. A remarkable view through the Gap is provided from the monument of Kaiser Wilhelm on one of its flanking hills and from the Bismarck statue on another hill across the river.

The district of Minden-Lübbecke has over 30 wind- and water-mills dotted around the area. They have been restored and a few, which are open to the public, are operating again. There are also an extraordinarily wide variety of types of mill, among them the classical "Holland" windmill with canvas sails, typical German "Bock-" mills made entirely out of wood and standing on a pedestal, some horse-powered, mills built from roof-tiles, and mills with thatched roofs. The water-mills stand on "Sieks", small valley-arms on the slopes of the Weser-Wiehengebirge heights, which are criss-crossed with streams, as well as on the larger rivers, such as the Werre, Aue, Gehle and Grossen Diekfluss. All the mills of the region are under national conservation orders and are being constantly renovated and put back into operation. In some, there are bakeries attached and you can sample bread baked by age-old methods with tea or coffee served in the openair in the mill grounds. In others, you can even try your own hand at bread-baking. A trip round windmill country by road is well worthwhile and a marked route can be obtained from the Minden Tourist Office, who also arrange special weekend packages in the area in cooperation with good hotels en route. Special tours of the operational mills are available and can be arranged by telephoning the relevant windmill caretaker. Phone numbers and addresses from the Minden Tourist Office.

To the southwest are Bad Oeynhausen, a pleasant spa with a casino, and Herford, with its beautiful medieval buildings, including the 13th-century Minster, and several 14th-century churches. Another spa lies east of the main road after we pass Herford, Bad Salzuflen, with its large Kurpark, 16th-century Rathaus (Town Hall), half-timbered houses, restaurants, numerous pensions and small hotels.

Southwest of the Teutoberg Forest is the broad plain of Münsterland, a region of moated castles and old manors, and of fertile countryside with red brick wide-gabled farm houses. Münster itself, the center of this region, can be reached from Paderborn direct, or from Bielefeld, Halle, and Osnabrück.

Münster and Environs

Münster, the regional capital and a bishopric for more than 1,100 years, has an old, medieval center. Together with Osnabrück it was host to the treaty of Westphalia, which ended the Thirty Years War in 1648. The period portraits of the treaty signers can be seen in the Peace Hall of the Gothic Rathaus, faithfully reconstructed after World War II. The Romanesque cathedral has a hall with big 13th-century carved figures of the apostles and saints and an astronomical clock with a Glockenspiel playing at noon. The Gothic St. Lamberti Church with interesting sculptures, the arch-windowed and arcaded houses in Prinzipalmarkt and several moated castles in the vicinity, among them particularly Burg Vischering in Lüdinghausen (about 29 km./18 miles away) and Wasserschloss Rüschhaus (eight km./five miles), are other top sights. The city has also a lively cultural life—the Westphalian University is here, housed in the Baroque residence palace of the former prince-bishops—and there are frequent theatrical and musical performances in the city theater.

There are four museums in Münster worth visiting: the Westfälisches Landesmuseum für Kunst und Kulturgeschichte (Provincial Museum of Art and Cultural History), with a good collection of medieval and modern art, displays of regional history and a library; the Westfälisches Landesmuseum für Vor- und Frühgeschichte (Provincial Museum for Prehistoric and Early History); the Westfälische Museum fur Naturkinde und Planetarium (Natural History Museum and Planetarium); and the Mühlenhof-Freilicht Museum, an openair museum with all kinds of historic windmills, early corn-grinding equipment, blacksmith's workshop, bakery, etc.

The latter two are both located at Aasee Lake recreation park, where you will also find the municipal zoo, the most modern of its kind in Germany, with a dolphinarium.

Münster is a good center for visits to the picturesque places in which this region abounds: Freckenhorst, to the southeast, where there is a fine medieval Romanesque church; to the northwest, Burgsteinfurt, with an important moated castle; Rheine, for St. Anthony's basilica; and west to Coesfeld, a Hanseatic city with its old walls and gates still standing; Borken with a 12th-century tower and the 15th-century Church of the Holy Ghost, among others, and Bocholt, an important center for more than 1,000 years, with many interesting buildings, including the 17th-century Rathaus, in the Renaissance style.

Münsterland is known for its abundance of castles, fortresses and particularly for its Wasserschlösse (moated castles). Originally, the moated castles were simple brick affairs. They then spread out into ponderous and imposing buildings of which there are many still extant.

One of the most beautiful castles of Münsterland, only a few kilometers from the Dutch border, is Anholt. It dates back to 1178 and belongs to the family of the Princes of Salm-Salm. The castle is now a museum and, above all, a hotel and restaurant of high standard. There is a valuable collection of paintings, including works by Rembrandt, while the park is landscaped rather like that of an English stately home.

Burg Vischerung is one of the oldest castles in the Münsterland and residence of the Droste zu Vischering family. Founded in 1270 by Bishop Gerhard von der Mark to secure his sovereign rights against the lords of Lüdinghausen, it was a mighty bastion. In spite of periodic destruction by fire Burg Vischering is still splendid, with a main building that is protected by a complicated system of ramparts and ditches. It contains the Münsterland Museum; concerts are given in the Rittersaal, or Knights' Hall. Throughout the Münsterland there are many open-air theaters.

At Steinfurt, the castle is a magnificent piece of architecture, built for the Princes of Bentheim-Steinfurt. The various sections date mainly from the 16th to 18th centuries, while the Romanesque castle chapel is from the 12th century and the Rittersaal from the 13th. The large park and gardens were laid out in the 18th century.

Southwest of Münster, reached via Lüdinghausen, is Nordkirchen, with its 18th-century moated-castle, the "Versailles of Westphalia." One of the most important Baroque structures in the region, its history dates back as far as the 14th century, when the site was a fortress to protect the bishopric of Münster. The castle itself is on an island with an adjacent formal garden to the west designed very much in the manner of those at Versailles. The building now houses the State Financial College, but the interiors are still open for visiting on Sundays.

Southeast is Soest, a medieval Hanseatic city with preserved walls and gates, among them the massive Osthofentor, containing a notable collection of weapons. The mighty tower of the Romanesque St. Patroclus Church was used not only for ecclesiastical purposes but served also as the armory for Soest citizens. St. Peter's Church, from the same period, contains important 13th-century murals. In the Gothic Wiesenkirche is a 16th-century stained glass window representing the Last Supper—with the menu composed of Westphalian ham, pumpernickel, and beer. The Burghofsmuseum (City History Museum) is housed in a 16th-century patrician house. The city also boasts the "Roman" house, which in fact dates only from 1200. South of Soest is Möhne Dam on the Ruhr river in the Arnsberger Forest nature park—a favorite recreation and excursion spot—on the northern approaches to Sauerland. West are the chimney forests of the Ruhr.

Industrial Cities

Dortmund is the largest city of Westphalia and as befits an industrial center, takes pride in its modern achievements rather than in those of the past. It is proudest of all of its tall TV tower with a rotating restaurant and magnificent view, and of the Westfalenhalle, the largest congress and sports hall in Europe, an oval building that appears from the outside to be made exclusively of glass, and which has seating for 23,000 persons. Dortmund is the greatest brewing center in Europe—and also turns out liqueurs. The industry is of respectable antiquity: St. Mary's Church has a medieval drawing of a man drinking from a cask of beer. The Ostwall Museum has a fine collection of modern German artists. There is also the Museum für Naturkunde (Natural History Museum), with valuable collections of zoological, geological and mineral exhibits, the Museum für Kunst und Kulturgeschichte (City Museum for Art and Culture), and the ruins of the medieval Hohensyburg castle above the Lenne and Ruhr rivers, on the site of a Saxon fortress dating back to 775.

Bochum is an important center of mining, steelworks, and of the automobile, machine, chemical and electronic industries, and home of the Ruhrland University. The city is characterized by the heavy solid mass of its modern city hall, but it is not completely without reminders of the past. The Evangelical Church in Bochum-Stiepel contains some first-rate medieval frescos. Bochum also harbors in its Bergbau Museum a unique exhibit, a model of a coal mine. In addition, the Planetarium and the Institute for Space Research are worth visiting. The grimness sometimes characteristic of industrial cities is here relieved by four major parks, of which the Stadtpark is the largest.

South of Bochum is Hagen, more industry and a nice location on the northern slopes of Sauerland, while to the north is smaller Recklinghausen, known particularly for its annual Ruhr Festival featuring orchestras, opera companies and theatrical groups from all over Germany as well as art exhibitions. It also has the Ikonenmuseum (Icon Museum), the only one of its kind in western Europe.

Gelsenkirchen is the second-largest city in Westphalia, one of the greatest industrial centers in the world and located next door to Essen in Northern Rhineland. But Gelsenkirchen is also known for its green parks, including the Ruhr Zoo, and several castles in the suburbs, for the quality of its musical and theatrical performances, and for the fact that it possesses two of the best horserace tracks in Germany. It is approximately one hour on the autobahn from Köln airport and less than half an hour from Düsseldorf.

PRACTICAL INFORMATION FOR WESTPHALIA

TELEPHONES. We have given telephone codes for all the towns and villages in the hotel and restaurant lists that follow. These codes need only be used when calling from outside the town or village concerned.

HOTELS AND RESTAURANTS. Farmhouse holidays are particularly popular in this region. Details from the respective tourist offices or the regional Westphalian office in Dortmund. Westphalian hams sometimes weigh as much as 33 pounds, and for breakfast a huge slice of it is served on a wooden board with rich dark pumpernickel which has been baked 20 hours, and a glass of strong *Steinhäger Schnaps* (juniper brandy). Bacon, as much in favor as ham, is served with giant beans and a good thick gravy. *Pfefferpotthast* is a deliciously spicy dish of pieces of beef boiled with bay leaves, cloves and onions, mixed with breadcrumbs and spiced with peppercorns.

Münster, the capital of Westphalia, has an equally highly seasoned stew of offal called *Töttchen,* and in Soest you must try the similar *Wamme* which must be consumed with *Braune Ecke,* a rye bread roll. A dish to look out for in the Teutoburg Forest area is *Pickert,* a dough made of grated potatoes and buckwheat flour and fried in a skillet. Another Westphalian specialty is a type of sausage baked in dough.

Anholt *Parkhotel Wasserburg Anholt* (E) Kleverstrasse (02874–2044). Beautiful castle-hotel located in Isselburg in the flatlands close to the Dutch border. Surrounded by a wide moat with formal garden, trees and lawns the castle dates back to the 12th century. Restored after World War II damage with original materials. Interiors are feudal with splendid tapestries and lovely porcelain. 29 rooms, all elegant and atmospheric, 1 suite. Restaurant with excellent cuisine and annual speciality weeks. Lakeside terrace in summer. AE, DC, MC.

Attendorn. In Sauerland. *Burghotel Schellenberg* (M), Am Biggesee (02722–6940). 45 rooms, most with bath. A castle hotel dating from the 13th century. Tennis, riding, hunting, fishing; medieval *Rittersaal* restaurant. AE, DC, MC. *Landhotel Struck* (I), Repetalstr. 245 (02721–1523). 28 rooms all with bath and W.C. In Niederhelden. Rustic style with good restaurant; special weekly terms. DC.

Bad Driburg. *Althaus Parkhotel* (M), Caspar-Heinrich-Str. 17 (05253–2088). 34 rooms. MC. *Gräfliches Kurhaus* (M), Am Bad 9 (05253–841). 135 rooms. In quiet Kurpark, an elegant 18th-century building with half-timbered facades; restaurant, outdoor café, horseback riding, golf. MC.

Bad Salzuflen. *Lippischer Hof* (M), Mauerstr. 1a (05222–3503). 70 rooms. *Maritim Staatsbad* (M), Parkstr. 53 (05222–1451). 190 rooms. Indoor pool, excellent restaurant. DC, MC. *Schwaghof* (M), Schwaghof 1

(05222–1485). 84 rooms. Three km. (two miles) outside town, very quietly located; good food. AE, DC, MC, V.

Bochum. *Am Südpark* (M), Höntroperstr. 103 (02327–73162). 20 rooms, all with bath. In nearby Wattenscheid, by the park's edge; good restaurant. DC. *Arcade* (M), Universitätstr. 3 (0234–33311). 168 rooms. At the main station. *Novotel* (M), Stationring 22 (0234–594041). 118 rooms. Heated pool, good-value restaurant. AE, DC, MC, V. *Plaza Hotel* (M), Hellweg 20 (0234–13085). 36 rooms, all with radio, T.V., beverage refrigerator. Near main station; grill specialties. DC, MC. *Savoy* (M), Huestr. 11 (0234–60886). 58 rooms with bath or shower. No restaurant. AE, DC, MC, V.

Restaurants. *Alt Nürnberg* (E), Königsallee 16 (0234–311698). Very good service. AE, DC, MC. *Bagatelle* (E), Leithstr. 11 (02327–35665). In Wattenscheid. Fine cuisine, good value. DC, MC, V. *Bochumer Brauhaus* (M), Rathausplatz 5 (0234–14215). Belonging to the brewery of that name; fine food. *Stammhaus Fiege* (M), Bongardstr. 23 (0234–12643). Old brewery with varied menu from hearty to *nouvelle cuisine*. *Wendenroth* (M), Castroper Str. 178 (0234–590011). Located close to the planetarium; good value. MC.

Detmold. *Burghotel Blomberg* (M), in der Burg (05235–2071). 22 rooms all with bath. 21 km. (13 miles) east of town in Blomberg, located in part of the former castle of the Counts of Lippe. Swimming pool, sauna, outdoor restaurant. V. *Detmolder Hof* (M), Lange Str. 19 (05231–28244). AE, DC, MC, V. *Lippischer Hof* (M), Allee 2 (05231–31041). 16th-century cavalier's house. AE, DC, MC, V. *Kanne* (I), Paderborner Str. 155 (05231–47212). On outskirts at Berlebeck. DC. *Zur Forelle* (I), Paderborner Str. 131 (05231–4922). Also at Berlebeck.

Restaurant. *Hirschsprung* (E), Paderbornerstr. 212 (05231–4911). In Berlebeck suburb. Family establishment in hunting-lodge style. AE, MC.

Dortmund. *Parkhotel Westfalenhalle* (E), Strobelallee 41 (0231–120 4245). 107 rooms, all with bath. Good restaurant. AE, DC, MC, V. *Römischer Kaiser* (E), Olpe 2 (0231–54321). 137 rooms. AE, DC, MC, V. *Parkhotel-Wittenkindshof* (E), Westfalendamm 270 (0231–596081). 65 rooms, all with bath. AE, DC, MC, V. *Landhaus Syburg* (M), Westhofener Str. 1 (0231–774471). 21 rooms. Central, quiet and comfortable. DC, MC, V. *Novotel* (M), Brennaborstr. 2 (0231–65485). 104 rooms. Swimming pool. AE, DC, MC, V. *Romantik Hotel Lennhof* (M), Menglinghäuser Str. 20 (0231–75726). 39 rooms. In Barop suburb. 150-year-old house in idyllic surroundings; atmospheric and notable restaurant (0231–75726). MC, V. *Esplanade* (I), Bornstr. 4 (0231–528931). 48 rooms. AE, DC, MC, V.

Restaurants. *Alt Horde* (E), Benninghofer Str. 4 (0231–414184). Fine food in local-style setting. *Grüner Baum* (M), Lübkestr. 9 (0231–430255). *Hövelpforte* (M), Hoher Wall 5 (0231–142803). AE. *Krone* (M), Alter Markt 10 (0231–527548). AE, DC, MC.

Gelsenkirchen-Buer. *Maritim* (E), Stadtgarten 1 (0209–15951). 265 rooms and apartments. Sauna, swimming pool, nightclub, bars; first-class service, fresh, imaginative food in *Parkrestaurant,* accent on business not tourism. DC. MC, V.

Restaurant. *Mövenpick-Schloss Berge* (M), Adenauer Allee 103 (0209–59958). A moated castle. Indoor and outdoor restaurant; tavern and café.

Minden. *Exquisit* (M), In den Bärenkämpen 2a (0571–43055). 81 beds. Swimming pool, sauna. AE, MC. *Schloss Petershagen* (M), Schlossstr. 5 (05707–346). 11 rooms. About 16 km. (ten miles) out in Petershagen on the banks of the Weser. Sports facilities, restaurant. *Bad Minden* (I), Portastr. 36 (0571–51049). 64 beds. Sauna. AE, DC, MC. *Victoria* (I), Markt 13 (0571–22240). 65 beds. Sauna, no restaurant. AE, DC, MC, V.

Restaurant. *Ratskeller*, Am Markt 1 (0571–25800). Two sections to choose from: one, an expensive wine restaurant; the other an atmospheric, moderate, beer tavern. AE, DC, MC.

Münster. *Kaiserhof* (E), Bahnhofstr. 14 (0251–40059). 109 rooms all with bath. Café but no restaurant. AE, DC, MC. *Parkotel Schloss Hohenfeld* (E), Dingbänger Weg 400 (02534–7031), in Roxel suburb. Former castle in its own grounds. Modern; indoor pool, sauna; bikes for hire. International restaurant. *Waldhotel Krautkämer* (E), Zum Hiltruper See 173 (0251–8050). 85 rooms. Beautifully-located luxury hotel with all facilities. v. *Conti* (M), Berliner Platz 2a (0251–40444). 65 rooms. At the main station; no restaurant. AE, DC, MC, V. *Romantik-Hotel-Hof Zur Linde* (M), Handorfer Werseufer 1 (0251–325002). In Handorf section. Annexe (E). 31 rooms, all with bath. Building dates from 1661 with antique furnishings. Game specialties in the fine restaurant. Boats for hire. *Schloss Wilkinghege* (M), Steinfurterstr. 374 (0251–213045). 40 rooms. Castle-hotel in park-like surroundings, with castle tavern and restaurant of note. MC. *Überwasserhof* (M), Überwasserstr. 3 (0251–40630). Picturesque. DC, MC. *Horstmann* (I), Windhorststr. 12 (0251–47077). 27 rooms all with bath. No restaurant.

Restaurants. *Kleines Restaurant im Oerschen Hof* (E), Königsstr. 42 (0251–42061). High-class cuisine in Münster's number one gourmet restaurant. *Pinkus Muller* (M), Kreuzstr. 4 (0251–45151). Only remaining "Altbier" tavern in town brewing and serving traditional Münsterland "Müller's Alt" and "Pinkus Pils" strong dark beer.

Paderborn. *Arosa* (M), Westernmauer 38 (05251–2000). 100 rooms all with bath. Swimming pool, sauna. AE, DC, MC, V. *Hotel Zur Mühle* (M), Mühlenstr. 2 (05251–23026). With exclusive restaurant. DC, MC. *Krawinkel* (I), Karlsplatz (05251–23663). *Südhotel* (I), Borchenerstr. 23 (05251–7805). AE, DC.

Restaurants. *Schweizer Haus* (E), Warburger Str. 99 (05251–61961). *Ratskeller* (M), Rathauspl. (05251–25753). DC, V.

Recklinghausen. *Barbarossahotel* (M), Löhrhof 8 (02361–25071). 58 rooms. Swimming pool. AE, DC, MC, V. *Parkhotel "Die Engelburg"* (M), Augustinessen Str. 10 (02361–25066). 31 rooms all with bath. Small, comfortable and quiet; fine food in atmospheric tavern. *Wüller* (I), Hammer Str. 1 (02361–41051). 65 rooms, most with bath or shower. Swimming pool. AE.

Restaurants. *Auerbach's Keller* (M), Heilig-Geist-Str. 3 (02361–182818). Open round the clock. *Die Engelsburg* (E), Augustinessen Str. 10. (02361–25066). In the hotel of the same name.

Schieder-Schwalenberg. *Schlosshotel Burg Schwalenberg* (M), auf der Schwalenburg (05284–5167). 16 rooms. Founded in 1231, combines modern comfort with romantic medieval decor. Lovely location. AE, V.

Soest. *Im Wilden Mann* (E), Am Markt 11 (02921–15071). "Romantik Hotel." In the center of town, a picturesque half-timbered house with an original beer parlor and elegant restaurant specializing in fish and game dishes as well as traditional Westphalian recipes. Reservations essential as hotel is small with only 11 beds. AE, DC, MC, V. *Andernach zur Börse* (M), Thomästr. 31 (02921–4019). 23 rooms. Good food in its colorful restaurant. *Haus zur Börde* (M), Nöttenstr. 1 (02921–13544). 8 rooms.

Restaurants. *Pilgrim Haus Anno 1304* (M), Jakobstr. 75 (02921–1828). Westphalia's oldest hostelry. Atmospheric. 10 rooms.

Willingen. Prominent winter sports resort, with several small, moderate hotels. *Hotel Der Sauerland Stern* (E), Kneippweg (05632–6041). 500 rooms, all amenities. AE, DC, MC, V. *Romantik-Hotel-Stryckhaus* (M), Mühlenkopfstr. 12 (05632–6033). 66 rooms, all with bath. Fine restaurant. AE, DC, MC, V.

CAMPING AND YOUTH HOSTELS. There is a good selection of campsites throughout the region, although there are more in the Teutoburger Forest and Tecklenburger Land than in Münsterland. The Sauerland offers a large variety of sites, but many are up to 80 percent full with long-term campers, while others are not of a high standard. Some of the best in this area are at Attendorn-Biggesee (on the lake), Delecke-Möhnesee (at the reservoir), Warstein in the Arnsberger Forest, and Meschede-Mielinghausen. There are Youth Hostels and campsites both in the countryside and around the cities and towns. Details from the local tourist offices.

TOURIST INFORMATION. The regional tourist office for Westphalia is *Landesverkehrsverein Westfalen,* 4 Balkerstr., 4600 **Dortmund.** Local offices as follows: **Bad Driburg,** Verkehrsamt, Lange Strasse 140, 3490 Bad Driburg (05252–88180). **Bad Salzuflen,** Kur- und Verkehrsverein, Parkstr. 20, 4902 Bad Salzuflen (05222–183205). **Bochum,** Verkehrsverein, 1 Kurt Schumacher Platz, 4630 Bochum (0234–13031). **Detmold,** Verkehrsamt, Rathaus, Lange Strasse, 4930 Detmold (05231–77328). **Dortmund,** Verkehrsverein, 1 Königswall 18, 4600 Dortmund (0231–54222174). **Minden,** Verkehrsamt, Ritterstr. 31, 4950 Minden (0571–89385). **Münster,** Verkehrsverein, Berliner Platz 22, 4400 Münster (0251–40495). **Paderborn,** Verkehrsverein, Marienplatz 2a, 4790 Paderborn (05251–26461). **Recklinghausen,** Stadtverwaltung, Rathaus, 4350 Recklinghausen (02361–5871). **Soest,** Verkehrsamt, Am Seel 5, 4770 Soest (02921–103323). **Willingen,** Kurverwaltung, Korbacher Str. 10, 3542 Willingen (05632–6023).

HOW TO GET AROUND. By air. The main international airports are Dortmund for the west of the region and the Ruhr area; Hannover for the northeast and the Münsterland; as well as Düsseldorf and Frankfurt. There are regular internal flights from Frankfurt and Munich to the airfield at Arden near Paderborn. Further, the new "Lufthansa's Airport Express" train now provides a regular direct rail service between Frankfurt and Düsseldorf airports complementing the already existing air service. It runs four times a day both ways and also links Bonn and Köln.

Charter flights from all over the world as well as inland flights from Frankfurt land at the domestic airport of Münster-Osnabrück in Greven.

By train. Owing to close proximity to the industrial Ruhr, the whole of Westphalia is served by a first-rate rail network. Dortmund, Paderborn, Bielefeld, Kassel, Gelsenkirchen, Bottrop, Munster and Recklinghausen all have excellent rail connections into the region. InterCity express trains stop at Dortmund, Bochum, Münster, Hamm and Minden. Bochum and Dortmund are linked by S-Bahn with Essen, Duisberg and Düsseldorf.

By car. For excursions by car, the regional tourist office in Dortmund (Balkenstr. 4, 4600 Dortmund) describes nine scenic routes in their magazine *Westfalen, Münsterland, Tecklenburger Land: Journal.* In addition, there is also the Westfälische Mühlenstrasse (Westphalian Mill Road). Information from the Minden tourist office.

By bus. Bus services are frequent in all parts of the region, with well-served terminuses in all the main cities. Several long distance bus lines (German Touring) traverse the region, too, such as the T91D linking Dortmund with Bochum and Düsseldorf (thence via Köln to Kehl on the French border and on to Barcelona); the T92 from Hamburg to Osnabrück, Münster, Duisburg and Düsseldorf (thence via Köln to Paris and Madrid); the T92B from Hannover to Bielefeld, Lippstadt, Soest and Remscheid (thence to Köln, Liège, Brussels, San Sebastián and Madrid); and the T92C. The T65 provides a direct bus service between Dortmund and London via the ferry at Zeebrugge or Oostende.

Full details from travel agents and tourist offices.

By boat. Dortmund, site of the largest canal port in Europe, provides direct links with other major European seaports. Steamer trips are arranged around the port as well as boat excursions to Henrichenburg ship lift. Passenger and pleasure boats also run services on the Dortmund-Ems Canal and the Datteln-Hamm Canal from May to October, departing from the landing stage bridge in Münster and from the north bank wharf in Hamm on the River Werse; on the Rhine-Herne Canal from Recklinghausen; also on the 20 lakes and reservoirs of the Münsterland, Weserbergland, Sauerland, Siegerland and Bergisches land.

By bike. Perhaps the most important and popular form of transport in the Westphalian Münsterland is the bicycle. The countryside around Münster is wide and open, interlaced by the characteristic hedges. Bicycles can be hired at 13 different railway stations in the Münsterland: Amelsbüren, Borken, Burgsteinfurt, Capelle, Coesfeld, Davensberg, Dülmen, Haltern, Handorf, Hiltrup, Lembeck, Maria Veen Münster itself and Rheine, and from rental agencies in most towns. Naturally, the main cities of Westphalia such as Dortmund, Duisburg, Bochum, Detmold, Paderborn, Soest and Willingen also have plenty of possibilities for hiring cycles, and you should inquire at the respective tourist offices. A map showing addresses and phone numbers of railway stations renting cycles, is available from the German Railways in Münster, Deutsche Bundesbahn, Bahnhofstr. 1, 4400 Münster. Tour suggestions and descriptions are available from the Regional Tourist Offices in Dortmund or Münster.

By post coach. Another charming means of transportation is the old romantic mailcoach along the 11 km. (seven miles) stretch linking the climatic health resorts of Nümbrecht and Wiehl in the Upper Bergisches Land. The vehicle seats nine passengers and is a replica of an Imperial mail coach built in 1871. It usually runs on Tuesdays, Thursdays and Saturdays and covers the distance in two hours. Further information can be obtained from the tourist offices in Wiehl and Nümbrecht.

EXCURSIONS. Local tourist offices organize many bus tours to the windmills, moated castles, parks, wild animal reserves and recreation areas throughout the region. Münster in particular has many interesting excursion destinations in the countryside surrounding it, as well as further afield to places of interest on the Dutch border. The tourist office has a selection of pre-arranged tours under the heading *Vor den Toren der Alten Stadt* (literally, "in front of the gates of the old city").

SPORTS. The most important sports' center of the region is the Westfalenhalle in Dortmund, the largest sport and multi-purpose hall in Europe, combining ice and roller skating rinks and with indoor tennis courts and riding school. Westphalia is particularly fond of **horseracing** and many international and national galloping and trotting events are scheduled especially in Gelsenkirchen, Dortmund, Recklinghausen (where the European World Championships are held on Hillerheide track), and riding tournaments in Dortmund, Münster, and Herborn. Bochum has a riding stadium. **Horseback riding** schools and facilities in Münster, Warendorf and several other localities. A full list of riding stables is available at the regional tourist office. **Golf** courses exist in Bochum, Dortmund, Lippetal, Bad Driburg, Münster, Neheim-Hüsten near Möhne lake, Recklinghausen, Bad Salzuflen and Burgsteinfurt. There are **tennis** courts in all spas and all larger cities.

There are **water sports,** including **sailing** and **sail-boarding, canoeing** and **rowing** on the Aasee lake in Münster, with its sailing school and boats for hire, on the Hiltruper See, and on the 20 or so reservoirs and man-made lakes of the Sauerland, including the large Möhnesee and Biggesee, as well as Diemel-, Henne-, Sorpe- and Beversee lakes.

Swimming in the many artificial lakes; in the swimming stadium and other pools of Dortmund; in the very modern pool at Wittenerstrasse in Bochum, and in numerous other pools scattered throughout the region. **Boat-trips** on the Weser and Mittellandkanal from Minden (Schlachtschleuse Lock) to Porta Westfalica, Vlotha and back; short trip lasts 40 mins, full trip 1½ hrs. There are also regular day-trips around the Biggesee from Olpe, Westphalia's largest man-made barrage dam.

The main **winter sports** are to be found in the Hochsauerland uplands and resorts include Brilon, Winterberg, Altastenberg, Neuastenberg, Fredeburg, Langewiese and Willingen, with between them some 40 ski jumps, 100 ski lifts, 1,600 km. (1,000 miles) of marked ski trails, 18 ski schools, etc. In the Eggegebirge hills near Bad Driburg are well-marked tracks for **cross-country skiing.** Full details from the Dortmund regional tourist office.

Gliding is available at Borkenberge near Haitern, Oerlinghausen near Bielefeld, Arnsberg, Greven, Dortmund, Hamm, Marl and Recklinghausen. Hot air **ballooning** at Ennigloh near Bünde and at Münster.

Walking. The countryside of the Münsterland, the Teutoberger Wald forest, and the "Lippische Schweiz" (or Lippisch Switzerland) around Heiligenkirchen are all good walking and hiking areas. In the fine nature parks of the woodland areas there is a dense network of marked hiking trails such as those of the Wiehengebirge, the northern part of the Teutoberger forest, and Arnsberger Wald forest, the Rothaargebirge, the Eggegebirge, or the Siebengebirge. There are also a good number of short (one to two hour) marked round-trip walking tours here.

There is a similar first-class network of trails and paths around Bad Driberg, also in the Eggegebirge region, a particularly interesting trek being the "Sachsenring" and "Steinbergrundweg", circular tour of about 20 km. (12 miles), or the "Eggeweg", which is part of the European long-distance trek from the North Sea to the Mediterranean. Information about these trails from the tourist office in Bad Driburg. Around Münster, too, you can enjoy pleasant hikes or walks along the paths on either side of the banks of the rivers Werse, Ems and Angel, and favourite starting points for walking in this region are Handorf, St. Mauritz Angelmodde and Wolbeck. For further information about walking and hiking contact either the regional tourist office in Dortmund, the Münsterland tourist office in Münster, or the local tourist or information office in the town in which you are staying.

FRANKFURT

Business as Usual

Frankfurt-am-Main, to give the city its full name, was transformed more radically than perhaps any other German city by the destruction and bombing of World War II. Before the war, Frankfurt was a charming, largely medieval town. A 20th-century Rip-van-Winkle, revisiting it today, would find it almost unrecognizable.

Massive allied bombing in March 1944 reduced much of the city to rubble. However, rather than restore the city to its original form, as happened in many other cities and towns throughout the country, it was decided to pull down much of what remained and rebuild it, as rapidly as possible, in an aggressively modern manner. The hope was that Frankfurt would be chosen as the new capital of Germany. In the event, it was Bonn that was selected, and the graceless modern city that Frankfurt had become has long since been a source of some embarrassment and civic blushes. However, only too well aware of the less-than-lovely modern Frankfurt, energetic efforts have lately been put in hand by the authorities to restore what little remains of the old city, the lavishly reconstructed 19th-century Opera House, reopened in 1984, being the most recent development.

Yet in many ways, Frankfurt would have made an excellent capital of the new Germany. Located in almost the dead center of the country, it has always been a major crossroads, and is now not only at the heart of the post-war autobahn system, but is a major air, ship and rail center. The super-modern airport is one of the biggest and busiest in Europe; there are five main-line railway stations, connecting the city with all parts of

Europe; and the three harbors—connecting with the mighty river Rhine—comprise the largest inland port in the country.

A crossroads always attracts trade, and this has been true of Frankfurt since the Romans first built a bridge across the Main here 2,000 years ago. The first customs house was built in the 11th century, providing a regular flow of trade taxes to the city coffers. By the 12th century the city was a major trading center, and the annual Summer Fair has been held ever since 1240. The Spring Fair is relatively new, dating only from 1330.

Trade brings finance houses, to provide credit and to arrange transactions of money for traders who do not want to carry cash. Following the example of the Flemish in Antwerp, the Frankfurt City Fathers set up their first Stock Exchange (Börse) in 1595. Banking became an important business and the oldest banks are still functioning today: Lauteren and Co., Hauck, and Bethmann. The Frankfurt Jewish community, though confined to a ghetto within the old town walls, was to produce some of the world's greatest financiers, including the Rothschilds, who opened their first bank in 1798. The bankers of Frankfurt played a part in the American Civil War when they financed the armies of the North at a time when Paris and London were helping the South. By one of the ironies of history, American bombs destroyed the Frankfurt Börse somewhat less than a century later. Today, Frankfurt is still the country's financial center and the city skyline is dominated by the skyscrapers of the major banks.

Trade always goes hand in hand with political power. In the 9th century, Charlemagne set up court here and subsequently the German Emperors of the Holy Roman Empire were elected and crowned here. The city was politically independent for several centuries until this special status was abolished by Napoleon's occupying army in 1805, but it was later re-established within the confines of the German Union, which had its first all-German Parliament in Frankfurt. The City Fathers fought a political battle with the Prussian Monarchy for supremacy of the united Germany, but failed to win, and in 1866 Frankfurt's free status was finally abolished for good.

The political power is gone, but a cultural power lingers on, a spirit of liberalism which has survived several wars. Even in the early days of Hitler's Third Reich, the city's major newspaper, the *Frankfurter Zeitung,* was a spearhead of resistance: sadly, it was also an early victim. Publishing has for centuries been important to Frankfurt, perhaps sparked off by Johann Gutenberg, the inventor of movable type, who set up shop here in 1454. Within decades, the city became the printing center of Europe and the Annual Book Fair is the largest of its kind in the world.

By an odd coincidence, Germany's greatest writer, Goethe, was born here. The remains of his house, lovingly restored after the last war, are now open to the public (see under Old Town). Frankfurt has for many years offered a Goethe Prize for Literature, which has been won by such eminent authors as Gerhart Hauptmann, Sigmund Freud, Albert Schweitzer and Thomas Mann.

Exploring Frankfurt

Frankfurt is not a tourist city: visitors usually have business here or are in transit for other destinations. Yet the city has a charm of its own, something that has survived the wholesale bombing and subsequent reconstruc-

FRANKFURT

0 miles ½

0 kilometers ½

Points of Interest

1 Alte Oper
2 Deutsches Architekturmuseum; Deutsches Filmmuseum; Deutsches Postmuseum
3 Dom (Cathedral)
4 Eschenheimer Turm
5 Fernmeldeturm
6 Historisches Museum
7 Goethe Haus und Goethemuseum
8 Hauptbahnhof
9 Hauptwache
10 Heinrich Hoffmann Museum
11 Katharinenkirche
12 Liebfrauenkirche
13 Liebieghaus
14 Leonhardskirche
15 Messe
16 Museum für Kunsthandwerk
17 Museum für Völkerkunde
18 Museum für Vor und Frühgeschichte (Karmeliterkloster)
19 Naturmuseum Senckenberg
20 Nikolaikirche
21 Paulskirche
22 Römer
23 Schauspielhaus
24 Städelsches Kunstinstitut und Städtische Galerie
25 Zoo

Pedestrian zone

tion work, something of the ancient spirit of Frankfurt. You may find it among the few streets that survived the war, or the painstaking reconstructions of major buildings, or—more simply and mysteriously—in one of the old teashops where Frankfurters still gather to read the newspapers and chew over a slice of cake. In addition, the city boasts some excellent museums, art galleries, and one of the best municipal theater companies in Germany.

The Old Town

The medieval town (Altstadt) in Alt Sachsenhausen was enclosed by a semi-circular wall on the north bank of the river. It was almost entirely destroyed during the last war, but some of the more interesting buildings have been carefully reconstructed with much of the original stone and iron work.

The most pleasant approach is from the west along Main Kai, separated from the river by a small, grassy park—it is here that many of the most important museums are sited, along the length of Schaumainkai or Museums Ufer. Just after the Eiserner Steg turn left into the cobbled square called Römerberg, dominated by the 13th-century Nikolaikirche: the tower is a reconstruction but some of the interior remains intact. Its forty-bell carillon rings out three times a day. Opposite the church is a group of three Gothic buildings, the Römer, for many years a symbol of Frankfurt. This has been the City Hall for over 500 years. Behind the church is the fine half-timbered Schwarzer Stern, and on the eastern side of the square, or Samstagsberg, are six painstakingly reconstructed 15th- and 16th-century houses. In the center of this almost completely restored square is a fine 17th-century fountain topped by a statue of Justice, one of four city fountains to have survived the bombing.

Beside the Nikolaikirche is the Historisches Museum, the History Museum. Here you can see a perfect scale model of the Old Town, complete with every street, house and church, and—on the floor above—the astonishing city silver. One piece in particular is worth examining, a vast table ornament in the shape of a ship, one meter high in solid silver, with a symbolic father at the helm, mother at the bow and two children trimming the gold-fringed sails. Carved across the waters is "Frankfurt als Freistadt," the free city.

Outside once more, you might take a little light refreshment before passing on east to the Dom (Cathedral). In the south west corner of the Römerberg is an original medieval inn. Half houses a traditional Frankfurt-style teashop, and the other a beer-hall and a restaurant. Schopenhauer, the philosopher, lived the last years of his life next door, in a house overlooking the river.

You will see the 90-meter (300-foot) red sandstone tower of the Cathedral of St. Bartholomew as soon as you leave the Römerhof. Built between the 13th and 15th centuries, it survived the bombs of the last war, along with some 14th-century carved pews and 15th-century murals, which had been bricked up in anticipation of disaster. These treasures now add dignity to an otherwise unremarkable interior. The German Emperors used to be crowned here in days gone by. One of the most interesting features of the tower is the view from the top. This is no longer open though you might get in during the low season.

Behind the cathedral is the Leinwandhaus (the old Cloth Hall), built in 1399 as a textile sample room for fairs. Later it became a court building and is now a small museum. Pass it on your right, and turn left towards Kurt-Schumacher Strasse, which will take you to the Karmeliter-kloster, faithfully reconstructed from pictures and plans of the original, which dated from the 14th and 15th centuries.

Now we turn left along Berlinerstrasse, passing the oval-topped Paulskirche, where the first all-German Parliament sat in 1848. A little further on is the oldest remaining building in the city, a 13th-century chapel once belonging to the palace constructed by Friedrich Barbarossa. Opposite stands the only wooded building to escape the British and American bombs, a fine half-timbered Renaissance house.

At the Kornmarkt, turn right and then left, which takes you onto the Grosser Hirschgraben, where the reconstruction of Goethe's house stands. Furnished and decorated in the 18th-century manner, it gives a good impression of how the great man's life-style might have been.

You are now outside the Old Town walls, and ready to embark on the next leg of your tour, which takes in the so-called New Town (Neustadt). If you are hungry, stop off at Stephan Weiss', a marvelous delicatessen two short blocks north, in Grosse Bockenheimerstrasse, and sample a *Zeppelinwurst* before continuing on your way.

The New Town

There are two possible routes now. Following one of them, you can walk east along the Zeil, the city's largest pedestrian zone, lined with one department store after another, and the site of the old cattle market, which leads you out of the New Town at Alfred-Brehm Platz to the entrance of the Zoologischer Garten (Frankfurt Zoo).

The Zoo is one of the chief attractions of Frankfurt, the oldest in Germany, except for that in Berlin. Its remarkable collection includes a Bears' Castle, an Exotarium (aquarium plus reptiles) and an aviary, reputedly the largest in Europe, where many of the birds can be seen in a natural setting. As is generally the case in Germany, the Zoo is a recreational center where animals are not the sole attraction. Others include a restaurant, a café, and afternoon concerts during the summer, while its Kleines Theater im Zoo offers plays.

The second route will take you northwards towards the Eschenheimer Turm, passing—at the northern end of the Rossmarkt—Frankfurt's original place of execution. It was here that Faust's Marguerite was put to death for infanticide.

Walking southwest, you pass the Alte Oper (Old Opera House) at Opernplatz, entirely renovated within the old walls, which were gutted during the war. The new complex contains conference halls, theaters and a cinema. Here you are also close to Frankfurt's financial center, the West End, where today over 365 international banks have their offices. The impressive office buildings which were built during the last 15 years are now dominated by the city's highest skyscrapers: the twin towers of the German Bank. Further south, along Neue Mainzer Strasse is the Municipal Theater (Schauspielhaus), which also contains an opera house: the productions here are first-class. A few minutes further south is the Untermainbrücke and the river.

For a quieter stroll, turn east at the Turm instead of west, and follow the parkway along Eschenheimer Anlage and Friedberger Anlage. There is little to see but everyday life in Frankfurt, which to many a visitor provides as interesting a time as the more sensational round of buildings and statues. When you come to the river, you will be well positioned to start a short visit to Sachsenhausen, which is just across the Obermainbrücke.

Sachsenhausen

Formerly a village separate from Frankfurt, Sachsenhausen is said to have been established by a colony of Saxons conquered by Charlemagne and resettled here. It is now largely a residential area and—having suffered far less from the war than the city itself—it contains much of authentic historical interest. It is, of course, more recent, mostly dating back less than 200 years, but there are pockets of 16th- and 17th-century houses, which give a fine impression of what the Old Town must have been like.

Once over the river, turn half-right along Frankensteiner Strasse, which leads into the old nightlife quarter around the eastern end of Schulstrasse. Here you will find a charming assortment of old and new, with nightclubs, discos and restaurants scattered among the half-timbered houses and narrow alleyways. You might take care to pick out a venue for the evening, returning after the theaters have closed. Then continue west along Kolb Strasse, past elegant 19th-century residential houses, into the busy shopping area of Schweizerstrasse. This is where many working Frankfurters live. There are several old inns where the specialty is apple cider, which the locals call *Apfelwein* (or *Ebbelwei* in dialect), a mild and highly distinctive brew.

At the north end of the Schweizerstrasse you arrive at the river again. If you have time, there is a pleasant walk along the Schaumainkai, where you can enjoy the river traffic and a view of the busier northern part of the city across the water. If you turn right and walk towards the Eiserner Steg (for pedestrians only) you'll soon come to the city's newest museum, the Museum für Kunsthandwerk (Museum of Applied Arts) at Schaumainkai 17, designed by American architect Richard Maier. Turning left at Schweizerstrasse you'll immediately pass the German Filmmuseum, while right next door is the German Architectural Museum, both occupying old houses. Further on you will see the Städel Art Institute, which contains a fine collection of paintings, including works by Dürer, Renoir, Monet and Vermeer, as well as Rembrandt, Rubens and other great masters.

A little further on is the charming 17th-century Liebieghaus, now administered by the Städel Institute to house their collection of classical, medieval and Renaissance sculpture. You can return to the northern bank of the river by way of the Friedens Brücke, which leads you, via Baseler Strasse, to the Main Station, in Frankfurt's West End.

The West End

From the Station (Hauptbahnhof) three avenues lead to central Frankfurt: Kaiserstrasse, Münchenerstrasse and Taunusstrasse. They are lined with shops, restaurants, strip clubs and cinemas, and once made up a lively and colorful district. Unfortunately, as in city playgrounds all over Europe, there is a rather desolate and seedy atmosphere here today, with blaring music and neon lights taking the place of the welcoming charm that once prevailed.

More interesting for the visitor on the lookout for something characteristic of Frankfurt, is to wander north along Friedrich-Ebert-Anlage to the Messe, a vast complex of exhibition halls where some of the world's greatest trade fairs are held. Apart from the two major fairs in spring and late summer, there are several important smaller ones, notably the Poultry Show in January, the Automobile Show in March, the Fur Fair at Easter and the Book Fair in early fall.

Further north still, along Senckenberg-Anlage, is the delightful Palmen Garten, one of the most complete botanical gardens in Europe. It includes a number of special collections—like the 2½-acre rock garden, the rose and rhododendron garden and a splendid cluster of tropical and semitropical greenhouses, which contain over 800 species of cactus and a magnificent Victoria Regia waterlily from the Amazon.

To the east of the Palmen Garten is the Grüneburg Park, the former Rothschild Estate which is now open to the public. It contains a sports center and a magnificent office complex designed by the architect Hans Pölzig in 1925. Originally a munitions factory, these offices were a target which the Allied bombers missed.

Excursions from Frankfurt

Höchst is Frankfurt's furthest western suburb, on the Main, and was once a medieval town in its own right, governed from Mainz before Frankfurt engulfed it. Thus it possesses buildings of the Middle Ages which, since they remained undamaged, are worth seeing now that the medieval part of Frankfurt itself has been laid waste. Its importance, however, is largely industrial, almost all of its citizens being employed in the machinery, electrical, shoe, and dye works of this quarter. The last named is the most important, the Höchster Farbwerke being the largest chemical plant in Germany; it produces not only the aniline dyes of which Germany once had almost a monopoly, but also such drugs as salvarsan and diphtheria serum. Höchst has long been an important manufacturing center. In the 18th century it was famous particularly for its porcelain. This industry is now being revived after a lapse of 150 years, by the Sudeten Germans who were expelled from Czechoslovakia. The famous porcelain manufacture works are in Dalberger House on Bolongaro Strasse.

Of the old buildings to be seen in this quarter, by far the most interesting is the Justiniuskirche, older than anything remaining in Frankfurt proper, since it goes back to the days of the Carolingians, that is to say, the beginning of the 9th century. Its older part is early Romanesque, while the 15th-century choir is Gothic. Some of the ancient town walls are still in place along the river, together with the customs tower; there are old timbered houses of the kind similar to those wiped out by the air raid in Frankfurt, as you climb the hill from the river; and you can also see the ruins of the old castle and the magnificent Bolongaro Palast, once the home of a family of Italian snuff manufacturers who established themselves here in the 18th century. The view over river, fields, and woods from this château is alone worth the trip.

A supermodern contrast to these old buildings is the Höchst Centennial Hall with its huge round roof, designed for use as a concert hall, theater, convention hall and sports arena. Another contemporary addition on the western border of Frankfurt is the Main Taunus Zentrum, a colossal shopping center, the largest in Europe, located in the middle of meadows and woods and featuring some 80 specialized stores along with two supermarkets, several restaurants, many service establishments ranging from gas stations to a kindergarten, parking space for 3,000 cars, fountains and flower beds.

For a more rural ride, take a day trip to the southwest of the city, where you will find the Stadtwald, the City Forest, which is threaded with lovely bridle-paths and roads, as well as containing one of Germany's most beautiful sports stadiums. It was a big forest before the war, when it covered 1,000 acres, but the necessity of replanting 42 acres started the local authorities on a reforestation program that is adding 3,000 acres to the original area.

There are many tremendous old trees in the Stadtwald, not unsurprisingly, as it is the first place in Europe where trees were planted from seed (they were oaks, sown in 1398, while 30 years later evergreens were started in the same fashion). There are a number of good restaurants in the forest, and it would be difficult to imagine a pleasanter place to eat and linger.

There are several other places that can be enjoyed on an excursion from Frankfurt. Among them is Hofheim, 18 km. (11 miles) to the west, on the Wiesbaden road, or 30 minutes by train. It is an old Roman town, with a parish church dating partly from the 15th century, a Kurhaus, trips to the beautifully located 17th-century Hofmeier Kapelle, ruins of an old fort, lookout tower and the old suburb of Marxheim, river and forest walks.

Königstein im Taunus, about eight km. (five miles) north west of Soden, is a favorite weekend spot with woods on three sides, and two mountains embracing the town. The old quarter contains many interesting buildings, and the town is dominated by the massive ruins of Königstein castle, usually floodlit during summer weekends.

Kronberg is a lovely old town about 16 km. (10 miles) north. It has a very interesting castle and animal park. Less than four km. (two miles) from Kronberg is Falkenstein, another small, hilly summer resort, with ruins of a 13th-century castle.

Eppstein im Taunus is 24 km. (15 miles) farther north from Kronberg, and is a place chiefly attractive to nature lovers, but there is also the 12th-century Eppstein castle and a 15th-century Protestant parish church.

Bad Soden is a spa with 26 hot salt springs, prettily located on the Sulzbach river. It has a Kurhaus, Kurpark and swimming pool.

Grosser Feldberg is the highest of the Taunus mountains. You can visit the remains of a Roman fort at Wellquelle, or stay at one of the neighboring villages—in Reifenberg (Ober-Reifenberg at 610 meters (2,000 feet) is the highest settlement in the Taunus region, with the ruins of an old castle and an 18th-century chapel); in Schmitten, a resort village with a swimming pool; at Arnoldshain, where there is a ruined castle and a 12th-century church; or in Glashütten. Each of these villages has several pleasant, quiet, and low-priced hostelries. While in the Grosser Feldberg neighborhood, you can climb the Altkönig to see the remains of Celtic fortifications there.

Bad Vilbel, to the northeast in the Nidda valley, has been a spa since Roman times. Its old buildings, pleasant walks in the parks and neighboring country, Kurhaus and swimming pool, make it a pleasant and easy (only 13 km./8 miles) excursion point from Frankfurt.

Offenbach, on the Main River, is virtually a suburb of Frankfurt, but is a city in its own right with a long history going back to the 10th century. The landmark of Offenbach is the 16th-century Renaissance Isenburg Castle, today housing a technical school, but the city is perhaps even better known for its German Leather Museum, unique in the world, containing objects made of leather of all types, from all ages and from all over the world; naturally, there is a large section devoted to the history of shoes. It is located here because Offenbach is the center of the German leather industry, in addition to supporting important machine and chemical plants. Those interested in printing and the graphic arts will want to see the Klingspor Museum, where some of the best specimens of world-wide book production from 1890 to the present are displayed.

The chief sights of Hanau, a little further up the river, are the extensive baroque Schloss Philippsruhe and the half-timbered Goldsmith's House with exhibits of local jewelry for which this area is renowned. In the market square is a monument to the famous Grimm brothers, the collectors and writers of fairy tales and folk stories, who were born here (Jakob in 1785, Wilhelm in 1786); Jakob Grimm was also an outstanding philologist.

The Kinzig River flows into Main at Hanau, coming from the nearby Kinzig Valley whose soft meadows are protected by the forested slopes of Vogelsberg and Spessart hills. In the upper section of Kinzigtal are Steinau, where the Grimm brothers spent their childhood, and two small and quiet spas, Bad Orb and Bad Soden (not to be confused with the spa of the same name in the Taunus).

At Gelnhausen, nearer to Hanau, you may visit the reddish and still impressive remnants of the 12th-century castle-fortress of Emperor Barbarossa. Philipp Reis, who invented the telephone in Germany at the same time Bell developed one independently in the United States, also lived in Gelnhausen.

A few miles up the Main from Hanau is Seligenstadt, where a Carolingian basilica, built about 825, rears one large and two small spires above the waters of the river.

PRACTICAL INFORMATION FOR FRANKFURT

TELEPHONES. The telephone code for Frankfurt is 069. To call any number in this chapter, unless otherwise specified, this prefix must be used. Within the city, no prefix is required.

HOTELS Most of the larger Frankfurt hotels are located in the vicinity of the main railroad station, not far from the fair grounds. This fact, and because the principal airlines have their offices near the main station, makes it very practical to stay in that vicinity. But it also has its setbacks: the business center of the city is quite a walk away (15–20 minutes) and at night some of the streets around the station have a noisy, unpleasant aspect, which doesn't improve very much by day. Since Frankfurt is a very busy commercial city, you are wise to reserve in advance in view of the fairs, exhibitions, conventions, and so on, that occur frequently. Prices are generally pretty high.

Do-it-yourself hotel reservation machines have been installed at Frankfurt's airport and the main railway station. It works this way: Arriving visitors push buttons to register their choice of accommodation, price range and length of stay. The computer responds by giving names of hotels that fit the bill and lights indicate their positions on a city map. You then decide on one hotel by pushing another button, insert a ten-mark note and out comes written booking confirmation of your hotel together with its full address. DM.6 constitute a deposit towards your hotel bill, the balance is the service charge due to the machine, nicknamed "Hot Resy" by the locals. Instructions for its operation are multi-lingual; 65 hotels in Frankfurt are programmed into this computer. Alternatively, the tourist office can also help with accommodations.

Deluxe

Airport Hotel Steigenberger. Unterschweinstiege 16 (69851). 350 rooms. Half a mile from the airport, though in attractive wooded setting. Quiet, spacious and comfortable, with an excellent and highly atmospheric old restaurant. In addition, the 14 conference rooms help make this an ideal businessman's hotel. Shuttle bus to and from airport. AE, DC, MC. V.

CP Frankfurt Plaza. Hamburger Allee 2–10 (770721). 591 rooms. Located on the 26th floor (and continuing upwards for quite a way) of the tallest residential building in Europe. Comfortable and well-run, and boasting a nightclub, three restaurants and magnificent views. Across the road from the Messe, the exhibition grounds. AE, DC, MC. V.

Frankfurter Hof Steigenberger. Am Kaiserplatz 17 (20251). 400 rooms with bath. Fine central location for vast and glittering hotel. Restaurant and cafe with inviting outdoor terrace, plus bar and excellent French restaurant. AE, DC, MC, V.

Frankfurt Inter-Continental. Wilhelm-Leuschnerstr. 43 (230561). 814 rooms. Spacious and comfortable highrise, though lacking in atmosphere, but fine views over the Main. Three restaurants, wine tavern, conference facilities and, the star exhibit, 64 two-room suites. AE, DC, MC, V.

Gravenbruch-Kempinski. 6078 Neu Isenburg 2 (06102–5050), 317 rooms with bath. Attractive hotel with excellent service, 11 km. out of town, past the spaghetti junction on 459. Its *Gourmet Restaurant* completes the pattern of recommendability. AE, DC, MC, V.

Hessischer Hof. Friedrich-Ebert-Anlage 40 (75400). 167 rooms with bath. Elegant one-time town house, with excellent personal service and attractive antiques throughout. Good restaurant. AE, DC, MC, V.

Holiday Inn. City Tower, Mailander Str. 1 (68020). 405 rooms. Located in Sachsenhausen, south of the river. Usual Holiday Inn amenities. AE, DC, MC, V.

Parkhotel. Wiesenhüttenplatz 28 (26970). 310 rooms. Elegant and gracious hotel in good central location near the station. Very attractively decorated, though note that rooms in the older wing are larger (and more expensive). Excellent gourmet restaurant, *La Truffe,* and bar. AE, DC, MC, V.

Ramada-Caravelle. Oeserstr. 180 (39050). 236 rooms. In western suburb of Nied, 10 minutes from the airport. Two restaurants, bar, pool, sauna. Comfortable if nondescript. AE, DC, MC, V.

Sheraton. Flughafen (69770). 820 rooms, including some suites. Located practically in the airport, with rail station in the basement and autobahn directly outside. Heavily sound-proofed, however. Extensive conference facilities, three restaurants, sauna, shops, disco, movie theaters complete the extensive facilities. Very convenient businessman's hotel, but not too much atmosphere. AE, DC, MC, V.

Expensive

An der Messe. Westendstr. 102 (747979). 46 rooms, no restaurant. AE, DC, MC, V.

Arabella. Lyonerstr. 44–48 (66330). 400 rooms. South of the river in Niederrad suburb. Three restaurants, bar, pool. AE, DC, MC, V.

Crest Hotel. Isenburger Schneise 40 (67840). 289 rooms. Located midway between city and airport. Airconditioned throughout. AE, DC, MC, V.

National. Baseler Str. 50 (234841). 95 rooms. Located at the main station. Comfortable, with good restaurant. AE, DC, MC, V.

Palmenhof. Bockenheimer Landstr. 89–91 (753–0060). 50 rooms with bath. Turn-of-the-century hotel, recently renovated. Cozy basement restaurant with expensive nouvelle menu. AE, DC, MC, V.

Rhein Main. Heidelberger Str. 3 (250035). 48 rooms. First-class comforts and personal service. Restaurant and bar. AE, DC, MC, V.

Savigny. Savignystr. 14 (75330). 130 rooms. Elegant modern hotel, full of atmosphere, located near the main station. Restaurant and bar. AE, DC, MC, V.

Turm Hotel. Eschersheimer Landstr. 20 (154050). 75 rooms; excellent restaurant. AE, DC, MC, V.

Moderate

Admiral. Hölderlinstr. 25 (448021). 52 rooms, all with bath. Quiet, but no restaurant. AE, DC, MC, V.

Ambassador. Moselstr. 12 (251077). 120 beds, all rooms with bath. AE, DC, MC, V.

Am. Zoo. Alfred-Brehm-Platz 6 (490771). 85 rooms. AE, DC, MC, V.

Arcade Hotel Frankfurt. Speicherstr. 3–5 (273030). 193 rooms with shower. Restaurant. MC, V.

Ebel. Tanusstr. 26 (230756). 35 rooms. No restaurant. AE, DC, MC, V.

Excelsior. Mannheimer Str. 7–10 (256080). At main rail station. AE, DC, MC, V.

Maingau. Schifferstr. 38–40 (617001). 100 rooms with bath. In Sachsenhausen but only five minutes from the Römer. Restaurant. AE, MC.

Neue Kräme. Neue Kräme 23 (284046). 21 rooms with bath. Very central and quiet. No restaurant. AE, DC, MC, V.

Post. Sindlinger Bahnstr. 12 (37010). In Sindlingen suburb. 120 beds. With pool and sauna. No restaurant. AE, DC, MC.

Royal. Wallstr. 17 (623026). 34 rooms. In Sachsenhausen district; no restaurant. AE, DC, MC, V.

Schwille. Grosse Bockenheimer Str. 50 (283054). 55 rooms. Close to the Alte Oper, with an excellent and famous café. AE, DC, MC, V.

Westfälinger Hof. Düsseldorfer Str. 10 (234748). 80 beds. Good value. V.

Zentrum Hauptwache. Rossmarkt. 7 (295291). 60 beds. No restaurant. AE, DC, V.

Inexpensive

Diana. Westendstr. 83 (747007). 29 rooms, 9 with bath. In a pleasant residential area convenient for fairground and downtown area. AE, DC, MC, V.

Pension Uebe. Grüneburgweg 3 (591209). 18 rooms with bath. On the top three floors of an office building, on a street with good restaurants. Cozy rooms with good atmosphere on top floor. AE, DC, MC, V.

Camping

Campingplatz Bärensee. 6450 Hanau-Bruchköbel (06181–12306).

Campingplatz Heddernheim. An der Sandelmuhle 35, Frankfurt 50 (570332).

Campingplatz des Wassersportvereins. Offenbach-Bürgel (862949).

Youth Hostel

Haus der Jugend. Deutschherrnufer 12 (619058). 470 beds.

HOW TO GET AROUND. From the airport. Frankfurt's international Rhine-Maine airport, located to the southwest of the city, is linked to the city center by an excellent S-Bahn (suburban electric railway) service (S15) which runs every ten minutes to the main station (Hauptbahnhof, Platform 21). The S14 line calls at the station, below ground and then continues to the Hauptwache, city center. The journey takes 11 minutes to the main station and 15 minutes to the Hauptwache. Single fare is DM.3.10 or DM.4.20 according to the time of day. Taxis from the airport cost about DM.35.

There are further direct connections by InterCity express to other main German cities, the principal service being the relatively new Lufthansa "Airport Express" which links Frankfurt with the airports and cities of Bonn, Köln and Düsseldorf. This runs four times a day and tickets cost DM.155 to or from Düsseldorf, DM.132 to or from Köln and DM.130 to or from Bonn (at the time of writing). The usual excellent Lufthansa in-flight service is provided on the train, and in addition your luggage is transferred to or from the train if you have a Lufthansa flight connection. And if you are in possession of a valid air ticket for the same route, but prefer to travel by train, then the service is free of charge. There is also the similar "Rail-Fly" service operated by German Railways.

City transportation. Frankfurt and its suburbs are well served by tram and bus lines. The trams are gradually being placed out as the U-Bahn is extended. For taxis dial 25001 or 230033; there are also some 50 taxi stands in the downtown area. Basic fare is DM.3.60 plus DM.1.80 per kilometer. Guided city bus tours start daily at 10 A.M. and 2 P.M. at the north side of the main railroad station from April 1 to end Oct. A roundtrip bus tour of Feldberg, Königstein, Kronberg begins daily at 2.30 from June 1 to Sept. 30 from the same place. Frankfurt is also served by an efficient network of fast suburban electric trains (S-Bahn) and the underground system (U-Bahn), at present with seven main lines.

The whole transport network interconnects, and tickets are valid on all forms of transport. These can be purchased from blue automatic machines ("automats") at all train stations and some streetcar stops, and it is always useful to have some small change handy. However, for tourists, a 24-hour ticket is recommended. This is good for unrestricted travel in the city and its immediate suburbs on all forms of transport, and costs DM.7.

The pleasant scenery around Frankfurt can be reached swiftly and economically by the city public transport. Information from the *Frankfurt Verkehrs Verein* (F.V.V.), tel. 26941.

The "Ebbelwei Express." The Frankfurt Municipal Transport Department runs a delightful "oldtimer" streetcar, brightly painted and offering a nostalgic city tour set to music. The "Ebbelwei Express" runs every Saturday and Sunday from the Ostbahnhof station through the city and Sachsenhausen and back. It departs every 40 minutes between 1.30 and 5.30 P.M., calling at the zoo. Theaterplatz, Opernplatz and Hauptbahnhof, among other stations, and costs DM.3. Information from *Stadtwerke Frankfurt and Main,* Postfach 102132 (13682425)

By boat. There are a variety of round-trips and excursions on the Main River. Steamers of the *Köln-Dusseldorf* line operate day trips and ferry services, as well as longer excursions. Information from the K.D. Pavilion, Frankfurt Mainkai am Eisernen Steg (282420), where the boats depart. In addition, the shipping companies *Fahrgastschiff Wikinger II* (282886) and *Frankfurter Personenschiffahrt Anton Nauheimer,* Mainkai 36 (281884) operate day trips to Rüdesheim and Assmannshausen, Seligenstadt and Aschaffenburg, and roundtrips on the Main. These also depart from the Eisener Steg landing stage. Combined steamer-trip/wine tastings are organized by the tourist office; details from Deutsche Touring, Am Römerhof 17, also.

Historic Railway. There is an historic railway with a steam-driven engine which runs along the river Main from Eisener Steg to Frankfurt-Griesheim (West) or to Frankfurt-Mainkur (East) on special weekends from Jan. to May and during the summer (Sat. 1–5 P.M., Sun. 10–12 and 2–5 every hour). The trip in both directions costs DM.5 one way, roundtrip DM.9. For information contact *Historische Eisenbahn Frankfurt e.V.,* Eschborner Landstr. 140 (539147).

TOURIST INFORMATION. For room reservations, general tourist information, city maps and tickets of all kinds for cultural performances, contact the *Verkehrsverein,* im Hauptbahnhof (in the main station), opposite platform 23 (2128849). Open mornings to evenings, Apr. to Oct., Mon. to Sat. 8–10, Sun. 9.30–8; Nov. to Mar., Mon. to Sat. 8–9, Sun. 9.30–8. Also in the Hauptwache Passage (212 8708/09). They issue a calendar of weekly events entitled *Frankfurter Wochenschau,* giving details of concerts, theater, special events, exhibitions, museums. They also arrange city tours, special tours and guides. Opening times are Mon. to Fri. 9 A.M.–6 P.M., Sat. 9 A.M.–2 P.M.

There are three information offices at the airport (in departure hall B, arrival hall B, and transit hall B). For information in advance of your trip, contact the Verkehrsamt Frankfurt/Main, Gutleutstr. 79, 6000 Frankfurt (069–212–8849).

USEFUL ADDRESSES. Car rental. *Avis,* Mainzer Landstr. 170 (230101). *Hertz,* Schwalbacherstr. 47–49 (75850); *Europcar,* Mainzer Landstr. 160 (234002); *InterRent,* Stephanstr. 15 (291028).

In addition, all the major car hire companies also have offices at the airport.

Consulates. *American Consulate General,* Siesmayerstr. 21 (740071). *British Consulate General,* Bockenheimer Landstr. 51–53 (720406).

Lost and found (Fundbüros). *Städtisches Fundbüro (Municipal Lost and Found Office),* Mainzer Landstr. 323 (7500 2403). Open Mon. to Fri. 7.30 A.M.–1 P.M. *Airport Lost Property Office,* Arrival Hall A (690 6359). Open 7 A.M.–7 P.M. *German Railways/S-Bahn Lost Property Office,* at the main station, northern entrance, opposite platform 24 (265 5831). Open 24 hours. *City streetcars, buses and U-Bahn,* Verkehrsbetriebe F.V.V., Stadtwerke, at the underground (U-Bahn) station Hauptwache, in the passage (1368 2258). Open Mon. to Fri. 7 A.M.–6 P.M.

Official Tourist Office for all Germany (Deutsche Zentrale Für Tourismus). Beethovenstr. 69 (069–75720).

Post Offices (Postämter). The post offices at the airport and the main railway station are open round the clock, and the city main post office is open 7 A.M.–9.30 P.M. Addresses for *post restante* mail; Hauptpostamt, 6000 Frankfurt 1, or Flughafen-Postamt, D-6000 Frankfurt, from abroad. The *Hauptpostamt* is on Zeil 108–110.

Trade fair information (Messe Frankfurt). Ludwig Erhard Anlage 1 (757 5222).

Travel agents. *American Express International,* Steinweg 5 (210548). *D.E.R. Deutsches Reisebüro,* Eschersheimer Landstr. 25–27 (156 6289). *Thomas Cook,* Kaiserstr. 11 (13470). *Hapag-Lloyd Reisebüro,* Rossmarkt 21 (2162286).

TOURS. The tourist office arrange guided city bus tours daily from Mar. 1 through Oct. 31, leaving from the north side of the main railway station at 10 A.M. and 2 P.M. The sightseeing tour lasts about three hours and costs DM.26 (children half-price). Tours out into the surrounding countryside are also available from May 1 through Sept. 30. These tours depart from the same point, on Sundays at 2 P.M., last about four hours and cost the same as the city tours. Information from the Tourist Information office at the Main Station (2128849).

EXCURSIONS. The Frankfurt travel companies *Dema-Reisen Sightseeing* and the *Deutsche Touring* offer a varied program of excursions into the countryside around Frankfurt as well as further afield. Excursion destinations include the Rhine Valley, with a river steamship cruise and winetasting, day trips to Heidelberg and Rothenburg ob der Tauber, or an evening "Cabaret" tour of some of the spiciest Frankfurt nightspots. A "Frankfurt Panorama Tour" organized by Deutsche Touring, departing from the south side of the main station, takes in both the city and surroundings, with visits to the "old town" of Höchst, Bad Soden spa and Kronberg in the Taunus, and there are also 2- and 3-day trips to Rothenburg and Heidelberg together with a tour of the Romantic Road. For full information, prices and departure times, contact: *Dema-Reisen Sightseeing,* Mannheimer Str. 7–9 Frankfurt (231322); *Deutsche Touring,* Am Römerhof 17 (79030); or inquire at the Tourist Office at the Main Station.

If you prefer to make your own excursions, the tourist office can suggest various destinations easily reached by public transport. For full information contact the office. They also produce a brochure, in English, "Bus tours," including seven tour descriptions and maps.

If you book a flight to Germany to or via Frankfurt, with Lufthansa or another I.A.T.A. airline, you will be given a brochure and a coupon which may be exchanged at the tourist office at the airport for a book of vouchers for a whole series of free or reduced-rate tourist services. These include city sightseeing tours, free entry to the museums and cheap rates on excursions organized by the Deutsche Touring.

SPORTS. The Waldstadion in the Stadtwald (City Forest), Mörfelder Landstr. 362, is the chief center for sports. There is a stadium with three **swimming** pools, 20 **tennis** courts, **archery** stand, **ice skating** rink in winter, and in the immediate vicinity an 18-hole golf course. There is a **horse race** course at Niederrad, with meetings from March to November.

Golf. Frankfurter Golf-Club, Golfstr. 41 (666–2118). Open from beginning of April to end Sept. Members only, or golf-players, with a handicap, already members of another club. Entrance fee during week DM.50, weekends DM.70.

Squash. *Squash-Zentrum Ost,* Ostparkstr. 35 (434756); *Squash 13,* Karl-von-Drais-Str. 5a (549099)

Swimming. There are eight openair pools open from May 15 through Sept. 15. *Brentanobad,* Rödelheimer Parkweg; *Eschersheim,* Im Uhrig; *Höchst,* Palleskestrasse; *Stadionbad,* Mörfelder Landstr.; *Hausen,* Ludwig-Landmann-Str. 314; *Nieder-Eschbach,* Heinr.-Becker-Str.; *Silobad Höchst,* Silostr.; *Berger-Enkheim,* Fritz-Schubert-Ring. Then there is the "Garden Indoor Pool" Rebstockbad, August-Euler-Str. 7 (708078). It boasts wave machines, diving tower, an 80-meter (260-foot) river flowing through the pool, linking the indoor hall with the garden area outside, children's pool, nudists' pool, massage, fitness rooms, solarium, sauna, and much more! Open Mon. 2 P.M.–10 P.M., Tues., Thurs. 9 A.M.–8 P.M., Wed., Fri., Sat., Sun. 9 A.M.–10 P.M. Price DM.11 for the day or DM.8 for three hours. Children half-price.

Tennis. There are more than 250 outdoor and 36 indoor courts throughout the city. At the following courts you can book in advance and do not have to be a member: *Waldstadion* (6708011); *Europa Tennis & Squash Park,* Ginnheimer Landstr. 49 (532040).

General information about sports facilities from Sport-und Badeamt der Stadt Frankfurt, Hochstr. 4–8 (2123565).

PARKS AND GARDENS. Historischer Garten. This is a sunken garden located at the Römerberg, bang in the city center. It contains the excavated remains of Roman buildings and a Carolingian Imperial Palace.

Mainuferpromenade. For a riverside walk, try a visit to the pretty Mainuferpromenade with its large expanses of lawn and exotic and local flowers and shrubs. Here, too, you can find boats to hire on the Main.

Nizza. A garden area of Mediterranean trees and shrubs, set out on the banks of the Main on either side of the Untermain bridge.

Palmengarten. Hothouses with tropical plants, palm-tree houses, orchids and cacti exhibition, plus playground and recreation facilities. Located at Siesmayerstr. 61, and named after the gardener who landscaped the park, Heinrich Siesmayer. Admission: adults DM.4, children DM.1.50. Open daily 9–7.

Stadtwald (Frankfurt City Forest). The largest municipal woodland in Germany. Bus no. 36 from Konstabler Wache to Hainer Weg. Marked forest nature paths (Waldlehrpfad), bird sanctuaries and wild animal enclosures.

Zoologischer Garten. Alfred-Brehm-Platz 16. One of the most important zoos in Europe, with 4,750 animals and 588 species. Founded in 1858. Zoo admission: adults DM.7, children DM.3; Exotarium admission: adults DM.3.50, children DM.1.50; combination ticket: adults DM.8.50, children DM.4. Open daily 8 A.M.–7 P.M. in summer, 8–5 in winter, with nocturnal animal house and "Exotarium" for exotic animals open till 10 P.M.

HISTORIC BUILDINGS AND SITES. Alte Oper (Old Opera House).

Opernplatz. One of the most splendid opera houses in Europe, built between 1873–80, completely burnt out in 1944, but recently and lavishly restored.

Börse (Frankfurt Stock Exchange). Börsenplatz. Built in 1879 by Heinrich von Burnitz and Oskar Sommer. Admission: free. Open Mon.–Fri. 11:30–1:30.

Bolongaro Palast. Bolongarostr (Höchst). Palace built in 1772 by the snuff manufacturer Bolongaro. Impressive facade. Now seat of the Höchst company's board of directors. Contains Höchst porcelain exhibition. Admission: free. Open Mon.–Fri. 9–3.

Deutschordenshaus. Brückenstr. 3–7. Baroque commander's building of the German Order of Knights, built in 1709 over a Gothic cellar. Open Mon., Tues., Thurs., Fri. 8–4, Wed. 8–8.

Eschenheimer Turm. Eschenheimer Tor. 15th century tower, the finest of the original 42 city towers.

Fernmeldeturm (Telecommunications Tower). Wilhelm Epstein Str. Known locally as "Ginnheimer Spargel" (Ginnheim's asparagus), this is the fourth highest tower in the world (331 meters/1,086 feet). Revolving restaurant and observation platform.

Goethe Denkmal. Kaiserstr. Monument to the great German poet, erected in 1844.

Goetheturm. Wendelsweg. Highest wooden tower in Germany (43 meters/141 feet). Located on the Sachsenhäuser Berg hill on the edge of the Stadtwald. Has 196 steps to the observation platform. Forest café nearby.

Hauptwache. A Baroque building erected in 1730, formerly the City Guard House, now a focal point of buisiness and commerce. Frankfurt's center of public transport is just underneath.

Höchster Schloss (Palace of Höchst). Bolongarostr. Built 1360 as seat and Customs House of the Archbishops of Mainz. Destroyed and rebuilt several times during its history; all that remains today is the medieval keep, the northeast wing and one section of the living quarters. Lies in park with bridge over the moat. Admission: free.

Kaisersaal (Imperial Chamber). In the Römer Rathaus. Between 1566 and 1792 showplace of the coronation banquets for ten German Emperors. Contains portrait gallery of 52 emperors from 768 to 1806. Admission: DM.1 Open Mon.–Sat. 10–6, Sun. 10–4.

Römer (Town Hall). The symbol of Frankfurt. Three Gothic gabled houses, Alt-Limpurg, Römer and Löwenstein, taken over by the city council and turned into the town hall. Other houses have since been added to the complex. Rebuilt after the war.

Saalhofkapelle (Saalhof Chapel). One of the oldest buildings in the city center, dating back to 1165. Located in the Historic Museum at the Römberg.

Steinernes Haus. Markt (at the Römerberg). Built out of stone in 1464 as a Patrician house and has also been a trading post. Now the seat of the Frankfurt Society of the Arts.

Zeil. One of the most famous shopping streets in Europe, dating back to 1330. It was a cattle market until about 1550, then in the 18th century inns and taverns were erected. After 1866 retail shops and then department stores appeared. A pedestrian zone since 1973, and completely redesigned in 1983.

CHURCHES. Alte Nikolaikirche (St. Nicholas). At the Römerberg. Built in the first half of the 13th century and formerly the chapel of the City Council. The chimes from the clocktower can be heard every day at 9.05 A.M., 12.05 midday and 5.05 P.M.

Dom (Cathedral of St. Bartholomew). On the Domplatz cathedral square. Built from the remains of a 9th-century chapel around 1315, it was then added to several times after damage by fire, and more recently after bomb damage sustained during the war. The cathedral served as the scene of election and coronation of German emperors in the Middle Ages. Open Mon.–Fri. 9–12 and 3–6. The cathedral treasury (Domschatz) and the election chapel can be visited upon prior application to the Cathedral Office, Domplatz 14.

Justinuskirche (St. Justin's). Bolongarostr./Justiniusplatz 2 in Höchst. Consecrated in the year 834; Frankfurt's oldest building.

Katharinenkirche (St. Catharine's). Hauptwache. Built in 1678, formerly a convent and hospital. Main Protestant church of Frankfurt. Goethe was christened and confirmed here.

Leonhardskirche (St. Leonard's). Mainkai. Gothic single-roofed church with five naves. Parts of the church date from the early 13th century.

Liebfrauenkirche (Church of Our Lady). Liebfrauenberg. Gothic church on the Marienberg, with Baroque chancel. Open Mon.–Fri. 7–7.

Paulskirche (St. Paul's). Paulsplatz. Built between 1787 and 1833 and in 1848 the meeting place of the German National Assembly. Used today for celebrations, exhibitions and important conferences, particularly during the fall international Book Fair when the German Publishing Association's Freedom Prize for literature is awarded here at the start of the Fair.

MUSEUMS AND GALLERIES. Deutsches Architekturmuseum (German Museum of Architecture). Schaumainkai 43 (2128472). Five floors of drawings, models and audio-visual displays chart the progress and development of international architecture through the ages. Changing exhibitions. Open Tues. to Sun. 10–5, Wed. 10–8.

Deutsches Filmmuseum (German Cinema Museum). Schaumainkai 41 (2128830). West Germany's first museum of cinematography, with an imaginative collection of film artefacts. Changing exhibitions. Cinema. Open Tues.–Sun. 10–5, Wed. 10–8.

Goethe Haus und Goethemuseum (Goethe's House and Museum). Grosser Hirschgraben 23 (282824). The birthplace of Goethe, and one of the most famous museums in the city. Located near the Hauptwache, it contains collections of maunscripts, paintings and memorabilia from his lifetime. Admission: DM.2. Open Mon.–Sat. 9–6, Sun. 10–1.

Heinrich Hoffmann Museum. Schubertstr. 20 (747969). Dedicated to the creator of the world-famous children's book hero *Struwelpeter.* Open Tues.–Sun. 10–5. Free admission for children up to the age of 14. The original drawings by Hoffman can be seen in the **Struwelpeter Museum** at Hochstr. 45–47.

Historisches Museum (Museum of History). Saalgasse 19 (2123370). Houses a collection of objects of historical and cultural interest, including displays portraying the local way of life from the 16th–20th century. The **Kindermuseum** (Children's Museum) is also housed here. Open Tues.–Sun. 10–5.

Liebieghaus (Museum alter Plastik) (Liebig Museum of Sculpture). Schaumainkai 71 (2128617). Contains the city's collection of sculpture from almost all historical epochs—Egyptian, Greek and Roman antique, German and French medieval, Italian Renaissance, Baroque, and a small collection of Far Eastern sculpture. Open Tues. to Sun. 10–5, Wed. 10–8.

Museum für Kunsthandwerk (Museum of Applied Arts). Schaumainkai 17 (2124037). All kinds of European handicrafts, furniture, porcelain, glass, silver and textiles ranging in style from Gothic to Art Nouveau. Large East Asiatic and Islamic section. Open Tues. to Sun. 10–5, Wed. 10–8.

Museum für Völkerkunde (Ethnological Museum). Schaumainkai 29 (2125391). Interesting exhibits from all parts of the world, with emphasis on the Americas, Africa, Indonesia and the South Pacific. Open Tues. to Sun. 10–5, Wed. 10–8.

Naturmuseum Senckenberg (Natural History Museum). Senckenberganlage 25 (75421). Largest natural history collection in Germany, with Europe's most impressive examples of dinosaurs and whales. Mineralogy, geology, botany but especially zoology. The most important single exhibit here, reversing the usual order of things, is an import from the United States—the only complete specimen in Europe of a diplodocus. Admission: DM.2. Open Tues.–Sat. 9–4, Wed. 9–8, Sun. and holidays 9–6.

Schirn Kunsthalle Frankfurt. Am Römerberg 6A (1545172). Exhibits and documentations on 20th-century art.

Städelsches Kunstinstitut und Städtische Galerie (Städel Art Institute and Municipal Art Gallery). Schaumainkai 63. A fine collection of old masters. Admission: DM.2. Open Tues. to Sun. 10–5, Wed. 10–8.

THEATERS AND CONCERTS. The tickets for the municipal theaters can be purchased at the tourist office in the Hauptwache or in the theaters themselves (11–1, Sundays 11–12, and one hour before the beginning of the performance).

Alte Oper. Opernplatz (13400). Orchestral and choral concerts, ballet, operetta.

Die Komödie. am Theaterplatz/Neue Mainzer Str. 18 (284580). Boulevard theater.

Die Schmiere. Seckbächer Gasse 2 (281066) A literary-political cabaret theater which disarmingly calls itself the "worst theater in the world." In the Karmelitenkloster monastery building.

Festhalle. Ludwig Erhard Anlage 1 (75750). At the Fair Grounds. Concerts.

Fritz Remond Theater im Zoo. Alfred-Brehm-Platz 16 (435166). Boulevard theater.

Kinder- und Jugendtheater. Niddaforum 2 (570596). Children's theater.

Palmengarten. Siesmayer- or Palmengartenstrasse (752093). Orchestral and choral concerts in the halls in the gardens.

Playhouse. Hansaallee 152 (151 8326). English-language plays.

Sendesaal Hessischer Rundfunk (Radio Concert Hall). Bertramsstr. 8 (1551).

Städtische Bühnen (Municipal Theaters). Theaterplatz 1–3 (236061). Opera, drama and comedy are performed on the various stages of the ultramodern City Theater. Box office opening hours Mon. to Fri. 10–6, Sat. 10–2; also evenings. Advance bookings through *Theaterkasse Sandrock,* Hauptwache-Passage (20115/116, 283738).

SHOPPING. Frankfurt's shopping center lies between Opernplatz (at the old opera house), Hauptwache (a square at the nexus of the city's public transport network with shops and boutiques on two levels, above and below ground), and Konstabler Wache. This entire area, including the Zeil—Frankfurt's so-called "shopping mile" and Germany's busiest shopping street—was completely redesigned a couple of years ago and is now a pedestrian zone lined with myriad shops, department stores, cafés and restaurants.

In the neighboring side streets a wealth of elegant fashion boutiques sell top-notch designer clothing, excellent shoes and leather goods (Goethestr./Steinweg); exclusive jewelry and watches (Goethestr./Rossmarkt/Kaiserstr.); glass and porcelain (Schillerstr.); modern furniture and accessories (Sandgasse/Berliner Str.); art and antiques (Braubachstr./Fahrgasse/Weckmarkt). There is an elegant shopping gallery on three levels in the BfG skyscraper on the corner of Theaterplatz and Neue Mainzer Str. Not the least bit elegant (but far livelier and a good place for a snack) is the Kleinmarkthalle (Ziegelgasse, at the corner of Hasengasse), an indoor fresh produce market offering a multitude of flowers, fruit, vegetables, spices, cheese, meats and sausages. The heart of Frankfurt's famous fur trade is in Düsseldorfer Str., opposite the main station.

The following are some typical Frankfurt souvenirs to look out for: Apple Wine *(Apfelwein)* can be purchased in the bottle in most supermarkets or taverns; *Bethmännchen und Brenten* (Marzipan cookies); *Frankfurter Kranz* (a creamy cake); or a *Struwelpeter* puppet or doll, after the famous children's book character invented by Heinrich Hoffmann.

Flea Markets (Flohmärkte)

Every Saturday at the Schlachthof (Deutschherrenufer corner of Wasserweg), open 8–2. Here you may pick up objets d'art, bric a brac, perhaps even antiques (but be careful if you are not sure of the piece's authenticity), but at all events an interesting souvenir to take home. There are also various antique markets held on weekends; check the local newspapers for details.

RESTAURANTS. Eating out in Frankfurt is expensive, often exceedingly so. Given the city's international nature and its proliferation of expense accounts—not to mention the out and out affluence of so many of its inhabitants—this is perhaps not altogether surprising. But be warned that you should expect to pay well above the average. It's a good idea also to make reservations in advance for all the pricier spots—most get very crowded—and for a good many of the less expensive.

The range and quality of restaurants in Frankfurt is immense, however, from the most sophisticated French *haute cuisine* to earthy and pungent local dishes in street corner Gasthofs. The most famous specialty is the *Frankfurter,* though many other varieties of sausage abound. However, perhaps the most characteristic local delicacy is *Rippchen mit Sauerkraut,* heavily-smoked pork chops with a lavish helping of sauerkraut. Equally fulsome game dishes also proliferate—venison and boar in particular—in all helping to make the city a happy hunting ground for those with a taste for red meat.

Finally, in keeping with its international flavor, you'll find large numbers of overseas restaurants, particularly Asian, throughout the city. The tourist office produces a very helpful booklet called *Eats and Treats in Frankfurt am Main.*

Expensive

Brückenkeller. Schützenstr. 6 (284238). Ancient, vaulted cellar with antique decor. Extensive wine list. Reservations recommended. AE, DC, MC, V. Closed lunch, Sun., and three weeks in July.

Le Cheval Blanc. Frankfurter Str. 1 (06102–4276). Excellent and atmospheric restaurant in Neu-Isenburg, 7 km. (4 miles) southeast of the city. Smoked eel and dry smoked ham specialties, and openair dining in summer. AE, DC, MC, V. Closed Sun.

Erno's Bistro. Liebigstr. 15 (721997). Small French restaurant, lavishly praised. Openair dining in summer. Reservations essential. AE, DC, MC, V.

Frankfurter Stubb. Bethmannstr. 33 (20251). Small, international restaurant in the basement of the Frankfurter Hof Steigenberger hotel. Also offers fine local specialties. Atmospheric and good. AE, DC, MC, V.

Gourmet Restaurant. Gravenbruch Kempinski hotel (06102–5050). In Neu-Isenburg Gravenbruch, 11 km. (8 miles) southeast of the city. Excellent, though expensive, spot, with openair dining in summer. Reservations necessary. AE, DC, MC, V. Closed weekends.

Hessler. Am Bootshafen 4 (06181–492951). 12 km. east, in Maintal (Dornigheim). Small, elegant; unique *nouvelle cuisine.* For lunch try the "Junior" restaurant.

Humperdinck. Grüneburgweg 95 (722122). Particularly good-value, first-class cuisine. Reservations advised. AE, DC, MC, V. Closed Sat. lunch and Sun.

Restaurant Francais. Bethmannstr. 33 (20251). Very superior French restaurant in the Frankfurter Hof Steigenberger hotel. Should be high on any list for excellent food and service. AE, DC, MC, V.

Rotisserie. Wilhelm-Leuschner-Str. 43 (230561). Elegant riverside French restaurant in the Inter-Continental hotel. AE, DC, MC, V.

Rotisserie 5 Continents. Flughafen B 40 (690 3444). The location in the Airport Hotel Steigenberger may not be very glamorous, but this is an otherwise excellent grill restaurant. Very convenient. AE, MC, V.

Waldrestaurant-Unterschweinstiege. Unterschweinstiege 16 (692503). Atmospheric farmhouse, some 200 years old, attached to the otherwise souless Airport Hotel Steigenberger. Excellent boar specialties. Reservations essential. AE, DC, MC, V.

Moderate

Bistrot 77. Ziegelhüttenweg 1–3 (614040). Alsatian specialties are served at this bright and cheerful French restaurant in Sachenhausen. AE, DC, MC, V. Closed Sat. lunch, Sun., and mid-June–mid-July.

Börsenkeller. Schillerstr. 11 (281115). French dishes dominate the menu of this centrally located eatery near the stock exchange. AE, DC, MC, V. Closed Sun.

Casa Nova. Stresemannallee 38 (632473). Superior Italian restaurant in the cozy interior of a Sachsenhausen house. Imaginative fish dishes. Weekend reservations essential. MC. Closed Sat. and two weeks in Aug.

Dippegucker. Eschenheimer Anlage 40 (551965). Centrally-located spot that's excellent for hearty local specialties. Rather a rustic atmosphere. Also at Am Hauptbahnhof 4 (234947). AE, DC, MC, V.

L'Escalier. Feuerbachstr. 23 (725480). The only place in town that will offer you real North African *Couscous.* AE, MC.

Henninger Turm. Hainer Weg 60 (606 3500). Tower-like grain elevator in Sachsenhausen, across the river, belonging to the Henninger Brewery. Two rotating restaurants on the top floor, both with excellent views. On the ground floor, there's the **Turmschänke** beer tavern. AE.

Neuer Haferkasten. Löwengasse 4 (06102–35329). Top-notch Italian food—not that you'd guess it from the name—and openair dining in summer; in Neu-Isenburg 7 km. (4 miles) southeast of the city. AE, DC, MC, V.

Scarlet Pimpernell. Krögerstr. 7 (292138). Russian food and balalaikas. Recommended. Reservations essential.

Strassburger Haus. Grosse Rittergasse 58 (610505). Rather more expensive, but scores for good food and atmosphere; in Sachsenhausen.

Tse Yang. Kaiserstr. 67 (232541). Leading spot for excellent Chinese food. AE, DC, MC, V.

Wine and Beer Restaurants

Generally less expensive than regular restaurants (though by no means always so—we've indicated below which fall into higher price brackets), and scoring highly for local atmosphere and specialties, are Frankfurt's wine and beer restaurants. In addition, they're among the few eating spots in town where the otherwise all-pervading and mostly nondescript internationalism of the city is absent. Anyone attempting to escape from what the Frankfurt tourist office have clumsily dubbed "Main-hatten" should take refuge in one (or more) of the following:

Haus Wertheym. Fahrtor 1, on the Römer (281432). Medieval inn serving bock beer and rustic meals in very picturesque surroundings.

Rheinpfalz-Weinstuben. Gutleutstr. 1 (233870). One of the best reasonably priced wine restaurants; near the City Theater. AE, DC, MC.

Schwarzwald-Stube. Mainkurstr. 36. Specialties from the Black Forest; plus good wines and beer. DC, MC.

Weinkrüger. Goetheplatz/corner of Junghofstr. (285130). Reliably good German food and wine.

Apfelwein Taverns

Even more indigenous are the city's Apfelwein taverns, mostly located in Sachsenhausen. They have for the most part escaped the creeping tawdriness that has overtaken this old district, and remain one of the city's last links with a simpler past. Mind you, the Apfelwein itself, a species of mild cider—called *Ebbelwei* by the locals—may well not be to everyone's taste. Put it another way, most people new to it are likely to find it rather unpleasant, though Frankfurters maintain that you can develop a taste for it quite rapidly. Still, for atmosphere, music and snacks—a characteristic one is *Handkäs mit Musik,* small pieces of cheese with "music," in this case represented by oil, vinegar and onions—try one of the following. Most, by the way, have a wreath of green leaves over the door; easy to spot.

Atschel. Wallstr. (619201). Characteristic and very inexpensive.

Zur Eulenburg. Eulengasse 46 (451203). One of the most original of them all; in Bornheim, north of the river.

Zum Fichtenkränzi, Wallstr. 5 (612778).

Zum Gemalten Haus. Schweizer Str. 67 (614559). Very old and atmospheric.

Zum Grauen Bock. Grosse Rittergasse 30. Very basic and typical family restaurant for hungry people.

CAFES. Frankfurt, like all German cities, boasts innumerable cafes. They are scattered throughout the city, though the center has more than its fair share. Here you'll find natives and visitors alike congregating (especially in the afternoon) to have coffee and rich cakes and pastries, the latter being more or less obligatory for all Germans, and yes, visitors too.

Three likely spots to try are:

Cafe Laumer. Bockenheimer Landstr. 67 (727912). Traditional meeting place for Frankfurt's intellectuals. Excellent cakes and light luncheons. Also in the Filmmuseum.

Cafe Schwille. Gross Bockenheimer Str. 50 (284183). Cafe in the hotel of the same name, serving breakfast from 6 A.M. Large terrace.

Hauptwache. 250-year-old building overlooking the busy square of the same name; summer terrace.

NIGHTLIFE. In much the same way that the Wall Street district wouldn't exactly be your first port of call if you were planning a trip around the flesh pots of New York City, so Frankfurt, for all its unashamed internationalism and sophisticated expense account living, is unlikely to win many votes as Germany's premier afterhours town. In fact, with the exception of the cheap sex clubs lining the Kaiserstr. and Münchenerstr. running east from the main station—all that passes for a red light district here—downtown Frankfurt outside office hours is about as diverting as a half-empty can of kerosene.

But if the city center isn't precisely pulsating with excitement, there's still plenty to do away from the downtown area. For more sophisticated, and expensive, amusements, the larger hotels all have bars, discos, nightclubs and so forth. There may not be much to distinguish them from thousands of similar haunts the world over, but they're tried and tested. We give details of the better ones below.

Alternatively, head over the river to Sachsenhausen, Frankfurt's left bank. It's hardly the quaint old Bohemian quarter it likes to sell itself as, but for bars, discos, clubs, beer and wine restaurants and, of course, Apfelwein taverns, this is probably the best place to try. It does get very crowded, however, being very much on the tourist track, and is also home to growing numbers of video-game arcades and sundry other rip off joints. A viable alternative to Sachsenhausen is provided by the even more fashionable Bornheim district to the northeast of the city center, where an almost equal number of bars, clubs, and the like, are located, and the atmosphere is much less forced.

Frankfurt does have one trump card, however: jazz. Indeed the city not unreasonably calls itself the jazz capital of the country. Fittingly, the city also plays host to the German Jazz Festival every fall. There are hundreds of jazz venues, from smokey backstreet cafes to concert halls. Details below.

Finally, do remember that, as with nightspots everywhere, those in Frankfurt can and do change quite unpredictably, bursting onto the scene and, sometimes, dying with little or no warning.

Nightclubs and Bars

Dorian Gray. Flughafen C, 0 Level (6902212). The leading nightclub. At the Rhine-Main airport; with internationally-known clientele, exclusive disco.

Fidelio. (725758). Bockenheimer Landstr. 1.

Jimmy's Bar. Friedr.-Ebert-Anlage 40 (745507). Good dancing spot.

Le Jardin. Kaiserhofstr. 6 (288956).

Paradieshof. Paradiesgasse 23 (624053). In Sachsenhausen; good for dancing.

Park-Cafe Odeon. Seilerstr. 34 (285055).

Sachs. Darmstädter Landstr. 119 (615002). In old brewery cellar, several pubs and a disco; for the younger tourist.

Stadt Wien. Weckmarkt 13 (288287). Dinner dancing to Austrian tunes.

UNO. Bibergasse 9 (287697). Disco.

Jazz and Rock

Der Jazzkeller. Kleine Bockenheimer Str. 18a (288537). Modern, hot and free jazz.

Jazzkneipe. Berliner Str. 70 (287173). Swing.

Jazz Life Podium. Kleine Rittergasse 22–26 (626346). Dixieland and swing.

Sinkkasten. Brönnerstr. 5 (280385). Rock, jazz, blues.

Schlachthof. Deutschherrnufer 36 (623201). Dixie and swing matinees.

In addition: **Batschkapp,** Maybachstr. 24 (531037); **Down by the Riverside,** Mainkai 7 (283677); **Niddapark-Terrassen,** Woogstr. 52 (520522), New Orleans to country; **River-Jazzkeller,** Kranengasse 2 (307591), old-time to modern jazz; **Jazzhaus,** Kleine Bockenheimer Str. 12 (287194), incredibly narrow 16th-century building with lots of atmosphere.

NORTH GERMANY

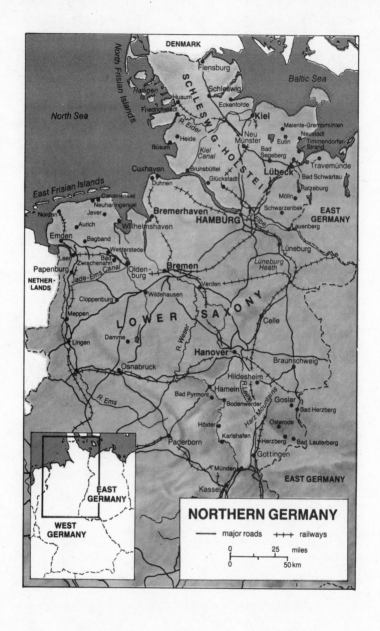

NORTHERN GERMANY

— major roads   +++ railways

0   25   miles
0   50 km

DENMARK

Flensburg

SCHLESWIG-HOLSTEIN

Baltic Sea

Schleswig

Eckenförde

Kiel

Malente-Gremsmühlen

Neustadt

Neu Münster

Eutin

Timmendorfer-Strand

Bad Segeberg

Travemünde

Lübeck

Bad Schwartau

Ratzeburg

Mölln

Schwarzenbek

EAST GERMANY

Lauenburg

Halligen Is.

Husum

Friedrichstadt

R. Eider

Heide

Büsum

Kiel Canal

North Sea

Cuxhaven

Brunsbüttel

Glückstadt

Duhnen

Bremerhaven

HAMBURG

Elbe

Lüneburg

North Frisian Islands

East Frisian Islands

Carolinensiel

Neuharlingersiel

Jever

Norden

Aurich

Willhelmshaven

Emden

Bagband

Westerstede

Leer

Bad Zwischenahn

Zwischenahn Canal

Oldenburg

Bremen

Verden

Lüneburg Heath

Papenburg

NETHER- LANDS

Jade-Ems Canal

Cloppenburg

Wildehausen

LOWER SAXONY

Celle

Meppen

Damme

R. Weser

Lingen

Hanover

Braunschweig

Osnabrück

Hildesheim

Hamelin

R. Leine

Goslar

R. Ems

Bad Pyrmont

Bodenwerder

Bad Herzberg

Höxter

Osterode

Harz Mountains

Karlshafen

Herzberg

Bad Lauterberg

Paderborn

Göttingen

Münden

EAST GERMANY

Kassel

EAST GERMANY

WEST GERMANY

HAMBURG

Germany's Greatest Port

The Elbe is one of Europe's greatest rivers and Hamburg, standing at its mouth, was for centuries the busiest port in Europe. The ships of Hamburg, and those of her partner cities in the medieval Hanseatic League—Bremen and Lübeck—brought fabulous wealth to their owners, and through them to thousands of their fellow citizens. From the splendid red-brick warehouses that still stand along the river's northern shore to the copper-domed churches and public office buildings, and beyond these to the palatial suburban houses of the wealthy burghers, the city is still an impressive sight. Every year some 15,000 ships sail up the lower Elbe from the sea, loaded with cargos which range from oriental gems and carpets to raw minerals and timber. Many tourists also arrive by sea.

Hamburg, or the "Hammaburg," was founded originally by Charlemagne in 810. From almost its earliest days, the city's prosperity has depended on its trading activities. The first port was built in 1189, and in the mid-13th century the city entered into a mercantile partnership with neighboring Lübeck that was to develop into the Hanseatic League, a commercial union of North Sea and Baltic cities of immense wealth and influence during the later Middle Ages, when Hamburg itself was a city republic and Free Imperial City of the Holy Roman Empire. Even today, Hamburg calls itself a "Free Hanseatic City."

In more modern times, the port and trade have remained the city's life blood. But Hamburg is also home to Germany's media. Nearly all the country's principal newspapers and magazines are based here, as are numerous press agencies and public relations firms. Similarly, Studio Hamburg, German's largest film and television studios, are located in the city. Finally, Hamburg is also the center of Germany's record and tape industries.

And yet the wealth and grandeur of Hamburg is not what it was. The elegant hotels still glitter with chandeliers, the best shops are still chic, but elsewhere the city is less grand. The war took its toll, of course, and the many new buildings are more functional and less ornate than the old. The way of life is more functional too: the traditional, rather rigid politeness of the people has given way to a more straightforward, friendlier approach. Pompous pride lingers on in the older establishments, but for the most part Hamburg is thoroughly cosmopolitan.

Water dominates Hamburg, not only because of the harbor but also by virtue of the tiny river, the Alster, that flows south, through the old city, into the Elbe. Once little more than an insignificant waterway, the Alster is central to the Hamburg scene, for during the 18th century it was dammed—just north of the old city—to form a lake. Divided into two at its southern end, this lake is known as the Binnenalster (Inner Alster) and the Aussenalster (Outer Alster), the two separated by a pair of bridges. Surrounded by gardens, grand hotels and private mansions, the lake is a fine sight. In spring, the gardens burst with rhododendrons, in summer there are openair cafés where you can take a meal and watch the boats. Sailing and windsurfing are popular, though the winds are unreliable. You can also ride the ferry boats, which stop at landing piers along the shore before plying north along the suburban canals, which are lined with the gardens of elegant 19th-century houses.

Water also plays a part in sustaining another Hamburg specialty—the lively nightlife. Like all ports, Hamburg has its rumbustious and rowdy side. But Hamburg has taken this traditional license to a new and in places staggering degree that can make a Klondike frontier town look like a temperance meeting. The St. Pauli district just to the west of the old town is where it all happens. Here you will find club after club, some no more than discos, others offering considerably more disreputable amusements, but all of them using sex—in one form or another—as a selling point. The atmosphere throbs with its own unique vitality. Passers-by are encouraged to part with their money, so don't take more than you intend to spend. But don't worry. The club owners, restaurateurs, waitresses, pimps and whores who work here are no less businesslike or dishonest than elsewhere. To preclude any opening for disagreement, order your own drinks, rather than letting a hostess do it for you, and pay as soon as they are served.

Exploring the City

The true city of Hamburg, the Alt-Stadt, can be seen on foot in a day, if you have stamina and a good pair of walking shoes. Only a small fraction of the city's 1.7 million people live here, but much of their historical tradition is found within the old city walls. The actual walls no longer exist, but where they stood the streets are called "wall," (or *Wallanlagen*), so you will easily be able to trace the old boundaries.

Begin at the main railway station (Hauptbahnhof), which is the terminus for every kind of train, from the local underground (U-bahn), the wider ranging suburban trains (S-bahn), the simple wooden-seated regional trains that stop at every station (D-zug), to the express trains south and west (InterCity) and the luxurious first-class transEuropean expresses (T.E.E.). Simply to stand beneath the vast vaulted glass canopy of the station roof and watch Europe's most efficient railway system is an experience. Return later for trips out of town, but now head out towards the Alster. Glockengiesserwall is a rather monstrous street, heavy with traffic—follow the example of the good citizen and stop when the pedestrian light is red. As with so many of the regulations that are observed in Germany, these lights will make your walk more relaxing.

On your right is the monolithic domed Art Hall (Kunsthalle), which is certainly worth visiting. It is a powerhouse of genius, and especially of the 20th-century German artists who—despite two wars, or perhaps because of them—have produced some extraordinary work.

When you emerge, cross the Alster by the Lombard Bridge (Lombards-brücke), pause to sample the curious blend of sea air and city smoke, then press on along the Esplanade, passing the ultra-modern Opera House (Hamburgische Staatsoper) on your left. The first opera house in Germany was built here in 1677 on the site of the old Gänsemarkt (Goose Market) and Hamburg has been closely linked with opera ever since. Straight ahead of you is the Botanical Garden, first laid out in 1821 on the site of the original Hamburg fortress. The Palmenhaus (Palm House) and the Victoriahaus with its water lilies from the Amazon are particularly interesting. Beyond the Botanical Garden and bordering Jungius Str, is the most famous park in Hamburg, the Planten un Blomen (Plants and Flower), laid out in 1936 and relaid in 1973 for the National Garden Show. The masses of tulips in spring are followed through the year by displays of flowers in season. After dark in summer, there is a water ballet played out by special fountains accompanied by colored lights and music.

You are now just outside the Gorch-Fock-Wall. Beyond the park stands the Fairground (Messe) with congress halls and exhibition grounds, where there is a year-round program of trade fairs. To the north of the railway—the line that runs from the Hauptbahnhof to Dammtor and beyond—is the University (an interesting area if you care to return there another day, with book-shops, student cafés and the Harvestehude area with some notable architecture).

But your tour follows the wall, and next you come to Karl-Muck Platz, with Hamburg's premier concert hall (Musikhalle), where the great composer Brahms heard his works performed before returning to his simple room north of the city. Continuing along the Holstenwall, with parkland on the right, your next important stop is at the Hamburg Historical Museum (Museum für Hamburgische Geschichte) with a splendid collection of marine models which demonstrate the development of the port and ships that have used it. In the Kaufmannsdiele, there are concerts once or twice a month.

St. Pauli and the Port

Swinging southwest towards the river, you enter the St. Pauli district. At night it is a buzz of neon lights, music and street life, but by day it is rather quiet, ideal for a first visit to acquaint yourself with the layout of the streets. Follow the Reeperbahn which runs parallel to the river.

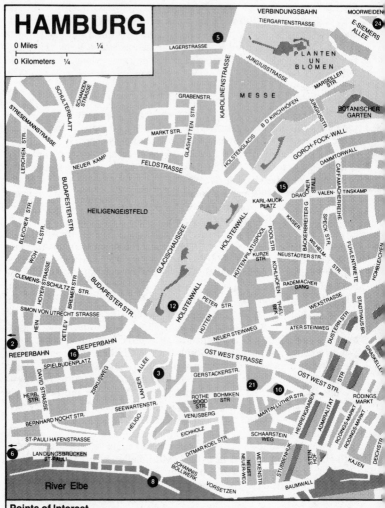

Points of Interest

1 Alster Cruise Tour	7 Hamburgische Staatsoper
2 Altonaer Museum	8 Harbor Tour
3 Bismarck Memorial	9 Hauptbahnhof
4 Deutsches Schauspielhaus	10 Krameramtswohnungen
5 Fernsehturm	11 Kunsthalle
6 Fisch Markt	12 Museum für Hamburgische Geschichte

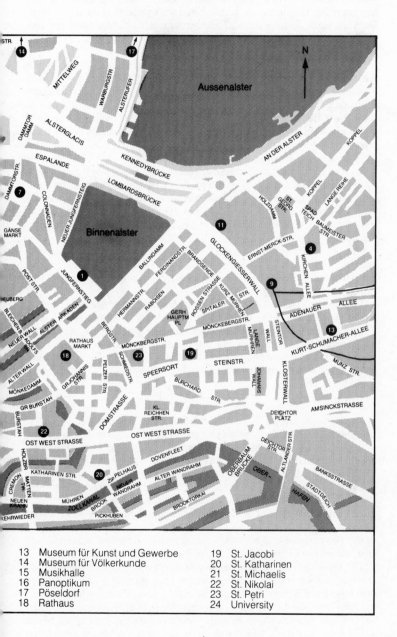

13	Museum für Kunst und Gewerbe	19	St. Jacobi
14	Museum für Völkerkunde	20	St. Katharinen
15	Musikhalle	21	St. Michaelis
16	Panoptikum	22	St. Nikolai
17	Pöseldorf	23	St. Petri
18	Rathaus	24	University

When you come to the crossing with Davidstrasse, where Hamburg's most famous police station stands, turn left and walk through towards the river. On your right is the walled-off Herbertstrasse, painted a lurid red and marked with a warning, "No ladies admitted"; though this is not strictly true.

Now the ground slopes down towards the Elbe, across what was once the most fascinating part of St. Pauli, the old huddle of riverside buildings which stood along the narrow streets is gone, and a new complex of offices, shops and flats has replaced it. Walk past it down to the waterfront. On the left are the St. Pauli Piers (Landungsbrücken St. Pauli), where local passenger ships and excursion boats tie up. Check the times of the tours around the port, a trip which takes in miles of quayside, hundreds of freighters, ocean liners and floating docks.

To your right, the road leads to Altona in the suburbs of the city, with its fascinating Sunday morning fish market and, above, the graceful town hall and the Altonaer Museum, which contains an interesting marine display. It is worth returning here another day and walking west along the river shore to Övelgönne, a narrow, riverside way with extremely beautiful old houses.

Near the St. Pauli piers, you can see the dome above the old Elbe tunnel, built in 1911. A new one, which is further west, was opened in 1975: three km. (two miles) long—the longest in Europe—it diverts much of the through traffic from the city center.

To get back to the Alt-Stadt, turn away from the river and go up Helgoländer Allee towards the Bismarck memorial. As so often happens with former heroes, Bismarck's Prussian warmongering during the last century has largely been romanticized. His statue stands, with its fierce moustache, huge jack-boots, spiked helmet and sword, as a reminder of the destructive forces that have swept across Europe—more than once.

The Inner City

As you approach the inner city, the fruits of war are all too apparent. The heart of Hamburg was ripped to shreds during the last war, and though construction speeds on there are still vast, gaping holes. One building that survived the holocaust was the 18th-century brick church of St. Michael's (St. Michaelis), which now comes into view on your right, surrounded by a cluster of small red-brick houses, the Krameramtsstuben, tiny, 17th-century houses that today are art galleries, inns and cafés. From the green-topped spire of St. Michael's, the watchman blows his trumpet every day at 10 A.M., to east and west, and again at 9 P.M. to all four directions. You can climb to his windy music stand, just below the clock, and gaze across the entire city and the port—a splendid panorama.

The Ost-West-Strasse now takes you into town, but first there is that maze of old warehouses, bridges, water-worn stairways and abandoned quays around Rödings Markt, and the canals, called Fleete, which connect the Elbe with the Alster. There is something here of Venice and Amsterdam. When you have seen enough, steer towards the high spires of the Town Hall (Rathaus), which will guide you to the Alt-Stadt center, her most elegant shops and restaurants, and the chance to rest your feet.

One of the most exquisite shopping arcades in Europe is in the Alster Arcade, alongside the canal that borders the Rathausplatz. Here you will find furs, diamonds, ancient apothecary boxes and modern manicure kits, Bavarian lederhosen and Chinese porcelain—in short, the best consumer goods from all over the world. If you have the money to spend, this is a good place to spend it.

The cheaper, larger department stores lie to the east of the Rathaus, but before you head in that direction, check the times when the Rathaus itself is open. This fine late-19th-century building, designed in a splendid neo-Renaissance style, has a fine festival hall, noble vaulted ceilings, elaborate doorways and offers a rare view of German official architecture at its proudest.

The Alster Lakes

If the weather is fine, now is the time to head for the Alster, a short walk which takes you out onto the elegant Jungfernstieg. Here there is a café on the lakeside, and the chance to check the boats that leave every few minutes to cross the Alster waters. On a gustier day, you might prefer to cross the Rathausplatz and explore Mönckebergstrasse. Largely rebuilt after the war, there are nevertheless a couple of architectural gems here— the Petrikirche (St. Petri's) dating from 1849 and, next door, a 300-year-old house which gives a startling impression of how this street might once have been before the invention of steel and plate glass. Across the road, in Gerhard Hauptmannplatz, is the Hamburg TIP, an information center where you can find out about everything from current concerts and excursion trips to Schleswig-Holstein, to who needs a drummer for his band and who is offering a ride to Berlin on Wednesday. Here, too, you find the Thalia Theater.

A little further along Mönckebegstrasse is the best hamburger place in town, entirely American in conception, for the universally useful meal-in-a-bun which takes its name from this city has truly nothing to do with Germany. For authentic local sausages, and fine local breads and cakes, continue a little further to the café/conditorei Otto Vernimb. Here, from a first-floor window, you can watch the city come and go, enjoying succulent desserts at acceptable prices. The pedestrian precinct below is full of shoppers and the atmosphere is always relaxed.

South towards the river from here, there are some interesting pieces of architecture, notably the Chilehaus, the Sprinkenhof and the Ballinhaus— built during the last century and happily survivors of the war. They deserve an afternoon on their own, as does the immense television tower, the Fernsehturm, 270 meters (890 ft.) high and visible throughout the city. From its summit, you will have a stupendous view of Hamburg, particularly at night.

At the end of Mönckebergstrasse is the main station again, and beyond it the Arts and Crafts Museum (Museum für Kunst und Gewerbe), in Steintorplatz. Also close by, in Kirchenallee, is the German Theater (Deutsches Schauspielhause). Originally built in 1889 it reopened in 1984 after extensive renovation, which uncovered the original murals, ceiling frescoes and gildings. The theater's accompanying stage is the Malersaal.

Excursions from Hamburg

Downstream from the city along the Elbe shore is the quaint riverside village of Blankenese, where narrow streets and winding step-ways (Treppe) connect the main road above with the waterside and beach below. There are several pleasant restaurants here, where you can sit and gaze at the ships as they rumble up and down the river. You can catch an S-bahn train from the main station, which carries you quickly and comfortably, but the most interesting ride is certainly by car along the Elbchaussee, with its elegant parks and attractive old mansions.

On the other, southern, side of the river, beyond the refineries which have made the Elbe unsafe for swimming with their effluence, lies the agricultural Alte Land, the Old Land. This can be reached by local ferry from St. Pauli Piers via Wedel (at Welcome Pier) to Lühe. A drive through this very traditional region, with its vast timbered farmhouses in which people, animals and crops are all housed under one roof, is a dip into history. Canals, simple taverns, fresh air and men hard at work are the characteristics of this flat Saxon land. One goal of this trip might be Stade, an old Hanseatic city, with many of its medieval buildings still intact. The best time to visit is April/May, when the fruit trees are in blossom, or in June for the cherry harvest.

For a look at the mouth of the mighty Elbe, which is fed by waters from Czechoslovakia over 1,125 km. (700 miles) away, take a boat from Hamburg to Cuxhaven and, beyond it, to the island of Helgoland. In fine weather, this is a delightful ride, and you can still get back to the city before nightfall. If you have the time, spend the night on Helgoland, which will refresh you for another bout of tourist life back in the city.

East of Hamburg, riding up the Elbe, lies the glorious wild Saxon Forest (Sachsenwald). You can get there by S-bahn through a series of rather dismal industrial dormitory towns like Bergedorf and Reinbek, stopping off, if you have a mind to, at the Bismarck Museum in Friedrichsruh, where the Iron Chancellor died, in the bosom of land presented to him by Kaiser Wilhelm in 1871, for services rendered. It is, however, much more pleasant to drive through these woods, in which case you might turn north, follow the little Bille through its valley, and make your goal the picturesque old watermill at Grander-Mühle or, a little further along, the bathing beaches at Grossensee and Lütjensee.

East of Hamburg, again, but further to the north, is Lauenburg, a pleasant little town at the point where the Elbe-Lübeck Canal leaves the river. It is reached by boat from the St. Pauli Piers or by suburban train, but the point is the boat ride through lovely country. On the way, you pass The Four Lands—Vierlande—large stretches of land, growing fruits and vegetables for the Hamburg market, separated by various branches of the Elbe, canals, and other rivers, that under the very eye of Hamburg have maintained their old customs and costumes (the latter particularly colorful, involving, for the women, a curious headdress that looks like an inverted bowl). Shortly before the goal is reached are Geeshacht, an old town creeping onto the hill above it, and several bathing beaches along the Elbe. Until less than a hundred years ago Lauenburg was the seat of an autonomous duchy of the same name and the half-timbered architecture of the lower town is witness to its historic past while the terrace of the former castle in the upper town provides a good view of the Elbe, bridged here for one of the main connections between north and south, at the point where it is joined by the Lübeck-Elbe canal.

If you have a spare afternoon, and the weather is good, take the U-bahn northwest to Hagenbeck, where the zoo is situated. The animals roam in open enclosures, with moats rather than cages to contain them. The great-great-granddaughter of the founder still runs the zoo, which was built up as a private business. Wild animals are still trained here for circuses.

PRACTICAL INFORMATION FOR HAMBURG

TELEPHONES. The telephone code for Hamburg is 040. To call any number in this chapter, unless otherwise specified, this prefix must be used. Within the city no prefix is required.

HOTELS. Prices are higher than elsewhere in Germany. Hamburg has many hotels but advance booking is necessary in summer and whenever large conventions or congresses are taking place—and this is quite often. Central booking offices (Hotelnachweise) can arrange this for you: there is one in the main station, on the Kirchenallee side (326917), and another at the airport arrival hall (24870240).

The Tourist Office offers a selection of all-in package deals and special arrangements, including, for example, "Happy Hamburg Package" which in conjunction with about 80 hotels of varying categories offers one, two or three days' accommodations (Mon. to Fri. only, bed and breakfast); a "Happy Hamburg Pass" with vouchers for reduced round-trips through the city, the harbor and on the Alster, a visit to the townhall, free entrance to the stately museums, and to some night clubs. Contact the Tourist Information office (see below).

Deluxe

Atlantic Hotel (Kempinski). An der Alster 72–79 (28880). 430 beds, most rooms with bath, 20 suites. Located on lakeside, elegantly furnished with glittering public rooms; roof-top swimming pool; nightclub. Fine *Atlantic Grill* restaurant, noteworthy *Atlantic Bar* and new, rustic beer tavern *Mühle.* AE, DC, MC, V.

Crest. Mexikoring (6305051). 270 beds, all with bath or shower; two restaurants and a bar. Situated near Hamburg City Park; convenient for airport and shopping. AE, DC, MC, V.

Hamburg Plaza. Marseiller Str. 2 (35020). 785 beds, most rooms with bath, color TV and radio. Swimming pool and sauna, two good restaurants and rooftop cocktail lounge with a fine view. AE, DC, MC V.

Inter-Continental. Fontenay 10 (414150). 600 beds, all rooms with own bathroom. Located on the lakeside, with several restaurants and bars, indoor pool, sauna, conference rooms, shops and large carpark. AE, DC, MC, V.

Ramada-Renaissance. Grosse Bleichen 36 (349180). 211 rooms, all with bath; 47 apartments. Situated in the heart of the city between Jungfernstieg and the Presseviertel. Sauna, solarium, *Noblesse* restaurant (E), and piano bar. AE, DC, MC, V.

Vier Jahreszeiten. Neuer Jungfernstieg 9 (34941). 300 beds, most with bath. Also on the lakeside, a hotel of the very highest class, with luxurious antique-style suites and excellent food. Impeccable service. The hotel even has its own farm. AE, DC, MC, V.

Expensive

Abtei. Abteistr. 14 (345–7565). 14 rooms, all with bath. An elegant period building on a quiet, tree-lined street near the Alster lakeside park. AE, DC, MC, V.

Ambassador. Heidenkampsweg 34 (230002). 200 beds, most rooms with shower or bath. Located in Hammerbrook district, near the Binnenbarbour and the Elbe Bridge; bars and swimming pool; grill restaurant. AE, DC, MC, V.

Aussen Alster. Schmilinskystr. 1 (241557). 27 rooms, all with bath. A small, tranquil hotel in a gracious 19th-century house. Located by the Alster lake. AE, DC, MC, V.

Bellevue. An der Alster 14 (248011). 103 beds, conference room, restaurant. Popular hotel on the lakeside, with splendid view of Alster; rooms at the front are larger but somewhat noisy. AE, DC, MC, V.

Berlin. Borgfelderstrasse 1–9 (251640). 120 rooms with bath and good view; suites with TV. Located near the autobahn exit, it is very modern and has excellent food. AE, DC, MC, V.

Europäischer Hof. Kirchenallee 45 (248171). 350 rooms, most with bath or shower; good restaurant; garage. Located opposite main station, near the Schauspielhaus and Hansa Theater. AE, DC, MC, V.

Garden Hotels Pöseldorf. Magdalenenstr. 60 (449958). 70 rooms, all with own bathroom; very well equipped. Located in a quiet side street in the pretty Pöseldorf section of the city, not far from the Alster and the center. An attractive garden is open for guests in summer. First-class service with a personal touch. V.

Moderate

Baseler Hospiz. Esplanade 11 (341921). Friendly and efficient service and neatly furnished rooms. Located near the State Opera House. AE, DC, MC, V.

Eden. Ellmenreichstrasse 20 (248480). 170 beds. Pleasant and modern. AE, DC, MC, V.

Kronprinz. Kirchenallee 46 (243258). 107 rooms, some with bath. Bar. AE, DC, MC, V.

Mellingburger Schleuse. Mellingburgredder 1 (6024001). 20 minutes' drive from city center in idyllic forest location. The *Alsterwanderweg* hiking trail passes the door. The hotel itself is over 150 years old, with a thatched roof, peasant-styled furnishings, and the restaurant serves regional northern German dishes. AE, DC, MC.

Metro-Merkur. Bremer Reihe 12–14 (247266). 104 beds, meals for guests. Located near main station.

Pacific. Neuer Pferdemarkt 30–31 (439 5094). 100 beds. Situated near Heiligengeistfeld. DC, MC.

Raphael Hotel Altona. Präsident-Krahn-Str. 13 (381239). 95 beds. Near Hamburg-Altona railway station in Altona. DC.

Steen's. Holzdamm 43 (244642). 11 rooms, all with bath. Small and intimate hotel located close to train station. AE, MC.

Wappen von Hamburg. Floating hotel-ship. In summer it plies the Hamburg–Helgoland route, but in winter is docked at the St. Pauli Landungsbrücken when it offers accommodations, dining facilities and entertainment. 63 beds in 29 cabins, all with shower and WC.

Wedina. Gurlittstr. 23 (243011). 23 rooms, most with bath. Old-fashioned but comfortable hotel. AE, DC, MC, V.

Inexpensive

Aachener Hof. St.–Georg–Strasse 10 (241313). 63 beds. Hotel-pension just outside the center.

Alameda. Colonnaden 45 (344290). Good, basic accommodations. AE, DC, MC, V.

Amsterdam Garni. Moorweidenstr. 34 (441419). Very clean and friendly pension, close to Dammtor station and the university. No restaurant.

Metro Merkur. Bremer Rehie 12–14 (247266). Convenient and functional hotel near the train station. No restaurant. AE, DC, MC, V.

Camping

For information call ADAC, Amsinckstr. 39 (2399246).

Camping Anders. Kieler Str. 650 (570 4498).

Camping Brünning. Kronsaalweg 86/Kieler Str. (540 4994).

Campingplatz Buchholz. Kieler Str. 374 (540 4532).

Campingplatz Ramcke. Kieler Str. 620 (5705121).

Youth Hostels

There are four main Youth Hostels in Hamburg for which you will need a YH identification card, though there's no age limit.

Auf dem Stintfang. Alfred Wegener Weg 5 (313488). Near the St. Pauli Landing Stages.

Hamburger Jugendpark Langenhorn. Jugendparkweg 60 (5313050). For groups only.

Horner Rennbahn. Rennbahnstr. 100 (651 1671).

Horner Rennbahn Gästehaus. Rennbahnstr. 100 (651 1671). Annexed to Horner Rennbahn.

HOW TO GET AROUND. From the airport. Buses leave the airport for the city center (main station) every 20 minutes from 5:15 A.M. to 9:30 P.M. The journey takes about 25 minutes. In the reverse direction, buses depart from the central bus station near the main station every 20 minutes from 5.20 A.M. to 9.20 P.M. Single ticket including luggage costs DM. 7.00, children half-fare. Another possibility is taking the HVV Airport-Express from/to Ohlsdorf tube station. These buses run every 10 min. and cost the normal HVV tariff.

City transportation. Hamburg has an excellent system of buses, electric suburban railways (S-Bahn) and metro or subway (U-Bahn). The whole public transport system is a combination of seven different transport services joining together to form the Hamburg Transport Combine (HVV). Fares are uniform for the entire system and tickets are purchased from HVV ticket kiosks and from automatic vending machines in each station and at some bus stops. These machines accept DM.2 DM.1, 50 and 10 pfennig pieces, but also dispense change. A map of all stations is available at tourist offices or from the HVV ticket kiosks. A day ticket for travel anywhere in the large central zone costs DM. 7. However we recommend that you buy a special tourist ticket from the HVV. These are valid on all types of HVV transport (including first class), for any number of journeys. As a city tourist ticket in the inner zone it is valid from 9 A.M. until 4.30 A.M. the following day and costs DM. 8 per person per day. As an area tourist ticket for Hamburg and surroundings, that is, for the whole HVV network, it is valid for the whole day and costs DM. 13 per person per day.

By bus. Hamburg is well served by street public transport, though it is helpful if you can speak a little German. The advantage of the bus over trains is that you can view the city as you travel, particularly from the double-deckers.

By boat. The Alster fleet of ferries and steamers has been taken over recently by a private tour operator, *Alster Touristik GmbH*, who have added a special Alster Cruise to the standard timetable.

Regular Alster "taxis" usually leave the Jungfernstieg pier for points along the lake and the canals. For inquiries call 341145. For harbor trips from St. Pauli Piers, with commentary in English, check the timetable of *HADAG* ships (3768024) or Harbor Launches (314 4644/4267). A round-trip lasts about an hour and costs DM. 11.00.

From Easter to Christmas there is a pleasure trip available, leaving from the St. Pauli Landing Stages, Brücke 2 (Bridge 2) at 8 P.M. The trip lasts about three hours, with a lavish buffet, unlimited draught beer and one schnaps as you cruise through the illuminated port, with music and singing. Price about DM. 50.00.

By taxi. Taxis, which can be hailed in the street, are expensive. Charges start at DM.3 and increase rapidly. You can call a taxi also by dialing 441011.

TOURIST INFORMATION. The Hamburg Tourist Information center is at Bieberhaus am Hauptbahnhof, 2000 Hamburg 1 (248700). They deal with all tourist inquiries, supply much printed material, give assistance to visitors, have an advance hotel-reservation service and sell theater tickets.

Another visitors' service center is at the airport in the Arrival Hall D, *Information am Flughafen,* open daily from 8 A.M. to 11 P.M. (24870240), also providing an accommodations service, information on sightseeing, entertainment, restaurants, plus information on Hamburg's public transport system (HVV) and the sale of tourist tickets.

A similar information point is in the city center at Gerhart Hauptmann Platz, (324758) open Mon. to Fri. 9–6, Sat. 9–2, or 9–6 on first Sat. of month.

There is another information pavilion at the main railway station (Hauptbahnhof), (24870230), and there is also one conveniently located between entrances 4 and 5 of the St. Pauli Landing Stages, which forms part of the Harbor Information Center (313977). Both are open Mon. to Fri. 9–6.

USEFUL ADDRESSES. ADAC Automobile Club Recovery Service. Amsinckstr. 39 (23999).

Car Hire. *Auto Sixt,* Ellmenreichstr. 26 (241466). *Avis,* Drehbahn 15–25 (341651). *Hertz,* Amsinckstr. 45 (230045).

Consulates. *American,* Alsterufer 28 (441061). *Canadian,* Esplanade 41–47 (351805). *British,* Harvestehuder Weg 8 (446071).

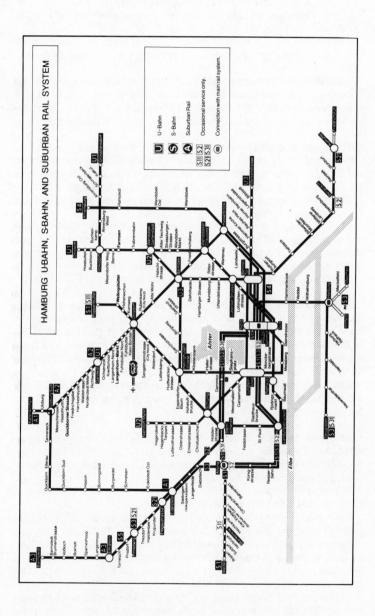

HAMBURG U-BAHN, S-BAHN, AND SUBURBAN RAIL SYSTEM

U-Bahn
S-Bahn
Suburban Rail
Occasional service only.
Connection with main rail system.

Lost property. *City lost & found office,* Fundbüro, Bäckerbreitergang 73 (351851). *Rail,* Stresemannstr. 114 (3918–5589).

Medical Emergency. 228022.

Police. Emergency tel. 110.

Post Offices. *Central Post Office,* Münzstr. 1 (23951), open Mon. to Fri. 8–6, Sat. 8–noon. *Post Office Main Station,* (239 5333), open 24 hours.

TOURS. City sightseeing buses start from Kirchenalle (opposite Hotel Phoenix) at the main railway station. A tour of the city (with English–speaking guide) lasts about two hours and costs DM.18. Tours depart at 11 A.M. and 3 P.M. in April and May; more frequently from June on.

There is an extended version of this tour available, which lasts two and a half hours; there are also combined "City and Harbor" tours, by bus and HADAG ship; and boat trips which depart from the Jungfernstieg quay Apr. through Oct., or from the St. Pauli Piers, Bridges 2 and 3.

There is a "Hamburg by Night" tour, which includes a boat trip, a bus drive, and visits to nightspots and a sex show.

Then there are canal cruises through Hamburg's waterways; trips by ship to the Blankenese quarter; boat trips out to the "Altes Land" around Hamburg; and boat trips to the Vierlande, which is Germany's largest flower-growing area on the Elbe upstream from Hamburg.

Information for all trips from the Tourist Information Offices.

EXCURSIONS. There are many interesting areas and quaint villages that can be reached easily from Hamburg, by car, ferry or day bus trip. Some examples of excursion goals are: the village of Blankenese; Stade, an old Hanseatic city with many of its medieval buildings still intact; the island of Helgoland; the Sachsenwald (Saxon Forest); or Lauenburg, a little town at the point where the Elbe-Lübeck Canal leaves the river.

Day bus trips are organized by the Tourist Information Office, and they will also supply additional information to help you plan excursions of your own.

SPORTS. Sports of all kinds—fishing, golf, sailing, swimming and tennis etc.—are available in Hamburg. Details on all can be had from either the Tourist Office or *Hamburger Sportbund* (Hamburg Sports Association), Schäferkampsallee 1 (41210).

Biking. The Tourist Office (Fremdenverkehrs-zentrale (248700)) rent bikes for DM.2.00 an hour. (Apr. through Sept.).

Golf. *Hamburger Golf-Club Falkenstein,* In de Bargen 59, (812177). *Golf-Club auf der Wendelohe,* Oldesloer Str. 251, (5505014).

Sailing. *Yacht-Schule Bambauer,* Schöne Aussicht 20a (220 0030). Sailing school. In addition sailing, rowing and pedal-boats can be hired during the summer from 10 A.M.–9 P.M. at average cost DM.9–12 per hour for two people, each additional person DM.3.

Swimming. Not in the Alster or Elbe please! Hamburg has a very large selection of indoor and outdoor pools, which can be found listed in the monthly *Vorschau* brochure available at all tourist offices and information points. For example: *Alster Schwimmhalle,* Ifflandstr. 21, *Blankenese,* Simrockstrasse, or *St. Pauli,* Budapester Str. 29. Because of school-party visits, inquire first about opening times.

Squash. Among many others, *Squash Point Hamburg,* Eimsbüttler Chaussee 63 (4301031).

Tennis. Information about tennis courts from *Hamburger Tennis Verband* (tennis association), Hallerstr. 89 (445078).

PARKS AND GARDENS. Alsterpark. On the Alster, with a splendid view of the city skyline.

Hagenbeck Zoo. In the northwest suburb of Stellingen and easily reached by U-Bahn or bus. Originally founded in 1907, the zoo has long enjoyed a reputation for modernity and innovation (it was the first zoo anywhere to house animals in openair pens).

Hirschpark. On the Elbe, with game enclosure and charming tea house with thatched roof.

Jenischpark. On the Elbe, with classical manor house and Barlach Museum.

Planten un Blomen. In the city center. Extensive park with many rare trees and shrubs; trips around the park on a miniature railway; plus concerts and illuminated water organ.

Stadtpark. North of the Alster. Houses the Planetarium; plus 19 miles of footpaths; rock concerts in summer.

HISTORIC BUILDINGS AND CITY DISTRICTS. Deichstrasse. Old merchants' street with self-contained groups of old burgher-houses in varying styles. The buildings date from the 17th century; inside, the office, warehouse and living quarters of the merchant were often to be found under a single roof. The buildings were largely restored to their original state after being almost destroyed in the great fire of 1842.

Eppendorf and Winterhude. Attractive and popular residential districts at the end of the Alster with magnificent private homes dating from the turn of the century. Any number of pubs and restaurants can be found in both districts.

Fernsehturm (TV Tower). Lagerstr. 2–8 (Sternschanze tube station). Superb view over the city and surrounding areas from the observation platform at 128 meters (420 feet) (though the height of the tower itself is a massive 270 meters [890 feet]). Good restaurant and self service cafe. Quite a steep entrance charge.

Fisch Markt (Fish Market). One of the city's most colorful attractions, located between Hexenberg and Grosse Elbstrasse. The market, held every Sunday, between 6 and 9.30 A.M., is by no means confined to fish, and everything from birds to bicycles is on offer.

Grossneumarkt. This area, located between the city center and St. Pauli, has blossomed into a delightfully atmospheric center of pubs and clubs. Take a stroll along Peterstr. to see the restored brick and half-timbered houses and the monument to Brahms, the city's most famous son.

Krameramtswohnungen. In the courtyard of Krayenkamp 10/11, opposite St. Michaelis. The houses were built by the Merchants' Guild for the widows of its members and they are one of the few relics of old Hamburg. Now a cultural center with an art gallery, a small museum, second-hand bookshop and a café.

Panoptikum (Wax works), Spielbudenplatz. Best wax works in Germany; everyone from Charlemagne to Elvis.

Planetarium. In the Stadtpark. Excellent and very modern Planetarium, capable of projecting up to 8,900 stars on to the roof of the dome. Also exhibitions on many aspects of space and space travel.

Pöseldorf. Small, very modern shopping area on the Outer Alster, with antique shops, boutiques, pubs and restaurants. Trendy and atmospheric and excellent for a night out.

Rathaus. To the south of the Binnenalster, this is Hamburg's City Hall. Built in the late-19th century in splendid Renaissance style, the building rests on some 4,000 oak piles, while the interior has a total of 647 rooms, many sumptuously furnished.

CHURCHES. St. Katharinen.

Am Zollkanal. Gothic church built between 1350 and 1420 with 105 meter (345 foot) spire, at the top of which is a statue of the saint.

St. Jacobi. Steinstr. 14th-century church with famous organ and three medieval altar pieces.

St. Michaelis. Ost-West-Str. Built between 1750 and 1762 and a great Hamburg landmark; this is the most important late-Baroque church in north Germany. Beautiful view of the port from the tower.

St. Petri. Mönckebergstr. The original church on this site was built in the 12th century, but destroyed by the great fire of 1842. The present building dates from 1849.

MUSEUMS AND GALLERIES.

Most Hamburg museums are closed on Mondays, and most also have one day a week when entry charges are dropped. However, like opening times (usually 10 to 5), these vary and it's best to check with the tourist offices for up to the minute information.

Altonaer Museum/Norddeutsches Landesmuseum (North German Regional Museum). Museumstr. 23, in the suburbs of Altona. Collections covering life and culture of North Germany; strong maritime collections.

The Kunsthalle. Glockengiesserwall 1. Hamburg's principal art gallery and contains some of the best works of art in northern Germany. The collections include paintings from the late Middle Ages to modern times. European and American (from the '60s onwards) schools are particularly well represented. Perhaps one of the finest pieces is the *Grabow Altarpiece,* executed by Master Bertram in the late-14th century.

Museum für Hamburgische Geschichte (Hamburg Historical Museum). Holstenwall 24. Hamburg's history, the development of the port and seafaring. The *Historic Emigration Office* is also housed here. Opened in 1984, it is Germany's first historical documentation center for the history of emigration. Between 1850 and 1914 almost five million people passed through Hamburg's harbor on their way to the "New World." The collection has a data store with the names of all those who left Germany between those years. Visitors interested in researching their immigrant forefathers need only provide the name and year of emigration from Germany. A search through the archives costs $30 and provides a certificate stating all personal data, family members and town of origin.

Museum für Kunst und Gewerbe (Museum of Decorative Arts and Crafts). Steintorplatz 1. Remarkable medieval gold and silver work, Renaissance furniture, 18th-century porcelain and art nouveau.

Museum for Völkerkunde (Ethnology Museum). Rothenbaumchaussee 64. Exhibits from all over the world; particularly good exhibits from Africa and South America.

Oevelgönne Museumshafen (Harbor Museum). Beim Anleger Neumühlen, Oevelgonne. A floating museum; sail boats, freighters, fire-ships, etc; in the harbor at Oevelgönne. Open until the Elbe freezes.

THEATERS. The theater season runs from Sept. through May. Traditional theater is well represented with drama and comedy, as well as numerous workshop, youth and boulevard theaters. A good knowledge of German is necessary to get full enjoyment from a theater visit, of course.

The ballet presents no language problems. In fact it occupies a very special place in Hamburg. The Hanseatic City has become the German metropolis of ballet in latter years, and it is worth the effort to obtain a ticket during the Ballet Festival weeks in July.

Full details of theater and concerts, with details of performances, box office opening times, etc. can be obtained in the monthly calendar of events *Hamburger Vorschau* available from tourist offices and information (1-Punkt) stands.

The three well-known orchestras of Hamburg—the Philharmonic, NDR Symphony and Hamburg Symphony—perform concert cycles with well-known conductors and soloists in the **Musikhalle** concert house. Church concerts likewise also rate exceptionally highly in Hamburg.

The following are some of the most important theaters:

Altonaer Theater. Museumstr. 17 (391545/46). Mainly classical.

Deutsches Schauspielhaus. Kirchenallee 39/41 (248713). One of the leading theaters in the German-speaking world. Modern productions of classical and avant-garde plays. The building has lately undergone extensive restoration and was reopened to the public only in October 1984. It is a delight to visit, the language barrier notwithstanding.

The English Theater. Lerchenfeld 14 (225543). Plays in English.

Hamburger Kammerspiel. Hartungstr. 9 (445162). Traditional theater offering mainly lighter fare.

Hamburgische Staatsoper (State Opera House). Dammtorstr. 28 (351555). Opera-house with international fame and world-famous ballet ensemble.

Hansa Theater. Steindamm 17 (241414). The only classical music-hall in the German-speaking world, with drinks and light meals served.

Kleine Komödie. Neuer Wall 54 (367340). Boulevard comedies.

Piccolo Theater im Fürsthof. Juliussstr. 13–15 (435348). The world's smallest theater (with restaurant).

Das Schiff. Anleger Holzbrücke (364765). A small theater on Germany's only theater-ship, moored at Holzbrücke near the corner of Ost-West/Deichstr.

Thalia Theater. Gerhart-Hauptmann-Platz 2 (330444). A theater with a great tradition; many stars of German-speaking stage appear here.

Theater im Zimmer. Alsterchaussee 30 (446539). For more experimental plays.

Theater für Kinder. Max Brauer Allee 76 (382538). Children's theater.

SHOPPING. Shopping malls—the city has nine—make shopping in the city a real treat, even when it's raining. The way through this dense network of arcades leads you through the cool, industrial-like architecture of the Gänsemarkt-Passage; the two adjacent passages of Neuer Gänsemarkt and Gerhof; the glass-roofed Hanse Viertel Galerie Passage, over 200 meters long; the Galleria with its marble pilasters; the classical building of the Alte Post; the passage in the 100-year-old office building Hamburger Hof; and finally through the Landesbankgalerie.

There is a useful book published (unfortunately in German only, but with the help of a simple dictionary you should be able to follow it easily) entitled *Hamburg Shopping* (Christians Verlag). Ask at a bookshop or the Tourist Information.

As an international port and city, Hamburg's specialties are naturally varied and the wares offered come from all over the world. For example, Spanish, Chinese and, perhaps above all, English. There is a particularly large choice of English clothing, furniture, antiques and, of course, tea, as well as lobster, smoked salmon and caviar. It is also well worth looking for some maritime souvenirs: ships in bottles, maps and charts, coins, uniforms. The following stores carry such goods:

J. Binikowski. Lokstedter Weg 68 (462852), For ships in bottles.

Gäth & Peine. Hermannsr. 46 (335586). Flags.

Harry's Hamburger Hafenbasar. Bernhard Nocht-Strasse 63 (312484). Close to the harbor, selling everything and anything.

Seifarth & Co. Robert-Koch-Str. 19, in Norderstedt section (5240027) (day and night). Europe's largest caviar mail-order company, with lobster, salmon and tea.

RESTAURANTS. Food in Hamburg is for the most part excellent and good value. Aside from the hamburger, the city is famed for sea food. Perhaps the most renowned fish dish is *Aalsuppe* (eel soup), comparable to the Marseille *bouillabaisse.* The city also produces some other excellent soups. Try the *Arfensuppe mit Snuten un Poten,* a thick pea soup with pig's trotters, and *Hamburger Frische Suppe,* made of beef, veal and vegetables. Other Hamburg specialties include *Stubenküken* (chicken), *Vierländer Mastente* (duck), *Birnen, Bohnen und Speck* (pears, beans and bacon), and the sailor's favorite, *Labskaus.*

Expensive

L'Auberge Francaise. Rutschbahn 34 (410 2532). Excellent French cooking, and delicious seafood recipes. (Closed Sun.). AE, DC, MC.

Bavaria-Blick. Bernhard-Nocht-Strasse 99 (314800). On the top floor of the building, a classy restaurant with Hanseatic atmosphere. AE, DC, MC, V.

Le Canard. Martinistr. 11 (460 4830). Has the reputation among regular customers of being the best restaurant on earth! The delicate French cuisine can boast a whole row of medals and prizes. The wine list is outstanding. DC.

Le Delice. Klosterwall 9–21 (327727). In the Markthalle, small elegant bistro; food exquisite and reservations are a must.

La Fayette. Zimmerstr. 30 (225630). Newly established top address for gourmets. Fine cuisine based on local specialties, plus excellent Bavarian dishes. AE, DC.

Fischereihafen-Restaurant. Grosse Elbstrasse 143 (381816). Fish specialties in every imaginable way they can be prepared. Hamburg's best fish restaurant by far. In an old house right on the Elbe, with panoramic view. DC.

Haerlin Restaurant. Neuer Jungfernstieg 9 (34941). In the Vier Jahreszeiten Hotel, it shares the hotel's high standards. A view of the Binnen Alster and marvelous cooking. AE, DC, MC, V.

Landhaus Dill. Elbchaussee 404 (828443). Former coaching house, now a top French restaurant specializing in *nouvelle cuisine*. There are over two dozen different brands of *Armagnac* on the wine-list. DC, V.

Landhaus Scherrer. Elbchaussee 130 (880 1325). Famous country-house-style restaurant. Very expensive, but a real Hamburg institution. With separate Bistro-Restaurant for lunch-time meals. Fine regional dishes in cosy surroundings. (Closed Sun.). AE, DC, MC.

L'Auberge Francaise. Rutschbahn 34 (410–2532). Traditional seafood and fine wines in what's regarded by many as the city's top French restaurant. DC, MC, V.

Nikolaikeller. Am Cremon 36 (366113). An old Hamburg tavern serving local specialties including several kinds of *Matjes.*

Schümanns Austernkeller. Jungfernstieg 34 (346265). Specializes in seafood; solemn wooden decor with pretty booths. Closed Sun.

Moderate

Ahrberg. Strandweg 33 (860438). Traditional German dishes and seafood specialties in a long-time favorite by the river in Blankensee. AE, DC, MC.

Alt Hamburger Aalspeicher. Deichstr. 43 (362990). Smoked eel dishes, sole, plaice and herrings, fresh daily.

Alt Hamburger Bürgerhaus. Deichstrasse 37 (373633). Traditional Hamburg specialties in gourmet restaurant in the historic Deichstrasse. AE, DC, MC.

Bologna. Hudtwalckerstr. 37 (460 1796). Near the Winterhuder Market Square. Small, select Italian specialties. DC, MC.

Le Château. Milchstr. 19 (444200). A traditional French restaurant in a 19th-century mansion in fashionable Poseldorf.

Gino Carone. Ruhrstr. 60 (850 6688). Italian delicatessen recommended especially for delicious lunches. Don't be put off by its location in a rather ugly industrial area.

Il Giardino. Ulmenstr. 17–19 (470147). An attractive courtyard makes summer dining here a delight. Italian and nouvelle specialties. AE, MC, V.

Nationalküche. Eppendorfer Weg 9 (437565). Light German food served in candle-lit cellar under glass roof.

Portugalia. Kleiner Schäferkamp 28 (417555). Original Portuguese specialties in atmospheric surroundings.

Ratsweinkeller. Grosse Johannistr. 2 (364153). Restaurant at the Rathaus with long tradition of good cuisine. Located in beautifully-vaulted cellar of the city hall. AE, DC, MC.

Skyline-Turm-Restaurant. Lagerstr. 2 (438024). In the Fernsehturm. A revolving restaurant (one turn an hour) 128 meters (420 feet) high up on the 270-meter (890-foot) TV tower, with outstanding view. Two sections: the upper section is a fine and higher-priced restaurant; the lower section is self-service. Also a café. AE, DC, MC.

Süllberg. Sullbergsterrasse 2 (861686). A vast indoor and outdoor restaurant and cafe in a castle-like structure on a hill above Blankenese. AE, DC, MC.

Tre Fontane. Mundsburger Damm 45 (223193). Fine Italian restaurant with a family touch. Portions are large.

Zum Alten Rathaus. Börsenbrücke 10 (367570). Noted for good food, sea-shanties and "salty" wisecracks—in vaulted-cellar tavern *Zum Fleetenkieker.* AE, DC, MC.

Inexpensive

At Nali. Rutschbahn 11 (410–3810). One of the city's oldest and most popular Turkish restaurants. Open till late. AE, DC, MC, V.

Avocado. Kanalstr. 9 (220–4599). Popular and modern restaurant offering excellent value and imaginative food.

Destille. In the Museum für Kunst und Gewerbe (Arts and Crafts Museum) (280 3354). Stylish museum-cafe in art-nouveau style. Excellent buffet, freshly served salads, cold cuts, good cheese and beer from the wood.

Die Hofküche. Hofweg 41 (223268). Former colonial stores premises, decorated with plenty of antiques. Today a delicatessen store and party service, serving good-value tasty lunches, particularly hearty soups.

Fischerhaus. St. Pauli, Fischmarkt 14 (314053). Located right at the fish market. Specialty of the house is marinated *Bratherringe* (grilled herring).

Fischkajüte. St. Pauli Landungsbrücken, Brücke 5 (314162). At the landing stages. Oldest fried-fish restaurant in Germany. AE, DC.

Inter-City Restaurant. At the Altona Railway Station. Particularly good value, serving wholesome traditional meals at realistic prices.

Kanzelmeyer. ABC Str. 8 (344296). Open Mon. to Fri., quick, clean and inexpensive.

Old Commercial Room. Englische Planke 10 (366319). Old Hamburg cooking. Open continuously from 11 A.M. to 1 A.M. DC, MC, V.

Schmitz. Marie-Luisen-Str. 3 (484132). Small, nostalgic eating-house serving plain fare in outsize portions.

Vegetärische Gaststätte. Over the Alsterarkaden passage (344703). Oldest establishment of its kind in the world for good-value vegetarian food.

Beer Restaurants

Anno 1750. Ost-West Str. (330070). Baroque building and one of the oldest structures in Hamburg. Newly-established rustic beer-tavern serving wholesome home cooking—a mixture of Bavarian and Hamburg dishes.

Nürnberger Bratwurstglöckle. Grindelberg 7 (449696). This rustic beer tavern serves the dark Nurnberg beer, and a mixture of Bavarian and Franconian home-cooking. Inexpensive.

Posemuckel. Bleichenbrücke 10 (344411). Beer village (the biggest in North Germany) with 13 types of draught beer, Sun. to Thurs. 7 P.M. to 1 A.M. Fri. and Sat. until 3 A.M.

Wine Taverns

Bistrot a Vin. Grosse Bleichen 36 (in the Mövenpick-Hanse Viertel) (351635). Has become the meeting place of the wine connoisseurs of Hamburg. Over 400 different vintages to try. Light snacks are served with the wine-tasting.

Weinstuben am Grossneumarkt. Grossneumarkt 10 (346689). Cellar tavern, with plenty of wood paneling. Mainly Alsatian, Pfälzer and Badischer wines. With the wines, wholesome dishes of *Matjes* and *Schwarzbrot* are served, and thick soups.

Zur Traube. Karl Theodor Str. 4 (390 9347). In a side street behind the Ottensener Market Square. Rustic decor, the same since 1936. Over two dozen different kinds of open wine, and 50 different bottled vintages. Small snacks.

CAFES. Alsterpavillon. Jungfernstieg 54 (345052). Traditional meeting place on the Alster. First-class confectionary and cakes.

Gustav Adolf von Schweden. Grosse Bleichen 32 (341944). Has the oldest tradition of confectionery in Germany. Closed Sundays.

Konditorei Vernimb/Mövenpick. Spitalerstr 9 (324455). Specialties are pyramid cake and confectionery for diabetics.

Schöne Aussichten. Im alten botanischen Garten (34013). Beautifully situated in the old botanic garden. Especially attractive for the younger tourist.

NIGHTLIFE. It goes without saying that the hottest spots are concentrated in St. Pauli around the Reeperbahn, in a little side street known as the Grosse Freiheit (or Great Freedom—that's putting it mildly). The shows themselves are expensive but to walk through this area is an experience in itself and you can soak up the atmosphere without spending anything. It's *not* advisable, however, to travel through this part of the city alone, especially if you're a girl.

Indeed, if you have any doubts about the St. Pauli district, but want a look anyway, the best bet is to join one of the organized tours arranged by the Tourist Office. They depart at 8 from Hachmannplatz (opposite the main station) and after stopping at several big hotels the tour will start with a visit to the Zillertal on Reeperbahn. It continues with a strip-show in a cabaret on Grosse Freiheit before returning to the point of departure. Price is DM. 80 per person including two drinks (DM. 70 without stripshow). Expensive, but safe.

The following is a small selection of the many nightspots on offer and, in the case of the sex shows, includes only the less bizarre and/or sordid. (It's not understating the case to say that while some of the sex clubs may be quite good fun and relatively harmless, a good many others are pornographic in the extreme. None gets going until about 10; all will happily accommodate you till the early hours. Order your own drinks rather than letting the hostess do it for you and pay for it as soon as it arrives, though check the price list again before handing the money over. If you order whisky, for example, you can be sure you will not get an inexpensive brand).

If you have difficulties on the "world's wickedest mile," the nearest police station (Davidswache) is not far away.

Bayerisch Zell. (314281). Respectable atmosphere.

Cafe Keese. Reeperbahn 19–21 (310805). Palais de danse with good bands. Ladies' choice. Gentlemen are expected to wear suits and ties.

Colibri. Grosse Freiheit 34 (313233). Sex theater with a magnetic attraction for many.

Crazy Boys. Pulverteich 12 (246285). Three shows a night. Boy strippers.

Kaiserhof. Spielbudenplatz 24 (314276). Here the not-quite-so-young meet at the "Lonely Hearts' Ball." Closed Mondays.

Pulverfass. Pulverteich 12 (249791). Superior drag show.

Safari. Grosse Freiheit 24 (315400). One of the top nightspots on St. Pauli.

Salambo. Grosse Freiheit 11 (315622). Sex theater with an amazing show.

Discos and Dancing

Alsterufer 35. Alsterufer 35 (418155). Bar, disco, restaurant and gallery. Latest "in" place.

After Shave. Spielbudenplatz 9 (319 3215). Jazz and rock disco, where more than the usual hits are played.

Bier Palast. Dammtordamm 1 (343825) Jolly dance-hall with long counters and intimate niches. Good music. Also closed Mondays. Live bands.

Blauer Satellit. Marseiller Str. 2 (35020). In the Hamburg Plaza Hotel. Hamburg's highest disco—over 300 ft. up.

Boccaccio. Kirchenallee 49 (299444). Near the main station. Elegant dance-hall with plush and cosy atmosphere. International bands. Closed Mon.

Chesa. Beim Schlump 15 (458811). Intimate disco. Hot meals served until the early morning hours.

Madhouse. Valentinskamp 46a (344193). Disco, always packed full from midnight onwards. Loud music and crazy people.

Offline. Eimsbütteler Chaussee 5 (439 8094). Disco with ingenious glittering light effects. Open Fri. and Sat. only.

The Seventh Heaven. Ballindamm 9 (330237). You can meet a lot of important personalities at this disco. Closed Mon. and Tues.

Top Ten Club. Reeperbahn 136 (314524). Disco relic of the Beatles' era of the sixties and still "in." Closed Mon. and Tues.

Jazz and Rock

Cotton Club. Alter Steinweg 27–31 (343878). Hamburg's oldest jazz cellar. Mainly traditional jazz. Closed Sun.

Fabrik. Barnerstr. 36 (391563). Jazz, rock, pop, blues and theater in a former munitions factory.

Logo. Grindelallee 5 (410 5658). A music club with the widest ranging programme. Stars of the music scene perform here, but also many young up-and-coming groups.

Markthalle. Klosterwall 9 (339491). Communication center in an old market hall. Music and theater. The main emphasis is on Punk, and *Neue Deutsche Welle* (New German Wave).

Grosse Freiheit 36. (319 3649). In the St. Pauli district. It was here that The Beatles played in Hamburg. Great place for live music and dancing.

LOWER SAXONY

The Land of Contrasts

Lower Saxony is bounded by the Elbe on the north, East Germany on the east, Holland on the west, and by Westphalia and Hesse in the south. It includes also the East Frisian Islands in the North Sea. This is a land of wide variety, containing within its borders sea-bound islands and coastal harbors, great river ports and vast heaths, medieval Hanseatic cities and university towns, forests, lakes and spas, and even, as a climax to the extremes, mountains high enough for winter sports.

Exploring Lower Saxony

Moving westward on the southern bank of the Elbe, the first place of importance we come to is Cuxhaven, the third-most important port in Germany after Hamburg and Bremen. It is also an important fishing town and, together with adjacent Duhnen, a beach resort. In the 700-year-old Schloss Ritzebüttel in the center of town is the Heimatmuseum with local history collections, while in nearby Stickenbüttel, in the Dorfstrasse, is the fascinating Wrackmuseum, exhibiting finds from shipwrecks in the Elbe estuary.

Cuxhaven calls its seaside bulwark, for some reason mysterious to outsiders, Alte Liebe (Old Love), and is inordinately proud of its Kugelbake—a stilt-mounted monster of a buoy which stands on the end of a jetty. This marks the beginning of Lighthouse Lane, as the heavily-traveled sea route northward from this point is called. The best fun from Cuxhaven is a sail by smack to the island of Neuwerk.

Passing down the coast from Cuxhaven you will come to Bremerhaven, which performs for Bremen the service Cuxhaven does for Hamburg—many ships dock here instead of sailing up the Weser to the bigger city. Bremerhaven is no mere suburb of Bremen. It is an important city in its own right. With the largest fisherman's harbor in the world (its auction hall is well worth visiting) it possesses a fisheries museum—Nordseemuseum, am Handelshafen 12—and a maritime museum, Deutsche Schiffahrtsmuseum, Van Rozelen Strasse, near the radar tower. This museum has a harbor with many old vessels including a 1380 Hanseatic trading ship, ancient lighthouses, and one of Europe's oldest dry docks. Bremerhaven also has a North Sea Aquarium, an institute of seamanship, the Morgenstern Museum, with prehistoric exhibits and folk art at Kaistrasse 6, and an openair museum at Parkstrasse 9 with traditional peasant houses and 17th-century furnishings. The well-equipped building on the dock at which liners tie up is the modernized and enlarged overseas passengers' terminal, 260 meters (850 feet) long and containing passenger waiting rooms, ship reservation and travel offices, shops, post-office counters, money exchange offices, several restaurants and lunch counters. It is interesting to note that the very first ship to use the newly-founded harbor of Bremerhaven was the U.S.S. *Draper* in 1830. Like most world ports, Bremerhaven enjoys a lively nightlife.

The Great Port of Bremen

About 65 km. (40 miles) up the Weser is Bremen, Germany's oldest and today her second port (Hamburg is the first), a great center of world trade since the days when, with Hamburg and Lübeck, it was one of the Big Three of the Hanseatic League. There is a landing stage in the harbor from where you can take a boat tour of the port. The sightseeing boats first pass by the great three-mast sail ship *Deutschland*, an outstanding beauty, employed today by the naval school and usually at anchor near the Stephans Brücke. Then you proceed to several sections of the great port where ship stands next to ship under rows of cranes.

Immediately upstream from the St. Martin's landing stage is the Great Weser Bridge and not far from it, a little further in from the right bank and tucked away from traffic, is the oldest part of the city, the idyllic Schnoorviertel (Schnoor quarter), with narrow streets and dozens of toy-like houses dating from about 1600, populated by artists and containing small galleries and craftsmen's shops.

European art from the 15th century to the present day can be seen at the Kunsthalle gallery, Am Wall 207. The Roselius Sammlungen in the historic Böttcherstrasse is a collection of German and Baroque art. The museum devoted to the art and cultural history of Bremen is the Bremer Landesmuseum für Kunst und Kulturgeschichte (known as the Focke Museum), at Schwachhauser Heerstr. 240. The Übersee Museum on the main station square, Bahnhofsplatz 113, reflects Bremen's importance in maritime history and overseas trade.

Outside of the moated Old Bremen and beyond the main rail station is the green expanse of the Bürgerpark at whose edge are the exhibition grounds with the ultramodern Stadthalle with several halls intended for

congresses, conventions, musical events, great social occasions and similar. In addition to many other modern buildings in the inner city, Bremen
possesses fine examples of modern architecture in such residential apartment settlements as Vahr and Neue Vahr in the eastern suburbs.

Oldenburg and the Stone Age

From Bremen, the picturesque land of East Frisia, with a fringe of fascinating islands off its coast, can be reached in a circular swing which takes
in a number of other interesting points. First stop is the garden city of
Oldenburg, where those glazed Klinker bricks you see in North German
buildings are produced. Oldenburg is also known for its 13th-century
Lamberti Kirche, its 15th-century St. Gertrud Kapelle and above all for
its Renaissance palace, the Grossherzogliches Schloss, built in 1604. This,
the former residence of the Grand Dukes of Oldenburg, contains the
Landesmuseum für Kunst und Kulturgeschichte (Regional Museum of
Art and Cultural History), with 66 rooms devoted to art through the ages.

Oldenburg is in the middle of Stone Age country—the region where
Stone Age man painfully gathered together the great boulders scattered
over the countryside by the glaciers of the Ice Age and heaped them up
into funeral monuments called here Hünengräber or Hünenbetten, giants'
graves or giants' beds. They are particularly numerous on the Ahlhorn
Heath south of Oldenburg, where the largest one stands—the Visbecker
Bridegroom, made of 150 granite blocks forming a structure 110 meters
(360 feet) long—Germany's Stonehenge. Oldenburg's Staatliches Museum
für Naturkunde und Vorgeschichte deals with the natural history and prehistory of the coastal area.

To the northwest of Oldenburg is a lake called Zwischenahner Meer
whose blue waters are dotted by sails, swans and seagulls and whose southern shore is presided over by the noted spa of Bad Zwischenahn. Further
in the same direction is the town of Westerstede, surrounded by meadows
and oakwoods, with its 12th-century Peterskirche (St. Peter's Church).
At nearby Ocholt is the Howieker Wassermühle, an historic watermill,
and an original Ammerland half-timbered house. To the north of Oldenburg, fast rooted in the land, make a swift transition to Wilhelmshaven,
standing on the sea, at Jade Bay, where the Ems–Jade Canal cuts across
the peninsula of East Frisia and makes it an island. Beside fine sunny
beaches, Wilhelmshaven's specialty is relaxing therapeutic mud baths.
From the Küstenmuseum, in the city hall, you may learn more about the
coastal region, its geology, archaeology and history. Wilhelmshaven is a
starting point for tours along the East Frisian coast and to the islands off
it, or across the East Frisian peninsula, with its many moated castles.

From East Frisian Islands to Osnabrück

From Wilhelmshaven we go to Jever, the center of a district studded
with castles, whose own is famous for the carved oak timbers of the ceiling
in its great hall. The castle, surrounded by a beautiful park, houses one
of the best local museums in North Germany; the town church contains
a rich Renaissance sarcophagus, the Rathaus dates from 1609 and Jever
traces its history back for over 1,000 years. Next you reach Carolinensiel
on the coast, which you can then follow through country which looks like

Holland—windmills, dikes and fat cattle grazing in the fields—or cut across to one or the other of the East Frisian Islands to swim from their sandy beaches, which the mainland, at this point, lacks.

The East Frisian Islands, reading from the Dutch border eastwards, are Borkum, Juist, Norderney, Baltrum, Langeoog, Spiekeroog, Wangerooge. They have been taken up in quite a big way as "back-to-nature" resorts, excellent for family vacationing.

These islands are really a kind of fringe of the coastline, several miles out, a necklace of sandy outcroppings, each one nearly all beach. They all have good ferry services, from whatever the nearest point on the mainland is, Norddeich for Juist, Norderney and Baltrum, Bensersiel for Langeoog, and so on. They are all of them attractive in their own ways.

Borkum is the largest of the chain, and very popular; here you will see holidaymakers riding horses along the vast expanses of beach at low tide, or walking for miles. In fact horse-riding is a favorite relaxation on several of the islands. Borkum is very well supplied with all sorts of accommodation, spa facilities and lots for families to do by night and day. Juist is very popular too, with even more of a family atmosphere. The special sport here is sailing land yachts on rubber-tired wheels across the long beaches. It has an interesting Küstenmuseum (coastal museum) and popular summer concerts.

Norderney is the oldest North Sea resort (since 1797), and has a slightly more international flavor. There is an indoor pool with artificial waves, for use when the sea is too cold, and a naturist beach here, too. The official museum of East Frisian culture, the Fischerhaus Museum, is on Norderney, as is a museum of marine life—Meeresmuseum—in the Haus der Insel in Langestrasse. Baltrum, the smallest of the islands, has an attractive fishing village. Langeoog has a notable bird sanctuary, and for holidaymakers the emphasis is on sport. Spiekeroog, reached from Neuharlingersiel or Carolinensiel, has an old church with mementos and objects from the 16th-century ships of the Spanish Armada, as well as East Frisia's highest peak—Dune 21, all of 75 feet high. Wangerooge has unusually wide, sandy beaches, an all-the-year-round season, air which relieves hay fever and the delight of stepping straight out of your hotel on to the beach.

Tea drinking is an unexpected feature of East Frisian life, but don't expect it to resemble the European concoction. It's even more an acquired taste—very dark brown though being so strong and taken with thick cream and a lump of sugar, rather like coffee. Seagull eggs are another novelty and no less strong.

These are not, by and large, sophisticated places for a holiday, but neither are they Coney Island or Blackpool. They are relaxed, essentially openair places, where a lot will depend on the weather, but, if it is good, you could have a healthy holiday to remember.

Back to Dry Land

On the mainland again, you might swing through Norden, notable for its Town Hall (1500) and Gothic Church of St. Ludger; Emden, home port of the herring fleet and a busy shipbuilding and shipping town (it is the trans-shipment point for the Ruhr, and at the mouth of the Ems–Jade Canal), with a fine museum containing a notable collection of medieval art, stained-glass windows, and old arms and armor; Aurich, from which you can visit Upstalsboom, where the medieval Frisian Diets met; Bagband, jumping-off point to see large-scale moorland cultivation at Wiesmoor; Leer, a picturesque old river port which is the largest cattle market in northwestern Germany; Papenburg, a typical moorland settlement; Meppen and Lingen, with their interesting town halls.

From here go southeast to Osnabrück, a lively city for centuries. Its cathedral, the Dom St. Peter, was built between the 11th and 13th centuries; the bishopric of Osnabrück is 1200 years old. Its Gothic Town Hall was the scene of negotiations involving Sweden and the Germanic Empire which led to the Treaty of Westphalia in 1648, ending the Thirty Years War. George I of England was born in Osnabrück in 1660 as the son of the Elector of Hannover, though he was not to be called until 1714 to found England's present ruling house, which changed its name to House of Windsor in 1917. Among the more recent achievements of this city are the production of highly-regarded pumpernickel and a potent variety of schnaps known as *Korn.*

Returning to Bremen you proceed north from Osnabrück through Damme, a pleasant old town and climatic resort in an area of wooded hills, half-timbered farmhouses, ponds and stone graves; a few miles east is the Dümmer Lake, known for the many species of birds and alive with sailboats during the warm season. North of Damme is Dinklage with a romantic moated castle and located in a fertile farm region rich in old customs. Cloppenburg, further north, is noted for its openair museum, Niedersächsisches Freilichtsmuseum, which has 50 historic buildings in traditional East Frisian style: farmhouses, windmills, craftsmen's shops, churches and schools, some dating back to the 17th century. Wildeshausen, on the Hunte River and the main road to Bremen, has preserved some of its walls, gabled houses and the Romanesque Alexander Kirche. Nearby is Ahlhorn Heath with the previously mentioned giant grave stones.

Launching out from Bremen once more, this time in a southeasterly direction, your first stop is Verden on the Aller River, noted for two things—its cathedral and its horseback riding and racing traditions. It has a museum, the Deutsches Pferdemuseum at Andreasstrasse 7 and Strukturstrasse 7, devoted to the horse and its place in the history of mankind. Verden is an excellent starting point for canoe or kayak trips. You come next to Nienburg, with its charming gabled houses, its fine town hall, its picturesque marketplace and the pleasant nearby lake, the Steinhuder Meer.

Industrious Hannover

Hannover (the English variant has one "n") is most animated in the spring, when the great international industrial fair, the most important of its kind in the world, is held here. But as a big industrial city with great cultural traditions, it always has many other fairs, exhibitions, conventions and continuous theatrical and musical programs.

The war left almost nothing of the old town but the little that remained has been sympathetically restored and reconstructed. The tower of the Gothic Marktkirche is the city's landmark; the church itself contains a notable wood-carved altar, a 15th-century baptismal font and bronze doors by the famous contemporary German sculptor Gerhard Marcks.

Nearby is the beautifully restored Altes Rathaus (Old City Hall), which together with Marktkirche now represents an island amid the modern, functional buildings of the surrounding shopping streets. Not far away is another survivor of the old town, the 17th-century Ballhof, a multi-winged, half-timbered building where the first opera in Hannover was performed in 1672, and a row of other half-timbered houses. The neo-Classical Leineschloss, standing on the bank of Leine, has acquired an ultramodern annex and now houses the Lower Saxon Parliament, for Hannover is the capital of Lower Saxony. Also on the bank of the Leine you can observe the round Beginenturm, the only fully preserved (and once the strongest) tower of the city walls. Across the river is the Neustädter Church with the grave of philosopher Leibniz.

The massive and vast Rathaus (the present City Hall), built during the first decade of the current century, is reflected in the small Maschpark lake, while the north shore of the large Maschsee lies only a few hundred yards away. Maschsee, which was made from 1934–36 with the assistance of the parallel-running Leine river, is the playground for sailing and rowing enthusiasts and there is a large swimming establishment on its south shore; passenger boats ply the lake during the summer months. Hannover's Art Museum, the Kunstmuseum Hannover mit Sammlung Sprengel, is by the Maschsee at Kurt Schwitters Platz and features 20th century art with works by Picasso, Beckmann, Ernst Klee, Leger, Nolde and many others. Hannover is known for its parks, among which Eilenriede, like Maschsee, is within easy walking distance of the city center. Eilenriede, lying beyond the main railroad station and railroad tracks, is the city forest and includes, among other features, the zoo which harbors some very fine and rare animals.

The most elegant street of Hannover is the section of Georgstrasse between Aegidientor Platz, where some of the most modern office buildings have sprung up, and Kröpcke square, the nerve center of Hannover's downtown traffic. The Opera House near Kröpcke on Georgstrasse was originally built in the mid-19th century by Georg Ludwig Laves, the favored Hannover architect of that period, and it has undergone extensive restoration. Georgstrasse continues from Kröpcke to Steintor square. Nearby in Goseriede street stands the Anzeiger Building, belonging to a publishing firm; from its top floor, reached by elevator, there is a fine view over the city.

Two other museums of interest are the Kestner Museum at Trammplatz 3 which has an especially good Egyptian collection and the Wilhelm Busch Museum, Georgengarten 1, which is dedicated to the famous painter and humorist, creator of Max and Moritz.

The Baroque Herrenhausen Gardens (Herrenhäuser Gärten) in the northwestern suburbs are among the most beautiful parks in Europe. They contain fountains, cascades, sculptures, several garden pavilions, orangerie and a Baroque theater. These unique Baroque gardens have remained unchanged since their completion in 1714. In summer they form the backdrop for the Hannover Openair Theater Festival (Sommerspielen) with son et lumière and concerts. In the museum in the Fürstenhaus residence (Herrenhausen Museum, Alter Herrenhauserstrasse 14) you can see furniture, paintings and etchings.

In the southeastern outskirts on the other edge of the city are the fair grounds (Messegelände), with three fair buildings, 22 exhibition halls and a vast outdoor exhibition area.

Only about 20 kilometers (12 miles) southeast of the Hannover fair grounds is the 1,100-year-old town of Hildesheim, a real treasury of old architecture; although most of it was destroyed in the war, much has since been reconstructed. The most interesting churches include the cathedral (Dom) begun in 852 with bronze doors dating from 1015, a 13th-century baptismal font, numerous other works of art and an outstanding treasury; the 11th-century St. Michaelis-Kirche (St. Michael's) and the 12th-century St. Godehardkirche (St. Gothard's) both in pure Romanesque style. Among the most beautiful half-timbered houses are Wernerhaus and Waffenschmiedehaus, both 16th century. The Pelizaeus-Museum has an outstanding Egyptian collection.

From Weser Hills to Harz Mountains

Now swing west to Hameln (Hamelin is the anglicized version) which would be worth visiting anyway, as the town with the finest examples of the Weser Renaissance houses, but which has a particular attraction as the city of the Pied Piper. You will see his house in Hameln, along with many other palatial private homes, whose timbered façades are likely to bear inscriptions addressed to you, with words of advice, criticism or irony, all in Old German. The Pied Piper's story is re-enacted every summer, usually on Sundays, when the Piper in his medieval clothes walks through the streets of the town followed by an army of delighted kids dressed as rats and performing the Rat Dance.

Hameln is situated on the Weser in the region called Weserbergland after the river. The Weser Hill Country, as its name could be translated into English, is formed by some 15 hill ranges located on both sides of the Weser and extending from Hannoversch Münden, where the Fulda and Werra join the way to Porta Westfalica where the Weser breaks violently through the last range in order to enter the North German Plain at Minden, flowing across it to Bremen and to the North Sea. Weserbergland is a region of beautiful scenery and fairy tales, of old monasteries, castles, and deep forests; the banks of the river are lined with attractive little towns and the interior is dotted with healing spas. Only a few miles south of Hameln is Bad Pyrmont, the most important one, a fashionable and well-known watering place. It has one of the most beautiful spa parks in Germany, once a favorite with Goethe. Its waters are beneficial for a number of disorders, ranging from skin diseases to blood circulation troubles. It also has a large, well-equipped riding center. A number of other spas are to be found in the area west of Bad Pyrmont, and we have already visited some of them in western Germany, since the Weser Hill Country forms a dividing area between northern and western Germany.

Proceeding up the Weser River from Hameln you come to Bodenwerder, the town where Baron Münchhausen, the teller of the world's tallest tales, used to live; to Höxter, an old Hansa town with outstanding half-timbered houses and the nearby famous Benedictine Abbey of Corvey, founded in 822; to Karlshafen with its fine Baroque buildings; to Hannoversch Münden, the "birthplace" of the Weser, with painted half-timbered buildings, a very fine Town Hall, and the remains of city walls.

Not far from here is the fairy-tale Sababurg Castle of the Sleeping Beauty, in Hesse.

To the northeast is the ancient university town of Göttingen, whose 14th-century Town Hall, medieval half-timbered houses, and particularly its old students' taverns should not be overlooked. Göttingen has a Stadtmuseum (municipal museum), dealing with prehistory and geology, as well as a Museum für Völkerkunde, Am Wall, devoted to folk arts and crafts. Nearby is the village of Ebergötzen with the Wilhelm Busch Mühle watermill, the setting for the famous Max and Moritz stories and illustrations.

Farther northeast you reach the Harz Mountains at Osterode, an enchanting walled town with fine 15th- and 17th-century buildings, and the birthplace of the famous woodcarver, Tilman Riemenschneider. Not far from here along the southern edge of Harz are Herzberg with the 13th-century castle-fortress and Bad Lauterberg, specializing in Kneipp cold water cures. At the northern edge of the Harz, and very near the border of East Germany, is the beautifully situated spa of Bad Harzburg with chloride and ferrous waters. The Grosse Burgberg hill above it can be ascended by chair lift. There is also a fine view from the Harzburg, the remains of a fortress built by Heinrich IV in about 1065. In winter Bad Harzburg becomes a skiing center, and there is now a year-round casino. Just south of Bad Harzburg is the Brocken summit, the highest in Harz (1,142 meters or 3,750 feet), where the witches hold their Sabbaths, now in East Germany.

The evergreen forests of the Harz Mountains appeal both to those in search of holidays and of health. Many of the places at the highest altitudes are climatic health resorts which in winter become skiing centers, for Harz is the only important skiing region of North Germany. The principal winter sports centers and summer resorts include, in addition to Bad Harzburg, particularly Braunlage, Hahnenklee-Bockswiese, Clausthal-Zellerfeld, Schulenberg, and St. Andreasberg.

Goslar, Braunschweig and Lüneburg

If you think you have already seen everything possible in the way of medieval towns, you are likely to revise your ideas when you come to Goslar. Nestled in the beautiful country of the Harz, Goslar is an encyclopedia of the domestic architecture of past ages, as well as of ecclesiastical and public architecture, which is less rare. From its own buildings, street after street of them, it can produce a multitude of examples for each of the clearly marked periods it represents—Gothic houses built between 1450 and 1550, transitional buildings combining Gothic and Renaissance features in the last quarter century of that period, Renaissance homes from 1550 to 1650, Baroque from 1650 to 1880. The 15th–16th- century guildhouses are magnificent. It has in addition some of the thickest towers of any defense works anywhere, several 12th-century churches, and the ancient (11th–12th century) Romanesque palace of the German Emperors. The latter is worth visiting if only for the grandiose, 19th-century murals depicting early German history and for its interesting chapel. The Goslarer Museum at Königsstrasse 1, has a fascinating model of the town as it was centuries ago, ecclesiastical treasures from the cathedral (demolished in 1819) and exhibits relating to Goslar's part in imperial history.

The ancient Rathaus on Marktplatz contains the Huldigungssaal, a fabulous room entirely covered (walls and ceiling) with tempera paintings done by an unknown artist in 1500, and still retaining all their brilliant color. This old meeting room of the city elders also has a secret chapel.

But Goslar is more than architecture and history. To stroll along the stream that still rushes headlong through the streets, to climb the tower of the Marktkirche (Market Church) just before its bells announce the hour of day, to linger in the marketplace, is to step back into another way of life. This is a corner of Germany to be savored and enjoyed. Plan to allow at least a day, and save some of that time for rambles on foot.

You now come to another old city, a famous one, Braunschweig (the English version is Brunswick), which is north of the Harz. The old capital of Lower Saxony, Braunschweig is symbolized by the bronze lion dating from 1166, which stands in its Burgplatz—itself symbolizing Henry the Lion, who built the city's historic Romanesque cathedral (Dom). One of Germany's finest examples of sepulchral art is the tomb of Henry and his wife in the cathedral. Don't miss the Gothic Altstadtmarkt (Old City Market) with its half-timbered Gothic and Renaissance houses, and the 13th-century Altstadtrathaus (Old Town Hall), one of the oldest in Germany. Lining the narrow streets of the Magniviertel, the area around St. Magni Kirche, are medieval high-gabled houses; Paulinerstrasse 6 is a half-timbered house dating back to 1495. Still in the center of town are the early Gothic Ägidienkirche and St. Martins Kirche (about 1200). The town museum (Städtisches Museum) is at Am Löwenwall, the regional museum (Landesmuseum) is near the Ägidienkirche, and the natural history museum (Naturhistorisches Museum) is at Pokelstrasse 10a. The Herzog Anton Ulrich Museum has paintings by Rembrandt, Rubens, Van Dyck, Holbein, Cranach and Jordaens.

Kloster Wolfenbüttel, the abbey at Wölfenbüttel near Braunschweig, now houses the 12th-century Gospel of Henry the Lion, purchased by the German Government at auction in London for an astounding DM.30,000,000.

Celle is a colorful old town, with fine half-timbered houses and with the oldest court theater in Germany. Its ducal castle is an imposing pile, its outstanding event of the year the Stallions' Parade in October. From this point you may take one of two routes—through Ülzen, where notable sights are the Rathaus, the Guild House, and the Marienkirche with the "Golden Ship"—or through Soltau, near the natural park preserve of Wilsede and the painters' colonies in Fallingbostel and Bispingen. Either way brings you to Lüneburg.

Lüneburg is thought of particularly as a sort of museum of brick architecture, and it is true that there are whole streets of 15th- and 16th-century structures of that material; but there are also plenty of half-timbered buildings, with carved and brightly-colored oak beams combined with the brick—mostly 14th century. The 14th-century Church of St. John (St. Johanniskirche) and that of St. Nicholas (St. Nikolai Kirche) are both fine examples of brick architecture, but the 13th–15th-century Rathaus is perhaps the finest structure in the city, with its elaborate carvings, the beautifully decorated beams and the wall painting in its banqueting hall, and the noble proportions of the Gothic Chamber of Justice. The old crane on the Ilmenau River harbor is a picturesque sight.

Lüneburg gives its name to one of the most ancient lands of Germany—the Lüneburger Heide (Lüneburg Heath), covering about 45 square miles and extending roughly between the Elbe in the north and the Aller River in the south, the border of East Germany in the east and the Bremen–Hamburg autobahn in the west. Here prehistoric man lived, and left the mark of his passage by the great stones he heaped into cairns or built into passage tombs or set up into chambered forms, like the Seven Stone Houses near Fallingbostel, the burial chamber of the later Stone Age in the Klecker Forests near Bendestorf, or the tomb in Schieringer Wald near Bleckede. This is a vast area of varying scenery: of flatlands and undulating hills; of tracts of heath proper with old juniper shrubs of bizarre shape, wild flowers and flocks of sheep alternating with large forests rife with game and rich farmlands where the horse is the main animal; of elevations offering panoramic views over sections of the Heide and of tiny, shallow valleys where all you can see is the edge of the next wood, or perhaps a rock thrown from nowhere, or a swampy pond; half-timbered thatched-roof farmsteads alternate with small and colorful old towns dotted with the monuments of the past, simple village churches topped by wooden steeples with medieval cathedrals and monasteries. Here you take an inexpensive vacation in a dozen or so climatic resorts, such as Bendestorf, Hanstedt, Jeteburg, Schneverdingen or Walsrode; or, in case you need a cure in such spas as Lüneburg (for Lüneburg is also a spa) or Fallersleben, or in the Kneipp-cure (cold-water cure) resort of Fallingbostel.

As well as its old towns, pretty villages, spas, lakes and forests, the Heath also contains the memorial to the victims of the Bergen-Belsen Concentration Camp. It stands in solitude in a clearing on the Lüneburg Heath, about four miles southwest of the nearest town of Bergen. (The name of Belsen is not found on most maps; the town is more usually referred to as Bergen-Belsen. It is roughly 50 kilometers (30 miles) north of Hannover and is northeast of Celle in the southwest of the Heath). After passing the mounds that mark the sites of the common graves, you will find the obelisk honouring the victims of the Holocaust. Further on, in a clearing thickly covered with heather, is the actual site once occupied by the camps themselves.

PRACTICAL INFORMATION FOR

LOWER SAXONY

TELEPHONES. We have given telephone codes for all the towns and villages in the hotel and restaurant lists that follow. These codes need only be used when calling from outside the town or village concerned.

HOTELS AND RESTAURANTS. The majority of hotels in Lower Saxony are in the Moderate to Expensive price range; similarly, it can also be costly to stay on the islands where a cure tax is also requested. As the bracing climate is considered just as therapeutic in winter as in summer there are few off-season rates. However, many resorts offer special package arrangements *(Pauschalangebote),* and the farther inland one goes, the cheaper it gets. Accommodations services are to be found at local tourist offices (*Verkehrsverein; Kuramt* in health spas). There is also an abundance of private accommodations: in pensions and in holiday apartments and cottages; ask for addresses of *Privatvermieter.*

Bad Harzburg. Spa and winter sports center in the Harz Mountains. *Bodes* (E), Am Stadtpark 48 (05322–2041). 90 rooms. Kneipp cures, cosmetic studio. Quiet location on edge of forest. AE, DC. *Braunschweiger Hof* (E), Herzog-Wilhelm-Str. 54 (05322–7035). 78 rooms. 150-year-old hotel in local rustic style; indoor pool; beer tavern, bar, restaurant. AE, DC, MC, V. *Seela* (E), Nordhäuserstr. 5 (05322–7011). 34 rooms, most with bath or shower. Indoor pool, sauna, solarium, Kneipp cures and massages. Good restaurant. AE, DC, MC, V. *Haus Eden* (M), Amsbergstr. 27 (05322–4733). 16 rooms. No restaurant. *Kurpark* (M), Kurhausstr. 5–7 (05322–2061). 55 rooms; modern building. MC. *Landhaus am Rodenberg* (M), Am Rodenberg 20 (05322–3058). 15 rooms. No restaurant. *Victoria* (M), Herzog-Wilhelm-Str. 74 (05322–2370). 80 beds.

Bad Pyrmont. Sap in the Weser Hills. *Bergkurpark* (E), Ockelstr. 11 (05281–4001). 57 rooms. Sauna, solarium, garden terrace; two good restaurants. AE. *Kurhotel-Kurhaus* (E), Heiligenangerstr. 4 (05281–151). 103 rooms, most with bath or shower; thermal baths, casino; very quiet. AE, DC, MC, V. *Bad Pyrmonter Hof* (M), Brunnenstr. 32 (05281–609303). 45 rooms. Near pedestrian zone. *Haus Neander* (M), Am Helvetiushügel 9 (05281–8295). 18 rooms. Centrally located, with large garden. *Waldecker Hof* (M), Brunnenstr. 34 (05281–608353). 20 beds.

Bad Zwischenahn. Modern spa resort on Zwischenahn lake, accessible from the Oldenburg–Westerstede autobahn or from the Bremen–Oldenburg–Norddeich rail route. *Jagdhaus Eiden am See* (E), Aschhauserfeld (04403–1022). Magnificent half-timbered former hunting lodge by the lake. First-class cuisine in Hunter's and Fisherman's rooms (regional) and in *Apicius* restaurant (gourmet). AE, DC, MC, V. *Seehotel Fährhaus* (M), Auf dem Hohen Ufer 8 (4711). Idyllic location on the banks of the Zwischenahner Meer lake in a peaceful setting but only five minutes away from town center. 100 beds, all rooms with bath; indoor pool. AE, DC, MC.

Baltrum. *Dünenschlösschen* (M), Wattenmeer, Ostdorf No. 48 (04939–234). Modern; fish specialties in restaurant. *Pension Strandburg* (M), Haus No. 139 (04939–262). Near main beach and cure house.

Bederkesa. Small town between Bremerhaven and Hamburg. *Romantik Hotel Waldschlösschen Bösehof* (E), Hauptman-Böse Str. 19 (04745–7031). 30 rooms, half with shower, in modern annex. Sea-captain's manor house built 1826, original rustic style. Indoor pool, sauna, fitness room, bowling, riding nearby; wonderful lake views. Ideally situated for exploring between the Weser and the Elbe. AE, DC, MC, V.

Borkum (East Frisian Island). Summer resort. *Miramar* (E), Am Westkaap (04922–891). 36 rooms. At main beach; indoor salt-water pool, sauna, solarium; first-class service. *Nordsee-Hotel* (E), Bubertstr. 9 (04922–841). 115 rooms, most with bath or shower. Package arrangements on request. DC, V. *Graf Waldersee* (M), Bahnhofstr. 6 (04922–1094). 28 rooms, all with shower or bath. Short distance from main beach and town center. Good *Kupferkanne* restaurant. DC. *Ostfriesenhof* (M), Jann Berghausstr. (04922–3612). 70 beds, most rooms with bath or shower. On promenade at main beach; fine sea view from sun terrace. *Haus Bettina* (I), Süderstr. 2 (04922–2022). All rooms with shower; central, near Kurpark. *Hotel-Pension Bruns* (I), Reedestr. 2 (04922–2320). 31 rooms. Breakfast only.

Restaurants. *Der Insulaner, Heimlicher Liebe,* in holiday village of same name at beach. *Stadtsschänke,* Franz-Habich-Str. 18 (04922–2225). *Störtebeker,* Reedestr. 36 (04922–629). Good-value lunches in the oldest fish restaurant.

Braunlage. *Maritim-Berghotel* (L), Am Pfaffenstieg (05520–3051). 300 rooms. Two pools, sauna, sports facilities; quiet location. AE, DC, MC, V. *Romantik Hotel Zur Tanne* (M), Herzog-Wilhelm-Str. 8 (05520–1034). 22 beds, most rooms with bath. Hotel in local style, one of the best in the region, with first-class cuisine in two restaurants and cafe. AE, DC, MC, V.

Braunschweig (Brunswick). *Deutsches Haus* (E), Burgplatz 1 (0531–44422). 84 rooms. Quiet, castle-like building next to the cathedral. AE, DC, MC, V. *Mercure-Atrium* (E), Berliner Platz 3 (0531–70080). 130 rooms, all with bath or shower. Central and very comfortable, and with first class restaurant. *Mövenpick-Hotel* (E), Welfenhof (0531–48170). 132 rooms, all with bath. Located in the heart of the city, next to the main shopping area. Excellent restaurant, indoor pool, sauna and solarium. AE, DC, MC, V. *Ritter St. Georg* (E), Alte Knochenhauerstr. 12–13 (0531–13039). 25 rooms, all with bath or shower. New hotel, opened only in 1985, with the unusual distinction of being located in the oldest timbered building in Brunswick; it dates back to 1454. Excellent restaurant.

Frühlings-Hotel (M), Bankplatz 7 (0531–49317). 66 rooms. No restaurant. AE, DC, MC. *Pension Wienecke* (I), Kuhstr. 14 (0531–46476). 17 rooms. No restaurant.

Restaurants. *Gewandhaus* (E), Altstadtmarkt (0531–44441). In former guildhouse of the influential sailmakers; 12th-century with Renaissance facade (1590). Parts of the cellar are over 1,000 years old. Elegant wine restaurant, cellar with old paintings. Seafood specialties, local and Bavarian beer. DC.

Das Alte Steakhaus (M), Alte Knochenhauerstr. 11 (0531–46606). MC. *Haus Zur Hanse* (M), Güldenstr. 7 (0531–46154). 16th-century half-timbered house; good fish and regional specialties. AE, MC. *Zum Bitburger* (M), Stobenstr. 15 (0531–43733). Pleasant, atmospheric. MC. *Zum Starenkasten* (M), Thiedestr. 25–27 (0531–874121). Fine local specialties. *Grüner Jäger* (I), Ebertallee 50 (0531–71643). In Riddaghaus suburb, located in wildlife reserve; good wholesome dishes, game specialties. *Löwen Krone* (I), Leonhardplatz (0531–72076). In the Stadthalle (City Hall). *Neustadt Rathhauss* (I), Küchenstr. 1 (0531–41904). Little changed in 700 years, interior illuminated by a sea of candles. A house specialty is herb wine *(Kräuterwein).* *Wolters am Wall* (I), Fallersleber Str. 35 (0531–41066). One of several good-value restaurants to be found all over town.

Cafés. *Café Tolle,* Bohlweg 69, with terrace. *Café Schlosspassage,* Schloss-passage, for pastries; *Stadtpark,* Jasperallee 42, in park, also restaurant; both with music.

Bremen. *CP (Canadian Pacific) Hotel Bremen Plaza* (E), Hillmann-platz 20 (0421–17670). New in 1985, 230 rooms, all with bath. *Crest* (E), August-Bebel-Allee 4 (0421–23870). 150 rooms, all with bath. Restaurant. In the suburb of Neue Vahr. AE, DC, MC, V. *Mercure-Columbus* (E), Bahn-hofplatz 5–7 (0421–14161). 153 rooms, all with bath; 8 apartments. Centrally located opposite the rail station, with excellent value restaurant plus a Chinese restaurant, *Peking Entenhaus;* bar and cellar tavern. AE, DC, MC, V. *Novotel* (E), Zum Klümoor, Achim-Uphausen (04202–6086). About 20 km. (12 miles) upstream on the Weser. 116 rooms, all with bath or shower. AE. *Park* (E), Im Bürgerpark (0421–34080). 150 rooms, all with bath. Suites; elegant restaurant, cafe, bar, terrace overlooking small lake. Magnificent setting. AE, DC, MC, V. *Zur Post* (E), Bahnhofsplatz 11 (0421–30590). 224 rooms, all with bath; 3 apartments. Built 1889; tradition and modern comfort side by side; parking; several restaurants; indoor pool. AE, DC, MC, V.

Bremer Hospiz (M), Löningstr. 16–20 (0421–321668). 76 rooms, all with bath or shower; particularly comfortable. AE, DC, MC, V. *Landhaus Louisen-thal* (M), Leher Heerstr. 105 (0421–232076). 58 rooms, 2 apartments. Most with bath or shower. Family hotel in Horn suburb; garden with pavilion. AE, DC, MC, V. *Strandlust* (M), Rohrstr. 11, Vegesack (0421–667073). About 16 km. (ten miles) downstream on the banks of the Weser. 27 rooms. Renowned restaurant with local specialties. AE, DC, MC. *Überseeho-tel* (M), Wachtstr. 27–9 (0421–320197). 142 rooms, all with bath or shower. Garni. Near Rathaus. Reception on third floor (elevators). AE, DC, MC. *Lütkemeyer* (I), Rockwinkeler Landstr. 83 (0421–259461). Small; near autobahn exit in Oberneuland suburb.

Restaurants. *Das Kleine Lokal* (E), Besselstr. 40 (0421–71929). Excellent cuisine and good wines in atmospheric surroundings. *Meierei im Bür-gerpark* (E), Im Bürgerpark (0421–211922). Beautiful location; wholesome cooking, fish and local dishes. AE, DC, MC, V. *Alte Gilde* (M), Ansgaritorstr. 24 (0421–171712). In the Schnoorviertel (artists' quarter), in deep, vaulted cellar of 17th-century "Gewerbehaus." DC. *Comturei* (M), Ostertorstr. 31 (0421–325050). In the Schnoorviertel; several vaulted halls and tavern rooms in building dating back to 13th century; local, international and French cuisine. DC, MC. *Deutsches Haus* (M), Findorffstr. 3 (04792–1205). In Worpswede artists' quarter. Specializes in teas, of which you can choose from over 30 kinds. Beautifully located. Also accommodations in 125-year-old hotel building. *Deutsches Haus und Haus am Markt* (M), Am Markt 1 (0421–321048). Old patrician house opposite the Rathaus; many atmospheric rooms; fish specialties. AE, MC, V. *Flett* (M), Böttcherstr. 3 (0421–320995). In the Haus St. Petrus. *Bremer Aalsuppe* (eel soup), fresh Weser salmon, *Bremer Kükenragout* with specially cured herring. MC. *Die Glocke* (M), Domsheide 6 (0421–327750). Next to cathedral. Summer dining in cloister courtyard. Local fish specialties. AE, MC, V. *Ratskeller* (M), City Hall, Am Markt (0421–3290910). In existence since 1408, reputedly the oldest German Ratskeller. In the 15th century the city fathers decided that only German wine would be served. The cellar is lined with wine casks, including an enormous one that has been holding wine since the 18th century. Unsurpassable selection of over 600 German wines.

Excellent seafood and other top dishes. AE, DC, MC. *Schnoor 2* (M), Schnoor 2 (0421–321218). Old gabled house in the artists' quarter. AE, DC, MC, V. *Martini-Grill* (I), Böttcherstr. 2 (0421–326002). For quick, good-value meals, excellent pastries and ice creams. DC, MC.

Cafés. *Konditorei Knigge,* Sögestr. 42. Excellent pastries and snacks. *Rhododendron,* Marcusallee. In the famous park. *Schnoor-Teestübchen,* Wüste Stätte 1 (0421–326091). Half-timbered house in the Schnoorviertel. Over 40 different sorts of tea. *Stecker & Co.,* Knochenhauerstr. 14. Half-timbered house dating back to 1742. Good pastries.

Bremerhaven. *Haverkamp* (E), Prager Str. 34 (0471–48330). 90 rooms, all with bath; 3 apartments. Indoor pool, sauna. AE, DC, MC, V. *Nordsee Hotel Naber* (E), Theodor Heuss Platz (0471–48770). 101 rooms, most with bath or shower; some suites. Modern and central; two restaurants; American-style bar. AE, DC, MC, V. *Parkhotel* (M), Im Bürgerpark (0471–27041). 46 rooms, all with bath; three apartments. Two restaurants; quiet location. AE, DC, MC. *Weser* (M), Weserstr. 132 (0471–71156). 74 rooms, most with bath. Restaurant. *Geestemünde* (I), Am Klint 20 (0471–28800). 14 rooms; garni.

Restaurants. *Columbusbahnhof* (M), Columbuskaje (0471–43220). Overlooking harbor, fine views from first floor. DC. *Fischereihafen-Restaurant Natusch* (M), am Fischbahnhof (0471–71021). At fish market rail station; particularly good value. AE, DC, MC. *Lehrke* (M), An der Geest 19 (0471–21177). Out near the yacht harbor. Local beers from the wood. *Seute Deern* (M), Am alten Hafen (0471–416264). Old time three-masted ship in the German Maritime Museum, offering fish specialties.

Small taverns specialising in fried fish: *Fischerstube,* Keilstr. 16; *Höpker,* Bismarckstr. 34; *Fischrestaurant am Theaterplatz* (M), Schleswigstr. 3 (46690). Traditional style; *Zum Fischbäcker,* across from the main station.

Cafés. *Café Bode,* Hafenstr. 91, beautiful cakes; *Columbusbahnhof,* Columbuskaje; *National,* Burger-meister-Smidt-Str. 101; *Pumpe,* Alte Bürger 159 (0471–414177).

Cuxhaven. *Badhotel Sternhagen* (E), Cuxhavener Str. 86 (04721–48280). 40 rooms; nine apartments; every comfort. At Duhnen beach, three km. (two miles) from town; quiet, fine view. Rustic interiors. Two indoor salt-water pools, solarium, sauna. Good restaurant, wine tavern. DC. *Golfhotel Strandhotel Duhnen und Seehotel Kamp* (E), Duhnerstrandstr. 7 (04721–4030). 60 rooms, most with bath; 42 apartments; eight holiday flats. Indoor pool, solarium, sports room. At Duhnen. Fine fish specialties; dancing. *Donners* (M), Am Seedeich 2 (04721–5070). In Grimmershorn section. 85 rooms, most with bath. Modern, fine view, pleasant bar. *Seepavillon* (M), Bei der Alten Liebe 5 (04721–38064). 47 rooms. Modern, beautiful location at the Alte Liebe lighthouse. Good restaurant. AE, DC, MC, V. *Strandperle* (M), Duhnerstrandstr. 15 (04721–47055). In Duhnen. 56 rooms, also apartments. Indoor pool, sauna; restaurants. AE, DC, MC. *Pension Glückskäfer* (I), Strandsstr. 57 (04721–47038). Eight beds, garni. Ideally located in Döse section at the Kurpark and 150 m. from beach.

Restaurants. *Duhner Fischpfanne* (M), Cuxhavener Str. 94 (04721–21655). Home-smoked fish. *Steakhouse Zum Rauchfang* (M), Am

Wattenweg 5 (04721–48104). In Duhnen. *Strandhaus Döse* (M). Modern, on Döse beach.

Goslar. *Der Achtermann* (E), Rosentorstr. 20 (05321–21001). 140 rooms, most with bath or shower. Built around one of the original (1501) towers of the old city wall. Excellent restaurant, good selection of wines. v. *Kaiserworth* (E), Am Markt 3 (05321–21111). 57 rooms, most with bath or shower. Former merchant tailors' guildhall built 1494. Terrace, inexpensive restaurant. AE, DC, MC, V. *Niedersächsischer Hof* (M), Klubgartenstr. 1–2 (05321–20064). 110 beds. *Schwarzer Adler* (M), Rosentorstr. 25 (05321–24001). 35 rooms. Noted evening restaurant. *Goldene Krone* (I), Breite Str. 46 (05321–22792). 26 rooms. Good restaurant.

Restaurants. *Brusttuch* (M), Hoher Weg 1 (05321–21081). In hotel of same name. Dates from 1526; famous for Harz specialties since 18th century. AE, DC, MC. *Ratsweinkeller* (M), in Hotel Kaiserworth; atmospheric. AE, DC, MC, V. *Zwinger* (M), Thomasstr. 2, historic fortress.

Göttingen. *Gebhards* (E), Goethe Allee 22–3 (0551–56133). 61 rooms, some with bath or shower. Terrace; garden. AE, DC, MC, V. *Beckmann* (M), Ulrideshuserstr. 44 (0551–21055). 26 rooms; no restaurant. *Central* (M), Jüdenstr. 12 (0551–57157). 45 rooms, most with bath. In pedestrian zone with access for residents' cars. Antique furnishings; no restaurant. AE, DC, MC, V. *Zur Sonne* (M), Paulinerstr. 41 (0551–56738). 41 rooms, many with bath or shower. Garni. DC, MC, V. *Hainholzhof-Kehr* (I), Borheckstr. 66 (0551–75008). 12 rooms. Half-timbered house in the forest, near rail station. Simple, pleasant, good food and wine.

Restaurants. *Junkernschänke* (M), Barfüsserstr. 5 (0551–57320). Atmospheric tavern. AE, DC. *Kreuzgang* (M), Markt 7–8 (0551–47322). Located in historic vaulted cellar. *Schwarzer Bär* (M), Kurze Str. 12 (0551–58284). Half-timbered house dating back to 1500; favorite with students. MC. *Marktstübchen* (I), Weender Str. 13–15 (0551–56640). Traditional students' cellar; "University Room" decorated with drawings, etc. *Rathskeller* (I), in the Rathskeller (0551–56433).

Hahnenklee-Bockswiese. Climatic resort and winter sports center near Goslar. *Harz-Stern Kur- und Sporthotel* (E), Triftstr. 25 (05325–720). 130 rooms. Luxurious, two pools, fine restaurant. AE, DC, MC. *Dorint Harzhotel Kreuzeck* (E), Am Kreuzeck (05325–741). Modern, comfortable, many facilities; attractive and well known. International restaurant, tavern and bar with dancing. *Diana (Café Seerose),* (M), Parkstr. 6 (05325–7030). 23 rooms. Indoor pool, sauna, solarium, fitness room. Restaurant-café. *Gästehaus Nagel* (M), Parkstr. 2 (05325–2031). 25 rooms, all with bath or shower. New, by lake; no restaurant. *Hahnenkleer Hof* (M), Parkstr. 24a (05325–2011). 32 rooms; pool. DC, MC. *Gästehaus Klose* (I), Rathausstr. 1 (05325–2422). 8 rooms with bath.

Hameln (Hamelin). *Zur Krone* (E), Osterstr. 30 (05151–7411). 70 beds, all with bath. *Börse* (M), Osterstr. 41 (05151–7080). 35 rooms, 1 apartment, most with bath or shower. Fine restaurant. AE, DC, MC. *Dorint-Weserbergland* (M), 164er Ring 3 (05151–7920). 103 rooms with bath. AE, DC, MC, V. *Gästehaus Ohrberg* (M), Margeritenweg 1 (05151–65979). In Berkel suburb. 18 rooms, most with bath. Outdoor pool; quiet and comfortable; no restaurant. *Sintermann* (M), at the rail station (05151–14248). 50 beds; good food, bar, beer tavern. AE, DC, MC.

Restaurants. *Klütturm* (M), Auf dem Klütberg (05151–61644). For excellent regional food, plus a delightful view over the Hameln. *Rattenfänger-Haus* (I), Osterstr. 28 (05151–3888). Located in a magnificent Renaissance building, dating from 1603. AE, DC, MC, V.

Hannover. It is advisable to reserve ahead, particularly during trade fairs. *Intercontinental* (L), Friedrichswall 11 (0511–16911). 285 rooms. Luxurious, eight-floor building opposite City Hall. Landscaped grounds, plaza with fountains, shops, café, cocktail lounge, grill restaurant, underground parking. AE, DC, MC, V. *Kastens Hotel Luisenhof* (L), Luisenstr. 1–3 (0511–12440). 160 rooms, all with bath or shower. Smart restaurant, bar, music and dancing. AE, DC, MC, V.

Am Stadtpark (E), Clausewitzstr. 6 (0511–810031). 252 rooms, all with bath. 2 restaurants; pool. AE, DC, MC, V. *Central Hotel Kaiserhof* (E), Ernst-August-Platz 4 (0511–327811). 67 rooms, some with bath. AE, DC, MC, V. *Crest* (E), Tiergartenstr. 117 (0511–51030). 108 rooms with bath. At the zoo. AE, DC, MC, V. *Georgenhof* (E), Herrenhäuser Kirchweg 20 (0511–702244). 17 rooms. Small country house in quiet location near Herrenhausen Gardens; outstanding food. *Grand-Hotel-Mussmann* (E), Ernst-August-Platz 7 (0511–327971). 100 rooms, many with bath or shower. Modern, central; café, bar. AE, DC. *Holiday Inn* (E), Petzelstr. 60 (0511–730171). 146 rooms, all with color T.V.; soundproof suites. Indoor pool, lounge, bar, disco, sauna, solarium. At the airport. AE, DC, MC, V. *Körner* (E), Körnerstr. 24 (0511–14666). 81 rooms. In quiet side street; back rooms have balconies and overlook park. AE, DC, MC, V. *Maritim* (E), Hildesheimer Str. 34 (0511–16531). New in 1984. 550 beds in rooms and apartments, all with bath. Indoor pool, sauna, solarium and sports room. AE, DC, MC, V. *Parkhotel Kronsberg* (E), Laatzener Str. 18 (0511–861086). 105 rooms, all with bath or shower. In trade fair complex; parking, gas stations. Two good restaurants. AE, DC, MC, V.

Am Rathaus (E), Friedrichswall 21 (0511–326268). 53 rooms. Recent, facing City Hall, with small inexpensive restaurant. AE, MC, V. *Am Thielenplatz* (M), Thielenplatz 2 (0511–327691). 90 rooms, most with bath or shower and balcony. AE, DC, MC, V. *Inter-City Hotel* (M), Ernst-August-Platz 1 (0511–327461). 52 rooms; at main station. AE. *Landhaus Köhne* (M), Seeweg 27, in Garbsen (05131–91085). 19 rooms. A real find, about 11 km. (seven miles) out on B6; good restaurant. *Thüringer Hof* (M), Osterstr. 37 (0511–326437). 59 rooms. With old-style cellar restaurant. AE, DC, MC.

Benther Berg (M), Vogelsangstr. 18 (05108–3045). Quiet hotel about 7 miles out of town, with indoor pool, sauna and solarium. AE. *Wülfeler Brauereigaststätten* (I), Hildesheimer Str. 380 (0511–865086). 45 beds. Small hotel, with hearty home cooking.

Restaurants. *Alte Mühle* (E), Hermann Löns Park 3 (0511–559480). In Kirchrode suburb. Dates back to 1637, with windmill from 1544. AE, DC. *Bristol Grill/Kanzleikeller* (E), Theodor-Heuss-Platz (0511–810031). Belongs to *Hotel Am Stadtpark*. AE, DC, MC, V. *Clichy* (E), Weissekreuzplatz 31 (0511–312447). High-class French cuisine. *Die Insel* (E), Rudolf von Benningsen Ufer 8 (0511–831214). Also café; on Maschsee lake. MC. *Leineschloss* (E), Heinrich Wilhelm Kopf Platz 1 (0511–326693). In super modern annex of the Leineschloss Palace; outdoor terrace. *Schuh's* (in Hotel Schweizerhof) and the smaller *Gourmet's Buffet,* Hinüberstr. 6 (0511–34950), both (E). The former with fine haute cuisine, the latter more casual in bistro style. Both AE, DC, MC, V. *Stern's Restaurant Härke Stuben* (E), Marienstr. 104 (0511–817322). Despite beer-tavern appearance, first-class restaurant, French and international cuisine. AE, DC, MC, V. *Witten's Hop* (E), Gernstr. 4 (0511–648844). In 400-year-old farmhouse about 15 minutes' drive from center. Hannover's top restaurant.

Mövenpick-Café Kröpcke (M), Georgstr. 35 (0511–326285). Fine *Baron de la Mouette* restaurant on first floor; standard restaurant and café down stairs. *Mövenpick im Casino,* am Maschsee, Arthur Menge Ufer 3 (0511–804018). On the lakeside with (E) *Bakkarat* restaurant on the first floor and *Restaurant Mövenpick* (M) and *Zipfel* (I) on the ground floor. Open from 6 P.M. to 4 A.M.

Beer restaurants. *Altdeutsche Bierstube* (M), Lärchenstr. 4 (0511–344921). Rustic atmosphere. *Rotisserie Helvetia* (M), Georgsplatz 11 (0511–14841). Pleasantly rustic Swiss atmosphere.

Wine taverns. *Fey's Weinstube,* Sopienstr. 6 (0511–325973). Dates back to 1880 as meeting place for artists, writers, army officers and scientists. Zither music; over 100 wines. *Weinloch,* Burgstr. 33 (0511–322748). In the old town. *Wein-Wolf,* Rathenaustr. 2 (0511–320788). In cellar; open Sat. until 1 A.M.

Cafés. *Café Meiffert,* Am Aegi. *Konditorei und Café Kreipe,* Bahnhofstr. 12. Good pastries. *Stadtcafé,* Grupenstr. 2.

Hildesheim. *Gollart's Hotel Deutsches Haus* (E), Carl-Peters-Str. 5 (05121–15971). 45 rooms; 3 suites. Indoor pool. AE, MC,

Restaurant. *Romantik-Restaurant Kupferschmiede* (E), Steinberg 6 (05121–263025). Outside town on the Steinberg heights. AE, DC, MC, V.

Lüneburg. *Residenz* (E), Munstermannskamp 10 (04131–45047). 35 rooms, most with bath. Small and modern, with good restaurant *Die Schnecke.* AE, DC, MC, V. *Seminaris* (E), Soltauer Str. 3 (04131–7131). 165 rooms. Super-modern, all comforts. AE, DC, MC. *Romantik Hotel Josthof* (M), Am Lindenberg 1, Salzhausen (04172–292). 30 beds. On the Lüneburg Heath in 300-year-old building with furnishings in original style. Swimming, fishing, riding nearby. Excellent restaurant. *Wellenkamp* (M), Am Sande 9 (04131–43026). 45 rooms, all with bath or shower. Former post-house. Good restaurant. AE, DC, MC, V.

Norderney (East Frisian Island). *Friese* (E), Friedrichstr. 34 (04932–3015). 45 rooms; good facilities, central. DC. *Hanseatic* (E), Gartenstr. 47 (04932–3032). 36 rooms. Modern, quiet location. *Kurhotel Norderney* (E), Weststrandstr. (04932–771). 33 rooms, all with bath; four apartments. DC. *Strand Hotel Germania* (E), Kaiserstr. 1 (04932–648). 47 rooms. Beautiful view; good-value restaurant; open Apr. through Sept. *Apart-Hotel Haus am Meer* (M), Kaiserstr. 3 (04932–8930). 10 singles, 37 apartment rooms, 6 holiday flats. Closed Nov. and Dec. *Georgshöhe* (M), Kaiserstr. 24 (04932–8980). 86 rooms. Traditional, near beach; tennis, salt-water pool, sauna, sunbathing lawn. New apartment house next door.

Oldenburg. *City Club Hotel* (E), Europaplatz 20 (0441–8080). 90 rooms, all with bath. Indoor pool, sauna, sports room, restaurant and café. *Heide* (M), Melkbrink 49 (0441–81001). 75 rooms; apartments and holiday flats. Pool, sauna, solarium, good restaurant. AE, DC, MC, V. *Sprenz* (M), Heiligengeiststr. 15 (0441–87033). 47 rooms, most with bath or shower; atmospheric *Balkan Grill.*

Restaurants. *Le Journal* (E), Wallstr. 13 (0441–13128). Excellent. AE, DC, MC, V. *Parkhotel* (M), Cloppenburgerstr. 418 (0441–43024). Colorful, in hotel. *Sartorius-Stuben* (M), Harbartgang 6 (0441–26676). Atmospheric. AE, MC, V.

Osnabrück. *Hohenzollern* (E), Heinrich-Heine-Str. 17 (0541–33170). 105 rooms, most with bath. At main station. Indoor pool, sauna, solarium, sportsroom. Good restaurant and cozy *Löwenbräukeller.* AE, DC, MC, V. *Parkhotel* (E), Am Heger Holz (0541–46083). 90 rooms, most with bath. Indoor pool, sauna, minigolf, bowling, riding; *Restaurant-Cafe Kampmeyer.* AE. *Residenz* (E), Johannisstr. 138 (0541–586358). 22 rooms, all with bath. Very comfortable. Garni. *Kommende-Lage Gastliches Ritterhaus* (M), Rieste (05464–5151). Near autobahn A1 (E5) in the direction of Bremen. 33 rooms. Former guesthouse of the Johannite nuns' convent; own grounds; medieval restaurant. *Klute* (M), Lotterstr. 30 (0541–45001). 22 rooms, half with bath or shower. Restaurant. *Kulmbacher Hof* (M), Schlosswall 67 (0541–27844). 41 rooms, all with bath. *Kulmbacher Keller* restaurant. DC, MC. *Welp* (M), Natruper Str. 227 (0541–123307). 20 rooms, most with bath. Restaurant.

Restaurants. *Chez Didier* (M), Buersche Str. 2 (0541–23331). French bistro in provincial style; Mediterranean fish a specialty. *Ellerbracke* (M), Neuer Graben 7 (0541–22811). *Der Landgraf* (M), Domhof 9 (0541–22372). AE, DC, V. *Niedersachsenhof* (M), Nordstr. 109 (0541–77535). In the suburb of Schinkel. Rustic garden-restaurant.

Cafés. *Café Brüggemann,* Bierstr. 13. *Café Leysieffer,* Krahnstr. 4 (0541–22755). *Romanisches Café,* Johannisstr. 46.

Rinteln/Steinbergen. *Grafensteiner Höh* (M), Grafensteiner Höh 42 (05751–5277). Located in nearby Steinbergen. *Zum Brückentor* (M), Weserstr. 1 (05751–42095). *Stadt Kassel* (I), Klosterstr. 42 (05751–2284). 18 rooms. In atmospheric timbered building.

Wangerooge (East Frisian Island). *Strandhotel Gerken* (M), Strandpromenade 21 (04469–611). 52 rooms; open May through Sept. AE, DC, MC, V. *Strandhotel Kaiserhof* (M), Strandpromenade 27 (04469–202). 55 rooms; open summer only. *Strandapartments Monopol,* 04469–248, hire apartments.

Wilhelmshaven. *Jacobi* (M), Freiligrathstr. 163 (04421–60051). 50 years of tradition, fully renovated. Good Frisian breakfast. AE, DC, MC, V. *Kaiser's* (M), Rheinstr. 128 (04421–42071). Central, modern, comfortable; good-value restaurant. *Silence Norse Hotel* (M), Olhafendamm 205 (04421–60073). With fine view of the port. AE, DC, MC, V.

Restaurants. *Artischoke* (M), Paulsstr. 6 (04421–34305). *Columbus* (M), Südstrand (04421–44088). At the Helgoland Kai (quay), maritime atmosphere, fish specialties. *Lagerhauskate* (M), Börsenstr. 25 (04421–43485).

Good wholesome local cooking. *Ratskeller* (M), Rathausplatz 1 (04421–21964). In the City Hall.

Bier-Akademie (I), Südstrand, for beers from the wood; snacks; café. For hamburgers: *Manni's Citystube,* Börsenplatz (04421–25038), to 3 A.M.

CAMPING AND YOUTH HOSTELS. There are campsites and youth hostels throughout Lower Saxony, the majority of youth hostels being in the Harz region and on the Lunebürger Heide. For a complete list of campsites write to: *Fremdenverkehrsverband Nordsee-Niedersachsen und Bremen,* Gottorpstr. 18, 2900 Oldenburg. A full list of youth hostels is available from the German Youth Hostel Association (DJH)—see "Camping" in *Facts at Your Fingertips.* Alternatively, contact local or regional tourist offices.

FARMHOUSE VACATIONS. Over 350 farmhouses in Lower Saxony offer accommodations, which may consist of an entire farmhouse, an apartment on a farm, or bed and breakfast in a farmhouse.

Write to *Arbeitsgemeinschaft Urlaub und Freizeit auf dem Lande,* Düsterneichen 303, 2725 Bothel, for details. State the area you are interested in, the number of persons and the dates for which you require the accommodation.

Farmhouse holidays in the Harz Mountains can also be reserved through the *Harzer Verkehrsverband,* Marktstr. 45, Postfach 1669, 3380 Goslar.

TOURIST INFORMATION. Bad Harzburg, Kurverwaltung, Herzog-Wilhelm-Str. 86, 3388 Bad Harzburg (05322–3044). **Bad Pyrmont,** Kur- und Verkehrsverein, Arkaden 14, 3280 Bad Pyrmont (05281–4627). **Baltrum,** Kurverwaltung, Postfach 120, 2985 Baltrum (04939–561). **Borkum,** Verkehrsbüro, Am Bahnhof, 2972 Borkum (04922–303316). **Braunlage,** Kurverwaltung, Elbingeröder Str. 17, 3389 Braunlage (05520–1054). **Braunschweig,** Verkehrsverein, Hauptbahnhof, 3300 Braunschweig (0531–79237). **Bremen,** Verkehrsverein, Bahnhofsplatz 1, 2800 Bremen (0421–36361). **Bremerhaven,** Verkehrsamt, Friedrich-Ebert-Str. 58, 2850 Bremerhaven (0471–21780). **Cuxhaven,** Kurverwaltung (in the Duhnen section), Cuxhavener Str. 92, 2190 Cuxhaven (04721–47044). **Goslar,** Tourist Information, Markt 7, 3380 Goslar (05321–704216). **Göttingen,** Fremdenverkehrsverein, Altes Rathaus, 3400 Göttingen (0551–54000). **Hameln,** Verkehrsverein, Deisterallee, 3250 Hameln (05151–202517). **Hannover,** Verkehrsbüro, Ernst-August-Platz 8, 3000 Hannover (0511–1682319). **Lüneburg,** Verkehrsverein, Rathaus, Marktplatz, 2120 Lüneburg (04131–32200). **Norderney,** Verkehrsamt, Bülow Allee 5, 2982 Norderney (04932–891156). **Oldenburg,** Verkehrsverein, Lange Str. 3, 2900 Oldenburg (0441–25092). **Osnabrück,** Verkehrsamt, Marktplatz 22, 4500 Osnabrück (0541–3232202). **Wangerooge,** Verkehrsverein, 2946 Wangerooge (04469–1411). **Wilhelmshaven,** Verkehrsbüro, Stadthalle im "Jade Zentrum," 2940 Wilhelmshaven (04421–26261).

The regional tourist office for Lower Saxony is *LFVV Niedersachsen,* Marktstr. 45 (Gildenhaus), 3380 Goslar 1 (05321–20031). For Bremen and the coast: *FVV Nordsee-Niedersachsen-Bremen,* Gottorpstr. 18, 2900 Oldenburg.

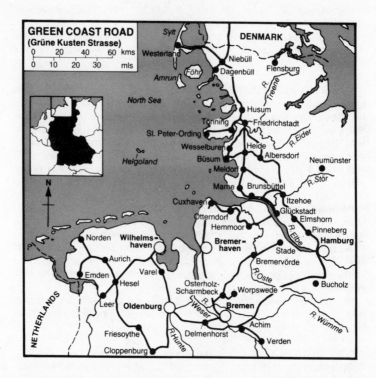

GREEN COAST ROAD
(Grüne Kusten Strasse)

HOW TO GET AROUND. By air. The main international airports serving Lower Saxony are Hannover, Bremen and Hamburg. Hannover is nearest the inland regions, the Weser Hills and the Harz Mountains. Hamburg and Bremen give access to the coastal regions and the East Frisian islands.

The East Frisian airline, *Ostfriesischer Flug-Dienst* (OFD), has direct flights twice a day in summer from Bremen and Düsseldorf to Emden, the main airfield for flights to the islands. Roland Air (ROA) operates direct to the islands from Bremen and Bremerhaven. The OFD operates regular services to Borkum, Juist, Norderney, Baltrum, Langeoog and Wangerooge, as well as flights linking the islands, and sightseeing trips. Contact: *Ostfriesischer Flug-Dienst,* 2970 Emden, Flugplatz (04921–42057).

There are several charter airlines operating in the region and flights are available to the islands from Dortmund, Münster, Osnabrück and Leer. For details of all air services write to the regional tourist office in Oldenburg.

By train. Bremen and Hannover are the main rail centers, Bremen being the link station for the coastal resorts. The most important rail stretches are: Bremen–Bremerhaven–Cuxhaven; Bremen–Oldenburg–Wilhelmshaven; Bremen–Oldenburg–Leer–Emden–Norddeich. Braunschweig,

Göttingen and Osnabrück are all on InterCity routes. Bad Harzburg serves the Harz Mountains.

Most East Frisian island resorts are some distance from their respective harbors and consequently railroads exist on all the islands except Borkum and Norderney, where buses and taxis serve.

By bus. *Europabus* (line No. EB 183) connects Hannover, Hildesheim and Göttingen on the Travemünde to Munich stretch of the Helsinki–Zagreb international route. Its sister company, *Deutsche Touring*, Am Römerhof 17, 6000 Frankfurt/Main 90 (069–79030), connects Bremen, Oldenburg and Leer (T41, Helsinki–Oslo–London); Hildesheim, Bad Harzburg and Goslar (T42, Hamburg–Bad Grund); Hannover, Hildesheim and Göttingen (T86, Helsinki–Oslo–Frankfurt or T91H, Hamburg–Frankfurt–Barcelona).

By car. The northern part of Lower Saxony—between the rivers Elbe and Ems—is traversed by a 1,750-km (1,090-mile) long scenic route from Scandinavia to Western Europe known as the Grüne Küstenstrasse (Green Coast Road—see map p. 411), passing through quiet hamlets as well as major cities. Information from *Arbeitsgemeinschaft Grüne Küstenstrasse, Gebiet Ems/Weser/Elbe,* Verkehrsverein Bremen, Postfach 100747, 2800 Bremen 1.

Note that cars are prohibited on all the East Frisian Islands, with the exception of Borkum and Norderney where they are limited to particular zones.

By boat. As befits a region with a large coastline, ferryboats play a large role in transportation. Year-round services, with increased frequency in summer, link the East Frisians to the mainland. Ferries for Baltrum sail from Norddeich or Nessmersiel (latter in summer only); for Borkum from Emden and Eemshaven in Holland; for Juist and Norderney from Norddeich; for Spiekeroog from Bensersiel and Neuharlingersiel; for Wangerooge from Harle or Wilhelmshaven. The crossings take between one and two hours. It is advisable to book ahead for all ferries in summer.

Boating is popular on inland waters with, for instance, motorboat trips on the Okersee lake near Altenau in the Harz (May–Oct.), the Bederkesaer See and the Geeste-Elbe canal at Bederkesa, and on Maschsee lake in Hannover (Apr.–Oct.). From May through Sept. the *Oberweser-Dampfschiffahrt* and *Weisse Flotte Warnecke* operate daily ferry services on the river Weser between Hameln, Bodenwerder and Bad Karlshafen. For further information contact *Oberweser-Dampfschiffahrt,* Inselstr. 3, 3250 Hameln (05151–22016); or *Weisse Flotte Wernecke,* Hauptstr. 39, 3250 Hameln (05151–3975) and at Weserstr., Bodenwerder (05533–4864).

By bike. As a large proportion of Lower Saxony is flat cycling is popular and there are many cycle tracks. Bikes can be hired almost anywhere, notably at rail stations. The regional tourist office in Bremen publishes a booklet *Radtours in Südliche Nordsee und Nordwesten* describing ten coastal and inland routes, listing places of interest. Details of a six-day tour (with luggage taken care of) over the Lüneburger Heide from the Lüneburg tourist office or from *Verkehrsbüro Gemeinde Bispingen,* Borsteler Str. 4–6, 3045 Bispingen.

EXCURSIONS. Several bus companies in Hannover operate excursions. There is a Museums Tour, a trip to the openair museum in Cloppenburg, and a tour of the Romanesque churches of southern Lower Saxony.

A five-day excursion takes in the Harz, Braunschweig and the Lüneburger Heide. Full details from the Hannover tourist office.

Try to see the Lüneburger Heide with its picturesque villages and churches, lovely heathland views, and old towns of Lüneburg and Celle, with the wild-life reserve, or the huge bird sanctuary at Walsrode. Day excursions are organized by the *Fremdenverkehrsverband Lüneburger Heide,* Am Sande 5, 2120 Lüneburg (04131–42006), and by the tourist office in Hannover.

SPORTS. Fishing. A license is required to fish in Germany. The Harz is a good fishing area. You do not need a license, however, to catch fish at fish farms (there is one near Hamburg between Winzenburg and Lampspringe) where you pay for each fish you catch. Deep-sea fishing trips, as well as excursions combined with fishing are organized from Cuxhaven (04721–35232).

Golf. The Hannover Golf Club is at Am Blauen See in the suburb of Garbsen. There are courses in Bad Harzburg, Am Breitenberg 107 (05322–6737), in Cuxhaven, Osnabrück and Buchholz on the Luneburger Heide. Norderney has a nine-hole course.

Hiking. The Harz Mountains are superb hiking country. Under a popular scheme arranged by the tourist offices—"Wandern Ohne Gepäck"— your luggage is sent on ahead of you. Walking tours are also organized for Sept. and Oct. on the Clausthal plateau (seven days) and in the Upper Harz (13 days).

Hannover's Eilenriede park offers pleasant walking, as does the 30-km. trail around the Steinhuder Meer lake. For details contact the *Wandern und Naturistenbund Hannover,* Beekestr. 107, 3000 Hannover 91.

For information about trails on the Lüneburger Heide contact: *Fremdenverkehrsverband Celler Land,* Schlossplatz 6a, 3100 Celle; *Landkreis Lüneburg,* Auf dem Michaeliskloster 4, 2120 Lüneburg; *Urlaubskreis Gifhorn, Amt für Wirtschaftsförderung,* Schlosstr., 3170 Gifhorn; *Tourist Information, Naturpark, Elbufer-Drawehn,* Postfach, 3130 Lüchow.

Cuxhaven's tourist office has prepared suggestions for 12 walking tours in the surrounding forests, moors and marshes and along coastal paths.

Wattwanderung—walking on the long stretches of tidal sands and wading across the shallows—is practiced from most island and coastal resorts. Because of the varying tides we strongly advise you to join an organized tour.

Horseback riding. The horse holds a special place in Lower Saxon tradition and there are numerous opportunities for holidays in the saddle. A large equestrian center at Löwensen near Bad Pyrmont (05281–10606) offers various activities including trekking. Riding is popular on the sands and mudflats of the mainland coast. You can also hire horses at many centers in the Harz region.

Sailing. Sailing is popular on most of the inland lakes, particularly on Hannover's Steinhuder Meer and Maschsee, Zwischenahner See by Bad Zwishenahn, on the River Weser between Bremen (where regattas are held) and Bremerhaven, on the River Aller and in the Ems estuary. At Cuxhaven sailboats and sea-going yachts can be hired, or lessons taken; information from Kapitän R.M. Dietzler, Wehrbergsweg 34, 2190 Cuxhaven (04721–46269).

Small boats of all kinds can be hired at most places where there are rivers or lakes. Canoes and rowboats can be hired at Bremen and at Hannover (tel. 0511–15236 for Maschsee lake), where canoeists can also contact the *Landeskanuverband,* Maschstr. 20 (0511–881500) for information on the best stretches of water. Information for the Lüneburger Heide rivers from the *Fremdenverkehrsverband Lüneburger Heide* in Lüneburg, Postfach 2160.

Swimming. All coastal resorts have pools, many with heated sea water and waves, both indoor and outdoor. The largest indoor sea water pool in Europe, with waves, can be found on Borkum. Large cities have many indoor pools. The health and ski resorts of the Harz also have indoor pools, including a glass-fronted one with artificial waves at Bad Pyrmont.

Tennis. All large towns and resorts have tennis courts.

WINTER SPORTS. The forested Harz Mountains are an important winter sports region in Germany and the one with the oldest tradition. Their slopes are much more gentle than those of the Alps, the highest peak, the Brocken, being only 1,142 meters. The terrain lends itself particularly to cross-country skiing and is mostly easy to medium/pleasant for ski-hiking through the woods. Another specialty of the area is ski-jumping. The snow is abundant and deep and normally lasts until the middle of March. The best pistes are at Schulenberg, the Lower Saxony Ski Alpinum, which has a 1,200-meter Olympic run. The principal centers are located at elevations of between 490 meters (1,600 ft.) and 790 meters (2,600 ft.), with skiing up to 975 meters (3,200 ft.).

The most important skiing center of Lower Saxony is made up of five attractive Kur centers, together known as the *Oberharzer:* Altenau/Torfhaus, Buntenbock, Clausthal-Zellerfeld, Schulenberg and Wildemann. All five resorts are connected by regular bus services with the fast train stop of Goslar. Skiing areas are situated between 550 meters (1,800 ft.) and 850 meters (2,800 ft.).

Other important resorts are: Bad Sachsa, Braunlage, HahnenkleeBockswiese, Hohegeiss and St. Andreasberg.

For information about snow and piste conditions (in German), telephone the *Harzer Schneetelefon* on 05321–40124.

SCHLESWIG-HOLSTEIN

Sand Dunes and Thatched Roofs

Schleswig-Holstein is Germany's northernmost province, the land that lies north of the Elbe, and the one most conscious of the sea. Its western limit is the North Sea, its northeastern boundary the Baltic, known to the Germans as the Ost See, the East Sea. This is Germany's flatland—a wide plain of soft green heaths, sandy dunes, rich fields, and blue waters. The land of several historic Hanseatic cities, Schleswig-Holstein abounds in architectural and artistic treasures. In the center, it is a rich agricultural area whose villages of thatched-roof cottages and windmills in green fields offer an attractive contrast to the wind-blown grass clinging to the sandy dunes of the coast.

Exploring Schleswig-Holstein

North of Hamburg in an almost straight west-east line and on the road which crosses the Schleswig-Holstein peninsula from Brunsbüttel in the west to Lübeck in the east lie three important spas: Bad Bramstedt, with new spa buildings located a mile or so out of town, which is traversed by several small streams operating two water mills in the center; Bad Segeberg, separated from Bad Bramstedt by the Segeberger Forest, whose chief attraction is the Kalkberg, a 90-meter (300-foot) rock formation, the only place in Schleswig-Holstein where mountain climbing can be practised and at whose foot is a large outdoor theater where plays based on Karl May's novels are performed every summer (Karl May was the romantic German writer who wrote adventure stories about the American Indians); and Bad Schwartau.

Lübeck

Lübeck, "Queen of the Hansa," owed its dominating position in the Hanseatic League—which made it an important influence in the development of all of northeastern Europe—principally to its favorable location on the Trave River, just above the point where it empties into the Baltic. The old harbor buildings and docks along the river give visible evidence today of the ancient prosperity of this port, which in the time of the Hohenstaufen Emperors became an Imperial Free City. Its wealth is obvious also from the fine old buildings in its center. Most spectacular of these is the City Hall. Lübeck is famous for its brickwork, and the Rathaus is probably the finest example of all, retaining in part the black glazed tiles characteristic of the region. It is a striking building, with its arches resting on pillars on the ground floor and curious rounded cylinders, each capped with a pointed spire like a dunce's cap, embedded in its walls. Lübeck is also well-known for its ceramic tiles (Lübecker Kacheln) and amber (Bernstein).

Other buildings worth visiting in Lübeck include its famous cathedral, founded in 1173 by Henry the Lion, in which you will find the *Triumphal Cross,* carved in wood by Bernt Notke, in 1477; the Holstein Gate, two massive towers, again with conical roofs, connected by a central section whose façade rises in a series of steps; the city walls; St. Mary's Church, also founded by Henry the Lion in 1159, at the same time the city was founded; and the Heilige-Geist-Spital (Hospital of the Holy Ghost), built in 1280 with an early Gothic church. Both the cathedral and St. Mary's Church, like so many other fine buildings in Lübeck, were badly damaged in the war, but both have been partially restored; some of their treasures have been returned, others are still in the St. Annen Museum, which contains North German art, specializing in medieval pieces. St. Peter's Church has also been restored and its tower can be ascended (by elevator) for a magnificent view of the city. Also in a special class is the Buddenbrookhaus, in the Mengstrasse; it provided the background for the famous novel by Thomas Mann, who was born in Lübeck. Also worth a visit is the Behnhaus in the Königstrasse, an 18th-century patrician house with 19th-century interiors and a modern art collection.

South of Lübeck along Die Alte Salzstrasse (The Old Salt Road) are several interesting towns. The first is Ratzeburg, huddled on a tiny island in the Ratzenburger Lake in the center of a lovely lake region. The top attraction of the town itself is the outstanding 12th-century Romanesque cathedral. The next stop is medieval Mölln, also on a lake and with a Romanesque church where Till Eulenspiegel is allegedly buried; the inscription on the tombstone says that he died in Mölln in 1350. South of Mölln is Schwarzenbek at the edge of Sachsenwald, and then we reach the Elbe at Lauenburg.

Travemünde and the Coast Resorts

Northeast of Lübeck is the beach resort of Travemünde. This is the most popular of all Baltic holiday spots, and it manages to keep up the jollity all year around, thanks to the luxurious gaming casino overlooking the beach. If Travemünde is the point where you first touch the Baltic, you will find beaches whose pattern is repeated all along this coast with thick pine woods running down to the sand. Where bathers concentrate, you will find the characteristic enormous wicker chairs, in which you can shut yourself up to change in your own individual bathhouse, each chair sitting in the middle of a crater scooped into the sand, to prevent it from upsetting in high winds.

Travemünde is the first of a whole string of beaches enjoying a sheltered position on the Baltic bay that cuts in behind the long peninsula running north from this point. It is a large, beautiful seaside resort with a nautical Cornwall or Massachusetts flavor, filled with restaurants, casinos, and hotels. If you arrive by sea, you will find one of the prettiest seaside locations around today, right in the town, with handsome craft from Finland and Sweden, gliding up the Trave, and lit up at night. Travemünde is a good place to visit, even if only for a day trip—it's 20 minutes from Lübeck and an hour from Hamburg. One of the colorful sights is a marvelous fish, fruit and vegetable market, held on Monday and Thursday mornings near St. Lorenz Church.

Across the bay is East Germany and an hour's drive away in the other direction is Hamburg's international airport. All the resorts along this part of the coast are lively. Next comes Niendorf, a little fishing village, which has preferred to stay that way instead of going cosmopolitan like its next-door neighbor to the north, Timmendorfer Strand, with its fine white-sand beach and extensive woods. Next come Scharbeutz, Haffkrug and Sierksdorf, all quiet vacation spots. From the old town Neustadt (with the name of "new town"), the railroad and main road run directly through Oldenburg to Grossenbrode from where you cross to the island of Fehmarn over a bridge; on the other side of Fehmarn you reach Puttgarden, the ferry port for Denmark. Along the coast, however, there are several important beach resorts, among them Grömitz, Kellenhusen, and Dahme.

Eutin, to the northwest of Neustadt, takes us away from the coast and puts us back on the road to Kiel. Eutin has several claims to fame: it's the gateway to "Holstein Switzerland," with its lake plateau and nature park; it's the birthplace of the composer Carl Maria von Weber; it's noted for its rose cultivation; there's an old moated castle set in a beautiful park; and, finally, it is on a charming lake.

This last is not much of a distinction here. We are now in the lake district. Our next town, Malente-Gremsmühlen, a health resort, offers a popular Five Lakes Tour. Plön with a castle known as a "miniature Versailles," which succeeds it, is completely surrounded by lakes. Across the Greater Plön Lake you can go by boat to the little resorts of Dersau and Bosau, the latter with a fine church dating from 1150. Next comes Preetz, where there is an old convent, and we exit from Holstein Switzerland without having seen anything remotely resembling an Alp.

Kiel

This brings us to Kiel, which happens to be a university town, but unfortunately it is difficult to think of that today since its old university, founded in 1665, was completely demolished in the last war, as well as the old castle of the Duke of Holstein-Gottorf. The world over, this name automatically brings to mind the Kiel Canal—except in Germany, where this great engineering achievement, which has converted the only mainland Denmark possessed into one more island, is known as the North Sea-East Sea canal. Its entrance—or exit, depending on your point of view—remains one of the major sights of Kiel.

Once the chief naval port of Germany (and the home of Germany's largest training schooner *Gorch Fock*), Kiel remains today one of the country's greatest centers for both inshore and deepsea fishing. Everyone knows of Kiel Week early in summer, the international regatta during which craft of all sorts, wind, motor, or muscle-pulled, race on the waters of Kiel Fjord. This is the gathering time of the international set, for the leading yachtsmen the world over compete.

There are a number of interesting trips to be made from Kiel. By boat there is a pleasant ride to Laboe, near the opening of the fjord at whose base Kiel itself lies. There is an impressive monument at Laboe, but its finest attraction is a flat sandy beach, protected by the lie of the land from the sharp eastern winds, which because of its gentle slope is particularly safe for children. On the same side of the fjord is Schönberg, with another fine beach, reached by a local railway line from Kiel.

There are a number of interesting places to visit in Kiel. These include the Kunsthalle (Art Gallery) on Düsternbrookerweg, with 19th- and 20th-century paintings; the Museum für Völkerkunde (Ethnological Museum), which concentrates on the peoples of the South Seas, East Asia and Africa; the Schiffahrtsmuseum (Nautical Museum), in the old fishmarket, which illustrates the history of Kiel's seafaring life; and Schloss Museum, which is a regional historical collection in Kiel castle. Not far away is the "living" Freilicht-museum Molfsee with many historic buildings.

Schleswig and Flensburg

From Kiel the direct road for Schleswig passes through Eckernförde, with its 500-year-old Rathaus and wine cellar hewn out of solid rock. But if you travel by train you have to pass through Rendsburg with an impressive bridge over the Kiel Canal.

If you come into Schleswig by car, you will pass a signpost bearing in small letters the name "Schleswig," and under them in larger characters, another and stranger title, "Haithabu." Surmounting the whole is the carved replica of a Viking ship. For Schleswig was a Viking city, and Haithabu was the name of this locality in Viking days. Today it is Haddeby, and you may visit it on Schleswig's outskirts.

The oldest city in Schleswig-Holstein, Schleswig, from the 9th to the 11th centuries, was an important center of foreign trade. It has two major attractions you must not fail to visit. One is St. Peter's Cathedral (St. Petri Dom), begun in 1100. It is a fine building, though its great drawing card is not the cathedral itself, but the fact that it contains one of the most famous Renaissance works of art in all Germany—the Bordesholm Altar. This is a remarkable example of the woodcarver's art, a richly ornamented altar piece containing no less than 392 figures, which was made by Hans Brüggemann in 1521. It originally stood in the Augustine abbey of Bordesholm, a small place in the Schleswig lake district, where very few persons saw it; so in 1666 the Duke of Schleswig had it removed to the cathedral of his capital. Concerts by organists of international repute take place in the cathedral during the summer.

The other great sight is Gottorf Castle, the biggest castle in Schleswig-Holstein, on an island in the Schlei, the largest and narrowest fjord of the region and which in the Middle Ages formed the border between Holstein and Saxony. The original building was constructed about 1150 for the Bishops of Schleswig, and became the residence in 1268 of the Dukes of Schleswig-Holstein-Gottorf, who held it for some four-and-a-half centuries. In 1713 it fell to the Danish crown and was stripped of its treasures; in 1842 it was completely destroyed. In 1864 Schleswig-Holstein was conquered by Bismarck and restored to Germany as the first act in the unification of Germany under Prussia and later the castle was rebuilt. The present building is a faithful restoration of the old one. It contains the great Landesmuseum of Schleswig-Holstein with a fine collection of medieval ecclesiastical art, of arts and crafts from the 16th to 19th century and of folk art, as well as the King's Hall and Castle Chapel. It also contains one of the largest and finest collections of prehistory and early history in Germany, including the only stone with a runic inscription ever found in this country, objects from Viking graves, and the Nydam Boat, an Anglo-Saxon craft of the 4th century, the sort of ship in which the Angles and Saxons sailed from this neighborhood for the conquest of Britain. As well as the museum in Gottorf Castle, Schleswig has its Städtisches Museum (City Museum), in the V. Günderoth's Hof, a 17th-century country residence.

The area between Schleswig, Flensburg, Flensburg Fjord and Schlei deserves mention since it gave its name to the language you are at this moment reading. It is called Angeln, and from it, 1,500 years ago, came the Angles, the men who crossed the North Sea to the British Isles and settled in England.

"The Gate to the North," Flensburg, is full of picturesque old houses. One of them is the Nordertor—built in 1595 and formerly a city gate—a Gothic brick structure with a series of stepped gables, which, gate though it is, harbors a house inside. So does the Kompagnietor (1603), which also served as a guildhouse. The Old Flensburg House and St. Mary's Church (1284), with a neo-Gothic tower added in 1880, the arcaded North Market (1595), and the fishing quarter of Jürgenby, with its picturesque boats and fishing nets, are also worth visiting. A more modern attraction of Flensburg is the fact that it produces rum. One of the local brands, of which there are some 128 produced by 28 distilleries, is known descriptively as "Flensburg Fire."

When in Flensburg, make the excursion to Glücksburg Castle, once the residence of the Glücksburg line of the House of Oldenburg and the cradle of the royal houses of Denmark, Norway, and Greece. Mirrored in the lovely lake that almost completely surrounds it, Glücksburg Castle stands in majestic solitude over the still waters and the encircling green forests. The castle itself, built between 1582 and 1587, houses one of the best collections of tapestries in Germany.

There are also the Naturkundliches Museum (Natural History Museum), with its fine collection of local birds, butterflies and pressed plants, and the Städtisches Museum (Municipal Museum), which contains ecclesiastical art, arts and crafts of Schleswig-Holstein from prehistoric times to the 19th century, furniture and medieval sculpture.

North Frisian Islands

At Flensburg, you are on the Baltic, but a drive to the west of less than 48 km. (30 miles) puts you in North Frisia, on the North Sea. Offshore lie the North Frisian Islands, the most famous and expensive of which is fashionable Sylt. Here you get your first taste of this healthy vigorous country—sometimes too vigorous, on the days when gales sweep in from the open sea, holding the dune grass flat against the ground and making the sand of the beaches ripple like waves. At Keitum you can see the answer of the old shipmasters to the wind, in the snug thatch-roofed homes they built in order to spend their declining days looking out upon the element on which in their younger years they lived. In Keitum they picked a propitious spot, for it is usually sheltered from the gales, for these islands; indeed it has a considerable reputation as a climatic health resort. Its immunity from the full force of the gales is shown by its numerous trees; most of the territory of the North Frisian Islands has been swept bare of them. To visitors, Keitum offers several spectacles—the old Frisian House, the Regional Museum (Heimatmuseum), and the 12th-century church at St. Severin, once the most important on the island and built on the site of a shrine dedicated to the Germanic goddess of marriage, Frigga.

Westerland, Sylt's most famous resort, is a busy center, with a casino, fashion shows, sporting events, and all the bustle of chic vacation spots. Some distance from the more frequented localities, however, Westerland has staked out a sector more in tune with the natural surroundings of the island—a nudist beach.

Another attractive stop on the Isle of Sylt is at Kampen, the most expensive and elegant "village" on the island. If you like horseback riding, a canter from Wenningstedt to Kampen along the shore will long remain in your memory. A favorite excursion from Kampen or Westerland is a boat ride to the islands where seals bask and play in the sunshine.

Two other delightful North Frisian isles are Föhr and Amrum. Föhr has the mildest climate of the North Sea Islands—roses bloom well into the winter at Wyk, its loveliest and oldest resort, a noted health center, where the traditional Frisian costumes are worn.

Amrum has three resorts, which, oddly enough, are quite widely known in the United States in spite of their remoteness, for many Frisians emigrated to America from here. They are Wittdün, whose ten-km. (six-mile) beach is sheltered by sand dunes 30 meters high; Nebel, with an interesting ancient cemetery and a local museum housed in a windmill dating from 1771; and Norddorf, just a beach and bird sanctuary.

Helgoland

Probably the most interesting of the North Sea Islands, however, is Helgoland, located about halfway between the North Frisian and the East Frisian Islands. Its red sandstone cliffs rising regally out of the green water have viewed a stormy past: originally a health resort of the early Frisians, it later provided secret shelter to sea pirates. Its strategic location has made it a long-fought-over prize to many seafaring nations, including Denmark and England. Although no longer the smuggler's paradise it has been in the past, particularly when much of this coast was blockaded during the

Napoleonic wars, it is today the shopper's paradise, for it is a duty-free oasis for the bargain-minded.

There is whisky galore on Helgoland and at the same prices that you would pay in the various duty-free airport shops. With the right set of vacationers Helgoland could easily become a "Tight Little Island." Since Helgoland is a duty-free area you have to pass customs when leaving for the mainland but the quantity you can take along customs free may change from time to time.

Sea swimming is mainly from the dune island (the north beach is a nudist colony) facing the port, connected with it by motorboat service, but there is also excellent swimming in the town itself, in the large twin swimming pool, filled with seawater and whose indoor and outdoor sections are connected by a water corridor. Not far from the swimming pool, which is located in the sports and recreation area, is the interesting aquarium containing almost all specimens of the North Sea fauna. Regular ships cannot dock in Helgoland and therefore you have to transfer to small boats which will take you in and out. Everything on Helgoland was blown up by the Allies at the end of the last war (although you will notice that some thick defense walls at the sea level below the red cliff remained almost unscarred by the dynamiting attempts) and therefore everything on Helgoland is new. An elevator now connects the lower part of the town with the upper part. The buildings, spotless and neat, designed along the most modern lines, and painted in pastel colors, almost give the impression of neatly arranged toys. The importance of Helgoland as a tourist center and health resort has increased tremendously during the past years and if you contemplate spending some time there during the summer you should make your reservations well in advance. Note, however, that there are no cars on the island—motoring is prohibited.

On the Mainland

Back on the mainland again, proceed south to Husum, opposite the small group of Halligen Islands, embattled against the sea, even more off the beaten track than those just visited. Places to visit in Husum include the Nissenhaus, containing a collection of natural history and agricultural objects from early North Frisia; the Ostenfelder Bauernhaus, an historically-furnished old Geest farmhouse; the Schlossmuseum, a 16th-century castle with a collection of furnishings and objets d'art from the North Frisian Islands; and the Theodor Storm Haus, former residence of a famous poet, containing an exhibit on his life and works.

South of Husum is Friedrichstadt, separated from the sea by the Eiderstedt peninsula which pushes into the North Sea at this point, into which you might want to make a side trip to the beach resort of St. Peter-Ording, with a year-round season, or the smaller one at the mouth of the Eider River, Tönning. From Friedrichstadt, our route passes through Heide, with an interesting museum (from here there is a side trip to Büsum, once a simple fishing village but now a bathing resort with horseracing on the sand flats and a spa which bathes its patients in the North Sea mud that is reputed, perhaps because of high iodine content, to have powerful health-restoring qualities); Meldorf, whose Church of St. John the Baptist, built in 1220–30 in early Gothic style, presides over a city where handicraft still flourishes; and brings you to Brunsbüttel, at the south end of the North Sea-Baltic Canal.

Crossing the canal, you proceed to Glückstadt, famous for its *Matjes,* a special kind of marinated white herring. The best time for tasting it is from the beginning of June to August: "Matjes Weeks." Here, where you might pause long enough to admire the six-sided Market Square, from which no less than 15 streets branch out, before taking the ferry over the Elbe to Wischhafen, we cross out of Schleswig-Holstein and into Lower Saxony.

PRACTICAL INFORMATION FOR
SCHLESWIG-HOLSTEIN

TELEPHONES. We have given telephone codes for all the towns and villages in the hotel and restaurant lists that follow. These codes need only be used when calling from outside the town or village concerned.

HOTELS AND RESTAURANTS. In addition to the more expensive hotels in the larger centers and in the popular North and Baltic Sea resorts (particularly Sylt), there are many inexpensive, modest accommodations in Schleswig-Holstein. Most establishments remain open all year round. However, resorts in Schleswig-Holstein, in common with many other German resorts and cities, offer off-season reductions.

A seaside resort complex, named (oddly to us) Damp 2000, is located between Eckenförde and Kappeln. Covering 15 acres, it consists of a year-round holiday complex of apartment houses and bungalows with every sort of indoor and outdoor sport imaginable. There are three heated pools, children's playgrounds, kindergarten, babysitter service. There is no through traffic.

For farmhouse accommodations, a list of farm addresses throughout Schleswig-Holstein offering bed and breakfast, holiday apartments or whole farmhouses for rent is available. Write *Sparkassen Verzeichnis Urlaub auf dem Bauernhof in Schleswig-Holstein,* Postfach 4120, 2300 Kiel, or the regional tourist office for Schleswig-Holstein.

Amrum (North Frisian Island). In **Nebel.** *Gästehaus "Kap Horn"* (M), Strunwai (04682–2338). Open all year round, 25 rooms, about half with bath. *Pension Steinbach* (I), Waaswai (04682–729). Right on the "Watt" beach.

Restaurant. *Ekke-Nekkepenn* (04682–2245). The island's best-known restaurant. Excellent for fish and seafood.

In **Norddorf.** On the northernmost tip of the island near the bird sanctuary. *Apartement Hotel Seeblick* (E) (04682–888). New 1983; 22 rooms and 15 apartments, indoor pool, sauna, solarium, restaurant. *Ual Oemreng Wiartshüs* (E) (04682–2003). The strange-sounding name alone gives an idea of its originality. Typical North Frisian-styled thatched house with 14 rooms, all furnished in local style, about half with own bath. Restaurant with fish and shrimp specialties. AE, DC. *Hotel-Restaurant Graf Luckner*

(M), Haus No. 80 (04682–2367). Game, poultry and fish specialties. Closed Nov. and Dec.

Also any amount of private and bed and breakfast accommodations in equally quaint-looking North Frisian houses.

In **Wittdün.** *Ferienhotel Weisse Düne* (E), Achtern Strand 6 (04682–855). 10 apartments, indoor pool, sauna, restaurant. *Haus Südstrand* (M), Mittelstr. 30 (04682–2708). With restaurant and garden; open all year. *Strandhotel Vierjahreszeiten* (M), Obere Wandelbahn (04682–2379). 40 rooms. Only hotel on the south beach. AE, DC, MC, V.

Föhr (North Frisian Island). In **Wyk.** *Strandhotel* (E), Königstr. 1 (04681–797). 14 rooms, 14 apts.; terrace, cafe and restaurant. *Colosseum* (M), Grosse Str. 42 (04681–961/2/3). 28 rooms, 4 apts., terrace, restaurant. Closed Mar. *Duus-Hotel* (M), Hafenstr. 40 (04681–708). 25 rooms. Recently renovated. Restaurant. *Kurhotel am Wellenbad* (M), Sandwall 29 (04681–2199). 55 rooms, pool, sauna. Well-run hotel, very good restaurant. Closed between Jan. and Mar., Nov. to Dec. AE, DC, MC.

Restaurants. *Alt-Wyk* (M), Grosse Str. 4 (04681–3212). Mussels a specialty. *Glaube-Liebe-Hoffnung*, Hafenstr. 28 (04681–2272). Original pub.

In **Nieblum.** *Haus Osterheide* (I), (04681–2895). 13 rooms, tennis and cafe.

In **Süderende.** *Landhaus Altes Pastorat* (E), (04683–226). A gourmet's mecca. Evenings only (7.30 P.M. precisely). Reservations a must. Some rooms.

In **Utersum.** *Zur Post* (M), (04683–897). With annexe, 14 rooms, some with bath, and 2 apartments; sports room and cafe, no restaurant. *Eckhüüs* (I), Dorfstr. 12 (04683–358). 10 rooms, most with bath, plus apartment; quiet.

Helgoland (North Frisian Island). All hotels on Helgoland are recent, as the entire settlement has been completely rebuilt. Small hotels and pensions are being added all the time. *Kurhotel/Seehotel* (E), Lung Wai 27 (04725–595). Two hotels in one; quiet, view, with all facilities and top comfort. Two separate first-class restaurants. AE. *Hüs Weeterkant* (M), Am Südstrand 5 (04725–642). All rooms with bath; tennis, water sports, fishing. *Rungholt* (M), Sudstrand 9 (04725–372). *Hanseat* (M), (04725–663). Facing the port at Südstrand. *Haus Stadt Hamburg* (M), Am Sudstrand 15 (04725–688). Fine view; breakfast only. *Felsen-Eck* (I), (04725–234). On the upland; small, with terrace cafe with beautiful view over the harbor. *Nickels* (I), Kurpromenade 33 (04725–554).

Restaurants. *Dünen-Restaurant* (M), (04725–644). Worth a visit. *Störtebecker* (M), (04725–622). On the uplands, good local atmosphere. DC.

There is a bungalow town on the dune island, where the swimming is best; small, inexpensive 2- and 4-person recently-built bungalows (without cooking facilities or running water) stand among sand dunes, protected from the wind. Next to them is a large camp site. A restaurant and tiny airport are located on the island, as well as some provision shops. Travel to and from Helgoland proper is by motorboat (daytime only), about a 10-minute ride. Privately operated ferry lines run until 11.00 P.M.

Sylt (North Frisian Island). In **Kampen.** (Accommodations office 04651–43300). *Hotel Rungholt mit Haus Meeresblick* (E), (04651–41041). 54 rooms, very comfortable, half-pension only. *Hotel Walter's Hof* (E), (04651–42000). 29 rooms, also apts., and holiday flats; pool, sauna. Excellent restaurant. For details of (M) and (I) pensions call the accommodations office. Most places open Mar. to Oct. only.

Restaurants. For a bit of local color, visit the tavern *Kupferkanne* (E), the "Copper Kettle," Stapelhooger Wai (04651–41010). An old converted bunker decorated in "seafaring modern" style; popular with writers and artists, whose special province Kampen is. Restaurant, bar, disco. *Sturmhaube* (M), Riper Stieg (04651–41140). Near the red cliffs, with a fine view of sand dunes and sea. *Dorfkrug Rotes Kliff* (M), (04651–43400). Restaurant with disco. *Village* (E), (04651–1035). Restaurant, bar, disco. *Vogelkoje Kampen* (M), (04651–1035). Thatch-roofed café and restaurant.

In **Keitum.** (Accommodations office 04651–31050). *Romantik Hotel Benen-Diken Hof garni* (E), (04651–31035). 30 rooms, 7 suites, 4 apts. Reduced rates in early spring and Nov. Delightful and typical. *Wolfshof Hotel garni* (M), (04651–3445). 15 rooms, pool, sauna, solarium. Small but very good.

Restaurant. *Fisch-Fiete* (E), Weidemannweg 3 (04651–32150). Very good and always crowded.

In **Morsum.** *Nösse,* Nösistig (E), (04641–422). Excellent gourmet kitchen; overlooks the Morsum cliff. Bistro is open at lunch-time.

In **Tinnum.** *Romantik Restaurant Landhaus Stricker* (E), Boy Nielsen-Str. 10 (04651–31672). 250-year-old Frisian timber house; maritime decor and first-rate menu. Wine-list with nearly 400 different wines. *Fränkische Weinstuben* (M), Täärpstig (04651–440). Very good local food.

In **Wenningstedt.** Hotels seasonal May through Oct. Most larger hotels offer half or full pension only. For accommodations office call 04651–43210. *Friesenhof* (E), Hauptstr. 16 (04651–41031). 17 rooms, 10 apartments. *Strandhörn* (E), Dünenstr. 1 (04651–42990). 16 rooms, all with own bath; small, exclusive hotel near the beach, with first-class *Kaminstübchen* restaurant. *Strandhotel Seefrieden* (E), (04651–41071). Also opposite the beach, 90 beds, most rooms with own bath; open all year. Restaurant *Admiral's Stube.* DC. *Pilz* (M), Hochkamp 9 (04651–41033). 25 beds; small and good. *Seehotel Heidehof* (M), Hochkamp 10 (04651–41047). 12 rooms, all with own bath, 9 holiday apartments. Garni. *Die Widmarckt* (I), Am Denghoog (04651–42282). 12 beds, open summer only. *Haus Herma* (I), Friesenweg 4 (04651–41438). 18 beds. Quiet location, heated openair pool; restaurant.

Restaurants. *La Bonne Auberge* (E), Am Dorfteich 2 (04651–41476). AE, DC. *Witthüs,* Alte Dorfstr. 9 (04651–42974). DC.

In **Westerland.** (Accommodations office 04651–24001). *Hotel Miramar* (E), Friedrichstr. 43 (04651–5091). 130 beds, pool, sauna, solarium. Modern hotel behind old walls. On the beach. *Stadt Hamburg* (E), Strandstr. 2 (04651–8580). 110 beds, all rooms with bath. Luxurious hotel, large rooms, antique furnishings. Excellent restaurant. *Hotel Monbijou garni* (M), Andreas Dirks-Str. 6 (04651–6081). 27 rooms, on the beach, open May through Sept. *Hotel Roth am Strand* (M), Strandstr. 31 (04651–5091). Modern and comfortable. Open all year. *Hotel Vier Jahreszeiten* (M), Johann Möller Str. 40 (04651–23028). 27 rooms, all with bath; on the beach.

Restaurants. *Käpt'n Hahn* (E), Trift 10 (04651–5461). Old Frisian house, with marine decor and excellent food; rather crowded. *Alte Friesenstube* (M), Gaadt 4 (04651–1228). North German and Frisian specialties. *Seekiste* (M), Käpt'n Christiansen-Str. 9 (04651–22575). Good local food in original surroundings.

In the *Kurzentrum* (Cure Center), there is a large café-restaurant with protected booth-tables so you can enjoy the sea air in any weather.

Flensburg. In city center. *Flensburger Hof* (M), Süderhofenden 38 (0461–17320). Good and comfortable. AE, DC, MC, V. *Hotel am Rathaus* (M), Rote Str. 32–34 (0461–17333). Modern. No restaurant. DC, MC. *Flensborg Hus* (I), Norderstr. 76 (0461–26105). 25 beds. *Hotel Europa* (I), Rathausstr. 1–5 (0461–17522). Restaurant, smoked eel a specialty. AE, DC, MC. *Hotel am Stadtpark* (I), Nordergraben 70 (0461–24900). Quiet location, good view overlooking the Flensburg Fjord. *Zoega* (I), Norderstr. 33 (0461–23508). 30 beds, good restaurant.

Restaurants. *Borgerforeningen,* Holm 17 (0461–23385). Local and international specialties in old merchant house. *Börsenkeller,* Grosse Str. 77 (0461–23338). Rustic, with local fish specialties. *Brasserie Napoleon* (0461–22022) and *Hofrestaurant* (0461–13110), Grosse Str. 42–44. Historic building and antique furnishings. *Piet Henningsen,* Schiffbrücke 20 (0461–24576). An unusual place at the harbor, practically a small sailing "museum."

In **Mürwik.** *Hotel "Am Wasserturm"* (M), Blasberg 13 (0461–36071). Modern, quiet, but still central. Good restaurant.

In **Glücksburg** (6 miles). *Intermar-Hotel Glücksburg* (M), Fördestr. 2–4 (04631–941). All rooms with bath; on the waterfront, indoor pool, sauna, riding, tennis, water sports, fishing. AE, DC, MC, V. *Kurparkhotel* (M), Sandwigstr. 1 (04631–551).

Restaurant. *Boysen's Gästehaus,* Grosse Str. 32 (04631–7007). Excellent restaurants on beach.

At **Oeversee.** *Romantik Hotel Historischer Krug* (E), (04630–3344). A 450-year-old thatched house with 32 rooms, sauna, solarium. The atmospheric restaurant offers fish, game, and fine German wines.

Kiel. *Conti-Hansa-Hotel* (E), Schlossgarten 7 (0431–51150). New in 1984, in a beautiful park near Oslokai on the Kiel Fjord; 338 beds, all rooms with bath or shower, some with terrace. AE, DC, MC, V. *Maritim-Bellevue* (E), Bismarckallee 2 (0431–35050). Beautifully-located on the fjord, 180 rooms with bath; pool, sauna, tennis, riding, water sports, fishing. AE, DC, MC, V. *Astor* (M), Holstenplatz 1–2 (0431–93017). 59 rooms with bath or shower and radio, rooftop cafe-restaurant. AE, DC, MC, V. *Berliner Hof* (M), Ringstr. 6 (0431–62050). 160 beds. AE, DC, MC. *Consul* (M), Walkerdamm 11 (0431–63015). 70 beds. AE, DC, MC, V. *Ring-Hotel-Kieler Kaufmann* (M), Niemannsweg 102 (0431–85011). 51 rooms; in park, new restaurant. AE, DC, MC, V. *Dietrichsdorfer Hof* (I), Heikendorfer Weg 54 (0431–26108). 45 beds; garni. *Friesenhof* (I), Kaiserstr. 63 (0431–731789).

Restaurants. *Restaurant im Schloss* (E), Wall 80 (0431–91158). Next to the Congress Hall, dates back to 1580. Rooms for larger groups in the cellar vaults. AE, DC, MC. *Friesenhof im Ratskeller* (M), Fleethörn 9 (0431–95494). In the Rathaus, typical Frisian-style rooms with cosy niches and corners. Wholesome dishes and Frisian specialties. *Jever Bőőn* (M), Dänische Str. 22 (0431–93909). Local specialties. AE, DC, MC.

Lübeck. *Altstadt Hotel* (M), Fischergrube 52 (0451–72083). Central new hotel behind old facade. Also has apts. Closed Dec. 22–Feb. 1. AE. *Hanseatic garni* (M), Hansestr. 19 (0451–83328). *Kaiserhof garni* (M), Kronsforder Allee 13 (0451–791011). 110 beds, most with bath, sauna. AE, MC. *Ringhotel Jensen am Holstentor* (M), Obertrave 4–5 (0451–71646). Atmospheric restaurant *Jagdzimmer.* AE, DC, MC, V. *Wakenitzblick* (M), Augustenstr. 30 (0451–791792). Small modern hotel, nice view over river. AE, DC, MC. *Schabbelhaus* (E), Mengstr. 48–52 (0451–72011). Atmospheric (frequented by Thomas Mann) and expensive. AE, DC, MC, V. *Stadtrestaurant* (E), Am Bahnhof 2 (0451–84044). Excellent international cuisine. AE, DC, MC. *Ratskeller* (M), (0451–72044). In the Rathaus; picturesque. AE, DC, MC. *Haus der Schiffergesellschaft* (M), Breite Str. 2 (0451–76776). Historic sailor's inn (since 1535). *Historische Weinstuben* (M), Koberg 8–9 (0451–76234). Beneath the Heilige-Geist-Spital; 12th-century wine cellar with first-class restaurant. AE, DC. *Cafe Niederegger* (M), Breite Str. 89 (0451–71036). Opposite the Rathaus; Johann Georg Niederegger first produced marzipan here in 1806. *Lübecker Hanse* (M), Kolk 3–7 (0451–78054). French specialties; closed Sun. AE, V.

Schleswig. *Strandhalle* (E), Strandweg 2 (04621–22021). Outstanding small hotel, 2 pools, beautiful garden, overlooking yacht basin. AE, DC, MC, V. *Waldschlösschen* (E), Kolonnenweg 152 (04621–32026). With covered pool, idyllic situation, excellent restaurant. *Skandia* (M), Lollfuss 89 (04621–24190). AE. *Waldhotel am Schloss Gottorf* (M), An der Stampfmühle 1 (04621–23288).

Restaurants. *Schleimöve,* Süderholmstr. 8 (04621–24309). Specialties— fish and seagulls' eggs. *Senator-Kroog,* Rathausmarkt 9–10 (04621–22290). Good local food.

In nearby **Treia** (10 miles): *Osterkrug,* Treenestr. 30 (04626–550).

Timmendorfer Strand. *Maritim Golf-und-Sport-Hotel* (E), An der Waldkapelle 26 (04503–4091). 250 rooms. AE, DC, MC, V. *Maritim Seehotel* (E), Strandallee (04503–5031). 241 rooms; pool, sauna; with outstanding restaurant. DC, MC, V. *Seeschlösschen* (E), Strandallee (04503–6011). 150 rooms; pool, sauna. *Holsteiner Hof* (M), Strandallee 92 (04503–2022). 21 rooms, with restaurants. *Krug's Hotel Meeresblick* (M), Strandallee 152 (04503–2305). 50 rooms, has an old-style beer tavern. MC. *Romantik Hotel Landhaus Carstens* (M), (04503–2520). Some rooms; has thatched-roof restaurant with beach terrace built around courtyard, with local specialties including seafood, home-brewed beer. V.

Restaurant. *Meyer's Speiselokal* (I), Strandstr. (04503–3893). Good quality cuisine.

In **Niendorf.** *Yachtclub Timmendorfer Strand* (E), Strandstr. 94 (04503–5061). 60 rooms, pool, sauna. AE, DC, MC, V. *Johannsens Hotel* (M), Strandstr. 150 (04503–2892). 50 beds.

Travemünde. *Kurhaus-Hotel* (E), Aussenallee 10 (04502–811). 104 rooms, all with private facilities; 19th-century elegance with 20th-century comforts. AE, DC, MC, V. *Maritim Strandhotel* (E), Trelleborgallee 2

(04502–75001). 500 beds, pool, sauna, thermal baths. Luxurious modern skyscraper. Amazing view from roof garden restaurant. AE, DC, MC, V. *Hotel Deutscher Kaiser* (M), Vorderreihe 52 (04502–5028). 45 rooms, some with bath. AE, DC, MC, V. *Hotel Strandperle* (M), Kaiserallee 10 (04502–74249). Very good small hotel with restaurant. AE, MC, V. *Strandhaus Becker* (M), Strandpromenade 7 (04502–75035). Directly on the promenade, quiet with fine view. 34 rooms, about half with bath; sun terrace, café and restaurant. *Seegarten garni* (M), Kaiserallee 11 (04502–71777). 20 rooms, 5 apts., pool. Very good find.

Restaurants. *Zur Sonne* (M), Vorderreihe 6 (04502–5153). Good local food and fish dishes. *Hein Mück* (I), Vogteistr. 48 (04502–2450).

In nearby **Ivendorf.** *Alte Kate anno 1748* (E). Historic, extremely expensive.

In 1983 the *Casino* next door to the Kurhaus was reopened. In addition to its former gaming rooms, the nightclub and terrace garden, it has a new gourmet restaurant, café and café-garden (afternoon Tea Dance), an elegant American Bar and *Musiksaal* for concerts.

Tremsbüttel. For a peaceful vacation in this region, a most exceptional hostelry is the castle hotel *Schlosshotel Tremsbüttel* (E), Schlossstr. 6 (04532–6544). 40 beds; lying about halfway between Hamburg and Lübeck (near Bargteheide). Built as a hunting castle for the Dukes of Holstein-Gottorf in 1644 and surrounded by a large estate, it has been converted into a hostelry offering period-furnished accommodations, from singles to suites; tennis, riding, hunting, and fishing. AE, DC, MC. There is a vintage car museum nearby.

CAMPING. There are numerous campsites throughout Schleswig-Holstein. The East and North Frisians, however, are not so well endowed. You can camp only on recognized sites. All sites fill up quickly in summer, and it is advisable to book in advance. All have washrooms, and most have shopping facilities and electricity points for caravans; some even have restaurants. Enquire at local tourist offices for locations and details, or write to: Verband d. Campingplatzhalter in Deutschland e.V., Landesverband Schleswig-Holstein Kiefernweg 14, 2361 Wittenborn, (04554–1757).

YOUTH HOSTELS. There are many Youth Hostels throughout Schleswig–Holstein, though again, the islands are less well supplied. Enquire at local tourist offices for locations and details.

TOURIST INFORMATION. The regional tourist office for Schleswig-Holstein is the *Fremdenverkehrsverband Schleswig-Holstein,* Niemannsweg 31, 2300 Kiel (0431–561061). In addition, there are local tourist offices at: **Amrum,** Kurverwaltung, Amrum (04682–544). **Flensburg,** Verkehrsverein, Norderstr. 6, 2390 Flensburg (0461–23090). **Föhr,** Kurverwaltung, Föhr (04681–3040). **Helgoland,** Kurverwaltung Lung Wai, 2192 Helgoland (04725–80850). **Husum,** Gross Str. 25, Husum (04841–666133). **Kiel,** Verkehrsverein, Auguste-Viktoria-Str. 16, Kiel (0431–62230). **Lübeck,** Verkehrsverein im Hauptbahnhof, Lübeck (0451–72300). **Schleswig,** Verkehrs-und Touristbüro, Plessensstr. 7, Schleswig (04621–814226). **Sylt/Westerland,** Fremdenverkehrszentrale, am Bundesbahnhof (04651–24001). **Sylt/East,** Kurverwaltung Sylt Ost,

Keitum (04651–31050). **Travemünde,** Kurverwaltung, Strandpromenade, 2400 Travemünde (04502–80432).

HOW TO GET AROUND. By air. The main airports for international flights are Hamburg and Bremen, from where there are interconnecting flights to the domestic airports of Kiel, Lübeck, and Flensburg. The North Frisian Islands of Sylt and Helgoland are served by seasonal services operated by regional airlines or airtaxi services.

By ferry. All the islands have good ferry services linking them with both the mainland and each other. Sylt is most easily reached from Hamburg via Cuxhaven and Helgoland. Föhr and Amrum have services from Dagebüll and Schlüttsiel, both easily reached by train and bus. Ferries to Pellworm and the Halligen islands run from Husum.

Ferry services to Helgoland operate all year round from Cuxhaven, while in summer there are services from Bremerhaven, Wilhelmshaven, and Hamburg (rail/sea connection via Cuxhaven). There are also frequent services from Hornum on Sylt, Wyk on Föhr, Wittdün on Amrum, Husum and Dagebüll on the North Sea coast.

By train and bus. Train services throughout North Germany are good. The main rail centers are Hamburg, Bremen and Flensburg, all easily reached from other parts of the country. From all three cities there are good connections to the Schleswig-Holstein coast, and to the ferries to the Frisians.

On the East Frisians most resorts are quite a distance from their respective harbors. Consequently island railroads exist on all the islands except on Borkum and Norderney, where bus and taxi services will take you around.

On the North Frisian islands there is a good rail connection to Sylt from Niebüll on the mainland over the Hindenburg Damm (rail only—cars are taken on the train). On Sylt there are good bus services linking all the main resorts and towns. Both Föhr and Amrum also have good island bus services.

By bicycle. A recommended form of travel on all the islands, where the roads are far less suited to automobiles, which in some cases, such as on Amrum and Föhr, are as good as prohibited. Schleswig-Holstein has more cyclists than anywhere else in Germany, and 60 percent of the highways, 20 percent of the municipal roads and 10 percent of other roads have cycle tracks. In addition, there is a vast network of side roads and tracks leading through the small villages and hamlets of the hinterland which makes cycling even more attractive.

Bicycles can be hired from private agencies in most of the resorts.

For full information about cycling in Schleswig-Holstein, contact the *Fremdenverkehrsverband Schleswig-Holstein,* Kiel (see above for address).

By car. Although cars can be a handicap on the islands, there are some very scenic routes on the mainland.

Schleswig-Holstein with its North Sea and Baltic coasts is traversed by the northern part of the long Green Coast Road (Grüne Küsten Strasse) (Norway–Denmark through Schleswig-Holstein and Lower Saxony to Holland), which enters the region at Niebüll, and covers the whole of North Frisian and the North Sea coastal resorts, until it crosses into Lower Saxony at Hamburg. (See map p. 388.) Information about the routes and places of interest along its way from *Fremdenverkehrsverband Schleswig-Holstein.*

A second scenic route, which will take you from the Baltic coast at Lübeck to Lüneburg, is the Alte Salzstrasse (Old Salt Road). It runs parallel to the Elbe-Lübeck Canal and traverses meadow and forestland with a total of 35 woodland lakes. It follows parts of the old salt-traders' route from the brine lakes around Lüneburg (where salt was first discovered in the 10th century) to Lübeck for shipping abroad. Information about the route from *Gebietsausschuss "Alte Salz Str." Fremdenverkehrsverband Schleswig-Holstein.*

EXCURSIONS. Owing to the relatively small size of the region—the fourth smallest state in Germany—excursions by bus, rail or car are possible to most places of interest for a day trip. However, the vast stretches of coast and the inland lakes and waterways make boat travel one of the most popular forms of excursion.

On the Baltic coast anyone in the vicinity of Kiel should not miss the opportunity to take a boat trip on the Kiel Fjord. Regular excursion ships and ferryboats depart from the station quay (Bahnhofs Quai) in Kiel, and you can also make day trips to Denmark from here.

Inland, the lakes of Holstein's "Little Switzerland" offer plenty of opportunities for boat trips. You can take a "Five Lakes Tour" from Gremsmühlen through the bays and narrows of the five adjoining lakes, or in the opposite direction on the larger Kellersee lake. On Plönersee, the largest lake in the area, motorboats operate regular round-trips from Fegetasche, which is worth a visit in itself.

From Lübeck you can take a harbor round-trip or a city sightseeing tour on the idyllic canals running through the center of the old town.

Crossing to the North Sea coast, the land behind the dykes of North Frisia is worth touring by bus or train (bus tours are run from the main tourist centers) for its picturesque villages and polderland.

There are also various organized excursions available to the islands and to wild life sanctuaries. For details of all these trips, contact the local tourist offices.

SPORTS. Yachting under ideal conditions is possible in the waters of the extensive Flensburg Fjord, which for some distance separates Denmark and Germany. There are more than 20 sailing schools along the North Sea Coast.

Boating and canoeing are very good on the Trave River. From Lübeck you can do the 23-km. (14-mile) trip to Travemünde, on the Baltic, or up the river making for Bad Oldesloe (35 km., 22 miles), or Bad Segeberg, another 23 km.

Swimming, motorboating, and other water sports are practised at these resorts. Indoor seawater swimming pools with artificial waves, nicely warmed, at Westerland, Büsum, St. Peter-Ording, Wyk, Grömitz, Haffkrug, Borkum and Eckernförde. Many have glass façades with a view of the sea. Helgoland has a unique twin seawater swimming pool where you can swim in winter. Travemünde's modern indoor glassed-in seawater pool is connected directly with the Kurhaus; has a sauna and sun terraces.

As well as all these water sports, there are other activities available. **Golf** courses at Kiel, Travemünde, Wyk and Lohersand. **Tennis** in Kiel,

Westerland, Kampen, Helgoland, Travemünde, all larger towns. **Horse-back riding** schools and instructors in Flensburg, Lübeck, Kampen and elsewhere. Riding-holidays on the farm can also be arranged through the local tourist offices, and the regional tourist office in Kiel issues a brochure. Riding across tidal sands is popular along the North Sea coast. **Fishing** Schleswig is one of northern Germany's best regions for freshwater trout. Shark fishing high sea excursions are organized from Helgoland. **Hiking** and walking trails in the region have been extended over the past years, since the appeal of hiking in non-mountainous, or flatland has increased, particularly walking around the dykes and polders of North Frisia, on the mudflats of the tidal sands around the islands, or around the countless lakes of Holstein's "Little Switzerland." Suggestions for hiking tours, information and maps from the regional and local tourist offices.

Ludwig van Beethoven
1770-1827

WEST BERLIN

Life in the Fast Lane

Berlin is like no other city in the world, which is hardly surprising, for there is no other city that has gone through the traumas that have afflicted Berlin for the last 40 years and, indeed, are not yet at an end. In spite of these stresses and strains—or perhaps because of them—Berlin is a city that is vibrantly, aggressively alive. We assume that no one considering a trip to Berlin can be unaware of its status as a beleaguered Western enclave, but it would be totally wrong to approach a visit to Berlin metaphorically wearing your helmet and gasmask, ready for a daring dash across no-man's-land. For, beset as Berlin is by endless day-to-day problems, and even darker long-term anxieties, it has evolved into an exciting, modern community that is a glorious amalgam of Las Vegas, the Left Bank, Hyde Park, the Via Veneto and a classy beer cellar, the whole pervaded by that unique quality of the Berliner character, which combines liveliness with a slightly cynical forbearance, sentimentality with a keen-edged wit. The schizophrenic quality of life for a Berliner, living as he does in the middle of a symbol of the world's division, has that slightly lunatic quality of having been conceived by a Cold War Lewis Carroll.

Background to Berlin

Berlin's peculiar and unique status as a little piece of the West lying deep within Eastern Europe dates from the immediate post-War period. Having been conquered initially by the Soviet Union in 1945, the city was subsequently administered by a four-power commission, or Kommandatura, consisting of the four victorious Allied powers, the United States, Britain, France and the Soviet Union, each responsible for one sector of the city. In June 1948, as post-War euphoria began to give way to Cold War, the Soviet Union walked out of the Kommandatura. In an attempt to force the Western Allies to relinquish their stake in the city, allowing them to gain complete control, the Soviets then instituted a blockade of Berlin, cutting off all communication between it and West Germany, some 177 km. (110 miles) away. In this, they failed signally. A massive and ultimately successful airlift was put into operation by the West, with more than three-quarters of a million flights bringing in almost two million tons of goods to the city. In May 1949, after 11 months, the Soviets were forced to lift their blockade.

The divisions between East and West were only further underlined by the blockade and airlift, and indeed remain the most distinctive feature of this extraordinary city. Any hopes that a reconciliation might be effected and some sort of normality returned were finally laid to rest in 1961 when the Berlin Wall was built by the Soviets. Ostensibly intended to protect the Eastern half from the malign influence of the West, it was in reality a brutal means of forcibly ending the massive flood of refugees that poured into West Berlin throughout the '50s.

Having survived such traumatic and severe birth pangs, it is hardly to be wondered at that the modern city has so pronounced an air of febrile excitement and moves at so fast and urgent a pace. But it has had to face other, almost equally testing questions. Its main problem has been to maintain a balanced population structure, or simply to prevent any decrease in population. Career opportunities are limited, and so an increasing number of younger people have moved away. In spite of all sorts of tax incentives for business many firms have transferred their headquarters to West Germany. The exodus of people in their late '20s to early '40s is reflected in the population image: the prevalence of older people in the streets is striking. The many universities and institutes ensure that there are vast numbers of young people as well, but the absence of people in their '30s and '40s, who are actually earning money and producing, is conspicuous. The city has tried to counteract this development by giving generous incentives to people who decide to work in Berlin. Also, there has been a development of the service industries which attract more people to the city. Similarly, with its new congress center, Berlin is now one of the foremost congress cities in Europe. Rather interestingly, a lot of successful artists who could afford to live elsewhere choose to live in Berlin. There is still something about the social atmosphere of the city that makes it preferable to some people to West Germany proper.

In Berlin you can live anonymously. There are many sub-cultures, and material pressures as well as pressures to conform generally are felt much less than in the rest of Germany. Since the 17th century, when the "Grosse Kurfürst" Friedrich Wilhelm gave asylum to the French Huguenots and the first Jewish community was established ("In my kingdom every man must find his own way to heaven"), there has always been a certain cosmopolitan tolerance in Berlin. Something of this still exists, although even Berliners themselves complain about an increasing provincialism, and they used to be notorious for their boastful arrogance. "If we had your mountains they would be bigger," a Berliner is supposed to have told a Bavarian.

Exploring West Berlin

For the visitor to postwar Berlin, the heart of the city is the Kurfürsten-damm, or Ku-Damn as it is generally called, the center of activity both by day and by night. For the American, it is Broadway and Fifth Avenue in one; for the Briton it is Oxford Street and Piccadilly.

Originally just an alley leading to the Prince-Elector's Hunting Lodge in Grunewald, the Kurfürstendamm is now a busy shopping street, and others lined with big stores are clustered about it—the Kantstrasse, which meets it at an acute angle at the Kaiser Wilhelm Memorial Church, the Tauentzienstrasse, which meets it at an obtuse angle at the same spot, the Joachimstalerstrasse, which cuts across it. The stores and office buildings that line these streets are mostly built on sites from which the ruins of war-destroyed buildings have been cleared away. You will find the best vantage point to watch the interesting and animated spectacle of the street in one or other of the sidewalk cafés, whose glassed-in terraces line the Kurfürstendamm.

At night, the quarter is just as lively, for this is a theater district as well. The Komödie is on the Kurfürstendamm, the new Schiller theater is near-by, the opera a block away, and there are a score or more of film palaces, not to mention nightclubs and bars.

The Kurfürstendamm starts at the Kaiser Wilhelm Memorial Church (the Gedächtniskirche), which was rebuilt in 1961 with only the badly damaged tower, "Berlin's finest ruin," remaining from the prewar church. Close to the church is the main railway station, Bahnhof Zoo on Harden-bergplatz. From here you can enter either the vast Tiergarten park or the beautiful Berlin Zoo, which also has another entrance through the impres-sive Elephant Gate on Budapesterstrasse. Even if you are not an admirer of zoos, don't disdain this one. It contains 1,825 different species in sur-roundings as close to their natural environment as possible. Germans are fond of zoos and provide other distractions than the animals for their amusement while they're there. You can eat or drink well within the zoo, listen to openair concerts, and take in various forms of amusement.

Entering the Tiergarten proper, you are in the great 630-acre park that was central Berlin's prewar pride—its Central Park, Hyde Park, or Bois de Boulogne. Originally intended for royalty only, it became the first pub-lic park in Berlin after major landscaping in the English style. The damage done to the Tiergarten during the war was not all the result of external attack, though some of it was. A good deal of the Battle for Berlin was fought here, but it was for fuel that the Berliners cut down the lovely old trees during the bitterly cold winter of 1945–46.

Trees that took a century to grow can hardly be replaced overnight, but Berlin did what it could to restore the Tiergarten. Trees and bushes were planted, new paths laid out, and today the park has regained its for-mer charm. One of the problems was that of disposing of rubble. The solu-tion adopted was to heap the shattered bricks and stones into artificial hills, cover them with soil and sow grass. Several of these rubble "moun-tains" have become part of the Berlin skyline, most notably the Insulaner at the southern tip of the Steglitz district, which is 79 meters (260 feet) high.

Siegessäule, Victory Column

Bisecting the Tiergarten from east to west is the Strasse des 17 Juni, named in memory of the Germans shot down by Russian tanks in 1953 when East Berlin construction workers laid down their tools in protest over greatly increased work "norms." Focal point of this broad avenue is a vast circle called the Grosse Stern or Great Star. From its center rises a 64-meter (210-foot) column of dark red granite, sandstone and bronze surmounted by a gilded figure of Victory. The Siegessäule, as it is called, was raised in 1873 to commemorate the Franco-Prussian War, and originally stood in front of the Reichstag.

If your legs are strong, climb the Siegessäule for a magnificent view of Berlin's heart. As you face east and look along the Strasse des 17. Juni towards the Brandenburger Tor, the English Garden will be practically at your feet, to the left. Because it was dedicated by Anthony Eden, the then Foreign Secretary of Great Britain, Berliners often refer to it jokingly as the Garden of Eden. East of this park-within-a-park you'll be able to pick out Schloss Bellevue, which has been restored and is the official residence of the President of West Germany; in summer months its interiors are open to the public. To the southeast you can see the concert hall of the Berlin Philharmonic Orchestra, the Philharmonie, the Museum of Applied Arts (Kunstgewerbemuseum), the National Gallery (Nationalgalerie), and the State Library (Staatsbibliothek), which with its 2.9 million volumes is the largest library of its kind in the world. Its outstanding collection of manuscripts comprises many rarities, particularly in the field of music. Its beautifully light and functionally designed reading-room can accommodate 600 readers.

Before returning to street level, look west along the Strasse des 17 Juni. Immediately on your right hand rise the gaily painted and fancifully balconied apartment houses of the Hansa Viertel, a district that has been revived by the best work of architects from a dozen nations of the world, during the Interbau exhibition of 1957. On your left is the Technical University plus the Hochschule für Musik and the Academy of Fine Arts.

But walk east along the Strasse des 17 Juni towards the Brandenburger Tor. On the left is the Soviet War Memorial, a semicircular colonnade surmounted by a massive statue of a Russian soldier and flanked by World War II artillery pieces and tanks. The road is closed in front of the monument, and changing of the guards can only be watched from a special area opposite. Continue walking towards the Brandenburger Tor and you'll reach platforms which will allow a view of the Eastern sector, which begins a few yards in front of the former city gate and Arch of Triumph of the German capital. Built in 1789, it was inspired by the Proplyaea of the Parthenon. The Victory Quadriga—the two-wheeled chariot drawn by four stallions—by Schadow, was added in 1793. Victorious Prussian troops used to parade through the Tor on their return from a successful campaign. The last troops to march beneath it, however, were not on parade. They were Red Army infantrymen who stormed through it in May 1945. By then, the famous quadriga was shattered seemingly beyond repair. For a dozen years the sole adornment of the shell-pocked gate was a red flag. Then, in 1957, East German workmen began the task of repairing the Brandenburger Tor, a job that was completed late the following

BERLIN
West and East

━━━ East/West border

Miles
0   ½
0   ½
Kilometer

Points of Interest

1 Ägyptisches Museum
2 Altes Museum
3 Amerika Gedenkbibliothek
4 Antikenmuseum
5 Berlin Museum
6 Bode Museum
7 Brandenburger Tor
8 Checkpoint Charlie
9 Dahlem Museums;Botanischer Garten

10 Deutsche Oper
11 Deutsche Staatsoper
12 Englischer Garten
13 Europa-Center
14 Funkturm; I.C.C.
15 Grunewald
16 Kaiser Wilhelm
     Gedächtniskirche
17 Kreuzberg

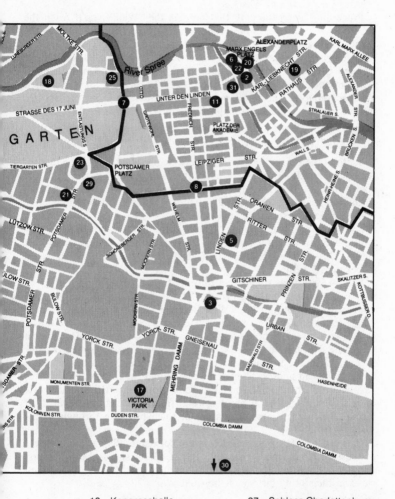

18	Kongresshalle
19	Marienkirche
20	Nationalgalerie
21	Neue Nationalgalerie
22	Pergamon Museum
23	Philharmonie
24	Rathaus Schöneberg
25	Reichstag
26	Schloss Bellevue
27	Schloss Charlottenburg
28	Siegessäule
29	Staatsbibliothek
30	Tempelhof Airport
31	Zeughaus
32	Zoologischer Garten

year. Meanwhile, the West Berliners discovered the moulds in which the original quadriga was cast. A new one was poured, gilded and hoisted to the top of the refurbished gate in a rare, remarkable instance of cooperation between East and West.

Proceeding along the path that borders the "Wall", you'll reach the Reichstag, which has now been reconstructed. It was burned down on the night of February 28, 1933, providing the Nazis with a convenient pretext for outlawing the opposition. All that remained was the shell of the florid Italian Renaissance structure that was built in 1884–94 to house the Prussian parliament, and later performed a similar function for the ill-fated Weimar Republic. The building was further damaged during the last war but has now been almost completely restored.

Potsdamer Platz

South of the Brandenburger Tor is Potsdamer Platz, where the British, American, and Russian sectors meet. It was once the busiest spot on the continent, but today it is the most desolate in Berlin. A few hundred yards to the northeast are the covered remains of Hitler's reinforced concrete bunker, where he spent his final days.

Half-an-hour's walk away is "Checkpoint Charlie." Beside Friedrichstrasse subway station it is the only entry point for foreigners into East Berlin. Do not miss the exhibition about the "Wall" in the Haus am Checkpoint Charlie.

If West Berlin has risen like a Phoenix from its pyre, cleared away its rubble, put up new buildings, so has East Berlin, though this looks even less like its prewar state than West Berlin. Except for the once splendid Unter den Linden, the renowned avenue of stately trees, impressive stores, embassies and famous hotels that used to lead to the Royal Palace (blown up by the Russians and paved over to form the Marx-Engels Platz), this was originally the working quarter of Berlin with row on row of solid, clean apartment houses. Though never a slum, it was congested and thus particularly vulnerable to bombing. Today you notice the Stalinist style of East Berlin's principal buildings and the newer high-rise apartment blocks, which are a faceless feature of town planning throughout the world.

Close by the western approaches to the Potsdamer Platz you'll probably notice a thicket of small shops selling food, candy, shoes, cheap clothing, and the like. Here, too, have taken place many of the most dramatic escapes in the stormy history of the Cold War.

The Rathaus, Tempelhof, Kreuzberg and Steglitz

From here, turn south and head towards the district called Schöneberg whose Rathaus or City Hall now houses the Senate and the House of Deputies, West Berlin's governing bodies, and the Regierender Bürgermeister or Mayor. The open square in front of the building is used for a market two mornings a week, one of those small-town activities that often give Berlin a peculiarly provincial air.

Each day at noon, however, the deep tones of the Freiheitsglocke ring out to remind Berlin and the world that "all men derive the right to freedom equally from God." If you can spare the time, climb the belfry and take a closer look at this replica of America's Liberty Bell, donated to Berliners in 1950 by the United States. In a room at the base of the tower are samples of the 17,000,000 American signatures that are stored behind a door carved with a text describing the events that motivated this expression of solidarity with the West Berliners.

Another symbol of Allied intervention is the Platz der Luftbrücke in front of the American Military Airport at Tempelhof. A soaring, three-pronged concrete monument salutes the 31 American, 39 British, and 5 German airmen who lost their lives flying in coal, food, medicine, and other necessities of life during the Blockade. The three arcs symbolize the three air corridors used during this critical period.

Walk north along Mehringdamm and turn right into the district of Kreuzberg, between Fidicin and Bergmannstrasse. There are several blocks of apartment houses here, built at the turn of the century and beautifully restored, which give an impression of what Berlin was like before the last war.

Further down Mehringdamm, on Blücherplatz, is the American Memorial Library. A magazine room with more than 1,000 periodicals and a music department equipped with booths for listening to records and tapes complete its facilities.

The Steglitz district is in south Berlin, and has outstanding botanical gardens and a botanical museum. The display of plants, flowers, shrubs, trees, and bushes, large and small, rare and common, is set among smooth green lawns, statuary, and little pools, in a triumph of the landscape architect's skill. Besides the museum there are hothouses for the cultivation of tropical plants.

Dahlem's Museums and the Free University

Close to the Botanical Gardens in the Dahlem district, is a cluster of museums, institutes and archives headed by the Gemälde Galerie, with an outstanding collection of paintings. Berlin is less rich in art than before the war. The state museums were in what is now East Berlin. Many of their treasures were removed to the West and distributed all over Germany.

The collection in the Gemälde Galerie is really splendid, for examples of work of most of the European masters are on view—Dürer, Holbein, Brueghel, Giotto, Raphael, Titian, Caravaggio, Guardi, as well as many French, Flemish and Dutch masterpieces, with, of course, the ubiquitous Rembrandt well represented, especially by his famous *Man in a Gold Helmet*. Also in this complex of museums is the Museum für Völkerkunde (Ethnographic Museum), with art from far regions of the world, brilliantly displayed; the Oriental art museums; and also the Skulpturengalerie (Sculpture Gallery), containing Byzantine and European sculpture from the 3rd century up to the 18th, and especially strong in medieval and Baroque sculpture. Nearby is the Free University, founded in 1948 with more than 25,000 students, almost entirely German. It is a vital center of German intellectual life.

To the northeast lies the Grunewald, Berlin's largest park and summer playground. The Havel river and the rubble mountain Teufelsberg (a winter sports center) are both popular parts of the park. Within the vast wood are the Kaiser-Wilhelm-Turm which allows a splendid view over the

Havel river and the Jagdschloss Grunewald (Hunting Lodge), built in 1542, and containing not only hunting trophies, but also a representative collection of Dutch and German painters, with emphasis on the Dutch 17th century. In summer candlelight concerts are held in the courtyard.

In the southwestern part of Berlin close to the bridge, curiously called the bridge of Unity, which marks the end of the American sector and the beginning of East Germany is the beautiful park and palace of Glienicke, dating from the mid-19th century. Close by is the delightful Blockhaus Nikolskoe, a log house built by Frederick William III for Crown Prince Nicholas of Russia in 1819, today a restaurant with one of the better views of the Havel River. Unfortunately part of it was destroyed by fire in 1984 but has been restored. A few hundred meters more bring you to the Pfaueninsel or Peacock Island (you can hear the screams of the peacocks from which the island takes its name) reached by ferry. Here Frederick William II built a château to resemble a partly-ruined Italian castle.

Charlottenburg

Going back to the city take the Avus autobahn, a stretch of motorway that penetrates Berlin as far as the Charlottenburg quarter. The end of the Avus marks the beginning of the Messegelände or Fair Grounds, a whole city of exhibition buildings grouped around the 138-meter (453-foot) Funkturm (Radio Tower). An elevator carries you to its top for an extensive view of the surroundings, including the Olympic Stadium to the west with the British compound and the openair Waldbühne theater—and, of course, the international congress center I.C.C., which makes Berlin one of the foremost congress cities in Europe. It has room for 5,000 people at a time, and there is a corresponding number of smaller rooms to enable large gatherings to split into reasonably sized working-parties. The I.C.C. is extremely well-sited, next to the exhibition grounds of the Funkturm complex and with direct access to the motorway.

One edge of the Messegelände impinges on Theodor-Heuss-Platz, in whose center burns an eternal flame on top of an altar-like monument to Justice, Liberty, and Peace.

If you leave Theodor-Heuss-Platz behind and turn east along Kaiser Damm and Bismarck Strasse, the Victory Monument glitters distantly in the sun. Before completing the circuit of West Berlin, however, branch off to the left on Schloss Strasse and immediately you will see the restrained proportions of Charlottenburg Palace, not only a lovely building in itself, but the home of yet another collection of museums. Berlin is a city of museums! A guided tour will take you through the state apartments with their memories of the great kings and queens of Prussia. The rooms are sumptuous, crowded with fine decoration and works of art. There is a porcelain collection, in the China Cabinet, which will startle you with the amount of plates and vases all over the walls and as if the variety wasn't enough, reflected in large mirrors. The Rococo Golden Gallery is a most impressive hall, with delicate plasterwork in gilt. Frederick the Great's rooms are close by. In the west wing is the Museum of Ancient History and space for exhibitions.

Opposite the front of the palace is the Ägyptisches Museum, with a rich collection of ancient Egyptian treasures, dating from 4 B.C.–A.D. 3, including what is probably the most famous portrait bust in the world, that of

Nefertiti. Beside this museum is the Antikenmuseum (Museum of Antiques), with a hoard of gold and silver pieces that are a must for anyone interested in jewelry from the classical world.

The park surrounding Charlottenburg is also worth visiting. Part of it is laid out as a French Baroque garden and another is designed in the English landscape tradition, which was so popular with the late 18th-century German monarchs. Tucked away in these extensive grounds are the mausoleum where some of the Prussian royal family is buried, and the Belvedere, a pretty retreat, built with a view of the lake.

As a parting thought for West Berlin it may please you to know that there are still two vineyards in this big city. One is in the district of Kreuzberg, the other in Neukölln. Unfortunately, the wine is not for sale, and it is offered only on special occasions to guests of the district authorities who own the vineyards.

PRACTICAL INFORMATION FOR WEST BERLIN

TELEPHONES. The telephone code for West Berlin is 030. To call any number in this chapter unless otherwise specified, this prefix must be used. Within the city, no prefix is required.

HOTELS. Berlin lost all of its great old luxurious hotels during World War II but has since acquired a number of top-class hotels with international reputations and more are being built every year. The city is also rich in small hotels and pensions. Because of the great business activity, frequent fairs, conventions and other periodic events, as well as the large number of tourists visiting the city throughout the year, it is recommended to wire or write for reservations in advance. At Tegel Airport there is a hotel indication board showing where rooms are vacant.

If you do not write direct to the hotel, or reserve your accommodations through your travel agent, then you might wish to contact the hotel reservation service of the Berlin Tourist Office (Verkehrsamt) in the Europa Center, Budapesterstr. (2626031). Also at Tegel Airport (41013145), open 8 A.M.–10.30 P.M.

Deluxe

Ambassador Berlin. Bayreuther Str. 42/43 (219020). 360 beds, sauna, pool, solarium, bar; all rooms with bath, color TV. 2 excellent restaurants. AE, DC, MC, V.

Berlin Penta. Nurnberger Str. 65 (240011). 850 beds, all with bath, color TV and video; pool, sauna, solarium; bar, 2 restaurants. Fully air-conditioned, comfortable and central. AE, DC, MC, V.

Bristol-Hotel Kempinski. Kurfürstendamm 27 (884340). 325 rooms with marble bath, color TV, air-conditioning; 20 apartments; 3 outstanding restaurants; bar. The "Kempi" is Berlin's most renowned hotel. Destroyed in the last war, rebuilt in 1952 and renovated in 1980, it offers the atmosphere of an old-established luxury hotel, with stylish furnishings and excellent service. Right in the heart of the city. AE, DC, MC, V.

InterContinental Berlin. Budapester Str. 2 (26020). 600 rooms with bath, bars, roof garden, pool, 3 restaurants. Modern and very comfortable. AE, DC, MC, V.

Palace. Budapester Str. 42, Europa Center (269111). 250 beds. French restaurant and a well-stocked bar. AE, DC, MC, V.

Schweizerhof Berlin. Budapester Str. 21–31 (26960). 876 beds; pool, sauna, solarium; 3 restaurants, 2 bars. Well-established modern hotel, comfortable. Restaurants offer Swiss cuisine. AE, DC, MC, V.

Seehof. Lietzensee Ufer 11 (320020). 120 beds; pool, sauna, solarium; restaurant, bar. Situated close to the fair grounds at the Funkturm overlooking the Lietzensee. Lakeside cafe-terrace. AE, DC, MC, V.

Steigenberger Berlin. Los-Angeles-Platz 1 (21080). 337 rooms with bath, pool, sauna, solarium; shops; 3 restaurants, 2 bars. Contemporary art exhibits. Restaurants offer gourmet dishes as well as Berlin specialities. AE, DC, MC, V.

Expensive

Alsterhof Ringhotel Berlin. Augsburger Str. 5 (219960). 250 beds; heated pool, sauna, solarium; bar, restaurant. AE, DC, MC, V.

Am Zoo. Kurfürstendamm 25 (883091). 200 beds; bar, no restaurant. Slightly staid businessman's hotel, but comfortable and well run, and with the benefit of an excellent central location just off the Ku-Damm. AE, DC, MC, V.

Berlin Excelsior. Hardenbergstr. 14 (3199–1). 320 rooms with bath, garden terrace, winter garden, bar, restaurant. Modern, comfortable, central. AE, DC, MC, V.

Bremen. Bleibtreustr. 25 (881 4076). 72 beds. Welcoming atmosphere. No restaurant. AE, DC, MC, V.

Hotel Arosa Berlin. Lietzenburger Str. 79–81 (880050). 147 beds; heated pool, bar. *Walliser Stuben* restaurant. AE, DC, MC, V.

Palace. Europa Center (269111). 160 rooms with bath. This hotel, popular with Americans, has comfortable rooms and a memorable view on the Budapesterstrasse. Sauna, whirlpool. AE, DC, MC, V.

Savoy. Fasanenstr. 9/10 (311030). 200 beds. Comfortable, modern, efficient. Very good service. AE, DC, MC, V.

Schlosshotel Gehrhus. Brahmsstr. 3–10 (8262081). 50 beds. We can enthusiastically recommend this former palace-style private residence, in an exclusive location in the park district of Grunewald. AE, DC, V.

Schweizerhof Berlin. Budapesterstr. 21–31 (26960). 430 rooms with bath. Rustic decor and high standard of comfort in this centrally located hotel. Large indoor pool, sauna, fitness room, hairdresser. Children stay free in parents' room. AE, DC, MC, V.

Steglitz International. Albrechtstr. 2 (791061). 429 beds. Modern, very comfortable. Sauna, solarium and restaurant. Near Rathaus Steglitz tube-station. AE, DC, V.

Moderate

Arosa Aparthotel. Lietzenburgerstr. 79 (880050). Attractive, modern, central. Excellent value. Some rooms with kitchenettes. AE, DC, MC, V.

Astoria. Fasanenstr. 2 (312 4067). Quiet, good value. Centrally located between the Zoo and the Technical University. Breakfast, but no restaurant. AE, MC, V.

Casino Hotel. Köningen-Elisabeth-Str. 47a (303090). 24 rooms with bath. Large, comfortable rooms in a former Prussian military barracks. In the Charlottenburg district. Restaurant serves Bavarian specialties. AE, DC, MC, V.

Pichlers Viktoriagarten. Leonorenstr. 18 (7716088). Small, good value, just south of the Insulaner complex. Good restaurant.

Ravenna. Grunewaldstr. 8–9 (792–8031). 45 rooms with bar or shower. Friendly hotel in the Steglitz district, close to Botanical Garden. Well-equipped rooms. AE, DC, MC, V.

Rheinsberg am See. Finsterwalder Str. 64 (4021002). In the north of Berlin; idyllic setting. Modern, comfortable. 2 heated pools, sauna, solarium. Good restaurant.

Riehmers Hofgarten. Yorckstr. 83 (781011). 21 rooms with bath or shower. In the interesting Kreuzberg district, with good connections to center of town. Elegant rooms. AE, DC, MC, V.

Studio. Kaiserdamm 80–81 (302081). 93 beds, all rooms with baths. Near Funkturm (radio tower and exhibition halls). AE, DC, MC.

Inexpensive

Dom. Hohenzollerndamm 33 (879780). Simple and adequate, good for the younger tourist.

Econtel. Sommeringstr. 24 (344001). 205 rooms with bath or shower. Families are well cared for at this hotel near Charlottenburg Palace. Also nice touches in the single rooms. Snack bar. MC.

Elton. Pariserstr. 9 (883 6155).

Hospiz Friedenau. Fregestr. 68 (851 9017). Small and quiet. Close to the subway.

Kurfürstendamm. Kurfürstendamm 68 (882841).

Metropol. Fasanenstr. 71 (881 7579).

Radloff-Rumland. Kurfürstendamm 226 (881 3331).

Camping

Details on camping in Berlin are available from the *Berlin Camping Club,* Ebersstr. 27 (782 4096).

Campingplatz Dreilinden. Albrechts Teerofen (805 1201). Open all year.

Campingplatz Haselhorst. Pulvermühlenweg (334 5955). Open all year.

Zeltplatz in Kladow. Krampnitzer Weg 111 (365 2797). Space for about 400 tents/caravans. Open all year round.

Zeltplatz in Kohlhasenbrück. Neue Kreis- Corner Stubenrauchstr. (805 1737). Space for approx. 300 tents and caravans.

Youth Hostels

C.V.J.M. (Y.M.C.A.). Einemstr. 10 (261 3791).
Jugendgästehaus Berlin. Kluckstr. 3 (261 1097).
Jugendgästehaus am Wannsee. Kronprinzessinnenweg 37 (803 2034).
Studentenhotel Berlin. Meiningerstr. 10 (784 6720). Good hostel with sauna, pub and food.

The following hostels offer rooms during school holidays:
Adam von Trott-Heim. Am kleinen Wannsee (805 3491).

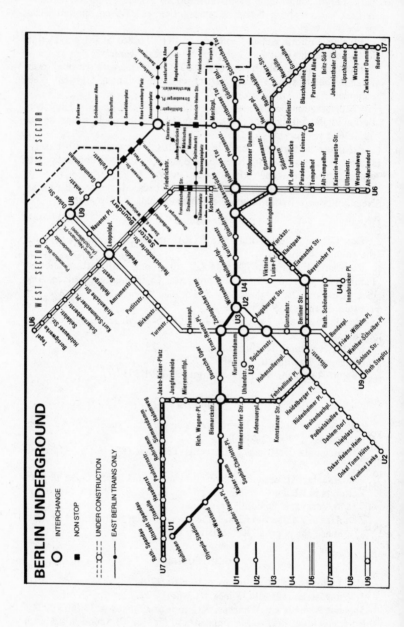

Studentendorf of the Free University. Potsdamer Chaussee 31 (801071). For students only.

HOW TO GET AROUND. From the airport. The main airport for West Berlin is Tegel. There are about 80 flights daily to and from West Berlin from the main cities of West Germany. The trip takes as little as an hour and there are special reduced excursion fares. Regular express bus services connect Zoo Station and Tegel.

City transportation. Because of its vast area, Berlin is not the kind of city that can be comfortably covered on foot. In fact you would find yourself easily exhausted if you tried to do so. But, luckily, Berlin has a really magnificent network of public transport, which is especially a blessing for the budget tourist, who is not likely to be hiring a car or wanting to invest in taxis.

B.V.G. (the Berlin Transport Corporation) has 83 city bus routes and 8 subway lines. You can get a special map with the entire system of bus, S- and U-Bahn trains and the timetable booklet containing all lines, fares, the first and last buses and underground trains, from underground ticket offices.

The U-Bahn (underground) and the S-Bahn (surface trains) provide high-speed services all over the city. There are two U-Bahn lines that go through to East Berlin and one S-Bahn; only stop, Friedrichstr. There are special reduced tickets available, the Touristenkarte (Tourist Pass), valid for use on all transport, including the ferrys from Wannsee to Kladow. These currently cost DM. 32 and are valid for 4 days, or DM. 16 for 2 days, and are available from the Berliner Verkehrsbetrieb (B.V.G.) main ticket office at the U-Bahn station Kleistpark or the Zoo station.

In the summer, special excursion buses operate from the Zoo underground station almost non-stop to Wannsee and the neighboring lakeside resorts.

TOURIST INFORMATION. The *Berlin Tourist Office*, Europe Center, D-1000 Berlin 30 (262 6031). This is the place to go with any problems you may have while in Berlin. There is another Tourist Office at Tegel Airport (4101314). Both are open daily from 7:30 A.M. to 10.30 P.M. For group bookings or information about the political situation of Berlin write to *Informations-zentrum Berlin*, Hardenbergstr. 20, D-1000 Berlin 12 (310040).

USEFUL ADDRESSES. Car rental. *InterRent*, at Tegel Airport (4101–3368) and Kurfürstendamm 179 (881 8093); *Hertz*, Budapesterstr. 39 (261 1053) and airport (4101–3315); *Avis*, Budapesterstr. 43 (261 1881) and airport (4101–3148).

Consulates. *American*, Clayallee 170 (832 4087). *British*, Uhlandstrasse 7/8 (309 5292). *French*, Stauffenbergstr. 14 (8818028).

Emergencies. *Police* (110). *Ambulance and emergency medical attention* (310031). *Dentist* (1141). *Pharmacies* (1141) for emergency pharmaceutical assistance.

Lost Property. *Polizei Präsidium*, Tempelhofer Damm 1 (Platz der Luftbrücke tube station) (6991); *B.V.G.* (for property lost on the public transport system), Potsdamerstr. 188 (216 1413).

Motorists. *ADAC* (German Automobile Club), Bundesallee 29 (86865); *AvD* (Automobile Club of Germany), Wittenbergplatz 1 (213 3033).

Post office. Open 24 hours a day at the Zoo railway station.

TOURS. One good form of tour is the one you work out yourself and then implement by getting a Tourist Pass. But if you want to get yourself orientated in the city before striking out on your own, the following companies offer several daily tours: *Berliner Baren,* Stadtrundfahrten (213 4077), departs from Rankestr. 35 opp. Memorial Church; *Berolina* (883 3131), departs from Meinekestr. 3 at Kurfürstendamm; *Severin & Kühn* (883 1015), departs from Kurfürstendamm 216 at Fasanenstr; *BVB Stadtrundfahrten* (882 2063), departs from Kurfürstendamm at Joachimstaler Str. Prices vary depending on the length of the trip. City trips of 2 hours cost around DM. 20, 3 hour trips around DM. 30, and combined West and East tours around DM. 50. Remember to have your passport with you if the tour is taking in East Berlin. Be prepared to pay an extra DM. 15 for an official East German guide.

VISITING EAST BERLIN. Formalities for Western visitors to East Berlin (or Berlin Capital of the G.D.R., as the East Germans prefer it to be called) are surprisingly few. Anyone planning just a day trip need take only their passport; visas are not required. To cross into East Berlin, you can take either the U- or S-Bahn, both to Friedrichstr., or, much more atmospherically, cross over at the famous Checkpoint Charlie. In both cases, permits costing DM.5 per person, will be issued to you by the East German authorities. You will also be obliged to change DM.25 per person by the East Germans.

Alternatively, a number of sightseeing tours from West Berlin are available (see *Tours* above). All formalities will be organized for you if you take one of these trips, though again don't forget your passport.

You may take as much Western currency with you as you like provided you declare it on arrival. Keep the currency declaration form you will be given or you won't be able to export the balance. East German currency may be neither exported or imported. You can bring out any goods, gifts, etc., you may have bought in East Germany provided their total value does not exceed 100 East German marks. Keep all receipts to show to East German customs.

Finally, if you are approached with offers to sell you East German marks at rates in excess of the official one you should *under no circumstances* agree. This is a criminal offence in East Germany and the consequences should you be caught far outweigh any temporary advantages, however tempting they appear.

For further information on what to see and do in East Berlin, see *Practical Information for East Berlin* in the East Berlin chapter.

SPORTS. Berlin is a big sports center. The Olympic Stadium on the Heerstrasse, completed for the 1936 Olympic Games, seats 95,000, and can provide standing room for 25,000 more. International football (soccer) matches are held here as well as gymnastic competitions, a sport of which Germans are fond. There is also a swimming pool, where championship meets take place, and athletic fields.

The favorite place for **swimming** in Berlin is the Wannsee Strandbad. The Wannsee, the Havel river, the Heiligensee and the Tegeler See are suitable for boating, sailing, rowing, even surfing in parts. On the Spree river one can reach the heart of Berlin by boat. If you try **boating** in Berlin, be careful to keep in the Western sector—there are parts of the Wannsee (more correctly, the Havel) that belong to East Germany. The efficient East German water police, using speedy motorboats, delight in pouncing—and keeping—any West Berlin craft that venture into their area. There is a thermal bathing establishment in the Europa Center, with underwater massage, sauna, various thermal baths, as well as swimming pools. In 1985 the "blub", a hyper modern bathing complex was opened at Buschkrugallee 64 (606 6060).

For information about playing tennis call the Berliner Tennis Verband (825 5311/825 8319) or book a court at the *Tennis & Squash City,* Brandenburgische Str. 31 (879097).

Also in winter Berliners, adults and children, get great fun out of **ice-skating** in the open air. There are several skating-rinks among them *Eisstadion Wilmersdorf, Eisstadion Neukölln,* and the *Eisstadion Wedding* and the *Eissporthalle Berlin* in Jaffestrasse. At all of them boots and skates may be hired.

Further information on all sports is available from the Tourist Office.

HISTORIC BUILDINGS AND SITES. Europa-Center. Breitscheidplatz. A symbol of post-war West Berlin. Inside are over 100 shops, cafés and restaurants. See the water clock and the new fountain in front of the building. A trip up to the i-Punkt on the roof of the 22nd floor is well worth it for a view over all Berlin—West and East! Observation platform open 10–midnight; elevator DM.1.

Funkturm (Radio Tower). Another of the city's trademarks, with an equally dazzling view of the city at night, and of course during the day, from the 126-meter (413-foot) high observation platform. The tower which is 138 meters (453 feet) high was constructed in 1926 for the Berlin Trade Fair. Open till 10.30 P.M. Entrance fee DM.3. Restaurant at 180 feet. Open daily 11–11. Elevator to restaurant, adults DM.2, children DM.1.

Grundelwaldturm. 180-foot high observation tower in the middle of beautiful Grundelwald forest, built in 1897. Offers a fine view over the Havel landscape. Open daily in summer 10–5. Admission: DM.0.70.

Hamburger Bahnhof. Invalidenstr. Berlin's oldest rail station built between 1845 and 1847. It proved shortlived, however, and was closed down in 1884. It was later used as a rail museum. Today, after extensive restoration it has reopened as an exhibition hall.

Kaiser Wilhelm Gedächtniskirche (Kaiser Wilhelm Memorial Church). Breitscheidplatz. Built in honor of Wilhelm I between 1891 and 1895, the bombed ruins of the church now stand as a memento of World War II and as a reminder to keep the peace. Admission: free. Open Tues.–Sat. 10–6, Sun. 11–6.

Olympiastadion (Olympic Stadium). Constructed for the infamous 1936 Olympics (but also used for numerous Nazi rallies after the games), this remains the largest sports arena in the country, seating 95,000 spectators. It was here that the legendary Jesse Owens won his four gold medals in 1936. Admission: free. Open daily 9–dusk, except during events.

Reichstag. Platz der Republic. Built in 1884–94, the inside was destroyed in an arson attack in 1933, and virtually the whole building destroyed at the end of the last war. It was restored and is now used for receptions and conferences. It houses a permanent exhibition on German history. Admission: free. Open Tues.–Sun. 10–5.

Siegessäule (Victory Column). Am Grossen Stern. 64-meter (210-foot) high column with a figure of winged Victory crowning it that commemorates the Prussian campaigns of 1864, 1866 and 1870/71. The view takes in the Brandenburger Tor and Unter den Linden in East Berlin and is definitely worth the 285 steps up. Admission: adults DM.1.20, children DM.0.70. Open Mon. 1–7, Tues.–Sun. 9–7.

Zitadelle Spandau. Impressive 16th-century moated castle incorporating an even older watch tower, the 12th-century Juliusturm. Also boasts a fine restaurant in the deeply atmospheric vaulted cellars. Open Tues.–Fri. 9–4:30, weekends 10–4:30; opening times vary in winter.

MUSEUMS AND ART GALLERIES. Entrance to the most important of the state-owned museums—those at Charlottenburg, at the Kulturzentrum Tiergarten, and the Dahlemer Museen, etc.—is free. All are open daily from 9 to 5 and closed Mon.

Schloss Charlottenburg (Charlottenburg Palace). Luisenplatz. The former summer residence of the kings of Prussia houses the following museums:

Museum für Vor- und Frühgeschichte (Prehistoric and Proto History Museum), West Wing. Contains archeological finds from prehistoric times to the early Middle Ages.

Galerie der Romantik. Masterpieces of 19th-century German painting; new gallery in the west wing. Admission: DM.6 for combined ticket to all buildings. Open Tues.–Sun. 9–5.

Opposite the Charlottenburg Palace are the:

Ägyptisches Museum (Egyptian Museum), Schlossstr. 70. The museum contains treasures from ancient Egypt including the most famous portrait bust in the world, that of Nefertiti, and finds from the excavations at Tell-El-Amarna. Admission: free. Open Sat.–Thurs. 9–5.

Antikenmuseum und Schatzkammer (Museum of Antiquities and Treasury), Schlossstr. 1. Greek and Roman treasures upstairs, glittering silver and gold—some dating back over 3,000 years—downstairs in the Treasury. Admission: free. Open Sat.–Thurs. 9–5.

Dahlemer Museen (Dahlem's Museums). **Gemälde Galerie** (Painting Gallery), entrance on Arnim Allee 23. One of Germany's great picture collections; with no less than 26 Rembrandts and 14 Rubens, as well as a host of works by other great masters. Admission: free. Open Tues.–Sun. 9–5.

Kupferstichkabinett (Etchings Gallery). Important collections of drawings, prints and illustrated books from the 15th to 20th centuries. Of particular note are the Rembrandt drawings and the works by Dürer, Holbein and Cranach.

Museum für Islamische, Indische und Ostasiatische (Islamic, Indian and Far Eastern Museum), Lansstr. 8. Fine collections from the Orient.

Museum für Völkerkunde (Ethnological Museum), Lansstr. 8. A marvelous collection of ethnic works from all over the globe. Sections are devoted to Ancient America, Africa, the South Seas and South and Southeast Asia. Includes Mayan carvings, masks from the South Seas, Benin bronzes and a whole host of other treasures.

Skulpturengalerie (Sculpture Gallery). European sculpture from antiquity to the 18th century. Particularly noteworthy are the German medieval works and those from the Italian Renaissance.

Kulturzentrum Tiergarten (Cultural Center). Several museums, some still under construction, are located on the edge of the Tiergarten park. Open to the public are:

Kunstgewerbemuseum (Museum of Applied Arts), Tiergartenstr. 6. Opened 1985, housing a wonderful collection from the Middle Ages to the late 19th century. The highlight is the Guelph Treasure. Admission: free. (Open Tues. to Sun., 9–5.)

Musikinstrumentenmuseum (Museum of Musical Instruments), Tiergartenstr. 1. Added to the Philharmonie in 1984, it is a fascinating collection of musical instruments. Admission: free. Open Tues.–Sat. 9–5, Sun. 10–5. Guided tours on Sat. at 11 with a noon presentation of the Wurlitzer organ, cost DM.3.

Neue Nationalgalerie (National Gallery), Potsdamer Str. 50. A wideranging collection of 19th- and 20th-century painting, principally German. Changing exhibits of contemporary art. Admission: free. Open Tues.–Sun. 10–5.

Zoo, Hardenbergplatz 8. Excellently housed and imaginatively displayed animals. (Open daily in summer 9–7, in winter 9–5). Zoo admission: adults DM.7, children DM.3.50; zoo/aquarium combination ticket; adults DM.11, children DM.5.50.

Other Museums. Bauhaus-Archiv/Museum für Gestaltung (Bauhaus Archives and Museum), Klingelhöferstr. 13–14. Collections concerned with the history of the Bauhaus (1919–33), Gropius' innovative school of arts and design in Weimar and Dessau. Admission: DM.3. Open Wed.–Mon. 11–5.

Berlin Museum, Lindenstr. 14. 300 years of Berlin arts and culture; also has good restaurant. Admission: DM.3. Open Tues.–Sun. 10–6.

Brücke Museum (Bridge Museum), Bussardsteig 9. Collection of Expressionist painting school (The Bridge) which was active in the city before World War I. Housed in delightful park-like residential area. Admission: DM.3.50. Open daily 11–5.

THEATER. The theater in Berlin is quite outstanding but of course except for operetta and the (non-literary) cabarets it is mostly for those who understand German well. Of the city's 18 theaters the most renowned both for its modern and for its classical productions is the *Schaubühne am Lehniner Platz,* Kurfürstendamm 153 (890023). Housed in the recently restored *Mendelsohnbau* of 1926/28 it is one of Germany's most modern and splendid theaters. Also important are the *Schiller-Theater,* Bismarckstr. 110 (319 5236) which has an excellent workshop, the *Werkstatt;* the *Schlosspark-Theater,* Schloss Str. 48 (791 1213); the *Renaissance-Theater,*

Hardenbergstr. 6 (312 4202); and the *Freie Volksbühne,* Schaperstr. 24 (881 3742).

Mainly for Boulevard plays there is the *Komödie,* Kurfürstendamm 206 (882 7893), the *Theater am Kurfürstendamm,* Kurfürstendamm 206 (882 3789), and the *Hansa Theater,* Alt-Moabit 47 (391 4460). Among the experimental and small intimate theaters is the *Tribüne,* Otto-Suhr Allee 18–20 (341 2600), a youthful enterprise.

Berlin has a long tradition of literary and political cabaret-theaters. The Berlin idiom is savage and debunking, and therefore admirably suited to social and political satire. Today there are the *Stachelschweine* in Europa Center (261 4795), *Die Wühlmäuse,* Nürnbergerstr. 33, corner of Lietzenburger Str (213 7047).

MOVIES. There are about 70 cinemas in Berlin, most of them round the Kurfürstendamm. *Arsenal,* Welserstr. 25 (246848); *Filmbühne am Steinplatz,* Hardenbergstr. 12 (312 9012), also has a restaurant; *Lupe 1,* Kurfürstendamm 202 (883 6106); and *Lupe 2,* Olivaerplatz 15 (8811170).

MUSIC. Berlin is a music center. The *Berlin Philharmonic,* under Herbert von Karajan, is the focus of musical activity. There are also several other good symphonic orchestras and internationally famous soloists and ensembles appear regularly. During the summer many open-air concerts take place. Particularly pleasant are the concerts in the *Eichengalerie* of the *Charlottenburger Schloss;* in the *Waldbühne* close to the Olympic Stadium; in the courtyard of the *Jagdschloss Grunewald;* and there is "Jazz in the Garden" of the *Nationalgalerie.*

Principal concert halls in West Berlin are the *Philharmonie* (254880) at the *Kulturzentrum Tiergarten;* the *Konzertsaal der Hochschule der Künste* (31852374) in Hardenbergstr. 34; and in the ultra-modern *ICC-International* Congress Center (30381) on Messedamm.

The Deutsche Oper Berlin stands on the site of the pre-war Opera House in Bismarckstr. 34–37 (341 4449). There are daily performances of the standard operatic repertoire. Musicals can be heard at the recently-restored *Theater des Westens,* Kantstr. 12 (312 1022).

Twice-weekly concerts are given in the glass-sheathed Memorial Church and Bell Tower next to the old Kaiser Wilhelm Memorial, (245053).

SHOPPING. The Kurfürstendamm is a curious mixture of prosperity and tawdriness. Streets branching off the Ku-damm offer good shopping, and at its end, where the Memorial Church stands, is Breitscheid Square with the Europa Center, a large intertwined group of buildings with dozens of shops on street level, below and above ground. A stroll down the adjacent Tauentzienstrasse takes you to the *KadeWe* on Wittenbergplatz. This is the largest department store on the Continent and a definite must for every visitor to Berlin. Other excellent shopping streets are Schloss Strasse (Steglitz) with several department stores and the Forum which houses a variety of shops, and Wilmersdorfer Strasse, a partially-roofed-over pedestrian precinct.

Antiques abound in Berlin. The best places to go are around Keithstrasse (close to Wittenberg Platz tube station); Suarezstrasse (between Kant- and Bismarckstrasse), and Eisenacher- and Motzstrasse close to

Nollendorf Platz subway station with the *Berliner Flohmarkt,* where 16 old U-Bahn cars serve as small shops. There are a couple of interesting Trödelgeschäfte (second-hand and junk shops) on Bergmannstrasse in Kreuzberg, where there is a good chance of coming across something unique. On Sat. and Sun. mornings there is an open-air fleamarket on Strasse des 17 Juni, right at Tiergarten S-Bahn station. Definitely worth a visit.

RESTAURANTS. The three favorite food specialties of Berlin are *Bockwurst* (a chubby frankfurter); yellow pea soup with *Bockwurst* and/or a slice of bacon; and *Eisbein* (pig hock) and sauerkraut. You will find these three specialties almost everywhere you drop in to eat. *Bockwurst* stands are as common as the proverbial hot-dog stand in America. *Berliner Kindl* restaurants are a sure bet for *Eisbein:* this chain is located all over West Berlin.

Berliners also like *Schlesisches Himmelreich:* roast goose or pork with potato dumplings, cooked with fried fruit in a rich gravy. *Königsberger Klops* are meatballs, herring, and capers—a wonderful combination of meat and fish. Fresh carrots, peas, asparagus, and mushrooms make a dish called *Leipziger Allerlei,* and there's wonderful smoked goose breast. *Kasseler Rippenspeer,* concocted long ago by a Berlin butcher named Cassel, is salted pork, fried golden in butter, then cooked slowly until well done. A traditional summer dish is *Aal grün mit Gurkensalat,* tiny pieces of eel from the nearby river, cooked in rich sauce, and served with boiled potatoes and cucumber salad.

Expensive

It is essential to make reservations for all Expensive restaurants.

An der Rehwiese. Matterhornstr. 101 (803 2720). Gourmet spot, located in the annex of a turn-of-the-century villa. AE, DC, MC, V. Closed lunch, Sun., Mon.

Berlin Grill. Kurfürstenstr. 62 (26050). In the Hotel Berlin. Excellent food and service. AE, DC, MC, V.

Conti Fischstuben. Bayreutherstr. 42 (219020). In the Hotel Ambassador. Good fish dishes and excellent cheaper dishes at lunchtime.

Kopenhagen. Kurfürstendamm 203–205 (881 6219). Central. Danish food a specialty. AE, DC, MC.

Alt Berliner Schneckenhaus. Kurfurstendam 37 (883 5937). Long established, lots of atmosphere. Not easy to find—entrance in backyard!

Park Restaurant. Los Angeles Platz (21080). In the Hotel Steigenberger.

Rockendorf's Restaurant. Düsterhauptstr. 1 (402 3099). In north Berlin, worth the long trip. Closed Sun. and Mon.

Moderate

Alter Krug. Königin-Luise-Strasse 52 (832 5089). Not far from the Dahlem Museums, certainly near enough for lunch when seeing the exhibits or the Botanic Garden. Attractive restaurant with outdoor dining. DC, MC, V.

Blockhaus Nikolskoe. Nikolskoer Weg (805 2914). 1819 Russian-style blockhaus in a charming spot at the southern end of the Wannsee (on the Havel) and a long, long taxi ride from downtown. Game dishes. Reservations not necessary. AE, DC, MC, V.

Chalet Suisse. Im Jagen 5 (832 6362). Out in Grunewald suburb. Has terraces and attractive dining areas. Not far from Dahlem. AE, DC, MC.

Drei Bären. Kurfürstendamm 22. You can't get more central than this very popular spot, it actually spills onto the sidewalk, right where all the world passes. Fine local food, especially dumplings filled with eels, and Eisbein.

Forsthaus Paulsborn. Am Grunewaldsee (813 8010). Right in the Grunewald, close to the Hunting Lodge. Game specialties. Reservations advised on weekends. AE, DC, MC, V. Closed Mon. and dinner Oct.–Mar.

Heckers Deele. Grolmannstrasse 35 (88901). Westphalian-style restaurant with Westphalian specialties. Also has 25 rooms. Reservations not necessary. AE, DC, MC, V.

Historischer Weinkeller. Alt Pichelsdorf 32, Spandau (361 8056). Vast choice of German wines in centuries-old wine cellar. Closed on Mondays.

Hongkong. Kurfürstendamm 210 (881 5756). On the second floor, overlooking the liveliest part of the Ku-damm. Excellent Chinese cuisine. AE, DC, MC.

Joe am Ku-Damn. Kufürstendamm 225. Central and very popular, and decorated with a multitude of artefects from the days of the Prussian Empire. This is the place to come for traditional and hearty north German specialties. Try *Schlachtplatte*—mixed variety meats and sausage, and very much better than it sounds—or *Eisbein*—boiled knuckle of pork, normally served in portions that would satisfy a caveman. Dancing after 8 P.M.

Le Bou-Bou. Kurfürstendamm 103 (891 1036). Bistro-type restaurant, art-deco interior, not too expensive and usually full of life.

Mampes Gute Stube. Kurfürstendamm 14 (881 7101). Old Berlin again, and excellent cooking, too. DC, MC.

Mövenpick. Europa Center, Breitscheidplatz (262 7077). 4 different restaurants in one, all above average. AE, DC, MC, V

Silberterrasse. Tauentzienstr. 21 (240171). Located in the huge department store *Ka-De-We,* not far from the Europa Center. A wide selection of gastronomic choices. AE, DC.

Wannsee Terrassen. Wannseebadweg (803 4024). Terraces overlooking Wannsee; a way out but good in summer. Near the Strandbad for a swim. Dancing, but not every night. Closed Mon.

Weinstuben Habel. Hohenzollerndamm 93 (826 1260). Pleasant restaurant with garden and quite close to the Schloss Gehrhus Hotel.

Zlata Praha. Meinekestrasse 4 (881 9750). Bargain-value food from Eastern Europe, washed down by huge range of beers.

Inexpensive

Berlin Museum "Weissbierstube." Lindenstr. 14 (251 0121) Serves typical local food and also has Berlin's popular beer, called Berliner Weisse, which is flavored with raspberry juice. No credit cards. Open Tues. to Fri, 11–6; Sat. to Sun. 11–4.

Hardtke. Meinekestrasse 27 (881 9827), on the corner of Kurfürstendamm. Perhaps the most typical of all Berlin restaurants, with bare wood steins and gargantuan portions of hefty fare. Recommended for atmosphere and value.

Ratskeller Schöneberg. (782 8326). At Schöneberg Rathaus. When visiting the Liberty Bell, have lunch here. Atmospheric and with excellent, filling set meals.

Schultheiss Bräuhaus. Kurfürstendamm 220 (881 7059). Full of life and high spirits. A solid, beer cellar setting with food to match. AE, DC.

Thürnagel. Gneisenaustr. 57 (691–4800). Located in the Kreuzberg district, this vegetarian restaurant is tasty enough to convert a seasoned carnivore. No reservations. No credit cards. Closed lunch.

If you are looking for a snack, or a coffee break, try one of the city's **Konditoreien** for delicious cakes and pastries. Three on Kurfürstendamm will tempt you, **Kranzler** at 18/19, **Leysieffer** at 218, **Möhring** at 213.

NIGHTLIFE. Berlin's nightlife has always been famous, not to say notorious. There are a number of small places of no particular distinction, but the specialty of Berlin is entertainment with shows of varying elaborateness. All Berlin tour operators offer either Illumination Tours of around DM. 75 or Night Club Tours which in their price of around DM. 100 include entrance fees to three different shows and three drinks. Be warned against taking the advice of a taxi driver and heading for Potsdamerstrasse or Stuttgarter Platz.

Chez Nous. Marburgerstr. 14. Near Europa Center. Empire style plush and Cabaret-Revue with world-famous drag show. Open from 9 to 3 with two shows a night. Reservations are recommended (2131810).

Dollywood. Welserstr. 24 (248950). Three shows a night, four on weekends. Closed Mon. Otherwise open from 8.30.

La Vie en Rose. Europa-Center (3236006). Spectacular show with light effects and international stars. Book ahead. Open from 9. Revue theater.

Metropol. Nollendorfplatz. For the younger tourist, a strobe heaven; if you can stand the decibels you'll love the price. A definite hot spot.

New Eden. Kurfürstendamm 71. Dancing to two bands, strip shows and reasonably priced drinks. Stick to beer if you can.

Riverboat. Hohenzollerndamm 177. Mississippi riverboat décor and Berlin liberation make it a great spot. (Closed Mondays.)

Kneipen

Berlin has roughly 5,000 bars, pubs, dives and such like which all come under the heading of *Kneipen*—the Berlin expression for the local on the corner where one calls in for a beer, a snack, a discussion and sometimes also to dance.

Cour Carree. Savignyplatz 5. Open daily from midday until 2.00 A.M. Art-Nouveau style with French food. Garden.

Dicke Wirtin. Carmerstr. 9 (on Savignyplatz). Open from midday until 6.00 A.M. Very lively inn with lots of nostalgia. A Berlin original.

Leydicke. Mansteinstr. 4. Another historic spot. Proprietors operate their own distillery and have a superb selection of wines and liqueurs; definitely the right atmosphere to enjoy a few glasses.

Lutter und Wegner. Schlüterstrasse. A peppy, colorful establishment; the barman (and innkeeper) is a painter and the waitress an actress.

Schiller Klause. Schillerstr. 10. Open Mon. to Fri. 4.00 P.M.–2.00 A.M., Saturday from 9.00 P.M.; closed Sun. Traditional theatergoers' pub next door to the Schiller Theatre.

Sperlingsgasse. Lietzenburgerstrasse. 12 different pubs right in the center of nightlife.

Wilhelm Hoeck. Wilmersdorferstr. 159. Berlin's oldest kneipe is also the most beautiful. The superb interior dates back to 1892—all original.

Frequented by a colorful cross-section of the public; definitely worth a visit.

Zwiebelfisch. Savignyplatz 7. Meeting-place of literary Bohemians of all ages. Good atmosphere for getting to know people. Small menu.

EAST GERMANY

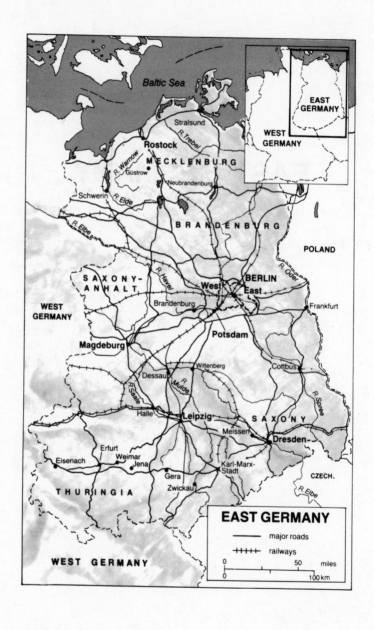

Baltic Sea

Stralsund

Rostock

R. Warnow
R. Trebel

M E C K L E N B U R G

Güstrow

Neubrandenburg

Schwerin

R. Elde

R. Elbe

B R A N D E N B U R G

POLAND

SAXONY-
ANHALT

R. Havel

West **BERLIN**
East

R. Oder

WEST
GERMANY

Brandenburg

Frankfurt

Magdeburg

Potsdam

Wittenberg

Cottbus

Dessau

R. Mulde

R. Saale

R. Spree

Halle

Leipzig

S A X O N Y

Meissen

Dresden

Erfurt

Weimar

Karl-Marx-
Stadt

Eisenach

Jena

Gera

CZECH.

Zwickau

T H U R I N G I A

R. Elbe

WEST G E R M A N Y

EAST GERMANY

——— major roads

+++++ railways

0   50   miles

0   100 km

EAST
GERMANY

WEST
GERMANY

FACTS AT YOUR FINGERTIPS

For general vacation information—Travel Agents, Passports, Health and Insurance, Student and Youth Travel, Hints for Handicapped Travelers, German Time, etc.—see the West Germany Facts at Your Fingertips *section.*

TRAVEL FORMALITIES. Formalities for visiting East Germany, though not prohibitive, are nonetheless strictly observed by the authorities and it is as well to follow them closely. Essentially, this means booking your trip through a travel agent officially accredited by the *Reisebüro der DDR,* the East German state tourist organization. This does not mean that it is necessary to take one of the several package tours offered; instead, the various formalities involved in arranging your trip (visas, hotel vouchers or booking, advice on currency exchange, etc), which in one way or another interlock, will be taken care of for you and you should have no (or at least fewer) hitches at the border or once in the country. Given the reluctance of the East German authorities to allow visitors to stay anywhere other than in officially-designated hotels or campsites—with friends or relatives, for instance—and the consequent delays and difficulties you will encounter in arranging a visit of this type—there is little real benefit in not booking via a travel agent. Note that a visa processing fee is charged for all visitors, however.

In the U.S. and Canada, you can obtain information from accredited travel agencies. You can find out which one is nearest you by writing to the **Consulate of the GDR,** 1717 Massachusetts Ave. N.W., Washington, DC 20036. The Washington consulate is also responsible for Canadian affairs.

Among accredited travel agents **in the U.S.** are:

Cortell Group, 770 Lexington Ave., New York, NY 10021

Koch, 157 E. 86th St., New York, NY 10028 (212/369–3800)

Orbis, 500 Fifth Ave., New York, NY 10110 (212/391–0844)

Lindblad Travel, P.O. Box 912, Westport, CT 06881 (800/243–5657 or 203/226–8531)

Security Travel, 1631 Washington Plaza, Reston, VA 22090 (703/471–1900)

Pecum Tours, 2002 Colfax Ave. S., Minneapolis, MN 55405 (612/871–6399)

Travcoa, 875 N. Michigan Ave., Ste. 3732, Chicago, IL 60611 (800/992–2003)

Maupintours, 1515 St. Andrews Dr., Lawrence, KS 66046 (800/255–4266)

Hemphill Harris, 16000 Ventura Blvd., Encino, CA 91436 (818/906–8086)

Love Tours, 15315 Magnolia Blvd., Ste. 110, Sherman Oaks, CA 91403 (818/501-6868)

In the U.K., GDR tourist affairs including visa assistance are handled by *Berolina Travel,* 20 Conduit St., London W1R 9TD (01/629-1664). Berolina can also give you the names of other U.K. travel agents authorized to make GDR bookings.

We give details on visiting East Berlin from West Berlin in the *Practical Information for Berlin.* For information on visiting East Germany by car or train, see *Getting to East Germany* below.

WHEN TO GO. The main tourist season runs from late April to early October, when the weather is at its best and most important tourist events are held. The advantages of off-season travel—lower prices and fewer crowds—are slight, however, given that prices are generally low anyway, even in the high season, and crowds are few and far between, added to which the winter weather is grim at the best of times.

The summer climate is delightful and settled. Winter, as we say, is not so much fun.

Average afternoon temperatures in degrees Fahrenheit and centigrade:

Berlin	Jan.	Feb.	Mar.	Apr.	May	June	July	Aug.	Sept.	Oct.	Nov.	Dec.
F°	35	38	46	55	65	70	74	72	66	55	43	37
C°	2	3	8	13	18	21	23	22	19	13	6	3

SEASONAL EVENTS. The first weeks of March and September see the Leipzig Trade Fair, the country's biggest single event (prices rise accordingly when the Fair is on, and accommodation is virtually impossible for non-business visitors). Weimar holds a Shakespeare Festival in April; in July the Hanseatic cities of Rostock and Stralsund stage a week of festivities, known as the *Ostseewoche;* September/October see the Berlin Festival of Music and Drama; June sees the Handel Festival in Halle dedicated to the composer George F. Handel who was born here. These dates may vary slightly.

CURRENCY. The monetary unit of East Germany is the *Mark der DDR,* referred to in West Germany as the "Ostmark" (East Mark), but more simply, just Mark, written as M. Like the DM of West Germany, the DDR mark is divided into 100 pfennigs. There are banknotes of 100, 50, 20, 10, and 5 marks, and coins of 20, 10, 5, 2 and 1 mark and 50, 20, 10 and 1 pfennig. The East German mark is officially pegged at 1:1 with the West German DM and the same exchange rates to other currencies apply. At the time of writing (mid-1988), the rate was about DM.1.7 to the U.S. dollar, and about DM.2.97 to the pound sterling. However, these rates will certainly fluctuate, so check before starting your trip.

Hold on to any 20 and 10 pfennig coins. The 20 pfennig piece is needed for a pay phone and the 10 pfennig coins are useful for the streetcar or bus where tickets come out of an automatic dispenser and no change is otherwise available.

You may import any quantity of foreign currency, provided you declare it on arrival. According to the rules, if you fail to declare what you have brought in, none of it may be taken back out. Keep the form you will be given as you must produce it when you leave along with all relevant documentation you will receive when you change money. Any remaining foreign currency you have may then be exported. Note, however, that you may neither import nor export East German currency.

Foreign currency may also be used in certain designated shops, restaurants and hotels. Indeed, some of these will take *only* foreign currency, even for such domestic items as postage stamps. Traveler's checks in a Western currency are of course acceptable; however, traveler's checks may only be exchanged for East German marks. Moreover, foreign currency can be exchanged for East German marks *only* at officially-designated exchange offices and banks. If you are offered East German marks at rates in excess of the official one, you should under no circumstances agree. This is a criminal offence in East Germany and the penalties, should you be caught, and you almost certainly will be, far outweigh any short term gains, however tempting these appear.

Bear in mind that you are required to change DM.25 or the equivalent in Western currency per day per person (DM.7.50 for children between six and 15 years). These amounts will be converted into GDR marks and must be spent in East Germany. If you have prepaid hotel or camping vouchers, you will probably have already met the minimum exchange requirement. When changing currency or paying for anything in Western currency (including with a credit card), be sure to get a receipt showing the exchange, as this is the only way you can prove that you have met the minimum exchange requirement and thus get excess GDR marks changed back into Western currency when you leave the country.

Credit cards. American Express, Diners Club and increasingly, MasterCard/Access are acceptable at better restaurants, hotels and shops. The usual signs are displayed indicating which cards are taken. In addition, Avis, Hertz and Europcar cards are valid for car rentals in the G.D.R.

LANGUAGE. English, while spoken in all centers where American or English tourists will be, is otherwise very much less widely spoken than in West Germany. However, visitors need have no worries, as they are unlikely to be able to travel much away from the well-trodden tourist routes.

GETTING TO EAST GERMANY. By train. There are numerous train routes to East Germany, and trips are easy to arrange. Again, it is easiest to fix up your trip via one of the officially-sanctioned operators or through a travel agent, but independent travel is perfectly feasible. If you do go independently, it is wise to get your visa before you leave. In theory it is possible to get a visa at the border, but in practice this is generally a courtesy offered mainly to business travelers headed for the Leipzig Fair. In order to get a visa at the border, you must have pre-paid hotel or camping vouchers. Transit visas can be issued at the border, but you must have a visa for the next country you plan to visit, if a visa is needed.

The most convenient train to Berlin for visitors from the U.K. is that from the Hook of Holland, connecting with the overnight ferry from Harwich. The *Ost-West Express* from Ostend, with train and jetfoil connections from London (Victoria) also provides a convenient overnight service for Berlin.

Virtually all major West German cities have good through connections to East Germany and there are also direct train connections from other West European cities, including Vienna, Brussels and Paris.

By car. Car travel to East Germany is similarly simple, but you must have hotel or camping vouchers in order to get a visa at the border. Once you are in the country, rules are strict and must be observed at risk of sudden and extravagant fines, always payable in Western currency. Tolls in the form of a road use tax of M5 for up to 200 km., M15 for up to 300 km., M20 for up to 400 km. and M25 for up to 500 km. are levied. This tax is payable in Western currency. Green cards for insurance and registration documents are required for all vehicles, except those registered in Britain, which require registration documents only.

In addition to the points of entry from West Berlin, there are ten highway borders (West German highway number/West German town/East German town): B104/Lübeck-Schlutup/Selmsdorf; A24/Gudow/Zarrentin; B5/Lauenberg/Horst; B71/Bergen (Dumme)/Salzwedel; A2/Helmstedt/Marienborn; B247/Duderstadt/Worbis; Herleshausen/Wartha; B19/Eubenhausen/Meiningen; B4/Rottenbach/Eisfeld; A9/Rudolphstein/Hirschberg. Your travel agent will be able to give you further details.

CUSTOMS ON ARRIVAL. Customs officials are courteous but thorough. You may bring into East Germany any reasonable amount of tobacco, spirits or wine for personal use. However, spare parts for cars may be imported only with permission. Although customs regulations have now been somewhat relaxed regarding publications, some Western magazines and newspapers may not be allowed in, and officials may hesitate over tape and video cassettes. The degree of strictness often depends on the general East-West political climate. If you have valuables such as a portable computer, special photo equipment, fur coat, or the like with you, you may avoid problems when leaving the country by having this noted in your passport when you arrive in the GDR. It may be useful to keep receipts, particularly for antiques or other valuables for which you have paid in Western currency, in case of questions upon leaving the country.

You may import gifts to the value of M200 duty free per person for visits of up to 5 days. If you plan to stay longer you may bring gifts to the value of M100 for each day of your stay. Note that the value of goods is based on their sales price in the GDR, which is not necessarily what you will have paid for them. When you leave, duties may be charged on purchased goods you take out, beyond the value of M20 per person per day's stay in the GDR for up to 5 days or M100 for a longer stay. For regulations governing the import and export of money, see *Currency* above.

HOTELS. Visitors to the G.D.R. are effectively obliged to stay in hotels belonging to the state-run "Interhotel" chain. These include all the major hotels in all cities and other tourist centers. The Interhotels such as the Grand, Palast and Metropol in Berlin, Merkur in Leipzig, and Bellevue in Dresden are fully up to international standards, prices included. Those seeking more moderately priced accommodations may try the "H.O." chain or the church-backed Evangelical hostels. The few private hotels are almost impossible to book as a Western visitor. G.D.R. travel officials will try to book you into one of the best hotels; if you seek more moderate accommodations you may have to argue your point at some length.

Our hotel grading system is divided into four categories. All are per person. Deluxe (L) M100 upward; Expensive (E) M90–100; Moderate (M) M70–90; Inexpensive (I) M40–70. A single room with bath will cost about M5–10 more than half the double rate.

CAMPING. There are over 30 "Intercamp" sites in East Germany, all with electricity, water, and sanitation and other facilities. They are open from May 1 to Sept. 30. Camps are located in Berlin, Zierow (Baltic coast), the Mecklenburg lake district, Dresden, Erfurt, Leipzig and the Hartz mountains. You must, however, book your campsite *before* arriving in East Germany. You will be issued with vouchers which you must surrender on entering the country in exchange for marks (M25 for adults, M10 for those 6–16 years) on entering the country. For those over 16 camping fees cost $11 per person per night or equivalent in other hard currency; those under 16 $4.50 per night; those under 6 go free. Your travel agent can give you full details. Fees may vary in dollar prices according to the exchange rate.

Note that Youth Hostels are not officially open to Western visitors, though in practice campers (under 30) may sometimes be allowed to use them if space is available. For a list of hostels, write *Jugendtourist,* 1026 Berlin, Alexanderplatz 5, DDR.

RESTAURANTS. Both the number of interesting restaurants and the quality of food has increased tremendously over the offerings of only a few years ago. Even the hotel restaurants have improved, adding such exotica as Japanese, Cuban, French, and Indonesian specialties. But most tourists will probably prefer to sample the fare elsewhere, where contact with the East Germans is more likely and the food more representative of the G.D.R. Many of the restaurants listed as inexpensive are either cafés or bars, with somewhat limited choices.

Our restaurant grading system is divided into three categories. Expensive (E) M30–40, Moderate (M) M20–30, Inexpensive (I) M10–20. These prices are for one person and do not usually include drinks.

Food and Drink. Dishes on East German menus in cities are heavily influenced by Eastern European cuisine. Explanations are usually given in several languages, including English, and generally speaking regional specialties manage to make themselves known. In Berlin, for instance, you will find the famous *Eisbein mit Sauerkraut* (knuckle of pork with pickled cabbage), *Rouladen* (rolled stuffed beef), *Spanferkel* (suckling pig), *Berliner Schüsselsülze* (potted meat in aspic), *Schlachteplatte* (mixed grill), *Bürgermeister-Suppe* (thick soup), *Hackepeter* (minced meat), and *Kartoffelpuffer* (potato pancake).

Just outside Berlin, in the haven and tranquility of Spreewald (the Spree woods) and their "streets" of waterways (much of this district has no roads, so boats are the only means of transport), freshwater fish specialties abound, as well as the familiar sausages peculiar to every spot of Germany,

East or West. Good ones to try are *Spreewälder Wurstplatte mit Meerrettich* and *Quark mit Leinöl* (various types of sausage with horseradish, or cream cheese with oil dressing). *Fisch in Spreewaldsosse* (fish in season with a local sauce) or *Aal mit Gurkensalat* (eel and cucumber salad) number among the best fish dishes. There are seafood restaurants throughout East Germany, many of them called *Gastmahl des Meeres*.

Thuringia specializes in venison, poultry and fish. *Röstbrätl* (pot-roast), *Thüringer Sauerbraten mit Klössen* (pickled roast meat and dumplings), *Bärenschinken* (ham) are typical, and *Thüringer Kesselfleisch, Würzfleisch, Schlachteplatte, Thüringer Wurstplatte* are all local sausage dishes.

In the Harz Mountains, you may come across *Halberstädter Käsesuppe* (cheese soup), or *Harzer Köhlerteller mit Röstkartoffeln* (meat cooked over a charcoal grill and served with roast potatoes).

Wines and spirits tend to be eastern rather than western,—Bulgarian wines and Polish and Russian vodkas. A local throat-scorcher, found particularly around the Harz Mountains, is *Schierker Feuerstein*.

TIPPING. Officially abolished, but generally accepted in hotels and restaurants. Tip in West German deutschmarks if possible, otherwise US dollars and coins. While tipping in local currency is, of course, acceptable it will seldom result in improved service, or much in the way of thanks.

MAIL. Postal rates are the same as in West Germany (see West German section). If you mail your cards or letters from one of the large hotels they may ask for West German currency in payment for the East German stamps. The post offices deal only in East German marks.

TELEPHONES. Local calls from pay phones require a 20 pfennig coin. However, it is not possible to make long-distance calls from pay phones. Inquire at your hotel instead. To call the U.S. or Canada, dial 012–1, followed by the area code and number. For the U.K., dial 0644 plus city code and number.

CLOSING TIMES. Banks are open from 8 to 11.30 on weekdays, closed Saturdays. Berlin shops are mostly open from 10 to 7 (8 on Thurs.), shops outside Berlin from 9 to 6. Only department stores and other large shops are open on Saturdays, and then mornings only. Restaurants are open from 10 to midnight, bars 9 P.M. to 4 A.M. Closing days of both may vary.

Museums are generally open from 10 to 6 Tues. to Sun., closed Mon.

National Holidays. January 1; Good Friday; Whit Monday; May 1 (Labor Day); October 7 (Republic Day); Christmas.

GETTING AROUND EAST GERMANY. The country is relatively small so there are no internal air connections. Train is the preferred means of travel and service is frequent and cheap. The system of highways is constantly being improved, but roads other than major routes are often in poor condition.

By train. East German trains, all operated by Deutsche Reichsbahn (or DR), have improved substantially in recent years. Moreover, rail travel here is very inexpensive, notwithstanding the supplements that have to be paid for the faster trains. These come in three grades: Express, the fastest, shown as "EX" in timetables; Fast, shown as "D"; and semi-fast, shown as "E." Their low cost does mean, however, that they get very crowded and it is as well always to reserve your seat ahead. Most long and medium distance trains have both first and second class carriages, and a good number also have either dining, buffet or refreshment cars, though these are unpredictable. Meals are not expensive, but it is rare to get a choice. Overnight trains generally also have first and second class sleeping cars and second class couchettes.

Main lines are being electrified, but steam lingers on in many areas, especially in the narrow gauge systems of Bad Doberan to Ostseebad Kühlungsborn, or the coast near Rostock and from Wernigerode to Nordhausen in the beautiful Harz mountains. Happily, the East German authorities have become increasingly tolerant of rail enthusiasts, but taking pictures of trains in and around stations is prohibited. Four-day tours are available out of Leipzig over the narrow gauge lines on trains drawn by steam locomotives. Your travel agent will have details.

By car. Close to 1,000 miles of motorway and nearly 7,000 miles of secondary roads crisscross the country. Roadways and routes are well marked, but detailed maps will be useful. A highway toll is charged, payable in West German marks. Traffic regulations are specific and strictly enforced, from parking rules to speed limits, for which radar traps have been contrived. Drivers would do well to get a copy of the rules in English before attempting to motor in the GDR, as the police levy fines for the slightest offense. Foreigners have to pay these in West German currency. Speed limits on the Autobahn are 100 k.p.h. (63 m.p.h.), on other roads 80 k.p.h. (55 m.p.h.), and in towns 50 k.p.h. (30 m.p.h.).

Gasoline (petrol) is available either at *Minol* or *Intertank* filling stations. Both chains sell regular and premium grades by the liter. Minol stations supply gasoline against GDR marks (you may be asked to show your currency exchange receipt) or against coupons which may be bought at a discount at the border. Otherwise the Intertank stations sell gasoline at reduced prices, but only for West German marks. Current price for a liter of premium gasoline at Minol is M 1.65; an Intertank station charges DM. 1.36. These prices are subject to adjustment. Unleaded gasoline is available at only a few filling stations.

Drinking and driving is strictly forbidden and fines are heavy for violators. You may even find yourself subject to an on-the-spot fine if you are seen getting into your car after leaving a bar, regardless of whether you have actually been drinking. It's better just to pay up rather than argue. Seat belts are required at all times, with fines for non-use.

Car rental. Cars can be hired at all Interhotels, and a good many other hotels. Rental cars may be driven into the West or into Czechoslovakia, although there is a fee if the car is not returned to the GDR. Rates are given in West German DM and are generally low, although the cars on offer tend to be less than the most luxurious or newest. The most expensive model, a Volvo 264, costs DM. 510 (about $305 at writing) a week, the least expensive, a Lada 1300, costs DM. 200 (about $120) a week, both plus mileage ranging from DM. 1 for the Volvo to DM. 0.35 per km. Widest choice of models is in Berlin, but reserve in advance if you prefer a more comfortable car. Car rentals may be charged to an American Express, Diners Club, Avis, Hertz or Europcar credit card.

EAST GERMANY

Where Past and Present Meet

East Germany, officially known as the German Democratic Republic (or G.D.R.), consists of that portion of the former German Reich between the Elbe and the Oder-Neisse rivers in Central Europe. It was founded in October 1949 from the Soviet-occupied zone of Germany, some six months after the creation of its western sibling, the Federal Republic of Germany. The division of Germany into two separate states after World War II resulted from the inability of Germany's victors to agree on its future. In April 1945, a mere month before the official end of the War, the Soviet leader Josef Stalin is reported to have said "whoever occupies a territory imposes on it his own social system, as far as his army reaches. It cannot be otherwise." This pragmatic statement was to prove accurate in the extreme, and it hardly needs stressing that the post-War division of Germany largely corresponds to the demarcation line between Soviet and American troops. (The American Army initially occupied a small section of the southwest part of the G.D.R., only to withdraw shortly thereafter in return for a foothold in Berlin.)

Geography and Economics

East Germany contains all or parts of the former German provinces of Brandenburg, Mecklenburg, Pomerania, Saxony-Anhalt and Thuringia. Covering an area of some 108,273 square km. (67,000 square miles), East Germany is less than half the size of the Federal Republic of Germany.

Whereas West Germany is about the size of the state of Oregon, the G.D.R. roughly corresponds to Missouri. The country consists of generally hilly to mountainous terrain in the southern regions of the Thuringer Forest and the Erzgebirge, a mountain range forming a natural boundary with Czechoslovakia, and in the southwest where the Harz mountains spill over into West Germany. In the central and northern regions the land flattens into a lake and marsh area, actually an extension of the immense Baltic Plain which stretches beyond Poland. Cold in the winter and hot in the summer, this sparsely wooded land is in fact a forerunner of the Russian steppes.

Although a small country, East Germany is densely populated with nearly 17 million people. It is also heavily industrialized and rates not only as one of the economic leaders of Eastern Europe, but among the ten most important industrialized countries in the world, perhaps adding some credence to the claim that Germans can make any system work. Major industrial centers are located around the capital East Berlin, as well as in and around southern cities such as Halle, Karl-Marx Stadt (formerly Chemnitz), Leipzig and Dresden. Poorly endowed with natural resources, the G.D.R. relies heavily upon Soviet imports of oil and other raw materials to help feed its industries. An exception is one of the world's largest concentrations of lignite or brown coal, the heavy mining of which helps account for the grayness and acrid smell of many large East German cities. Major industries include steel production, chemicals, heavy machinery, electronics, cameras, and an array of manufactured goods. Living standards are quite high for Eastern Europe, but continue to lag considerably behind those in the West and the average East German worker is about a third less efficient than his West German counterpart.

The Modern State

Politically and economically, East Germany is closely modeled on the Soviet Union, with all decision making concentrated in the hands of the East German communist party, officially known as the Socialist Unity Party, (SED). Although several other political parties and a parliament also exist, the country is actually run by a small group of leaders in the communist party's leading organs. As the Soviet Union's leading trading partner, East Germany is closely integrated not only politically (member of the Warsaw Pact) but economically with the USSR. An estimated 400,000 Soviet troops are stationed on East German soil to ensure compliance with Moscow's dictates and to guard this strategic outpost of the Soviet Union's Eastern European empire.

The history of East Germany is closely intertwined with that of the East-West conflict. Located on the demarcation line between East and West, East Germany was the focal point for some of the most dramatic crises in East-West relations, such as the Berlin Blockade of 1949. As the "other" German state East Germany provided a classic test case in the competition between Western capitalist democracy and Soviet-style socialism. It has been a competition in which the G.D.R. has not always fared well. In June 1953 East German workers in East Berlin and other major cities rose up in revolt to protest against the regime's policies, an uprising which had to be suppressed by Soviet tanks. Then, throughout the '50s nearly four million East Germans expressed their dissatisfaction with existing conditions by "voting with their feet" and escaping to the West via West Berlin. A brutal end was to put to this mass exodus on August 13, 1961 through the construction of the Berlin Wall, with the partition of Germany's former capital drastically symbolizing the final division of the German nation.

Just as the Cold War left its imprint on the '50s and '60s, so detente in the '70s left its mark on the G.D.R. Following the conclusion of a series of treaties between East and West in the early '70s on matters such as the status of Berlin and relations between East and West Germany, the G.D.R. finally achieved international recognition and was admitted to the United Nations. Domestically, the ruling authorities started to relax at least some controls and openly pursued a policy of "goulash communism," attempting to increase their popularity by raising living standards. Similarly, East German writers were allowed limited freedoms, while contacts with the West, above all with West Germany, increased considerably. No longer an international outcast, the G.D.R. started to expand its foreign ties.

Despite overwhelming economic and political dependance on the Soviet Union and the banners seen almost everywhere proclaiming loyalty to the Soviet cause—"We greet the soldiers who safeguard our peace"—the Russian influence in East Germany is in many ways more superficial and does not go nearly as deep as the American impact upon West German social lifestyles and culture. East Germans remain deeply interested and fascinated by the West. Even the East German government acknowledges this interest. Until recently, all but a small area around Dresden could receive western television. In a concession to those who lived in the "valley of the uniformed," the government now carries the popular West German stations on local cable.

Yet in many other ways, the G.D.R. remains very German. Scratch the surface and you'll find another side of the country that will tell you much more about its German past than its Soviet-dominated present. Despite three-and-half decades of ostensibly revolutionary rule, there's a quiet conservatism and identification with old traditions and customs in many small East Germany towns and villages that is in marked contrast to the much more hectic and cosmopolitan pace of life in West Germany. Time, while not having stood still, has taken much less of a toll on this side of the border. Likewise, although a communist and therefore officially an atheist state, religion continues to play an important role, with some 47% of the population officially Protestant and another 8% Catholic. East Germany also boasts many a great figure from Germany's grand but often tragic past, and indeed the communist regime subtly encourages identification with this monumental heritage, as witnessed for example by the official celebrations in 1983 of the 500th anniversary of the birth of Martin Luther. In this and in many other ways, the past remains the present in East Germany.

Treasures of the East

In no other sphere of East German life is this more neatly illustrated than by the range and numbers of artistic treasures the country possesses, eloquent testimony to the affluence and cultural significance of the region before it was sucked into the Eastern bloc.

Berlin has the greatest share of this artistic richness, though much is now in the Western half. Frederick the Great's superb collection of Watteaus, for instance, though intended for display in Sans Souci Palace, today in the G.D.R., is now in West Berlin's Charlottenburg Palace. Similarly, the Dahlem Museum has finished up with most of the great Prussian art treasures. But the Pergamon and Bode Museums in East Berlin still have the largest collection of classical architectural structures in the world housed inside buildings; and, in the Bode Museum, highly important Egyptian collections. The German State Library is also here.

Aside from Dresden, Weimar is the other great cultural treasure house. Bach, Goethe, Schiller, Luther, Herder, Liszt and Wagner are just a few of the great men who spent many years in this deeply historic city. There is good documentation on the private as well as the public side of their lives and works to be found in hotels and museums.

Dresden has 16 other important museums besides the Zwinger; Leipzig, synonymous with Bach, has a magnificent Bach archive, while the University has the largest Egyptian collection of its kind in Europe. And anyone devoted to the medieval poets and the romantic revival of the 19th century will find a haven in Wartburg Castle, primarily, of course, associated with Luther.

Money for maintenance is one of the serious drawbacks facing East Germany, but much restoration has been done, and quite as beautifully and as lovingly as any in West Germany. There is considerable public appreciation of music, opera, drama and art, and the official attitude is positive, with the result that East Germany has 86 theaters and opera houses functioning. Newest amongst these is the restored Semper Oper in Dresden. Berlin and Dresden are the best testimony to the reconstruction of churches, cathedrals and art galleries, so much so that one tends to forget that they *have* been restored, at great cost in time, money and effort, and to notice instead the no-man's-land around the frontier with West Berlin and the rather "anonymous international" style of contemporary hotels and public buildings.

Pergamon Museum

EAST BERLIN AND POTSDAM

Museums and Memorials

East Berlin, Capital of the G.D.R.—as the East Germans insist the city be called—has been given a thorough scrubbing and sprucing up to mark the 750th anniversary in 1987 of the city's founding. Most visitors will see the reconstructed Friedrichstrasse, the renovated opera house and other central parts of the city which have been given loving care with you in mind. Wander off the beaten path, however, and you will find the drabness and communist sameness for which the eastern zone of the city is better known. Alas, some of the showcase housing and other communal projects hastily built in the '50s and '60s are now more than showing their age and shoddy construction. West Berlin on the other side of the Wall remains a potent example of Western free enterprise, very much alive in contrast to the quieter atmosphere in the Eastern zone.

However, the appeal of East Berlin goes deeper than the contrasts it presents with West Berlin, and vice versa, of course. Rather, there is something fatally attractive about the city itself, a quality shared, albeit in very different form, by West Berlin.

What precisely this quality is, however, remains elusive. But it is doubtful that any other European city has quite the same aura of once-gilded and doomed mystery, or lends itself so easily to the faintly haunted atmosphere that pervades Berlin. Or indeed, if anywhere else has witnessed so much tragedy and been the scene of so many of the 20th century's more terrifying and poignant dramas. In East Berlin, the ghost of a war-torn Europe still stalks the streets.

Exploring East Berlin

The major starting point for tours around East Berlin, whether you visit the city from West Berlin or are staying in East Berlin itself, is Unter den Linden. (If you are visiting from West Berlin, walk north along Friedrichstrasse from Checkpoint Charlie, the principal crossing point between West and East Berlin, to reach Unter den Linden). Unter den Linden, a long and much-loved avenue running east–west through the heart of the city, was one of the major sights of pre-war Berlin, a sort of Fifth Avenue and Champs Elysées rolled into one. The main landmark at its western end by the Berlin Wall is the Brandenburger Tor, a massive and heroic triumphal arch built in the late-18th century, topped by a splendid chariot drawn by four stallions. For long, it was perhaps the most potent and evocative symbol of the city, much as is the Statue of Liberty in New York or the Eiffel Tower in Paris, to continue the metaphor. These days, lying just inside the eastern half of Berlin, its symbolism is rather different, serving instead as a tragic reminder of the sundered state of the city, a condition underlined when the East Germans turned the statue around to face east.

The western end of Unter den Linden is lined principally with government buildings, though as you approach the eastern end of the street you will find a number of historic and generally rather splendid buildings clustered together. These include the German State Library (containing over four million volumes) with behind it the 18th-century Humboldt University; the impressive 17th-century Museum of German History (Museum für Deutsche Geschichte), housed in what was originally the city arsenal, or Zeughaus, and the most famous Baroque building in Berlin; the 18th-century German State Opera (Deutsches Staatsoper) last year splendidly restored and now reopened; and, just to the south, St. Hedwig's Cathedral (St. Hedwigs Kathedrale) in Bebelplatz, another fine 18th-century structure.

To the south of Unter den Linden is the Platz der Akademie, a sizeable square notable for the neo-classical Schauspielhaus, dating from 1820 and recently beautifully rebuilt as the city's leading concert hall. On either side, also undergoing restoration, are the "French" and "German" cathedrals, the French reformed church evidence of the massive Huguenot presence in Berlin at the beginning of the 18th century, and now housing a Huguenot museum. Restorations have brought the whole square to life.

Unter den Linden then bends slightly north as it passes over the river Spree and onto Museum Island, where it runs into Marx-Engels-Platz, a somewhat dreary square that is today the site of the Ministry of Foreign Affairs, the State Consul and the massive Palace of the Republic (Palast der Republik). Originally, the Royal Palace, begun in the Renaissance and one of the city's most famous and beautiful buildings, was here. Sadly, it too was a casualty of wartime bombing and in 1951 what remained of the building was pulled down, and the Palace of the Republic built in its place.

Moving on to Museum Island, the major attractions are, naturally enough, the series of museums it boasts. These are: the Old Museum (Altes Museum), an austere neo-Classical pile just to the north of Marx-Engels-Platz; the National Gallery (Nationalgalerie), a fine classical building containing mostly 19th-century works; the Bode Museum, located at the northern tip of the island; and the magnificent Pergamon Museum, opposite the Bode Museum. This last is perhaps the city's star attraction, containing the Pergamon Altar, dating from 180 B.C. and one of the Seven Wonders of the World. Like the Bode Museum, however, there are also sizeable collections of Egyptian, early-Christian and Byzantine works.

Heading northeast from Museum Island onto the right bank of the Spree along Liebknechtstrasse, you will see the futuristic T.V. tower, the Fernsehturm, rising upwards on your right. It's 365 meters high (1,197 ft.) and boasts a revolving restaurant and observation platform at the summit; the view is predictably sensational. A little to the south of the T.V. tower in Rathausstrasse is the Red Town Hall, the Rotes Rathaus, a late-19th-century Italianate building crowned with a 74-meter (240 ft.) tower. There's also a 400-meter-long frieze (1,310 ft.) running round the entire building on the second floor illustrating famous events from Berlin's past.

Back of the Rotes Rathaus is the beautifully restored Nikolai Kirche (although no longer used as a church, but a museum) and the surrounding square, replete with cafés, restaurants and shops, spilling over into the Poststr. Cross the Spree river on the Mühlendamm bridge and you'll be on the Fischerinsel, Fisherman's Island. Press along the Gertraudenstr. and you'll find a host of tiny and fascinating streets alongside the Spree canal to your right. You'll think you're in Amsterdam, not Berlin.

Headed back northeast again brings you alongside the TV tower, the focal point of Alexanderplatz, a huge square and the postwar architectural showplace of East Berlin, although in truth most of the newer buildings, despite their apparent modernity, are slab-like and dated. In addition to the hotels and restaurants here, this is also the shopping center of the city. A uranium clock, surrounded by fountains, lies in the middle of the square. Running away southeast from Alexanderplatz is Karl-Marx-Allee, originally Stalin-Allee, a monumental and rather dull avenue lined with apartment blocks. It was here that the riots of June 1953 took place.

The last stop on most tours of the city is generally to the Soviet military cemetery at Treptow, another monolithic construction, built with marble taken from Hitler's Reich Chancellery among other places. On either side of the broad avenue leading up to the massive statue of a Russian soldier that forms the heart of the complex are stone reliefs portraying episodes from World War II, lauding the heroic Soviet troops who defeated the fascist forces of the Nazis.

Potsdam

Potsdam, some 30 km. (20 miles) southwest of Berlin, assumed significance in German history in 1660 when the Prince Elector of Prussia, Friedrich Wilhelm, determined to make what had until then been no more than a small settlement the site of his palace. He duly built a palace there and the town thereafter became the principal seat of the Hohenzollerns, later Kings of Prussia, and in the 18th century the dominant power in German affairs. As the influence of the Hohenzollerns grew, so they built ever more lavishly, largely in imitation of the French kings, in particular of their magnificent palace at Versailles. This French influence, in part at any rate the result of the influx of Huguenots from France at the beginning of the 18th century but owing as much to Frederick the Great's admiration for all things French, is most evident at Sans Souci, a delightful Baroque palace dating from 1745. Its Concert Room is particularly fine, but there are also a number of magnificent picture galleries, containing works by Rubens, Van Dyck and Caravaggio among others. In addition, the rooms where Voltaire lived, most celebrated of all French 18th-century philosophers and greatly admired by Frederick the Great who invited him to Potsdam, have also been preserved. A visit to the Cecilienhof, a modern palace built in a medieval mode, also presents certain features of interest. Here Truman, Stalin and Churchill signed the Potsdam Agreement in 1945 which effectively sealed the fate of post-war Germany, enabling the Soviet forces to remain in control of those areas of Germany that their drive into Germany had won for them; in other words, East Germany. The significance and meaning of the Agreement tends, not unnaturally perhaps, to be seen in a somewhat different light by the East German authorities, as your guide will no doubt make clear.

As well as its architectural treasures, Potsdam today is also a substantial industrial center, with a population in excess of one million. Nonetheless, areas of the center and much of the surrounding countryside are generally unspoilt, the latter being densely wooded in parts.

PRACTICAL INFORMATION FOR
EAST BERLIN

HOTELS. As most visitors to East Germany and its capital will be taking some sort of package tour, or will at any rate have made reservations in advance, the problem of searching for a hotel won't be encountered. The tourist office does operate a reservations service—see below for address—but will only accept bookings if you write in advance, meaning that you might as well book through a travel agent before you leave.

Generally the standard of East Berlin hotels is high, certainly the city boasts most of the best hotels in the country—a conscious decision by the East Germans and part of their aim to make their capital a showpiece for the nation. The top hotels each have their own character and are the equal (in price as well) to equivalent accommodations in the West. Facilities—restaurants, bars, fitness rooms, T.V., private baths and toilets, etc.—are good.

Very Expensive

Grand. Friedrichstr. 158–162 (2–20920). Grand in every sense, from atrium lobby to garden restaurant and unusually attractive accommodations. Opened in 1987 to mark the city's 750th anniversary. Centrally located; 300 rooms, studios and suites, all with full facilities. Amenities include four restaurants, an assortment of bars, swimming pool and sauna, squash, shops, car rental and business facilities. AE, DC, MC, V.

Metropol. Friedrichstr. 150/153 (2–22040). Centrally-located a short distance from Unter den Linden. 320 rooms, all with bath or shower; some studio rooms and suites are also available. Every possible facility and service is available, including fitness center, special business facilities and own yacht. There's also a travel agent on the 11th floor where you can book tours. Although the oldest of Berlin's best hotels, preferred by many for its more intimate and personal atmosphere. AE, DC, MC, V.

Palasthotel. Karl Liebknechtstr (2–2410). 600 rooms, all air-conditioned and with all facilities. 12 restaurants, a fitness center, Banquet and Conference center, shops, travel agent, and a yacht, complete the amenities. Groups tend to be booked in here; individuals may prefer the Metropol or the Grand. AE, DC, MC, V.

Expensive

Berolina. Karl Marx Allee 31 (2–210 9541). Less central. 350 rooms with bath or shower, roof garden restaurant, cafe, bar, shops. AE, DC, MC, V.

Stadt Berlin. Alexanderplatz (2–2190). Located right in the middle of the city center. 600 rooms, all with private facilities; 40 stories high. Several restaurants, the one on the top floor is for residents only. Travel agency, bank, sauna. AE, DC, MC, V.

Unter den Linden. Unter den Linden 14 (2–220 0311). 300 rooms all with private facilities. Comfortable, and good location. Restaurant, conference rooms and bar. Theater and nightclub reservations. AE, DC, MC, V.

Moderate

Adria. Friedrichstr. 134 (2–282 5451). 70 rooms with bath or shower. Because of the lower price range and decent location, this hotel tends to fill up far in advance. Popular restaurant. No credit cards.

Newa. Invalidenstr. 115 (2–282–5461). 57 rooms, some with bath. An older hotel, but good restaurant and service. No credit cards.

Inexpensive

Hospiz am Bahnof Friedrichstrasse. Albrechtstr. 8 (2–282–5396). 110 rooms, some with bath. This evangelical hostel is very popular with families, so it gets booked up months in advance and public areas are not particularly restful. Restaurant. No credit cards.

Hospiz Auguststrasse. Auguststr. 82 (2–282–5321). 70 rooms, some with bath. Comfortable, friendly, church-run hotel. Breakfast is the only meal served here. No credit cards.

HOW TO GET AROUND. By U-Bahn. The U-Bahn, or subway, is fairly extensive. Route maps, details of fares and special one-day tourist tickets are available from the Alexanderplatz rail station and the tourist office. Some newsstands also have time tables. A normal streetcar, bus or subway trip costs M.20; a reduced-price tourist ticket for all means of transport is available for M2.

By tram and bus. Tickets are very inexpensive, but buses can be rather uncomfortable and crowded, and hot in the summer. Tram routes are displayed on all tram stops; these are marked *Halt.*

On foot. This is the best way to get to know the city. Maps (Stadtplan) are available at hotel information desks, newspaper kiosks and at the main tourist information office on Alexanderplatz. Jaywalking is frowned upon and pedestrians are expected to observe the walk/wait lights at intersections.

TOURIST INFORMATION. The main tourist office in East Berlin is located at Alexanderplatz 5 (215–4328); it is operated by the Reisebüro der DDR. The office can provide much useful information on the city, and you may also book sightseeing trips in and around the city, theater and opera tickets and trips to other parts of the country. A special counter giving information in English is located on the second floor (215–4402). It is open Mon. to Fri. 8 A.M.–8 P.M., Sat. and Sun. 9 A.M.–6 P.M.

Some of the more expensive hotels also have tourist information offices. There is one at Schönefeld airport as well (678–8248).

USEFUL ADDRESSES. Embassies. *American Embassy,* Neustädtische Kirchstr. 4–5, 108 Berlin (2–220 2741). *British Embassy,* Unter den Linden 32–34 (2–220 2431). There is no Canadian Embassy in East Berlin, but if circumstances demand, call the Canadian Embassy in Warsaw at Ulica Matejiki 1–5, PL-00481 Warsaw, Poland (064–822–0298–051 from East Berlin). Alternatively, try the Canadian Military Mission in West Berlin (849–261–1161). If that fails, the British Embassy will help, provided they know you have made an effort to contact the other two.

Emergencies. *Police,* 110. *Ambulance,* 115. *Doctor, dentist,* 1259 or call the U.S. or U.K. embassy and ask for assistance. *Pharmacies,* 160. *Driver assistance,* 524–3565, 6 A.M.–10 P.M.

Lost property. Wilhelm-Pieck-Str. 164 (2–282 9403). The railroad lost property office is at the rail station at Marx-Engels-Platz (2–587 21671).

Main post office. Corner of Ostbahnhof and Strasse der Pariser Kommune; open day and night for telegrams, express letters, and small express parcels.

TOURS. Eleven different guided city tours ranging from one to three and a half hours can be booked via your hotel or the Reisebüro der DDR. Fares range from M 3–12. Taxi sightseeing tours of the city cover six fixed routes, starting and ending at Alexanderplatz. Tours last from 40 minutes to two and a half hours and cost DM 16.50–55 depending on the route, for up to four people; tel. 246–2255 for details. Tours are also given in English.

PARKS AND GARDENS. Plänterwald Park. Extends from the Zenner restaurant up to the Baumschulenweg S-Bahn station. Bordered by the river Spree on one side and Neue Kreugallee on the other, this park has an openair theater, playgrounds and sports fields. There is also an amusement park on the north side with a huge ferris wheel from which you have an excellent view of the area. Take the S-Bahn out to Baumschulenweg for a convenient breather.

Volkspark Freidrichshain. Laid out in the 19th century, this is the oldest park in the city center. It was further developed when its green hills were created by covering up the one million cubic meters of rubble from buildings destroyed in this part of the town during the war. There is a charming fairy tale fountain located in the western corner of the park.

Zoologischer Garten (Zoo), Friedrichsfelde. Accessible by the S-Bahn, the Zoo is regarded as one of Berlin's most popular attractions. There are over 5,000 animals generously grouped in natural surroundings and often separated from visitors only by moat.

HISTORIC BUILDINGS AND SITES. Brandenburger Tor (Brandenburg Gate). Designed by Carl Gotthard Langhans in the late-18th century and intended to act as the architectural conclusion to Unter den Linden. It is crowned with a giant quadriga—a horse-drawn chariot—driven by the Godess of Peace. Today, it is a poignant symbol of the divided city.

Gedenkstätte Berlin-Karlshorst (Berlin Karlshorst Memorial Site). The building in which Germany signed the unconditional surrender on May 8 1945 that marked the end of the European theater of World War II. The great hall in which the surrender was signed and some 15,000 documents, principally stressing the Soviet role in the struggle, are the main attractions. Open Tues. to Fri. 9–1 and 3–6, Sat and Sun. 9–6.

Marienkirche (St. Mary's Church). Karl Liebknecht Str. Gothic hall church dating originally from 1294, but much restored and rebuilt since, though the choir is original. The spire, despite its Gothic style, dates from the late-18th century.

Neue Wache (New Guard House). Unter den Linden. Monumental neo-Classical building, designed by the ubiquitous Schinkel, originally the Royal Guard House. Today, it houses the Memorial to the Victims of Fascism and Militarism. An eternal flame burns in a glass cube in the center of the hall, while in the tomb beneath stand urns containing the ashes of an unknown resistance fighter and an unknown soldier. The guard is changed every hour, but every Wednesday there is a more lavish parade, rather more in keeping with the euphemistic and grandiloquent name given to the memorial.

Nikolaikirche (Church of St. Nicholas). Spandauerstr. Berlin's oldest building, dating from about 1200. It was heavily damaged in the war but has been beautifully restored.

Palast der Republik (Palace of the Republic). Marx-Engels-Platz. Massive building housing the plenary hall of the "People's" Chamber, in addition to theaters, restaurants and an electronic T.V. guide providing information on the facilities. The main entrance hall is lit by more than 9,000 lamps, and is jokingly-known as the "lamp shop."

Rotes Rathaus (Red Town Hall). Rathausstr. Interesting Italianate building, built in 1861–69. The giant 74-meter tower and massive frieze running round the entire building are the dominant features.

St. Hedwigs Kathedrale (St. Hedwig's Cathedral). Bebelplatz. Baroque building dating from 1747. It was bombed during the war, and though the exterior has been carefully restored, the interior is predominantly modern.

Schauspielhaus (Main Concert Hall). Designed by the architect Schinkel and beautifully restored in 1984 to be the center of the city's concert activities and home to the East Berlin Symphony Orchestra.

Sowjetische Gedenkstätte der Sowjetarmee (Soviet War Memorial). Treptow Park. Giant size memorial dedicated to the millions of Soviet soldiers who lost their lives in the war; 5,000 officers and men are interred here.

MUSEUMS AND GALLERIES. Altes Museum (Old Museum). Marx-Engels-Platz. Neo-Classical building designed by Schinkel and completed in 1830. Works by East German artists, plus print room, and drawing collection. Open Wed. to Sun. 10–6.

Bode Museum. Am Kupfergraben. Egyptian, early-Christian and Byzantine departments; plus special exhibits of Italian old masters. Open Wed. to Sun. 9–6, Fri. 10–6.

Brecht House. Chauseestr. 125. Berlin working and living quarters of author Bertolt Brecht and his actress-wife Helene Weigl; Brecht archive. Admission: DM 3. Open Tues. and Fri. 10–12, Thurs. 5–7, Sat. 9.30–12 and 12.30–2.

Kunstgewerbemuseum (Arts and Crafts Museum). Köpenick Palace. European arts and crafts; special exhibits. Open Mon. to Sat. 9–5, Sun. 10–6.

Märkisches Museum. Am Köllnischen Park 5. Everything you've ever wanted to know about Berlin's cultural history. Admission: DM 3. Open Wed. and Sun. 9–6, Thurs. and Sat. 9–5, Fri. 9–4.

Museum für Deutsche Geschichte (Museum of German History). Unter den Linden. Former city arsenal in magnificent Baroque building. It was later used as a hall of fame glorifying Prusso-German militarism. Today, it charts German history from 1789 to the present, though with a pronounced Marxist bias; interesting but different. Admission: DM 3. Open. Mon. to Thurs. 9–7, Sat. and Sun. 10–5; closed Fri.

Museum für Naturkunde (Museum of Natural History). Invalidenstr. 43. Paleontological, mineralogical and zoological departments. Open Tues. to Sun. 9.30–5; closed Mon.

Nationalgalerie (National Gallery). Bodestr. 19th- and 20th-century paintings and sculptures. Open Wed. to Sun. 9–6, Fri. 10–6; closed Mon. and Tues.

Pergamon Museum. Am Kupfergraben. The name derives from the principal exhibit here and number one attraction, the Pergamon Altar, a magnificent and vast altar dating from 180 B.C. Just as impressive is the Babylonian Processional Way in the Asia Minor department. There are also Egyptian, early-Christian and Byzantine collections, plus a fine collection of sculptures from the 12th to the 18th centuries. Pergamon Altar and architectural rooms open daily 9–6, Fri. 10–6. Other sections closed Mon. and Tues.

MUSIC AND THEATER. East Berlin enjoys an enviable reputation in the musical and theatrical worlds, with opera in particular very highly rated. However, theater productions will be in German, so non-German speakers will find a visit rather limiting. The tourist office at Alexanderplatz can advise on current productions; alternatively, consult the monthly magazine *Wohin in Berlin?* Ticket sales are from theaters, generally from 12 to 6, or from the central box office in the Palast Hotel. Concerts generally take place in the *Schauspielhaus* on Platz der Akademie (2–227 2156) or in the *Palast der Republik,* Marx-Engels-Platz (2–238 2354). Opera, operetta, ballet and musicals are performed at the *Deutsche Staatsoper, Komische Oper, Metropol Theater,* and *Palast der Republik.*

Among leading theaters are:

Berliner Ensemble. Bertold Brecht Platz (2–288 80).

Deutsche Staatsoper. Unter den Linden (2–205 40).

Deutsches Theater. Schumannstr. 13a/14 (2–287 1225).

Distel (cabaret). Plays various locations; (2–207 1291).

Kammerspiele. Schumannstr. 13a/14 (2–287 1226).

Komische Oper. Behrenstr. 55 (2–220 2761).

Maxim Gorki Theater. Am Festungsgraben 2 (2–207 1843).
Metropol Theater. Friedrichstr. 101 (2–200 0651).
Puppet Theater. Greifswalder Str. 81–84 (2–365 0696).

SHOPPING. American Express and Diner's Club credit cards are accepted in government-owned Intershops and elsewhere where sign is displayed. The Palast Hotel, Berlin has the biggest and best Intershop, accepting only hard currency plus credit cards. Dolls' tea services are beautiful; try at Centrum Department store, Alexanderplatz, Berlin. Locally made jewelry can be found at Skarabaus, at Frankfurter Allee 80. For antiques try the state-run shop at Friedrichstr. 180/184. Books (try Unter den Linden), sheet music, records and cassettes are cheaper than in West Berlin but if touring Eastern Europe the East German Centrum, Budapest, has East German records even cheaper. Dresden china is actually made at the nearby and very lovely town of Meissen, and examples can be bought by visitors there. The workshops can be viewed as well, as can the exhibition hall, which has examples of old and new Meissen porcelain on display.

RESTAURANTS. All the hotels listed above have restaurants, and most of the larger ones have several, all serving generally good food. In addition, the city also has a number of reasonably good eating out spots, though certainly in nothing like the same numbers as West Berlin. Prices are low. Restaurants and cafés are usually open from 10 A.M. to midnight, bars from 9 P.M. to 4 A.M. Most restaurants close one day a week, so check.

Expensive

Ermeler Haus. Märkisches Ufer 10–12 (2–279 4036). A stately restaurant located in a 16th-century building and one of the top spots in the city. Good wine list. Reservations advised. AE, DC, MC, V.

Forellenquintett. Friedrichstr. 158–162, in the Grand Hotel (2–20–920). Fish specialties prepared in the style of the nearby Spree Forest. Reservations advised. AE, DC, MC, V.

Ganymed. Schifferbaudamm 5 (2–282 9540). Central location and good service. No credit cards. Closed Mon. Reservations essential.

Jade. Karl-Liebknecht-Str. 5, in the Palast Hotel (2–241–2333). Chinese/Asian specialties, in comfortable, modern surroundings. Reservations advised. AE, DC, MC, V.

Roti D'Or. Karl-Liebknecht-Str. 5, in the Palast Hotel (2–241–2245). French cuisine in a fine setting, but this restaurant caters only to those paying in Western currency, so it is often uncomfortably empty. AE, DC, MC, V.

Schwalbennest. Am Marstall (upstairs), Rathausstr. at Marx-Engels-Platz (2–212 4569). New and extremely attractive. Outstanding service and food, with wide choice, but avoid the overpriced flambéed extras. Reservations essential at noon as well. AE, DC, MC, V.

Zur Goldenen Gans. Friedrichstr. 158–162, in the Grand Hotel (2–209–20). Regional specialties, game and venison dishes. Reservations advised. AE, DC, MC, V.

Moderate

Historische Weinstuben. Poststr. 23 (2–212 4122). Cozy little wine restaurant with historic atmosphere. Small meals only are available. Reservations essential, but ask your hotel to set them up.

Lindencorso. Unter den Linden 17 (2–220 2461). Wine tavern and "concert" cafe, plus Havana Bar (open till 4 A.M.). Special evenings for young people. Reservations essential on weekends. No credit cards.

Operncafe. Unter den Linden 5 (2–200 0256). Located in what was originally the Princess' Palace; atmospheric and traditional, with cafe, restaurant and wine tavern. AE, DC, MC, V.

Sofia. Leipzigerstr. 46 (2–229 1831). Good Bulgarian cuisine and a Bulgarian band in appropriate setting.

Telecafe. T.V. Tower, at Alexanderplatz (2–210 4232). The view is better than the food, but still worth the trip up.

Inexpensive

Alt-Cöllner-Schankstuben. Friedrichsgracht 50 (2–212–5972). Beside canal in old Berlin; friendly and charming. Limited menu, but good quality. No credit cards.

Haus Budapest. Karl Marx Allee 91 (2–436 2189). Hungarian folk music helps put you in the mood for good Hungarian food. Fine wine list.

Haus Warschau. Karl Marx Allee 95 (2–430 0814). Poland provides the food here. Terrace cafe in summer is an extra bonus. Good value.

Zenner. Alt-Treptow 14–17, in Treptower Park (2–272 7211). One of the oldest beer gardens in the city. Pleasant surroundings and a great view of the Spree. Reservations advised. No credit cards.

Zum Goldbroiler. Rathausstr. 5 (2–212 3290). Variety of chicken dishes. Right next door is the *Cafe Rendezvous* for that much-needed coffee break.

Zur Letzten Instanz. Waisenstr. 16 (2–212 5528). Historic restaurant dating back to 1525. Good atmosphere and splendid food, if limited variety. Reservations essential. No credit cards.

Zur Rippe. Poststr. 17 (2–212–4932). Rustic beer tavern in a restored house dating back to 1672. Small and intimate. Specializes in spare ribs. Reservations advised. No credit cards.

NIGHTLIFE. Though hardly on a par with West Berlin, East Berlin nonetheless offers a diversion or two after hours. On the other hand, neither are the prices on a par with those across the wall, and an evening of dancing, entertainment and wine at the Stadt Berlin can cost as little as DM.20. A number of the larger hotels offer dinner-dancing. For nightclubs with music and good atmosphere, try one of the following:

Club Metropol. Hotel Metropol, Friedrichstr. 50.

Hafenbar. Chauseestr. 20. Centrally-located and good ambience.

Haifischer. In the Opern Cafe, Unter den Linden 5.

Lotos Bar. Schönhauser Allee 46. Variety program.

Panorama Bar. Hotel Stadt Berlin, Alexanderplatz. Up on the 37th floor; great view of the city.

Pinguin Bar. Rosa Luxemburg Str. 39. Lots of plush and intimate lighting.

PRACTICAL INFORMATION FOR POTSDAM

Hotels and Restaurants

Interhotel Potsdam (E), Lange Brücke (33–4631). 17-story block beside the Havel river; 350 beds, all rooms with private facilities. Good restaurant, plus shops, sauna, grill-bar and water sports facilities. *Hotel Cecilienhof* (E), Neuer Gartern (33–32141). 42 rooms with bath or shower. Located in a beautiful and quiet setting.

Restaurants. *Café Rendezvous* (M), Friedrich Ebert Str. 114. Good concert café—worth a try. *Klosterkeller* (M), Friederich Ebert Str. 94. Central location. *Kulturhaus Hans Marchwitza* (M), Am Alten Markt. Choice of restaurant proper, wine restaurant, or bar with dancing. *Weinbergterrassen* (M), Gregor Mendel Str. 29. Offers a wine pub, bar, and restaurant with dancing.

TOURIST INFORMATION. *Reisebüro der DDR,* Friedrich Ebert Str. 115 (corner of Yorckstr), tel. 33–4221.

Johann Sebastian Bach 1685-1750

THE REST OF EAST GERMANY

Europe's Youngest State

Splendidly situated on the banks of the Elbe, Dresden was the capital of Saxony as early as the 15th century, though its architectural masterpieces, heavily damaged during the war and now restored, date from the 18th century. The most outstanding Baroque buildings are the Zwinger Palace, the Opera House, the Cathedral, with a fine Silbermann organ, and the National Gallery, which once again houses a unique collection of paintings. The magnificent Semper Oper (opera house), restored and rebuilt, was reopened in 1985; most of Richard Strauss' operas were first performed there. The Picture Gallery in the Semper Building of the Zwinger Palace complex is one of the most highly concentrated exhibits of magnificence in the world. In addition to its most famous masterpiece, Raphael's *Sistine Madonna,* there are 12 Rembrandts, 16 Rubens and 5 Tintorettos, to mention only a few of the masters. In short, for Italian and Dutch paintings of the 16th and 17th centuries, few museums can match the Zwinger collection. There are over 20 other museums here, however. Combine your visit with the cable-car trip to Weisser Hirsch, a hill overlooking the city, where you can dine at the famed Luisenhof restaurant. From the T.V. tower, where there is a café, there is a splendid view to the Albrechtsburg Castle in Meissen, including the Karl May Foundation's Red Indian Museum, illustrating the history of the North American Indians.

The Zwinger apart, you have to look fairly hard for reminders of Dresden's former architectural glory, but indicative of this and the modern concept of town planning is a walk through Weisse Gasse where the statue of the Goose Thief (Gänsedieb) stands, Webergasse, now a shopping center and Gewandhausstrasse with its Children's Frieze (Kinderfries). Prager Strasse connects new with old Dresden and leads to the arcades of the Altmarkt, through Baroque Schloss-strasse with its expertly restored Georgentor and over the Dimitroff Bridge to the right bank of the Elbe.

A short trip down-river brings us to the city of Meissen, famed for its porcelain. Its castle and late-Gothic cathedral (an excellent Cranach in the latter) are vivid reminders of the town's ancient history. Halfway, a few miles inland, the Baroque Mortizburg Castle, former hunting lodge of the Saxon kings, houses a fine museum. Turning upstream by river boat, you can enjoy the scenery of flat-topped sandstone mountains rising steeply from both banks of the meandering Elbe, sometimes to a height of 395 meters (1,300 ft.). The most impressive of all hills is the Lilienstein, opposite the fortress-town of Königstein. Bad Schandau, near the Czechoslovak border, is a major tourist center.

Leipzig, Trade Center

As a center of the printing and book trade, as well as of the European fur trade, Leipzig acquired world renown soon after the Napoleonic Wars. One of the greatest battles, which led to the Emperor's fall, was fought here in 1813 (the Battle of Nations), commemorated by the ponderous Völker-Schlachts-Denkmal. Richard Wagner was born here in 1813 and was molded by a long-established musical tradition which boasts such names as the Gewandhaus Orchestra, founded in 1781, and the St. Thomas Church Boys' Choir, closely associated with Johann Sebastian Bach. Astride great trade routes, Leipzig became an important market town in the early Middle Ages. Thus the scene was set for the twice yearly Trade Fair (March and September) which has brought together exhibitors and buyers from all over the world for more than half a century. Today the Fair is the most important single meeting place of East and West for commerce and industry. Little is left of old Leipzig, but among the places to see are—the 12th-century market place, with a Renaissance Town Hall now housing the Town Museum, which possesses valuable documents about Leipzig, including a diorama of the Battle of Nations. You can go through a gateway in the Town Hall to the Nasch Market, Leipzig's most famous square, formed by the façade of the 17th-century Old Trade Exchange.

There are many associations with Goethe in Leipzig—he was a student here—and also with Johann Sebastian Bach, notably the Thomas Church, originally the center of a 13th-century monastery and rebuilt in the 15th century. This church, with its tall Gothic roof over the nave, is Bach's burial place. Today it is still the center of Bach tradition in Germany and the home of the Thomaner Choir. More Gothic ecclesiastical architecture in the early 16th-century Paulinen Church. You can walk through it—it's the sole remnant of a 13th-century Dominican cloister.

Of recent vintage are the new cubistic Gewandhaus with its several concert halls, the New Opera House in Karl-Marx-Platz, and the enormous sports stadium. Train-lovers will like to know that here is Europe's largest station—26 platforms.

Today Leipzig has the biggest German-language library, hosts the International Book Art Exhibition, and trains personnel in book production. Book production goes with music and art production too. Seven million packs of playing cards are made and exported yearly.

Fur processing, from East German mink and fox, and fur auctions are still important features. Most enterprising, though, is the successful breeding and export of wild animals, including lions, bears, hyenas and Siberian tigers.

In Gohlis, a Leipzig suburb, stands a small farmhouse, now a museum, which tells you that Schiller wrote his *Ode to Freedom* here in 1785. Gohlis Castle, set behind a magnificent wrought-iron gate in a fine park, was a meeting place for Leipzig's intellectual and artistic world under Goethe's teacher, Böhme. Today it houses the Bach Archives. Close-by is the Zoo, where they breed animals for export. Southwest, and following the Martin-Luther-Ring, stands the Georgi Dimitroff Museum, the Supreme Court of the Reich from 1895 to 1945. In the Great Hall in 1933 the Dimitroff (Reichstag Fire) trial took place. Dimitroff was the leader of the Bulgarian Communist Party. Behind this museum is the music center of Leipzig, focused on the Gewandhaus.

Other excursions that can be made from Leipzig are to Lutherstadt Wittenberg, Halle, Eisleben, Namburg and Altenburg.

Lutherstadt Wittenberg was the center of the German Reformation, whose history is exhibited in the early 16th-century monastery of the Augustines and former residence of Luther. Humanist Philipp Melanchthon was born in a Renaissance house here and in the Town Church, Wittenberg's oldest building (14th and 15th centuries), are paintings by Cranach (the Elder), and Vischer, better known as a contemporary of Dürer's in Nürnberg. Luther and Melanchthon are buried in the 15th-century Schlosskirche (Castle Church), totally destroyed in the Seven Years War and rebuilt only in the 19th century. From the tower you have a fine view of the old town and its narrow streets. Statues to the two men stand in front of the 16th-century Town Hall.

Halle is the birthplace of Händel (statue in the market place). His house is an important musical instrument museum, spanning five centuries.

Further trips can be made to the medieval towns of Naumburg and Altenburg—where they make playing cards and where the Castle Museum has a collection of playing cards.

Harz Mountains

The Harz is the best known of mountain districts in central Germany. Delightful surroundings help to enhance the medieval character of Wernigerode, dominated by a feudal castle. The thousand-year-old Quedlinburg is a dreamy little town, with its half-timbered houses, winding lanes and its outsize cathedral. It's well worth visiting, though accommodations are very limited and it may be advisable to stay at the Magdeburg Interhotel and make excursions from there. Magdeburg has Germany's first Gothic cathedral, some fine Baroque buildings, and several theaters, including a puppet theater.

From here one can also visit the timber-framed houses of Halberstadt. Thale is best reached via Quedlinburg and the Devils' Wall. Thale's surroundings include the beautiful Bode valley, the witches' dancing place

(Hexentanzplatz) and the Harz mountain theater, also accessible by cable railway. So on to Rübeland with stalactite caves, and Stolberg in the southern Harz with fine Renaissance houses, Baroque castle and museum.

Thuringia

This region, 100 km. (62 miles) long and between 10 and 35 km. (6 and 22 miles) wide, lies at the most southwesterly point of East Germany, vying with the Harz (to the north) and Erzgebirge (east) in sheer unspoiled, undeveloped wooded mountain slopes, forests, clear streams, rare plants, and traditional craftsmanship, notably glass and wooden toys. Walkers will enjoy particularly the Schwarztal, Inselberg and Rennsteig regions; the air is the most remarkably heady in all Germany. At the two extremities of the Thüringer Wald lie two historic cities: Eisenach and Saalfeld, the latter with the most beautiful stalactite caves in East Germany—really fairytale grottos. Eisenach is dominated by the 900-year-old Wartburg Castle, mentioned in many a German legend. Here minstrels like Tannhäuser, Walter von der Vogelweide and Wolfram von Eschenbach sang of noble lords and lovely ladies. During the stormy days of the Reformation it served as a refuge for Martin Luther, who translated the New Testament into German here in 1521.

Bach was born in Eisenach in 1685; and incidentally the Wartburg car is manufactured here. Further east, Erfurt, seemingly untouched by history, remains one of the finest of German cities, with its cathedral and the church of St. Severin, its matchless Gothic and German Renaissance houses, and its 600-year-old bridge, with 33 houses built on it. Erfurt has long been associated with flowers and there is a summer horticultural show (of plants from Communist countries) in the grounds of Cyriak Castle.

Only a few miles away, Weimar retains the atmosphere of the old residential town of German princes. Lucas Cranach lived and worked here. Its greatest period came at the turn of the 18th century when Goethe, Schiller, Wieland and Herder, giants of the era of German humanism, made this town famous in the realms of literature and philosophy. Later on, Böcklin and Lenbach founded the Weimar school of painters here. For historical significance, true peace and graciousness, Weimar is unsurpassed in East Germany.

Among the intersting places to visit are—Goethe's residence in Frauenplanstrasse, and his summer house in the beautiful park on the Ilm; the Dower Palace of the Duchess Anna-Amalia; Schiller's house opposite the Gänsemännchen (Little Goose Boy) well; his and Goethe's vault; the Liszt Museum; the Herder Church with Cranach Altar. This is a town where history can be observed and felt, unimpeded, for the most part, by contemporary comment.

That is more than can be said for Buchenwald, the Nazis' terrible concentration camp a little to the north, on the Ettersberg. This is not a place for the over-sensitive and the horror endured by the 56,000 people murdered here is made no easier on the eye and mind by the whitewashing messages purporting that the blame for these vile camps must really be laid at the West German door alone. The wretched victims are loosely described as anti-Fascist, which they most probably were. But mostly they were Jews, and that is why they were there.

Near Weimar are Apolda, with Germany's oldest bell foundry and bell museum, the 13th-century cathedral town of Naumburg, and Jena, with its 16th-century university. Schiller was a professor and Karl Marx wrote his doctor's thesis on philosophy here. Also here is the Zeiss planetarium which should be visited even if you find this subject dull. Gera is a very beautiful patrician and Renaissance town where one can still see the 16th-century town hall, a 17th-century chemist's shop, patrician houses spanning four centuries (1500–1900) and fine botanical gardens and orangery. Several castles are nearby: the 600-year-old Osterburg at Weida and the 1000-year-old Ranis Castle.

Oberhof, a year-round resort, is the tourist center of Thuringia and in winter the scene of bobsled and toboggan runs, skating and skiing. Suhl is the capital of the Thuringian Forest, known for gun manufacture for four centuries. Suhl country comes second only to that of the Baltic coast for popularity as an East German holiday region.

Christmas decoration fanatics should visit the glass-blowing town of Lauscha, home of such delights—with a glass industry museum.

The Erzgebirge

This most powerfully dramatic, wooded mountain landscape forms a natural barrier with Czechoslovakia and is idyllic for walkers and motorists, both rejoicing to find even less traffic than elsewhere in East Germany. However, the forests of Erzgebirge have suffered terrible pollution, and vast areas of leafless trees now stand where healthy green once prevailed. Extensive use of brown coal as fuel, particularly in the industrial area just northwest of the forests, has caused this pollution.

Karl-Marx Stadt is the principal city. Badly damaged in World War II it is long since re-established as a center for heavy industry, turning out modern automatic weaving machines and everything to do with the knitting, spinning and calico printing industries, plus bicycle manufacture. If you have to be here—and most people prefer the countryside—there is a 250-million-year-old petrified tree trunk in front of the Textile Museum on Theaterplatz.

The Schlosskirche and Schlossberg museum are nice to look at, likewise the Siegert House with its carefully restored Baroque facade. Of the former 25 medieval military towers only the Rote Turm still stands today. There are also some fine patrician houses but the jewel is the late Gothic cathedral with wooden sculptures and its Silbermann organ from 1714, the oldest of the still existing 31 organs he made. The Golden Door of the Marienkirche, dating from the 13th century, is built into the south side of the cathedral.

Freiberg is attractive and still has the remains of its ancient fortifications as well as tiny miner's houses in narrow streets—"Erzgebirge" means "ore mountains." The highest located East German town is hereabouts, Oberwiesenthal, which lies at the foot of the Fichtelberg. Spas figure highly in East as in West German recreation and round here they have Bad Brambach and Bad Elster, the latter in a charming parklike setting.

From Karl-Marx Stadt, you can take a trip to the 800-year-old Burg Rabenstein and the Rabenstein group of rocks, a network of caves hollowed out by mining, with also the remains of a 17th-century castle. 10 km. (6 miles) away is Pelzmühle with pleasure steamers.

At Küchwald is an openair theater if what is on is understandable to you. The Augustusburg is a formidable Renaissance building, built in 1572 as a hunting center and now houses a museum of the creatures caught in these mountains. In the castle church is an altar painting by Lucas Cranach the Younger and many people get pleasure from a well here which is 170 meters (555 ft.) deep. Water sportsmen head for the Kriebstein Dam 25 km. (15 miles) distant, a relaxing area, or to Sachsenring, the international motorcycle race course.

Seiffen, deep in the mountains, is not to be missed: famous, like mountain villages the world over for woodcarving, its toy museum is a joy, as are the workshops of the turners and carvers.

Close to Annaberg in the Sehma valley is the Frohnauer Hammer, an iron processing installation from the 15th century and framework house of the former owner of the forge, today a local art museum with bobbin-lace room. Musicians may know the names Klingenthal and Markneukirchen, for centuries centers for musical instrument manufacture. A large collection of musical instruments is at the museum in Markneukirchen. Annaberg is a bobbin-lace center but was formerly famous for silver mines, long since closed, but there are some houses which indicate local prosperity. The church dates from 1520.

The Baltic (Ostsee)

Crossing the northern lakeland district we soon reach that part of the coast known as Ostsee, or Baltic. Old Hanseatic cities alternate with well-known beach resorts. Largest of East German ports, Rostock lies almost in the geographical center of the coastline. Its architectural unity has been broken by war damage, but there are still several items of interest to see. The Town Hall has seven towers, spanning 13th to 18th centuries. Medieval Rostock can still be seen in the Stone Gate and parts of the old town wall. The Kröpelin Gate is now a museum for local history and important examples of ecclesiastical architecture are Kreuz Church, St. Mary's Church and the 13th-century Nikolai Church. The busy modern harbor is also of interest. The train and car ferry for Denmark (about the cheapest in Europe and thoroughly comfortable) leaves the coast at Warnemünde, one of the best-known seaside resorts.

To the west, Wismar, for nearly two centuries a Swedish possession (1648–1803), gives evidence of old Hanseatic traditions, but architecturally the most enchanting place is Stralsund, with its quaint streets and venerable, red-brick public buildings and churches, fine examples of northern Gothic. Further inland, Schwerin was the seat of the Dukes of Mecklenburg and is typical of the old German provincial capitals, with its stately castle (with lovely silk tapestries in the hall and superb gardens) and opera house. In fact throughout the north of East Germany, right down to Frankfurt/Oder and Potsdam, you meet the red-brick Gothic architecture now so much admired but favored in the Middle Ages solely because of the lack of natural building stone.

Excursions that can be made from Rostock include a trip round the port and boat trips to Hiddensee Island and to the beach at Warnemünde; to Bad Doberan with 14th-century Gothic cathedral and numerous art treasures; narrow gauge railway to seaside resorts of Heiligendamm (the first German bathing resort, established in 1793) and Kühlungsborn. Also to

Wismar, second largest seaport with an attractive 14th-century market square and Alte Schwede burgher house.

Neubrandenburg is another old town with many fine churches, the east gable of one (St. Mary's) being in Gothic brick and in imitation of Strasbourg Cathedral. From here you can make a side trip to Lake Müritz with East Germany's biggest nature reserve on the east bank, excellent for hiking on marked paths.

The woodlands of the Darss Peninsula represent perhaps the last example of primeval forest formations in Europe and are now a national park. To the east, the narrow island of Hiddensee was always a favorite summer haunt of artists and bohemians. Gerhart Hauptmann, the playwright, came here every year from the turn of the century and was buried on the island in 1946. The highlight of the coast is Rügen, Germany's largest and most beautiful island. It is dented by hundreds of bays and creeks. The vast Bay of Lietzow, protected from all sides, is ideal for sailing. Chalk cliffs of Stubnitz, 400 feet high, and dropping almost vertically into the sea, are the landmark of Rügen. Of the many fishing villages and beach resorts, Binz is the best known and has some good hotels. The Munich-Berlin-Stockholm train reaches the ferry-boat at Sassnitz. Southwest of Rügen is the island of Usedom, with a string of seaside resorts, some famous, like Heringsdorf and Zinnowitz, some infamous, like Peenemünde, cradle of the World War II V1 and V2 missiles.

PRACTICAL INFORMATION FOR
THE REST OF EAST GERMANY

HOTELS AND RESTAURANTS

Dresden. *Bellevue* (L), Köpkestr. (51–56620). With 320 rooms plus suites and apartments, Dresden's newest hotel opened in 1985; all facilities including fitness center, sauna, restaurants. Hotel incorporates an old, restored, town house. AE, DC, MC, V. *Newa* (E), Leningrader Str. 34 (51–496–7112). Near main rail station; city's second best hotel, 315 rooms with bath. Good restaurant (open to guests only), café, bar, and gift shop. AE, DC, MC, V.

Astoria (M), Ernst Thälmann-Platz 1 (51–475–5851). 88 rooms, some with bath, simple but comfortable. Located near zoo; café, gift shop. AE, DC, MC, V. *Gewandhaus* (M), Ringstr. 1 (51–496–286). 99 rooms, some with bath. Central location and good café. No credit cards. *Interhotel Prager Strasse* (M), Prager Str. (51–48560). Consists of two hotels, the *Königstein* and *Lilienstien,* near the main rail station. 300 rooms each with bath. Restaurants, sauna, parking. AE, DC, MC, V.

Parkhotel Weisser Hirsch (I), Bautzner Landstr. 7 (51–36851). 50 rooms in pleasant surroundings, though none with bath. Restaurant, cafe, dancing. No credit cards. *Waldpark Hotel* (I), Prellerstr. 16 (51–34441). Quietly-located with good restaurant and dance bar.

Restaurants. *Canaletto, Elbterrassen, Wackerbarths Keller* (wine restaurant) and *Buri Buri* (Polynesian restaurant), all (E) and all located in Hotel

Bellevue. Köpckestr. (51–56620). Reservations recommended for all but Elbterrassen. AE, DC, MC, V.

Café Pöppelmann (M), Grosse Meissner-G. 15 (51–56620). Baroque atmosphere in a restored old city house incorporated into the Hotel Bellevue. Reservations advised in evening. AE, DC, MC, V. *Café Prag* (M), Altmarkt. Central location; very popular. Evening shows. *International* (M), Pragerstr. 15. Nice atmosphere and the food is quite good. *Luisenhof* (M), Bergbahnstr. 8 (51–36842). Reached by cable, overlooking the city and the Elbe. Reservations advised. No credit cards. *Meissner Weinkeller* (M), Strasse der Befreiung 1 (51–55928). Good food; wide variety of local wines. Reservations advised. No credit cards. *Sekundogenitur* (M), Brül'sche Terrasse (51–495–1435). Wine restaurant with view of the Elbe. Especially nice on the terrace, weather allowing. No credit cards. Closed Mon.

Äberlausitzer Töppl (I), Strasse der Befreiung 14. Regional specialties. The fish is quite good, and they serve a great dark beer. *Kügelgen Haus* (I), Strasse der Befreiung 14 (51–52791). Choice of a grill, coffee bar, restaurant proper, or an historic basement bierkeller. Popular, so book ahead. No credit cards. *Pirnaisches Tor* (I), Pirnaischer Platz. Choice of fish grill, restaurant proper, terrace café, or mocha bar.

In **Meissen,** the following restaurants are recommended: *Am Tuchmachetor* (M), Lorenzgasse 7; *Ratskeller* (M), Marktstr. 1; *Vincenz Richter* (M), An der Frauenkirche. Definitely worth a visit. *Winkelkrug* (M), Schlossberg 13. Also very nice.

In the vicinity of **Moritzburg,** with its baroque hunting lodge, the historic *Räuberhütte* and *Waldschanke* offer local specialties in a rustic setting.

Eisenach. *Parkhotel* (M), Wartburg Allee 2 (623–5291). 42 rooms, all with bath or shower; restaurant and gift shop. No credit cards. *Stadt Eisenach* (M), Lusienstr. 11–13 (623–3682). Restaurant and gift shop. *Auf der Wartburg* (M), (623–5111). 30 rooms with bath or shower. Charming hotel in Wartburg Castle, with an excellent view of the city. Historic restaurant with all the trimmings. Bus service to and from the rail station. No credit cards.

Erfurt. *Erfurter Hof* (E), Am Bahnhofsvorplatz 1–2 (61–51151). Top grade hotel, all rooms with private facilities. Good restaurants, bar, nightclub, cafe with dancing. AE, DC, MC, V. *Kosmos Interhotel* (M), Juri-Gagarin-Ring 126–127 (61–5510). 320 rooms, all with private facilities. Huge hotel with three restaurants and many amenities; panoramic view. AE, DC, MC, V.

Gera. *Hotel Gera* (L), Strasse der Republik (70–22991). 300 rooms, all with private facilities. Good restaurant serving local specialties, cafe, dancing. Nondescript but comfortable. AE, DC, MC, V.

Jena. *Hotel International* (E), Ernst Thälmann Ring (791–8880). Typical Inter hotel; some rooms with private facilities, central location, good restaurant, bar and cafe. *Schwarzer Bär* (M), Lutherplatz 2 (791–22543). 60 rooms, some with private facilities. Excellent restaurant and cafe, and good service.

Karl-Marx-Stadt. *Chemnitzer Hof* (L), Theaterplatz 4 (71–60421). 100 rooms, all with bath. Centrally-located; comfortable, with friendly service. Restaurant, cafe, bar. Building is a fine example of Bauhaus architecture. AE, DC, MC, V. *Kongress* (L), Karl-Marx-Allee (71–6830). Giant-size block with numerous facilities including the best Intershop outside the "Palast" hotel in East Berlin. AE, DC, MC, V. *Hotel Moskau* (E), Strasse der Nation 56 (71–60311). Some rooms with private facilities. Restaurant and cafe; adequate. AE, DC, MC, V.

Leipzig. *Astoria* (L), Platz der Republik 2 (41–71710). 309 rooms with bath. Across from the rail station, so convenient but noisy; good restaurant. AE, DC, MC, V. *Hotel Merkur* (L), Gerberstr. (41–7990). 440 rooms with bath. The most prominent, expensive and massive hotel in town. Three restaurants, plus fitness center, shops, bars (including one on the 27th floor); much above average. AE, DC, MC, V. *Hotel am Ring* (E), Karl Marx Platz 5–6 (41–79520). 276 rooms with bath. Centrally-located and good; a reasonable alternative to the Merkur. AE, DC, MC, V. *Stadt Leipzig* (E), Richard Wagner Str. 1 (41–288814). 340 rooms, all with bath. Restaurant, cafe and bar and helpful service. AE, DC, MC, V. *Interhotel zum Löwen* (M), Breitscheiderstr. (41–7751). 108 rooms with bath. Cheerful and pleasant with good facilities, though not opulent. AE, DC, MC, V. *International* (M). Tröndlinring 8 (41–71880). 104 rooms, some with bath. Charming older hotel, central location. Restaurant, beer stube, bar. AE, DC, MC, V. *Parkhotel* (I). Richard-Wagner-Str. 7 (41–7821). 174 rooms, few with bath. Good location across from rail station, but spartan accommodations. Restaurant, parking. No credit cards.

Restaurants. *Sakura* (E), Gerberstr., in Hotel Merkur (41–7990). Japanese cuisine. Reservations essential. AE, DC, MC, V.

Altes Kloster (M), Klostergasse 5 (41–282252). Specializes in game. Quite popular, so book ahead. Reservations advised. No credit cards. Leipzig's most famous restaurant is *Auerbach Keller* (M), Grimmaische Str. 2 (41–209–131). Historic setting immortalized in Goethe's *Faust.* Reservations essential. AE, DC, MC, V. *Burgkeller* (M), Naschmarkt 13 (41–29–5639). Good restaurant; also, Doina restaurant serves Romanian national specialties. No credit cards. *Falstaff* (I), Georgiring 9. Wine restaurant in an historic setting. *Gastmahl des Meeres* (M), Dr. Kurt Fischer Str. 1. (41–29–1160). Wide variety of seafood. No credit cards. *Paulaner* (M), Klostergasse 3 (41–28–1985). Attractive and quiet, with good food. Reservations advised. No credit cards.

Regina (I), Hainstr. 14 (41–282052). Cozy wine restaurant; book ahead. No credit cards. *Kaffeebaum* (I), Fleischergasse 4. Reportedly the oldest café in the country, in a Bürgerhaus well over 450 years old. Worth visiting. No credit cards. *Kaffeehaus* (I), Hainstr. 20. Nice café in which to sip a mocha and relax. *Panorama Café* (I), University Tower on Karl Marx Platz. Located on the top floor, it commands a fine view of the city. No credit cards. *Stadt Kiew* (I), Messehaus am Markt. A variety of Ukrainian specialties. Central location.

Rostock. *Warnow Interhotel* (E), Lange Str. (81–37381). Giant-sized hotel, all rooms with bath. Restaurants, nightclub, bars, shop; clay pigeon shooting and horse-back riding arranged. Try local Mecklenburg dishes in the restaurant and visit the old "Teepott" restaurant in the lighthouse.

AE, DC, MC, V. *Hotel am Bahnhof* (M), Gerhart-Hauptmann-Str. 13 (81–36331). 82 rooms, some with bath. Central location but few amenities. No credit cards.

Restaurants. *Jägerhütte* (M), Barnstofer Wald (81–23457). This rustic restaurant lies hidden in the woods near the zoo. Good atmosphere and game specialties. Reservations essential. *Restaurant-Komplex* (M), Schillerstr. 14 (81–5371). Four different restaurants in one building: Asian, Cuban, Russian and Scandinavian. Book ahead.

Schwerin. *Stadt Schwerin* (E), Grunthalplatz 5 (84–5261). All rooms with bath; restaurant, cafe and sauna. No credit cards. *Hotel Polonia* (I), Grunthalplatz 15 (84–86405). Some rooms with bath; reasonable alternative to the Stadt Schwerin.

Suhl. *Thüringen Tourist* (E), Ernst-Thälmann-Platz 2 (66–5605). 180 beds, all double rooms with shower, balcony and bath. Restaurant, cafe, nightclub and shop.

Weimar. *Elephant Interhotel* (E), Am Markt 19 (621–61471). 115 rooms, some with bath or shower. Dates back to 1696, though vastly modernized. Goethe, Schiller, Herder, Liszt—and Hitler—stayed here. Several restaurants, bars, garden with terrace, nightclub and shop. Reserve well in advance. AE, DC, MC, V.

Restaurant. *Zum Weissen Schwan* (M), Frauentorstr. 23. Historic inn right next to Goethe's house.

TOURIST INFORMATION. All local tourist offices are run by the Reisebüro der DDR. They have offices at the following places: **Dresden,** Prager Str. 11 (51–495–5025). **Eisenach,** Bahnhofstr. 3–5 (623–5161 5165). **Erfurt,** Angerstr. 62 (61–5700). **Gera,** Strasse der Republik 29 (70–23783). **Jena,** Spitzweidenweg 22 (791–25428). **Karl-Marx-Stadt,** Strasse der Nation 56 (71–60331). **Leipzig,** Katharinenstr. 1 (41–79210); or, Leipzig Information, Sachsenplatz (41–79590). **Rostock,** Hermann-Duncker-Platz 2 (81–3800). **Schwerin,** Leninplatz 1 (84–83635). **Suhl,** Ernst-Thälmann-Platz 1 (66–23012). **Weimar,** Marktstr. 4 (621–2173).

TOURIST
VOCABULARY

TOURIST VOCABULARY

The German language follows very strict rules of pronunciation which are designated by the spelling of the words. The vowel sounds are either long or short. Long vowels are indicated when they are doubled—Aal, Tee, Boot; when followed by "h"—Bahn, Sohn, Uhr; when followed by one consonant only—gut, Hof, Tal; before a single consonant followed by a vowel—Leben, Name, Rose. Thus a long "a" as in Tal (valley), "ah" as in Hahn (rooster) or "aa" as in Aal (eel) will be pronounced as in father; a long "e" as in Esel (donkey), "eh" as in mehr (more) or "ee" as in Tee (tea) will be pronounced as in fey; a long "i", "ih" as in ihr (her), "ie" as in Tier (animal) or "ieh" as in Vieh (cattle) will be pronounced as yield; a long "o" as in rot (red), "oh" as in Sohn (son) or "oo" as in Boot (boat) will be pronounced as in bone; a long "u" as in Bruder (brother) or "uh" as in Stuhl (chair) will be pronounced as in rude.

Short vowels are indicated when they are followed by more than one consonant. Thus a short "a" as in Mann (man) is pronounced as in man; a short "e" as in Welt (world) is pronounced as in pelt; a short "i" as in Kind (child) is pronounced as in lint; a short "o" as in Motte (moth) is pronounced as in knot; a short "u" as in Butter (butter) is pronounced as in foot. The "e" in words ending in -e, -el, -en and -er, is also short.

There are also modified vowels which are those qualified by umlaut (..): "ä," "ö," "ü," and "äu." A long "ä" or "äh" as in während (during) or spät (late), is pronounced as in late; a short "ä" as in Wände (walls) is pronounced as in pet; a long "öh" or "ö" as in Söhne (sons) is more difficult as there is really no English equivalent—the nearest would perhaps be yearn, or the French "deux"; a short "ö" as in Göttlich (divine) is pronounced as in fir; a long "üh" or "ü" as in kühn (bold) is again difficult to translate in English—perhaps prune with a Scottish accent! A short "ü" (as in Müller, miller) is similar to the long sound—only shorter!

And then there are diphthongs—but there are only three! Firstly "au" as in Frau (woman) is pronounced like the "ou" in house; "eu" and "äu" as in Leute (people) and Bäume (trees) are pronounced like the "oy" in boy; and "ei," "ai" and "ay" as in Ei (egg), Kaiser (emperor) and Bayern (Bavaria) are pronounced like the "i" in flight.

The consonants are pronounced as they are in English with the following exceptions:
"b" as in English except when it is followed by another consonant or at the end of a word in which case it is pronounced as an English "p," e.g. Obst (fruit) or Grab (grave)
"ch" is pronounced like the "h" in huge
"d" as in English unless it appears at the end of a word as in Land (land) in which case it is pronounced as the English "t"
"g" always hard (as in good). If it appears at the end of a word it is pronounced as a "k" as in Ring (ring)
"j" always pronounced as the "y" in young
"r" is usually "rolled" from the back of the palate

"s" before and between vowels as in Sohn (son) and Rasen (lawn), pronounced as in wise

before consonants and at the end of a word, as in Geist (ghost) and Gras (grass), pronounced as in son

"sp"and "st" at the beginning of a word, as in Spiel (game) and Stuhl (chair) is always pronounced "shp" or "sht"

is a signal for a sharp "s" following a long vowel, as in Stra e (street). It is used instead of "ss" at the end of a word, as in na (wet). In this book we have used "ss" throughout

"sch" as in Schiff (ship) is pronounced simply as "sh"

"th"as in Thron (throne) is pronounced as "t" alone

"v" as in Vater (father) is pronounced as "f"

"w" as in Wagen (car) is pronounced as "v"

"z" as in Zucker (sugar) and "tz" as in Katze (cat) is pronounced like the "ts" in cats

Tonal stress is practically always on the first syllable (as in the English words cooker, Albert or bacon)—there are exceptions as there are to pronunciations, but they are too complex and numerous to go into here. Nouns are always given capital letters, as are adjectives and verbs when they are used as nouns. Best get yourself a complete German Grammar or language course if you want this sort of detail.

USEFUL EXPRESSIONS

Hello, how do you do?	Guten Tag (gootn tahg)
Good morning	Guten Morgen (gootn mohrgn)
Goodnight	Gute Nacht (goota nakht)
Goodbye	Auf Wiedersehen (owf veederzayn)
Please	Bitte (bitta)
Thank you	Danke (danka)
Thank you very much	Vielen Dank (feelen dank)
	Herzlichen Dank (hairtslihen dank)
Yes	Ja (ya)
No	Nein (nine)
You're welcome	Bitte (bitta)
	Gern geschehen (gairn geshayen)
	Keine Ursache (kyna oorzaha)
Excuse me	Entschuldigung Sie mir, bitte (entshooldegoong zee meer, bitta)
Come in!	Herein (hairine)
I'm sorry	Es tut mir leid (ess toot meer lite)
My name is . . .	Ich heisse . . . (ih hyssa)
Do you speak English?	Sprechen Sie Englisch? (shprehen zee English)
I don't speak German	Ich spreche kein Deutsch (ih shprehen kine doitsh)
Please speak slowly	Bitte, sprechen Sie langsam (bitta, shprehen zee langsam)
I don't understand	Ich verstehe nicht (ih fershtayer niht)
Please write it down	Bitte, schreiben Sie es auf

Where is . . . ?	Wo ist . . . ? (vo ist)
What is this place called?	Wie heisst dieser Platz?
	(vee hyst deeza plats)
Please show me	Bitte, zeigen Sie mir
	(bitta, tsygen zee meer)
I would like	Ich möchte gern (ih merhta gairn)
How much does it cost?	Wieviel kostet es?
	(veefeel kostet ess)

(bitta shriben zee es owf)

SIGNS

Entrance	Eingang (inegang)
Exit	Ausgang (owsgang)
Emergency exit	Notausgang
Toilet	Toiletten
- men	Herren (hairen)
- women	Damen (dahmen)
- vacant	frei (fry)
- occupied	besetzt (bezetst)
Hot	Heiss (hise)
	Warm (varm)
Cold	Kalt
No smoking	Rauchen verboten (rowhen fairboten)
	Nichtraucher (niht-rowher)
No admittance	Kein Eingang (kine inegang)
	Kein Zutritt (kine tsootritt)
Stop	Halt
Danger	Gefahr (gevehr)
Open	Offen
	Geöffnet (gayerfnet)
Closed	Geschlossen (geshlossen)
Full, no vacancy	Voll (foll)
	Belegt (beleht)
	Kein Zimmer frei (kine tsimmer fry)
Information	Auskunft (owskoonft)
Bus stop	Bushaltestelle (bus-halte-stelle)
Taxi stand	Taxistand
Pedestrians	Fussgänger (foos-genger)

ARRIVAL

Passport check	Passkontrolle (passcontrolla)
Your passport, please	Ihren Pass, bitte
	(eeren pass, bitta)
I am with the group	Ich gehöre zu der Gruppe
	(ih gehera tsu dair groope)
Customs	Zoll (tsoll)
Anything to declare?	Etwas zu verzollen?
	(etvas tsu fairtsollen)
Baggage claim	Gepäckausgabe (ge-peck-ows-gahbe)
This suitcase is mine	Das ist mein Koffer

(dass ist mine koffer)

A porter, baggage carrier	Einen Träger, Gepäckträger
	(inen trayger, gepecktrayger)

TRANSPORTATION

to the bus	zum bus (tsoom boos)
to a taxi	zu einem Taxi (tsu inem taxi)
to the Hotel . . . , please	zum Hotel . . . , bitte
	(tsoom Hotel . . . , bitta)

MONEY

Currency exchange office	Wechselstube (vehsel-stooba)
Do you have change?	Können Sie wechseln?
	(kernen zee vehseln)
May I pay with	Kann ich mit (can ih mit)
- a traveler's check	einem Reisescheck (inem rises-sheck)
- a voucher	einem Gutschein (inem gootshine)
- this credit card?	dieser Kreditkarte
	(deeza kreditkarta)
	bezahlen? (betsahlen)
I would like to change some traveler's checks	Ich möchte gerne Reiseschecks eintauschen (ih merhte gairn rises-shecks eintowshen)

THE HOTEL

I have a reservation	Ich habe vorbestellt (reserviert)
	(ih hahba forbeshtellt (reserfiert)
A room with	Ein zimmer mit (ine tsimmer mit)
- a bath	bad (baht)
- a shower	einer Dusche (ina doosha)
- a toilet	einer Toilette, w.c. (ina toiletta, vay tsay)
- hot running water	fliessend warmen Wasser (fleesent varmen vasser)
What floor is it on?	In welchem Stockwerk ist es?
	(in velhem shtockverk ist es)
- ground floor	Erdgeschoss (aird-geshoss)
- second floor	Zweiter Stock (tsviter shtock)
Elevator	Aufzug (owftsoog)
Have the baggage sent up, please	Lassen Sie das Gepäck nach oben bringen, bitte (lassen zee dass gepeck nah oben bringen, bitta)
The key to number . . . , please	Den Schlüssel für Nummer . . . , bitte (dayn shloosel fur noomer . . . , bitta)
Please call me at 7 o'clock	Bitte, wecken Sie mich um sieben Uhr (bitta, vaecken zee mih oom zeeben oor)
Have the baggage brought down	Lassen Sie das Gepäck herunter bringen (lassen zee dass gepeck hair-oonter bringen)

| The bill | Die Rechnung (dee rehnung) |
| A tip | Ein Trinkgeld (ine trinkgelt) |

THE RESTAURANT

Restaurant	Restaurant
	Gaststätte (Gast-shtette)
Waiter!	Herr Ober! (Hair ober)
Waitress!	Fräulein! (froiline)
Menu	Speisekarte (shpiza-karta)
I would like to order (this) . . .	Ich möchte gerne (das . . .) bestellen (ih merhte gairn (dass . . .) beshtellen)
Some more . . . , please	Noch etwas mehr . . . , bitte (noh etvass mehr, bitta)
That's enough	Das ist genug (dass ist genuht), Das genügt
The check, please	Der Scheck, bitte (dair sheck, bitta)
Breakfast	Frühstück (fruh-shtook)
Lunch	Mittagessen (mittag-essen)
Dinner	Abendessen (abent-essen)
Bread	Brot (brote)
Butter	Butter (booter)
Jam	Konfitüre (Marmalade)
Salt, pepper	Salz/pfeffer (salts)
Mustard	Senf
Sauce, gravy	Sosse
Vinegar	Essig (essih)
Oil	Öl (oel)
Bottle	Flasche (flasha)
Wine - red, white	Wein (vine) - rot, weiss (vice)
Water	Wasser (vasser)
Mineral water	Mineralwasser (minerahl-vasser)
Milk	Milch
Coffee, with milk	Kaffee, mit milch (kaffay mit milch)
Tea, with lemon	Tee, mit Zitrone (tay, mit tsitrona)
Chocolate	Schokolade, Kakao (shockolahda)
Sugar, some sugar	Zucker, etwas zucker (etvass tsooka)
Spirits	Alkoholische Getränke (alkoholisha getrenka)

MAIL

A letter	Ein Brief
An envelope	Ein Umschlag (oomshlahg)
A postcard	Ein Postkarte
A mailbox	Ein Briefkasten
The post office	Das Postamt

A stamp	Eine Briefmarke
By airmail	Mit Luftpost
How much does it cost	Wieviel kostet es (veefeel . . .)
- to send a letter	- einen Brief
- to send a postcard	- eine Postkarte
by airmail to the United States (Great Britain, Canada)?	mit Luftpost nach Amerika zu schicken (England, Kanada)?
To send a telegram, cable	Ein Telegramm zu schicken

LOCATIONS

. . . Street	. . . Strasse (shtrahsa)
. . . Avenue	. . . Allee (alleh)
. . . Square	. . . Platz (plats)
The airport	Der Flughafen (flooghafn)
A bank	Eine Bank
The beach	Der Strand (shtrant)
The castle	Die Burg, das Schloss (boorg, shloss)
The cathedral	Die Kathedrale (katedrahla)
The church	Die Kirche
The coffee house, café	Das Café
The garden	Der Garten
The hospital	Das Krankenhaus
The movies, cinema, film	Kino, ein Film
The museum	Das Museum
A nightclub	Ein Nachtclub (nakhtkloob)
The palace	Der Palast
The park	Der Park
The station	Der Bahnhof
The theater	Das Theater (tayarta)
- a play	- ein Schauspiel, Theaterstück (showshpeel, tayartastook)
The (official) travel bureau	Das Reisebüro (rizabooro)
The university	Die Universität (ooniverzitet)

TRAVEL

Arrival	Ankunft
Departure	Abfahrt
- airport	- Abflug

The Airplane

I want to reconfirm a reservation on flight no. . . . for . . .	Ich möchte mir eine Reservierung für Flug Nummer . . . für . . . bestätigen lassen (ih merhta mir ine reserfieroong fur floog noomer . . . fur . . . beshtetigen lassen)
Where is the check-in?	Wo ist die Flugscheinkontrolle?

       (vo ist dee
       floog-shine-kontrolla)

I am checking in for . . .   Ich fliege nach . . . (ih fleega
       nah)

Fasten your seat belt   Bitte anschnallen

The Railroad
The train   Der Zug (tsoog)
From what track does the   Von welchem Bahnsteig fährt der
train leave?   Zug? (fon velhem bahn-shtige
       ferht der tsoog)

Is this seat free?   Ist diese platz frei? (ist
       deeza plats fry)

Which way is the dining car?   Wo geht's zum Speisewagen?
       (vo gate's tsoom shpise-vahgen)

Bus, streetcar
Does this bus go to . . . ?   Fährt dieser Bus nach . . . ?
       (ferht deeza boos nah)

  trolleybus   - O(berleitungs)bus
       (ober-lite-oongs-boos)

I want to get off at . . .   Ich möchte an der . . . steigen
       (ih merhta an der . . . shtigen)

. . . at the next stop   . . . an der nächsten Haltestelle
       (an der nehshten halte-shtella)

Taxi
I (we) would like to go to   Ich (wir) möchte(n) nach in die
. . . street, opera, zoo,   . . . Strasse, zur Oper, zum Zoo
. . . , please   . . . , bitte
       (ih (veer) merhte(n) nah
       in dee . . . shtrassa, tsoor Opper,
       tsoom Tsoo . . . , bitta)

Stop at . . .   Halten Sie bei . . .
       (halten zee by)

Stop here   Halten Sie hier (haltn zee heer)

NUMBERS

1	eins (ains)	25	fünfundzwanzig (foonf-und-tsvantsig)
2	zwei (tsvy)	30	dreissig (dryssih)
3	drei (drai)	40	vierzig
4	vier (fier)	50	fünfzig
5	fünf (foonf)	60	sechzig
6	sechs (zeks)	70	siebzig
7	sieben (zeeben)	80	achtzig
8	acht (akht)	90	neunzig
9	neun (noyn)	100	hundert (hoondert)
10	zehn (tsen)	200	zweihundert
11	elf	300	dreihundert
12	zwölf (tsveulf)	400	vierhundert
13	dreizehn (drai-tsain)	500	fünfhundert
14	vierzehn		

15 fünfzehn	600 sechshundert
16 sechzehn	700 siebenhundert
17 siebzehn (zeeb-tsain)	800 achthundert
18 achtzehn	900 neunhundert
19 neunzehn	1000 tausend (towzent)
20 zwanzig (tsvantsig)	

DAYS OF THE WEEK

Sunday	Soontag (zontahg)
Monday	Montag (montahg)
Tuesday	Dienstag (deenstahg)
Wednesday	Mittwoch (mitvoh)
Thursday	Donnerstag
Friday	Freitag (frytahg)
Saturday	Samstag or Sonnabend (zamstahg or zonahbent)

Index

The letter H indicates Hotels and other accommodations.
The letter R indicates Restaurants and other eating facilities.

WEST GERMANY

General Information

Fodor's Travel Guides

U.S. Guides

Alaska
American Cities
The American South
Arizona
Atlantic City & the
  New Jersey Shore
Boston
California
Cape Cod
Carolinas & the
  Georgia Coast
Chesapeake
Chicago
Colorado
Dallas & Fort Worth
Disney World & the
  Orlando Area

The Far West
Florida
Greater Miami,
  Fort Lauderdale,
  Palm Beach
Hawaii
Hawaii (Great Travel
  Values)
Houston & Galveston
I-10: California to
  Florida
I-55: Chicago to New
  Orleans
I-75: Michigan to
  Florida
I-80: San Francisco to
  New York

I-95: Maine to Miami
Las Vegas
Los Angeles, Orange
  County, Palm Springs
Maui
New England
New Mexico
New Orleans
New Orleans (Pocket
  Guide)
New York City
New York City (Pocket
  Guide)
New York State
Pacific North Coast
Philadelphia
Puerto Rico (Fun in)

Rockies
San Diego
San Francisco
San Francisco (Pocket
  Guide)
Texas
United States of
  America
Virgin Islands
  (U.S. & British)
Virginia
Waikiki
Washington, DC
Williamsburg,
  Jamestown &
  Yorktown

Foreign Guides

Acapulco
Amsterdam
Australia, New Zealand
  & the South Pacific
Austria
The Bahamas
The Bahamas (Pocket
  Guide)
Barbados (Fun in)
Beijing, Guangzhou &
  Shanghai
Belgium & Luxembourg
Bermuda
Brazil
Britain (Great Travel
  Values)
Canada
Canada (Great Travel
  Values)
Canada's Maritime
  Provinces
Cancún, Cozumel,
  Mérida, The
  Yucatán
Caribbean
Caribbean (Great
  Travel Values)

Central America
Copenhagen,
  Stockholm, Oslo,
  Helsinki, Reykjavik
Eastern Europe
Egypt
Europe
Europe (Budget)
Florence & Venice
France
France (Great Travel
  Values)
Germany
Germany (Great Travel
  Values)
Great Britain
Greece
Holland
Hong Kong & Macau
Hungary
India
Ireland
Israel
Italy
Italy (Great Travel
  Values)
Jamaica (Fun in)

Japan
Japan (Great Travel
  Values)
Jordan & the Holy Land
Kenya
Korea
Lisbon
Loire Valley
London
London (Pocket Guide)
London (Great Travel
  Values)
Madrid
Mexico
Mexico (Great Travel
  Values)
Mexico City & Acapulco
Mexico's Baja & Puerto
  Vallarta, Mazatlán,
  Manzanillo, Copper
  Canyon
Montreal
Munich
New Zealand
North Africa
Paris
Paris (Pocket Guide)

People's Republic of
  China
Portugal
Province of Quebec
Rio de Janeiro
The Riviera (Fun on)
Rome
St. Martin / St. Maarten
Scandinavia
Scotland
Singapore
South America
South Pacific
Southeast Asia
Soviet Union
Spain
Spain (Great Travel
  Values)
Sweden
Switzerland
Sydney
Tokyo
Toronto
Turkey
Vienna
Yugoslavia

Special-Interest Guides

Bed & Breakfast
  Guide: North America
  1936...On the
  Continent

Royalty Watching
Selected Hotels of
  Europe

Selected Resorts
  and Hotels of the U.S.
Ski Resorts of North
  America

Views to Dine by
  around the World